RELIGIONS OF THE WORLD

RELIGIONS
OF THE WORLD

THEIR NATURE AND THEIR HISTORY

BY PROFESSOR CARL CLEMEN

UNIVERSITY OF BONN

in collaboration with

FRANZ BABINGER, LEO BAECK, HEINRICH HACKMANN
F. E. A. KRAUSE, KARL H. MEYER, FRIEDRICH PFISTER
GÜNTHER ROEDER, ALBERT SCHOTT, FRANZ ROLF
SCHROEDER, ERICH SEEBERG, OTTO STRAUSS

TRANSLATED BY THE REV. A. K. DALLAS M. A.

With one hundred and thirty-five illustrations

Essay Index Reprint Series

BOOKS FOR LIBRARIES PRESS
FREEPORT, NEW YORK

STANDARD BOOK NUMBER:
8369-0011-1

LIBRARY OF CONGRESS CATALOG CARD NUMBER:
69-17570

PRINTED IN THE UNITED STATES OF AMERICA

TRANSLATOR'S NOTE

The last decades have witnessed a distinct revival of interest in the study of comparative religion. Many books on the subject have appeared within recent years, and most modern commentaries on the books of the Bible have sought to utilize the results gained by labourers in this field. There is still room, however, for such an account of the religions of the world as that of which an English translation is here presented. The book is avowedly intended for general readers, and an endeavour has been made to bring out clearly the broad outlines of the various faiths. At the same time, as Professor Clemen says, it contains fresh contributions to the understanding of its great subject.

As might be expected, the original presents various styles of writing. This may account for some unevenness in the translation. Owing perhaps to the special nature of the subjects dealt with, the style of some of the contributions lacks the clearness that is conspicuous in others, and many of the sentences are unusually long and intricate. The chapter on Hebrew religion is written in a style of great dignity. No attempt has been made to reduce these differences to anything like uniformity. The translator has been content to endeavour to make the meaning clear.

Quotations from Scripture have been given according to the Revised Version, except where the author's point requires another rendering. All the footnotes, with the exception of those on pages 48 and 58, have been supplied by the translator.

A. K. DALLAS

RHYND LODGE
SEAFIELD, LEITH
February 1930

v

027563

PREFACE

The main purpose of this work is to provide the general reader with an account of the history of the various religions of the world. The writers have therefore tried to avoid all unnecessary technicalities of expression, and have refrained from enlarging on unessential details. They have preferred to confine themselves to the main features of the various religions, and have emphasized chiefly those aspects of them which are really important for their adherents. It is, after all, by these that a religion must be judged.

If from this point of view the book may be considered a supplement to larger special works on the same subject, there are several respects in which it can claim an independent value. In the first place, in addition to a description of primitive religion, the national religions, and what is commonly understood under the name of the world religions — the two last-named groups being dealt with in chronological order — the work contains a discussion of prehistoric religion, which has never before been included in any similar book, and of Judaism and Christianity, which are also usually omitted. Secondly, in dealing with those religions whose history falls into several periods the writers have sought to avoid emphasizing some of these at the expense of others. They have even indicated where necessary their influence on other religions or on popular superstition. Lastly, the contributors are specialists in the subjects that have been assigned to them, and have therefore been able to add something not easily found elsewhere. They have all been allowed a free hand — a liberty including the use of the spellings of proper names which they individually prefer — and each is responsible only for his own contribution.

The illustrations are not meant to be mere decoration which might have been dispensed with; they are intended to illustrate the text, and have been carefully chosen for this purpose.

CARL CLEMEN

vii

CONTENTS

ILLUSTRATIONS

I. PREHISTORIC RELIGION

I. PREHISTORIC RELIGION

by Carl Clemen

It is only in connexion with mankind that we can speak of religion at all, and therefore when we set out to trace the history of religion back to its origin our first question must be, When did man make his first appearance in the world? To be sure, the question whether he already existed in the Tertiary Period or, for that matter, earlier need not concern us here, for even if he did exist we can know nothing about his religion. The same is the case with the earliest man of the Quaternary Period or of the Glacial Age with its various sub-periods. The *homo* of that time certainly did not exactly resemble the man of the present day, and it is little we can say about him. Up till now it is only in Europe that any trace of him has been discovered. Our information begins with the Mousterian Age, which probably coincided with the last European Ice Age but one — *i.e.*, say, from 350,000–225,000 B.C. The entire Palæolithic or older Stone Age was succeeded about 5000 B.C. by the Neolithic or later Stone Age, which in turn was followed by the Copper and Bronze Age about 3000 B.C. and by the Iron Age from 1500 B.C. onward. In this chapter we are not to speak of the later Iron Age — the so-called La Tène Period — nor of the earlier Iron Age — the so-called Hallstatt Period — nor even of the later Stone Age. The civilization of all these periods was represented, entirely or in part, by actual peoples concerning whom we have other information and of whom we shall speak in the next chapter. Here we are concerned only with prehistoric religion. This cannot be traced back to definite peoples, although some attempts have been made to do this. We have no information about it other than that which can be gathered from archæology, and therefore its reconstruction is difficult, but still it is possible to say something about the various periods of prehistoric religion. These periods cannot be dealt with successively; they can only be treated in connexion with separate aspects of the subject and by means of careful comparison with the historical religions, especially the religion of primitive man.

Using the word ' worship ' in a quite general sense — we shall define it more exactly afterward — prehistoric religion consisted in worship of the dead. As far back as Palæolithic times the dead were actually interred. This is proved by the fact that numerous remains have been found in cavities which must have been specially prepared to receive them. Further, similar remains have been found in various places lying on stones or bones or else covered with stones, and this again points distinctly to burial. Remains found in the so-called 'crouching' posture — although, as a matter of fact, one does not adopt this posture when going to sleep, but lies down on one side and draws up the knees so as to conserve the heat of the body as much as possible — might of course be those of men who had been suddenly overwhelmed, but in that case it is not clear why the arms and legs often lie so close to the body that they must have been tied to it, after the manner still common among primitive peoples. Again, many of the bones, especially those found in caves, are coloured red. Red liquid was poured or red powder strewn over the corpse, and precipitated on the bones after the flesh had decayed. This is, of course, a specially clear proof that the dead were actually interred. Again, the flint utensils and ornaments so often found beside human remains cannot in all cases have been in their possession by chance when the owners were overwhelmed, but must have been laid beside them by others as gift-offerings.

These are some of the considerations — other even clearer indications will be added later — that go to prove that as far back as the Palæolithic Age the dead were buried. But the presence of the gift-offerings just mentioned takes us farther. It indicates that the dead were originally believed to survive corporeally. Only on this supposition could these offerings have any meaning. As we shall see later, some other prehistoric customs can be explained only in the same way, and the same belief must underlie various other practices which have continued (with another meaning) down to the present day. This belief in a bodily survival, however, cannot have originated in the slight difference observed by prehistoric man between a dead person and a person asleep, for this difference must very soon have been seen to be a fundamental one. Nor can Palæolithic man merely have inferred a bodily after-life for his dead from the dreams and visions in which he saw dead men as living, for he had other dreams besides to which even he could not possibly ascribe actuality. If he drew this inference in this case it can only have been because he could not believe that the last breath meant the end of all. This has an important bearing on our estimate of their belief on that subject. If prehistoric man conceived life after death as a bodily survival, it must have been because he could not conceive an after-life of any other kind. It was only gradually — otherwise this oldest conception would not have endured so long as it did — that prehistoric man became convinced that the body did not continue to live and that he tried to differentiate between it and a spiritual entity — a soul, if we may here use the word — which of course he could not at first conceive as purely spiritual. That the existence of a soul was, occasionally at least, assumed as far back as the Palæolithic Age is perhaps a legitimate inference from facts such as those now to be adduced. All the skulls found in the Ofnet cave near Nördlingen lay facing westward. Was this in order to indicate, not to the skulls, which could not survive by themselves, but to the souls the way to that realm where all the dead were gathered together, a realm which, as men so often thought afterward, was to be sought where the sun went down? This is of course only a probable explanation. But what seems more certain is that the hole frequently found chiselled in the transverse slab of the megalithic monuments or barrows belonging to the Neolithic Age was meant to provide the soul (it is often called the ' soul-hole '), even if only temporarily, with a way of escape from the grave. This indicates that the existence of a soul was assumed, although it was not yet conceived as incorporeal. The practice of cremation also, which occurs in Europe in the Neolithic Age and is common in the Bronze Age, would be consistent with a belief in a life after death only if this after-life had ceased to be conceived as necessarily connected with the dead body.

Of course all this comes far short of proving that the dead were worshipped. That such worship was actually paid to the dead is only an inference from the fact that the dead were feared. Men sought to keep them at as great a distance as possible. This is the most probable explanation of many of the practices that were followed. Stones were heaped on the dead body; the huddled-up bodies were tied with cords, crammed into urns, and mutilated. These practices are attested for the Bronze Age and among many primitive peoples. Many other customs which are still current among uncivilized peoples (and which still exist even among civilized peoples in the form of superstitious practices) served originally the same purpose. Among civilized peoples these are, of course, interpreted differently to-day, but, as we shall see, these later interpretations help to explain why these means were used to keep the dead at a distance. That illness or other evils were at that early time ascribed to the dead, or that superhuman powers were attributed to them, cannot be proved; but the converse — viz., that superhuman aid was expected from them when they were appeased or conciliated — may be inferred from the attentions that were paid to them.

Among these attentions to the dead we include, first, the red colour which was applied to the bodies. This practice is common to this day among uncivilized races, and even among many civilized peoples, where it takes the form of burying several dead bodies together in a red coffin or in red clothing. The red colour was no doubt meant to represent the blood, which even at that early time was esteemed " a quite special juice," whose virtues Palæolithic man thought he could secure for his dead by imparting to their bodies a red colour. In a grave near Mentone was found in front of the mouth and nose of the dead man a depression filled with powdered blood-stone. Evidently he was meant to sniff this powder and thereby acquire the powers resident in it or in the blood. Similarly, when the dead man was buried near the fireplace the intention apparently was to provide him with warmth, just as the gifts of food and drink indicate the desire to supply his need for these. Above the grave in the cave at Chapelle-aux-Saints,

Corrèze, numerous bones of animals were found, but no utensils of any kind except three very fine flint knives. This no doubt means that the grave was the scene of feasts of which the dead man was supposed to partake, although he did not dwell there. At the time of interment utensils and ornaments were given to the dead, and in the Neolithic Age human beings were buried alive or killed at the grave of their masters or husbands..

At a still later time worship of some kind was certainly paid to the dead. This is shown by the custom of allowing the space in front of the grave to lie waste. This was not done to allow others to be buried there afterward. In particular, however, this continuous worship of the dead seems to prove that they were credited, not only with the powers that might be thought natural to dead men in a future life, but also with superhuman powers, which were believed to be reinforced, or at least preserved, by the red colouring. This whole way of regarding the dead cannot be explained as being due to ideas derived from dreams and visions. It can only mean that an already existent conception of higher beings was transferred to the dead, who were believed to exist in an after-life, and to whom therefore this conception could be transferred.

It is only this belief that the dead possessed superhuman powers that explains many of the customs which must be postulated for the Stone Age. It was believed that the special powers of the dead could be passed on to those who survived. To be sure, the discovery of numerous single bones, especially mandibles (lower jaw-bones), which probably had been coloured red, and were specially preserved or actually worn on the person, does not prove that prehistoric man attributed to them *supernatural* powers. Many primitive men did that, at least originally; they would not otherwise have worn lower jaw-bones round their necks, or fastened them to their war trumpets or used them in religious ceremonies. But when prehistoric man deliberately preserved and even wore these bones he may have wished thereby only to acquire their *natural* powers. Similarly, when he transformed skulls into drinking-cups he may have done so not because they were useful for that purpose or because he wished to show scorn of his foes, but because he believed that he could thus acquire the powers resident in them. Again, although in Scandinavia in the Neolithic Age scalping was customary, and the scalp was looked on not only or not mainly as a trophy, but as the *locale* of the powers resident in the hair, we need not suppose that these powers were believed to be superhuman. But the case is different when we find that at the same period in many districts in France portions of skulls were worn which evidently had been trepanned during the lifetime of their original owners. How such an operation — which is not rare among primitive men — could have been performed by Neolithic man we need not consider, nor does the question whether a man's skull was opened in order to let out an evil spirit that dwelt in it concern us at this point. In any case the idea must have been that a man who had been delivered from his sufferings by this operation was not only himself protected for the future against them, but after his death could also protect others through the virtue of the portion of skull that had been thus treated. This means that superhuman powers were actually attributed to these bones and that they were worn as amulets.

With this we pass from prehistoric worship of the dead to the magical customs of the prehistoric period. The conception of magic essentially involves the belief that a man can by some means or other actually acquire powers that transcend experience. If merely natural powers are in question the matter does not belong to religion. Only that kind of magic is religious which enables one to obtain for oneself or for others supernatural or, as the case may be, superhuman powers. Whether in prehistoric times the acquirement of superhuman powers was believed to be possible in any other way than that which has been described we do not know. For even if (as is proved by the broken or split human bones which have been found among similar animal bones) cannibalism was certainly practised in the Stone Age — though surely not by those who honoured their dead in the ways already described, but by others — it is still a question whether this was done in order to acquire the superhuman powers of those thus dealt with. If these powers were believed to reside in the blood they might, of course, be obtained by eating the flesh, although that is not quite certain. The peculiar tattooing which is found on some figures of idols belonging to the Neolithic Period, and which will be discussed later, was certainly practised by men on themselves first, but that it had any magical significance is again only *probable*: it *may* have merely been a remarkable form of ornament. But that cannot be the case with the T-shaped marks found on many female skulls of the same period in the department of Seine-et-Oise. These marks were branded so deeply that the skulls still show the scars. Similar branding occurs among civilized peoples, ancient and modern. Its special original significance we shall see later.

It is uncertain whether the ornaments which were given to the dead and ordinarily worn by the living had talismanic significance. At a later time, of course, that was — and, indeed, still is — the case, and partly explains why those ornaments (which were not originally *ornaments* at all) were worn on the hands and the feet — the parts of the body that chiefly come into contact with hostile influences — and with quite special frequency at the openings in the head — ears, nose, and mouth — through which harmful powers could gain entrance to the body. A later time even attributed supernatural powers to the material of which the prehistoric ornaments were made — *e.g.*, to the teeth of animals, rare stones (which occur as early as the Palæolithic Age), gold (which emerges in the Neolithic Age), and to corals, which appear for the first time in the Hallstatt Period. Without any doubt magical significance was attached to the multifarious objects belonging to the mineral, vegetable, and animal worlds which, in the Bronze Age, were not only worn as ornaments by the living, but were heaped together into bronze vessels or leather pouches and given to the dead. They cannot be explained in any other way. Even the small axes of stone and bronze which in the Stone Age and in the Bronze Age were buried with the dead, and which were quite unsuitable for practical use, must certainly have served as amulets, and the same is true of the bronze figures of bulls, made to be worn as pendants, which have been found in France and Posen. That these were supposed to transfer to their human wearers only the *natural* powers of these animals is highly improbable.

That already in prehistoric time there existed a belief in the transference of supernatural powers by contact — for that is the point at issue in the last-mentioned cases — may perhaps be inferred from the further fact that there existed already in the Palæolithic Age a form of magic that was even less natural. We mention it here for the sake of the inference that is to be drawn from it. Both among uncivilized and civilized peoples the idea prevails that an image or picture can be a substitute for the object represented by it. As we shall see, this idea underlay the branding or stigmatization already mentioned. But many primitive peoples further believe that when they copy an animal they thereby conjure up the animal itself, or at least bring it under their power. This must be the meaning — at any rate, the original meaning — of those faithful and artistic pictures of animals which are found in caves going back to Palæolithic times. Some of these animals are represented with the point of a spear or an arrow sticking in their body and surrounded by missile weapons. In some cases armed men are attacking them, in others human hands are stretched forth to seize them, and there are also huts into which they are to be dragged. Seeing that animals are alone in question, all this is not strictly relevant here, but it shows that we are justified in attributing to prehistoric man a form of magic that is, if we may put it so, more natural than this, and, further, that just as prehistoric man thought that by making representations of animals he could conjure them up or bring them under his power, so he may have entertained the same ideas regarding higher beings.

From the Neolithic Age onward we frequently find on the top or sides of stones bowl-shaped depressions, some of which may perhaps be natural, but most of which are certainly artificial. Of course, only depressions on a horizontal surface could have served as receptacles for offerings, but depressions of this kind are frequently found on a perpendicular surface. They must therefore have another meaning, and the same is true of those complete or half circles, spirals, and other figures which frequently occur. What that meaning is is still in dispute, but the most probable explanation is that all these figures represent the sun. This is also the meaning of the spoked wheel sometimes found with them. That does not imply that it was the original meaning. The spoked wheel, like other implements to which reference will later be made, might originally have been looked upon as possessing supernatural powers in itself, because it had proved to be much more useful than had been at first expected. Nevertheless, at a later time — not so late as the historical period, when the wheel was frequently used symbolically, but already in prehistoric time — it may actually have been understood to be an image of the sun. And from this spoked wheel, which from the Bronze Age onward is found as a pendant or as ornamentation on needles and knives (Fig. 1), was probably evolved the simple cross and the hooked cross which are also found on rocks in the Bronze Age. This cross may therefore also have been an image of the sun.

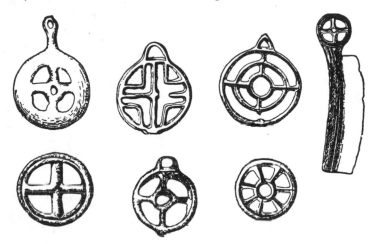

FIG. 1. WHEEL-SHAPED PENDANTS AND WHEEL-SHAPED ORNAMENTATION
ON A KNIFE
From Clemen, " Religionsgeschichte Europas," vol. i

Of course all this does not yet prove that the sun was conceived as a higher being. It is quite possible that, just as animals were copied merely as animals, the sun was copied merely as a heavenly body, to the intent that it might shine for a longer time or with greater effect or fulfil its *natural* effects in some other special way. We shall, however, see later that at least from the Bronze Age onward actual *worship* was paid to the sun, and we may perhaps legitimately infer that similar ideas were entertained regarding it in prehistoric time, because similar representations of it are found on megalithic graves. In such cases they certainly had a magical signification; that is to say, they were meant not merely to conjure up the sun, but to convey its powers to the dead, and, further, these powers were not those natural to the heavenly body, but the supernatural powers of a higher being.

On the monument at Kivik, in Sweden (Fig. 2), which belongs to the Bronze Age, there appears with the spoked wheel what seems to be a representation of the moon. If this interpretation is correct, then the inference is that at that early period the moon also was looked upon as a higher being. But this interesting monument takes us no further. Leaving out of account meantime its other two slabs, whose meaning is not clear, we find represented on it a stone pyramid (similar to several others found on megalithic graves in South-west Europe, in the Caucasus and in India),

FIG. 2. SLABS FROM THE KIVIK MONUMENT
From Clemen, " Religionsgeschichte Europas," vol. i

two other mysterious objects, and two metal axes with handles. The object appearing below these is probably a sledge, although it may be something else. The hook-shaped figures found on many French graves have also been explained as axes with handles, while some of the yoke-shaped objects also found there have been interpreted as horns and the comb-shaped figures as ships. These last, however, seem ultimately to stand for the sun. In Norwegian rock-drawings similar ships are found along with the sun. But these interpretations are by no means certain. Only the T-shaped scar found on many female skulls in France can be as yet confidently interpreted as a double-headed axe.

The indubitable representations of axes found elsewhere and the diminutive hatchets already mentioned, as well as the stone pyramids on the Kivik monument and elsewhere, were without any doubt — originally, at least — conceived as possessing special powers which were meant to be transmitted to the dead. Similarly, those axes of stone or bronze, too large and too brittle for practical use, which have been found may have been merely fetishes, worshipped for the same reason as the spoked wheel was worshipped. Like the wheel, the axe, which was the principal tool of prehistoric man, had proved to be more useful than had been expected, and it too was therefore looked upon as a higher being. The worship of stone pyramids is not so easily explained. Was it the result of their peculiar shape or the striking manner in which they were put together? Or did men in course of time come to believe that special experiences associated with them pointed to supernatural powers? Even then we should still be far from a real explanation either of the worship of such fetishes or the worship of the dead or other higher beings with which we have still to deal. In any case, supernatural powers were presupposed, and attributed to the dead only because the dead were believed on the grounds already given to survive after death, or to natural objects because these were in some way striking or mysterious.

A similar explanation holds good for the worship of trees, of which there are traces as early as Neolithic times. At Skjelmoor, in Jutland, was found a tree-trunk that had been hollowed out and filled with small pieces of wood. It stood upside down on a cairn of stones, and was encircled by vessels and potsherds that were probably connected with sacrifice; that is to say, it was an object of worship. But it would hardly have been such had the living tree not been previously similarly esteemed. And we have already seen that in the Bronze Age animals also were probably regarded as higher beings.

That the sun, that part of nature whose worship we can most readily understand (Goethe declared it — of course in a different sense — to be absolutely natural), was actually worshipped as far back as the Neolithic Age could be proved from Stonehenge (Fig. 3) if that monument could be shown to have been a sanctuary of the sun. And as the opening of the horseshoe which forms the centre of the whole plan points almost exactly toward that point in the sky where the sun rises at the summer solstice, it is quite possible — indeed, it is very likely — that Stonehenge was such a sanctuary. Of course, the whole structure may be merely a grave monument. Actual worship of the sun cannot with certainty be proved till the Bronze Age. The earliest proof of it is provided by the vehicle unearthed at Trundholm, in Zeeland, on which stands a gold-mounted disk drawn by a horse (Fig. 4).

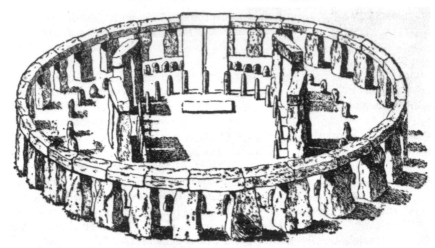

FIG. 3. STONEHENGE, AS RECONSTRUCTED BY BROWNE
From Clemen, " Religionsgeschichte Europas," vol. i

Probably the reason why the disk, although drawn by a horse, is represented as standing on a vehicle along with the horse is that it was taken from place to place (at fixed seasons of the year and in a larger form) in order to bring the blessing of the sun to the districts visited. The smaller replica of this

FIG. 4. VEHICLE FROM TRUNDHOLM
From Sydow, " Kunst der Naturvölker "

processionary vehicle certainly represents a gift to the sun bestowed in order to induce him to traverse each new day his apparent path in the sky. Similar gifts to the sun are attested for a later time. A like explanation probably applies to other chariots and other objects of the Bronze Age which at first sight certainly seem to have no connexion whatever with the

FIG. 5. VESSELS FROM DENMARK AND HUNGARY
From Clemen, " Religionsgeschichte Europas," vol. i

sun. But the discovery on Italian, Teutonic, and Scandinavian vessels — although some of them belong to a later period — of the sun-disk conjoined with swan necks (Fig. 5) justifies us in seeing in the chariots with the same ornamentation and even in the birds on wheels (Fig. 6) representations of the sun. In later times the sun is frequently found in conjunction

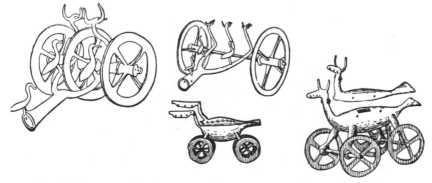

FIG. 6. CARRIAGE FRAMES WITH BIRD-NECKS AND BIRDS ON WHEELS
FROM LAUSITZ AND ITALY
From Clemen, " Religionsgeschichte Europas," vol. i

with swans; the birds are sometimes hollowed out. Sometimes only a vessel is set on wheels (Fig. 7); this also probably represents the sun, for the sun is frequently conceived as such a vessel moving across the sky. Hence we may perhaps legitimately interpret the chariot from Strettweg, in Hungary (Fig. 8), which is at least as late as the Hallstatt era, as a sun-chariot —

FIG. 7. VESSEL ON WHEELS FROM
MECKLENBURG
*From Clemen, " Religionsgeschichte Eu-
ropas," vol. i*

i.e., the shallow bowl held in position
by the central female figure (of more
than life size) must have formed the
bottom of a vessel that was meant to
represent the sun. By this time, however, the sun was no longer pictured
as moving on wheels or drawn by a
horse, but as borne by a deity depicted
in human form. The horse-heads,
originally four in number, but now
only three, attached to the frame of
the chariot, and the horses on which
four men are seated, might of course
point back to the earlier representation
of the sun as in motion. Even the two
stags standing at the front and rear of

FIG. 8. CHARIOT FROM STRETTWEG, IN HUNGARY
From Sydow, " Kunst der Naturvölker "

the platform possibly refer to the sun — if we are justified in presupposing that it is the sun that is indicated by the wheel drawn by two stags found in the rock-drawing at Lilla Gerum in Sweden (Fig. 9). Even if the stags on the chariot from Strettweg are sacrificial animals — behind each of them is a man with an axe in his hand — this interpretation is not rendered impossible: they might have been offered to the sun in order to equip him for his daily march through the heavens. If our explanation thus far is correct, this would also be the purpose of the entire chariot. As in the case of the other chariot already described, a larger form of it must have been taken from place to place — this is the only conceivable reason why all these structures are set on wheels — a smaller replica

FIG. 9. ROCK-DRAWING IN SWEDEN
*From Clemen, " Religionsgeschichte Europas,"
vol. i*

FIG. 10. HORSE FROM BECKERSLOH,
NEAR NÜRNBERG
*From " Abhandlungen der Naturhistori-
schen Gesellschaft in Nürnberg," vol. xxi*

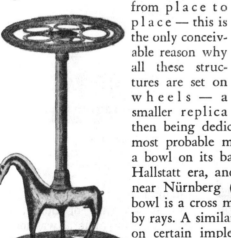

FIG. 11. BRONZE HORSE
FROM CALACEITE, SPAIN
*From " Abhandlungen der
Naturhistorischen Gesell-
schaft in Nürnberg," vol. xxi*

then being dedicated to the sun. This is also the most probable meaning of another horse carrying a bowl on its back which likewise belongs to the Hallstatt era, and which was found at Beckersloh near Nürnberg (Fig. 10). On the bottom of the bowl is a cross mounted on wheels and surrounded by rays. A similar cross is still found in that district on certain implements, and is universally understood to indicate the sun. The same applies also to the bronze horse which probably belongs to the same time and was found in the Spanish province of Terual. It stands on one disk and carries another (Fig. 11). It too was probably a votive offering to the sun, and was dedicated for the purpose already often mentioned. The same must be said of the bronze bowl containing small vessels of gold adorned *au repoussé* with concentric circles which was found near Lavindsgaard, in Finland, and of the hundred small golden ships decorated with the sun-disk which were dug up at Nors, in Jutland.

Whether (in addition to the sun, which may have been thus represented at a later time) prehistoric man also believed in the existence of other deities with a human form cannot be definitely decided for Palæolithic times. The figures in the round and in relief (most of them female and extremely corpulent) which we have from this period might represent

FIG. 12. THE SO-CALLED VENUS OF WILLENDORF

From Clemen, " Religionsgeschichte Europas,"
vol. i

FIG. 13. RELIEF FROM LAASSEL
From Clemen, " Religionsgeschichte Europas," vol. i

human beings sacrificed to the dead at the time of burial, no longer in reality, but, as was sometimes done at a later time, only in effigy. (See Figs. 12 and 13.) This suggestion finds some support in the fact that several of these figures were found in a layer of red ochre. This, as we saw, was meant to convey to them higher powers. On the other hand, the small, extremely corpulent figures discovered in Malta, belonging to the Neolithic or perhaps to the Bronze Age, might represent dead people. Some of them are depicted as asleep (Fig. 14), and a deity could hardly have been conceived in this way. But the objects, certainly of Neolithic Age, found in French megalithic graves (Fig. 15) cannot possibly represent dead people, for in that case it is difficult to see why in graves which contained several bodies, never more than one person (and that a woman) was represented. In those cases where the breasts were not actually chiselled they had apparently been indicated by paint. Although many of these figures are carrying a double-headed axe or some other implement — the brow and nose are frequently axe-shaped —

FIG. 14. SLEEPING WOMAN FROM HAL SAFLIENI, MALTA
From Hörnes, " Urgeschichte der bildenden Kunst "

this does not contradict this interpretation, for, as has been said above, the axe might have actually come to be a symbol of deity. The four horizontal lines under the eyes of some of the figures probably point to tattooing, which must have been already practised by the people of that time. But of course this does not exclude the possibility that it is a deity, a deity of the dead, and therefore of life, that is here depicted. Again, the boulders of stone with female breasts which occur in Sardinia certainly represent higher beings, whereas the very imperfect male figures which belong to the Later Stone Age may quite well be representations of dead men. Only those found in almost every house in Jablonica (in Serbia) and in Thessaly can be household deities. This is certainly the case with the roughly cut wooden male figures from the Broddenbjärg Moor, in Jutland, and from Alt-Frisack, in Brandenburg (Fig. 16). These are lifesize, while most of

FIG. 15. GRAVE MONUMENTS FROM FRANCE

From Clemen, " Religionsgeschichte Europas," vol. i

FIG. 16. WOODEN FIGURES FROM JUTLAND AND BRANDENBURG

From Clemen," Religionsgeschichte Europas," vol. i

the others are very small, and can therefore hardly have been images to which worship was paid.

In what manner these deities were worshipped in the Later Stone and Bronze Ages and in the Hallstatt Period we do not know. We have already spoken of a votive offering to the sun. That was perhaps the purpose served by the round cakes of resin from the Bronze Age. In particular the so-called depot discoveries were not valuables that had been buried to hide them from robbers, but votive offerings, first to the gods that lived under the earth and afterward to other deities. This seems to be the only explanation why implements, ornaments, weapons, and wind instruments are so often found in pairs. Things that men themselves highly valued they thus sought to bestow on others in at least double measure, and this same modest generosity they afterward practised toward the gods also. That other things were similarly devoted to them, and that prayers were offered to them, is certainly probable, but it cannot be directly proved.

Many other features in prehistoric religion are still obscure, and will probably always remain so. All the same, more is known about the religion of that time than most people are at first inclined to believe, and we are thus able to trace the history of religion farther back than has usually been done. In particular, belief in a life after death and in the supernatural powers of the dead certainly existed in the Palæolithic Age, together with a belief in the transference of such powers to others. In the Neolithic Age this latter belief is even more evident, especially the belief in the existence of higher beings. And in the Bronze Age we find evidence of several such beings to whom worship was really paid. Of course, it is possible that religion in the Neolithic Age and in the Bronze Age — especially in Europe — was influenced by other countries in which, as we shall see later, religion was more highly developed at an earlier time than on our continent.

BIBLIOGRAPHY

There is as yet no complete account of prehistoric religion, for Mill's *Prehistoric Religion* (1918) deals chiefly with other matters and of Mainage's *Les Religions de la préhistoire* only the first volume has as yet appeared; it treats of the Palæolithic Age. Reference may be made to Hörnes, *Urgeschichte der Menschheit* (1895; fourth edition, 1912; re-edited by Behn in 1921); *Natur und Urgeschichte des Menschen* (2 vols., 1909); *Kultur der Urzeit* (3 vols., 1912; also re-edited by Behn in 1921–23); Obermaier, *Der Mensch der Vorzeit* (1912); Burkitt, *Prehistory* (1921); MacCurdy, *Human Origins* (2 vols., 1924). The following deal specially with Europe: Sophus Müller, *Urgeschichte Europas* (1905); Forrer, *Urgeschichte des Europäers* (1908); Hahne, *Das vorgeschichtliche Europa* (1910); Schuchhardt, *Alteuropa* (1919; second edition, 1926); also Hörnes, *Urgeschichte der bildenden Kunst in Europa* (1898; re-edited by Menghin in 1925), and Déchelette, *Manuel d'archéologie préhistorique, celtique et gallo-romaine* (2 vols., 1908 and 1914). For the national religions of Europe see Clemen, *Religionsgeschichte Europas* (vol. i, 1926).

II. PRIMITIVE RELIGION

II. PRIMITIVE RELIGION

by Carl Clemen

That there are now no primitive men in the strict meaning of the word is well known. Earlier writers used the term 'people in a state of nature' or even 'savages.' Strictly speaking, there is little justification for contrasting them with civilized peoples, for those with whom we are now to deal do possess civilization of a kind. In detail there are cultural differences among the various primitive peoples which enable us to arrange them in a rough kind of chronological order. Certain elements of civilization which do not stand in any sort of genetic relation to each other frequently occur in combination, and constitute what have been called 'culture zones.' These must have shifted or have been subsequently broken up. In such cases the civilization that separates them is of course younger, whereas the civilization which has been thrust back into the outlying corners of a continent may be regarded as the oldest.

In keeping with these principles, and taking the Oceanic realm first, the oldest civilization is that of the Tasmanians. It became extinct as long ago as 1876, and we are already within sight of the time when many other civilizations will have shared the same fate. Therefore not much is known about Tasmanian civilization, for the well-known difficulties that confront all research into the mentality of primitive men were of course even greater at a former time than they are now. In various parts of Australia we find a so-called ancient Australian civilization, which is also met with in Africa (among the Bushmen) and in South America (among the Ges tribes, the Patagonians, and, more recently, among the Fuegians). In Australia it is broken up by the totemistic civilization — so called because it is dominated by the peculiar view that between certain peoples on the one hand and certain beings, objects, or phenomena on the other hand — especially animals — there exists a relationship. It is hardly possible to give a more exact definition of the meaning of totemism. This totemistic civilization is also found in other regions — in the South Seas, Indonesia, Near India, Africa, and America. In Australia it is broken up by a different civilization — that of the two-class or dual system based on mother right. It is so called because society there falls into two exogamous classes — i.e., classes whose members are not allowed to marry members of their own class, but only those of the other class — and, further, because family kinship is determined not by paternal, but by maternal relationship. This civilization is again met with in the South Seas and South-east Asia, in the Central Asiatic and Northern countries, in Africa and America. In Central Asia and in the North it is combined with elements of the ancient Australian civilization, in South America with totemism, in Africa with the latest civilization of Australia, the South Seas, Indonesia, and Farther and Near India — that is, the so-called Melanesian bow civilization, in which a special kind of bow is a characteristic feature. The youngest Oceanic civilization is the Polynesian, which is also found in Indonesia and Farther India, and has in Africa a kind of analogue in the civilization of the pastoral peoples.

In Africa the youngest primitive civilization is that of the Zambezi district, while that of the Sudan (especially in Benin) may have been influenced by the civilized peoples of North-east Africa and of Asia. The influence of Northern civilization has extended on the one hand as far as Arabia and on the other as far as the New World, and the advanced civilizations of Central America betray influences from the Old World. How such reciprocal influences were possible it is difficult to explain.

Vice versa, in the advanced civilizations (especially the religions) of the Old World, in its popular superstitions and customs, we meet with numerous primitive elements which have outlasted all changes. Just as in a forest which has been planted repeatedly with different trees the lowliest type of plant continues unchanged, so many elements of the most primitive civilizations and religions either reappear in the later civilizations and religions or seem at least to give rise to similar phenomena in them. Therefore (as various attempts have shown), unless we are to break up what are really units, we cannot exhibit the civilization and religion of primitive men according to periods. It is impossible not to hark back to what preceded and to anticipate what came later. It will therefore be better to discuss the religion of primitive men from the point of view of what is essential and inherent. Of course we begin with the oldest elements.

Even among the Tasmanians there was a kind of worship of the dead. The desire to prevent them from molesting the living underlay many of the Tasmanian customs. If this cannot be said of the practice of cremation, it is certainly true of their other customs of loading the dead body with stones (which goes as far back as prehistoric time) and raising a cairn or even building a pyramid over it. These practices imply a belief in the survival of the body, and this belief also explains the prehistoric and primitive custom of tying up the dead body with cords. Even in many parts of Europe it is still the practice to tie together the feet of the dead in order to render them unable to walk; and down to quite recent time in certain cases which will be referred to later a stake was thrust through the breast in order to fix the body to the ground. Many primitive men also break the bones of the dead or mutilate the body in some other way. The Greeks used to cut off the arms and legs, and until quite recently other peoples decapitated the dead bodies immediately after death, or did so afterward because the dead were reported to have 'walked.' Whether this was the original motive for placing the dead in a coffin or gathering the ashes in an urn or burying the body in some vessel, we are unable to say. The Cheremiss people give this explanation of the practice of fencing in a grave. To achieve the same end some Congo races strew thorns on the path to the grave to prick the feet of the dead should they try to return; some European peoples stretch a rope across the road after the dead man has been borne away, or, if the body has not been carried across water, they pour water on the path after it has passed. In Greece to-day this custom may be intended to alleviate for the dead the pains of hell, but this idea is patently an afterthought. The common modern practice of closing the eyes of the dead is explained — and perhaps rightly — by the inhabitants of the Nicobars as being due to the desire to prevent the dead man from seeing his way back, and this must certainly have been the original meaning of our custom of carrying the dead out of the house feet foremost. In totemistic civilizations platform burial is practised — *i.e.*, the dead are exposed in an elevated position or on a tree. This is no doubt only another means of protecting the living from their malign influences.

The dead, who are thus conceived as still surviving in the body or at least as retaining the powers they had in life, are also regarded as being inimically disposed toward the survivors. This is especially true of those dead who have been denied any form of good fortune enjoyed by others *e.g.*, women who died in childbed or who died unmarried, or those who died at the hands of others or by their own hands through the compulsion of others. By and by this conception was stretched to include those to whom it was not vouchsafed to live as long as others. Unpleasant experiences, too — especially nightmare — were attributed to the dead under this same implied belief that they survived in bodily form, and such experiences did much to strengthen that belief. By and by, however, the idea prevailed — it had already existed in prehistoric time — that the dead, especially one's own ancestors, were responsible for *pleasant* experiences, and must therefore be animated by friendly feelings toward those who survived them — or might at least be appeased and won over. Even among civilized peoples at the present day not only inanimate objects that belonged to the dead, but also their animals and servants and wives are dedicated to them. The probable explanation is, not that these are considered to be taboo — for why in that case should they be thus sacrificed to them? — but the fear that the dead might return and fetch them. It may be to prevent this that some civilized peoples to this day kill a dead man's domestic animals, even his bees. But when such gifts to the dead include things of a different kind, whether they are given at the time of burial or later, then it is clearly a different matter. Many primitive peoples (and if we may judge from the Old Testament prohibition against cutting one's skin for the sake of the dead [1] the ancient Hebrews practised that rite) allow their blood to drip upon the dead or place some of their hair on the dead body; and several civilized peoples of ancient and modern times did and still do this. These practices seem to supply further proof of the existence of the belief already mentioned that special powers reside in the blood and hair. But these gifts could be serviceable to the dead only if the latter were conceived as surviving corporeally. Many Lapps and Indians therefore bring offerings only as long as the corpse shows no signs of decay, while the Polynesians, Peruvians, and Egyptians embalmed their dead in order to preserve their bodies as long as possible. The motive no doubt was that the living might thus be enabled to continue to worship the dead and thereby win their favour.

FIG. 17. FRAMEWORK MADE OF SKULLS FROM NEW GUINEA
From Vatter, " Religiöse Plastik der Naturvölker "

In the dual system of civilization already referred to a single bone is carefully prepared and preserved. More frequently the skull of the dead man after suitable treatment is modelled to form a complete head (Fig. 17) and preserved. Underlying this practice is the belief that in the head reside not only the powers of the living man, but the supernatural powers which he has acquired by dying. Indeed, head-hunts are regularly organized in order to secure skulls for this purpose. The scalp, which has taken the place of the skull among the Indians, is now nothing more than a trophy, but originally, as we have seen, it was no doubt regarded as the means of conveying to its holder the powers of the dead man to whom it belonged.

In this same dual system of civilization, however, a distinction is drawn between the body, which after all does not survive, and a spiritual entity, although this latter could not at first be conceived and represented as other than corporeal. As the dead man was buried in the huddled posture ·(see

[1] Leviticus xxi, 5; *cf.* Deut. xiv, 1.

Fig. 18), so he was believed to live on in the same attitude, or if he had died of hunger he was represented as emaciated (see Fig. 19). The fact that the head is always pictured as disproportionately large indicates that a superior value was attached to it, and the same fact explains why the dead were so often represented by heads that can be donned by living men, or by masks that can be worn over the face. The occasions on which these are used will be enumerated immediately.

Even among peoples who believe that even the dead man, although he can subsequently take up his abode again in a human being, survives incorporeally, such survival is not always assumed as holding true for everybody. Sometimes it is only distinguished people, in other cases it is only males, who are supposed to survive; and their place of abode and their lot in the life beyond are regarded as varying according to the manner of their death or even their behaviour while on earth. Similar variety is believed to prevail with regard to the attitude they take toward those who survive them. Like the other dead, who are regarded as surviving in bodily form, they may be either hostile or friendly to those that remain, and when they enter into a man they may either bring illness upon him or render him valuable services. In the former case the survivors attempt to keep the spirit at a distance by carrying the body out of the house, not through the door, but through an opening made for this sole purpose and afterward closed up again. Even some civilized peoples do this, for in respect of the dead the converse holds true of what Mephistopheles says to Faust:

For Devils and for spectres this is law:
Where they have entered in, there also they
    withdraw.
The first is free to us; we're governed by the
    second.

Or, again, as is still done in some parts of Germany, the footprints of the bier-carriers are

FIG. 18. ANCESTRAL FIGURE
FROM THE PHILIPPINES
*From Vatter, " Religiöse Plastik
der Naturvölker "*

carefully effaced lest they should guide the dead man in finding his way back to the house. Or, finally, in case he should after all succeed in returning, the survivors disguise themselves by changing their mode of hairdressing or their clothing or even by assuming a different name. To the primitive mind a man's name, to quote *Faust* again, is not mere

" smoke and noise." It is so important a part of the personality that to change the name involves a change of the personality. On the other hand, when the souls of the departed are regarded as amicably inclined to those who outlive them, especially to their children, or at least as capable of being appeased by them, homage is paid to the dead by means of images

like those already mentioned, and prayers are offered to them. The heads and masks — the effigy of a being represents that being — are worn by the survivors in order to acquire for the time the personality of the deceased, and to convey to others also the helpful powers of the spirits of the departed. Sometimes it is difficult to decide whether in such cases it is really the spirits of the dead or other spirits that are meant. But before we pass on to consider this form of worship there is still another religious belief that remains to be noticed. It is found in the ancient Australian and kindred civilizations.

Probably the supreme being whose existence is assumed by these tribes had originally no religious significance. That supreme being is merely the originator of man, of his entire environment and of the customs and usages of which he has any knowledge.

FIG. 19. ANCESTRAL FIGURES FROM EASTER ISLAND

From Vatter, " Religiöse Plastik der Naturvölker "

In Australia, indeed, a plurality of such originators is assumed, and therefore no single one is regarded as the supreme being. When these people speak of a supreme being, however, belief is implied that he superintends the observance of the laws he has imposed, and he is therefore credited with a permanent importance at least in one definite direction. Among the Bushmen this conception of the supreme being has not been found, but they address to him their prayers for food. The Fuegians ascribe to their supreme being all the deaths that occur. This seems a logical inference from what we have taken to be the original conception of such a being. If they think that this being has created them and their environment, their customs and usages, superintends the observance of these usages, and supplies their food, then it is very likely he who calls men hence. But the Fuegians also feel that they are dependent on him in other ways. Yet it is perhaps no mere chance that very many of the prayers used by one of these Fuegian tribes, the Yamana, speak of their supreme being not in the second, but in the third person, so that there seems to be no real personal relationship between them and him. Even threats are sometimes used toward this supreme power. A woman whose child has died will urge her husband to kill some animals by way of re-prisal — she therefore hardly looks upon the originator of her grief as a *supreme* being. Among other tribes these originators are rarely worshipped, and when they are worshipped they are conceived to be gods of the sky or the sun-god, of whom we shall hear more further on. On the other hand, the idea that many gods of this kind, such as the god of the sky of the Indo-Germanic peoples, are originators or creators may be due to their having been confused with a being of this nature already known. Among primitive men themselves, however, the supreme being, even when he was really regarded as a *god,* was never looked upon as the *sole* deity. He was less important, indeed, than the other higher beings, and we shall now turn our attention to these.

Although the Fuegians undoubtedly believe in spirits as such, it is equally certain that this was not always the case, for other ultra-primitive peoples know nothing of such spirits. It is only when we assume that the original conception was one of higher beings possessed of special powers that we can understand the manner in which these were treated in later times. It is only powers and not personal beings that can be acquired or fended off by the help of magic, and the use of magic arts to influence personal beings must have been a later development. These powers, which were at first merely unusual and later became supernatural, have special names among many peoples. The best-known name is perhaps the Melanesian and Poly-nesian word *mana*. As we shall immediately see, these powers may reside in all kinds of objects in which for one reason or another they might suitably be thought to inhere.

It is only in rare cases — chiefly in West and Central Africa and in the West Indies — that stones were regarded in this way. Probably there was something striking about their shape or colour or composition, and they were looked upon as higher beings because some fortunate or sorrowful event took place in their vicinity. Similar veneration of stones is also attested among many civilized peoples, in particular among the Western Semites. In the Old Testament [2] the Hebrews are reproved for pouring libations and bringing food offerings to smooth stones. The best-known example is, of course, the Ka'ba at Mecca, the structure into which has been built the

[2] Isaiah lvii, 6.

Sacred Stone, whose powers are sought to be acquired by touch. Worship of stones is also found among many Indo-Germanic peoples, who may have borrowed it from the populations that preceded them. In Southern India we frequently find a group of four or five stones painted red, and until quite recent times similar fetishes were known to exist in Teutonic and Celtic territories.

Among primitive peoples in Oceania, Farther India, Africa, and America we frequently meet with the veneration of those tools or implements which are of great importance in daily life. In some cases it is simply a method of restoring to these objects their natural powers, but there are other cases in which it can only be called actual worship. This also occurred in primitive times, and is still found among some civilized peoples. It was widespread among the ancient Indians, and is general among the modern Japanese; and the axe, an implement which was worshipped as far back as prehistoric time, seems to have been an object of veneration among the Babylonians, Syrians, and Egyptians, and was certainly worshipped also both by the ancient and later population of Greece. Worship of the axe still exists here and there in Teutonic countries.

The worship of plants and trees requires no special comment. It is universal among primitive men wherever such vegetation is found, and also among almost all civilized peoples. Detailed examples need not be adduced. Dead trees and tree-trunks were also venerated — we need only mention the so-called Irminsul. And, finally, worship was paid to poles, although most primitive peoples now regard them as images of ancestors or of deities. The Ainu people cut a notch in them to represent the moon, and attach below the notch a small piece of charcoal that is just ceasing to glow (representing the heart). At the top they fasten strips of bast from the willow-tree to represent the long hair worn by the Ainu themselves. The worship of these poles is intelligible only if they were already regarded as higher beings. But there is a still more direct connexion between tree-worship and the wooden ear and lip plugs worn as amulets by many primitive peoples, especially the Botocudo, whose name is derived from this practice. And the same explanation applies to the belief cherished by various civilized peoples that the future can be foretold and hidden things revealed by the rustling of trees in the wind [3] and by the use of small wooden sticks in casting lots.

Every possible kind of animal is regarded as a higher being by both primitive and civilized peoples, and it is not always easy to give a reason in the various cases. Especially frequent is the worship of the snake, whose power of locomotion without feet, as well as its repeated sloughing of its skin, its fixed gaze, and its poisonous fangs, no doubt attracted special attention. Where a totem — very frequently an animal — belongs not to a group but to an individual, it too is regarded as a higher being, although totemism had

[3] Cf. 2 Sam. v, 24.

originally no religious significance. Among many civilized peoples the worship of animals gave rise to the belief that in some way or other they could deliver oracles, and it has led many primitive peoples to wear parts of animals as amulets.

Of the elements in the popular sense of the word (fire, water, air, and earth), fire especially is regarded by primitive men as a higher being. That needs no explanation, for many civilized peoples hold the same belief. This is especially true of the Persians (whose fire-worship will be discussed in a later chapter), but it is also true of many sections of the German people down to the present day. Natural as such a thing would be, water as such is not specially venerated by primitive men. Worship is reserved for certain manifestations of it — chiefly for fountains and springs; and several civilized peoples also regard these as higher beings. Still more frequent, alike among primitive and civilized peoples, is the worship of rivers. This is specially common among the Chinese and Indians, but it was also general not only among the Celts and the Slavs, but also among the ancient Germans, and has left traces there to this day in certain superstitious beliefs. The idea which still prevails that this or that stream demands sacrifices from time to time reflects a belief that was, to begin with, taken literally. Finally, the sea was regularly worshipped by numerous primitive peoples — occasionally by the Greeks and Romans — and is still so venerated by people on the coast of Palestine. The story of the ring of Polycrates and the practice that prevailed in Venice during the Middle Ages, when the Doge was wedded anew every year to the sea in order to regain its favour, are expressions of a similar feeling. These ideas regarding both water and fire are further reflected in the still prevalent belief that omens can be read in them. If fire burns brightly it indicates good fortune; when it emits smoke it portends misfortune. In the roaring of water human voices are heard. In water itself images are discerned that foretell the future, or when one has drunk of it he is believed to be able to give direct information regarding coming events.

We have already (*supra,* p. 8 ff.) spoken of the worship of the sky and of the sun by primitive men, and we saw that even in prehistoric time there was adoration of the sun and moon. In the custom of greeting the sun and moon at certain times we find an echo of this worship still, and the ancient veneration of the sky can yet be traced in the superstition that it is unlucky to point one's finger at it. The sky, sun, and moon were all three regarded as animate, just as primitive men regarded the already mentioned natural phenomena, beings, and objects as spirits. But before we consider this, the so-called 'animistic' view of the objects of religious faith, we must first look at the 'dynamistic' view — viz., that certain men are endowed with special supernatural powers.

Among many primitive peoples the chiefs, the priests, and magicians are so regarded, either because they themselves are believed to possess special powers or because they are in close touch with others who possess them.

Examples of this view are found in the once prevalent worship of the Mikado by the Japanese, of the Emperor of China by his subjects, and of the King by the ancient Persians. Just as the last-mentioned potentate could never go out on foot, or, if he did, must walk on a carpet which no other foot dare touch, and just as the clothing and the food utensils of the Mikado could never be used by anyone else, so the chiefs of many primitive peoples were and are surrounded by similar observances. These chiefs were believed to possess supernatural powers by virtue of which they could influence even the weather; these powers would, however, be forfeited if they were exposed to the gaze of others or if anyone else touched their clothing or their food utensils (into which their powers had passed) or stepped upon the floor or carpet which their feet had touched and to which their powers had thus been communicated. Another reason for these precautions was that their powers were regarded as too potent for other mortals and fatal to them. It is on record that a man who had unwittingly eaten what was left over from the meal of a New Zealand chief died of convulsions when he learned what he had done. If a native of Kisembo, in Angola, has of necessity touched the chief he lays the backs and palms of his hands four or five times on the backs and palms of the chief's hands, snapping his fingers each time in order to dispossess himself again of the powers communicated to him by the contact. In Tonga those who have touched the chief become charged with his uncanny powers, and must not touch even their own food, but must lap it from the ground or be fed by others. Evidently the act of eating does not count as touching the food, but they must not pick their own teeth — that also must be done for them by another. Whatever a chief has touched or trod upon becomes absolutely taboo, and fugitives who have taken refuge on any such spot find sanctuary there. It is remarkable, however, that these supernatural powers of the chief are not regarded as permanent. They are understood to have been withdrawn as soon as he begins to show signs of weakness. Nor is that all. After the lapse of a given time it is assumed that his powers have failed, and he is put to death. This noteworthy custom left traces among some civilized peoples to a comparatively late day. The Spartans believed that the fall of a meteor on a clear starry night at the end of the eighth year of a king's reign indicated that the monarch had sinned against the deity, and they suspended him until he was reponed by a Delphic or Olympian oracle. By the green lake at Nemi, in the Albanian hill-country, the priest-king always kept his sword in his hand, because he had good reason to fear that as he himself had killed his predecessor, so some other person would kill him. That is to say, he held his position only as long as he possessed sufficient physical strength to maintain it. In this case a priest is involved, and in many other places priests were and are believed to possess supernatural powers. But others besides priests are sometimes so regarded. For example, among the Toda the keepers of the Dairy, officials whom no other person may touch, and in whose presence their own fathers must prostrate themselves, give out oracles, and in Dutch Guiana toward the end of the nineteenth century a woman whose crippled legs bore some resemblance to serpents was for that reason regarded as a higher being. Similar instances are met with elsewhere.

As a matter of fact, however, *all* individuals are believed to be at certain times charged with supernatural powers, which they retain for a time. During that period they must live apart, and others must not approach them. In some places the newly born child and its mother must dwell for a time in the woods or in a special hut, which is afterward demolished, and in other places a person who is about to die is taken to such a hut. A death or a birth makes the usual dwelling taboo and therefore unfit for further use. A woman in childbed, like the man who has touched his chief, must not touch her food, and must therefore eat with the help of a small stick or fork. In some cases precautions are carried so far that others must not even see her. Before she can resume her place among others she must first dispossess herself of the powers with which she has been for the time endowed.

The peculiar custom known as the *couvade,* or 'the father brought to bed,' probably also rests on the belief that the birth of a child to a man puts him in possession of supernatural powers. This custom seems to be followed in Africa, and it is certainly common in Southern India, China, and Central and South America. It was also known among the Tibarenes in the Caucasus, the Ligurians in Corsica, and the Iberians in Spain. When a child is born the mother returns to her toil, while the *father* takes to his bed or to his hammock, and refrains from bathing until he wishes to return to his ordinary way of life.

The attainment of puberty is also attributed to similar powers, and therefore at that time young people go into retirement. In some places they may not even touch their food. That is probably because such contact would communicate the powers to the food, whence in turn they would be imparted to the young people, and be too potent for them. These young people are further forbidden to scratch themselves lest they should in this way dispossess themselves of the powers, or to walk on roads used by others lest the powers should thus be communicated to these others, to their hurt. Similar restrictions are laid down for women during their menstrual periods, which are also referred to the same powers. After such a period is over women must bathe, and the like regulation applies to young people when the time of attaining puberty is past.

Finally, those who have been in contact with the dead, especially those who have killed or buried them, become thereby charged with power and come under similar restrictions. Among the Agutainos on Palawan, one of the Philippines, a widow has to stay indoors for seven or eight days, and must not be seen by others for a further period. If she goes out she must warn others of her approach by rapping with a stick against the trees as she passes, and the trees thus touched are believed to wither away. On this same island a widow, and in other places all mourners, must bathe previous to the resumption of relations with other people.

Civilized peoples who also practise these restrictions speak of them as rites of purification, and regard the antecedent condition as uncleanness. This implies that they draw a contrast between the deities whom they wor-

ship and the powers of which we have been speaking. But even these peoples must have originally believed in the existence of such powers — otherwise all these practices would be unintelligible. As far back as the dual system of civilization based on mother-right the objects worshipped included the souls or spirits of the human beings to whom worship was paid. On certain occasions the King of the Matabele worships his own soul; the Pharaoh of Egypt worshipped his own *ka;* and among the Romans not only did each individual worship his own *genius,* but the dependents of a household paid homage to that of the master of the house, and at a later time the *genius* of the Emperor was worshipped by his subjects generally. We need not speak of the other souls or spirits which are assumed to exist in the objects of adoration and to which alone actual worship is paid, but we cannot omit to mention those spirits which, although they are supposed to be invisible, are depicted in human form. While they are represented in the crouching posture, they are not con-

FIG. 20. NAIL FETISH FROM LOANGO
From Sydow, " Kunst der Naturvölker "

ceived as resembling the dead; a *motif* has been borrowed from the dead and applied to the spirits in question. But

these figures, like the idols in civilized religions, are in many cases themselves regarded as higher beings, and are therefore sometimes subjected to rough usage and disrespectful treatment. That is the idea underlying the so-called nail fetishes (Fig. 20). Attached to the body of the fetish is a small box containing a •supernatural substance. By means of nails and pieces of iron hammered into its image the spirit is supposed to be brought into subjection to the will of the worshipper. Probably there is also sometimes involved the idea of an intensified destructive magic. An enemy or an illness can, it is thought, be got rid of by thinking of him or it while hammering in a nail, and success is all the more certain if this is hammered into a fetish.

There is also a rain magic, but, like destructive magic, it contains n o religious element, and therefore need not be enlarged upon here. It too is believed to have more certain success if it is performed in the presence of a fetish. The masks and d i s g u i s e s (Fig. 21) which, as we have seen, are used to represent not only the spirits of the departed, but other spirits also, serve strictly magical purposes. They produce the same helpful or injurious effects as the spirits themselves, and therefore both spirits and effects are represented by the masks. The spirits were originally believed actually to partake of the sacrifices presented to t h e m , and therefore among the Indians and some other peoples these sacrifices consisted of tobacco, and among the East Yaks of snuff, with the addition of peeled willow-bark to p l u g

FIG. 21. DISGUISES OR MASKS FROM NEW BRITAIN
From Danzel, " Kultur und Religion des Primitiven Menschen "

the nostrils. Frequently, however, primitive as well as civilized peoples offer sacrifices merely as signs of homage, although, as we shall see immediately, a special original conception is found later.

In the later primitive civilizations, side by side with spirits that are mostly conceived as pluralities and as generic beings, there are actual deities who are regarded as individuals, and who therefore bear proper names. They manifest themselves also in certain natural phenomena, or control definite spheres — sometimes more than one. In many cases one deity is regarded as the highest, and is conceived after the fashion of those originators of which we have already spoken, or is regarded as a creative deity. This con-

ception sometimes finds expression in the representations of them. Human beings constitute their ears, eyes, nose, and mouth, and are also distributed over their bodies (Fig. 22). The worship paid to them is practically the same as that paid to the spirits; but, as we have just hinted, the sacrifices offered to them perhaps serve another purpose, and in some cases are not sacrifices at all.

The Mexicans, for example, in whose religion human sacrifices played a large part (although perhaps not so large as later Spanish historians claim), cut out the heart of the human victim and offered it to the deity. The process is actually illustrated in Mexican manuscripts (Fig. 23). The original conception was that such a sacrifice fortified the deity — human life had its seat in the heart. But it should be added that the same procedure was also followed on occasions where all idea of sacrifice was absent.

Just as it was supposed that the supernatural powers of a king gradually became exhausted, so the annual withering and regrowth of vegetation was interpreted as the death and rebirth of a deity. Indeed, it was believed that the change of the seasons could be brought about only by killing the god of vegetation. He was put to death both to prevent him from dying of old age, and to utilize his power further either for one's own benefit or for that of another.

FIG. 22. STATUE FROM THE AUSTRAL ISLANDS

From Vatter, " Religiöse Plastik der Naturvölker "

Every year in Mexico the image of a deity was made of dough mixed with the blood of children. The priest shot an arrow through its heart — *i.e.,* the deity was symbolically killed — and then the image was eaten by the people. (Originally this rite must have been carried out with an actual human victim, just as in the cults of other Mexican deities human beings were killed at least once every year.) The skins of the male or female representatives of still other deities were put on other human beings, who were destined to play the part of sacrificial victims the year following. Among the Muysca such a human representative of deity was slain every five years, but this was merely a mitigated form of a former rite.

Similar mitigations a r e met with elsewhere. This rite of slaying the god of fertility in the person of a human victim is found among civilized races of the Old World, and it is impossible to believe that such a remarkable and peculiar practice can h a v e arisen independently at different places so far apart. As the first known attestation of it in America dates from the beginning of modern times, I believe that it first arose in the Old World, and that while in other cases primitive

FIG. 23. MEXICAN HUMAN SACRIFICE
From Danzel, " Kultur und Religion der Primitiven Menschen "

conceptions have left their impress on civilized religions, here we have an instance in which civilized religions have given rise to a practice among primitive men. It occurs only in advanced primitive civilizations, although, as has already been admitted, it is difficult to explain how such an influence could have been exerted.

BIBLIOGRAPHY

Réville, *Les Religions des peuples non civilisés* (1883); Brinton, *Religions of Primitive Peoples* (1898); Le Roy, *La Religion des primitives* (1909; 3rd ed., 1911); Nilsson, *Primitive Religion* (1911); Lowie, *Primitive Religion;* Tylor, *Primitive Culture* (3 vols., 1871; 5th ed., 1913); Visscher, *Religion und soziales Leben bei den Naturvölkern* (2 vols., 1911); Graebner, *Das Weltbild der Primitiven* (1924); Danzel, *Kultur und Religion des Primitiven Menschen* (1924). Primitive religion is also discussed in the general works, which should also be consulted for the chapters that follow: Chantepie de la Saussaye, *Lehrbuch der Religionsgeschichte* (2 vols., 1887 and 1889; 4th ed., 1926); von Orelli, *Allgemeine Religionsgeschichte* (1899; 2nd. ed., 2 vols., 1911 and 1913); S. Reinach, *Orphée* (1909); Turchi, *Manuale di storia delle religioni* (1912; 2nd ed., 1922); Huby, *Christus* (1913; 2nd ed., 1923); Moore, *History of Religions* (2 vols., 1914 and 1919); Jeremias, *Allgemeine Religionsgeschichte* (1918; 2nd ed., 1924); Richter, *Die Religionen der Völker* (1923); Lehmann, *Die Religionen* (1924).

III. ANCIENT NATIONAL RELIGIONS

1. BABYLONIAN RELIGION

by *Albert Schott*

The monuments from which we derive our knowledge of the Babylonian religion cover a period of something like three thousand years — from 3500 to 500 B.C. It is obvious that any account of such a long-lived religion cannot be true even to the leading features unless it conforms to the historical method, which, however, for various reasons it is still far from easy to follow.

Of the numerous ruined sites where remains of the ancient communities of that time lie buried comparatively few have been excavated and made accessible to expert investigation, and the material thus brought to light and examined represents only a number of more or less fortuitous relics of bygone religious activities.

Further, the peoples who professed the religion with which we are now concerned were probably at all periods in constant intercourse with their neighbours. These included the Elamites in the east, the Hittites in the north-west, and kindred Semitic tribes and the Egyptians in the west and south-west. We may certainly assume that such intercourse, even although it may not have been at all times equally active, was accompanied by an exchange of religious ideas. But, important and decisive as the reciprocal effects of this exchange must have been on the religious life of the time, it is meantime rarely possible to show what they were or even to determine their direction and extent.

This difficulty is in large measure due to the fact that our knowledge of the religion of some of these peoples — *e.g.*, of the Hittites and, to a still larger degree, of the Elamites — is still very imperfect. Further, the decipherment of the languages is still far from complete, although the Accadian language, the common mother-tongue of the Babylonians and Assyrians, now presents no great difficulties.

But even if we agree to leave out of account the connexions that must have existed between the Babylonian religion and the religions of adjacent peoples, it is still a task of extreme difficulty to write a history of it. Our knowledge of the Babylonian religion is chiefly derived from epic and lyric poetry, exorcisms, and instructions for the conduct of public worship, but the copies in which these have been handed down rarely enable us to determine the period to which the writings belong.

On the other hand, the age of most of the extant inscriptions by which the kings of Babylonia and Assyria sought to commemorate their achievements in peace or in war is known. And the economic and legal documents of ancient Mesopotamia contain information that nearly always enables us to assign them to definite dates. In view of the important part played by religion in the public and domestic life of Mesopotamian peoples, these monuments and documents throw much light upon many of the moving forces and conceptions of contemporary religious life. Our present task is, with the aid of these accurately dated writings, to arrange in order the conceptions and modes of expression that were peculiar to each period of Babylonian religion, and then to trace these conceptions in those religious writings whose age has been till now unknown. In this way we can gradually lay bare the history of the Babylonian religion so far as it has come down to us in written tradition.

Next to the literature, the plastic art of the Babylonians and Assyrians, which deals almost exclusively with religious subjects, is an important source of our knowledge of Babylonian religion. Fortunately, the age of most of the products of Mesopotamian plastic art is definitely known, because they contain inscriptions of those kings on whose initiative they were made. Occasionally, of course, it is still impossible to make out with certainty the objects and events which are represented. This is particularly the case with the seal cylinders. An immense number of remarkable figures are found on these cylinders — figures probably of demigods and deities — but unfortunately many of them contain no indication of their date, especially when they lack any inscription.

These preliminary remarks may serve to indicate the nature of the difficulties with which all research into the history of Babylonian religion has to reckon. They will also make it clear that this study is still in its infancy. Our present sketch of Babylonian religion can therefore claim to be only a brief statement of what is at present known, and it is possible that the near future will clear up much that is still obscure and supply much that is lacking.

As far as we can at present see, the most ancient representatives of religious life in Mesopotamia were the non-Semitic Sumerians, who lived on the lower reaches of the Euphrates and the Tigris. They invented (before 3000 B.C.) cuneiform writing, which was used by them and — both simultaneously and subsequently — by numerous peoples in Nearer Asia. One of the principal uses of this script was to hand down the religious writings. A Sumerian prince, Lugalzaggisi of Uruk (before 2700 B.C.), united many small Sumerian city-states under his own sway, and thus inaugurated the long series of Nearer Asiatic Great Powers, whose importance for the development and expansion of Babylonian religion can hardly be over-estimated.

From the most ancient times onward the civil law of the Nearer Asiatic peoples was promulgated in the form of religious formulas. Already in the centuries previous to Lugalzaggisi each city was regarded as belonging to a definite deity, whose 'representative' the ruler of the time felt himself called to be. It was at the behest of his city-god that a Sumerian ruler over-threw his neighbours; at the same behest he concluded peace with them. Accordingly, when he succeeded in conquering a city his own city-god was regarded as having overcome the god of that city. It may, indeed, have been these incessant feuds between Sumerian princes that brought at an early time the worship of some gods into more than one city, or even ex-tended it over the whole country. For example, Enlil of Nippur and his consort Ninhursag, Enki of Eridu, and later Nanna of Ur and Utu of Larsa probably enjoyed greater honour in most cities than the local city-gods. Lugalzaggisi, however, acquired for Anu, the god of his new capital Uruk, the supreme place in the Sumerian pantheon, and similar happenings took place more than once in after days.

Many of the same deities who thus presided over political events were also believed to be at work in the phenomena of nature. For example, Enlil (at least in the earlier period) was regarded as the lord of the atmosphere, Anu as the ruler of the sky; Enki was the god of fresh water; Enzu and Utu were the gods of the moon (or the sun). It is important to notice, how-ever, that the gods were not identified with the natural phenomena; they were always understood to be rather the exalted guiding powers of the world and of its component parts. Further proof of this is found in the fact that the images of the gods of Mesopotamia are, practically without exception, purely human in form (but see p. 51). The occasional occur-rence of metaphorical names for gods, like 'bull' and others, does not in-validate this statement.

Of the female deities, some ranked far below the gods whose consorts they were supposed to be, and these were of comparatively little impor-tance in the religious life. Others, however, were held in high esteem, some of them being actually city-goddesses, like Namašše (or Ninâ) in Lagaš, while others were mother-goddesses, like Baba (Gatumdag) and Ninhursag (Ninlil). Prayers were offered to Ninni (called in Accadian Ištar), and Nidaba, the city-goddess of Umma, was a goddess of wisdom.

Various sagas symbolize the activities of the gods in nature. The annual decay of vegetation was symbolized in the saga of the youthful god Tammuz, a lover of Ištar, who was the goddess of love as well as of war. It is still uncertain whether *all* the Sumerian (and Babylonian) sagas of the gods were at bottom allegories of the processes of nature.

The intercourse of men with the gods was variously conceived. The gods might either reveal themselves to men in dreams and visions or commune with them through the mediation of priests and priestesses of various ranks. Kings or their relatives also frequently held exalted priestly offices. The large majority of the rulers boast that they have built splendid temples to the gods and laid rich offerings on their shrines. To express their feelings of humility toward the gods many rulers caused themselves to be depicted in the act of taking part with their own hands in the building of a temple (Fig. 24). On the other hand, kings were understood to stand nearer to the gods than other mortals. Numerous rulers called themselves the children of some definite deity — indeed, some rulers of the third millennium claimed equality with the gods, and others even asserted their right to be called gods. This extreme claim was, of course, made only by those kings who ruled over a vast realm and whose domains included some outstandingly important temple city. (The case would be quite different if, as seems probable, it was believed that the personality of a king either in his lifetime or after his death could be immortalized in a statue, and if the gifts offered to these statues in the temple were believed to infuse life into them.

FIG. 24. UR-NAMAŠŠE, THE PRINCE OF LAGAŠ
(c. 2900 B.C.)

He is carrying in a basket the foundation stone for the temple.

From Meissner, " Babylonien und Assyrien "

But even this practice does not imply that the king was regarded as divine.) For example, Eannatum of Lagaš (c. 2800 B.C.), after having conquered Kiš, where there was a highly venerated sanctuary of the goddess Ninni, calls himself the "beloved spouse" of that goddess, and toward the end of the third millennium several rulers acted in a similar manner. As a rule the possession of Nippur, the sacred temple city of Enlil, was considered to be a prerequisite for a king's claim to deification. Narâmsîn of Accad, a king of Semitic lineage (of the twenty-sixth century B.C.), who had received a mighty empire from his predecessors, was the first who wrote his name with the divine symbol ✻, and numerous rulers of the twenty-second and twenty-first centuries did the same. Narâmsîn's famous monument of victory (Fig. 25) shows the king with a crown of horns, an ornament which only gods were supposed to wear.

Similar conditions are indicated in the epic of Gilgameš, but this must not be understood to determine anything regarding the date of this poem, which is the most outstanding literary product of the cuneiform period. It is a heroic lay, of truly royal greatness and genuine philosophic depth, which seeks to solve the eternal problem of the relation between men and the gods. Gilgameš is described as two-thirds divine. Only one-third is human, but this renders him mortal like all other men, and his mortality is unaffected by the fact that he contracts marriage with a goddess. All his efforts are directed to the performance of deeds that will outlive him and make his name immortal. He clings to his purpose in despite of the people and of the gods, neither of whom can approve his ambition. His contempt for the gods finds expression in serious crimes, which he commits with the aid of his only friend, Engidu. To punish the pair the gods contrive the death of Engidu. Now for the first time Gilgameš exhibits fear of death, and sets out on a journey of adventure in search of eternal life. He fails, and returns home bereft of all hope. The gods show him no mercy (with the exception of Ea, who appears in other legends also as well disposed toward men), but his pride remains unbroken. The poem presents the gods in an unfavourable light. Their behaviour is marked by injustice, caprice, vacillation, self-sufficiency, and voluptuousness, whereas the super-man, Gilgameš, is loyal, truth-loving, and full of a tireless zeal for action. It is prob-

FIG. 25. NARÂMSÎN, THE VICTORIOUS KING OF ACCAD (*c.* 2570 B.C.)
Depicted as a god.
From Unger, " Sumerische und Akkadische Kunst "

ably in this epic that the Promethean spirit first appears in human history, embodied in a figure of imperishable, tragic dignity. An increasing number of scholars are recognizing that this same subject-matter reappears in numerous sagas and folk-tales that are current to this day, especially in stories that have been woven round the names of outstanding religious heroes. The fact that we possess at least four Accadian versions of this

poem, as well as two in the Hittite and one in the Hurrite language, testifies
to the high esteem and widespread popularity which this work enjoyed in
Nearer Asia in ancient times.

It is worthy of special notice that Gilgameš shows profound reverence
toward the god Lugalbanda and also toward the sun-god. That is because
Lugalbanda was the tutelary deity of the kings of Uruk (he is not to be
confused with Anu, the sovereign lord and guardian deity of the *city* of
Uruk), and because as far back as the earliest Sumerian era every royal
dynasty of Lagaš had its own tutelary deity, to whom all the rulers felt
themselves more closely bound than to the mighty gods of the land or even
to the very important city-god. The guardian deity was looked upon as the
mediator between the city-god and the King (see Fig. 26). In any case, these

FIG. 26. GUDEA, PRINCE OF LAGAŠ (*c.* 2300 B.C.)
He is being led by his tutelary deity, Ningišzida, into
the presence of the city-god Ningirsu.
From Unger, " Sumerische und Akkadische Kunst "

domestic gods, perhaps just
because intercourse with them
was so intimate, rarely appear
in any official inscriptions of
the time other than those connected with Lagaš. It would
seem, however, that in Mesopotamia in the early Sumerian
period every one was believed
to have his own guardian god
(or goddess). This is attested
for a somewhat later time in
the numerous proper names
compounded with ' my god '
which were used in addressing the deity. It may be mentioned in passing
that the worship of these tutelary deities greatly increased in the course of
the centuries.

Toward the end of the third millennium the Sumerians were absorbed
into the Semitic empire which had been extending and consolidating its
power in Mesopotamia from the time of Sargon of Accad, the Semitic conqueror and successor of Lugalzaggisi of Uruk (see p. 42). The Sumerian
language seems to have survived only as a dignified medium for the expression of religious thought — like Latin in Western Christendom.

The last days of the Sumerian race coincided with a time when Mesopotamia was rent by civil wars. A foreigner, the powerful Elamite prince
Rîm-Sîn, ended this state of affairs by incorporating a large tract of the
contending territories into his own domains. He met his master, however, in
Hammurabi (1955–13). This king, the scion of a young royal dynasty, rescued Semitic Mesopotamia from the foreign Elamite dominion, unified it,
and made Babylon, which had hitherto been of little importance, the capital
of the new empire.

To this outstanding feat of martial genius and statesmanship Hammurabi added a brilliant achievement in the sphere of theology. Utilizing the numerous beginnings that had been made toward transforming the city deities into universally recognized gods (see p. 43), he gathered all the Sumerian and Babylonian deities into a comprehensive pantheon. With great sagacity he took measures for the preservation of the local places of worship. The celebrated catalogue of these holy places, with their gods and goddesses, which is contained in the introduction to his famous law code (Fig. 27) shows a carefully thought-out regard for the precedence of various deities, and bears witness to his extremely delicate respect for the religious views that were traditional among the peoples of Mesopotamia. Especially skilful is the stroke by which he sets Marduk, the hitherto unimportant city-god of Babylon, in the exalted position that had previously been held by Anu and Enlil. He declares that Anu and Enlil have handed over to Marduk the dominion over all peoples, and given him a leading place among the gods. In the eyes of his contemporaries this theology and the actual political position — both of which were his own creations — fully justified each other.

FIG. 27. HAMMURABI, KING OF BABYLON (TWENTIETH CENTURY B.C.), RECEIVING HIS LAW FROM THE SUN-GOD ŠAMAŠ

From Jeremias, " Das Alte Testament im Lichte des alten Orients "

We may mention at this point two writings which, judging from their linguistic peculiarities, belong to or near to Hammurabi's time. They contain a large collection of cup or goblet vaticinations. A priest of the exalted guild of soothsayers, of whom we also hear from other sources, both in Hammurabi's time and later, has to pour oil on water in a bowl, and to foretell coming events according to the shapes assumed by the oil. Apparently, however, it was not till a later time that such inquiries into the will of the gods were systematically made in this and in other ways.

Hammurabi had thus brought both his empire and its religion into a remarkably compact form, and amalgamated the two in very thorough fashion. But when, in the days of a much less vigorous descendant, his empire collapsed before the attack of the Hittites and the Kassites his religious institutions also inevitably fell into disruption.

A Kassite dynasty, which ere long successfully adapted itself to its Babylonian environment, now reigned over Babylonia from 1746–1171 — that is to say, for more than five hundred years. Of the condition of religion during the first half of this period we know next to nothing. King Agum II (c.

1600 B.C.) declares that he has rescued the images of the divine spouses
Marduk and Sarpânîtum from the hands of barbarian robbers, restored them
to Babylon, and repaired their sanctuaries.[1] He prefaces the inscription with
a notable catalogue of the gods, which agrees in all essentials with the
list made by Hammurabi. At the head of this otherwise purely Babylonian
catalogue, however, Agum places the Kassite deity Šukamuna; this is
the first instance of the adoption of foreign deities into the Babylonian
pantheon. It is an indication also that that pantheon was on the point of
dissolution.

In the period from 1350 to 1250 we find again and again that the names
of Kassite kings, when they occur in legal or economic documents, are
preceded by the divine symbol ❋. The religious meaning of this practice
is doubtful, because no recognizable rule is followed. Perhaps it is merely
due to the caprice of obsequious writers. In any case, the kings of that
time never write their names in their own inscriptions with the symbol
of deity.

Some information regarding the religious conditions in the later Kassite
period (from c. 1300 B.C. onward) and in the centuries that followed it is
found in the so-called kudurrus. These are chiselled duplicates of documents
giving details of the gifts made by the king to his subjects. The same period
has also left us economic texts which are important for our purpose because
of the numerous proper names that occur in them. In keeping with the usual
Mesopotamian practice, most of these names are derived from names of gods.
Lastly, we now know that about 1400 B.C. Babylonia had begun to cultivate
a more or less regular commerce with Egypt, Assyria, the Hittite empire, and
other countries — i.e., with all the civilized Great Powers of the day — and
to this must be added her frequent, though largely hostile, intercourse with
her Elamite neighbours. When we keep in mind the close and intricate
connexions that had grown up between political and religious life, we can
understand that this widening of the horizon and this increase of intercourse
could not fail to have decisive effects on Babylonian religion. Recent investigation goes to show that it is probably to this same later Kassite period
that we owe not only the Maklu and the Šurpu, the two celebrated collections
of incantations, exorcisms of evil spirits, etc., but also a large number of
religious documents of a similar nature.

These are the sources from which the following account of Babylonian
religion during the second half of the second millennium B.C. has been
gathered, but it should again be carefully remembered that the account
here given of this period represents only the present state of our knowledge.

---

[1] Theft of images of the gods is attested repeatedly in ancient Mesopotamia. The thieves
probably believed that possession of the foreign image would give them power over the god
in question, and therefore over his city. Perhaps also they did not clearly differentiate between
the god and the image.

When once Babylonian religious thought had crossed its own frontiers the immediate and inevitable result was that the lands outside these frontiers were recognized as being independent of the power of the Babylonian gods. This meant that the hitherto undoubted omnipotence of the Babylonian pantheon now began to be questioned. In view of this new situation, the Babylonian priests realized the necessity of becoming acquainted with all the conceivable powers in the universe and their effects, in order to have them as far as possible under their control.

It is only in this way that we can explain the extraordinary diversity of the powers — both friendly and hostile to man — that are addressed in the exorcisms and incantations. Foreign gods are named side by side with native gods; city gods and land-gods of ancient renown are enumerated in lengthy lists along with gods of unimportant places; sometimes, even, appeals are addressed to an ancient god-man like Gilgameš. A special and important part is now played by all kinds of evil spirits (spirits of the dead, etc.), and the aid of the good gods and good spirits is entreated against them. Human sorcerers and witches are credited with the sinister power of injuring their fellow-men in body and soul by means of incantations, magic, and the evil eye.

FIG. 28. DEMON HEAD

From Jeremias, " Das Alte Testament im Lichte des alten Orients"

It was probably from popular superstition that the priests borrowed this belief in the evil activities of magicians and demons, and they did this only when they became anxious to obtain an exhaustive knowledge of all the efficient powers in the universe. The demons were represented as creatures in animal shape (see Fig. 28 and Fig. 29, second row of figures). To many minds, however, this conception seemed far too definite to include all the imaginable and unimaginable forms in which evil could be embodied. They therefore conceived the idea of combining seven evil spirits to form a unit, the 'evil seven,' and to this they attributed all the evil in heaven and on earth. This 'evil seven' fills a large space in the religious literature of the time. It is evidence of the widened environment of that period that this sevenfold deity — who, strangely enough, was also regarded as a protective deity — was occasionally identified with the seven principal gods of the Elamites. Mention is also made of a sister of theirs, Narudu by name, who was probably an Elamite goddess. (Perhaps Narudu was regarded as an adversary of the lion-headed female demon Labartu, who is shown in the lowest row of figures in Fig. 29). On the other hand, exorcisms were addressed to evil women by whom people thought themselves bewitched. These exorcisms began with the words " Women of Elam, Sutû, Lulubu, Hanigalbat [etc.] . . . ," all these being names of countries outside Babylonia, the intention apparently being to include the entire genus of witches, conjunctly and severally.

The fear of the incalculable, malignant attacks of numberless evil spirits, always and everywhere on the watch to do hurt, could not fail to awaken in anxious hearts the longing for a reliable, powerful, and watchful comrade and protector. The guardian deity already mentioned (p. 46) seemed fitted to meet this need, and as a matter of fact the expression 'my god' now occurs in proper names more frequently than in earlier times. In the formulas of exorcism and incantation complaints are constant that the suppliants have been forsaken by 'their god.' The unhappy souls ascribe this to the fact that they have displeased him, or that evil spirits have prejudiced him against them. Evidently it was now believed that evil spirits could take up their abode in a man and do him hurt.

FIG. 29. RELIEF ILLUSTRATING THE PRACTICE
OF EXORCISM

From Meissner, " Babylonien und Assyrien "

The great importance ascribed to sorcery in all cases of human misfortune or illness is best shown by a text which is found in the collection known as Šurpu (see p. 48). Here Marduk, who from the time of Hammurabi was incontestably the most powerful deity in all Mesopotamia, fills the *rôle* of a sorcerer saviour who has been sent by his father Ea to the help of man. (It should be said, however, that it is uncertain whether this text really belongs to the period before us. It is in two languages, Sumerian and Accadian, and the former had become extinct long before the later Kassite period.)

Naturally these graphic conceptions appealed more strongly to the common people than did the ancient, official, priestly faith in the gods. Every addition to the number of the gods must have confused the minds and taxed the memories of simple people. Even the priests would in course of time have lost count of the deities in their pantheon if they had not taken measures to draw up a catalogue of the gods. Lists of deities had already been begun in the late Sumerian period, but such enumeration was more in keeping with the fondness of the Kassite period for the exhaustive collection and orderly arrangement of all existing material. The Šurpu and many of the *kudurrus* (p. 48) contain numerous lists of this kind though many of them disagree with each other. Efforts were of course made to remove these inconsistencies and produce a fixed and comprehensive catalogue in which the gods were arranged so as to exhibit their complicated relationships to each other. The adjustment of these lists shows careful sifting on the part of the priests, but their labours in this direction show little trace of living religious power.

This purely academic conception of the gods is also reflected in the way in which they are depicted on the *kudurrus*. In the pre-Kassite period the individual gods, when they were not otherwise recognizable by their activities, were distinguished from each other by a traditional distinctive badge, which was depicted as growing out of their shoulders. For example, Ningišzida had dragon heads (see Fig. 26); Šamaš had sunbeams (see Fig. 27). On the *kudurrus*, however, the deity was omitted altogether, and *only* the distinctive badge was shown (see Fig. 30). Thus the crescent moon indicated Sîn (the Sumerian Enzu); the eight-rayed star indicated Ištar, who was, *inter alia,* the goddess of the constellation Venus (*cf.* p. 43); the rayed disk indicated Šamaš (the

FIG. 30. KUDURRU OF THE KASSITE KING MELI-ŠIPAK II OF BABYLON (TWELFTH CENTURY B.C.)

From Unger, " Sumerische und Akkadische Kunst "

Sumerian Utu); the two divine headdresses set on thrones meant Anu and Enlil; and the goat-fish indicated Ea (the Sumerian Enki). Similar methods of distinguishing different deities are found on later Assyrian inscriptions and on exorcism reliefs (see Fig. 29, the top row of figures, but compare Fig. 25).

Soothsaying also was 'scientifically' cultivated during this period. Comprehensive lists were made of the results of the examination of entrails and

of observation of the constellations and of reports concerning miscarriages —
all showing unmistakably the attempt to reach some intelligible system. Each
result has appended to it a vaticination. All sorts of absurdities were gravely
considered, and the oddest relationships were boldly asserted to exist between
the things in the universe.

Remarkable also is the odd use of numbers, each deity being duly 'ticketed'
with a number. The number assigned to the moon-god was 30; 20 was that
of the sun. This practice was carried so far that instead of Sîn they wrote
✳ ⟨⟨⟨ and instead of Šamaš ✳ ⟨⟨ (⟨ = 10).

The widening of knowledge in the Kassite period and the mental elaboration and digestion of the new knowledge proceeded in two opposite directions. One of these led to the perfecting of a very superficial system of magic
and incantation, whose adherents believed that with these aids they could
ward off any form of disaster and alleviate illness or grief. (See Fig. 29,
second row of figures, where two priests in fish-like attire are exorcising
illness from a sick man.) But concealed in this system were the germs of
something quite different and far more significant. For one thing, it was
this same longing for a complete knowledge of the world and its powers that
produced the later Babylonian science; and, further, some important exorcism
texts show that Babylonian moral philosophy was now rising to a new
and higher stage. Even at an earlier period the gods, especially Šamaš, were
looked upon as the guardians of justice and law (Fig. 27) and as the avengers
of injustice and crime. The second table of the collection Šurpu gives an
extremely comprehensive list of all the offences likely to call down the divine
wrath. Some of these are juridical, but others are of a kind that no state law
can reach — that is to say, they are not crimes, but sins. Perhaps we see here
the birth of a new conception. The Egyptians have a similar 'catalogue of
sins' in the hundred and twenty-fifth chapter of their *Book of the Dead*.
That is all the more remarkable because the worship of Šamaš, which like
the worship of Marduk and Ea, was intricately connected with the system
of exorcism, produced truly poetical songs of praise to the sun-god closely
resembling the Egyptian hymns from Tell el Amarna, especially the hymn
of praise to Amenhotep IV (fourteenth century). It almost looks as if in the
second millennium B.C. there existed not only political and commercial intercourse, but also currents of religious thought and feeling connecting the
valley of the Nile with Mesopotamia.

In Babylonia the belief prevailed in some periods or perhaps at all times
that a man could move his guardian deity to anger by sins and crimes.
But as time went on this conception developed further. The desire to know
all things introduced into religious thought in every direction the conception
of the unknown. The magic texts speak not only of witches and wizards who
are known, but also of others who are unknown. The exorcism texts make
mention of unconscious sins, and in particular we constantly meet with
appeals addressed to the unknown god and the unknown goddess. That these

ideas reflect a deeply felt religious need is proved by the passionate language of the *Penitential Psalms to every God.*

But belief in the power and righteousness of the well-known gods of old no longer stood on a firm foundation. We possess a poem (probably from the second half of the second millennium) which recalls the ' dances of the dead' familiar in the Western world during the Middle Ages. It describes how the 'evil seven' urge Era, the god of pestilence, to seize the dominion over Babylon and over the whole earth. By a stratagem Era mounts the throne of Marduk, and then a terrible pestilence lays low man and beast, old and young, male and female, pious and sinful, amid the overwhelming horrors of suffering and death. Not until Era sees the expiring gods grovel-

FIG. 31. PROCESSION OF ASSYRIAN GODS

From a rock wall near Maltaja, showing the King (Sennacherib, *c.* 700 B.C.), Ašúr, Ninlil, Anu (?), Sîn, Šamaš, Adad, Ištar, the King.
From " Revue d'Assyriologie," vol. xxi

ling at his feet is his lust of dominion satiated and is he moved to lay aside his wrath. The sombre tone of this *Lay of Era,* the power and majesty of its descriptions, its elevation of language, reveal a great poet. His veiled contempt for the universally accepted views of the relationship between gods and men shows that he had the courage to follow out his thoughts to the end, without, however, disparaging the true reverence due to the divine powers.

In the second half of the second millennium the Babylonian state had lost all its former power. About 1250 B.C. Babylon was conquered by the Assyrians, a younger branch of the Babylonian people, under the leadership of an energetic king. The Assyrians did not retain their conquest long, but till their empire fell their kings unceasingly strove to maintain a powerful influence over Babylon; ultimately that proved impossible, in face of the great power Babylon had acquired in the religious life of Mesopotamia. Indeed, Assyria itself, lying far to the north, could not, even during the time when it had full command over the political fate of Babylon, escape the strong religious influences exerted by that city.

FIG. 32. ASSUR AS GOD
OF WAR

Cf. the winged sun-disk in Fig. 29 (top row of figures). *From Morris Jastrow, " Die Religion Babyloniens und Assyriens "*

Throughout their whole existence as an empire (2100–600 B.C.) the Assyrians entertained the same anthropomorphic conceptions of the gods as were held by the Babylonians. (See Fig. 31.) Ašur, the city-god of the capital, was the god of war (Fig. 32). That is not to be wondered at in view of the martial qualities of the Assyrians. Next to Ašur, the gods Anu, Adad (see Figs. 31 and 33), Sîn, Šamaš, and Ninurtu enjoyed the highest honours. Ištar, especially in her character as goddess of war, was highly revered in Assyria.

In the first half of the fourteenth century B.C. we hear for the first time of a temple of Marduk in Assyria — a proof of the increasing religious influence of Babylon, which, as has already been shown, led to the conquest of the city. The religious influence of Babylonia on Assyria, however, does

FIG. 33. ASSYRIAN TEMPLE WITH STEPPED TOWERS, DEDICATED TO ANU AND ADAD
Twelfth century B.C. Attempted reconstruction by Andrae.
From Meissner, " Babylonien und Assyrien "

not seem to have lasted to any strong degree beyond the ninth century. Of all the new thought of which we have spoken there are only a few traces in the Assyrian royal inscriptions. These include occasional allusions to the *Lay of Era*. Also in the ninth century we find the name of Marduk in a list of Assyrian deities, and we know that Shalmaneser III of Assyria (859–825), after occupying Babylon, offered sacrifice to the gods of the captured city. But too much stress should not be laid on this last fact, because it is an example of a practice that was frequently followed. (Compare, however, p. 48.)

On the other hand, for the middle of the eighth century it is from Assyrian royal inscriptions that our knowledge of the history of Babylonian religion is derived. (We have almost no Babylonian inscriptions.) They frequently mention by name Babylonian religious poems and imitate their style, but it is possible that what in Babylonia were genuine religious utterances had in Assyria come to be a matter of fashion or diplomacy or even of literary appreciation.

The despairing sense of sin expressed in the *Penitential Psalms to every God* (which has already been mentioned — p. 53) reappears in the beautiful poem of *The Innocent Righteous Man,* but there it is purified by the clear and distinct conception of deliverance. This same idea, though not so profoundly grasped, had already been hinted at in the collection Šurpu and in similar texts of earlier centuries (*cf.* p. 50). In the poem of *The Innocent Righteous Man,* as in the Book of Job, overwhelming misfortunes overtake a righteous man. In his sickness and helplessness he is despised and forsaken by all, but he retains his unshaken faith in the divine wisdom. In the end he finds deliverance.

Although here and there mention is made of ' gods ' (in the plural), and although some of these are even mentioned by name, the poem shows a great advance from the polytheism of the ancient Babylonian period; indeed, it comes very little short of a faith in *one* god of infinite knowledge, power, and goodness. The poet addresses this deity as " my god " or " my goddess " — probably an echo of the ancient idea of a guardian deity — but he also speaks simply of " [a] god " or " [a] goddess."

There are lists belonging to the first half of the first millennium containing, *inter alia,* phrases such as these: " Sîn is Marduk as giver of light in the night "; " Šamaš is Marduk in the sphere of the law "; " Adad is Marduk with reference to rain "; etc. This shows that even the ' theologians ' of the time felt it necessary to simplify the populous pantheon, and transferred to Marduk all the powers of the other gods; that is to say, although the existence of these gods was not denied, they had begun to lose their importance.

This tendency to award to Marduk a greatly increased power at the expense of the other gods is especially evident in the so-called *Hymn of the Creation of the World.* The observation of the constellations, which, in keeping with the spirit of the time, had been diligently pursued in Babylonia since the close of the second millennium, led in the first half of the eighth century to the revolutionizing discovery of the regularity and calculability of the courses of the planets and of other fundamental facts of astronomy. Without doubt the learned priests of the time gathered from this the conception of a comprehensive divine government of the world, and this found its poetical expression in the great *Hymn of the Creation of the World*. In that poem it is Marduk, the youngest of the gods, who conquers Tiâmat, the mother of Chaos, and out of her constructs the world, appoints to the constellations (which are here called images of the gods — compare the star-disks on the headdresses of the gods in Fig. 31) their orbits, and finally creates mankind to be the servants of the gods.

It is remarkable that, although this poem magnifies the god of their own capital city, the Babylonian (Chaldean) kings of the seventh and eighth centuries make no mention of it in any of their numerous inscriptions, although it was certainly known not only in Assyria, but also in Babylonia. Remarkable also is the reproach hurled against Nabonidus, the Chaldean king overthrown by Cyrus, contained in the recently discovered satire written by a Babylonian priest in the year 538 B.C. Nabonidus is upbraided for having degraded Bêl (= Marduk) in favour of Sîn. All the same the inscriptions of the Chaldean kings of Babylon reveal a profound piety. These monarchs, some of whom were great soldiers and all of whom were indefatigable temple builders, are shown here bending in deep humility before Marduk, the Merciful One, to whom chiefly they look for help, and before Nabû, his rightful son, who is believed to intercede with Marduk on their behalf. Although they rear temples to other gods and pay them homage, still it is Marduk (with Nabû) who is the chief object of their religious faith. While it was only in the beginning of the first millennium B.C. that this divine pair began to play an important part both in Babylonia and in Assyria, such worship is modelled to a large degree on very much older conceptions. The relationship of the Father God to his divine son was already assumed by Ea toward Marduk (see p. 50), and the thought of a divine mediator between a higher deity and mankind goes back to Sumerian time (see p. 46).

The last Babylonian monarchy received its death-blow at the hands of Cyrus, but many of the conceptions which had grown to maturity during the course of the centuries in Sumeria and Accadia, in Babylonia and Assyria, continued to influence the minds of the people.

It is a matter of great importance that in Mesopotamia at all times the gods were conceived in human form. Even in the periods of dreariest superstition this lent to the conceptions of deity something that was wholesome and unartificial, something that brought the gods near and made them real to the human heart. This was a soil on which man's sense of responsibility to the powers to whom he owed his existence could thrive, and out of this grew a strict moral doctrine, which included the conception of sin. The thought of being led by the gods or by one's guardian deity filled an important place in the life of the people of ancient Mesopotamia. As time went on this thought became so refined that it seems closely akin to a profound faith in one faithful, wise creator of the world. It must be admitted that at all times, in spite of an increasing tendency to see in every perishable thing only a parable or a mystery, the religion of the cuneiform peoples never ceased to be merely a religion for this life; and it is certainly no mere chance that it never showed any trace of mysticism — that is to say, of the tendency to identify the worshipper with his deity.

BIBLIOGRAPHY

Morris Jastrow, *Die Religion Babyloniens und Assyriens* (2 vols., 1905 and 1912); Ungnad, *Die Religion der Babylonier und Assyrer* (1921); Meissner, *Babylonien und Assyrien* (vol. ii, 1925); also De Sarzec and Heuzey, *Découvertes en Chaldée* (1887–1905); *Délégation en Perse: Mémoires publiés sous la direction de M. J. de Morgan,* vol. ii, " Textes Élamites-sémitiques," (1900); Jeremias, *Das Alte Testament im Lichte des Alten Orients* (1904; 3rd German ed., 1916); Frank, *Babylonische Beschwörungsreliefs* (" Leipziger Semitistische Studien, III, No. 3) (1908); Andrae, *Der Anu-Adadtempel in Assur* (No. 10. " Wissenschaftliche Veröffentlichung der Deutschen Orientgesellschaft ") (1909); Morris Jastrow, *Bildermappe zur Religion Babyloniens und Assyriens* (1912); Unger, *Sumerische und Akkadische Kunst* (in " Jedermanns Bücherei," Section " Bildende Kunst ") (1926).

2. EGYPTIAN RELIGION [1]

by Günther Roeder

Introductory Remarks. The land of Egypt was marked by such peculiarities that it could not fail to exercise a decisive influence on the history of the religion that grew up and flourished in it. The first outstanding feature of the country is the great length of the Nile valley. From the Mediterranean Sea to the First Cataract it is about 1000 kilometres (say 625 miles) long, while its maximum width is only a few miles. In many places there is only a narrow strip of fertile soil along the banks of the river. This unusual configuration compels the inhabitants of Upper Egypt to form small districts or cantons, each having only one neighbour to the south and one to the north. The people of Upper Egpyt have always been and still are somewhat inferior to those of Lower Egypt in civilization and development. The Delta, which forms the other half of the country, is an extensive plain, open toward the sea and offering free entrance to the influences of the countries that border on the Mediterranean.

The second characteristic feature of Egypt is the contrast between desert and corn-land. The desert which covers the interior of the whole of North Africa has, it is true, a few hollows where subterranean water and springs make tillage possible, but, speaking generally, it is a barren waste. It consists of sand and rocks exposed to the pitiless glare of the sun, and its parched, waterless soil renders it unfit for habitation except by caravans and nomads. The stock-raising people who dwell there can only make the best of the grass that springs up after the scanty rains. They know the water-holes, worship the isolated trees that are visible from afar, and dread the naked rocks of the mountains. For them one day is like another. Their chronometer is the moon, which gives them the month of twenty-seven days. In sharp contrast to the 'red sand' of the desert is the 'black soil' of the corn-lands, which are laboriously won by the toilers in ceaseless struggle with the sand, ever drifting to and fro before the wind. The weapon of the peasant in his constant fight is water. This he draws from the Nile and transports to where it is required. The rise and fall of the Nile and the course of the sun across the sky are the two powers that determine his year. It has three seasons —

[1] The majority of the illustrations in this section are taken from the Pelizaeus Museum in Hildesheim; Figs. 42, 43, and 44 are from the Berlin Museum; Fig. 45 is from the excavations at Gizeh.

that of the inundation, spring, or the time of sprouting, and summer, which brings the harvest. Diligence, justice, and respect for what belongs to another are the virtues of the Egyptian peasant. His daily work demands from him co-operation with his neighbours; the management of the Nile water necessitates organization; communal life, which sets the same goal before each man, promotes the growth of writing and arithmetic out of pictures and numbers, and produces a calendar whose dates are fixed.

It cannot be said that the Egyptians have any clearly marked racial characteristics. They include Hamites, whose settlements extend from the Mediterranean to the interior of Africa. To them perhaps, and to their Libyan neighbours, is due the development of higher civilization, and probably it was they also who determined the broad lines of the religion of the peasants. The Nile valley has again and again been overrun by Semites. These Arabian Bedouin have certainly given to Egypt some elements of their desert religion, and have also contributed a distinct colouring to the language and civilization of the country. The Egyptian religion has thus been deeply influenced from various quarters, but its vitality and variety are mainly due to the peculiar character of the land of Egypt, which has forced every immigrant people to adapt themselves to its unique conformation and laid upon them its spell.

The Egyptian religion, both in the most ancient period and later, contains features which, either by their wide distribution or by their nature, convey the impression that they are part of the original and universal dower of the people. In view of what has been said of the nature of the country it is difficult to speak of *universal* features of the religion. All the conditions — at least in Upper Egypt — encourage the growth of local variations, and perhaps much that at first sight seems to be the common property of the Egyptians proves afterward to have been the ancient possession of some small group. But we will first indicate the features which probably go back to the early period (prior to 3000 B.C.), and subsequently attained a wider distribution.

All over the country, both in the desert and in his fields, the Egyptian lives in the sunlight. The sun is a male deity and so is the moon. Female beings play in the heavens the same subordinate *rôle* as they do in the mundane life of Egypt. The souls of the dead soar to the stars, which are spirits, some of them good and others evil. The objective world, in which earth, air, and sky are superincumbent, is regarded as in various degrees animate, but the powers of nature, the Nile, the trees, and mountains have always been looked upon as living beings. Gods, or the animals specially associated with them and in whose guise they usually appear, protect man throughout the whole of his life, and also preserve his body after it has been laid in the grave from the decay which would render it impossible for the soul again to animate the body with all its powers. The ancient belief of the Egyptians in a life beyond the grave led at a very early time to careful construction of the grave and to great solicitude in providing the departed with all that was necessary for the life beyond. At a very distant period, also, the thought must have emerged that the sins of this life are punished in the future. The foremost helper given to man amid all the cares of his life here and hereafter was the god of his tribe or of his city. This deity was variously regarded as an incarnation of the powers of nature, the totem animal of his ancestors, the guardian of the burial-place, or some other divine being.

A great variety of influences governed the transformation and combination of these original conceptions. The various districts of Egypt attached themselves to the two states of Upper and Lower Egypt, and these were welded into one empire by the strong hand of Menes, the founder of the First Dynasty (c. 3300 B.C.). This development toward political unity is reflected in the religion. The sun-god becomes king of the gods and ruler of the world, and to him the moon-god, his representative and highest official, submits his reports. The moon-god is the inventor of writing, arithmetic, the keeping of archives, and other administrative activities. High above all the old inter-tribal conflicts now rises the majesty of the godlike Pharaoh, and his Court provides a pattern for the heavenly government. The various local gods are reconceived and redefined. Certain of their characteristics are emphasized and regarded as their special features, the others being made subordinate to these. The chief god is given a family, and round him are grouped his kindred and friends as a kind of ennead. In this manner the great temples have each a separate group of gods. These groups are at first not always on amicable terms, but under the pressure of circumstances they gradually modify each other. The dynasty of the reigning Pharaoh installs its own district deity as the King's god, and imposes his worship throughout the whole country. This deity, thus raised temporarily for political reasons to the dignity of the god of the empire, has long been a supreme king of the gods in his own district. When thus introduced into other temples and given a place beside the local deities this imperial god tends to displace the latter, to assimilate them to himself and ultimately absorb them.

Thus in every separate temple influences are at work producing from within organic developments in the personalities of the gods. On the other hand, influences from without force their way in and rob the various deities of their distinctive character by adding to them new features originally alien to them. Divine personalities arise which possess qualities that are inconsistent with each other, and it is not easy now to determine in every case whether certain features, attributes, and symbols, myths, and satellites really belonged to the deities originally or were only subsequently transferred to them. The merging of the temples in the national organization of religion, with its unified administration, also helped to hasten this process of assimilation. When the rulers of Thebes made Amon, the god of that city, the state-god of the Middle Kingdom (c. 2000 B.C.) of united Egypt, all the temples immediately adopted the new deity, and his influence was so overwhelming that the great gods of old were completely displaced. After Osiris, the god of the dead of Busiris, in the Delta (Fig. 34), had finished his triumphal course through the whole Nile valley he was everywhere entrusted with the protection of the bodies of the dead, and thereafter the ancient gods of the dead entirely disappeared.

This development of Egyptian religion was no doubt frequently interrupted by reactions. In spite of all the repressive measures employed by the priests there is clear evidence of internal disturbances. Sceptics and individualists arose from time to time, and several writings have come down to us which are no less than revolutionary in character. In one case a man, who was in a position to wield more influence than a mere writer, brought about an actual reformation of epoch-making importance. The author of this movement was King Amenophis IV (1375–58 B.C.), who called himself Aknatôn. After the manner of a true Oriental ruler, he sought to impose his own faith on the whole country. First of all he banished from the temples deities of every kind, whether they ruled in the world above or protected the bodies of the dead. As far as the King's power could achieve it, their names were erased, especially that of Amon, who had been the state-god of his predecessors. The royal reformer also sought to compel all temples throughout the land to worship the new god — perhaps at a separate altar. Nevertheless the temples of the ancient gods still survived, and the changes and the destruction wrought by him were not so very important.

FIG. 34. OSIRIS AS AN ERECT MUMMY

Osiris was the god of the dead and the type of every dead person who, like himself, desired to partake of illumination in the beyond.

The god of Aknatôn was the sun — the star itself, the creator and preserver of man, beast, and planet. Under the influence of Heliopolis the new faith arose with its centre at Tell el-Amarna, the royal city founded by the King. So far all this was genuinely Egyptian in the old sense, and the *Hymn to the Sun* written by the reformer contains many phrases and ideas which are also found in earlier hymns. But it was something new, indicating a break with the past, when the sun star was declared not to be a god, to have neither human nor animal shape, to possess neither attributes nor symbols, neither family nor ennead. The sun was depicted as a disk with rays terminating in hands (Fig. 35). Sacrifice was paid to this new ruler of the worlds not in an enclosed temple in subdued light, but on an altar under the open sky.

As might be expected, the introduction of the new faith met with determined resistance. The highly organized priesthood could not possibly allow their gods to be abolished at one stroke. Moreover, the once flourishing empire of the Eighteenth Dynasty was evidently falling to pieces year by year. The negroes and the Syrians, who, to quote the King's hymn, were brothers of the Egyptians, and no longer prostrate enemies of Pharaoh and

FIG. 35. THE SUN-DISK WITH AKNATÔN
AND HIS CONSORT

*From Haas, " Bilderatlas zur
Religionsgeschichte "*

wretched barbarians, ceased now to be confined within the Nile valley by strong armies and stern governors. With the King's death the driving power of the reformation disappeared, and although his sons-in-law remained faithful for a few more years to the new sun-god, ere long, in the short reign of Tutankhamen, who died young, a return was made to the national form of religion and Amon of Thebes was again recognized as the national deity. Aknatôn's name was now in turn erased from the temples and removed from the lists of kings, so that posterity might never hear of him. In later days only a few knew anything of the ' heretic of Amarna.' The same thing must have happened (although perhaps on a smaller scale) whenever anyone of independent spirit tried to give outward form to thoughts which deviated from the paths of official dogma.

The religious conceptions which, as we have seen, were originally current among the people remained in all essentials the popular ideas throughout the lifetime of the Egyptian religion. In all the periods men must have felt burdened by the sense of sin, and belief in the efficacy of incantations and amulets must have been universal. The keepers of the gate of the world beyond — greedy demons with long knives — were dreaded, and trust was placed in the intercession of sacred animals with the gods. But in the theological systems that have come down to us these popular conceptions are overgrown by priestly speculations that reveal little power of thought. Only to a slight extent has research succeeded in laying bare the ancient ideas. In the historical period we occasionally see deities belonging to the people's faith being adopted into the temple-worship — *e.g.,* Bes, the aged dwarf with foreign visage, and the Toeris, the helpers of women. To the priest the tree is the abode of a good goddess, who produces from it food and drink, but only an unlettered peasant ventures to direct a prayer to the mountain-peak.

The Pyramid texts (*c.* 2500 B.C.), our oldest source for religious conceptions, make little mention of ethical and moral questions, but we can occasionally read between the lines that the righteous man finds his reward in a happy life and that stern spirits punish the wicked. In chapter 125 of the *Book of the Dead* of the New Kingdom (middle of the second millennium) the dead man makes the negative confession — that he had not committed this or that sin. Similarly, autobiographies constantly insist that the ruler or official concerned had protected the weak and the widow, clothed the naked, and fed the hungry. In books of proverbial philosophy instructions are given regarding behaviour toward parents, teachers, and sages. But, speaking generally, the literary texts reflect the consciousness of innocence and of a claim to be pronounced just and like the gods. It is in the misspelt scribblings of simple people that we find a sense of sin and confession of it, a feeling of remorse and prayer for forgiveness, and also the confidence that the god will hear the cry of the oppressed. In these texts the suppliant knows that though the god may punish, he can also graciously forgive.

It is not easy to draw a line of division between magic and religion in Egypt. If we stretch the meaning of the word, ' magic ' also lies behind the prayers addressed to the gods in the temples or said for the purpose of securing some good gift for the dead in their graves. Accuracy of expression and attention to the prescribed ritual guarantee the efficacy of the prayer — woe to the gods if under such circumstances they refuse to hear! Incantations are in the hands of the priests, the servants of the great gods, who are frequently addressed in them. The gods themselves use such formulas against each other, and these are full of mythical tales and allusions. In any case, Egyptian magic has nothing to do with lower powers, nor is it classed among the forbidden arts. Incantations were used to fend off thunderstorms, illness, wild beasts, and wicked men. The former they keep at a distance; to the latter they bring harm, or annihilate them altogether. Besides these protective and aggressive forms of magic, there is also a love magic. In addition to incantations, the means of inducing magic included figures, either drawn or modelled. The ritual prescribed fire, water, drugs, and strange ingredients. Amulets fashioned in the appointed way could protect both the living and the dead. With the help of a list of good and bad days, efforts were made to choose a day that would be favourable for an undertaking. Measures were taken to secure protection against the evil eye, and when one was at one's wits' end the divine oracle was consulted.

The influence of Egyptian religion on other religions can be plainly seen in all the adjacent countries. In Nubia, with its kindred population, we find in later times established conceptions — prayers to the sun, falcon-deities, and sages — which are probably very old. From the time of the Middle Kingdom onward we find numerous Egyptian deities widely established on the Upper Nile. The later Nubians and the people of the kingdom of Meroe in the Roman period believed that they were the true adherents and the actual creators of the Egyptian religion. (This belief was already known to Herodotus.) The Libyans in the desert regions to the west probably introduced into Egypt the use of salt, soda, and pitch as preservatives of the dead body. It was they also who brought the goddess Nect from Sais, and built megalithic graves, and afterward spread Egyptian burial customs, amulets, and images of gods and animals over the whole of North Africa. An Egyptian choir-leader crossed the Mediterranean Sea to Crete. In Syria we find Byblos, which plays a part in the Osiris myth, in long possession of a

FIG. 36. COFFIN OF IDU, MADE OF CEDARWOOD
Found in his grave at Gizeh.
From Haas, " Bilderatlas zur Religionsgeschichte "

Hathor. In Greek times Sidon was full of mummy coffins made of marble. From ancient times Lebanon sent its cedars and supplied Egypt with material for beams and plants for buildings, furniture, utensils, and even for coffins (Fig. 36), while Syria's oils and resins contributed to the spread of the practice of embalming the bodies of the dead in the Nile valley. In return Syria received into its temples the gods and the rites of its Egyptian conquerors. The Old Testament contains Psalms closely akin to Egyptian songs.[2] Among the Proverbs of Solomon are literal translations from an Egyptian book of proverbial philosophy. The Hellenes carried far afield — even into Russia and France — deities of Egypt in Greek attire, especially Osiris, Isis, and

[2] Especially Psalm civ, which closely resembles the hymn to Amenophis IV.

Horus. The Roman Empire thereafter established them in Italy, and the Roman legions took them with them across the Rhine and into Asia. Christianity modelled its group of Mother and Child on that of Isis with her son Horus (Fig. 37), and shaped its cross from the Egyptian symbol of life (St Anthony's cross); from the Gnostics and the Sects — *e.g.*, the Sethians — it also borrowed some elements.

The later history of the Egyptian religion resulted in a lengthy struggle between the popular faith and the priestly doctrine. Victory inclined now to one s i d e and now to the other. The Renaissance of the Nubian-S a i t e-P e r s i a n period (seventh to fourth centuries B.C.) originated in the priestly circles, and revival of the literature and art of the ancient empire cannot have b e e n of popular origin. Nevertheless, the Egyptian religion must still have possessed great strength and vitality. It was the shield used by the priests under the Ptolemies against the invasion of Hellenism. New buildings continued to be erected down to the time of the emperors of the third century A.D., and Egyptian d e i t i e s were worshipped by the Blemmyes in Philæ

Fig. 37. Isis suckling her Infant Son Horus
From Haas, " Bilderatlas zur Religionsgeschichte"

down to the middle of the sixth century. The Egyptian gods were gradually merged into those of Greece, but when Christianity came it extirpated all that was pagan. Still, their ancient faith was long kept fresh in the minds of the Egyptian people by magicians and soothsayers.

Egyptian symbols were rescued from ancient literature — much of which is unknown to us — by the Renaissance. But when modern scholarship began to occupy itself with Egyptian religion scholars had to gather their material from the Old Testament, from Greek and Roman travellers, poets, historians, and philosophers. The 'illumination' of the eighteenth century brought critical methods to bear upon the subject, but the Egyptian sources became accessible only when the hieroglyphics had been deciphered. In recent years the science of comparative religion, especially the ethnological branch of it, has enabled us to understand Egyptian conceptions far better than before.

The sources for Egyptian religion are too numerous to be separately mentioned. Almost all the memorials from the Nile valley that we possess come

FIG. 38. BRONZE FIGURE OF A
SEATED CAT

The sacred animal of the goddess Bastet, queen of
the city of Bubastis, in the Delta.

from temples and graves, and of course they reproduce the priestly interpretations of the religious conceptions. For that reason religious buildings constructed from the ruins of cities, national monuments, and memorial stones are all the more important. Hieroglyphic inscriptions have nearly always a decorative purpose, and the papyri are mostly in the handwriting of young people. In both we have the utterances of professional writers, and not seldom the accounts are marred by the influence of some motive. The manuscripts that have been preserved are often so faulty that parallel passages are necessary before the meaning can be made out. The texts available are therefore not so numerous as they would seem to be at first sight. As a rule only single copies of these documents have come down to us, and very few of them were actually used in public worship. Unfortunately there is almost an entire lack of manuals and systematic treatises.

Gods and Temples. To the Egyptian mind all parts of nature were animate, and the powers that found expression in them were conceived as indwelling in the deities. Nature-gods like the sun, moon, constellations, and the Nile were everywhere worshipped, and were not regarded as having any local habitation. The theology of a later time manufactured other gods. Deities in ram shape represented the winds from the four chief points of the compass, and each district had its own sacred tree, animal, and symbol. In some temples nature-gods were combined with the local deities, and found permanent place there. This was most frequent in the case of the sungod, who became identified in early times with Atum of Heliopolis, in the Middle Kingdom with Amon of Thebes, and later with Thoth, Khnum, and others. Of many animals there was believed to be a supernatural species which was regarded as a manifestation of divine powers. The animal worshipped at any given place was allotted to the god who was likewise worshipped there, although animal and god had nothing else in common. One or more specimens of the sacred species was kept in the temple, and often regarded as the 'soul' of the deity.

Conceptions of the world varied greatly. The sky was always regarded as a female — cow, woman, ocean, bird-wing, etc.; the earth was a man, on whose back the plants grow; the air was a man with uplifted arms supporting the sky. The origin of the world was also variously imagined in different districts. From the dark primeval ocean grew a lotus flower, out of which sprang the sun; or, again, Ptah made the form of the earth, Khnum turned it on his potter's wheel, Thoth created it by the power of his word.

In each of the great temples of Egypt we find a local deity established, and in every case he is the lord of the whole district and the protector of the tribe. The duties of the local gods differ widely. In one place his myths tell how he created the world, in another he ministers to the dead, in a third he presides over some part of nature or some natural process (such as procreation), in a fourth he is the inventor of writing or the builder of temples. His shape varies also from place to place. The tribal totems are trees, animals, and fetishes of all kinds, and these are associated with the deities as their symbols. Later the gods are depicted in the general outline of a man or woman, with an animal head, a distinctive crown, and other attributes. Animal-worship also varies in different places. In one district the cat is worshipped (Fig. 38) or the crocodile, while in other districts these are detested. Prohibitions against killing lions and hippopotami, serpents and scorpions, rats and mice, can only have been due either to the hoary theory that they were sacred, or to the fact that the animals were rare and innocuous. The only other possible explanation of

FIG. 39
THE PILLAR OF DED
The symbol of Osiris.
Faïence.

the worship of animals is that it was a measure of protection against them.

The worship of some of the local gods spread farther afield, or was carried into other districts, and occasionally imitations of it were introduced elsewhere — *e.g.,* in the Nubian colonies, in the oases of Lybia, and in Syria. A good example of such an extension of influence, due to the inherent strength of the qualities symbolized, is that of Osiris, the god of vegetation and of the dead. His seat was at Busiris, in the Delta, where he had a fetish, Ded (Fig. 39), in the form of a tree (or perhaps of his vertebral column?). He moved to

FIG. 40. TEMPLE WALL PICTURE SHOWING KING PTOLEMY I SACRIFICING TO THE GODS

For the burning of incense see Fig. 41.

Memphis and displaced Anubis, the local god of the dead. In Abydos, in Upper Egypt, he became identified with the 'first of the westerns,' a dog, as protector of the dead. In the late period he was regarded as almost the sole god of the dead throughout the whole country, and gradually assumed ethical and even cosmological features.

In the early period the temples of the various local deities differed greatly. They were tabernacles of varied form and structure, and bore distinctive marks. From the Old Kingdom (about 2500 B.C.) we know only the sun sanctuaries at Abusir, which have been excavated by the Deutsche Orient-gesellschaft. There was an altar for sacrifice under the open sky in front of a mighty obelisk. In the New Kingdom (from 1600 B.C. onward) the prevailing type was a uniform structure with gateways (pylons), an open courtyard with colonnades, a roofed hall with pillars, and a holy of holies where semi-darkness reigned. The entire building was surrounded by walls

FIG. 41. CENSER USED IN THE TEMPLE FOR THE INCENSE OFFERING
From Haas, " Bilderatlas zur Religionsgeschichte "

without an opening. From the late period (seventh century B.C.) down to the time of the Roman emperors the temples were rebuilt in this style, although there are also examples of places of worship with windows and half-covered courtyards. The reliefs illustrate the worship of the gods by the King as representative of the people. Such a service must really have been held in the presence of all the statues in the temple. The daily ritual of public worship was performed in the holy of holies by the King (Fig. 40), or in his stead by the chief priest. The ministrant proceeded in ceremonial fashion to cleanse the image, anoint it, adorn and clothe it, offer incense to it (Fig. 41), and present gifts of food and offer prayers. The image, which stood in a chapel of stone, was small and portable. It was made of costly wood, mounted with precious metals, and inlaid with stones, and was arrayed in garments of choicest material. On great occasions it was carried in a shrine resting on a boat (Fig. 42), the populace accompanying the procession through the district, giving vent to unrestrained joy, which was increased by the per-formance of mythological events — 'mystery plays.'

Each independent place of worship had one priest, and each temple had several. These regular officials were assisted by laymen who served in turn for a month. From ancient times there had been priestesses. In the service

Fig. 42. Priests carrying the Boat with the Shrine
containing the Image of the God

of goddesses, whose natural handmaids they were, they played a different *rôle* from that which they performed for the gods. In the latter case the priestesses had to minister to their pleasures in the harem. In Thebes during the late period the " god-wife of Amon " stood at the head of a priestly hierarchy. At all periods the great temples included the priesthood of the whole district. The high priests bore ancient titles: in Memphis " great leader of the artists "; in Heliopolis " great scanner " (of the sky); in Sais " the great physician." They enjoyed independent powers, and frequently became a source of danger to the State. The members of the ordinary priesthood were divided into tribes ($\phi \acute{v} \lambda a \iota$) — the divine servants, the clean, the readers, the divine fathers, the keepers of the secret (or perhaps initiates of the mysteries), etc. The importance of the various temples depended on their political and economic position. The greatest power came to be held by the priests of Amon of Thebes, and far below these ranked Heliopolis and Memphis, not to speak of ancient gods like Thoth and Osiris. They controlled agriculture and stock-raising, the import and export of raw materials and manufactures, the movements of troops, etc. Apparently as far back

FIG. 43. JUDGMENT OF THE DEAD BEFORE THE THRONE OF OSIRIS

as the period before the New Kingdom the temples had been combined into a stable organization under a president, and this of course hastened the unification of the theological systems. Attached to the temples, with the rank of priests, were not only the various administrative officials, but also physicians and astronomers, historians and philosophers, architects and workers in relief. They were distinguished from the laity by a special uniform and — at least in the later period — by ritual regulations.

In every great temple there were several deities, and these formed a family. By the side of the lord, the *paterfamilias,* stood his consort and his son. Such an arrangement was not suitable in every case — *e.g.,* if the temple belonged to a goddess, such as Hathor of Dendera, or if a god had two consorts, like Thoth of Hermopolis and Khnum of Esna and Elephantine. In addition, the local system included animals, demons, fetishes, and certain cosmogonical conceptions, as well as incarnations of powers of nature. Heliopolis first formed a " great ennead," and included in it, somewhat forcedly, a select number of deities; in order to include the remainder a " small ennead " was formed, which was as little homogeneous as the other. The formation of enneads was imitated in other localities, and these represented the successive dynasties of primeval deities. Theological speculation and the requirements of organization brought them into uniformity. Deities were established in other localities and identified with each other. Myths and epithets, animal figures and attributes, were transferred to deities with which they had originally no connexion. Foreign deities crowded in from Nubia, Libya, and Syria, and were gradually identified with the native gods of Egypt. All this

FIG. 44. PREHISTORIC CORPSE IN HUDDLED POSITION
Found in the burial-place at Abusir el-Melek.

resulted in a confusion so complete that even the most learned priests were frequently at a loss to find a way out. The originally simple and uniform deities had become complex and many-sided, and their personalities had been greatly obscured by widespread assimilation. It is difficult for us now to see clearly the original features, which have been covered up by subsequent disfigurements and erroneous additions.

The Dead and the Grave. According to a belief which certainly goes back to a very early time in Egypt, the spiritual part of man does not die — it survives either alone, hungering constantly for its body, or in union with some other being, into whose body it has entered (the transmigration of souls). The abode of the dead lies far to the west, and in that direction the suppliant turns his face. There were, however, numerous local differences of belief with regard to the dwelling-place of the dead and their lot. In some localities the dead were believed to pass to one of the constellations, and thither soared a dead king, perhaps to fill the part of a ruler of that world. Elsewhere the realm of the dead was the Duat, which lies below the earth and is traversed by the sun-god at night. In it are doors with bars, rivers and chasms in which are serpents and other perils, while huge demons with knives guard the entrance. On a throne in the judgment hall sits

FIG. 45. BURIAL-GROUND WITH MASTABAS AT GIZEH
In the background is the pyramid of King Khafra.

Osiris, with the forty-two judges, before whom the dead man must make his negative confession, in which he enumerates the sins that he has not committed (see Fig. 43). If he is declared just, the fields of the blessed are open to him; if he is condemned, he falls a prey to the hound of hell. When a king dies he becomes the god Osiris, and lives all his experiences over again. Gradually this conception was extended to every individual, although it is not easy to see how every one could sit on the throne of the king of the gods and wear the royal robes. The ideas regarding resurrection that pervaded the Osiris myths were adopted with various modifications into the faith regarding the dead.

Like everything else in the Egyptian religion, the gods of the dead are variously conceived in different districts. In Memphis the protection of the departed and of their graves is in the keeping of a recumbent falcon called Sokar; in Thebes they are under the care of the cow Hathor. In several places their guardian is a recumbent dog, called Anubis in Siut and in Abydos "the first of the westerns." When the Ptolemies created the Græco-Egyptian deity Serapis they gave him features borrowed from Osiris. Osiris

FIG. 46. MUMMY-SHAPED COFFIN OF WOOD
From Haas, "Bilderatlas zur Religionsgeschichte"

(Fig. 34), who in his own city, Busiris, in the Delta, played other parts as well, was recognized as the god of the dead throughout all Egypt from the close of the Old Kingdom (c. 2400 B.C.). From the Saite period (seventh century B.C.) he was the only god of the dead, and he reappeared in the Roman Empire along with Isis and Horus. According to the myth about him, Osiris was a king who was murdered by his enemies. His widow tearfully searched for his corpse till she found it. From the revivified body she conceived Horus. The corpse was brought to Byblos in Syria, where it was torn to pieces by Set. Isis buried the parts in different places. New life awoke in Osiris, and he became king of the realm of the dead, while Horus ruled over the living. The events narrated in the myth were the subject of mystery plays. His worship was performed on the island that held his grave (Abaton). The myth came later to be interpreted ethically, Osiris and Set representing the contrast between good and evil. A cosmic meaning was also read into it — Horus and Set typified the struggle between light and darkness. The rising from the dead of the deity was represented by figures of Osiris made of earth containing grains of corn, so that the green sprouts symbolized the new life.

The graveyards were situated on the edge of the desert, if possible on the

western edge. The graves, originally shallow pits (Fig. 44), took the form
of chambers entered by a shaft. Over the grave was built a heap of stones,
called the mastaba (Fig. 45). It developed into the pyramid — at first for
kings and later for private individuals. In front of both pyramids and mastabas were places of worship. These were also provided in the rock-graves,
and contained, in the case of a king, images showing his deeds and his life
with the gods, in the case of a private individual his family, possessions, and
the offerings bestowed upon him. The coffin represented on a small scale,

FIG. 47. GRAVE SLAB OF PRINCE ONU, FROM HIS MASTABA AT GIZEH
Fourth Dynasty.
From Haas, " Bilderatlas zur Religionsgeschichte "

and the grave on a larger scale, the world in which the departed now lived.
In the older period it was shaped like a house or box (Fig. 36), in the later
period like a body (Fig. 46). In the spaces for worship in front of the
graves the relatives assemble for sacrifice and prayer (Figs. 47 & 48). Priests
for the dead were provided by means of endowments, although in the first
instance it was the duty of a son " to see that his father's name was kept
alive." Homage to the dead kings was long maintained by endowments, and
the Saitic period evinced its regard for the past by again providing priests
for the worship of the great Pharaohs of the Old Kingdom.

From hints contained in the Pyramid Texts (*c.* 2500 B.C.) it would seem that originally the dead bodies were allowed to decay, or were dismembered and the bones buried apart from the rest of the body. The oldest interments that have been found (the fourth millennium B.C.) show the body in the huddled posture (Fig. 44). From the time of the Old Kingdom onward (Fourth Dynasty, c. 2800 B.C.) the bodies are outstretched, with the face turned toward the rising sun. By and by the body was opened and mummified by means of increasingly elaborate methods. This practice was continued till the advent of Christianity put an end to it. Elaborate rituals pre-

FIG. 48. TABLE FOR SACRIFICE, SHOWING GIFTS TO THE DEAD
From Haas, " Bilderatlas zur Religionsgeschichte "

scribed the methods to be used for embalming and swathing the mummy and for the arrangement of amulets, and there were further instructions regarding the actual interment, at which a priest wearing a dog's-head mask represented Anubis, the god of the dead. Pictures show that previous to interment the mummy was transported to Abydos in order to hold fellowship with Osiris at the grave of that deity. The same desire found expression in the erection of a grave-stone in Abydos. We see the feast for the dead in the garden, the guarding of the mummy outside the grave, the process of " opening the mouth and the eyes," and then the coffin is lowered into the shaft in the presence of priests, readers, and incense-burners. Even prehistoric graves (Fig. 44) contain jars with food and favourite articles like weapons, tools, and ornaments. From the Old Kingdom onward we find figures of workmen preparing food for the departed or standing ready to take his place when the call to work comes. Women are shown ready to minister to him, and amulets are there to ward off dangers. At a later time we find large models of cattleyards and slaughter-houses, spinning and weaving sheds, entire dwellings, and even ships. The pictures of grave-chambers show similar scenes depicted with an increasing elaborateness that reveals the joy of the sculptor in his work. All reference to the future disappears, and only activities of this life are depicted, so that the departed can recall vanished joys and still find delight in them.

BIBLIOGRAPHY

Maspero's essays reprinted in *Bibliothèque Égyptologique* (vols. i–vi, 1893–1912); Brugsch, *Religion und Mythologie der alten Ägypter* (1885–90); Wiedemann, *Die Religion der alten Ägypter* (1890); Erman, *Die ägyptische Religion* (1905; 2nd ed., 1909); Breasted, *Development of Religion and Thought in Ancient Egypt* (1912); Roeder, *Urkunden zur Religion des alten Ägypten* (1915; 2nd ed., 1923); Kees, *Totenglaube und Jenseitsvorstellungen der alten Ägypter* (1926); monographs of the gods in Roschers' *Lexikon der griechisch-römischen Mythologie* and in Pauly-Wissowas' *Realenzyklopädie des klassischen Altertumswissenschaft*.

3. CHINESE RELIGION

by F. E. A. Krause

Among the Chinese, religion occupies a position essentially different from that which it fills in the case of other great civilized peoples. It has neither been content to control only one side of the activities of life nor claimed a place of its own apart from everything else. It was fitted into the civilization as a whole, and was at all points bound up with the general view of the world held by the ancient Chinese.

Especially when contrasted with what is usually met with in the Western world, Chinese civilization is distinguished by the way in which it has been completely unified and reduced, as it were, to a common denominator. All phenomena and events are harmoniously related to each other; none stand apart from the rest. Therefore the inter-relations of the different spheres and aspects of life are of the most varied kind. The religious life is not an exceptional condition. It is not contrasted with man's daily life. It pervades all the aspects of human life here below, and suffuses the whole social and political structure. Religion has a natural and necessary place in every aspect that Chinese life can assume.

In the ancient Chinese mind the sense of religion is not regarded as an awakening to the knowledge of something different from ordinary thought and life. Religious motives are not considered as something distinctive — they lie inconspicuously in the totality of thought and life. Therefore in China religion is so interwoven with the mechanism of life as a whole that the two can never be sorted out or disentangled. Religion is not looked upon as something belonging to a higher sphere — in the sense of something 'numinous' — a something which a man merely fears and worships. It is a constituent part of mundane life, with effects that are directly and everywhere felt.

The basic fact from which Chinese thought starts is the reciprocity that exists between the cosmos and human life. Man has to frame his life after the pattern of nature. But heaven also is affected by human actions. Human life has cosmic relations, and these give to every event a moral meaning. Therefore every separate detail of life, which to the Western mind has nothing specifically religious in it at all, has quite naturally for the Chinese mind a religious aspect. Together with the conceptions of the universe and of the relations of man to nature, it was the conceptions held regarding the soul that determined the development of the religious forms. Even these are not regarded merely as the soil on which a definite cult has grown up. Like the sense of dependence on the cycle of nature, they constitute the broad basis for the social structures of family and nation. It is only *one* of the results of this way of looking at things that the cosmic views and the conceptions of the soul found expression in nature-worship and ancestor-worship. The total effect has a much wider range, and found vent in numerous manifestations of a grosser religiosity. It is an essential feature of what we must call Chinese religion that it considers vague superstition just as important as any of the well-marked forms of worship. There has always existed a connexion between the systems that have in the historical period gained wider acceptance and the superstitious elements that have always been more or less present in the minds of the Chinese people. There is, it is true, hardly any trace of superstition in the oldest period, and very little sign of it, but the effect of a more primitive religiosity surviving from a more distant period is clearly apparent in the growth of the popular religion. This popular religion is not merely a mixture of different systems; it includes many peculiar forms of superstition which were afterward excluded from these systems.

A history of the Chinese religion must always start from the general fund of thought contained in the oldest literature. But in contrast to that of other civilized peoples, this ancient literature of China contains no works that are specifically religious. The religious material is contained in writings that are predominantly philosophical, ethical, social, or historical in character. In particular it is never possible to draw a line of demarcation between Chinese philosophy and Chinese religion.

The world of thought of the Chinese never found complete expression in any one literary document. It had already developed in various directions before it had become possible to write it down. Thus, owing to different emphasis having been laid on certain aspects, various views of the world have arisen in China which, although they were originally based on the same written source, gradually diverged, and finally took on an appearance of antagonism to each other. Careful and thorough investigation shows that Confucianism and Taoism, although they came later to be separate systems, grew up on the common soil of the ancient Chinese fundamental conceptions. If we had a better knowledge of many ideas and practices which belonged to the most ancient period, and which have been overlaid or obliterated by the ascendancy of practices that were later accepted as orthodox, we should be able to fit many elements that now seem out of place in later Taoism and in popular superstition into the great framework of ancient Chinese thought.

In this great fund of ancient Chinese thought lay many different possibilities of development. The centuries before the Christian era saw the rise of numerous schools of thought which, despite their diversity of form, continued to exist together, and even justified their existence. Some of these systems failed to gain wide acceptance because liberty of thought was greatly obstructed by very powerful official teaching. The result of this obstruction was that by and by, out of numerous possible developments of thought, one definite direction was taken — that represented by official writers and protected by the Government — to the exclusion of all others. This unification of Chinese thought put the stamp of rigidity on the intellectual life of the classical period and all the periods that followed it; it was aided, too, not only by the popular preference for a practical, ethical view, but also by other influences, especially the desire of the Government to consolidate the political situation.

Out of all the systems which had arisen from the placing of varying emphasis on certain aspects of universally accepted opinions, two attained outstanding importance. By their different attitude (sometimes amounting to antagonism) toward the problems which the world and life offered to the Chinese, these two ways of thought could not but seem to represent two entirely dissimilar views of the world, although all their doctrines were the truly logical outcome of ancient Chinese ideas. Their authors were Lao-tse and K'ung-tse, and they have been worked out by their respective schools into the systems of Taoism and Confucianism.

The two great men who lived in the sixth and fifth centuries were not the founders of a philosophy or a religion, nor did they in any sense produce anything new. Both merely rearranged the ancient views in an orderly way, but the points on which each laid the chief stress were not the same. Whereas Lao-tse dealt with his material in a theoretical and speculative fashion, K'ung-tse emphasized the practical conduct of life. The one founded an individualistic philosophy of pessimistic indifferentism, while the other taught a practical morality and laid the chief emphasis on life and conduct.

Diametrically opposed to each other as Lao-tse and K'ung-tse thus seem to be in the chief tenets of their doctrine, there are many points of connexion between them. They share many views received from the common stock of ancient Chinese thought, and accepted as valid by both. Their systems also contain that characteristic conception of the universe and of the relation of man to nature, or the interdependence between events and human life, of the moral connexion between nature and life, which has been called Chinese universism. Further, it is this common basis that constitutes the actual religious element in both cases, because, apart from this, neither the teaching of Lao-tse nor that of K'ung-tse has any distinctively religious element at all.

The doctrines of both teachers should always be distinguished from the outward forms which they afterward assumed in the hands of their respective disciples. It is just when we come to the religious contents that we see that the two systems were originally quite different from the external shape given to them at a subsequent period. It was only at a much later time that they became religions in the real sense, and this transformation did not come from within. In the one case it was brought about by political and constitutional influences; in the other it was due to the admission of popular ideas and the influence of the alien Buddhism.

The after history of the Chinese schools of thought makes it very difficult for us to speak briefly and broadly of Chinese religion or the Chinese religions. The various phases exhibit changes so profound that they cannot be included under one comprehensive formula. In any study, however brief, of the actual religious element in Chinese life and thought it is essential to keep clearly in mind the strong influence exerted on religion by the Chinese method of thought generally and in particular by the view of the world peculiar to that people.

The substance of ancient Chinese religious conceptions was derived from two sources, (1) observation of nature and the sense of man's dependence on it, and (2) theories of the soul and beliefs regarding the dead. These were embodied in the two fundamental aspects of Chinese religion, worship of nature and ancestor worship.

With the transition to settled life, which in the case of China took place in prehistoric time, the soil, on whose produce the population depended for their sustenance, had become a matter of prime importance. The cornland was regarded as under the care of special deities, and worship was paid to these in order to induce them to grant abundant harvests. These gods of the soil were closely connected with the fields over which they watched, so that from the very first there was a plurality of deities. These gods, who represented in themselves the properties of the soil, gradually developed into deities of the political divisions, of the principalities, of the kingdom. Their names and characteristics might change with change of ownership, with the rise of a new royal house, with the dominion of a new dynasty. They were strictly local, and their sphere of influence was strictly limited in its range.

The life of the agricultural population had always been regulated by the yearly cycle. The various forms of field-work had to be done at the times prescribed by the climate and the weather. Observation gradually led to the formation of a calendar, whose fixed dates came to have a religious significance. The celestial sphere exercised a decisive influence on the life of the terrestrial world. Men realized that they were dependent on the alternations of day and night, light and darkness, heat and cold, drought and moisture, wind and rain. Atmospheric conditions were therefore assumed to be powers of nature, and were duly worshipped. The heavens ruled the earth, and the various heavenly bodies exercised their appropriate influence. Thus the sun, moon, planets, and constellations were regarded as filling a religious rôle, and were worshipped. In a similar manner, men came to see that life was conditioned by the conformation of the earth's surface, the various configurations of which were ascribed to powers of nature, so that mountains, rivers, valleys, trees, and rocks became objects of religious veneration.

In this connexion we come upon a peculiar feature of Chinese thought. All phenomena were classified in two contrasted categories — that of *yang* as the male, the celestial, bright, warm, procreating principle and that of *yen* as the female, the earthly, dark, cold, and conceiving principle. This classification of all things found its strongest expression in superstitious beliefs, and gave rise to the system of geomancy, which has played so important a part in Chinese life.

The ancient Chinese saw a *collectanea* of all the powers of nature in the sky, which was therefore worshipped as the epitome of nature. It was not, however, looked upon as a supreme personal deity, but merely as the sum of the manifestations of power in the universe. In the speculative philosophy of Lao-tse heaven ranks equally with Tao as the original power of the universe. Here religion and philosophy merge into each other. They are simply different languages seeking to express the same thought by means of different projections.

In the classical texts the highest conception of the heavens is frequently identified with Shang-ti, a god who is described in a somewhat anthropomorphic way. He is perhaps an ancient constellation (the pole-star), and his exceptional position may be due to territorial and political considerations. As a matter of fact, the conceptions of the Supreme Ruler (Shang-ti) and of the Sublime Heavens (Huang-t'ien) afterward coalesce or absorb each other.

All nature was regarded as animate and charged with force. This bred in the popular mind a universal belief in spirits. From one point of view this was merely a way of expressing the connexion between man and nature, but, side by side with it, there emerged another kind of belief in spirits, which had its root in the ideas held regarding the soul. Human nature was believed to contain an element which in some undefined manner existed both pre-natally and posthumously, and which constituted the point of connexion between man and the powers of nature. It is quite clear that several conceptions regarding the creation and the separation of the soul were inter-crossed in these beliefs, and the statements in the sources are not always reconcilable.

The soul of man, which thus somehow continued to exist after death, afterward came to be identified with the spirit of the dead, and the very ancient practice of ancestor-worship is based on the attentions bestowed upon these spirits and the reverence with which they were regarded. The departed constitute an integral part of the great family circle. They take part in all that happens, and reward the attentions of the living with their protection and favours. The graves are their dwelling-places, and must therefore be carefully chosen and tended. In the soul-panels of the domestic shrine the spirits of the family ancestors are present, and the fortunes of the family — its weal or its woe — depend on the beneficent or injurious activities of these ancestors. Worship of the dead is thus a social duty which every family must perform in its own interests, and this practice affects profoundly the entire life of the people. It is the domestic analogue of nature-worship. Ancestor-worship constitutes the religion of the individual, and every member of the Chinese race without exception practices it as a family rite under the leadership of the head of his family.

FIG. 49. A CHINESE DOMESTIC SHRINE
From Kern, " Das Licht des Ostens "

On the other hand, nature-worship has always been a cult of special deities or powers limited to definite localities or to particular strata of the people. The worship of the supreme powers of nature, especially the sky, was the prerogative of the supreme head of the state; the worship of certain other powers was the privilege of the territorial princes, and other ceremonies were conducted by State officials. Nature-worship in ancient China was thus a religion of the governing classes, in which the mass of the people had no share. Observance of it formed part of the duties of the upper classes, who thus were the people's representatives as toward the sky and nature, and who therefore assumed all responsibility for the regulation of the due relations between man and the universe.

This worship of nature by and by developed into a State religion, while ancestor-worship continued to be the religion of the people. Apart from the domestic worship of ancestors, religion in China was entirely a concern of the State. Naturally, therefore, the religion *of* the State could easily come to be a religion *for* the State, and this is exactly what happened when Confucianism came to be the accepted and established form of State religion in China.

But all that has been said by no means exhausts the sphere of religion in China. It also includes the ordinances which are implicit in the reciprocal duties of man to man, and which are set forth in a scheme of a fivefold relationship — that of father to son, older brother to younger brother, husband to wife, monarch to subject, friend to friend. On this basis is built the entire life of the individual, which is governed by fixed principles that determine exactly his conduct in his family, in any organization of which he is a member, and in his position as a member of the corporate body of the state. The demands of piety are binding upon all. They frequently take the place of legal principles, and for the Chinese they have quite definitely the character of religious sanctions. The forms of propriety and social conventions are not merely a matter of breeding. They are an essential part of religious life. The Chinese word *li* is almost synonymous with *religio*. It means the binding power of an inward law that has a universal validity, expressed both in nature and in every human activity.

It is a national characteristic of the Chinese that outward form should all along have been so strongly emphasized that it has to a large extent eclipsed the inward meaning. Hence arose the natural tendency to pronounced ritualism that is so evident both in the religion and in other features of Chinese life. It is just this restraint, this discipline imposed by outward form on the Chinaman, that makes it so difficult for the Western mind to understand the mind of the Chinese. Much of what piety demands of them may seem to us unimportant, but in the eyes of Chinese piety it is indissolubly connected with ancestor-worship, and it is this that provides the religious basis for many things that are merely matters of form.

It is not too much to say that in China all religion — so far as it is genuinely Chinese and free from foreign influence — is through and through *moral*. The religious sanction is always based on the moral relation by which all things are governed — the processes of nature, the divisions of time, fieldwork, family kinship, the social bond, state government, belief in the spirits of the dead, symbolic ceremonies, and everything else that concerns life. The connecting link is in every case a moral responsibility. This fundamental importance attached to morality is most clearly apparent in ancestor-worship, the real religion of the people, but it is also present and active in the conception of the reciprocal dependence between man's life and the sky, in the mutual influences between nature and human life, and is, too, the cause both of the strange and complex forms of superstition and of the abstruse principles of the geomantic Fêng-Shui.

The limited space assigned to us makes it impossible to examine here how ancient Chinese religious thought is reflected in the literature, or to see how the teachings contained in the *Tao-tê-King,* the *I-King,* and the other Classics supplement or contradict each other and whether they can be combined to form a complete picture. Of profound importance was the work of K'ung-tse in arranging and sifting the oldest literature, and the object with which he undertook this labour had of course momentous consequences for the religious content of the ancient writings. His selection was made with the purpose of handing on the traditional doctrine, and his work was destined to determine by and by what was to be considered classical. His omission of those portions which did not serve his ends had a profound effect on all later thought. K'ung-tse rejected much that the religious needs of the people constrained them to retain. Little is known of the divergent views which did not fit into the system of Confucius, or of the subjects concerning which K'ung-tse deliberately kept silence. But it was inevitable that these rejected or suppressed portions should be adopted into other systems and thus pass over into later Taoism.

In course of time K'ung-tse's value-judgments obtained official recognition and all that contradicted them was rejected with increasing strictness. The subsequent adoption of Confucianism, with its practical morality and its political doctrine, as the sole orthodox creed had the effect of prohibiting all philosophical speculation and many aspects of the ancient religious teaching. Confucius was so far from being the founder of a religion that he deliberately omitted from his teaching a considerable part of the ancient religious faith of his people. But reaction was bound to come, and the gaps in the system of Confucius, which were perceptible to the national consciousness, were filled up at a later time by the insertion of much that he had rejected, by the revival of superstitious views, and by the reception of ideas borrowed from other countries.

It was for purely historical reasons that Confucianism was selected in preference to other competing systems. The Han Dynasty (206 B.C.–A.D. 221) declared Confucianism to be the sole permissible doctrine, decreed that it embodied the national view of the world, and made it the State religion. It was only when the Han Dynasty achieved the consolidation of the entire state that the teaching of Confucius, which had till then lacked any real religious element, was transformed into a religion. Necessarily, therefore, it was a religion that completely suited the political purposes of those in authority, a typical State religion.

The two component parts of this new State Confucianism were, as before, nature-worship and ancestor-worship. Nature-worship, however, which found its supreme expression in the sacrifice to the heavens, was now combined with the worship of the ancestors of the Imperial house. The emperor worshipped the heavens as his ancestor. As the " Son of Heaven " he was the mediator between the laws that govern the world and mankind. In the name of the entire nation — and to the Chinese mind the Chinese nation comprised all the inhabitants of the world — the emperor craved from the celestial and earthly powers blessing and prosperity, rich harvests and favourable weather. He became responsible for the well-being of his subjects, and in his sacred person he became surety for the necessary agreement between the eternal Tao of the universe and man's earthly lot. On the Chinese emperor rested the most tremendous moral obligation that can be conceived — viz., the reconciliation of mankind with the Reason of the world through the power of the supreme virtue which was supposed to indwell in him as emperor. This was the symbolical meaning of the sublime sacrifice to the heavens — the supreme expression of the State religion and the strict prerogative of " the Only Existing One."

Next to the heavens as the universal deity came the numerous heavenly bodies and constellations, mountains and rivers, the powers that controlled the weather, and the guardian deities of the soil. In the worship paid to these the ancestors of the emperor had their share. Through this association of the Imperial ancestors with the ancient gods of nature the emperor and his house became themselves divine. For him the cultus of the State religion was also a service of worship in honour of his ancestors. The ceremonies which the emperor had to perform for his people thus acquired a double significance — they were for him the family worship which was practised by every family throughout his realm.

In view of this fact, that religion was a State concern, it is clear that the mass of the people could have no share in the ceremonies of the State worship. These required the intervention of the emperor or of some one representing him. The Imperial privileges and prerogatives were entrusted to State officials in a carefully arranged order of precedence. The same religious duties which the emperor had to perform in the capital for the whole empire fell to be performed by each official for his administrative district in virtue of the due share of divine authority delegated to him by the ruler.

A special feature was added to the State religion when the Master, Confucius, was elevated to divine rank. A special form of worship, which was classed as ancestor-worship, was held in his honour. The rank of Confucius, next to that of the supreme heavens and on a level with the other deities, was settled differently by the emperors of the various dynasties. This expansion of ancestor-worship beyond the sphere of the family into a cultus for a larger community or for the whole nation became thenceforward a characteristic feature of the State religion. Virtuous and meritorious men could now be elevated to the rank of local deities, and receive their share of the State sacrifices. This honour was not confined to disciples of Confucius and many ancient sages; it was extended to prominent statesmen of later days. The important point in this connexion is that all such elevations were made by the emperor's command. In the Chinese religion the emperor

FIG. 50. MONUMENT TO CONFUCIUS AT CH'Ü-FU

is not only the lord of all men, but also the lord of the gods. The emperor thus determines the religion of the State by virtue of his own divine authority. This adumbrates a later development. With the approval of the emperor representatives of other systems — of Taoism or of minor popular beliefs — could be adopted into the pantheon of State Confucianism, and prominent statesmen could be raised to the status of national heroes.

The cultus consisted of prayer and sacrifice, and these were carried out with all the simplicity and dignity of the most ancient times. For nature-worship there were no temples. The ceremonies were conducted in the open air, on mountain-tops or on river-banks. For the worship of Confucius, how-ever — which was, as has already been said, classed as ancestor-worship — structures were erected in imitation of the domestic ancestral chambers. The supreme expression of the State religion was the great sacrifice to the heavens which was annually celebrated with great solemnity by the emperor on the Altar of Heaven in the capital (Fig. 51), three victims being offered in that ceremony.

Another characteristic feature was the absence of a priesthood. All religious

FIG. 51. ALTAR OF HEAVEN IN PEKING
From Kern, " Das Licht des Ostens "

celebrations were undertaken by the monarch and the State officials as part of their duties. The rites connected with ancestor-worship were performed by the head of the family, who united in his own person the sovereign au-thority of the *paterfamilias* and the office of priest for the spirits of the dead of his house. It was this restriction of the performance of all religious cere-monies to the representatives of the family and of the State that explains why in China religion never acquired a governing body of its own, such as is found wherever there is an organized religion with a hierarchy and a priest-hood. The State established religion as one of its own manifestations, and this same point of view was always taken by the Imperial Government in its dealings with other religious tendencies in the empire. These were tolerated only as far as they did not conflict with the State principle. When once a dogma had been declared orthodox there could no longer be any question of complete toleration. Official China had become Confucian in the time of the Han Dynasty, and all official powers and duties were determined by the instructions laid down in the·classical literature.

The study of this literature formed part of the training of all officials, and all candidates for Government appointments had to undergo examination in the contents of the classical writings. This democratic tendency of Confucian education gained its greatest triumph when Chu Hsi (1130–1200) declared that the orthodox principles were henceforth to be binding dogmas.

In the hands of Lao-tse and his successors the universalistic teaching of Tao, the oldest expression of ancient Chinese thought, had become a speculative philosophy whose abstract doctrines were of course beyond the grasp of the mass of the Chinese people. As time went on the philosophic meaning faded, and a less refined interpretation took its place. Tao, as the power of nature, had been the central theme of the teaching, and through passive union with this primordial principle of nature the perfect man was made a partaker of the powers of the universe and became immortal. This pantheistic conception now received a practical application, and Tao was regarded as a magical power by which the elixir of life could be produced. This of course meant that the philosophical Tao doctrine had become an alchemistic superstition. The possibility of such a development had always been latent in the teaching of Lao-tse, but this result was due to his successors, and was a complete contradiction of the original spirit of his doctrine.

Contemporaneously with this deterioration of Taoism, Confucianism gained its special status as the State religion with fixed dogmas. This could not fail to bring about great changes in the attitude of the two schools to each other. A different view of the world, although rooted in the common soil of ancient Chinese thought and owing its peculiar teachings merely to a different elaboration of that thought, was bound to sink into heterodoxy, although it showed no actual hostility to the doctrines of K'ung-tse. The common origin of the two systems and their originally equal claims to acceptance were forgotten as soon as the Confucian school, with its deliberately selected literature, became the State religion. Confucianism was merely the outcome of certain historical influences, yet when it attained sole dominion it proscribed all other opinions, even although these had been legitimate readings of Chinese thought since far back times.

The after history of Taoism was determined in two ways — externally by its increasingly apparent contradiction to the established dogma and internally by its own continual deterioration. As a result, all the views which had been rejected by Confucianism tended to attach themselves to the structure of Taoism, and round what was left of the ancient Tao doctrine were now grouped the multifarious, ever-changing forms of popular superstition. Some of these had existed from early times without being officially recognized, while others had been created by the unsatisfied cravings of the people. The play of imagination, for which there was no room within the State form of religion, produced within the framework of Taoism a rank growth of superstitions. The sources of information regarding these are inaccessible, and it is impossible to give further details regarding them.

We are also in the dark regarding the process by which Taoism became an actual *religion*. The only thing that can be safely said is that this process was strongly influenced by the alien Buddhism, which began to find its way into China at the beginning of the Christian era. The resemblance between the mystical element in the teaching of Lao-tse and the ascetic aspect of the Indian religion made it *a priori* probable that the two might gradually converge and ultimately coalesce. Although there was no real affinity be-

FIG. 52. TUTELARY DEITIES IN THE VESTIBULE OF A TAOIST TEMPLE
IN LU-FU-SHAN

tween the two systems, but merely a fortuitous identity of results that had been reached from entirely different starting-points, this gradual convergence profoundly affected the after history of both Taoism and Buddhism in China.

As a result of the influence of the ideas of northern Buddhism the ancient Chinese gods of nature were now regarded as possessing human shape, and images of them began to be made. On the analogy of the populous celestial pantheon of Mahāyāna, Taoism as a religion devised an equally varied galaxy of stellar deities, genies, and tutelary deities (see Fig 52). The adoration of national heroes was introduced, and saints, ascetics, outstanding men, and imaginary figures were worshipped as local deities. Lao-tse himself and many prominent personalities mentioned in the philosophical literature were deified, and legendary careers were invented for them after the manner of Buddhist narratives.

The ethical aspect of Taoism was also profoundly influenced by Buddhism. The doctrine of rewards and punishments for good and evil deeds was elaborated in a manner that was utterly un-Chinese. Hell and Paradise, with their deities and satellites, were borrowed from Buddhist teachings, although the doctrines of Lao-tse on the subject of immortality were to a large extent retained. The ecstatic asceticism of the Buddhists merged with the unpremeditated passivity of the Taoists, and the component parts of both systems were worked up into a pseudo-science of magic, geomancy, and exorcism which appealed so strongly to the popular superstition that it drew the entire life of the people under a religious influence.

In particular it was from Buddhism that the religion of Taoism borrowed its external organization, including its priesthood, its monastic life, its temple services, its idol-worship, the formulas of sacrifice, and many other things. Taoism, indeed, went so far as to institute a hierarchy, which, although it was to some extent tolerated by the Government, never received actual recognition. The supreme head, although he was not acknowledged as such by the monasteries, had the oversight of the *lay* brethren, whose activities were chiefly concerned with exorcism. He was, however, always subject to State control, and his activities were restricted to matters in which he could do no harm.

Both Taoism and Buddhism were regarded by the Confucian State as heretical. The Government interdicted, oppressed, and even persecuted their monasteries, and both systems suffered the same untoward fortunes. This oppression naturally drew them still more closely together, until the monastic side of Taoism was completely absorbed by the more popular Buddhism. What is left of it now has practically no influence on the life of the people.

The question how far Taoism and Buddhism have influenced each other in the course of the centuries cannot be further pursued here, important as it is for a full understanding of the present religious condition of China. Such a discussion would carry us into a sphere which belongs to northern Buddhism, a subject assigned to another section of this book.

The religion of the Chinese people is essentially a syncretism. It includes elements derived from the ancient belief in the powers of nature, the conceptions of the soul, the official State religion, Taoism proper, and pure Buddhism, and contains also features derived from the superstition that is so widespread among the Chinese people and some survivals of aboriginal customs. These are so intermingled that the component parts cannot now be disentangled.

The influence of the alien Buddhism on the thought of the people and on every aspect of their religious life has been very great throughout the centuries, so that the popular faith seems now to be completely permeated by Buddhist conceptions. The religious life of China really belongs for the most part to the sphere of Buddhism, and that lies outside our present subject, the typical Chinese religion.

BIBLIOGRAPHY

Plath, *Die Religion und der Kultus der alten Chinesen* (1862–64); Legge, *The Religions of China* (1880); Edkins, *Religion in China* (1884); de Harlez, *Les Religions de la Chine* (1891); de Groot, *The Religious System of China* (1892–1912); and *Universismus* (1918); Grube, *Religion und Kultus der Chinesen* (1910); Kern, *Das Licht des Ostens: Die Weltanschauungen des mittleren und fernern Asiens, Indien, China, Japan* (1923 — also to be consulted for the religions of India and Japan); Krause, *Ju-Tao-Fo, die religiösen und philosophischen Systeme Ostasiens* (1924).

4. INDIAN RELIGION [1]

by Otto Strauss

It is no longer necessary to emphasize the importance of India for the significance and history of religion. Scientific research on the subject has long been followed with keen interest, and there are many people to-day in war-shattered Europe who in their search for new spiritual values have turned longingly to the wisdom of India, and are looking expectantly to the East for fresh stimulus and the fulfilment of their hopes. In many cases this search is the expression of a deeply felt need; in others it is merely a new form of dilettantism. But science must ever keep clearly in view its high duty of sober, unbiased observation.

The following sketch, which must be brief owing to the limited space, should therefore be regarded not as an attempt to inoculate the Western mind with the spirit of India, but as an endeavour to give a historical account of the spiritual life of a foreign people.

That we may start with a clear view of the extent of our task, let us first look at the figures given in the latest *Census of India* (1921, vol. i, p. ii). The total population of India to-day (including Burma, but omitting Ceylon) is stated to be 316,128,921. The following table gives in round figures the numbers of the various religious confessions:

Hindus	216,700,000
Sikhs	3,200,000
Buddhists	11,600,000
Jainists	1,200,000
Parsees	101,800
Mohammedans	68,700,000
Christians	4,750,000
Jews	21,800
Primitive religions, etc.	9,800,000

In order to keep to the plan of the present work, we include here, under Indian religion, only the variations of the first group, who may be classed

[1] *Pronunciation of Indian words: a, c, u* are short; *ā, ī, ū* are long; *e* and *o* are always long; *r* is pronounced *ree* as in ' reed '; *c* as in English ' chin '; *j* as in English ' jungle '; *y* as in English ' yes '; *v* as in English ' very '; *ś* and *ṣ* like English *sh*. *Accentuation:* If the penult (last syllable but one) is long — *i.e.*, if it contains a long vowel or a short vowel followed by a group of consonants — it carries the accent (*e.g.*, ' Ṛgvéda,' ' Caitánya '); if the penult is short, the antepenult (last syllable but two) is accented (*e.g.*, ' Púrusa,' ' Bráhmaṇa ').

together as Brahmanic Hindus. As the table clearly shows, this group comprises by far the largest part of the population of the Indian peninsula.

The small community of Sikhs can be regarded as an addition to this
group, and will be dealt with in due course.

Buddhism, which arose in India in the sixth century B.C., and flourished in
its native land for fifteen hundred years, has now almost entirely disappeared
from India proper. Of the 11,600,000 Buddhists, 11,200,000 live in Burma,
which is part of India only in a political sense, because of the British conquest,
and does not belong to it in respect of situation, race, or language. In India
proper Bengal holds the first place, with 275,000 Buddhists. The Buddhists
of the Himalaya states, Kashmir (38,000) and Sikkim (27,000), are connected with Tibet, and therefore are not to be reckoned as belonging to
India proper. These modern conditions and the present-day importance of
Buddhism in Asia have led the editor of this volume to assign separate articles to the consideration of Buddhism and of the Indian religion. Therefore little will be said here about ancient Indian Buddhism, in spite of its
great importance for Indian religion in ancient days and in the Middle Ages.

On the other hand, owing to the fact that it has survived in India down
to the present day, the religion of the Jains, which is closely akin to Buddhism in origin and nature, falls within the limits of this section, although,
in view of its inferior importance and the small number of its adherents
(1,200,000), it cannot claim a large space.

The Parsees profess the ancient Iranian religion of Zoroaster, which in its
most ancient prehistoric form shows close connexions with the faith of the
Aryan Indians. For their faith's sake the Parsees left their former home in
the beginning of the eighth century after the Mohammedan conquest of
Persia, and settled chiefly in and around Bombay. An account of their religion therefore belongs to that part of this book which describes the religion
of Persia.

Islam, with its 68,700,000 adherents, stands easily at the head of the confessions which have no kind of connexion with Indian religion. Of that
large number Bengal claims 25,200,000 and the Punjab 11,450,000. Only a
minority of the Mohammedans in India can be traced back to foreign conquerors who brought their faith with them. The majority were originally
Hindus who, owing to political events which culminated in the dynasty of
the Mohammedan Mogul emperors (from 1500 to 1700), adopted Islam,
some by compulsion and some voluntarily. Of course this great extension
of the foreign religion was bound to have effects on the faith of the Hindus,
although, as we shall see, these were confined to certain periods and certain
men or groups of men. Present-day students of Islam are far from being in
agreement as to the counter-influence of Indian mysticism on the Mohammedan view of the world, but the discussion of that subject belongs to the
section on Islam. Even after the Mohammedan domination of India had
ceased, however, the religious differences between Hindus and Moham-

medans continued to play a large part in the life of India. The British Government has exploited them to the utmost. To bring about harmony by political means is one of the chief aims of the leaders of the modern Nationalist movement in India, just as it was the life aim of Tilak (who died in 1920) and is still to an even greater degree that of Gandhi (born in 1869, and still alive).

As far as numbers are concerned, Christianity plays a comparatively unimportant part. The great majority of its adherents belong to the lower strata of the population. But the number and type of baptized Indians are no indication of the influence exerted by Christian doctrine since the beginning of the nineteenth century on the religious life of India; a study of this influence will occupy us at the close of this sketch.

We can leave out of account as quite negligible the small number of Jews. They came mostly from Arabia and Mesopotamia, and half of them live in Bombay.

Lastly, the primitive religions, which are found in various parts of the Indian peninsula, will also be omitted here.

We must be content with these few comments on the religious census of the year 1921. The figures will give the reader who is unacquainted with Indian conditions of the present day some idea of the numerical importance of Brahmanic Hinduism. This is what is meant by the expression " the religion of India," and it is our task now to give an account of its historical development from the earliest times.

Turning now to this gigantic task, it will help the reader to find his bearings amid the confusing events of four thousand years if we divide our material into three historical periods.

The first will deal with the religion of the Aryan Indians at the time when it was still comparatively free from foreign admixtures. Chronologically this period extends from the beginning of the second millennium B.C. to about 300 B.C. Geographically it includes the entire northern plain of India — i.e., to use modern names, the country south of the Himalayas and north of a line drawn from the peninsula of Kāthiāwār to Calcutta.

In the second section we shall discuss the religious characteristics of Hinduism. The conquest of the north was followed by the Brahmanic colonization of the south, from about 300 B.C. onward. The theatre of the history in this period is therefore the whole of India, from Kashmir to the southern point; in time, we are brought down to the present day. The intrusion of non-Aryan elements in this period is indisputable, although it is impossible to show it in detail. The large number of outstanding religious personalities who belong to the Dravidic south is itself a sufficient proof of such influences.

In the third section we shall speak of the influence of two world religions on India. Islam began to gain ground in the fourteenth century, and Christianity, as a representative of Western civilization, in the nineteenth century.

The Indian attitude toward Christianity has given rise to a religious Nationalism, and brought about that struggle for spiritual and political independence which we are witnessing to-day.

I

The oldest document of Aryan India has come down to us in a state of marvellous preservation. It is a collection of rather more than a thousand hymns, mostly of a religious character. The name of this collection, *Rgveda,* means the " sacred knowledge [*veda*] of the verses." Of the age of this unique literary source nothing is definitely known, but it seems probable that it has existed — not of course in written form, but retained in human memory — exactly as it is to-day since the first half of the second millennium, B.C.

The gods whose praises are sung in the *Rgveda,* who are invited to the sacrifice, and to whom prayers are offered for victory, sons, wealth, and long life, do not all go back to an equally remote time. Research can to some extent trace their development, and the positions they occupy in the ritual provide some indications of their varying antiquity. The structure of the hymns presupposes long practice in the art of poetry on the part of the priests, and the very large number of stereotyped, frequently recurring lines proves that there was plenty of material available. This helps us to understand the part played by these priestly poets. They handed down in their families a finely developed art which was at the service of their royal patrons in return for payment. When they invite Indra, the god of war, to drink of the intoxicating beverage *soma,* that he may gather courage to annihilate the enemies of the Aryans, when in laudatory lines they remind him of his mythical exploits or praise his generosity to his loyal bards, it is evident that they feel themselves to be in the presence of a well-known power. The divine Indra or his divine high priest, Brhaspati, the lord of the sacred formula (*brahma*), who aids Indra in his mythical exploits just as the priest on earth aids his earthly king; Agni, the god of fire, who in his quality as sacrificial flame mediates between men and gods, and in his quality as hearth flame is the kindly friend of domestic life; the Asvins (the Indian Dioscuri), who send deliverance from danger; or Uśas, the attractive goddess of the dawn — these and many others are to the Vedic priests genuinely living beings, but they are not in any degree 'religious experience' to him. There is absolutely no trace of any sense of awe, although, of course, profound respect and reverence are always present. These cannot but be felt toward beings who are so much more powerful and more richly gifted than men. But the priest on his side does not come to them empty-handed. He, too, has something that they desire. He has the sacred word, the sacred formula, that strengthens and cheers the god, and he has the sacrificial food that stills the divine hunger and the *soma* beverage that brings good cheer.

Thus the relationship of the priest to his ancestral gods is clear and assured. The gods are great and good, but the priest is their friend. There is no problem, no mystery here. Nor is there any doubt concerning the world beyond the grave. Those who thus reverence the gods are the pious, and after death — may it be long in coming! — they will hold high revel among their kindred under the presidency of Yama, the king of the dead, in the shade of a leafy tree. All this breathes assurance and confidence in a priestly technique that can be relied on in the presence of good and great, but not overwhelmingly great, gods.

But there is one exception to what has been said. Intercourse between man and deity is not always purely material and objective, consisting in giving and receiving. There is one deity in whose presence the priests lose their confidence — viz., the great Varuṇa, with his near kinsman, Mitra. The spies of King Varuṇa are everywhere: from them nothing is hidden. When two men hold secret converse in the dark Varuṇa is present as the third. In the presence of this omniscient deity the singer becomes conscious of his littleness. Of Varuṇa he has no mythical stories to tell; in presence of that dread deity he offers fervent prayers for the forgiveness of his sins:

> Whatever sins we have committed against son-in-law, against friend, companion, or brother, against bondsman or stranger, from these absolve us, O Varuṇa! If we have been deceitful, like players at their play, whether wittingly or in ignorance, absolve us, O God. Let us be thy friends, O Varuṇa! [2]

Thus in the presence of this mighty ruler the usual confidence of the priests in their sacrifices deserts them, and here we see an ancient touch of profound solemnity projected into the daily routine. For Varuṇa keeps guard over the order of the world (*rta*). All the gods do so, but he in a more profound manner. In the way that has been foreordained — this seems to be the literal meaning of *rta* — day follows day, the sun runs his course, the rivers flow into the sea. In accordance with *rta* must man's behaviour also be if he is to stand his ground before Varuṇa. This overwhelming thought of the One Order, which is higher than the gods and under their guardianship, and which governs both the macrocosm of the external world and the microcosm of the human heart, seems to go back to the primeval Indo-Germanic people, and may even have formed part of the primitive conception of a law above nature. Like a giant of the past, it rises up in the age of the *Ṛgveda*; thereafter for a time it gradually fades away, but reappears in a new but not less magnificent form in the vision of unity of the *Upaniṣads*.

With regard to the intercourse between god and man, we have seen that side by side with trustful reliance on the good-will of the great and good gods (between whom and man there is a strictly regulated fellowship that is advantageous to both parties) there is also the less assured relationship to

---

[2] *Ṛgveda*, V, 85, 7-8, from the German translation by Hillebrandt.

Varuṇa. Doubts and fears trouble the poet when he comes into the presence of this moral power, behind which stands the impressive conception of *ṛta*. But we also find in the hymns of the *Ṛgveda* a feeling of actual dread toward a deity whose name is rarely mentioned. This is the god Rudra, who, whatever else he may be, differs from all other gods in this — he is *not* a good, benevolent power.

> Strike not great or small, neither sire nor offspring, neither father nor mother. Harm not our life. Harm us not in our children or children's children, nor in our pious ones, our cattle or our horses. Strike not, O Rudra, in thine anger our bondsmen.[3]

The fear here expressed toward the forerunner of the later great god *Śiva* rarely appears elsewhere in the *Ṛgveda*. The class of society that produced these hymns — recognized poets who sang in the service of kings and wealthy devotees — knew nothing of the fears felt by the lower classes of the people. That deep dread finds vent in the incantations of the *Atharvaveda*. This collection, which was later than the hymns of the *Ṛgveda* in being received as canonical, contains the substance of the primeval incantations against all the great and small contingencies that affect human life everywhere. Here we find the plain man seeking protection in minor magic against the innumerable dangers that surround him in a world that teems with evil spirits and malevolent powers. But we cannot pursue this line of thought further here, as our subject is merely the outstanding features of the Indian religion.

We revert, therefore, to the great circle of the good gods and the routine laid down for their worship. This cultus, which followed the lines laid down by tradition, was the age-long expression of simple devout feeling, but in profounder minds it left abundant room for the search after new inward experience. In the latest hymns of the *Ṛgveda* we can see the approach of the crisis that always occurs when a cultus threatens to stifle the living sense of religion. There is a perceptible striving after a unity above the multiplicity of the accepted gods. This search was stimulated by the fact that the figures of the gods were gradually losing their sharpness of outline. The poets had slipped into the habit of repeating the same praises in their worship of each god, and ascribed now to this and now to that deity not only all the works of creation and all possible great and good qualities, but also the same mythical exploits. Their chief interest no longer lay in a plastic conception such as the populace love. For the priest the god was sufficiently identified by his place in the ritual, and his personality gradually faded into an abstract conception. This tendency was further helped by the fact that the ancient Vedic worship knew neither idols nor temples. The numerous deities who were all invisibly present at the sacrifices were no longer differentiated, and their names were now interpreted as so many aspects of one being. A hymn in the last book of the *Ṛgveda* (X, 121) clearly betrays this tendency by its refrain, which is

[3] *Ṛgveda*, I, 114, 7–8, from the German translation by Hillebrandt.

repeated nine times. " Who is the god, that we may serve him with sacrifice? " Here we see the need felt for *one* supremely great deity who will
unite in himself all that is wont to be said in praise now of this god and now
of that, and who can be worshipped in a higher sense than, say, the warlike,
potulent Indra. The grudge felt by this poet against Indra, who is so popular
with other hymn-writers, finds subtle expression in the form of this hymn. It
is an imitation of a lay in praise of Indra, but it is to the new One god that
it is addressed. Two others actually name this new deity, and it is significant
that his name, Viśvakarman (" He whose Work is the Universe "), is a new
coinage, expressing an abstract thought.

In addition to the hymns that thus seek for or name the one god, there is
another that is specially noteworthy (X, 129). It also deals with the unity
of the deity and with the cosmogony, but, unlike the new ones, it sets at
the beginning of all things not a god, but a neutral principle, not further
defined. I have translated and discussed this hymn in my *Indische Philosophie*
(p. 24 f.) and must content myself here with this reference to it.

We now leave the period of the *Rgveda* and turn to another part of the
history of the Indian religion. Our sources here are the numerous sacrificial
texts called the *Brāhmaṇas*. While the hymns belong geographically to
Northwest India, the home of the *Brāhmaṇas* is North Central India. The
advance of the Aryan conquest was accompanied by a great development of
religious life. The ancient pantheon, which, as we have seen, had fallen into
discredit at the close of the *Rgveda,* had by this time lost still more of its
influence. The names of the deities had become mere counters in a priestly
game, and sacrifice now occupied the centre of interest, with a machinery so
elaborate that little room was left even for new deities like Prajāpati, the lord
of all creatures. Gods were no longer felt to be necessary; at least, personal
relationship to them was no longer essential. A complicated ritual of sacrifice
now gave men a magical power which produced the desired results with all
the certainty of natural laws if it was correctly used and properly understood. Even divine beings could now be compelled to obey man's will. The
place of sacrifice had become a symbol of the cosmos — what happened at
the altar had its parallel in the great world. That is to say, it was systematic
magic on a large scale. The magical work of the Brahman (that is, a man
qualified by virtue of his descent from a strictly exclusive caste and by his
laboriously acquired mastery over the formal side of sacrifice and its efficacy)
is like that of an experimenter in a modern physical laboratory. The powers
of such a recognized and successful expert in sacrifice could have no rival,
and the claims of the Brahmans passed all bounds. They even called themselves " men-gods."

During this period of the *Brāhmaṇas* religion was lifeless — at least, that
is the impression conveyed by our sources, which were written by pedantic
sacrificial experts. The great mass of the people stood outside of it. They
showed no interest in it, and still loyally worshipped not only their old gods,

but also many minor spirits. The dominant priestly class had little to give the people. Their fondness for speculation, however, their mania for discussing the inter-relations of the most heterogeneous things, their love of finding comparisons and identities everywhere, were not entirely fruitless. They brought clearly into view the conception of Brahma, which had already been adumbrated in the *Ṛgveda* — *i.e.,* the power that becomes efficacious in the sacred incantation and in the sacred person of the Brahman. Finding in Brahma the central motive power at the place of sacrifice, they saw also in it the central force of the world, the world unity. They further extended this search for unity into their own hearts, and after much groping they found in the word for ' self ' — *Ātman* — the term which, better even than ' speech ' or ' spirit ' or ' breath,' expressed the essence of human nature.

Their pioneer work in this direction was accompanied by an advance in their conception of the hereafter. Just as there are sacrificial rites which secure sons and cattle, prosperity and victory, in this life, so there are means by which hunger and other ills can be warded off in the world to come. Mention is made of the " second death," which can be evaded by sacrifice. This was another piece of groundwork which must be put to their credit. It paved the way for something that was to come.

This whole system as laid down in the *Brāhmaṇas* with its excessive emphasis on the formalities of sacrifice, its close caste ritual, and its prescribed life, was swept away in the ninth and eighth centuries B.C. by a new wave of spiritual life, which has left its deposit in the *Upaniṣads*. In these texts, many of which take the form of dialogues, we see the Indian mind in the act of springing up into fresh new life. This new life included new strata of the population. Kings, women, and men of uncertain descent now took their part, and frequently showed themselves superior to the official priests in their grasp of the new ideas which now occupied the centre of interest. At the same time, the connexions between the new ideas and the achievements of the *Brāhmaṇas* are everywhere apparent in the *Upaniṣads*. These writings, indeed, rank as the last portions of the *Brāhmaṇas*. Spiritual revolutions are never radical. They never extirpate root and branch what went before. Though the old is pushed aside, it frequently lives on and reappears strangely mixed with the new. But while we must not lose sight of that fact, a sketch like the present must naturally emphasize the new element, especially when it is the more valuable of the two.

This novel ingredient is usually called philosophy, and whoever has heard of the philosophy of the *Upaniṣads,* either from Schopenhauer or from Deussen, will be inclined to ask how this philosophy can be described as the culminating point of Indian religious life. It provides a classical illustration of the inseparable connexion between philosophy and religion in India. The fresh knowledge contained in the *Upaniṣads* is not merely intellectual; it is something that can be experienced. The goal is not a mere understanding of the truth for its own sake; salvation lies in the truth that is understood, in realizing the true core of human nature, which is hidden by the things that are objectively experienced.

We have seen how the search for unity found a twofold satisfaction in the *Brāhmaṇas*. In sacrifice was found the unity of the cosmos — that is, Brahma; the unity of human nature was found in the self, in the Ātman. The new knowledge is the identification of these two factors — Ātman and Brahma are identical. Brahma is the ego of the All, the Absolute Ego; the individual ego is a part of this universal Ātman, it *is* this Absolute Ego, "in whom and from whom and to whom are all things." The conception of Brahma is the fulfilment of the longing of the old reformers in the *Ṛgveda*. They sought the one great god behind or above the gods, because the limited powers of the ancient deities did not satisfy the need for something worthy of worship. Now has been found the Absolutely Great, that beside which there is none else, which knows no limitations, not even the limitation of individuality.

> He is my Ātman in my inmost heart, smaller than a grain of rice or a grain of barley or a grain of mustard or a grain of millet or than the kernel of a grain of millet. He also is my self in my inmost heart, greater than the earth, greater than heaven, greater than these worlds. He from whom all works, all desires, all sweet odours and tastes proceed, he who embraces all this universe, who never speaks and is never surprised — he is my soul in my inmost heart. He is Brahma. When I depart hence I shall obtain him. For him, to whom this comes, for him in sooth there is no doubt. [4]

Whoever reads these words, which are among the oldest of the kind that have come down to us, will at once feel that they disclose a vision that fills and gladdens the whole heart. We feel the original experience of the man to whom this came. It is not the outcome of brooding thought, but the power of vision. It involves, therefore, no estrangement from the world, no pessimistic attitude toward it. Brahma is, to be sure, that which is beyond sorrow, age, and death, but that is only the natural obverse side of Brahma as it is experienced. To have a vision of the Absolute, to *be* the Absolute — that is the central experience. And it is only when one has sated himself with this breadth and depth that the thought comes, "Whatever is other than this is full of sorrow."

Two other important new discoveries are accompaniments of the central vision of Brahma. These are *karma* and *saṃsāra*.

Karma means literally "performance," "work done," and denoted originally the sacrificial acts. Even in the *Ṛgveda* such performance was regarded as fruitful, and the same thought is even more prominent in the *Brāhmaṇas*. The benefits might appear in this life — as wealth, victory, health, etc. — or they might be reaped after death. In that case they consisted in the attainment of heaven or in the fending off of the second death. When the horizon widened beyond the limits of the ritual — and that is what we see taking place in the *Upaniṣads* — the conception of performance or work done also

[4] *Chāndogya-Upaniṣad*, III, 14.

widened, and every action of man in its moral aspect came to be regarded as profitable. The power which resulted from the performance of sacrifice, and which bore its fruit when the sacrifice was long past, was now conceived as residing in every human action that has a moral significance. *Karma* now means the influence of human action, which may remain long in suspension before it is realized in its result. The other conception was that of *samsāra*. This word (from the root *sr*, " to run ") means literally " to run about." As the conception of a second death in the hereafter had developed into the idea of being born again after death in a new incarnation, *samsāra* means the incessant return in ever new births. The nature of these reincarnations is determined by the deeds of the former life. That is to say, my fate after death depends on my *karma*. " Who does good reappears as a good man; who does evil as an evil man." Does the good life, then, lead to entrance into Brahma? No. Each *karma* bears empirical fruit. Whoever, therefore, aims at union with the Absolute, whoever wishes to realize the true nature of his ego, which is subject to no change, must be freed from *karma,* and this is effected by the vision of Brahma, that profound inward experience of which we have just spoken. In union with the Absolute, individuality is of course extinguished, for individuality is possible only so long as an ego is confronted by a non-ego. But when everything has been transmuted into one's own self all such distinctions vanish. He who has come to know Brahma becomes Brahma, is lost or absorbed in Brahma.

It was only gradually that some of the details and problems implied here were recognized and discussed. These views first clearly emerged in the *Upanisads,* and formed the basis of every higher type of religion in India. The good life brings good fruit, either in the form of an abode in heaven — interrupted, however, by a new reincarnation — or in the form of an immediate reincarnation. But the advantages of the favourable reincarnation are by no means always merely material prosperity or social well-being. Better than all else is the inward disposition which qualifies one for ever higher experience. To anticipate here what may be said about Buddhism, which has all its roots in these conceptions, rebirth as a *bhodisattva* — *i.e.,* as one who will attain the highest enlightenment in this existence — is conditioned by innumerable previous lives, in which are summed up all the merits which qualify one for the highest. On the other hand, an evil life leads a man downward to births in animal form, and in extreme cases involves a sojourn in hell.

The oldest *Upanisads,* with their vision of the Absolute, with their new epoch-making conceptions (*karma,* transmigration of souls, and salvation), became the starting-point for many developments. These raised structures of various kinds out of the newly found spiritual building-stones, and the religious life of India after the eighth century B.C. was enriched and diversified by a late series of *Upanisads* and by the rise of various sects, such as Buddhism, Jainism, and many others. These later *Upanisads* contain the first mention of a path which has continued to be a characteristic feature of Indian mentality ever since — the path of Yoga. But Yoga must be taken along with *tapas* if we are to understand the history of the religion. *Tapas* is mentioned as far back as the hymns of the *Ṛgveda* and in the most ancient ritual. It means literally "heat," thence coming to mean mortification of the flesh by watching, fasting, chastity, etc. This idea has been excellently summed up by Oedenburg:

> In this manner the ascetic gathers up in his own person "the blue-black dark, the power that grips," or, to use the language of earth, the nervous over-excitement, the susceptibility to visions, the diminution of the sense of reality. The line of division between the Possible and the Impossible, all limitations of will-power, are banished, and the ascetic reaches a plane where he feels that he and his environment are raised above the life of others and dwell in a higher world.

A similar condition is ascribed to the original creative force at the time of its own self-origination in the famous *Hymn of Creation* (*Ṛgveda*, X, 129). The same condition is reached by the offerer of sacrifice when he prepares himself for his task by initiation or consecration (*dīkṣā*). It was *tapas* that enabled the ancient seers to sing the eternal hymns of the *Ṛgveda,* and it was through the same practice that the pious attained the felicity of heaven. It is as a further development and a later stage of *tapas* that Yoga is best understood. The word comes from a verbal root, *yuj,* which means "to harness" or "to yoke" and is used of horses. Metaphorically it means the harnessing of psychic force. This gives rise to wondrous powers that transcend the limits of space and time circumscribing human life, yet these powers are not the really essential element in Yoga. That essential element lies in its special goal, in salvation, in liberation from the conditioned and the attainment of the Absolute. A series of instructions full of ethical charm is given as an introduction to the Yoga exercises, but these moral rules are not an end in themselves. They merely help to remove the grosser obstacles presented by man's lower instincts and bar his way to higher things. These ethical rules are followed by instructions concerning the treatment of the body, and include rules that prescribe the correct sitting posture, the withdrawal of the senses from the external world, and the control of the process of breathing. Then comes the spiritual aspect of Yoga — inward calm and concentration, which lead to ever higher planes of life, beyond the empirical. But even the experiences thus enjoyed in realms above the present life, where many truths are revealed that lie far beyond the reach of normal thought, are not yet the last or highest. The supreme goal is found in the attainment of the Absolute, of the completely Unconditioned. It may bear many names and be variously described, but it ever wears the same feature of Absolute Existence, differing essentially from all else that can be conceived. It must be admitted that this description goes far beyond the views of the older period, especially in the details and the arrangement, but the essence of Yoga was exactly the same even in the early stage.

Tapas — *i.e.,* purely bodily asceticism — has also been all along an outstanding feature of Indian religion. The chief differences between *tapas* and Yoga are these: Yoga rejects self-torments as such, and seeks rather to promote bodily well-being as providing a suitable basis for higher spiritual effort, whereas *tapas* always aims at power. A favourite theme is an ascetic who practises *tapas* to such good purpose that the gods, dreading his power, try to divert his energies in other directions. This idea is almost entirely absent from Yoga, the devotees of which are warned not to develop power lest it endanger the higher aims. Thus, like the Buddhist doctrine, in which it plays a great part, Yoga is a *via media* between the pleasures of the body and self-torture. The path of Yoga to planes of higher consciousness and to the sphere of absolute truth that transcends all thought became an important educational instrument in Indian life, and has left its mark on Indian mentality down to the present day.

What thus emerged in Yoga as a characteristic of the period that followed the oldest *Upaniṣads* reappears in another aspect of the religious attitude of the time — viz., the tendency to turn away from all that natural life offers. For the vision of *Brahma,* as we have seen, no reincarnation, not even the highest, was the *summum bonum*. Union with the Absolute was the one true good; compared with the brilliance of this goal, everything on earth and in heaven lost its colour. It is not, however, till the period with which we are now dealing that, as the result of further reflection, emphasis came to be laid on the insufficiency — nay, the paltriness — of the non-absolute. Now emerged that pessimism which lies at the root of all genuine redemptive religion. But this pessimism is not to be confused with resignation, for it is just this pessimism that underlies the new aversion from the world. This was what Buddha meant when he taught that suffering was a necessary part of all conditioned existence, and pointed out a path that led from sorrow and suffering to the life where these no longer existed — that is, the Unconditioned, Nirvāṇa. This was also the message of another new school, closely akin to Yoga, which advocated a similar way to freedom, and declared that the restraining of the senses was like the bridling of the wild horses that draw the chariot of life. The suppression of the senses was to be followed by the suppression of consciousness of the self, the constant danger of which lies in its affinity for all that is earthly. Thus one attains to Reason, whose continual activity is the direct outcome of the great dynamic power which man has learned to set up as an eternal material principal in opposition to the Absolute Spirit.

This strict differentiation between material and spiritual was quite alien to the oldest periods. Even ancient Buddhism analyzed the self (*ātman*), whose finality it denied, into five components — one a material factor and the others psychical. But now the soul, under the somewhat novel name of *puruṣa* — literally " man," *vir* — is clearly differentiated from all that is non-psychical. All action belongs to the non-psychical side; gross matter, the senses, the ego sense, thought — in Yoga they are all seen to be essentially different from the eternally unmoved spiritual light, which, though perfectly the same in all men, seems to be individualized and drawn into the vortex of life only by the delicate material of the body which accompanies it through the entire series of reincarnations. But this only *seems* to be so, for the truth of the Absolute Spirit can only be experienced by treading the path we have already spoken of: it can never be reached by discursive thought.

Salvation is thus the liberation of the soul from the mechanism of the forces of life. When this state has been reached the reincarnations cease. That this teaching was originally a Yoga experience, an inward experience, not a product of the intellect — although numerous different systems have adopted it, under the name of Sāṃkhya (*i.e.,* " Number," " Enumeration "), as their philosophical basis — is shown by the many difficulties which arose later when the factors of the Sāṃkhya series were regarded as cosmical grades and the structure of the world was traced back to the germinal creative force, *prakṛti.*

In these last paragraphs we have been dealing with the loftiest and most advanced efforts of the Indian mind. But no one who is familiar with the phenomena of religion can imagine for a moment that these speculations represent the average level of the ordinary Indian. We find a much more *naïve* and human way of looking at things in the traditional canon of a sect that flourished contemporaneously with Buddhism (sixth century B.C.), although it originated much earlier — viz., Jainism. Jainism — so called after the *soubriquet* of its restorer, Jaina (*i.e.,* " Conqueror ") — cannot, it is true, be compared with Buddhism in the magnificence of its conception or in its fertility of ideas, any more than in its numerical distribution, but it has excelled Buddhism in one respect. It has managed to survive in its native India down to the present day, whereas Buddhism has had to counterbalance its extinction in India by a widespread extension throughout the whole of Asia.

The clear distinction between matter and soul of which we have spoken is a prominent feature of Jainism. But whereas in Sāṃkhya this contrast cannot be bridged, any interconnexion between the two being regarded as merely apparent, in Jainism matter exerts a direct influence on the soul, this influence being expressed by a peculiarly primitive interpretation of *karma.* The very *naïveté* of the interpretation makes it not improbable that the sect, as its own tradition declares, was founded, under the leadership of Pār-svanātha, several centuries prior to Buddhism — *i.e.,* at a time when the conception of *karma* was still novel enough to be understood in a somewhat primitive way. The interpretation was this: a rarified *karma* matter was postulated which penetrates the soul and destroys its natural qualities or infuses new qualities alien to its nature. In order to become free from this infection by *karma,* in order to shake off the wretched chain of reincarnations, in order to be redeemed from all that is material, the soul must put forth ethical activity, and by means of the merit thus attained prevent the entrance of the poisons or destroy them if they have already entered. This theory of ethics, with its general rules for the laity and more detailed rules for the monks (like Buddhism, Jainism is first and foremost a monastic system), cannot be described in greater detail here. Like all other forms of Indian ethics, it contains not only the general moral commandments common to all higher views of the world, but also instructions on introspection and an extremely ascetic attitude toward property and sensuous enjoyment. In contrast to Buddhism, it awards high merit to bodily asceticism on the part of those that seek salvation. Indeed, deliberate starvation of the body is regarded as especially meritorious. When the pious Jainist has done his utmost to free his soul from the poison of *karma* he does not need to be reborn, but, as Von Glasenapp puts it, exists

> to all eternity in the highest part of the sacred region Īshatprāgbhāra, neither light nor heavy, without visible form, without a body and therefore permeable, but with a spatial (immaterial) extension of two-thirds of what he had in his last existence.

He is a 'redeemed' one (*siddha*), possessing infinite knowledge, infinite intuition, infinite power, and infinite bliss.

A religion such as Jainism, which, like Buddhism, teaches a self-redemption by the man who treads the appointed path, cannot logically have any cultus — *i.e.,* any outward form of worship. The only possible cultus would be a kind of memorial service in honour of the teacher of the way of salvation. This was the case in the oldest Buddhism, when honour was paid to the remains of Buddha, and this must have been the case also in the oldest form of Jainism. Gradually, however, images of Jaina and of his three-and-twenty predecessors were erected and worshipped, and there were further added twenty-four 'ford-finders' (Tīrthaṃkaras) as attendant deities, although, according to the doctrines of the sect, the gods are merely highly placed beings within the Saṃsāra. Thus Jainism, which in ancient times and in the Middle Ages was widely distributed not only in its native North-east and in its citadel Gujerāt (in the North-west), but also in Central and Southern India, has been compelled to give way since the eighth century B.C. to Hinduism, to which it had made too great concessions. It is only in modern times that Jainism, taking advantage of the general national movement of which we shall speak later, has again begun to spread propaganda, and to emphasize its antiquity and its completeness. This forward movement has been greatly facilitated by the enormous wealth of many of its adherents.

Before we turn to the study of Hinduism, something further must be said about the idea of deity in the religious thought of ancient India. After the ancient pantheon of the *Ṛgveda* had faded away no complete substitute appeared in the sacrificial texts. There were many divine beings, but the place of living personalities to whom a personal relation was possible was taken by the mechanical service of sacrifice, with its semi-natural and semi-magical rites. The rise of the theory of *karma* drove the idea of a personal deity still farther into the background. If a man's moral deeds automatically determine the fate of his soul in the next life, if his external and inner fate is thus self-determined, there is no room for that cry for help addressed by weak man to superior powers which gives such strong support to the faith in a deity. And the worship of a god was further weakened by the vision of Brahma as taught in the oldest *Upaniṣads*. To the impersonal Absolute, of which man is himself a part, there can be no such relation as that implied in personal worship.

There were also, of course, hints of a higher faith in a deity. Not only is there a tendency to personify the All-Ātman, but a mystical union with the Absolute, which, although it had no rational basis, came over the meditating soul like a sudden illumination, was regarded as a divine favour. It was natural to seek after an infinitely exalted Some One who could grant such a favour. We see here the first beginning of a new type of religious faith, which will occupy us later.

Both ancient Buddhism and ancient Jainism sternly denied the existence of a God. They did not deny the existence of numerous higher beings who inhabited the various grades of the celestial regions. These were worshipped in Yoga, and comprised many new names, as well as some old ones, such as Indra. But they did deny the existence of an absolute deity who can help men to obtain salvation or even grant it to him, and who hovers over the universe which he has made according to his good pleasure. By 'god' these religious sects mean unredeemed beings who, by virtue of their high merits, inhabit wondrous worlds, but who require a new, final reincarnation before they can be absorbed into the Absolute. For the series of reincarnations can only be closed from the human side.

Thus, although the lofty teachings of the *Upaniṣads* and of the various Indian sects place the divine on a lower level, it would be a mistake to think that the old gods were forgotten. They still lived in the minds of the populace, to whom the high knowledge of the *Upaniṣads* was inaccessible. In a similar manner the lay adherents of the numerous monastic religions (Buddhism, Jainism, etc.) did not accept the extreme conclusions of the official teaching. That faith in the ancient gods still survived is proved by the oldest *Upaniṣads* themselves in certain ceremonial and mythical passages and by the manuals of domestic ritual (the *Gṛhya-sūtras*) and of law, including religious and social duties (the *Dharma-sūtras*). There we find all the ancient names and ideas. Varuṇa, who punishes lying, Yama, who dwells in man's heart and judges him, and all the other ancient deities, as well as new ones, who must be appeased by the performance of religious and social duties by all who desire welfare here and hereafter. The conception of salvation is familiar to the populace also, although the search for the highest is now relegated to the end of one's days, when all parental duties have been fulfilled. But what did the plain man mean by " entrance into Brahma "? He clung to the prospect of heaven or a favourable reincarnation, and the priest could advise him how to attain these, without being false to his own higher insight, because his wide priestly experience enabled him to make allowances for all grades of attainment. If we may take all this as meaning that for each man only those gods and that goal are real which he can understand, then we have here the basis on which the great philosopher and practical theologian Śaṃkara (c. 800 A.D.) was able without opposition to conjoin an illusionistic monism of the most pronounced type with a living religion. This liberalism proved to be a source of strength to Indian religion, for it enabled it to unite the most diverse stages of civilization into one real whole, although of course to our ideas it was far from being uniform or consistent.

II

We come now to that phase of Indian religion which goes under the specific name of "Hinduism." That term is extremely comprehensive. It has not only a religious, but also a social meaning, for the caste system is a very important constituent of it. As the name of a religion, it excludes those religious societies which do not recognize the Veda as authoritative — e.g., Buddhism, Jainism, etc. — but includes practically all other shades of Indian religion from the first centuries B.C. down to the present day. As it is impossible in this short sketch to give even a faint idea of all these varieties of belief, we shall content ourselves with a study of the main aspects of two great

FIG. 53. VIṢṆU

He has his four attributes, the lotos, club, discus, and shell-horn, in his hands, and is accompanied by his spouses, Laksmi and Sarasvati.

From Zimmer, " Kunstform und Yoga "

deities which have occupied the chief places in Indian religion since the first centuries of our era. These two deities also typify the two qualities which characterize the Indian mind as the product of Aryan and non-Aryan (chiefly Dravidian) components. The god Viṣṇu (Fig. 53) embodies the softness and gentleness of the Indian national character, typifying kindness

FIG. 54. ṢIVA DANCING
From Cohn, " Indische Plastik "

and love toward all creatures, as well as a love toward God, which is akin to the erotic impulse and can actually take the erotic form. Ṣiva, on the other hand, is the embodiment of the dark, savage element. He is the great ascetic, who, adorned with his dread badges (a chain of skulls), meditates in the icy solitudes of the Himālayas or dances wild cosmic dances (Fig. 54).

Irritable and dreadful, like the human ascetic, he is a powerful ally, but also a terrible enemy thirsting for blood. This bloodthirsty side of his nature is specially embodied in his spouse, of whom we shall speak later. Next to these two great deities come numerous others who are worshipped by the people — the wise god Gaṇeśa, with the trunk of an elephant (Fig. 55), Kabera, who guards the treasures, Skandha, the god of war, etc.

FIG. 55. GAṆEŚA WITH THE ELEPHANT HEAD, GOD OF
THE ART OF WRITING AND REMOVER OF OBSTACLES

This atmosphere, so different from that of former days, which surrounds Viṣṇu and Śiva, finds further expression in the outward forms of the worship paid to them; whereas neither temple nor image was known in Vedic times, both now become prominent (Fig. 56). The suggestion that this change in the cultus is to be ascribed to non-Aryan, Dravidian influences finds some support in the fact that down to the present day the celebrants in the temples are despised, while the teaching Brahmans are held in as high respect as ever.

The conception of Viṣṇu has gathered various other deities around it. Local deities, deified heroes, beings of animal shape, and even Buddha have

all been brought by the Brahmans into the same circle as Viṣṇu and declared
to be incarnations of that deity (*avatāras,* literally ' descents '). One especially
important *avatāra* must be discussed first here. It is a fusion of Vāsudeva, the
deity of a western tribe, with *Kṛṣṇa,* the deified chieftain of a pastoral tribe.
This *avatāra* is important because it is here that we meet with the first mention of *bhakti,* the love of God, which plays such a large part in the history
of Indian religion. The first literary attestation of *bhakti* is in an episode from
the epic poem *Mahābhārata.* This was originally a heroic lay, but in the first
centuries of our era it became a storehouse of knowledge of all kinds. The
episode in question is related in *Bhagavad-gītā — The Lay of the Saint —*

FIG. 56. TEMPLE OF VIṬṬHAL VIṢṆU

' Viṭṭhal ' is the Kanaran form of the name ' Viṣṇu.' The temple is in the South Indian
city of Vijayanagar; it was destroyed in 1565.

From Longhurst, " Hampi Ruins "

and recounts the conversation between Arjuna, an outstanding warrior, and
his cousin and charioteer *Kṛṣṇa,* who in the course of time turns out to be
the incarnation of the Universal God. In its seven hundred verses the poem
deals with philosophical, religious, and ethical subjects, and by its popular
style, its tolerant spirit, and its warm tone won all Indian hearts to such an
extent that from the time it appeared (previous to our Christian era) down
to the present day it has been one of the best-known books of India, and
has even been called the Bible of the followers of Viṣṇu. Of its philosophy
we can say here only that it unites the dualism of Sāṃkhya with the supreme
unity of Brahma. The important fact for us here is that while the path *via*
knowledge to salvation is recognized as possible and legitimate, it is declared to be more difficult than the path *via* believing devotion to God. The

latter is open and accessible to all, and leads unfailingly to salvation. Here is an extract:

> Greater labour awaits those who cleave in their thoughts to the Unknowable, for the goal that is unknowable is difficult to reach by incarnate beings. But those who refer all works to Me, who consecrate themselves to Me, and serve Me in their heart with a devotion that they bestow on nothing else, those whose thoughts are dedicated to Me, I immediately save from the sea of this world's life that leads to death. Only incline thine heart to Me, set thy mind on Me, and thou shalt dwell with Me hereafter. Of that there is no doubt.[5]

This deity, absolute devotion to whom is the true way of salvation, is so completely absolute and alone that all worship offered to other gods is in effect addressed to him and acknowledged by him. This appeal to every pious heart of every confession, even to those who tread the independent paths of philosophy or of Yoga, was perhaps intended to attract new adherents, but it is also the first appearance of that tolerant spirit which recognizes all possible varieties of piety.

The Universal God of the *Bhagavad-gītā* demands for himself no prescribed form of worship. All the commandments of morality, both those that are ethical, enjoining gentleness, patience, love toward all creatures, and those that are social, determined by birth in a definite caste, along with faith, trust and love toward the divine — these are the requirements whose fulfilment brings salvation. But the sensuous element in the new faith is betrayed in the impressive apparition, with many mouths and arms, and with the insignia of Viṣṇu (club, coronet, discus, and lotus flower), which Arjuna may see, thanks to the grace of the god, who is visible to the ordinary eye only in the form of his human charioteer. The theophany, which occupies the middle part of the poem, is clearly meant to be its culminating point. It brings before the eye of the worshipper the surpassing greatness of the Universal God, whereas the ineffable majesty of Brahma is much more difficult to understand. To love and worship this god, to do all things for his sake as a matter of duty and with no thought of reward, to cast all consequences on the Universal God and leave them with him — this is a living, attractive conception such as earlier ages never knew. It has been suggested that these exhortations to the love of God are due to non-Aryan, Dravidian influences. Some have even ascribed the growth of *bhakti* to influences from Western Asia, especially as the Buddhism of North-west India at the time when Christ was born also shows strong traces of *bhakti*. But there is no clear proof of such influence, and it must always be remembered that complete consecration to the Universal Soul, who is declared in the *Upaniṣads* to be more worthy of love than son or wife, must have been at least one of the sources of *bhakti,* not to speak of the innate longing of the human heart to consecrate itself to something higher than itself, even if that something is unknown.

[5] XII, 5–8.

A full account of the life-history of Kṛṣṇa belongs to a later period. An appendix to the great epic the *Harivaṃśa* (*c.* fourth century A.D.) tells how in the city of Mathurā, which was always a centre of Viṣṇu-worship, the wicked King Kaṃsa is informed by a seer that he is threatened with death at the hands of a son of his aunt Devakī. Thereupon, at the command of Kaṃsa, all the children of Devakī are put to death. (This has no bearing whatever on the massacre of the children of Bethlehem, because the broad outlines of this legend are found in Indian literature as far back as the second century B.C.) Young Kṛṣṇa, however, is saved by his father, who exchanges him with a shepherd's daughter of the same age. The girl is killed by Kaṃsa, but Kṛṣṇa grows up among the shepherds, who look upon him as one of themselves. Even as a child Kṛṣṇa performs astounding feats, plays pranks, and has many adventures with demons and serpents, even with Indra. This part of his life is especially popular with all classes of the people. Perhaps the favourite passages of the narrative are those summed up by Winternitz in these words:

> In the beautiful autumn nights his heart rejoices as he watches the young shepherdesses dancing in the moonlight. They of course are all in love with the daring youth. They sing of his deeds, and playfully imitate his ways, his sports, his bright glance, his gait, his dancing, and his songs.

This is the first appearance of that erotic feature which is so prominent in the Vishnavite faith, that ardent love toward the god, the Viṣṇu-*bhakti*, that fills the soul of the worshipper. It is the counterpart of the sensuous love for the brave youth that fills the hearts of the shepherdesses. This erotic element can of course assume various guises. Symbolically it is a parable of true religious feeling, and a real psychical experience, but it sometimes completely replaces the religious faith by sexual feeling, and the history of Viṣṇu-worship provides many examples of this.

This relation of Kṛṣṇa to the shepherdesses exemplifies a feature of Indian religion of which we shall hear more when we come to speak of Śiva — viz., the great place occupied by female deity. In Vishnuism this cannot be said to be prominent. Where it does appear it centres round the name Rādhā. At first merely the *belle* among the shepherdesses (*Bhāgavata-Purāṇa, c.* A.D. 900), Rādhā afterward becomes the eternal spouse of Kṛṣṇa, and lives with him in the cow-world high above all the heavens. The somewhat dubious sect founded by Vallabhācārya (1479-1531) holds out as the highest hope of the faithful the prospect of sharing in the sensual delights of this divine pair, but excrescences of this kind have always been rare in Vishnuism. As a matter of fact, the erotic element, so far as it was not meant merely to tickle the ears of the populace (and here we must keep in mind the very great difference between the Indian and European attitude toward this subject), has done much to infuse warmth and intensity into genuine religious feeling.

An example of this is provided by the *Bhāgavata-Purāṇa*. The name 'Bhāgavata' denotes the sect that worshipped Kṛṣṇa under the title of Bhagavān, " the Saint." The same word occurs in the name *Bhagavad-gītā, The Lay [Gītā] of the Saint*. In this great work, which seems to have originated about A.D. 900 in Southern India among an ascetic group belonging to the Bhāgavata sect, intense love toward the god is combined with an undeniable erotic strain. Contemplation of the boundless devotion of the shepherdesses toward the beloved youth is supposed to rekindle passionate love in the heart of the worshipper of Kṛṣṇa. Here, therefore, love for the divine finds vent in a manner that closely resembles outbursts of sexual passion. As Farquhar puts it:

> *Bhakti* in this work is a surging emotion which chokes the speech, makes the tears flow and the hair thrill [this expression recurs frequently in erotic poetry] with pleasurable excitement, and often leads to hysterical laughing and weeping by turns, to sudden fainting fits and to long trances of unconsciousness. This excitation is produced by gazing at the images of Kṛṣṇa, singing his praises, keeping company with his devotees, hearing them tell the mighty deeds of Kṛṣṇa and talking with them about his glory and his love.

The way for the introduction of these features of the *Bhāgavata-Purāṇa* was prepared by religious poets in Southern India from the seventh to the ninth centuries. Under the name of " Āḷvārs " these men occupy an honoured place in the religious history of India. Going from temple to temple, they sang hymns declaring their ardent love to the great deity. In their ecstasy they even crossed the strictly guarded barriers of caste, and carried their message to those who had none. This breach of the caste restrictions has been witnessed again and again in India in times of great religious zeal. In the oldest *Upaniṣads* we read of a Brahman teacher who took as a disciple a youth who declared that he did not know who his father was, because this love of truth qualified him to be a genuine Brahman. Buddha received into his order every morally clean man, whatever his descent, if only his heart was set on salvation. In the didactic portions of the great epic it is said again and again that it is not lineage, but a moral life that makes a Brahman, and the *Bhagavad-gītā* also places little stress on differences of caste. This attitude has continued to be a characteristic feature of the best type of Vishnuism from that time down to the modern champion of freedom, Mahātmā Gandhi, who is waging war against the orthodox opinion of his country for the amelioration of the lot of the many millions of ' untouchables.' There is, of course, a difference between Gandhi's efforts and the purely religious movements of which we have been speaking. Gandhi is aiming at the complete abolition of the barriers of caste. He is, in fact, a social reformer. These ancient movements, however, were not directed at social reform. It was only in connexion with the religious goal that they recognized no differences of caste. Caste was not disregarded in daily life, but only for the vision of Brahma, for Nirvāṇa, for union with Kṛṣṇa. There is, too, another respect in which the Āḷvārs recall the times of the *Upaniṣads,* of Buddha and of the didactic epic — one of the twelve honoured Āḷvārs was a woman.

Among the adherents of the enthusiastic Āḷvārs were men who not only collected their hymns and made them a regular part of their worship, but also did much by their learned labours to strengthen the intellectual side of the movement. The Southern Indian town of Śrīraṅgam became a kind of intellectual centre, and the president of the temple there was one of the great men of India — viz., Rāmānuja (born in 1016). In him were combined profound religious experience and a strong desire to provide for that experience a philosophical basis. This desire was greatly strengthened by the fact that from another direction a great man had outlined an attractive view of the world which threatened the existence of the *bhakti* religion.

In the first centuries of the Christian era the various philosophical schools had summed up their doctrines in collections of aphorisms, or *sūtras,* as they were called. The doctrines of the *Upaniṣads* had been condensed and summarized by Bādarāyaṇa in the *Brahma-sūtras,* or *Vedānta-sūtras.* (' Vedānta ' means " End of the Veda," because the *Upaniṣads* formed the end of the Veda.) The brevity of these *sūtras,* which were meant to be committed to memory, necessitated explanatory oral commentaries. By and by these were written down, and the oldest commentary on the *Brahma-sūtras* that has come down to us is that of Śaṁkara (*c.* A.D. 800). The standpoint taken by Śaṁkara in this masterly work is that of ' illusionist monism.' The idea that the world and the deity who created it have a separate existence is only relatively true — in reality it is an illusion (*māyā*); Brahma alone is absolutely real, eternal, immutable, and one. This Vedānta doctrine, which is called *advaita* (' non-duality '), because of the grandeur of its conception and the personal influence of Śaṁkara found widespread acceptance, and became a strong rival to the more emotional Vishnuism, especially as the inclusion of the living god (*īśvara*) in the sphere of the truth of illusion was calculated to undermine the foundations of the *bhakti* of the followers of Viṣṇu.

To meet this danger Rāmānuja resolved to write a commentary on the *Brahma-sūtras* from his own point of view. He was able to utilize for this work previous writings, which have not come down to us. The obscurity and brevity of the *Brahma-sūtras* of course opened the door for varying interpretations, and, besides, Śaṁkara's illusionist monism had not been read into the sūtras without some violence. But it was not only hostility to Śaṁkara's point of view that urged Rāmānuja to teach a Vedānta of his own. He also wished to bring back Vishnuism, which had gathered many doctrines that were heterodox — *i.e.,* that deviated from the Vedic tradition — into closer touch with the venerated *Upaniṣads* and the highly esteemed *Brahma-sūtras.*

Rāmānuja also taught a form of monism, a unity, but this unity was qualified — hence its technical name, "qualified non-dualism." Material things, individual souls, and the Supreme Soul — *i.e.,* God — are three eternal principles, whose unity lies in the fact that things and souls constitute the body of God. They are his attributes or *modi.* God is free from all defects. He is the material and efficient cause of all, creates, upholds, and destroys the world, and is the goal for all souls, for the afflicted, for the seeker after truth, and for the enlightened. He manifests himself in manifold forms. As supreme Vāsudeva, or Nārāyaṇa (these are special names of Viṣṇu), he dwells in a celestial city in great glory, with all the attributes ascribed to him in the Viṣṇu mythology. In his self-transmutation he manifests himself in the various *avatāras* ('descents'), such as fish, tortoise, etc. As inward guide he dwells in the human heart, and is the constant companion of the soul in its journeys from birth to birth on earth, in heaven, and in hell. As incorporeal spirit he lives in the images of himself made by his worshippers out of any material whatever.

In the relation of man to God *bhakti* plays the chief part, but there is far less excitement in it than in that type of it cultivated by the Āḷvārs. Purity of food, chastity, performance of the ceremonial rites, virtue, and confidence — these constitute the *bhakti* discipline, but essential, too, is the study of the Veda, of the Vedānta philosophy as taught by Rāmānuja, and of the theory of ritual as laid down in the *Karma-Mīmāṃsā.* These requirements are interesting because they indicate Rāmānuja's return to orthodoxy; it is also noteworthy that only the three upper castes are qualified to practise this *bhakti.* But the full strictness of orthodox Brahmanism, which excludes the caste of the Śūdras from the higher religion, Rāmānuja neither could nor would adopt. For the Śūdras too there stands open a direct way to the divine, consisting in pious devotion, reflection on one's own helplessness, and personal prayer. As a substitute for the sacred cord over the left shoulder, which only the three upper castes were privileged to wear, he gave the Śūdras and the casteless adherents of his sect a special cord of purity, and also permitted them under certain conditions to visit the temples.

By and by, in the South of India, where the adherents of Rāmānuja are chiefly to be found, two schools arose holding different views as to the help which God gives to man on the way to salvation. According to one view, the initiative rests with man. He must first bestir himself before he can receive divine aid — just as a young ape must cling to its mother before she can carry it with her. The other school held that passive willingness is sufficient to win the divine assistance — just as a young kitten remains quite inactive while its mother carries it about.

The *bhakti* as taught by Rāmānuja was a meditative adoration rather than a spontaneous love for the divine, and it therefore exhibited greater sobriety than the type cultivated by the Āḷvārs. But a few centuries later there arose in Bengal a new movement, once more giving the central place in religious life to an extreme erotic passion, which found vent in songs of praise to Hari, as Viṣṇu was locally called. By means of a cultus consisting of dance and song, Caitanya (1485–1533) succeeded in bringing a large section of the people under his influence, although he did not seek to organize the sect or provide the new doctrine with a literature. That was done by his disciples and successors, who were held in high respect as spiritual teachers (*gurus*). The personal influence of Caitanya was so great that even in early manhood he was regarded as an incarnation of Kṛṣṇa. Of course, this is not an isolated case. Down to quite recent times men have been similarly deified in their lifetime. The temples of the sect contain images of Caitanya and the early *gurus* side by side with those of Kṛṣṇa and Rādhā.

This exceptionally high respect for spiritual teachers is a pronounced feature in one other Viṣṇu sect, that founded by Vallabha (1479–1531). The great regard entertained for such teachers has of course, been all along a characteristic feature in India, but nowhere has the authority of the *gurus* led to such abuses as have appeared among this sect in the course of the centuries. The *gurus* of this religious body have to be descendants of the seven grandsons of the founder, and they alone may own the temples, which every member of the sect must attend. The *gurus* are thus in a position to exert a financial and moral pressure that has resulted in the many scandalous abuses, such as those revealed in the law-courts of Bombay in 1862. These unpleasant incidents (which fortunately are confined within comparatively small limits) are mentioned here only in order to show the tremendous contrasts that are met with in the religious history of India and to illustrate the danger of judging it as a whole from a partial knowledge.

The attempt that has been made in these pages to indicate the main features of Vishnuism without giving anything like a systematic and complete account of all the sects requires to be supplemented in one respect. This is a matter of fundamental importance for the whole Indian attitude toward religion. I mean the tendency to combine separate divine beings and identify them with each other. Some would ascribe this to the power of the Indian imagination, which has been likened to luxuriant tropical vegetation, where innumerable growths are so intertwined that it is frequently impossible to disentangle them. Others are inclined to credit even the plain, unsophisticated Indian peasant with a profound consciousness of the ultimate unity of the divine. Perhaps there is something to be said for both of these explanations, but there is a third factor which has also had a large share in bringing about the result. I mean the deliberate exploitation of this tendency by powerful personalities. By means of such identifications these men have managed to bring under the recognized forms of religion conceptions of God altogether alien to Indian thought and utterly irreconcilable with it.

Vishnuism affords many examples of this tendency to identification. We shall leave out of account here cases like that of Nārāyaṇa and Viṣṇu, or

Vāsudeva and Kṛṣṇa, where the amalgamation has amounted to complete coalescence. We shall mention only those cases where the combination is still felt as such, and is deliberately retained.

We take first the theory of the four impersonations or *vyūhas* of Viṣṇu. They have been recognized from the first centuries of the Christian era, and appear in the most modern speculations of the various sects. The names of these *vyūhas* are Vāsudeva, Saṃkarṣaṇa, Pradyumna, Aniruddha. From the personal point of view Vāsudeva is identified with Kṛṣṇa, Saṃkarṣaṇa is regarded as his elder brother (under the name of Balarāma he also plays a prominent part in the history of the pastoral life of the youthful Kṛṣṇa), Pradyumna is Kṛṣṇa's son, and Aniruddha is his grandson. These four are interpreted either philosophically, as incarnations of principles in the evolutionary series of the Sāṃkhya system, or theologically, as impersonations of the divine power in its creative or ethical manifestations. Besides these four divine *vyūhas* there are female deities, as well as other sub-impersonations. In this sense the *vyūhas* play a part in authoritative works of Vishnuism and in many of the sects (*e.g.*, in that of Rāmānuja), although, of course, the qualities and characters assigned to them vary in keeping with the special opinions of each sect (*e.g.*, in that of Caitanya).

It is not quite clear whether these *vyūhas* have been evolved from human beings or local deities, but there is no doubt in the case of the *avatāras* or "descents" of Viṣṇu. In number these vary between six and twenty-three; in form they are animal or a mixture of human and divine. The animal forms, some of which go back to myths from the *Brāhmaṇas* period, are really no more objects of religious veneration than are the founders of heterodox religions — Buddha and the oldest Tīrthaṃkara of the Jainists — who have been included in the number of the *avatāras* with an evident purpose, but without practical result. On the other hand, worship *is* paid to the *avatāra* as a man-lion who has become an object of worship of one sect. It is unnecessary to enlarge here on Kṛṣṇa as an *avatāra,* because we have already pointed out the central position which he holds in Vishnuism, but we must say something about Rāma, the hero of the epic called *Rāmāyana*. This epic, which dates from pre-Christian days, has been translated into several modern Indian languages, and has exercised a great moral influence on large sections of the Indian people. Rāma, the pure youth, has been unjustly banished from his father's kingdom, and lives in the woods with his beautiful and virtuous wife, Sītā. Sītā is abducted by a demon and carried to Ceylon. With the help of an army of apes Rāma brings her back, and, after her virtue has been established by the ordeal of fire, finally ascends with her the throne of his fathers. This tale of heroic deeds, adventures, and conjugal fidelity has always been a favourite in India, and this royal pair, Rāma and Sītā, illustrate the virtues of purity and faithfulness, just as Kṛṣṇa and Rādhā stand for erotic passion. The actual deification of Rāma belongs to a later period.

In view of the limitations of our space we must be content to recapitulate very briefly the features of Vishnuism to which we have already referred. Its leading feature is love to God, with a tendency now toward pious devotion and now toward erotic passion. That there is here a great deal of intensive religious experience cannot be doubted. The erotic strain, apart from some undeniable excrescences, cannot be judged from the ordinary European point of view. Even missionaries who are intimately acquainted with Indian life corroborate this statement. The outward worship of Vishnuism differs from that of Shivaism by the absence of living sacrifices. Socially, it has always tended toward mitigating the harshness of caste; in modern times, indeed, it has come very near to the entire abolition of caste differences. Its liberal tendency is further shown by its use of the vernacular languages side by side with Sanskrit, which now occupies a position comparable with that of Latin in Europe during the Middle Ages. Philosophically, all the more important sects of Vishnuism since the time of Rāmānuja have restated their attitude toward the hostile monism of Śaṃkara. New commentaries on the *Brahma-sūtras* have been composed, and these have emphasized the relation of God to individual souls and to the material world as the chief differences between the various Viṣṇu sects.

We now turn from Vishnuism to Shivaism, the second prominent religious manifestation of Hinduism. Its basis in the Veda is the figure of Rudra, already mentioned, Rudra being the incarnation in divine form of the dread powers of nature. In some of the *Upaniṣads* an epithet is applied to Rudra which gradually became the most popular name of the god — *śiva*. The word *śiva*, which is an adjective and means "gracious," afterward became the name of the god. It was perhaps selected as a *captatio benevolentiæ* of the dreaded deity, but the choice of the name also indicates that this dread deity can, if proper means be used, be appeased, and can then be as gracious toward those who worship him as he is full of dread to others. Śiva has many other appellations. The epic *Mahābhārata,* where he is often spoken of at great length, mentions quite a large number of names. Some indicate his outstanding position: Īśa = " Ruler "; Mahādeva = "the Great God "; Devadeva = " God of Gods." Others are descriptive of his attributes: Triśūlin = " the Trident-bearer "; Tryakṣa = " the Three-eyed One." Some include the name of his wife: Umāpati = " Husband of Umā."

The name 'Umā' means " Mother," and the wife of Śiva is thus the mother-goddess. Like her husband, she has two sides to her nature. She is fierce and terrible to her foes (hence the epithet *durgā*) and kind and good toward those who worship her. Down to modern days she has been a very prominent figure in the religious life of the Hindus; indeed, as we shall see, she has frequently eclipsed her husband. Another of her names, Pārvatī, " Daughter of the Mountain," indicates that she loves the mountains, especially the Himālayas, whose daughter she is supposed to be (see Fig. 57).

FIG. 57. ȘIVA AND PĀRVATĪ
Copied from an ancient fresco.

But Śiva himself is frequently mentioned in connexion with mountains, and this reflects one of his natural characteristics. The world of rocks and glaciers on the top of the highest mountains of the world, in its wildness and inaccessibility, its majesty and its virgin snow, is a fit symbol of the savage god, who is variously pictured in the religious imagination as a gloomy ascetic, as a god who is fond of cosmic dances, or as a playful lover of his dread consort. Since olden times the bull has been sacred to him — the bull which unites in himself strength, rage, and reproductive power. There is no

FIG. 58. NANDIN OF TANJORE
From Cohn, " Indische Plastik "

temple of Śiva in front of which or within which the stone image of Nandin, the sacred bull, cannot be seen (Fig. 58), and to this day the sacred bulls of Śiva walk unmolested as honoured citizens through the streets of Benares.

Reproductive power, as symbolized in his sacred animal, is an essential characteristic of Śiva. He is regarded as the supreme creator of all that is. The symbol of this power is the male member (lingam), which figures in every temple of Śiva, along with the female organ of sex (*yoni*). These, however, are represented in such a manner that the unsophisticated observer

could not recognize them. (See Fig. 59.) The widespread use of this symbol — in one South Indian sect both men and women wear it on a cord
round the neck — must therefore not be taken as meaning that the sexual
element is specially prominent in the worship.

FIG. 59. LINGAM-WORSHIP
Miniature from the seventeenth or eighteenth century.
From von Glasenapp, " Brāhma und Buddha "

It is generally supposed that some ideas current among the lower classes
and uncivilized peoples have entered into the conception of Śiva and his
consort. In view of the close contact between the Aryan Indians and subjugated aborigines and other foreign elements this can hardly be doubted,
but it cannot be said to have been as yet conclusively proved. It cannot be
definitely said that even the lingam-worship, which was unknown to ancient

Brahmanism and even to the earlier portions of the *Mahābhārata,* was borrowed, because this method of symbolizing the divine creative energy was natural enough among the *naïve* and far from prudish Indians of the Middle Ages. In any case, all that may have been borrowed from other sources has been so intermingled with what is old and indigenous in the variegated religion of Shivaism that we are justified in speaking of it as a unified system. The worship of this god, great and terrible and yet kind, along with that of his consort, has lasted all through the centuries, down to the present day. It need hardly be said that various sects exist side by side with the ordinary cultus, and we shall now look at some of the most important features of these.

One early sect of Shivaism is called Pāśupata — *i.e.,* "Worshippers of Pāśupati" (the lord of domestic animals), an ancient name of Śiva. A Shivaite ascetic seems to have played an important part in the history of this sect. He came ere long to be regarded as an incarnation of Śiva, and was worshipped in the temples under the name of Lakulīśa or Nakulīśa — *i.e.,* "the God with the Club." In contrast to the usual figure with numerous arms, this deity had only two arms, and this has been regarded as a clear example of the deification of a man. An excellent description of the sect was given in the fourteenth century by a clever South Indian, who wrote an account of the sixteen most important systems. We give from this Sanskrit text, the *Sarvadarśana-saṃgraha,* a few extracts, in which the sect describes its own strong points:

> In the other systems the end of suffering [aimed at] is merely the cessation of suffering, but in our sect one also attains to supreme divine glory.

Here therefore we have the theistic system claiming to provide a better reward than the philosophical systems, which seek only the cessation of suffering, without any prospect of positive benefit. Again:

> In our doctrine God is completely independent, whereas in the others, while he is the source of all that happens, he is dependent on the law of Karma.

Further:

> In our system the worshipper of God attains after death to fellowship with God, and does not require to be reincarnated, whereas other doctrines promise a heaven which is not regarded as final. The ultimate hope held out by them is an isolation of the soul which lacks the bliss of nearness to God.

A special feature of the cultus is the smearing of the body with ashes. Other means for pleasing the deity are laughter, singing, dancing, the utterance of a certain sound, which has to be imitated from the sacred bull, and many other ecstatic manifestations. All these orgiastic performances are evidently peculiar to the god himself, and are therefore specially pleasing to him. At the same time, worshippers are recommended not to perform these ceremonies in the presence of unauthorized spectators, because their adverse criticism might tempt weak members of the sect to desert the good path. These extravagances, however, are outdone by another sect, which emphasizes the repellent and coarse aspect of Śiva. Quaffing wine out of human skulls, smearing the body with the ashes of cremated bodies, human sacrifices with horrible accompaniments — these form part of the cultus of this degenerate group, who thus do homage to Śiva as Bhairava — *i.e.,* "the Dreadful One" — and to his wife Caṇḍikā — "the Savage One."

Representatives of another type of Shivaism can best be taken together under the name of Śaiva-Siddhānta (*i.e.,* the "system that refers to Śiva"). It has produced a considerable Sanskrit literature, which in turn has become the basis of the remarkable South Indian literature of Śaiva-Siddhānta in the Tamil language.

On its theological and philosophical side the Śaiva-Siddhānta treats of God, souls, and the fetters of the soul. In contrast to the doctrine that we have just been discussing, the creative activity of God is limited by the law of *karma* — *i.e.,* by the effects of men's actions. (This represents the views of the purely philosophic systems.) The body of the deity is not like the human body, but consists of five elements (*mantra*), which are regarded as his powers. Souls are eternal, and, when freed from their fetters, are identified with Śiva. According to the nature of the fetters that bind them, the unredeemed souls are classified in groups varying in value. The fetters referred to are three in number: dirt, which conceals the true nature of the soul, the moral fruit of the deed done, and matter. A fourth or additional fetter is the power of Śiva as lord over the three, and this power (*śakti*) constitutes the female element of the god. *Śakti* is, so to say, the intermediary link between deity and all else. The cultus consists of dedication, the recitation of set forms, sacrificial burnt offerings, etc. Of interest also is the Yoga, which in this case is associated with a mystical theory of the body, but we shall speak of it later in connexion with the Tantras.

These same ideas are also fully developed in the South Indian Śaiva-Siddhānta. In this case, however, we have in addition a rich poetic literature, whose outstanding representative is the writer of hymns, Māṇikka-Vāsaga (about A.D. 900). Like the Vishnuite Āḷvārs (see p. 116), Śiva-worshippers have here celebrated in religious poetry an ecstatic love to God (*Śiva-bhakti*). The images of the god kindle within the singers the consciousness that to belong wholly to this one Supreme Being is the highest bliss, and the influence of the images is reinforced by fellowship with other worshippers and ascetics, for these also, like the images, are manifestations of the great deity.

The Śaiva-Siddhānta has also developed a distinct form in North India. In the ninth and tenth centuries there arose in Kashmir a literature that proclaimed the identity of the soul with God, and made this belief its distinctive tenet. This monistic tendency perhaps dates back to the influence of the great monistic philosopher Śaṃkara, who is said to have visited Kashmir in the course of his extensive missionary journeys.

We now come to that sect of Śiva-worshippers whose adherents wear, as has been said, a lingam (phallus) round their necks, and are therefore called Lingāyats. The sect originated in South India in the eleventh or twelfth century, probably to strengthen the Shivaite part of the population against the Jainists, who were very powerful at that time. The importance which the Lingāyats attach to monasteries — there are three principal ones, with other village monasteries dependent on them — is regarded as an imitation of the Jainist organization. A large part is played by the spiritual teachers, called *gurus,* and elaborate ritual honours are paid to them when they visit the homes of the people. Every Lingāyat must have a *guru,* solemnly chosen by himself as soon as he attains manhood. Attendance at the temple is not required; the restrictions of caste are less severe; the dead are buried, not cremated. Child-marriage, which became general in India after the Moham- medan conquest, is on the whole disapproved by the Lingāyats, and widows are allowed to marry again. Many social reformers are fighting to-day on behalf of these causes, because large numbers of widowed girls frequently fall into prostitution as a result of the infamous manner in which they are treated by their families.

We cannot here go into detail regarding the complicated theology of the sect. It closely resembles the qualified monism of Rāmānuja (see *supra,* pp. 115–18). The theophanies of the deity are determined by the *śakti* (see p. 124). A prominent feature is *bhakti,* which in its highest form brings the soul to blissful union with Śiva. These doctrines form the basis of a special sectarian commentary on the *Brahma sūtras.* The moral standpoint of the sect is lofty, and is entirely free from the objectionable features found among other worshippers of Śiva.

We will conclude our study of Shivaism with a reference to a school of thought whose origin can be traced back to about A.D. 600, and which is of very great importance for modern India. Its name is 'Tantraism,' derived from the word 'Tantra.' In its wider sense 'Tantra' means any literary pro- duction dealing with religion, philosophy, and natural science which is of later date than the Vedic literature. In its narrower acceptation it means writings which treat in a certain way of religion, ritual, conduct of life, medicine, magic, etc. The history of these Tantras, which go back to the seventh century and come down to the nineteenth, has not yet been com- pletely studied, and we must therefore confine ourselves to a short account of the leading thoughts which are more or less common to all the Tantras.

One such common feature is the idea of *śakti,* divine energy, which is represented under the image of a great mother-deity. In the Tantras this *śakti* is the wife of Śiva, some of whose numerous names we have already mentioned.

This conjugal relationship of the supreme divine powers appears in widely differing aspects. In one the sexual element is prominent, especially in that which goes by the name of "left-handed intercourse." Perhaps this is an attempt to counteract the ascetic leanings which have always been powerful in India — to bring men's natural impulses into touch with the religious life and to find in daily life the divine meaning which asceticism thought could be reached only by turning away from normal life. That these efforts are not new is proved by a passage from the oldest *Upaniṣads,* in which instructions are given for indulgence in sexual intercourse to the accompaniment of religious formulas. Other concomitants to worship recommended by the Tantras, but strictly forbidden elsewhere, including intoxicating drink, meat, and fish, seem to confirm the opinion that an attitude of opposition was intended.

The use of means and methods like these in connexion with religious ceremonies is of course fraught with danger, and excesses do occur. But even these do not justify a sweeping condemnation of the whole system. At a very early period a monastic interpretation of the relation between Śiva and Durgā drove the sexual element into the background. According to this interpretation, the divine spouse in the supreme sense is the god himself. Incapable in his absoluteness of any activity, he is transformed in his spouse into an active power, and through her becomes the material cause of the world. Thus understood, the ideas of sex take on a profound cosmic and symbolic meaning. Further, their use in worship is reserved for those who have advanced far on the religious path. They are strictly forbidden to laymen and novices. When the conjugal relationship of god and goddess has thus been interpreted as a mystical union, with the goddess as the active factor, it is the goddess who occupies the whole of the foreground in the mind of the worshipper, the god becoming little more than a subject for higher meditation. As Tantraism is a practical religion, it is the goddess that is the actual centre of its emotion and its life.

Her presence awakens those feelings of inward love (*bhakti*) which we have already described. In her honour are sung hymns which rival the best productions of the kind. In the worship of Durgā, as in that of Viṣṇu, all barriers of caste disappear. This is a result of the modernism of the sects when compared with the strictness that prevailed in ancient Brahmanism. For many centuries an ever-increasing multitude were excluded from Brahmanic worship and ritual because they did not belong to the three ancient privileged castes. These despised classes the newer sects had to keep in view if they were to secure a membership sufficient to ensure their own existence. A young man who wished to join in the worship of the goddess underwent a solemn obligation, called by the ancient Vedic name *dīkṣā,* although this had been open only to the upper castes. The spiritual teacher (*guru*) occupied a position as important as that of his ancient forerunners. Owing to the high respect enjoyed by the female sex in Tantraism, women were admitted to the ranks of the *gurus.*

The candidate for initiation received from the *guru* the *mantra,* the sacred text or spell which consecrated him to the service of the goddess, just as the youthful Brahman was consecrated by the *gāyatrī*, a verse from the *Ṛgveda*. But the *mantras* played a much larger part than this in the very elaborate worship of Durgā. This is another proof that the disciples of Tantraism were anxious to use modern methods to fill the ancient faith with new life.

This belief in the power of the sacred word goes back to the times of the *Ṛgveda,* and post-Vedic orthodoxy held the Veda to be eternal. The connexion of the word with its meaning, and therefore the word itself, was also eternal; the spoken word dies away. The utterance of the sound is in the Tantra system an image of the cosmic creation. The formation of language and the creation of the material world and of the human body, with its mystical ducts and centres, are revelations parallel to those seen in the divine creative power. Ancient and continually recurrent in the history of the Indian mind is the parallelism between the macrocosm (the world) and the microcosm (man); but new and peculiar to Tantraism is the addition of spoken sounds, although there are adumbrations of it in earlier times. The eternal sounds, meaning by that the fifty letters of the Sanskrit alphabet, are co-ordinated with the powers that inhere in the world and in man. They are distributed over the mystical centres in the human frame. In the lowest of these rests the mother of the world, in the shape of a coiled snake (*kuṇḍalinī*), waiting to be aroused in order that she may rise by means of a Yoga peculiar to Tantraism to the highest centre in the skull and be united with the Absolute. The sounds themselves, being correlated with the centres in the body, lend themselves to this, for they also are direct manifestations of divine power.

These remarks will perhaps give the reader some idea of the religious importance in Tantraism of the *mantras,* even of those which contain combinations of sounds linguistically meaningless. As the mystical importance of the sounds arises from the connexion with the Yoga of the six centres of the body, we must be careful not to reject as nonsensical even *mantras* which are linguistically unintelligible. It will be clear to anyone who is familiar with such matters that ideas of this kind open the door to practices that border on primitive magic. The Tantra system has by no means always kept clear from practices of that kind, but here again we must be careful not to condemn the whole system as nonsense.

Idol-worship in the temple, including the sacrifice of living victims, forms an important part of the worship of Durgā. In answer to sceptical objections to idol-worship, modern adherents of Tantraism have pointed to the psychological and mystical significance of the worship of images, and have successfully met the attacks along the lines of the latest national and religious movements. (More will be said of these in the next section.) A strong element of Tantraism has become manifest in the Indian Mahāyāna-Buddhism, and has spread far outside the borders of India. In India itself the chief stronghold of Tantraism is Bengal.

Looking back over what has been said about Viṣṇu, Śiva, and *śakti,* it will be seen that we have been dealing chiefly with sects. To describe these sects, with their special doctrines, seemed the best method of bringing out the chief points. But it must not be imagined that the dividing lines are rigorously drawn. Round the nucleus of actual adherents there is always a wide circle of less strict followers who, while they recognize the god of the sect as supreme and worship him in his temple, by no means deny the existence of other gods or profess intimate knowledge of the special theology of the sect with which they are thus loosely connected. And the farther we go from the centre toward the circumference of the circle, the fewer sectarian features do we find, until we reach a universal worship of Viṣṇu, Śiva, or Durgā. These deities tower above all the other members of the Indian pantheon merely as 'elect' deities, deities who are preferred to the others. These difficult distinctions are not always recognizable to-day, and probably the commonest form of worship in the first centuries of the Christian era was not regulated by these sectarian ties. Then followed a period when sectarian religion was more prevalent. In recent days the current is again flowing in a direction away from sectarianism. A modern native of Bengal voices this attitude in these words:

> I fast on the holy day Śivāratri, because it is sacred to Śiva, and I fast on Ekādaśi day [*i.e.*, on the eleventh day of each half-month] because it is sacred to Viṣṇu. I plant the bel-tree because it is dear to Śiva, and the tulsī shrub because Viṣṇu loves it. The great mass of Hindus are not sectarians. The sects, it is true, scribble a great deal and make much din, but they are only a small minority.

Of course this statement is disputed by the sects, but we do not profess to decide the question here. What interests us is merely the breadth of religious view which has always characterized the Indian people, although there has been a great deal of sectarian animosity. The idea that every form of worship has its justification is frequently expressed in even stronger terms, and each worshipper claims that all other cults, when compared with his own, are inferior approximations to the universal religious ideal. Besides the sects and apart from the great masses who are more or less indifferent to all forms of religion, there is another movement, which follows the Vedic ritual as laid down in the Gṛhya-sūtras (see *supra,* p. 107).

The adherents of this movement, who are found mostly in the South and West of India, are usually called "Smārta," from *Smṛti,* meaning "tradition." All through the centuries they have possessed an abundant literature, and outstanding men are found in their ranks. The philosophy of Śaṃkara suits their views particularly well, for it admits not only a strict monism which regards the absolute, sole Brahma as the only true reality and all plurality as merely apparent, but also a practical view of the world that has relative truth and enables them to perform the ancient traditional ritual. They have also adopted the worship of five gods of Hinduism: Viṣṇu, Śiva, Durgā, Sūrya (the sun-god), and Gaṇeśa (god of wisdom and remover of obstacles). This worship seems to have become universal among the Smārtas in the seventh or eighth centuries. It can be performed at home, and the gods can be represented by symbols (stones, metals, diagrams, earthenware vessels). One of these five gods is usually preferred to the other four. The philosophic theories of the Smārtas are as free to individual preference as is the choice of a god, although Śaṃkara's doctrines are accepted by the majority.

A description of the outward forms of worship might suitably close our account of the religion of this period. But the entire public and private life of India is so pervaded by religion that there is hardly any aspect of daily life that is devoid of religious meaning or reference. Want of space forbids anything like a systematic account of this huge amount of material, and we can refer only to a few points that are closely connected with what has already been said in this section.

The images of the gods in stone vary from the simplest symbols to the finest productions of the sculptor's art. For example, there are the earthenware vessels for the domestic worship of the Smārtas and the metamorphosed lingam that has already been mentioned (*supra, p.* 121). Moulds made of butter, wreaths of flowers, and red paint are the simple adornments spent on the lingam, and the same forms of homage are paid to the recumbent stone bull in or in front of the temple, to the riding animal and symbol of Śiva. The human figures of the gods immediately strike the European by their numerous arms. Many of the images have also several faces, looking in different directions. Special attributes indicate the deity represented. The discus, the diadem, the club, and the lotos flower are the traditional badges of Viṣṇu, the origin and meaning of each of which are explained in the written legends. Durgā, in keeping with her fierce character, usually carries a sword in her hand, or stands with her foot on some hostile demon whom she has overthrown.

The worship paid to a god in his temple closely resembles the homage paid to an earthly prince. The image is bathed and anointed; the flies that hover round him are fanned away; food is presented to him; he is cheered with music and dancing, or he is borne through the city in a gay procession or conveyed to special summer quarters at the beginning of the hot season. Hymns are chanted in his honour, particularly among the Vishnuite sects, who, like the Caitanga sect, have a kind of congregational worship. On special days of the year pilgrimages are made to certain temples, and exceptional merit attaches to the exertions incident to these journeys. In former days some of them lasted for months. Numberless places of pilgrimage are scattered all over the Indian continent, from the summit of the Himālayas to the plains. The present writer ascended the Himālayas to a height of more than 13,000 feet, and saw in a grotto there a lingam made of ice, which had drawn numerous pilgrims in August to an exhausting Alpine climb. And down in the southern point of India there is a famous temple of Rāma.

Another way of paying homage is to bathe at holy places, especially at the junctions of rivers (the Ganges and the Jumna at Allahabad) or at the places where rivers flow into the sea (the mouth of the Hugli, a tributary of the Ganges) or where the Ganges rises in the mountains (Hardwār), etc.

Among the sects marks on the body are frequently worn to indicate their particular allegiance. Lines on the forehead, vertical, horizontal, or curved, in white, yellow, or red paint, tell any informed person the sect to which the worshipper belongs. But many zealots for their faith are not content with simple marks like these. They tattoo their breasts and arms with special symbols of their chosen deity. Among themselves the members of a sect have an even surer mark by which they can recognize each other — viz., the sacred text (*mantra*) which they received at their initiation from their *guru* or spiritual teacher. This *mantra* usually consists of three words. The first is the ancient sacred syllable *Om;* the third is the word for worship; and the second is the dative case of the name by which the members of the sect call their god. In addition to this *mantra* there are others, used in meditation or as a mystical expression of their speculative opinions or religion or even for purposes which are more or less magical in their nature.

III

The foreign influences which have affected the development of Indian religion have differed greatly both in kind and in degree. Limitations of space compel us to confine our attention to two of these, and we must omit all reference to other extremely important factors, such as (among others) the lasting influence of primitive times and of the aboriginal inhabitants and the effect of Persian religion on the sun-worship in India.

Of the two great religions which have affected India as a result of political events, Islam exerted far less influence — apart, of course, from conversions and secessions — than did Christianity.

It was in the beginning of the fourteenth century that the Mohammedans gained a footing in the Deccan, and it was here, among the Vishnuite poets in the territory of the Mahrattas (Central and West India), that the effects of the Mohammedan hatred of idols were seen. Nāmdev, a tailor by descent and by calling, composed hymns in the first half of the fifteenth century for the purpose of spreading religion among the Mahrattas and in the Punjab. These hymns extol the divine Omnipresence, and pour scorn on the foolish idea that the deity dwells in his image of stone. Pilgrimages, ceremonial purifications, ascetic practices of all kinds, are pronounced unnecessary; only sincere faith in Vāsudeva's infinite greatness and goodness, purity of heart, and an upright walk are declared to be the essentials of religion. Thoughts like these are frequently found in Hinduism, but there was a constant effort to reconcile the call to inwardness with participation in the external forms of religion. Nāmdev, on the other hand, rejected the entire cultus of Hinduism, and thus introduced an alien note that echoed the spirit of Islam. Another trace of Mohammedan influence is found in the ancient sect known as Jainists. The middle of the fifteenth century saw the rise of the separate sect of Loṅkas, who rejected idol-worship as contrary to the oldest Jainist scriptures. In the seventeenth century the Loṅkas were absorbed into the sect of Sthānakavāsins, who denounced pilgrimages as well as idol-worship. This latter sect comprises to-day something like one-third of the Indian Jainists. Later poets carried on Nāmdev's work, among them being the popular singer Tukārām (1608–49), whose profound and pure religious spirit deeply impressed the national Mahrattan hero Śivāji when he led his people against the Mohammedan oppressor. This is another proof that the doctrines taught by these poets were not really opposed to Hinduism.

While these poets thus betray some slight Mohammedan influence, we find in the works of Kabīr (1440–1518) an actual commingling of Hinduism and Islam. Kabīr is interesting not only for his own sake, but also because of the influence he exerted on the founder of the Sikh religion, of which we shall later have something to say. Grierson says of Kabīr:

> What an extraordinary man Kabīr must have been! A poor Mohammedan weaver, who gained admission to membership in a Viṣṇu community by a clever trick, universally despised and hated both by Mohammedans and Hindus, maltreated by a Mohammedan emperor (Sikandar Lodi of Delhi, 1488–1517) and persecuted by the Brahmans of Benares, he had the unprecedented boldness to make a stand against the two great religions of India in the fifteenth century, and achieved his purpose.

His attack in both cases was directed against all ritualism, and, in the case of Hinduism, against idol-worship, belief in divine incarnations, and asceticism. If in these respects, as in his strict monotheism, he showed some leanings to Islam, on the other hand he adopted some of the leading ideas of Hinduism — for example, transmigration of souls (metempsychosis), the law of Karma, Brahma, etc. — and called his god Rāma, without, however, regarding him as an incarnation or mentioning a divine spouse. Eleven sects, whose founders lived between 1470 and 1750, are traced back to his teachings. The principles held in common by them all have been stated by Farquhar as follows:

> God alone is worshipped, and idolatry is strictly prohibited, so that Hindu worship is completely abandoned; men of any caste may exercise religious functions. The sect is open to all Hindus, and to Muslims also. Great stress is laid on the value of the *guru*. The literature is in vernacular verse, not in Sanskrit.

Gradually, however, all the Hindu practices and views have made their way in again.

Among the eleven sects just mentioned there is one that deserves further notice. It was founded in 1500 by a *guru* called Nānak, and is mentioned in the statistical table given at the beginning of this sketch under the name of

"Sikhs." Nānak takes up the same religious standpoint as Kabīr. Rejecting the entire cultus, he combined the leading conceptions of Hinduism with the monotheism of Islam, into which, however, he fitted the Indian *bhakti*. God is known by the name of Hari, one of the appellations of Viṣṇu. The history of the sect during the ensuing century contains two events worthy of notice; the first is the foundation of a central sanctuary, "the Golden Temple" (Fig. 60), in the middle of the second lake at Amritsar from which the modern city takes its name, and the second the production of a sacred book, *Granth Sahib* (*granth* = "book," *sahib* = "master"), in which are col-

FIG. 60. THE GOLDEN TEMPLE AT AMRITSAR
From von Glasenapp, " Brāhma und Buddha"

lected the hymns of the most eminent *gurus,* as well as some by Kabīr and poets of a kindred spirit. This book not only provides forms for private prayer and congregational worship, but, as the tenth *guru* (who died in 1708) had failed to nominate a successor, it is accepted as the canon of the sect, which recognizes no distinctions of castes. The necessity of defending themselves against the oppression of the Mogul emperors compelled the sect to adopt a military organization, which it has retained down to modern days. Thus in the beginning of the nineteenth century there was an independent Sikh dominion, which existed until it was annexed in 1845 by the British Empire. Since that time Hindu elements have continued to enter into the

Sikh religion, but in recent days a desire has been manifested for their expulsion. This is another symptom of the national Indian movement for self-determination.

The extension and consolidation of the British sovereignty in India at the beginning of the nineteenth century meant the introduction of Christian and European influence. An important movement began in Calcutta about that time. Its leader was Rām Mohan Ray (1772–1833). His father's family had long been followers of Caitanya, while his mother was the daughter of a Śākta family. At school he had been brought into contact with Islam, but after entering the British Government Service and coming into touch with missionaries he was led to study Christianity, even learning Hebrew and Greek for this purpose. He then conceived the idea of founding a purely spiritual religion, which should combine what was best in Hinduism with Christian faith and manner of life. To this end he founded a religious community called Brāhma Samāj — that is to say, "the Brahman Society." In this he had the support of his friend Dvārkanāth Tagore, the grandfather of the well-known writer Rabīndranāth Tagore. The texts of the *Upaniṣads,* Vedānta ideas, and the Christian Gospels were the basis of the new society, and their worship resembled a Protestant religious service. Besides studying purely religious matters, they interested themselves in social and ethical questions. Always a keen opponent of the burning of widows — although this practice was confined to certain classes and districts — Rām Mohan was largely responsible for the edict of 1829 which forbade it. He also actively opposed polygamy and the marriage of children, but he could not make up his mind to abolish caste differences. His society, whose headquarters were in Calcutta, was afterward carried on by Debendranāth Tagore, the son of Dvārkanāth. Under him the organization was strengthened by the imposition of a number of vows as a condition of reception. These were to refrain from the worship of idols, to love God, and do works well pleasing to Him. He also drew up an order of public worship, and sent out missionaries to gain new adherents in Bengal.

In 1857 young Keśab Candra Sen joined the movement, and soon displayed great activity. The Hindu domestic birth and marriage rites were discontinued, because they involved idol-worship, and new ceremonies — called Brāhma rites — were introduced in their stead. Caste was definitely abandoned, and Christian works of charity were inaugurated during times of famine and epidemics. Missions to Madras and Bombay led to the foundation of new branches of the society, and aroused in Keśab's mind the idea of a universal Indian Brāhma Samāj. All this, however, was too much for Debendranāth, who could not agree to the complete abolition of caste, marriage regardless of caste, or the remarriage of widows. Keśab, on the other hand, in view of his Christian convictions, could not waive these points, and the two men had to separate. Debendranāth Tagore and his party now constituted the original community, calling it Ādi [Original] Brāhma Samāj.

Its members still retained much of their sympathy with Hinduism. They merely aimed at the spread of theism among Hindus, and left the attitude to traditional Hindu practices and all questions of social reform as matters of individual choice. This lack of definiteness has resulted in a continuous diminution of their numbers, and the society to-day includes only a handful of families.

In 1866 Keśab founded a new society, and infused new life into it by the introduction of the methods of Caitanya (see *supra,* p. 117). These included chorus-singing with instrumental accompaniment, street processions with dancing and singing, banners and drums, meetings for prayer, worship, and preaching. The younger members eagerly took up the question of abolishing the custom of secluding women. They devised new marriage services after the model of the Christian service and encouraged the remarriage of widows. At this point, however, Keśab found himself in difficulties. He shrank from carrying through the complete emancipation of women, although it was logically involved in his other reforms, and, besides, he became so autocratic that many of his followers began to fear a recurrence of the abuses that, as we have seen, had formerly prevailed among the *gurus.* Their fears were strengthened when Keśab declared that on some special matters he had received personal commands from God.

In this difficult situation Keśab received fresh stimulus from an ascetic named Rāmakṛṣṇa, with the result that he turned once more to Hindu ideals, and joined a few of his missionaries in a life of meditation under ascetic conditions in a forest near Calcutta. He divided his companions into four classes, and trained them to forms of service that accorded with their natural gifts. Some of them sought fellowship with God by the path of Yoga, some by the way of *bhakti,* others by intellectual study, and others by practical service to humanity. Even this failed to reconcile many of his followers, and his influence in his community was hopelessly lost when he diverged from his own principles by permitting his daughter to marry the son of a reigning Hindu family according to a service in which Hindu ritual was employed. Another new society was now founded, under the name of Sādhāran [Universal] Brāhma Samāj. This has survived down to the present day, and has some thousands of adherents.

In 1881 Keśab founded a new league, called Naba Bidhān — *i.e.,* the New Rule — a peculiar mixture of Hinduism and Christianity. On the one hand, Hindu practices were reintroduced and the worship of Durgā and Viṣṇu was recognized as bringing salvation and interpreted as a kind of comprehensive theism; on the other, the character of Jesus, the Christian conception of sin and all that it involved, as well as Christian social ethics, were held up as the ideal. This remarkable league did not survive the death of its founder in 1884; the community broke up almost immediately.

A movement similar to the Brāhma Samāj in the east arose in the west, with Bombay as its centre. Beginning as a secret society, it became public in

1867. It has never had much influence, and its missionary activity is inconsiderable. It has retained its sympathy with Hinduism, but has been active in urging forward social reforms.

This description of Brāhma Samāj is intended to show the difficulties that lie in the way of any attempt to combine Hinduism and Christianity. These efforts were not due to any pressure from without. They came spontaneously from prominent Indians. The question thus arises, What induced these men to launch such endeavours? In trying to answer this question we must distinguish between two factors contained in Christianity: the religion taught in the Gospels, and the system of social ethics with the customs and practices prevailing in Christian countries. The leaders of Brāhma Samāj were irresistibly attracted by the figure of Christ, and were to that extent acting under religious influence, but they also saw the defects of the social organization that had gradually been evolved in India, and found a new ideal in Christian social ethics.

We have now to describe some movements which, unlike Brāhma Samāj, aimed at defending Hinduism as a valuable religious possession against Christianity. With this end in view they sought to purify their religion from all the dross they found in it as compared with Christianity. This complicated process may perhaps be described as follows. The first stage is an overwhelming sense of the majesty of the Gospel; then comes a recovery of the faculties, in which the value of the inherited religion is again felt, this sense of its value, however, being modified by the conviction that it needs to be purified or reinterpreted. The influence of Christianity as a religion thus operates indirectly, whereas the influence of the Christian social ethic is direct. No clear eye can fail to see the grandeur of this when it is compared with blots on Indian social life like caste restrictions, child-marriage, maltreatment of widows, and indifference to the wretchedness of the casteless.

A good example of this line of thought is presented in the person of Dayānanda Sarasvati (1824–83). Sprung from an orthodox Hindu family — the name given is not his original but his ascetic name — even in his boyhood he was repelled by the worship of the image of Śiva. While still a youth he became an ascetic in order to evade the marriage enjoined by his parents, bending all his energies to acquiring Yoga. Later he abandoned this path, studied grammar and philosophy, and renounced more and more the Hindu practices in which he had been brought up. After fruitless attempts by means of addresses in Sanskrit to propagate among the educated classes his views of pure monotheism without idolatry, he came into touch with Keśab Candra Sen in Calcutta, and was encouraged by him to try to reach the masses by speaking to them in the Hindu vernacular. His success led him to found in Lahore a community like that of Brāhma Samāj; this he called Ārya Samāj — i.e., " the Society of the Aryans." " Back to the Vedas " was his slogan, for in them he claimed to have rediscovered the Aryan faith in its pristine purity. In emphasizing the absence of idol-worship in the Veda he was faithful to historical truth, but when he claimed to have found a pure monotheism in the Vedic hymns he was violating the ancient texts by a phantastic interpretation. He denied that the Vedas were subject to limitations either of space or time, and declared that they contained the true knowledge of God. He claimed that they taught transmigration of souls and *karma* (although neither doctrine can be found there), and discovered in them the germ of all science, including the technical inventions of modern days! Hence the duties of the members of the Ārya Samāj are to worship God without images, to read and hear the Vedic hymns, to serve and help men in every possible way, and to extend their knowledge in every direction, including modern sciences. Caste is rejected; all men and women can be members of the society; divine incarnations are denied; animal sacrifices (and, indeed, every kind of material sacrifice) come under the same condemnation as idolatry; offerings to the dead and pilgrimages are denounced as superstitions. This society has attained a powerful position in the Punjab, and has done splendid work in the education of the young.

The self-determination advocated by the founder of the Ārya Samāj was more pronouncedly Indian than was that of the movement known as Brāhma Samāj, and Dyānanda Sarasvati had emphasized its political side as the logical correlate of its religious side. In both movements the defence and glorification of a national religion combined with a demand for political self-determination to attract increasing attention. In illustration of this we may refer to a man whose name has been already mentioned (p. 134) in connexion with the later activity of Keśab Candra Sen. Rāmakṛṣṇa, born in 1834, belonged to a poor orthodox Brahman family. The name just mentioned is not his family name. It was adopted later as his ascetic name, and to it was added the honourable title " Paramahaṃsa " (literally, " the Supreme Goose " — the goose had been the symbol of Brahma since an early period), which is awarded only to men of special sanctity.

This remarkable man was characterized by an outstanding religious optimism, and provides an example of that profoundly religious feeling which is so often met with in the Indian of to-day. He was evidently an expert in the ancient practice of Yoga, and his nature qualified him in an unusual degree for that highest grade in which the devotee by meditation attains a condition transcending all thought. The metaphysical value of this condition has always been estimated very highly in India. With equal intensity he pursued the search for the ultimate revelations of his religion. We are told of his struggles to see the dearly beloved goddess Durgā in all the glory of her ineffable majesty. We see him, in his ardent endeavours to overcome all ordinary human prejudices, undertaking the tasks of the most despised castes, and eating the food left over by the poorest of the poor that he might uproot all pride from his heart. He even tried to realize the spirit of other religions. For a time he lived like a Mohammedan. He tried to absorb the spirit of Jesus, and meditated on the message of His love. These experiences gave him the conviction that all religions were true — that they were all different paths to the one goal. Therefore he declared that every man should travel the path that has been appointed for him. For the Hindu there is nothing better than his own religion, which has come down to him through thousands of years. This extraordinary man, whom his admirers called " god-intoxicated," died in 1886. He left no writings — he knew no Sanskrit and very little English — but left instead a circle of admirers, in whose hearts he had engraved deeply his message of the unique value of Hinduism for the Hindus.

Among these admirers of Rāmakṛṣṇa the most distinguished is Svāmi Vivekananda (1862–1902), who laboured not only in India, but also in other countries, especially in America, in the cause of Hinduism. His inspired and inspiring love for his inherited religion as preached by his master led him to condemn Western civilization as materialistic and selfish. Thus in his hands the teaching of Rāmakṛṣṇa has taken on a political colour. Political self-determination has given birth to religious Nationalism. This is a matter of present-day history into which we cannot enter here. But we may close with a brief reference to two leading figures of our own day whose lifework is an expression of this national feeling based on religion.

In this movement for political independence, which has its roots in strong religious convictions, the names of two men stand out above all others — those of Bal Gangadhar Tilak, who died in 1920, and of Mohandas Karamchand Gandhi, who was born in 1869 and is still alive. Both have laboured earnestly for the external and internal independence of Mother India, but they have chosen entirely different methods of reaching their goal. They exhibit once more the two aspects of the Indian character which we have already seen illustrated in the conceptions of the two great deities Viṣṇu and Śiva.

Tilak, a man of choleric temperament, keen intellect, and profound learning, shrank from nothing that he thought would enable him to achieve his ends. The gloomy, fierce character of Śiva was reflected in the manner in which Tilak incited the populace to commit the bomb outrages that were so common in India in his lifetime. He and his supporters promised to any youth who sacrificed himself in the sacred cause eternal bliss in the arms of Mother Durgā, who found delight in sacrifices of blood. To bring home to the ignorant masses the disgrace of foreign dominion and the dangers that threatened their most sacred possessions, he made the ancient inviolability of the cow the symbol of the national inheritance which it was their duty to guard, and thus stirred the Indian heart to its depths. The cow was the symbol of the ancient wealth of India, which foreigners were stealing — of the nation's food, which a foreign power was denying to the starving people. The cow was the symbol of Mother India, of her civilization and her sanctity.

Gandhi's methods have been of an entirely different kind. They have been characterized by gentleness, love of humanity, and a shrinking from doing hurt to any living creature. In a word, he typifies the Viṣṇu side of the Indian nature. In his youth he studied law in London, and his residence in England enabled him to understand Christianity. He thought of accepting it, but on further reflection he believed that the ancient writings of his native land contained all that was lofty and valuable in it. With heightened patriotism and a deeper understanding of India, he abandoned a successful law career in South Africa in order to lead to liberty without bloodshed his compatriots oppressed by harsh laws, and ever since he has laboured in India in that cause.

"Without hate toward their adversaries, but with wills steeled and disciplined by an ascetic life, through the power of spiritual greatness, let Indians render foreign dominion morally impossible." That is Gandhi's message. Love and devotion toward God will give birth to a power which Europe, sunk in materialism, will not be able to resist. But liberty can be attained only by those who are worthy of it. Moral and social reforms are necessary before Indians can become thus worthy: the amelioration of the lot of women in general and of widows in particular; the abolition of caste privileges; the uplifting of the fifty millions who, owing to their castelessness, are reckoned 'untouchable'; love toward all men, especially Mohammedans, the brethren of the Hindus in the common cause. These are the main lines of Gandhi's teaching. How far they are in accordance with ancient Vishnuite views, how far they betray Christian and European influence, the reader will now be able to judge for himself. Nothing more need be said to show how deeply religion has entered into the political sphere. This, indeed, is the visible token of the vitality of the Indian religion down to the present day.

BIBLIOGRAPHY

For the religion: von Glasenapp, *Der Hinduismus, Religion und Gesellschaft im heutigen Indien* (1922), and *Brahma und Buddha, die Religionen Indiens in ihrer geschichtlichen Entwickelung* (1926). For the religious literature: Winternitz, *Geschichte der indischen Literatur* (2 vols., 1908 and 1920); Farquhar, *An Outline of the Religious Literature of India* (1920). For philosophy: Strauss, *Indische Philosophie* (1923). For illustrations of religious art: Cohn, *Indische Plastik* (1921); Diez, *Die Kunst Indiens* (1925); von Glasenapp, *Die heiligen Stätten Indiens* (1927). For the relations between the conception of the world and artistic productions: Zimmer, *Kunstform und Yoga im indischen Kultbild* (1926).

5. PERSIAN RELIGION

by Carl Clemen

Although, like the Indian religion, the religion of Persia has endured down to our own day, its literary monuments do not date back as far as those of India. In the course of the centuries, especially among certain classes of the people, it has changed as much as the Indian religion, but many views and practices have lasted throughout its whole history, so that a strictly historical description would involve considerable repetition. To avoid this we must occasionally look back and occasionally anticipate, but otherwise we shall endeavour to keep to a chronological arrangement of our material.

Concerning the most ancient form of the Persian religion, previous to the time of its reformer, Zoroaster, we have no contemporary information, and any attempt at reconstruction must be based on what we know of it in after days. We cannot help drawing certain inferences when we come upon features which not only do not fit in with its later forms, but are identical with or similar to those found among the Indians and even among other peoples akin both to Indians and Persians. One very ancient practice of this kind is fire-worship. Not only does it exist in India to this day, but it existed among the Scythians and Sarmatians, a people whose religion was closely akin to that of the Persian; it has also survived down to the present day (although now with a higher meaning than that which it had originally, fire being now a symbol of deity) among the so-called Guebres in Persia and among the Parsees in India. Among these last to this day a fire is kept continually burning in a room set apart for the purpose. Five times a day, with prayers and other religious exercises, a priest replenishes it with fragrant sandalwood. When he leaves the room he smears his forehead with ashes. A modern Parsee writer justifies this by saying that man himself will one day become ashes, and just as fire spreads light and fragrance all around, so should man now shed virtue and good works like an aroma about him. We shall see by and by the connexion between this ancient fire-worship and the peculiar Persian manner of disposing of the dead. There is a similar continuity in connexion with the equally ancient worship of water and of earth. Among the Persians it presented no peculiar features worthy of special mention. On the other hand, the worship of certain trees and plants, which also goes back to Indo-Persian prehistoric time, had a special meaning, which has endured down to the present day, and must therefore be discussed here.

No doubt the soft grass or clover on which the Persians, according to Herodotus, laid the flesh that was to be offered to the gods was, like the Indian *barhis,* merely litter for the sacrifice. Strabo tells us that the magicians, as the Greeks called the Persian priests, touched the victim with thin rods. The evident explanation is that supernatural powers were ascribed to these trees. Similarly, according to the *Avesta,* the sacred book of the Persians, of which we shall have more to say immediately, the priest holds in his hand twigs of baresman, although they are now always spoken of as being " spread." In India to-day they are in most cases made of wire, and rest on a stand, but they are still regarded as sacred, and are part of the apparatus of the only ancient sacrifice that still survives out of all those that have been mentioned. This goes back to the prehistoric time anterior to the separation of Indians and Persians, and therefore requires to be dealt with here. It is the sacrifice of *haomo,* which corresponds to the Indian *soma. Haomo* is an intoxicating beverage prepared — at a later time according to definite rules and with prescribed prayers — from the stems of a plant belonging to the genus *Ephedra,* and from other ingredients. Marvellous effects were attributed to it, as may be seen from the following hymn in its praise:

> I call down upon me thy intoxicating inspiration, O golden one; send down power, victory, health, well-being, prosperity, increase, strength to fill my whole frame, knowledge of all things.

Evidently this beverage was drunk by *all* the faithful. Nowadays it is consumed by the priest alone, who also pours a part of it into a well — in order, apparently, to extend its blessings to nature. In this *haomo* sacrifice (see Fig. 61), at which no layman may be present, the opening part of the *Avesta,* the so-called *Yasna,* is always recited. On special occasions the *Visprat* and the *Videvdat,* later parts of the *Avesta,* are also read aloud. The so-called *Khorda Avesta* is used in private worship. This explains why these portions of the sacred book have come down to us, while so much else has perished.

Greek writers make occasional mention of animal-worship among the Persians. This probably goes back to primitive times, and does not call for special description here. The views regarding certain powers affecting both the living and the dead occupied a prominent position among the Persians at a later period, and will be best discussed later on. At this stage we have still to mention the actual deities who were known in the earliest time, and were still worshipped in the period subsequent to Zoroaster.

Chief among these was Mithro. He was worshipped by the Indians under the name of Mitra, and he is mentioned under the name of Miidraashshiil in a document belonging to 1400 B.C. found in Asia Minor. He is called the god of the Mitanni, who were probably an Aryan tribe that had remained there after other tribes had left. Like the Indian Mitra, he was first and foremost the god of loyalty (*mitra* means " a treaty "), and praises are sung to

FIG. 61. PERSIAN WORSHIP
From Darmstete, " Le Zend Avesta"

him in that character in the opening lines of the hymn or *yasht* dedicated to
him. The *yashts* form part of the *Khorda Avesta* already mentioned. He was
also regarded as the god of war,

to whom the princes pray when they go forth to battle against the bloodthirsty hosts of the enemy, those who gather themselves together in battle array between the two countries that are at war.

In that character he turns against the deceivers, with the result that

the steeds of the deceivers refuse to bear their riders; though they run they do not advance, though they ride they make no progress, though they ride in their chariots they gain no advantage; backward flies the lance hurled by the enemy of Mithro. Even if the enemy throw skilfully, even if his lance reach his enemy's body, the stroke does not hurt. The lance from the hand of Mithro's enemy is borne away by the wind.

Prosperity is another gift of this god.

The spacious houses are inhabited by clever wives, provided with excellent scales, furnished with large cushions and spreading pillows.

Lastly, this *yasht* speaks of him as the god of light, and he was therefore identified by the Greeks and Romans with the sun-god, though, as we shall afterward see, the Mithra mysteries do not support this identification.

Along with Miidraashshiil in the treaty with the Mitanni referred to in the foregoing paragraph mention is made of Uruwanaashshiel, Intar or Indara, and the deities known as Nashaadtianna. All these must likewise have been worshipped before the time of Zoroaster. As we shall see, these Nashaadtianna, the heavenly twins, were afterward reduced to one, and, like Intar or Indara (the Indian Indra), were regarded by the Persians as evil spirits. On the other hand, Uruwanaashshiel, the Indian Varuṇa, was probably the origin of the deity whom Zoroaster proclaimed as supreme — Ahuro Mazdâ.

This evolution cannot be exactly dated. It was certainly earlier than the time mentioned in later Persian tradition — a few centuries before or shortly after 600 B.C. Others would place it still later, but it must have been much earlier. Xanthos (*c.* 450), the first Greek writer who mentions Zoroaster, places him more than six thousand years before the crossing of Xerxes into Europe (490 B.C.), while others date him six thousand years before Plato, or five thousand years before the fall of Troy. Of course these are round numbers and are far too high, but a writer in the middle of the fifth century could not possibly have placed Zoroaster so early if he had in reality lived only a hundred and fifty years before. He must have lived much earlier, probably as early as 1000 B.C., but even that must be taken as merely a rough approximation.

Whatever his date, Zoroaster stands out as the oldest prophet or reformer, next to Moses, of whom we know anything. Our sources tell us less of the circumstances of his life than of his religious teaching, and our information is gathered chiefly from the *gathas* or hymns contained in the first part of the *Avesta*, the *yasna* already mentioned. They are written in an older dialect than the rest of the *Avesta* and in a special metre. They probably date back to Zoroaster himself, or perhaps to some of his contemporaries. According to these *gathas,* Zoroaster was conscious of having been called by God himself, and therefore demanded faith in himself and in his teaching, which he declared to be a perfect religion. He permitted the continuance of fire-worship (although only in a symbolical sense), but condemned the drinking of the *haomo* beverage. In the *gathas* that have come down to us he makes no mention of Mithro or of any of the other older deities. He proclaimed as the supreme deity a god akin to the Indian Varuṇa, called Ahuro Mazdâ or Mazdâ Ahuro. The names also occur separately as Ahuro or Mazdâ.

This name, which appears later as Ormazd, means " the Wise Lord," and although Zoroaster sometimes speaks of Ahuro Mazdâ as the One who Knows, the name was probably not coined by him. It is not sufficiently characteristic of his conception of God. To Zoroaster God was pre-eminently the Strong and the Holy One, and to him as the Strong One Zoroaster ascribed the creation of the world.

> Who appointed the path of the sun and the stars? Who is it by whose power the moon waxes and wanes? Who founded the earth beneath and the heavens above in such wise that they do not fall? Who created water and plants? Who gave the wind and the clouds their speed? Who in his goodness made light and darkness, sleep and wakefulness? Who made morning, noon, and night, to remind the wise man of his duty?

According to this teaching, the two spirits who seem to have existed from the beginning — the holy one and the deceiving one — were subordinate to Ahuro Mazdâ, as were also the so-called Ameshâ Spenta (later the Amshaspands), the glorious immortals, or the immortal glorious ones, who are sometimes identified in the *gathas* with Ahuro Mazdâ, and are even designated, like that deity, as " wise lords " (Mazdâ Ahurângho).

Like Mithro, they are personifications of abstract ideas, and are sometimes spoken of as such. The Ameshâ Spenta were later differentiated, but the only passage in the *gathas* where they are mentioned together must be translated thus:

> for the holy spirit and for the thoughts, deeds, and words that best accord with divine justice, prosperity and immortality are given to us by Mazdâ Ahuro together with Xshathra and Armaitish.

But in other passages Right Thought (Vohu Mano), Divine Justice (Asha), Prosperity (Haurvatas), and Immortality (Ameretas) are, like Xshathra and Armaitish, divine beings who stand beside the supreme deity. Vohu Mano, right thought both in a moral and religious sense, is properly a human quality; Asha, justice or righteousness, is a divine principle; Xshathra, dominion, is an activity put forth by Ahuro Mazdâ; Armaitish, the right way of thinking, is again a human quality; while Haurvatas (prosperity) and Ameretas (immortality), which are always named together, are divine gifts.

Other similar personifications of abstract ideas are mentioned in the *gathas,* but hardly anywhere do we find an indication that these divine beings were regarded as having a natural side such as they have in other religions.

The later *Avesta,* which was only completed under the Sassanid king Shapur II, in the fourth century A.D., shows an advance. The Ameshâ Spenta, now reduced in number to six, have become connected with certain aspects of nature in ways which are only distantly hinted at in the *gathas.* In them Vohu Mano is asked by the cattle who is to plead their cause with men, and (in keeping with Zoroaster's interest in agriculture, to which we shall refer later) various agricultural functions are assigned to him, but in the later period of which we are speaking he has become the guardian lord of cattle. Asha, from whom, according to the *gathas,* fire has its power, has become the god and guardian of fire. Xshathra is now lord of metals, because riches are an appanage of dominion. Because a right way of thinking (this is hinted at in the *gathas*) includes a due interest in tillage and due care for the cattle, Armaitish is now the goddess of the soil. And, finally, seeing that prosperity and immunity from death are dependent on water and vegetation, Haurvatas and Ameretas have become the guardian deities of these. Other personifications of abstract ideas adopted by Zoroaster also received new interpretations, but the main point for us here is that further deities have been added to their number. Some of them, like Mithro, were probably worshipped in previous times, but some of them had become known to the Persians only at the time of their conquests under Cyrus and his successors.

Among these new deities the most important was the female deity Aredvi or Anahita — *i.e.,* " the Spotless One." This goddess is named along with Mithro on inscriptions of Artaxerxes II (404-358), who is said to have been the first to erect images of her in various parts of his dominions. There seem to be allusions to these images in the hymn dedicated to her — one of the longest and most beautiful — for it can hardly be a mere flight of imagination on the part of the author when he speaks of the goddess as a beautiful, stalwart maiden, with her dress girt high, clad in a beaver-skin and a magnificent voluminous cloak of gold, wearing splendid footgear fastened with ribbons of gold, holding sprigs of baresman in her hand, and decked with golden earrings and a necklace, and having on her head a coronet set with a hundred gems. The coronet, which is of gold, consists of eight parts, and is shaped like a chariot decked with ribbons. There is no mention of images of this kind in earlier times, for even the winged sun-disk which appears on many of the inscriptions of Darius I (for example, that at Persepolis shown in Fig. 62), and which is meant for Ahuro Mazdâ, is not properly speaking an image, but only a symbol of that deity. It has, however, such a strong resemblance to Assyrian representations that influence from that quarter is almost certain, and the same must be said of the description of Aredvi given above. In fact, Herodotus identifies the alleged Persian goddess Mitra — by whom he must really mean Aredvi (he probably confused her with Mithro

FIG. 62. RELIEF FROM PERSEPOLIS

because the two are often mentioned together, although they had not been as yet worshipped for any length of time) — with an Assyrian goddess whom he calls Mylitta, and by whom he probably means Ištar. This is corroborated by the fact that Anahita's worship included the so-called sacral prostitution of girls who thus yielded themselves in her honour. This flatly contradicts other Persian views. Plutarch, indeed, tells us of a priestess of Anahita who was bound to chastity. Originally Aredvi was a goddess of fertility or of water, and so the hymn of which we have spoken begins with the words:

> She has a thousand bays and a thousand outlets, and each of these bays and each of these outlets is forty days' ride for a mounted man who can ride well, and the outlet of this one stream is distributed over all the seven parts of the earth, and is full of water both in the summer and in the winter.

The reference here is undoubtedly to the waters above the heavens.

One of the festivals of the later Persians must have been borrowed in part at least from the Babylonians, and one of their customs was a survival from the primeval Indo-Germanic period. The name of the Sacæ, which means "Feast of Fools," and that of their king Zoganes, which means "Governor," are of Babylonian origin. In Babylonia on New Year's Day master and slave exchanged places, and for the king too a substitute was elected. Among the Persians, however, this substitute was subsequently hanged, the reason being, apparently, that the occasion was marked by sexual excesses among the Sacæ, which were committed in the temples of Anahita, the goddess, as we have seen, of fertility. The Persian King of Fools must originally have represented the spirit of vegetation, who not only dies every year when vegetation dies, coming to life again in the following year, but who *had* to be put to death at the right time in order that he might at the right time come to life again. This conception is attested among the Mexicans and the Muyscas, and we shall find traces of it later among the Celts, so that we are justified in holding that it existed (and in its original meaning) as far back as the time of the undivided Indo-Germanic people.

Among the later Persians that evil spirit whom Zoroaster adopted had developed into a real dualistic principle in opposition to Ahuro Mazdâ, the good spirit. According to Diogenes Laertios, it was in this sense that Aristotle understood the teaching of Zoroaster (this is the Greek form of the name Zarathustro), and it is thus that we find it reproduced in the later *Avesta*. In the first section of the *Videvdat* (here it differs from Zoroaster's own teaching) only the good is referred to Ahuro Mazdâ. Evil, including the reddish snake and winter, the horsefly and despair, weeping and groaning, a sorceress and the wicked rich, evil deeds and wicked sorcerers, untimely ailments, unseasonable heat, and non-Aryan lords of the land — all these are referred to the evil spirit, who is now called Angro Mainyush, and later Ahriman. While Ahuro Mazdâ dwells in light, Angro Mainyush dwells in deepest darkness.

Just as Ahuro Mazdâ has the company of the Ameshâ Spenta, so Angro Mainyush is accompanied by six arch-demons, among whom are Indro and Mânghaithem — *i.e.,* Indra and the heavenly twins. An earlier time had probably found in them a kind of contrast to the other deities. Numerous other demons were known to a later time — among them the planets, with names resembling those by which they were known in Babylon. Whereas they were worshipped in the latter country, they had been degraded to demons in Persia, apparently because they were believed to disturb the order of nature.

But this pure dualism had been a gradual evolution, and early attempts were made to combat it. Eudemos, who lived at the close of the fourth century B.C., tells us that the magi looked on space or time as the Supreme Unity, out of which a good and an evil spirit had arisen, and the latter opinion, known as Zervanism, was actually the prevailing view in Persia in the fifth and sixth centuries A.D., and had supporters at a still later time. Even when the doctrine of an initial dualism was taught, the evil principle was regarded as subordinate and destined to ultimate extinction; therefore opposition to the evil was preached with the same urgency that characterized the teaching of Zoroaster himself.

In fact, Zoroaster's reform was based even more on this tenet than on his spiritual view of God. He declares the supreme duty of man to be *good moral conduct.* One of the *gathas* says: " As his votive offering Zoroaster presents the life of his own body, the choicest of all thought, deed, and word, to Mazdâ; to Asha obedience and dominion." And, similarly, in the later *Avesta* we find again and again the same insistence on these three ways by which the good man must prove his worth. And all our information regarding the Persian religion reveals the same moral emphasis. In the great inscription at Behistun, Darius I declares: " For this reason was I aided by Auramazda and the other gods who exist, because I was not hostile, nor untruthful, neither I nor my family." And another inscription found at Naksh i Rustam concludes with the words: " O man, let not Auramazda's commandment be displeasing in thine eyes. Forsake not the straight path. Sin not." Again, Herodotus says of the Persians — and many later writers repeat his words — that they taught their sons to ride and to shoot with the bow and to speak the truth. They looked upon lying as the greatest possible disgrace, and getting into debt as the second greatest. The later sources for the Persian religion, written in the Pehlevi language, lay the greatest stress on morality of life, and condemn all offences against it. They even include in the condemnation many habits which were regarded as excesses or forms of sorcery, such as the use of cosmetics, the wearing of false hair, warm baths, wailing and weeping, and the fashion of wearing only one shoe. It has often been said (but present-day Parsees dispute the statement) that this Pehlevi literature expressly recommends marriage with one's nearest relatives, mother, sister, and daughter, although all other peoples condemn it as the grossest incest. The explanation, no doubt, was that inheritance was in the female line, for other offences of the kind, such as unchastity and adultery, were, and always had been, condemned. Although Herodotus accuses the Persians of having become addicted to pæderasty, this was at all times condemned by their religion. Indeed, apart from some sectarian practices (of which one at least will be referred to later), marriage and domestic life were held in high esteem. According to Herodotus, the king sent annual gifts to families where children were numerous, and Strabo says that the Persians married several wives in order to have many children. Some magi refrained from partaking of certain foods, but that also was a contravention of religious teaching. The

FIG. 63. TOMB OF CYRUS

Videvdat says: " Those who do not eat are unable to do the strenuous works of Asha " and, again, " Of any two men, he has chosen the better part who fills his belly with meat, rather than he who does not eat." In the *Saddar* we read: " With us fasting means fasting from sin with our eyes and tongues and ears and hands and feet." In particular, however, Zoroaster's interest in agriculture was kept up in later times. The *Videvdat* says: " That ground does not rejoice which lies long fallow, any more than the fine-looking wife who is long without children." And the work by Arda Viraf, which will be mentioned again farther on, promises the tiller of the soil and the shepherd a special reward in heaven. This explains why in later days — like the ox in the earlier time — the dog and two other animals considered to be closely related to him, the hedgehog and the otter, were commended to the special protection of the faithful, whereas other creatures, like snakes, frogs, ants, maggots, and flies, were killed in thousands by the magi. A Byzantine writer, Agathias, speaks of a celebration of which this was a chief part. At a later time the killing was replaced by the manufacture of magical means for extirpating such pests.

Why these animals were looked upon as having been created by Angro Mainyush or Ahriman is not quite clear. Many snakes are of course dangerous, but maggots, and perhaps also flies and ants, were classed with them merely because they arise or seem to arise in dead bodies. They were regarded as specially unclean, and were therefore got rid of by the magi in the way just described. The dead were exposed to the birds, because the Persians, like other peoples who disposed or still dispose of their dead in

FIG. 64. TOWER OF SILENCE
From Weute, " Leitfaden der Völkerkunde "

this way, attached absolutely no importance to the corpse. Later times continued the practice because it was believed that the dead passed into these creatures or were conveyed by them to the realm of the dead. And a still later motive was the desire to avoid desecrating the earth by burying the dead in it or fire by cremating the corpse. The *Videvdat* further enjoins that the corpse be placed on a layer of stones or lime or some similar material. In ancient times it was covered with wax or, as is shown by the still extant tomb of Cyrus in the plain of Murgab (Fig. 63), enclosed in stone. The burial-places of the modern Parsees, the Towers of Silence, still consist of stone. Further, the corpse had to be securely wrapped up, lest any portion of it should be lost and thus render any part of the earth unclean. Any water into which a dead body falls is thereby rendered unfit for use.

The *Videvdat* further enjoins that any severed, and therefore dead, parts of the human body, including the nails or the hair, which have to be cut in the ordinary course of events — they are still regarded as parts of the body — must be buried with special precautions lest they cause harm to anyone, even to the evil spirit himself. Excreta are looked upon as causing uncleanness, and must therefore — as Greek and Latin authors tell us — not be allowed to pass into a stream or ultimately to reach the sea. Nor must one spit, especially in the presence of another person. According to Xenophon, the passing of wind in any form was forbidden, and even the breath was regarded as defiling. Hence to this day the priests while on duty wear a cloth over their mouths (see Fig. 61). To be sure, the *Videvdat* says incidentally: "The napkin is a mere pretence if one is not girt with religion. Even a hypocrite can call himself a priest." All the same, these ordinances show that morality was in part at least understood to have an external side. This point comes out even more clearly in the same section of the *Videvdat,* where harshness toward a co-religionist is put on the same level as two infringements of the injunctions just referred to, and neglect on the part of anyone over fifteen years of age to wear a girdle and a shirt — a quite frequent omission with broad-minded Parsees to-day — is roundly condemned, the last-mentioned infringement alone being declared to be inexpiable!

There are, of course, other sins which are considered beyond forgiveness, but for most sins, if they are confessed and repented of, expiation is possible. It consists for the most part of purely external means, chiefly ablutions. These can be carried through not only with water, but with a liquid that is used for the same purpose in India — viz., the urine of cattle, animals which are held in high esteem there to this day. Further, we read in Herodotus of the transference of sins to a slain man. Those whose sins were to be expiated passed between the two halves of the severed body. Those whose duty it was to handle the dead, and who could not fail to make themselves repeatedly unclean, were, according to the *Videvdat,* to be absolved from their sins by being ultimately put to death in a specially horrible fashion. Less heinous sins were to be punished by a varying number of blows — up to one thousand — delivered with two specified instruments. Probably, however, these blows were not actually inflicted, the number of blows assigned merely indicating the seriousness of the sin in question. Prescribed prayers had to be recited several times in succession, but this religious exercise could easily become a formality. And, finally, the same has to be said about the concluding words of this section of the *Videvdat:* "Thou shalt verily make thy nature perfect: Thus does salvation come to every human being who perfects his nature by good thoughts, good words, and good deeds." These good deeds consist in killing the animals of Ahriman to the number of ten thousand, in bringing the same number of loads of firewood for the sacred fire, stems of baresman, and drink-offerings. It is only incidentally that mention is made of good works that will really benefit others, such as gifts or the building of bridges. And all these serve only to ward off punishments *in this life:* future punishments await the man after death.

To a certain extent a man's lot depends on the behaviour of those whom he leaves behind, but it is determined to a far greater degree by the life he himself has lived. Man's future fate is described in greatest detail in a part of the *Avesta,* the *Hadocht Nask,* the rest of which is lost. We give a few sentences from it, in a slightly abbreviated form:

Zoroaster asked Ahuro Mazdâ: " Ahuro Mazdâ, holiest of spirits, creator of the corporeal world, when a just man departs this life, where does his soul dwell the first night? " Ahuro Mazdâ made reply: " The whole day it sits beside his head, repeating these words, ' Blessed is he who brings blessing to anyone: to him will Ahuro Mazdâ give the desire of his heart.' During this first night his soul craves for joy equal to all the joys of the animate world, and the same is true of the second and third nights. At the end of the third night, when rosy dawn appears, the soul of the just man believes itself set among flowers and fragrances: from the south are wafted to him fragrant winds, sweeter than all others, and the soul of the just man inhales them. Whence comes the wind that I thus inhale, the sweetest I have ever known? And in this wind there comes toward him his own religious faith in the guise of a maiden, radiant and glorious, with shining arms, strong and handsome, beautifully formed, full breasted, nobly born, of high lineage, fifteen years of age, and fair as the fairest of creatures. Her the spirit of the just man addresses: ' Who art thou, maiden, fairest of all that I have ever seen? ' She, who is his own religious faith, replies, ' O man of good thoughts, words, and deeds, I am thy religion, thy own personal faith. Me, who was loved, thou hast made dearer still; beautiful though I was, thou hast made me more desirable; desirable as I was, thou hast made me more so; set high, thou hast set me higher still through these good thoughts of thine, through thy words and deeds.' "

Later writings tell us that the wicked man is also confronted by his conscience in the form of an ugly old woman. The just man is conducted by the fair maiden across the bridge of division, which is also mentioned in the *gathas.* There a court sits to judge the dead. According to our latest sources, the wicked is thrown headlong from this bridge, which turns the moment he sets out to cross it. It is as thin as a razor-edge — a conception also found in Islam, from which it is probably borrowed. According to *Hadocht Nask,* the further fate of the just and the wicked unrolls in four stages (in heaven and in hell for good and wicked thoughts, words, and deeds, and in endless light or in endless darkness). It is described in closer detail in the book of Arda Viraf already mentioned, where we read of the visit of a good man in the ecstatic condition to these abodes of the wicked and of the just. But Arda Viraf comes first to Hamestagan, of which Zoroaster himself spoke — *i.e.,* the place where all things are settled, and where the scales are held by good and evil deeds. That place (with those who dwell in it) lies between heaven and earth. The only change known there is a change of weather. Thereafter, into the heaven of good thoughts and words, which lies in the stars and the moon, pass those who have offered no prayers, sung no *gathas,* and married no relative, but who have performed other good works (presumably in thoughts and words). The heaven of good deeds that is in the sun is reserved for kings and princes. In heaven, too, these privileged ones are destined to a better fate in virtue of their exalted position. Finally, in the highest heaven of light dwell the souls of the just, divided into various categories. We have already seen that tillers of the soil and shepherds receive special treatment, but the nature of their bliss is not distinctly defined. A more detailed description is given of the tortures of the wicked. These vary with the nature of the wicked deeds committed. These include not only moral and religious offences, but also infringements of ceremonial law and offences against good manners. Some of the decisions are merely arbitrary, and others seem to be based on tradition, as is the case among other peoples. Most terrible of all is the description of the blackest hell, which occurs in an account of the various punishments inflicted there. The wicked are crowded as closely together as ear and eye, and are as numerous as the hairs in a horse's mane, but they neither see nor hear. Each one reflects: " I am alone." And when a man has spent only one day in hell he exclaims: " Are the nine thousand years not yet past after which we shall be set free? "

Elsewhere, too, mention is made of a cessation of the punishments of hell, and of the sufferings in Hamestagan — viz., at the end of the days, which will come nine thousand years after the creation of Ahriman (and occurs again three thousand years after the creation of the good spirits). Zoroaster also had predicted this end of the days, and had even spoken of it as imminent. There is a similar reference to it in the later *Avesta.* But no further mention of it occurs till we come to the later literature, the *Bundahish* and the *Bahman Yasht.*

Signs of many kinds, some of them due to Jewish and Christian influence, are to herald the approach of the end. First will appear two forerunners, and then the actual " saviour," all three being miraculously born, posthumous sons of Zoroaster. The appearance of this saviour ushers in the general resurrection of the dead — first that of the first human beings, and then that of those born later. Relatives will recognize each other. The wicked will reproach the just with whom they formerly lived that they failed to teach them to do the good works they themselves did. Then they are separated (even although they are related) and rewarded or punished according to desert for three days and three nights in heaven or in hell. This conception was probably adopted because there was at first no belief in a retribution immediately after death, and punishment for the wicked there must be. But even the wicked too are purified by molten metal. Originally this was supposed to destroy the whole world, and afterward came to be interpreted as a method of divine judgment. The just man will feel as if he were walking through lukewarm milk. To the wicked man it will be as if he were traversing molten metal. The reason why the temporary meeting of kindred was placed so late was probably that fathers, sons, brothers, and friends should now for the first time have the opportunity to ask each other: " Where hast thou been these many years? And what was the judgment passed upon thy soul? Wert thou just or wicked? " Ultimately, however, it makes no difference. All are to attain bliss and join together in everlasting praise to Ahuramazda and his archangels. Ahriman and the other evil spirits and even hell itself will be consumed by fire — a proof that this was the original purpose of fire — and all creation will be restored to its pristine condition. The victory of good is thus ultimately due to an intervention of the deity, but each man must have the necessary strength always to conquer the evil again.

Manichæism, which arose in the third century A.D., and held its ground in China till the fourteenth century, represented a different view. According to this system, evil is so closely bound up with good that they can be separated only by divine intervention or by special participation of individual men. We cannot go further into this theory at this stage, because Manichæism involves other theories which must first be discussed. But this may be said: Manichæism, like the Persian religion, expects the destruction of the world by fire. For some inexplicable reason, this conflagration will last for 1468 years, yet it will not avail to purify the wicked. Together with all the powers of evil, they will be fused and formed into a round mass.

This is another point of difference between Manichæism and the Persian religion. After being tolerated for a short period, the former was bitterly persecuted by the latter. On the other hand, Manichæism was tolerated by Islam, which penetrated into Persia immediately after the death of Mohammed, and it came to occupy an inferior position only because Islam happened to be the religion of the ruling class. To this day, however, there are in Persia something like ten thousand Guebres, whose name is derived from the Arabic *kafir,* meaning " unbeliever." Many emigrated to India in the eighth century, and a hundred thousand of them still live in and around Bombay. We have already said something about their religious belief, and some customs have grown up among them which may be briefly described here.

Of the events of personal life the celebration of marriage is especially bound up with religion. Some of the marriage customs have really nothing to do with the Persian religion proper. The bridal couple sit facing each other. Between them hangs a muslin curtain, beneath which they join hands. Bride and bridegroom are separately enveloped by the priests in a piece of muslin, which is tied by a cord that passes seven times round their bodies and seven times round their hands. This is to indicate their union, and was perhaps in earlier times supposed to effect it. The curtain between them is dropped to the floor amid the applause of those present and the newly married pair pelt each other with rice. This was originally a charm to produce fertility. The pair now sit down side by side, and two priests seat themselves on their right and left and recite the marriage prayers. Afterward the priests are replaced by two laymen, as representing the fathers of the bride and bride-groom. These declare that they consent to the wedding. Finally a priest de-livers a brief address recommending the young couple to emulate famous spouses of bygone days, and then recites other prayers, some of them being in the language of the *Avesta,* which neither he nor anyone else present under-stands. The celebration concludes with a banquet.

The most important festivity among the Parsees is the celebration of New Year's Day. They go to the temple of fire and burn sandalwood, distribute alms to the poor, and exchange greetings. In other respects the celebration is domestic in character, and is marked by universal good cheer. On the other hand, the feast for the dead which precedes it is of course of a more mournful character. It probably goes back to the period before Zoroaster, and is per-haps even of primeval Indo-Germanic origin.

The priests, who take part in all these celebrations, still constitute a caste apart. Originally they married only into families of their own caste, but in recent days they occasionally marry girls of other castes. The candidate for priesthood must receive a twofold consecration, and must first have studied the *Avesta* and the various rituals. Specially erudite priests are called *dasturs,* and the chief priest bears the title *dasturan dastur.* In Persia there is similarly a high priest, who each year allocates all the members of the faith to the other priests for attendance and oversight. Only the appointed priest is entitled to perform priestly functions in any given district, but he can if need be delegate his rights to another.

As a matter of fact, the Parsees in India avail themselves of the services of the priests merely in obedience to ancient habit and tradition. Large num-bers of them have become agnostics, while others have gone to the opposite extreme and have become Theosophists. The well-known benevolence of the Parsees — there are said to be very few destitute people among them — is explained by their wealth. It is also said that there are no prostitutes among them, but probably there are special reasons for this, as also for the vaunted honesty of the Guebres, which procured them employment in the gardens of the Shah, where no one could oversee their behaviour. Clearly their religion is still marked by the strong ethical strain which distinguished it from all other ancient religions except that of the Hebrews. It is not surprising therefore that, as will be shown later, the Persian religion deeply influenced the religion of Israel.

BIBLIOGRAPHY

Lehmann, *Zarathushtra, en bog om Persernes gamle tro* (2 vols., 1899–1902); Jackson, "Die iranische Religion," in *Grundriss der iranischen Philologie* (vol. ii, 1900–4, pp. 612 ff.); Henri, *Le parsisme* (1905); Dhalla, *Zoroastrian Theology from the Earliest Times to the Present Day* (1914); Pettazzoni, *La Religione di Zarathustra nella storia religiosa dell' Iran* (1921). On Zoroaster specially: Jackson, *Zoroaster, the Prophet of Ancient Iran* (1899); Bartholomä, *Zarathustra, Leben und Lehre* (1924). On earlier Persian religion: Moulton, *Early Zoroastrianism* (1913). On modern Parseeism: Menant, *Les Parsis* (1898).

6. GREEK AND ROMAN RELIGION

by Friedrich Pfister

The religion of the Greeks and Romans — what a variety of religious manifestations is connoted by these words! The religion of Greece: the brilliant pantheon of Olympus described by Homer and depicted by the artists of later days; the circle of graves on the castle hill of Mycenæ, a primeval site of an elaborate worship of the dead; the varied mythology that speaks to us from statues, transformed by the tragic poets, reduced to system by Hesiod and the historians; the ecstatic Mænads serving their god in orgiastic worship; the religion of Eleusis, with its promise of eternal bliss to its devotees; the prayer of Socrates for a beautiful soul; the magic papyri, revealing a great array of superstitions gathered from all lands; the introduction of Oriental gods — Serapis, Mitra, and the deities of the Semites; and, finally, the Lord's Prayer, for this too began its conquering career in the Greek tongue. And on the other hand the entirely different Roman religion, a religion destitute of imagination and devoid of myth, bearing deep marks of the influence of the Greek religion and with a history that runs parallel with it through many periods.

I. THE RELIGION OF THE GREEKS

The endless variety of the manifestations of Greek religion was implicit in it from its beginnings. Ethnologically the Greeks are not one race. They are the product of a mixture of Indo-Germanic and non-Indo-Germanic constituents, and their religion is a similar combination of elements taken from the religions of both. Besides, foreign influences found easy access to the inhabitants of the Balkan peninsula because the nature of the Greek coastline facilitated communication, and because highly civilized countries like Asia Minor and North Africa lay at no great distance. Therefore not only in the early period, but throughout its whole history, the Greek religion has adopted foreign elements — from Babylonia and Egypt, Phrygia, Thrace, Persia, from the Jews, Romans, and other peoples. Further, the Greek mind itself was as susceptible and receptive as the country, and the lack of political unity contributed its share to the variety of religious life and especially of the outward observances. In addition to the deities that were universally acknowledged, each city-state had its own local deities and legendary heroes, so that the number of gods who were worshipped on Greek soil was incalculable. Further, the history of Greece was not without influence on the shape of the religion. The religion of the small city-states was completely transformed in the empires of the Diadochoi, and again later in the world-wide empire of Rome. Further, religious faith — and this is true of other religions besides the Greek — was far from being uniform among all classes of the people. The lower classes had not the same attitude toward religion as educated men and philosophers. The faith of a Plato differed from that of a contemporary peasant of Bœotia, but "the religion of Greece" includes both. Finally, we cannot leave out of account the influence exerted by outstanding men. The Greeks, it is true, had no great founders of religion or prophets who left their mark on their country's religion after they themselves had passed away. Nevertheless, Greek religion owed much to men of genius like the authors of the Homeric poems, the great sculptors and painters and philosophers, as well as to men like Alexander the Great and Augustus. But even all these together do not completely account for the variety of which we speak. Its ultimate cause lay in the Greek genius itself, which created the religion and expressed itself in it.

In view of this variety no one will look here for a systematic account of the 'doctrines' of Greek religion. We can give only a sketch of its historical development. Greek history itself begins to be clear only from the point when our sources become fuller — that is, from the time of the Persian wars in the beginning of the fifth century. At that date only a short interval separated the religion of ancient Greece from that mighty cleavage in Greek civilization which was of such epoch-making importance for the religion. That cleavage took place in the fourth century, the century of Plato and of Alexander the Great, and behind it lay already a development of many hundreds, if not thousands, of years. The period prior to the Persian wars, in which ancient Greek religion reached its full stature, grows more obscure the farther back we go. What is apparently the most outstanding monument of Greek religion, equally important in itself, as a work of surpassing power, and in its effect on the religious development of all after time, belongs to this period. We mean the Homeric epos. And in spite of this eloquent witness — nay, just because its supreme attractiveness has drawn all attention to itself — the older Greek religion has remained shrouded in obscurity. It is mainly because we have been so dazzled by the brilliance of the Homeric poems that we have so long entertained a false conception of Greek religion. We have all along identified Homeric religion and Greek religion, and have characterized Greek religion as the religion of beauty. Only in modern days have we begun to place a different value on Homer as a source for the history of Greek religion, and called in other means for the elucidation of its earlier history.

Among those new aids come first the archæological discoveries made by Schliemann, Evans, and Halbherr in Crete, by Dörpfeld, Bulle, Frickenhaus,

Rodenwaldt, and others in Troy and on the mainland of Greece, in the inter-pretation of which many scholars, including von Duhn, Karo, Nilsson, Paribeni, and others have done great serivce. But the discoveries speak an ambiguous language. They provide bases for hypotheses rather than supply us with facts, and this is even more true of the architectural remains than of the cut stones and jewels, which are especially important for a knowledge of the religion. The numerous written characters found in Crete have not yet been deciphered, so that the excavations have so far told us nothing of the speech of the people. On the other hand, the Greek language itself con-tains much that is of non-Indo-Germanic origin, and therefore tells us something about the aborigines, their civilization, and also their religion. These elements of the Greek language have shown that the Greeks adopted a large number of names of gods from the aboriginal population, and they thus give a clue for the solution of the important question as to what is pre-Greek in the Greek religion. Further, we can draw inferences from the re-ligion of later times regarding that of earlier days. In the earlier religion we find primitive elements which have survived, so to speak, as fossils into later time. Our chief aid in recognizing these is ethnology, which shows us religions more primitive than that of Greece in the historical period. When we find in Greek religion elements that are essentially ancient, and hardly intelligible to later times, ethnological comparisons frequently enable us to interpret them as survivals from the prehistoric religion of the Greeks, and thus help us to understand the religious ideas of those early times.

1. The Religion of the Cretan and Mycenæan Civilization

Down to the close of the third millennium the Balkan peninsula, like the mainland of Asia Minor and the intervening islands of the Ægean Sea, was inhabited by a non-Indo-Germanic population. These people represent the Stone Age, which lasted in these districts down to 3000 B.C., or perhaps into the first half of the third millennium — and even longer in outlying parts. The Stone Age was followed by the Bronze Age, sometimes called the Helladic Period (in the Balkan peninsula), with its three subdivisions, the Early Helladic (c. 2500–2000 B.C.), Middle Helladic (c. 2000–1600 B.C.) and Late Helladic (c. 1600–1100 B.C.). In Crete, whose early civilization is better known, there was the Minoan Period, contemporary with the Hel-ladic Period, and similarly subdivided into Early, Middle, and Late. The Early Helladic civilization saw the first immigration of Indo-Germanic tribes into the Balkan peninsula. These were the ancestors of the later Ionians and Æolians. As the immigrants were nomadic tribes, their civi-lization was much inferior to that of the settled aboriginal population, but they conquered and intermingled with them. As time went on, in spite of being the dominant element, they adopted the civilization which they found, and even incorporated into their own language parts of the tongue of the native people. These borrowed elements, which consisted of words, place-names, and names of deities, survived into the later Greek vocabulary, and cannot be explained from Indo-Germanic languages. This collision of two peoples and civilizations gave rise to the first mixed religion on Greek soil of which we know anything. In other words, from the time when a Greek people emerges from complete obscurity into the twilight of pre-historic time their religion is a mixture of Indo-Germanic and alien elements.

FIG. 65. TABLE FOR SACRIFICE
From Evans, "The Palace of Minos"

The representatives of the so-called Mycenæan civilization were also Indo-Germans, while those of the Minoan civilization in Crete were non-Indo-Germanic. One of the main tasks of research is to disentangle these two elements of Greek religion. A similar problem is presented by the religion of Babylonia, in which there is a mixture of Sumerian and Semitic elements. The first step toward the solution of the problem will be the interpretation of the archæological finds that have been made at the two most important centres of civilization during the second millennium—viz., Crete and Argolis. The former provides evidence for the Minoan, the latter for the Helladic (Mycenæan) civilization. We must admit, however, that when all that is of doubtful interpretation is omitted, it is not very much that we learn from these witnesses, though the evidence from Crete is more illuminating than that from Argolis.

For one thing, we have learned something negative—there were no actual temples and no large images of the gods. These were characteristic features of Greek religion in after days.

red   green   yellow   blue

FIG. 66. SACRIFICIAL SCENE FROM THE SARCOPHAGUS OF HAGIA TRIADA
From Evans, "The Palace of Minos"

Now let us examine the Cretan evidence more closely. First of all, it tells us something about the sites of worship. Worship was celebrated in caves, in uncovered sacred precincts on mountain-tops surrounded by low walls dividing the sacred from that which was profane, or in small chapels in houses and palaces. These last, however, were in most cases so small that they can hardly have been used for great ceremonies, and must have served as places for storing the sacred utensils and idols. The ceremonies themselves were conducted in the open air, and consisted mainly of round dances and processions. A few scattered small chapels have been unearthed, containing apparatus and sacred objects, such as altars, sacrificial tables (Fig. 65), vessels, idols, and fetishes (chiefly double-headed axes). The things found also included votive offerings in the shape of imitations of parts of the human body, offered to some deity as thank-offerings for restoration to health, garments made of faïence presented to the goddess whose image stood in the place of worship, small statues showing men and women at prayer, and other representations of the ceremonies. The sanctity of a utensil — say, of an altar — was frequently indicated by the sacred horns attached. The sacrifices

were animals, or bloodless offerings which were poured into the depressions of the tables (see Fig. 65) or into large vessels (see Fig. 66). From the representations that have been found it is clear that women took an important part in the services.

Although there were no large temples with images, it should be stated distinctly that the beginnings of these already existed: small, detached, independent chapels, like those found in Gurnià, and small images, which no doubt, like the double axe and the sacred horns, were believed to be charged with sacred power, and were therefore worshipped. It is beyond all doubt that worship was offered here to personal gods. But there were fetishes also, like the double axe, the *labrys* (Fig. 67). This is also found in Asia Minor as the attribute of a Hittite god (Fig. 68), and later as that of Jupiter Dolichenus (Fig. 69), while in Crete its image, like that of the sacred horns (Fig. 70), was used to indicate that an object or a place was taboo — that is, consecrated. Sacred stones, too, and trees, animals, and birds (the dove) were worshipped, and occasionally a deity revealed himself in the form of a bird. Of personal deities, three appear most frequently in the discoveries. First is " the mistress of the animals," perhaps akin to the Kybele of Asia Minor. She is seen standing

FIG. 67. DOUBLE-HEADED AXE
From Haas, " Bilderatlas zur Religions-geschichte "

at a height from the ground between lions, or holding animals by the neck or legs (Figs. 71 and 72). Second is the goddess of snakes. Several examples of these have been found. The image is a female figure wearing a long skirt, with snakes coiled round her (Fig. 73). Third comes the shield-goddess, armed with a large shield or a lance (Fig. 74). The numerous idols found in graves do not represent goddesses; they are gifts to the dead, and were supposed to minister to the needs of the departed. Worship of the dead was also general at the time of the Minoan civilization.

The dead were not cremated, but were committed to the earth and provided with offerings.

About 1400 B.C. the Cretan palaces were conquered by Indo-Germanic hosts from the mainland of Greece, who settled down in Crete. They were the descendants of the first Indo-Germanic settlers in the Balkan peninsula, who had carried thither with them the Mycenæan civilization. The archæological finds cast less light on their religion than on that of ancient Crete. We have many evidences of Mycenæan civilization in the Balkans, especially from Argolis, but they tell us little about the religion, as no actual sanctuaries have as yet been found. What was presumably a domestic chapel in the palace of Mycenæ does not tell us much. The religion of the Mycenæan civilization was a mixture of non-Indo-Germanic elements (adopted from the aborigines and akin to the Cretan religion) and the Indo-Germanic elements of the invaders. From about 1600 onward Minoan civilization began to have a considerable influence on the Mycenæan, and still other non-Indo-Germanic elements probably found their way into the religion about this time. The shield-goddess, the double axe, and the sacred horns now appeared also on the mainland. Worship of the dead was more prominent than in the Minoan civilization. In particular the royal graves of Mycenæ exhibit great luxury and rich offerings. The more ancient of them, the shaft-graves in the castle, date from about 1600 B.C. The offerings were extraordinarily rich, and many of the bodies were actually hidden under gold and jewels. About two hundred years later, when the Cyclopean castle-wall was built, a rearrangement of this burial-place was necessary. The graves of the old kings and their families were placed together, and the whole area was fenced with a large circle of stone slabs. Inside this circle stood the stele on which

FIG. 68
HITTITE WEATHER-GOD
*From Haas, " Bilderatlas zur
Religionsgeschichte "*

were depicted the kings riding in their chariots, fighting in battle, or pursuing the chase (Fig. 75). An altar and a sacrificial pit were used in the worship; the graves of the departed now lay inside the castle-walls, quite close to the castle-gate, guarded by the stiffly erect lions (Fig. 76). The later rulers, from the end of the sixteenth century B.C. onward, erected for themselves and their families the large domed tombs that lie outside the castle. The bodies were laid under the dome, or, if such a place was available, in an adjacent mausoleum. The numerous bodies which were gathered in such a grave in the course of time made it literally a charnel-house, a huge heap of relics. In one such domed tomb in Crete were found the remains of nearly two hundred bodies, including possibly those of slaves slaughtered at the funeral of their masters, just as Achilles offered human victims at the burial of his friend Patroclus. The chambered graves in the vicinity of Mycenæ in which the common people were buried contained many corpses, sometimes large numbers of them, as well as offerings that point to worship of the dead.

The Mycenæan religion is the first phase of " Greek religion." It received additional non-Indo-Germanic elements as a result of the conquest of Crete, and the influence of non-Indo-Germanic religion continued into later times. A similar influence affected the Greek colonies in Asia Minor, and even the Greeks of the Hellenistic period. Apparently, however, still other peoples left traces, direct and indirect, although perhaps not so strong, on Cretan and Mycenæan religion — viz., the Egyptians and Babylonians, and perhaps also the Hittites. The two first-named peoples had already reached the zenith of their power when the first Indo-Germans invaded the Balkan peninsula. Egyptian influence on Crete is specially clear in various directions. Sphinx figures, the sistrum, and perhaps also the practice of mummifying the dead seem to have reached Mycenæ from the land of the Nile, and all

Fig. 69. Jupiter Dolichenus
From Haas, " Bilderatlas zur Religionsgeschichte "

sorts of fabulous animals were introduced from Babylonia. Whether Greek mythology was influenced by Babylonia — say, through the Gilgameš epic — is more than doubtful. Any such influence would certainly have left traces in this second millennium.

That the later movements of peoples which set in about 1200 B.C., and which are usually grouped under the names of the Dorian, Æolian, and Ionian migrations, failed to destroy this Mycenæan religion goes without saying. There are numerous sites of worship where religious rites can be proved to have been uninterruptedly performed from the Mycenæan era down to a time far beyond that of the migration of nations. These include two sacrosanct places of the ancient world, Delphi and Delos, where worship undoubtedly existed from the Mycenæan time onward. In Crete a number of sanctuaries were taken over by the invading Greeks, and were used even in later Greek times as places of worship. Among these are the cave sanctuary at Psychro and that on the Mount of Juktas, where in later days the grave of Zeus was shown. At Menidi, in Attica, worship of the dead was carried on at a Mycenæan domed tomb till well into the historical period. And, finally, the ancient castles themselves at Mycenæ, Tiryns, Megara, on the Acropolis at Athens, and on the Kadmeiá at Thebes were holy places in historic time, sacred to Hera, Athene, or Demeter. Therefore in the later religion, which we know better, we may look for numerous remains of an older faith, older conceptions of deity, older rites and myths, and we can thus use the later forms of faith to complete our picture of the religion of the Mycenæan period.

The means of doing so are supplied by the sciences of ethnology and comparative religion. The latter proves that certain fundamental types of religious thought, which appear in conceptions of deity, in cultus, and in myth, are common to all religions, and take the same form at similar stages of civilization. One of the most important findings of comparative religion is that nearly all primitive

FIG. 70. STRUCTURE WITH HORNS, MADE OF
SHEET BRONZE
From Haas, " Bilderatlas zur Religionsgeschichte "

religions include a belief in power — a belief in impersonal powers which can inhere in any perceptible object, such as men, animals, plants, stones, artifacts, etc. This belief is usually called " orendism," from the word *orenda* by which the Iroquois denote that power. This orendism is met with even in higher religions — in those of Greece and Rome till the end of the ancient era and even in Christianity. We may therefore assume that it existed both in the Mycenæan and Cretan religions, and it is our first task now to study these orendistic Greek conceptions, which lasted unchanged for thousands of years.

To the primitive mind all that is charged with orenda is taboo; in other words, all that possesses any special power, all that is set apart by having this name attached to it, is holy. This sanctity may be due either to the presence of orendistic powers or to a relation to personal gods. In any case, the epithet 'holy' presupposes the belief in powers which are manifested in whatever is regarded as holy. Temples and sacred precincts, altars and images, ritual utensils and all that belongs to the gods, are holy because they are charged with power, because they are the dwelling-places of deity or belong to deity. The essence of the holy consists in the power which works in it. It need not be a personal deity in whose power faith is placed; frequently

FIGS. 71, 72. THE GODDESS OF ANIMALS
From Haas, " Bilderatlas zur Religionsgeschichte "

it is an impersonal, marvellous, supernatural, magical power. The holy is filled with a kind of *fluidum* which radiates from it, and can be transferred or communicated by touch, like magnetic or electric energy. The holy must be kept apart from the profane, and any intercourse with it demands from man a state of holiness, increased power, cleanness, and chastity.

Even externally, therefore, the ancient sanctuary had to be strictly and clearly fenced off from profane territory. The word used for the sacred precinct expressed this idea. *Temenos* means a portion of ground which is cut off from the profane. It comes from *temnein,* "to cut" (*templum,* 'temple'). Similarly, "to consecrate" means etymologically "to set apart for sacred use." This setting apart was carried out by means of boundary stones, hedges, walls, or even a cord stretched round the sanctuary. All that was impure was excluded from this territory; only the pure man dare tread the holy ground. There were precise regulations concerning pure and impure, differing according to the holy place in question. There were ordinances forbidding entrance to all save the priest, or specifically excluding women, slaves, strangers, and the uninitiated. Others permitted the entrance only at certain times, or prescribed ablutions, chastity, fasting, refraining from certain foods, or the wearing or not wearing of certain garments. Any transgression of these rules or any desecration of the sanctuary called down divine vengeance or involved legal punishments.

While the whole temple area was thus holy, the altar was specially sacred.

This was the place of sacrifice. It was raised above the ground, forming a platform for the offerings, which must not be laid on ordinary soil. The altar was charged with sacred power. The suppliant who touched it came into immediate contact with the holy. The same was true of the image of the god. Wondrous stories were told of its power: how this or that image had wept or perspired or turned round to punish or hurt or heal, how on this image the welfare of the city depended, so that it was chained in its place lest it should be removed. The temple vessels too and all that belonged to the

deity were holy and withdrawn from profane use. When anything was no longer suitable for its sacred purpose, or when for any reason it could no longer be kept in the sanctuary, it was buried in the ground, and thus preserved from desecration. Two large stone chests belonging to the Minoan period were found buried in the palace at Knossos. These were crammed full of the furniture of an older temple which could not be utilized in the new building and which was thus saved from profane use.

Seeing that the Mycenæan period knew no actual temples with large images, the most ancient sites of worship were places and natural objects that were considered holy — mountain-tops, caves, rocks and stones, trees and groves, springs and rivers. The stone, tree, or stump was worshipped because some special power was believed to dwell in it. Such fetish-worship is originally not homage paid to a personal being,

FIG. 73. THE GODDESS OF SNAKES
From Evans, " The Palace of Minos "

but is purely orendistic: the fetish is charged with a power — it is itself the god. Similarly, the Cretan double axe is not originally a quality or symbol of a deity; it is itself a sacred, efficient object charged with power. A gem bearing the figure of the double axe was worn as an amulet (Fig. 77); a house on the stones of which the axe was chiselled was under sacred protection (Fig. 78). Nor are these figures the only means of imparting power to an object. The cutting of letters in it could likewise consecrate it: the Minoan period knew the use of writing, although we are still unable to decipher the numerous inscriptions. All the conceptions mentioned above formed part of the faith of the second millennium, as well as of the later time.

Innumerable other fetishes and gods of non-human figure survived also

FIG. 74. THE SHIELD-GODDESS

From Haas, " Bilderatlas zur Religionsgeschichte "

into historical time, and bear witness to primeval belief — boulders and stone pillars, wooden stumps and posts, trees and animals. Most of them were of course associated with personal gods and heroes, and some legend awakening interest by its antiquity explained the form of worship. Thus a wooden post

was looked upon as the sceptre of Agamemnon; a stone was the one that
Kronos swallowed by mistake instead of the boy Zeus and vomited forth
again: trees were pointed out which Agamemnon and Menelaus had planted;
the Thebans worshipped the weasel, because it played a part in the birth-
story of Herakles.

In addition to these forms of animal worship which continued into later
time there are other features of later Greek religion which prove that animal-
worship was widespread
in olden days. Many he-
roes, like Erechtheus and
Kecrops in Athens, Ky-
chreus in Salamis, Sosipo-
lis in Olympia, were de-
picted in serpent or in
semi-serpent shape. Nu-
merous sanctuaries con-
tained animal-shaped im-
ages; in Kyzikos there
was a bull image of Dio-
nysos, and in Phigaleia an
image of Demeter with
the head of a horse. Other
animals became the sym-
bols of the great gods —
the eagle for Zeus, the owl
for Athene, the pigeon
for Aphrodite; or their
former worship left traces
in their cult-names or even
in their poetical epithets.
Thus the cult of Athene
and Hera Hippia points
back to a worship of the
horse, and that of Apollo

FIG. 75. GRAVE STELE AT MYCENÆ
From " The Annual of the British School at Athens "

Lykios to a worship of the
wolf. The epic epithet ap-
plied to Athene, " the owl-eyed," and that of Hera, " the cow-eyed," likewise betray former animal-worship. Other animals were regarded as the
favourites of various gods, and were kept and fed in their temples — pea-
cocks for Hera and mice for Apollo Smintheus. The priesthood also contains
frequent hints of ancient animal-worship — priests of Dionysos were called
" cattle-herds," and priests and priestesses of other deities were called " bulls,"
" bears," " foals," and " bees," and are often depicted in animal masks or animal disguises. Legends too point in the same direction. Many of them tell of

FIG. 76. THE LION-GATE OF MYCENÆ

gods who appeared in animal form to help and guide men, as when dolphins saved Koiranos and Arion from the sea.

Tree-worship also flourished in the second millennium as well as later. According to a belief which, although primitive, still lived in later time, trees could be charged with marvellous power, with *orenda*. Each twig on such a tree shared in this power, even the twig which was broken off and wound into a circlet for the head. Thus the religious custom of wearing such a garland during worship meant that the sacred power that resided in the tree and in the garland was communicated to the wearer and consecrated him. Among the Greeks the worshipper wore this garland, and the suppliant fleeing to the altar for refuge wore the consecrating twig which brought him under the protection of the higher power, making him holy and inviolable. The same belief is seen in the custom of striking a person with the "rod of life." In Sparta at the festival of Artemis Orthia the boys were touched with twigs of the chaste-tree (*agnus castus*). The original meaning was that the power of the holy twig was thus communicated to the boys. Later the orendistic tree came to be regarded as the abode of a personal deity: tree nymphs or hamadryads peopled the woods; the oak was sacred to Zeus, the plane to Dionysos, the myrtle was worshipped as Artemis Soteira. Cult-names of the deities also reflect this ancient tree-worship. Dionysos was Endendros, Dendrites, or Sykites; Artemis was Daphnia, Karyatis, or Kedreatis; Apollo was Daphnites or Platanistios.

FIG. 77
CARVED STONE WITH
DOUBLE-HEADED
AXES

*From Haas, " Bilderatlas
zur Religionsgeschichte "*

Two other customs further illustrate ancient orendistic beliefs and show how the later religion casts light on the faith of the Mycenæan period. The first is the use made of sacred skins in the ritual. Many animals were regarded as holy, and in a similar way the sacrificial victim, being the property of a god, was looked upon as sacred — *i.e.,* filled with power. This power resided in every part of the animal, but especially in its hide. The priest therefore frequently wore a skin as a garment in order to acquire the power that resided in the animal. This is frequently shown on pictures of Cretan and Mycenæan civilization (see Fig. 66). The same belief meets us in the legend of the Nemean lion strangled by Herakles. This lion was invulnerable, and this marvellous quality was imparted to Ajax when as a child he was wrapped by Herakles in the skin. Skins of this kind, taken from sacrificial animals, were used for sleeping on in the temples; whoever wished to dream in a holy place lay down on such a hide and came thus into immediate contact with the divine power. But the power in the skin could also be used apotropaically, — *i.e.,* to cleanse from guilt. He whose hands were stained with blood, or who had otherwise become defiled, could by means of the skin purify and reconsecrate himself. Thus in the time of greatest heat the most prominent citizens clothed themselves in sheepskins and climbed Mount Pelion to the temple of Zeus in order to expel the demon of heat by the power that resided in the hide. Similarly, a goat-skin, such as is shaken by a Mongolian magician to bring rain, became, as the *ægis,* a symbol of Athene.

The second custom calling for mention is that connected with the olive

FIG. 78. STONE BLOCKS WITH DOUBLE-HEADED AXE
From Evans, " The Palace of Minos "

branch, the *eiresione.* This was an orendistic rod or branch, usually of olive, whose power was still further intensified by the attachment of bands of wool and fruits. It was carried by a boy, and its fertilizing virtue was imparted to the place over which it was borne or at which it was set up. Originally these branches were fertility fetishes, but gradually they evolved into personal deities or were specially associated with such. The fetish rod known as *korythale* became Artemis Korythalia, and was worshipped in ritual dances. The lad who carried the *kopo,* the olive branch, was also filled with the sacred power of the fetish, and was called *daphnephoros,* a name which in course of time became an epithet applied to Apollo. The fetish rod, too, which as a charmed rod played a part in the magic not only of the Greeks in all periods, but of other peoples also, was an orendistic rod of this kind, and the same is true of the sceptres of the kings and heralds. Similarly the amulets, which gave increased power to their wearers and warded off evil from them, and of which we now possess many specimens from the Minoan period down to late times, were likewise charged with power, which they owed to the inscriptions or images engraved on them.

We thus see that certain beliefs and ritual observances were current in all periods of the Greek religion, and maintained their ground through all the centuries from the Mycenæan period onward. The anthropomorphic conceptions of deity which were held up before men's eyes by the plastic arts and by poetry were unable to displace these survivals of ancient faith. As late as the second century A.D. worship was still paid to Eros as a block of stone in Thespiæ, in Bœotia, although the famous statue by Praxiteles had stood there for centuries. Even among the Greeks beauty made less appeal than holiness to religious feeling. The gold and ivory image of Athene by Phidias in the Parthenon at Athens called forth admiration, but religious homage was always paid only to the insignificant but sacrosanct image of Athene which had come down from olden time. The gods of the Homeric Olympus were familiar to every one from the epic, the tragedies, and countless other representations, but in his time of need the Greek preferred to have recourse to the deities which had been worshipped in his own village or in his native city since the days of old. In many cases these were quite different from the gods of Homer.

There is still another important group of phenomena that reveals the continuance of orendistic ideas into the historical period, and from which we can draw inferences regarding the view that prevailed in prehistoric time. In man too is evidenced a power, varying in strength in different individuals. Special strong *orenda* was possessed by the medicine man, the magician, the priest, the chieftain, the king. If two clans meant to war against each other, each considered it essential to seek out a doughty man whose *orenda* was great — just as, according to the Greek epic, Troy could not be taken till Achilles had been brought from Skyros. This power resided in quite a special degree in the *head* of the man in question. This is the belief that underlies the head-hunting of the South Sea races: they are eager to procure as much power-substance as possible. A man eats the brain of his foe in order to reinforce his own *orenda,* and he preserves a collection of heads. This is the meaning of the Greek myth that tells how Tydeus broke the skull of the slain Melanippos and ate his brains. Kyknos, son of Ares, lay in wait for wayfarers, killed them, and built a temple to Apollo out of their skulls. Oinomapos in Olympia slew his daughter's wooers, who had undertaken to run a race with him, and nailed their heads to his house or to the pillars of the temple. He even wished to build with them a temple to Ares. These and similar legends show that this belief and practice were not unknown to the Greeks. There are even traces among them of actual cannibalism. It was originally regarded as a means of acquiring the enemy's *orenda*. We find it in the tradition regarding Zeus Lykaios in Arcadia, and in the stories about Tantalos, Atreus, and Prokne.

This *orenda*, which is present in every person, the Greeks named *daimon*. It was conceived as possessing a more or less shadowy kind of personality. Just as primitive man endeavoured to strengthen his *orenda*, so did the Greek. To this *daimon* ritual worship was offered, at first once a month, then once a year, on the anniversary of its reception into the worshipper's body — that is to say, on his birthday. This is the origin of the celebration of the birthday — it was a service of worship to the *daimon* actively present in the man. But this power was not equally strong in each man. The king's *daimon* was specially potent; therefore the ritual in his case was performed on a larger scale, and the whole people took part in it. In virtue of his strong *orenda* the king was a sacred person: he was beloved and nourished by Zeus; it was through his power that the nation increased in strength. Sacral functions were therefore assigned to him, and mythical tradition implies that he was believed to be able on occasion even to control the weather. From the historical period of the Greeks we have only scanty proofs of this ascription of divinity to kings, because by that time kingship was for the most part abolished. But where it survived — as, for example, in Sicily — we have isolated traces as late as the fifth century which point to this kingly quality. From the time of Alexander the Great this worship of kings flourished in renewed strength, and its existence must be postulated for the kings of the Mycenæan period. The awe in which they were held can still be read in their Cyclopean castles, and in the huge grave monuments, for whose erection the labour of innumerable subjects was at the kings' disposal. The royal palace bore the same name as the sanctuaries of the gods, *megaron* and *anaktoron*, and the royal domain, like the sacred enclosure, was called *temenos*.

To the Greeks at all periods the priest too was a sacred personage — *i.e.*, he was in possession of special power, which had to be carefully guarded. That is the meaning of all the ordinances that regulated taboo and enjoined purity and chastity. The priest wore a special costume, a chaplet and woollen bands, and all these reinforced his sanctity. His special power included certain specific kinds of knowledge — of ritual and magical formulas and prayers. His special name in the epic was *areter*, " he who offers prayer," — *i.e.*, he who knows and can use the correct, efficacious sacred words and formulas. The seer's gift was also a specific endowment of many priests. Like any other *orenda*, such knowledge was hereditary in the family, and was handed on from father to son. Like kingship, priesthood was originally hereditary. Like the king, the priest could also command the weather; he knew the spell that brought rain and wind and hail, and his aid was invoked when the sun or moon was eclipsed. In many parts of the ritual he actually played the part of deity: he put on the mask and appeared in the dress of the god. If the god had an animal's shape, the priest disguised himself accordingly.

Even after his death a man's *orenda* did not lose its efficacy. It was still associated with his body, and, seeing that it might be either good or evil, it could be helpful and useful or hostile and injurious. Thus an element of contradiction pervades all worship of the dead, and this can be shown to have existed among the Greeks as among many other peoples. The dead were held in fear, and this fear was shown in efforts to render their power innocuous or even to make use of it. The Greeks too knew the practice of mutilating the dead, *mashalismos*. It was intended to weaken the slain man, so that he could not harm his murderer. They also constricted the corpse with cords, to confine its powers — a practice which was learned from the huddled bodies found in prehistoric graves. But on the other hand the Mycenæan graves prove the existence of a widespread actual worship of the dead, which lasted throughout the whole of antiquity. Everywhere this worship was orendistic — *i.e.,* men believed in an impersonal power associated with the corpse. The actual remains were charged with *orenda*. It was only later that this developed into animistic worship of the dead, or worship of the souls of the departed, involving a belief in a personal soul separable from the body. But among the Greeks in the historical period, as among other peoples, this soul-worship was based on the orendistic belief. Indeed, the latter idea gathered strength again at a later time, with the result that while the ancient worship of heroes and of the dead was predominantly animistic, the Christian regard for the dead betrays the renewed prevalence of orendistic conceptions. The grave was regarded as a holy place — especially the graves of those legendary heroes whose deeds had proved that special power dwelt in them. Graves were inviolable. They were marked off from profane ground and guarded against profane use. This is still seen in the ring of slabs set round the grave circle in the castle at Mycenæ. While it is certain that in historical time the dead were usually buried at a distance from human dwellings and outside the cities, many discoveries indicate that in Neolithic and Mycenæan times the dead were occasionally buried in the house. This practice is also attested for many primitive peoples.

All the features that have been briefly sketched in the foregoing paragraphs represent religious conceptions that were *universally current*. They were especially prominent in the cultus, which is the most conservative aspect of religion, and they existed both in prehistoric time and in later Greece. But there are numerous other points on which we are justified in drawing inferences from the Greek religion of historical time regarding the conditions that prevailed in older days. What we know of the gods and myths of later time casts light on the beliefs of the Mycenæan civilization. Homer mentions a large number of names of gods and legendary heroes which were not invented by him, but were in existence before his day. Some of these names and myths were perhaps already familiar to the Indo-Germanic invaders; others may have been known to the earlier non-Indo-Germanic population; some may have been formed subsequent to the migrations of the Mycenæan period. A few may even have been added after the downfall of Mycenæan civilization in the Greek middle era, and a very few may perhaps be regarded as inventions of the poets. It is impossible now to disentangle these in every case, but, speaking generally, it may be safely said that the large majority of these names and myths already existed or arose in the Mycenæan period and that only a small number were added under the influence of Dorian and Ionian migrations or were derived from alien sources. The epic poets elaborated material already existent rather than created new names and myths. The science of philology has decided that only some of the names are Indo-Germanic. These include very few of the names of the greater gods — only Zeus, Ares, Hera — and only a few of the names of the legendary heroes to whom a ritual was dedicated. All the other names of gods and heroes are pre-Indo-Germanic. Very few of the names of legendary heroes are inventions of the epic poets, and these of course are Greek.

But in deciding whether a name is to be pronounced Indo-Germanic or otherwise, it must be kept in view that in the course of development the name may have come to be associated with many other conceptions and myths and rituals that were originally alien to it. As a matter of fact, this took place to a very large extent, with the result that the more important deities gradually attracted a large number of accretions. In this way a divine name became connected with rituals and practices which really belonged originally to other deities, with epithets which were formed out of other divine names, with ideas about the activities and attributes of a deity which originally did not belong to him at all, and with myths which were formerly associated with other figures. Thus all the greater Greek deities of historical time were credited with Indo-Germanic and alien elements which it is impossible for us now to identify. Gods between whom certain resemblances were perceived were identified with each other — for example, the Indo-Germanic Dioscuri with the alien Tyndarides, an identification which resulted in giving the sons of Zeus a second human father, Tyndareos. In most cases it is therefore impossible to separate the original significance of a deity from the complex tradition. It can, however, be taken as certain that the greater gods mentioned in Homer were already worshipped in the Mycenæan period, although the worshippers of that period had a conception of them quite different from that which appears in the epic. In the case of the goddesses already named, Hera, Athene, and Demeter, to whom worship was still paid in the Helladic castles, their cult was either adopted by the conquerors of the castles at the close of the Mycenæan period, or, without any change of masters taking place, their cult was continued in the post-Mycenæan period. Certainly the cult of Athene goes back to pre-Indo-Germanic times. The myths and names of most of the legendary heroes likewise go back to the Helladic epoch, for it is very improbable that the Homeric poets 'invented' them all. Apart from other reasons, there is, as Nilsson, one of the best authorities on ancient Greek religion, has recently shown, one circumstance that points to this ancient origin of the Greek myths. The main centres of the Greek myths are also the main centres of Mycenæan civilization, and the greater the power and importance of a city of the Helladic epoch was, the greater also is the cycle of myths associated with it. It is true that we possess only doubtful pictorial representations of myths from the Mycenæan period, and it must be admitted that the recently published illustrations of cut stones from Thisbe, in Bœotia — showing, according to Evans, scenes from the stories of Œdipus and Agamemnon — cannot be absolutely depended on, for these stones may be forgeries. But even if we had no mythological representations from the Mycenæan period, this would not disprove the origin of the myths at that time. They might have arisen then and still contain some reminiscences of historical events of that period, even if these are few and have to be cautiously pieced together.

The process by which orendistic powers came to be ascribed to personal deities is hidden in the obscurity of the far past. It came about in Greek religion in the same manner as in that of Rome, but in the case of the latter the process was simpler. The orendistic 'gods' were inanimate objects, men, animals, or plants charged with power. They were therefore, as Herodotus justly calls them, nameless deities — fetishes, if we understand that term broadly enough and extend it to include orendistic men and animals. The deities were inherent in the substance, and as matter is perishable, and as primitive men always destroyed the fetish that had ceased to be effective, they were continually changing. But the conception remained that certain powers or certain men could cure disease, conjure up a storm, or ward off hail. This belief was manifested in all the ritual and magic ceremonies connected with objects that possessed such powers. Further, these powers, which manifested themselves in many ways and inhered in many objects and men, always had the same effect, and therefore the multiple manifestations could in each case be summed up under one head. The healing efficacy could be called Iatros, power to summon up a storm could be called Eudanemos, the hail-repelling power Chalazios. The common element in the separate manifestations was recognized and designated by a word — a self-interpreting or transparent name. Thus arose the 'transparent' special gods Eudanemos, Iatros, Chalazios, Eiresione, Kopo, Daphnephoros, Salpinx, just as among the Romans we find Janus, Robijo, Vervactor, Reparator, Strenia, and others.

This was the first step toward unification. In place of the almost unlimited multiplicity of external objects and separate manifestations in which the impersonal *orenda* was active came the unifying conception which was indicated by a word. The *orendas* of the numerous separate phenomena became special gods with transparent names. As yet, however, there were no proper names, but merely names whose meanings were self-evident. Many of them afterward became names of legendary heroes or epithets of the greater gods. These special gods were still very numerous, and they differed in different localities. While they were no longer mere impersonal powers, they were not as yet fully developed personalities. They still lacked a proper name and a myth. The third step of the process was taken when the gods were provided with these. The names whose meanings were originally self-evident gradually ceased to be understood. Some portion of the verbal stems from which the names were formed became obsolete. The appellation, now untransparent, became a proper name, and the god indicated by it was now a distinct personality. Usener has shown this very clearly. The names that had been borrowed from the religion of the aborigines, and which were in themselves strange to the Greeks, could easily become personal names. Thus most of the divine names of the later time are not self-interpreting. They are not ' speaking ' names. Those deities whose names continued to require no interpretation never attained the stage of clear personality, filled out by numerous myths and worshipped with ritual — deities like Uranos, Helios, Hestia. It was to the personality that the myth (which was often produced by the cult) attached itself, and the myth itself was further amplified and extended by the epic poems.

2. The Homeric Epos

The period of the Mycenæan civilization, which reached its close about the end of the twelfth century B.C., produced not only the myths, but also the lays in which they received their poetic dress and on which the subsequent so-called Homeric epos is based. The amplification of the myths into lays took place neither at the same place nor at the same time as the composition of the great epics which go under the name of Homer. The lays were composed on the Greek mainland during the Mycenæan period by minstrels who lived in the castles of Argolis, in the Kadmeia, and at other Mycenæan royal Courts. The Homeric poems were composed and written down on Ionian soil, and were recited by rhapsodists at the religious festivals which were held by the aristocratically ruled populations of the cities.

Beginning with the twelfth century, a new migration of nations poured over Greece, partly destroying the Mycenæan civilization and rasing its strongholds. The Dorians occupied large tracts of the Balkan peninsula, down to the southernmost point of the Peloponnesus. Before their advance portions of the older population fled eastward over the sea and settled on the west and south coasts of Asia Minor. Here they founded a Greek colonial dominion which for many years, down to the fifth century, surpassed the motherland in wealth and civilization. Naturally these emigrants took with them their ancient religion, their myths and heroic lays, but they also adopted many cults and legends of the ancient peoples of Asia Minor among whom they had settled. These new elements soon became known in the motherland. It was in this colonial dominion, especially on Ionic soil, that the Homeric epics arose. Owing to the long period during which these epics and the antecedent lays were taking their shape — in round numbers eight hundred years — they naturally contained many anachronisms.

The epics which have come down to us, the *Iliad* and the *Odyssey,* are only a small part of the treasures of the epic poetry of the Greeks. All the important myths were dealt with by the epic poets, and the available sources still bear witness to the extensive character of the epic tradition. For example, we know that a cycle of Theban epics gave the story of Œdipus, the march of the seven against Thebes, and the punitive expedition of the Epigonoi that captured the city. Another epic cycle dealt with the Trojan legends, the antecedents of the Trojan war, and a number of scenes and episodes of the war itself, such as the wrath of Achilles, his combats with the Amazon queen Penthesileia and with the Ethiopian king Memnon, the death and funeral of Achilles, the capture and destruction of Troy, the return of the heroes, and the wanderings of Odysseus. But, besides these, there were other myths, not belonging to the great cycle of Trojan and Theban legends, which were worked up by the epic poets. We know of one epic that dealt with the Argive story of Danaos and his fifty daughters, and others that were based on that of Herakles. By the sixth century at latest all the more important myths had found their epic minstrels. The subject matter of these epics — *i.e.,* the Greek mythology — was for the Greeks of all succeeding time (apart from a few sceptics) the accepted historical tradition of their early days before the Dorian migration. This tradition contained all that was believed to be known of that antiquity — the exploits of those who fought before Thebes and Troy, the deeds of Herakles and Theseus, the tales about Meleagros and Perseus, the voyage of the Argonauts, and much else. All this was put into prose form by the older Greek historians in the fifth century. Taking the epic tradition as their basis, they arranged the material in a fixed chronology and genealogy, and gave it forth as the ancient history of the Greeks. Nor was this all. The local traditions current in smaller towns and districts, which also existed in poetical form, were gradually adopted into the higher literature, and found their way into plastic art. Only a few sceptics and scholars doubted the truth of this epic tradition or questioned the historicity of all these heroes and of the exploits attributed to them by the poets. It was all accepted as *true* tradition, and everything that went under the name of Homer became the Bible of the Hellenes. To them the tradition was not only true, but also sacred. These epics were not composed merely for entertainment, or even for instruction concerning the great past. The heroes whose exploits were sung were also " godlike men," objects of religious worship and ritual homage.

Later time supplies proof that ritual worship was paid to nearly all the great figures in Greek mythology, and we now come to the extremely important but much-disputed question. Are these cults older or younger than the epic poetry? Seeing that as a rule the cult of a hero was celebrated at the place which the epic tradition assigned to him as his home, we can put the question in this way: Was the cult of a hero celebrated in a given city because according to the epic tradition this city was his birthplace, or was this city declared to be his birthplace because his cult was celebrated there? Does the cult of Agamemnon, Menelaos, Achilles, Helen, and Iphigeneia go back to the Mycenæan period, or was it only introduced in the seventh century or later because these heroes, of whom Homer had sung, were considered worthy of a cult? If the latter were the case, we should expect to find that the cult awarded to them followed the usual lines of such worship.

When we look into the subject of Greek ritual we find a clear classification of cults into two kinds, the uranic and the chthonic. The former, the celestial cult, is directed upward, and is addressed to deities who dwell in the heavens; the latter is addressed to deities on earth or under the earth or to the dead. In the case of uranic sacrifices the head of the victim was raised and the animal was slain by an axe-stroke. The blood that spurted from its neck was smeared on the altar. Only small portions of the victim were burnt; the rest was eaten by the worshippers. This was a meat-offering. In the chthonic sacrifices, on the other hand, the head of the victim was pressed down. From a deep incision in the throat the blood poured to the ground or into a pit. The blood was the chief thing, and these sacrifices were sometimes called " blood-satings." The flesh was entirely burnt on the low chthonic altar. None of it was eaten, as it was completely taboo, and belonged to the gods below. These two types of ritual were the natural expression of the thoughts involved. The sacrifice was directed to the object of the ritual — upward to the celestial gods, downward to the deities below. It would therefore be absurd to offer an uranic sacrifice to deities whose abode was beneath the earth. But in the faith of the Greeks the legendary heroes were dead men, the great dead of the past. Their bodies lay in the earth, in their graves. Their cult therefore, one would think, should be a chthonic cult and be directed to the earth, to the grave. But in many of the cults addressed to Homeric heroes this was not the case. They were worshipped by means of a uranic cult; they were honoured as " gods." And in every case this was explained by a special ' ascension legend.' The hero no longer dwelt below the earth, but in heaven or in the Isles of the Blest: he had been ' caught up.' Further, these hero-cults were marked by other practices which differed from those followed in the worship of the dead and resembled those used in worshipping the celestials; and in the pious belief of the Greeks the Homeric heroes played a part that raised them far above the level of a mere hero-cult and placed them on a level with the gods. Agamemnon was worshipped as Zeus Agamemnon; others as Zeus Amphiarios, Zeus Aristaios, Zeus Trophonios; Achilles as Lord of the Black Sea or as Pontarches; Helen as a tree-goddess, Dendritis. This could not possibly have been done in deference to the epic tradition, which spoke of them as *men* who had lived long ago. We are forced to the conclusion that the heroes who are presented in the mythical tradition as brave men of olden time were originally deities transformed by the poets into men of the past and regarded therefore by religious faith as legendary heroes. Their cult is older than the epos. It goes back to the Mycenæan period, and the forms of the cult in historical time prove that it was all along a cult addressed to gods and not to dead men. That is to say, the epos sings of legendary heroes to whom from of old ritual worship was paid, and so these songs were in the truest sense sacred poetry to the Greeks. The catalogue of the ships in the second book of the *Iliad,* which contains the names of the brave men who marched against Troy, was a list of legendary heroes and of the places at which they were mainly worshipped and which were looked upon as their native places — in other words, it is a systematic arrangement that was of outstanding religious interest. The name given to the catalogue, *Boioteia,* points to the country where hero-worship was specially prevalent, the country where flourished the poetic school of Hesiod, with its systematic theology.

From these considerations we can draw still another inference regarding the religion of the Mycenæan period. Side by side with the so-called greater gods of the later Greeks (Zeus, Hera, Athene, Poseidon, Apollo, etc.), other deities like Agamemnon, Menelaos, Helen, Achilles, and many others were worshipped, originally as gods, though in the course of the Mycenæan period they became human beings, brave men of the past, and legendary heroes. As such they were sung by the poets, and these poems had their effect on the popular faith. From the point of view of religious history there is no essential difference between Zeus, Apollo, and Athene on the one hand and Achilles, Agamemnon, and Helen on the other. The student of history sees in all of them beings who were looked upon as divine. But to the Greeks of the historical period the latter were men of old and legendary heroes and the former were gods, until they also were transformed by the teaching of Euhemeros into men of old. Thus the Greeks of post-Homeric time had a fixed order of precedence for the figures to whom ritual worship was paid: first, the greater gods; then lower deities like Eileithyia, the river-gods, nymphs, dryads, Pan; lastly, legendary heroes and the ordinary dead, ancestors. This order of precedence was settled once for all in the Greek mind by their epic poetry and by Hesiod's theology. These authorities fixed the precedence of the most important figures of the Greek cult. Even the absence of mention in the epic poetry was not without its meaning for the order of precedence. And what was the basis on which the epic tradition rested its precedence? It can be sought only in the ritual; not, to be sure, in the *type* of ritual, for many legendary heroes were worshipped in a uranic cult and many gods in a cult of chthonic type; but if the decisive element was not qualitative, it must have been quantitative — *i.e.,* the distribution of the cult and the importance that was attached to it. The merely local deities, whose cult was comparatively insignificant, became legendary heroes, while those whose cult was more generally known continued to be deities, and among these latter were included those gods who were worshipped at those places where epic poems arose. It goes without saying that local tradition had a strong influence in the matter, and the sphere over which the various gods held sway also played a part in it. But not all these old divine figures retained their personality: many of them sank to mere epithets. While in certain districts Agamemnon and Hyakinthos retained their personality, in some rituals they became mere epithets of a deity, like Zeus Agamemnon and Apollo Hyakinthos; and there were other divine names that shared the like fate. Some orendistic fetishes were similarly degraded — the trumpet supplied a cognomen for Athene Salpinx and the fetish of fertility gave its name to Artemis Korythalia.

This shows clearly the quite special position occupied by the Homeric epos in the history of Greek religion. That epos stood far apart from the religion of the past and of its own day, and had a very powerful effect on the religious development of after days; and, further, its basic characteristics were a tendency to systematize, to transform tradition into history, to rationalize former faith.

Thus the Homeric epos contains little or nothing of worship of the dead, of faith in a future life endowed with power and consciousness, or of a belief that the dead had any influence on life here. It has little or nothing to say of the numerous chthonic and local gods or petty demons, of animal-shaped gods and fetishes, of catharsis and magic, of mysticism and orgiasm — religious phenomena which held a prominent place in men's minds both at and after the time when the epos arose and most of which had existed in full strength long before. Only the primeval orendism still lives side by side with the new anthropomorphism. The Homeric gods, now few in number, are all conceived in human form. Though immortal, they are human — sometimes very human in their thoughts and emotions and desires and actions. Though superior to mortals in strength and freedom of action, like men they are in the grasp of fate, *moira*. They often visit earth, and are seen of men and intervene in their lives. Sometimes they are invisible or veiled in mist; at other times they are visible, when they may be recognized as gods or their divine quality be hidden from human knowledge. The gods of the epos constitute a commonwealth at whose head is Zeus, father of gods and men. They dwell on the divine Mount Olympus or in heaven, and come down to visit men and share in the sacrificial feasts. Their names have long been familiar to every one from Greek literature and plastic art, and the impression has long prevailed that Greek religion consisted in the worship of these gods. They included Zeus, the god of heaven, who no longer walked in person among men, but directed their lives from afar; his spouse Hera and her daughters the Eileithyia, who presided over human birth; his daughter Pallas Athene, virginal, warlike, and wise; his other daughter Aphrodite, fair and sweetly smiling; his son Hermes, who, with Iris, ran the errands of the gods; Apollo, Leto's son, whose arrows brought the plague, but who could also bestow wisdom; his sister Artemis, whose joy was in the chase; the god of savage war, Ares, his sister Eris, and his sons Deimos and Phobos, Dread and Fear; Hephaistos, the artist among the gods; Poseidon, the sea-god; the gods of the earth and of its depths — Demeter and her daughter Persephone and Hades, the god of the underworld. These were the main deities of the epos — some of them, however, were comparatively unimportant — a small company, allied to each other by lineage and marriage.

" As a man is, so is his God." This saying holds true of the Homeric gods only to a certain extent. They were fashioned in imitation of the nobles who ruled the cities of Ionia: their creator, however, was not the noble, but the poet. The noble boasted that he was descended from the gods or was at least " god-nourished," and he stood as high above the common people as the gods stood above men. Possibly, too, he lived as loosely as the gods of Homer, and his thoughts were as rationalistic as the conception which is reflected in this religion. But the Homeric religion was by no means his religion, and still less was it the religion of the people. Although that religion had undergone great changes on the soil of Asia Minor, it was still more akin to the faith of the Mycenæan period than to that of the Homeric epos. Just as the language of Homer is an artificial language which was never spoken anywhere, just as the entire civilization it portrays never existed anywhere, so also the religion of the epos was one that never lived in the hearts of any people. But just as the Homeric language had a tremendous influence on the language of after days, especially on the higher literature, on poetry and prose, so the Homeric religion had an incalculable influence on the subsequent development of the Greek religion. That influence was most marked on the religion which is reflected in the best Greek literature, lyric and tragic, and which was afterward attacked by philosophy, but it also profoundly affected the official religion of the *polis,* as well as the faith of the people at large. It is owing to the epos, therefore, that from this time onward a cleavage appeared in Greek religion greater than that which is found in other religions — the cleavage between the religion that found expression in literature and art and that which was manifested in popular faith and practice, with its primitive ingredients. Midway between the two, favouring perhaps the Homeric pantheon, stands the official religion of the state. As might be expected, the Homeric religion had less influence on the ritual of the cults than on the faith in the gods and men's conceptions of them. In these respects it gradually brought about the spread of anthropomorphic views, and led to the establishment of a recognized order of precedence. As time went on the Homeric pantheon gained general acceptance. On the other hand, the Homeric epos was the chief source for the legendary mythology of later days.

3. *Greek Mythology and the Beginnings of Science*

Homer has been called the Bible of the Hellenes. The Bible is a book of religion, not a manual of theology, and the same is true of Homer. But just as the Bible produced a theology, so did Homer, and the first stage of this theology appears in the poems which pass under the name of Hesiod and his school. The whole epos contained the sacred history of the Greeks, the tales about the legendary heroes, the history of the time prior to the Dorian migration. But the Homeric poets were neither historians nor scientists nor theologians. Hesiod, however, was all three. At least, the Greeks looked upon him as such, just as they reckoned the writers of myths like Pherekydes and Akusilaos, as historians. The only difference between the latter and Hesiod was that Hesiod wrote not in the scientific medium of prose, but in the epic medium of hexameter verse.

The *Theogony* as we have it now is not as it was when it left the poet's hand: it underwent numerous alterations and intercalations up to the fifth century. But the fundamental plan of it — the course of the generations and the close, showing the consolidation of the rule of Zeus — can still be clearly made out. Hesiod's work was not the only cosmogony and theogony available. Several other poets dealt with the same material in epic style.

Hesiod asks, whence came the world, gods, and men? He answers these questions in detail, utilizing as his sources the great mass of mythical tradition that had been put into epic form. He begins with the primeval powers. In the beginning was Chaos; then followed the broad-breasted Earth, with Tartaros and Eros. Out of Chaos came Erebos, the dark netherworld, and Nyx, Night; from Night came Ether and Day, whom she bore to Erebos. The Earth of itself produced the starry sky. Then the poet enumerates the posterity of Uranos and Gaia — *i.e.,* Heaven and Earth, the first parents and most important pair found in the myths of nearly all peoples. The history of the three generations, those of Uranos, Kronos, and Zeus, is then given: the myth of the mutilation of Uranos by Kronos, then, interrupted repeatedly by long genealogical lists, the deception of Kronos by Rheia and Zeus, the myth of Prometheus, and the war of the Titans. This forms the kernel of the *Theogony,* which ends with the consolidation of Zeus's ascendancy. Then follow a number of genealogical appendices, dealing with the marriages and descendants of the gods. Another attempted to reduce to systematic form the genealogy of the legendary heroes by drawing up a list of legendary heroines who had borne sons to gods and heroes. This *Catalogue of Women* was interspersed with many detailed narratives taken from the legends — the story of the Argonauts, and that of Meleagros, and others. This catalogue was thus the golden book of the ancient noble families, who traced their descent back to a god or to one of these 'heroines.' It was the Gothic calendar of the Greek nobility, but it was also a handbook to the heroic legends scattered throughout numerous epics. and a manual for the rhapsodists, who could choose a section of the catalogue as the starting-point of a heroic lay. In addition to the epos, which dealt chiefly with heroic legends, Hesiod utilized other poems which contained the stories of the gods. A considerable number of similar poems — mainly from a later time — have come down to us. They include the so-called Homeric *Hymns,* the *Hymns of the Muses* which form the introduction to the *Theogony,* and the *Hymn to Hekate* which stands in the middle of the *Theogony.* These all belong to the same poetical type — hymnody. Many lines recur in different poems. Hymns of this kind were certainly sung at the celebrations in honour of the gods as early as the eighth and seventh centuries, as a kind of prelude to a rendering of heroic incidents from the epos. There is a tradition that Homer and Hesiod competed in person at Delos, and sang in honour of Apollo the two hymns to Apollo that have come down to us. In these hymns the gods are represented as being subject to ordinary human weaknesses, and their doings are frequently described with touches of humour. This is exemplified in the *Hymn to Hermes,* which supplied Sophocles with the motif of the satyr play *The Bloodhounds,* and in the lay of Demodokos among the Phæacians, which tells of the adultery of Aphrodite and Ares and of the punishment inflicted on both, to the delight of the other gods, by Hephaistos, the deceived husband. Besides these hymns to the gods and the great epics, there were also minor epic poems dealing with isolated incidents from the heroic legends. There has come down to us a short poem, attributed to Hesiod, which describes one exploit of Herakles, his combat with Ares' son, Kyknos, whom he slays.

Thus the Greeks possessed a large poetical literature that covered the entire field of their mythology and their stories about gods and men. This literature comprised the great epics — part of which went under the name of Homer — the poems of Hesiod's school, the hymns of the gods, and some minor heroic epics — all in the Homeric metre. These formed the basis of the later expansion of Greek mythology, by far the largest portion of which is known to us in the form it assumed under the hands of poets, writers of myths, and sculptors. Later centuries worked up this material, but they created no new myths. All the works of lyric poets like Stesichoros, Pindar, and Bakchylides and of the three Attic tragedians were based on this religious foundation. Their poems were recited or performed at festivals of the gods or at celebrations held in honour of victorious national leaders, many of whom were after their death ranked with the legendary heroes. The homage thus paid to these paved the way to the Hellenistic worship of kings. These poems therefore took their material from sacred tradition. When a tragedian like Phrynikos ventured to bring on the stage a historical event of recent date his action was resented, or in any case rarely imitated. Only Æschylus followed his example, with his *Persians.* This attitude was very pronounced in the case of the Attic tragedians. On every possible occasion they introduced in their dramas religious institutions and rituals, and as Athens had few local myths they sought to associate the city and its holy places with myths from elsewhere. Æschylus, for example, mentioned Attic cults and festivals in his Prometheus trilogy and the divine institution of the Areopagus in his *Orestes*. The *Œdipus at Kolonos* of Sophocles was produced to inaugurate the cult of this Theban hero on Attic soil, and Euripides never missed an opportunity of glorifying Attic cults and festivals and the sacred local tradition, or of making solemn reference to these at the conclusion of his tragedies. At the same time, Euripides did much to detract from the solemnity and lofty tone of the myth. His heroes are reduced to mere men and shorn of their dignity.

The catalogue poetry of Hesiod and his school, with its theological, systematic, and didactic treatment of myth, was the close of epic poetry. Occasionally it took passages from the epos and arranged them according to definite points of view, and became thereby the starting-point for something that was quite new — namely, a purely scientific treatment of myth, using prose as its medium. The same Ionic soil of Asia Minor that produced the Homeric epos gave the world the further gift of science, and science, the child of religion and mythology, ere long laid critical hands on religion.

It was not for the first time that in the sixth century questions were raised with regard to the origin of the world and the past history of man, but it was the first time that an endeavour had been made to answer them scientifically. In this attempt the epos contributed much to both the matter and the form. The dialect employed was the Ionic, with occasional Homeric flowers of speech, and the contents of the epic tradition also passed over into the works of the new Ionian science. Like all mythology, that of the Greeks had frequently tried to answer questions about nature and civilization, and its answers had long sufficed for the needs of historians and metaphysicians. But the enlightened Ionians now demanded different answers. Voyages of discovery and commercial journeys had taught them a great deal about the world, and brought them into touch with foreign peoples, foreign customs, and foreign religious practices. The needs of navigators had led to the making of astronomical, geographical, and climatic observations, and people were now familiar with the animals, plants, and minerals of other lands. Their horizon was widened both geographically and intellectually.

It was the same two main problems that occupied the interest of Ionian science. One was the question about the nature of man — not the individual man, that came later — but the nature of mankind as a whole, the peoples, their history, manners, and physical constitution, the countries in which they lived. This question produced the sciences of history, ethnography, geography. The second main problem was the nature of the cosmos, its origin and its present condition, and thus arose natural philosophy and natural science. These five sciences produced the Ionic scholars, but their pioneer, at least in the spheres of cosmology and history, was Hesiod. Pherekydes of Syros (sixth century) illustrates this close connexion between Ionic science and myth. He stands intermediately between the two. Like Hesiod, he wrote a theogony, but, like the Ionians, he wrote in prose. According to him, the elements out of which the cosmos is formed are partly mythical (as in Hesiod) and partly real (as in Thales, Anaximander, and Anaximenes). Similarly, as early as the first half of the fifth century Akusilaos of Argos wrote a cosmogony, a theogony, and a heroic genealogy much after the manner of Hesiod. He and others drew up complete genealogies of the legendary heroes, supplemented the lists of the mythical city-kings, and tried to reconcile the conflicting traditions. An attempt was now made also to discover the meaning of the myths. Hera was the air, Poseidon the sea, Artemis the moon. Agamemnon the ether, Achilles the sun, Dionysos the spleen, and Demeter the liver; and this allegorizing tendency found its counterpart in an attempt to read historical facts into the marvels of mythology and to rationalize the three-headed hound of hell into a poisonous snake. Ere long religion and mythology were openly and directly assailed. Xenophanes of Kolophon poured scorn upon the current anthropomorphism, casting the blame for it on Homer and Hesiod, who, he said, had attributed all manner of vileness to the gods; and he ridiculed the fabulous creatures of which the myths were so full, declaring them to be inventions of former days. He was the first to voice the idea — which has become familiar in modern days through Feuerbach's dictum — that man had created God in his own image. Heraklitus went so far as to declare that he would like to see Homer banished from the festivals and whipped with rods, and had many severe things to say about the mystery religions and catharsis and other popular practices. The Sophists followed on the same lines. They were the true representatives of Greek enlightenment and free thought, and sought to guide the people into their own path. Protagoras declared that he did not know whether there were gods or not, and Diagoras of Melos brought upon himself the opprobrious epithet of atheist. The rhetoricians of this period took the myths as the subject of their declamations and exercised their wit after the manner of Gorgias in his mocking allusions to Helen and Palamedes. It should, however, be added that learned men were still found who continued to accept implicitly the historical truth of the myths. In their efforts to magnify the renown of Athens orators like Perikles and, at a later time, Isokrates culled their illustrations impartially from mythology and from historical tradition, and recognized no distinction between the two.

4. *The Religion of the Polis*

It may be taken as certain that in spite of the disturbances caused by the migrations, in spite of the destruction of Mycenæan civilization, and even in spite of the general downfall of civilization on the mainland of Greece, much of the religion of the second millennium survived in the religion of the time that followed. The religion of historical time exhibits only too many 'primitive' ingredients dating back to prehistoric time. This need cause no surprise. For what was there that could suddenly have wiped out Mycenæan religion? There was no missionary religion to drive it out, no great reformer to divert its development into other directions. There can be no doubt whatever that in remote districts the religion of the Mycenæan period survived unchanged for many centuries, just as remnants of the ancient Laconian dialect are heard to this day in outlying parts of the Peloponnesus. Gradual changes, however, affected religion in the centres of commerce and learning, and this period, the "Greek Middle Ages," saw the development of the religion of the city — *i.e.,* an official State religion — the Homeric epos still playing an important part even in this transformation.

According to the opinion usually held, the characteristic features of Greek religion in general and of this city-religion in particular were the absence of dogma, the lack of religious instruction, and the absence of a recognized priesthood. Put thus broadly, this is very far from being true. The correct way to put it is that there was no comprehensive religious organization with a uniform dogma, no unified priesthood to teach that dogma, and no religious instruction imparting it. Instead of one religious organization there were numerous separate cults dedicated to special deities. Each city had an immense number of such deities, and the deities of one city were by no means the same as those of another. These separate cults had their separate priests. There was a priest of Poseidon, a priest of Apollo, a priestess of Athene Polias. These priests possessed certain specific powers, and had specific knowledge of their own ritual and sacrifice, the tradition of their temple, and the myth of their own deity. There were also other cults, with numerous priests and regulations. The place of dogma in the cult was taken by the myth — without myth there could be no cult — and by the theological doctrines specifically associated with the cult. For example, the story of Amphiaros, his descent to the underworld, and his deification is to be regarded as the 'dogma' of the Amphiareion in Oropos. Whoever came to worship in his temple, seeking an oracle or healing, received from the attendant priest all necessary guidance and instruction as to the ordinances concerning abstinence from wine and the sacrifice that was required. He was told of the marvellous power that resided in the skin of the sacrificial victim, and was instructed to lay himself down on it to sleep. That is to say, the priest knew the 'dogma' of his own temple, the story of Amphiaros, the cult ceremonies and their meaning, his own duties, and the temple arrangements, particulars of which are still to be found in inscriptions. If the worshipper was unacquainted with any of them, the priest was there to instruct him. The legend itself anyone could learn from the epos. When we keep in mind the reciprocal relations that connected epos, myth, and cult, and remember that a knowledge of the epic poetry and therefore of the myth formed part of elementary education in the schools, we can see that there *was* something that could be called "religious instruction," — *i.e.,* instruction in sacred tradition about the gods and heroes worshipped in the cult, and about the things that underlay the 'dogma' of any given sanctuary. Of course, there were cults dedicated to figures whose names did not appear in the great epics, but in these cases the local tradition furnished the basis for the dogma of the cult.

But although the more important myths at least were thus fairly well known, all the intricate and complicated ritual forms could not possibly be familiar to every one — not even to all the priests. To have an intimate knowledge of these was a matter for the priests and officials concerned, and as a rule their knowledge was limited to the cult of their own deity and their own temple. How much of the ritual was in written form, at what time it was reduced to writing, by whom it was arranged, how far the state was interested in it, and, indeed, what was the whole attitude of the state to religion and ritual — on all these matters we possess a great deal of evidence which has not yet been sufficiently investigated. It is certain that the state did superintend the performance of the official cults and festivals, and that the relevant rules were laid down by law. The piety of the ordinary citizen consisted in worshipping the gods after the conventional, legally prescribed manner and in attending worship as required by the law. It was part of the duty of the Athenian citizen to take part in the worship of Zeus Herkeios and Apollo Patroos. No one who neglected to do so could ever hold the office of archon. Sacrifice must be offered at the appointed time, and no celebration must be omitted. The priests and state officials saw to it that the worship demanded by the law was duly rendered. It was, further, the duty of the state to see that the property of the gods was not injured or removed from the sanctuary, and that the temple itself was not damaged or destroyed or desecrated. All that belonged to the gods was protected by a curse that fell upon the impious man and upon anyone who sinned against the ordinances of the cult.

Within the confines of any given city the cults thus celebrated were very numerous and varied. There were large temples built in honour of this or that deity of the Homeric pantheon. In most cases, however, these deities were not worshipped under their simple name. To this was added a special cult-name denoting the distinctive characteristic of the deity to which honour was paid — *e.g.,* Apollo Alexikakos, the fender-off of evil, or Athene Polias, goddess of the city. In some cases the epithet was borrowed from an older deity, who had been replaced by one of the more important gods of Homer — *e.g.,* Apollo Hyakinthios or Artemis Iphigeneia or Zeus Agamemnon; in others it was derived from a local name — *e.g.,* Apollo Aktios or Artemis Ephesia. Apollo had more than two hundred such names. Further, there were sanctuaries dedicated to legendary heroes — chiefly those whose birth was laid by tradition in the city — to the ancient city-kings, to the founder of the city or the hero after whom the city had been named, or to heroes who, although born elsewhere, had served the city or in some way had been honoured with a cult. Besides these, numerous minor local deities and demons were worshipped who belonged neither to the Homeric pantheon nor to the company of legendary heroes. The principal cults and festivals were officially fixed, and were under state supervision. But gods and heroes, cults, festivals, and calendar varied in each city. The sole feature common to them all was some connexion with the gods, heroes, and myths of the Homeric epos.

In the midst of all this variety, however, there were already the beginnings of attempts at greater unification. There were religious currents that sought to transcend the narrow limits of the city and embrace a larger membership. There were germs of ' churches ' that claimed sole authority and manifested missionary zeal, aiming at larger organizations, at festivals and cults that would include the whole nation.

Chief among these were the Mysteries. Their principal deities, Demeter and Dionysos, are mentioned in Homer, but they are far less prominent there than the other gods, and were worshipped more by peasants than by nobles. They were not gods of war or of the educated classes, like those sung by Homer, but gods of toil, like those praised by Hesiod. They were, in fact, gods of the hard toil of the field-tiller, and they were worshipped in ways that the peasant knew and loved. And just because of this invincible power which they drew from the soil, the same power that filled the hearts of their worshippers and by and by elevated them in the political scale, they afterward conquered the world and commanded a more universal worship than the gods of Homer themselves. Their worship was bound to spread in proportion as men began to cherish in their hearts the longing, not merely for life in this world, but also for the life that is to come and to look in hope to the Beyond. For these deities promised to their worshippers a blessed life in an after world and union with the divine.

The starting-point of the victorious career of the Demeter Mysteries was Eleusis, which was at first an independent community, but came afterward under the dominion of Athens. The dogma of this Eleusinian cult is given in the so-called Homeric *Hymn of Demeter,* but many of its details will never be known, because the countless initiates of Eleusis faithfully kept its secrets throughout a thousand years. In outline it was as follows. The god of the underworld had carried off Persephone. Demeter travelled far, seeking her daughter, until at length, in the guise of an aged woman, she arrived at Eleusis. Unrecognized by anyone, she was received by the king and queen and put in charge of their little boy. To make him immortal she anointed him with ambrosia and breathed into him her own divine breath. Following the ancient, widespread custom, she was secretly bringing him into touch with purifying and sanctifying fire when she was discovered by the child's mother. This frustrated her purpose. She now revealed her identity, and commanded that a large temple should be built in her honour. She even retarded the yield of the earth till Hades, at the request of Zeus, restored Persephone. The latter could spend only two-thirds of the year on the earth; for the rest she had to return to the underworld, because she had tasted of the food of that

realm and now belonged to it. Demeter herself instituted the temple ceremonies. At the close of the hymn the man is declared blessed who has seen
the worship. The uninitiated can have no happy lot in the underworld. For the
initiates, however, Hades becomes Plutos, the giver of riches. That is to say,

FIG. 79. AN ELEUSINIAN RELIEF
From Brunn, " Denkmäler griechischer und römischer Skulptur "

wealth in life and bliss after death are promised to the worshippers of
Demeter; and these were in the gift of the authorities at Eleusis. It was,
however, only in the seventh century, when Eleusis came under the dominion
of Athens, and some changes were consequently made in the cult, that the
temple entered upon its prosperous career, and from the fifth century onward,

when the Attic empire was created, the world was gradually conquered by
the Eleusinian Mysteries. (See Fig. 79.) Eleusis became a place of pilgrimage
for all nations. It was visited by Greeks and Romans — even by Roman
emperors. The Christian emperor Valentinian I allowed his subjects to go
to it, but the Church Fathers vigorously objected. It was ultimately destroyed
by Alaric.

The cult of Dionysos also promised its initiates a rank above that of other
men and union with the deity through the sacrament. (See Fig. 80.) By
means of orgiastic dances, loud cries, and wild music ecstasy was produced,
and in this condition the devotee ate the god, — *i.e.*, the animal in which the
deity was believed to be embodied. The worshipper thus became filled with
the god, and attained the condition of ecstasy or inspiration. Probably

FIG. 80. DIONYSOS AND HIS ATTENDANTS
From Furtwängler and Reichold, " Griechische Vasenmalerei "

the name Dionysos was that of a Greek deity, to whom at a later time foreign,
perhaps Thracian, elements were attributed — orgiasm, in fact — and it
seems likely that a cult of this kind, so little akin to Greek religion, met
with considerable opposition. Many legends mention it; one such legend is
referred to in the Homeric epos. This orgiasm did not invade all the Dionysian cults. It occurred only here and there, in varying strength. Erwin Rohde,
to whom we owe a brilliant account of this religion, declares that it was
gradually Hellenized and humanized, but that is not the case. It was even
excluded from many of the Greek sanctuaries where Dionysos was worshipped, and the Attic drama, which was the product of Dionysian festivals,
had its roots, not in the orgiastic cult — which was a mere foreign accretion —
but in the native, rural festivities which had from time immemorial been celebrated with choral accompaniments in honour of the deity.

Orphism was a special form of the Dionysian cult. It was a religious movement which resulted in the formation of a large and widespread sect. The Orphic religion also appealed to the human longing for salvation, but it included in addition an explicit dogmatic doctrine on catharsis and asceticism, cosmology and eschatology, the destiny of the soul, and a moral life. The Orphics believed in the immortality of the soul, in the transmigration of souls, and in future rewards and punishments. They developed the conceptions of a future life, and their views regarding hell were entirely their own. Orphic sources were utilized by Pindar, Empedokles, and Plato, and some of their ideas were current in the Pythagorean communities. Some of them were even adopted at a later time by the Christians. In their ascetic rules the Orphics, like the Pythagoreans, were forerunners of Christianity. The Greek philosopher who did most to pave the way for Christianity — viz., Plato — was deeply impressed by Orphism, and those of his doctrines which are most nearly akin to Christianity have also the closest affinity to Orphic dogma.

Although Dionysian orgiasm was not a native product of Greece, but came to the Greeks from outside, ecstasy in itself was not alien to them, any more than to any other people. They believed that it was possible to attain inward union with the divine, and taught various ways by which this could be achieved. These included sexual intercourse, eating and drinking, touch, and dance and music leading to ecstasy. The seer was pre-eminently ecstatic. He became filled with the god, and when he was in this condition the god spoke through him. The name given to him, *mantis,* comes from the same root as the Greek word that means "to be mad, insane, possessed."

Dionysos bestowed this gift of inspired prophecy, sacred madness, but Apollo also had it in his gift. Whether as Rohde maintains, the Delphic oracle of this god owed anything to the Dionysian religion in its style of prophecy, in its manticism, is certainly open to doubt. At any rate in the historical period the Pythian priestess was inspired by the god in her prophecies — it was Apollo that spoke through her lips. The god of Delphi and his oracle contributed far more than even Demeter and Dionysos to the unification of Greek religion. If we are to regard the Homeric epos as a uniform Bible, and if we are to see in the Mysteries an attempt to achieve a unified religious society, then we can see in the sanctuary at Delphi a kind of ancient Papacy, whose power was felt both in religion and in politics. As early as the eighth and seventh centuries the fame of Delphi was international. Non-Greek kings of Asia Minor sent embassies to its oracle, and presented costly gifts. Its influence extended to the distant colonies of the west and to North Africa. Its power was felt on the external and internal policy of the states, on their legislation and alliances, on the foundation of colonies and cities, on constitutional changes and complications caused by wars. In matters of religion Delphi was the leading authority, and was consulted in connexion with special events and in times of pestilence and famine and similar misfortunes. Its advice was sought also in the sphere of morals. Numerous cults were established in obedience to its behests, and details of the ritual were settled in accordance with its guidance.

Delphi was associated also with one of the great Hellenic national festivals — the Pythian Games. Although each city had its own special cults and festivals, there were also a few sacred places in which all Greece gathered — Olympia, Delphi, Nemea, in Argolis, and the isthmus of Corinth. In his-

FIG. 81. APOLLO
Burlington Fine Art Club, 1904

torical time the feasts of Olympia and Delphi were held every four years, those of Nemea and Corinth every two years. The centre of interest at these gatherings was the contest, the *agon,* which included all kinds of physical exercises (*agōn gymnikos*) and horse-racing (*agōn hippikos*), as well as poetry and music (*agōn musikos*). These occasions gave powerful expression to the pan-Hellenic idea — *i.e.,* the solidarity of all Hellenes and their superiority to the 'barbarians.' This idea derived ever new strength from the religious ground on which the Greeks assembled to hold their great festivals, to practice their cults, and to give exhibitions of their physical and intellectual powers in honour of Zeus, Apollo, or Poseidon.

There were also other gathering-grounds where the people assembled in larger numbers than at the various city celebrations. These were the sacred places that constituted the religious centres of the city federations, such as the sanctuary of Poseidon Helikonios on Mykale, off the coast of Asia Minor, or the Panionion, the federal sanctuary of the Ionian cities, and south of it the Triopion, dedicated to Apollo, the religious centre of the six federated Dorian cities. There were also common cults in which mother and daughter cities were alike interested. The colonists regularly took the cults of their native cities with them to their new homes. To mention one example, in Megara they celebrated the cults of Demeter Malophoros, of Apollo Karinos, and of Artemis Orthosia; the Megarian colony of Byzantium had the cult of Artemis Orthosia and the month names Malophorios and Karinos, and the 'granddaughter' city of Selinus had the cult of Demeter Malophoros. A small island near Megara was called after the hero Minos, and Minos was associated with the city through the myth; the Sicilian 'granddaughter' city of Megara was called Minoa, and there the grave of Minos was shown. The legend explained how the grave came to be there — Minos pursued Daidalos as far as Sicily and died there.

To sum up, this first historical period of Greek religion, which brings us to the fourth century, the century of Plato, Aristotle, and Alexander the Great, presents a large number of features which prove that the Greek religion passed through the usual stages from multiplicity to unity, from the numberless powers of orendism to the final stage in which Christianity proclaimed dogmatic monotheism.

Speaking generally, Greek religion evinced no inclination to aggressive activity, no desire to enter upon propaganda. On the contrary, it showed great tolerance toward alien religions. Nevertheless, Greek cults spread as far as Spain and India and to the shores of the Black Sea. The agents in this expansion were not apostles of religion, but disseminators of Greek civilization. In contradistinction to the method followed by Christian missionary activity, the spread of Greek religion was the result of the spread of Greek civilization. When they left the motherland the colonists took with them their native faith and their rituals, and raised in their new homes temples to the same gods and heroes as they had worshipped in Greece. In this way alien peoples received certain Greek cults along with Greek culture in general.

Greek colonial expansion also affected the development of Greek mythology. A large proportion of Greek heroic stories belonged to the migration type of legend, in which the exploits of the hero are set in a framework of travel — e.g., those of the Argonauts, Herakles, Odysseus, and the returning Trojan heroes. These stories grew with the growth of Greek civilization.

As the Greeks carried with them to the colonies their rituals and myths, the heroes took new root there also, and the legends soon began to tell how the heroes had once touched these coasts or lived in these districts, instituted worship, founded rituals, built cities, and ultimately received worship there. All round the confines of the Græcized world were memorials that recalled the presence there of Odysseus, the Argonauts, Herakles, Diomedes, Menelaos, etc., and when Alexander the Great opened up India the story arose that Dionysos, the missionary deity, had also visited that country. Wherever Greek civilization spread, there the heroic legends followed it. In an exactly similar way later centuries expanded the Apostolic legends, which grew *pari passu* with the spread of Christianity.

II. THE ROMAN RELIGION TILL THE TIME OF AUGUSTUS

From the point of view of history the most important field of Greek colonization was Lower Italy and Sicily — Magna Græcia, as it was already called in antiquity. From the eighth century onward numerous Greek colonies and flourishing cities were founded, and the Greeks thus became the nearest neighbours of Latium at a time when that country was still divided into numerous communities, of which Rome was one. This close neighbourhood of the Greeks had important effects on the history of the Roman religion, and promoted its gradual Hellenization. Like the Balkan peninsula, the Apennine peninsula was originally inhabited by a non-Indo-Germanic population, who left traces, visible in historical time, both on the people and on their civilization. Further, as in the Balkans, so also in Italy there was an incursion of Indo-Germanic tribes from the north. At the time when the Greek colonists set foot on Italian soil that country was inhabited by a large number of Indo-Germanic and non-Indo-Germanic tribes, whose languages — even those which belonged to the Italic branch of the Indo-Germanic group — differed far more from each other than did, say, the Dorian and Ionian dialects of Greek. Both for the history of the Apennine peninsula and for the shaping of the Roman religion the most important of these tribes were the Indo-Germanic Latins and the non-Indo-Germanic Etruscans. From the eighth century onward these were joined by the colonists from Greece.

The origin of the Etruscans has been a matter of dispute since ancient times. Many share the opinion of Herodotus that they came over the sea from the east, from Asia Minor. Others maintain that they came from the north across the Alps. Still others, including Schuchardt, the modern historian of the prehistoric era, believe that they formed part of the pre-Indo-Germanic population who were already settled in Western Europe in the Ice Age, and afterward spread eastward. This population included the pre-Indo-Germanic peoples of the Balkan peninsula and the islands of the Ægean Sea, as well as the representatives of the Minoan civilization in Crete, who also made their way into Asia Minor. If this last opinion be correct, the relation of the Latins to the Etruscans resembles that of the invading Achæans to the pre-Greek population. It is, however, also possible — a dubious tradition supports this opinion — that the Etruscan influence on Rome dates from a comparatively

FIG. 82. ODYSSEUS AND THE SIRENS

late time, a time when the Etruscans were lords of Rome. Whatever be the true opinion — personally I agree in the main with Schuchardt, and at the same time I regard, with Beloch, the Etruscans as the pre-Indo-Germanic population — Etruscan influence on Roman religion is indubitable. Indeed, the earliest event in Roman history to which even an approximate date can be assigned — it is characteristic of the Roman religion that it should be the consecration of a temple — the consecration of the Capitoline temple of Jupiter Optimus Maximus, Juno Regina, and Minerva about the year 507, is closely associated with Etruscan influence, and the very name of the city of Rome, like many other Roman proper names, seems to be of Etruscan origin.

In connexion with Etruscan religion it is noticeable that at a very early date it too betrays a mixture of Etruscan, Italian, and Greek elements, and it was through the Etruscans that the Romans became acquainted with many features of Greek civilization. Etruscan religion (of which our knowledge is very imperfect) is distinguished by the existence of a clearly defined system, which strictly determines the relation of men to the gods, the meaning of the divine symbols, the *prodigia,* the work of the haruspex, the control of lightning, and the entire sacrificial system. It also prescribes how the affairs of the state and the life of the individual here and hereafter are related to religion. All these features can be seen in Roman religion, and it is a resemblance that points less to influence from without than to an inward penetration such as is conceivable only among a mixed population. A similar phenomenon can be seen in Greece in the Mycenæan period. This "Etruscan discipline," which was regarded as a divine revelation, was laid down in detailed writings, which were afterward translated into Latin and discussed by Roman authors, and this whole doctrine profoundly affected Roman religion. The names of the Etruscan gods are partly Etruscan (like Tinia and Turan, who were afterward identified with Jupiter and Venus, Tuchulcha, the demon of the underworld, and perhaps also Satre, who was adopted by the Romans as Saturnus), partly Greek (like Hades, Persephone, Charon, and Hercules), and partly Italic (like Juno and Minerva). Besides, we find quite a number of Greek myths depicted on Etruscan works of art (Fig. 82). Worship of the dead was very widely practised, and the ideas entertained regarding the world to come can be read in the wall-paintings of the grave-chambers, which show the rewards and punishments that were expected after death. It has recently been maintained that these betray Orphic influence, but this is not correct. (See Fig. 83.)

In Latium, which was contiguous to Etruria on the south, there were originally numerous communities. One of these — and not the most important one — was Rome. These Latins had a number of cults in common, in particular that of Jupiter Latiaris on the Alban Hill, where the annual festival of the Feriæ Latinæ was celebrated in his honour. When Rome took over the political hegemony of Latium it also took control of this festival, which continued to be held till the fourth century A.D. To Diana also temples were dedicated by all the Latins, the most famous being that in the grove of Aricia, on Lake Nemi. For a time it was the sanctuary of the whole Latin federation, and it lasted till far into the time of the Empire. The Romans adopted the cults of these two deities into their state worship, and it is equally certain that the cults of other deities were similarly of common-Latin origin.

All these elements, common-Latin, Etruscan, and Greek, were at an early date — probably in the time of the kings — mingled with others that were purely Roman; and there were, too, other influences, emanating from the rest of Italy. To separate all these is a task similar to that which had to be faced when we were dealing with the ancient Greek religion. We shall see by and by that new ingredients were continually being added from external

FIG. 83. DEMON OF THE UNDERWORLD AND THESEUS
From " Monumenti del Instituto," vol. ix

sources. The Roman religion assimilated them all, and although many of the later accretions can be easily detected, it is more difficult to discover the origin of those that were adopted in the most ancient period. In many cases, indeed, as we saw in connexion with Greek religion, the task is impossible. Deubner, one of our best authorities on Roman religion, says:

> The Roman religion reveals a development from the lowest stage to the highest. It starts from the primitive level of magic and fetishism and ends in the

victory of Christianity. During this unique development it did not at each new stage discard and reject the old. It tenaciously clung to it, with the result that the earlier strata can be plainly detected even in those forms that show spiritual advance, and we can follow the course of its evolution under unusually favourable conditions.

To these words we can heartily subscribe, but we would omit the word " unique." For Deubner's statement is also true word for word of the Greek religion. There are far more resemblances between the two — though there are also fundamental differences, which will be referred to afterward — than Wissowa, who laid the foundations of our knowledge of Roman religion, seems inclined to admit.

For our knowledge of ancient Roman religion we have one excellent source — viz., inscriptions which enable us to reconstruct the ancient Roman calendar known as the calendar of Numa, the order of the festivals of the kingdom. In all probability the oldest calendar was one of ten months, like that of many primitive peoples. The year of twelve months was introduced at the same time as the innovations at the end of the sixth century, and these were largely due to Greek and Etruscan influence. A further reform of the calendar took place under Julius Cæsar. For the older time we can thus distinguish between the primitive calendar of the kingdom and the pre-Cæsarean calendar of the republic. The last named, however, adopted the oldest, the ' Numanic,' arrangement of the festivals. That arrangement we know from the inscriptions already mentioned — so much of it at least as belonged to the official state religion. Other sources and general considerations complete our picture of Roman religion at its earliest stage.

Among the Roman gods of that time three stand out pre-eminently, and in their service were the three priests, the *flamen dialis, flamen martialis,* and *flamen quirinalis.* Next to the *rex sacrorum,* these three occupied the highest rank in the Roman priesthood. As his name indicates, Jupiter was originally an Indo-Germanic god, and was connected with the Greek Zeus even in the the derivation of his name. All the days of full moon were sacred to him, because on these days light did not cease even when the sun had set; for Jupiter was the god of light. On each of these days his priest sacrificed to him a white sheep in the fortress of the Capitol. There too was the Auguraculum, an open square, meant for the work of the augurs, who were also servants of Jupiter, and whose task it was to learn his will from the signs in the sky. On the opposite side, on the southern peak of the Capitol, where at a later time the temple of Jupiter Optimus Maximus towered up, stood in the earliest days the temple of Jupiter Feretrius, the god who strikes down the guilty with his thunderbolt. His priests were called *fetiales.* This temple contained the primeval fetish, a stone, the thunderbolt, from which the god took the name of Jupiter Lapis. Beside it lay the staff, a wooden fetish, on which oaths were taken. With the thunderbolt the sacrificial animal was killed when treaties were concluded. The implication was that just as the priest slew the pig, so should Jupiter strike the Roman people if they did not keep faith. This indicates that even at this early period ethical and political conceptions were associated with Jupiter. Three other festivals, which indicate that viniculture was under Jupiter's protection, belong to the oldest calendar; of these, two go back to ancient times — that of Jupiter Elicius, who had an altar on the Aventine and to whom processional prayer for rain (*aquælicium*) was made in time of prolonged drought, and that of Jupiter Fulgur, the god of lightning, to whom were consecrated the places that had been struck by lightning.

Like Jupiter, Mars also was a deity common to all Italic peoples. He was the god of war, the defender of the people, the city, and the fields, and with his month Martius the ancient Roman year began. From immemorial time his altar stood on the Campus Martius, and there at intervals of five years the lustration of the citizens took place. There were similar sacred processional rites for the city, the fields, and for the farm of the individual husbandman. The essential feature in these ceremonies was the drawing of the charmed circle round the plot of ground that was to be consecrated, purified, and sanctified. The victims for the sacrifice were led round in the processions. All that lay within the circle was consecrated and guarded against evil influences. Horses, weapons, and war-trumpets were consecrated at these festivals of Mars. The god himself was originally worshipped under the fetish of a lance. His servants were the *flamen martialis* and the *salii,* who performed with their sacred spears and shields the dances demanded by the god and who made known by appointed means the beginning and end of the season when war could be waged — viz., March and October.

Of Quirinus, the third deity, we know very little. His temple stood on the hill called after him, the Quirinal, and he seems to have been a deity after the likeness of Mars.

The rest of the ancient Roman deities and festivals were such as appealed to the practical needs of the people. Next to war, agriculture, stock-raising, and domestic affairs absorbed their interest. Honour was paid therefore to the two deities Tellus and Ceres, the former being the goddess of the tilled soil and the latter the guardian goddess of the fruits of the fields. In the spring-time, in order to secure good growth, cows big with calf were sacrificed to Tellus, and a few days later the festival of the Cerealia was held in honour of Ceres. Rust was averted from the grain crops by the festival of the Robigalia. Flora was the protectress of the blossom and Pomona of the fruits of trees; Consus and Ops were relied upon for a good harvest and its safe ingathering. Practically every aspect of the farmers' daily labour was in the keeping of special deities, whose names are known. Although taken as a whole they show an excessive systematization pointing to theological affectation, many of these were doubtless rooted in ancient faith and ritual. At the festivals of Ceres and Tellus the *flamen cerealis* called on the names of twelve other deities, who watched over an equal number of agricultural operations.

Vervactor superintended the first turning of the soil, Reparator the process of manuring, Imporcitor the ploughing, Insitor the sowing of the seed, Obarator the second ploughing, Occator the harrowing, Sarritor and Subruncinator the removal of weeds, Messor the mowing, Convector the getting-in of the crop, Conditor the garnering, and Promitor the removal of the crop from the garner. There were many other deities with analogous functions, and the ordinary activities of daily life were likewise under the protection of special deities.

Daily life and the home were also brought into relation to higher powers. Janus was the god of the house-door and the threshold. Originally the name denoted the door itself, in which, according to primitive faith, special powers dwelt. Similarly, Vesta was the domestic hearth, charged with power, and afterward the goddess of the hearth and the fire that burned there. Both deities, however, had a place in the official state cult. The priest of Janus was the *rex sacrorum,* and stood first in precedence among all priests. Vesta had her priestesses in the Vestal Virgins, whose duty it was to maintain the ever-burning fire on the hearth of the circular temple of Vesta, the shape of which was an imitation of the ancient Roman house. Both in the home and in the temple of Vesta rites were paid to the gods of the storeroom, the *penates.* Domestic religion also took account of the gods who were associated with the worship of the dead and of some living persons. Like the Greeks and other peoples, the Romans believed that in every man there dwelt a special power, an orenda. In the case of a man this was called his *genius,* in the case of a woman her *juno.* The *genius* of the head of the house was worshipped. A man's birthday is the festival day of his *genius,* just as among the Greeks it was the festival of a man's *daimon.* After death the souls of men, still charged with power, bore the general name of *manes,* and in their honour the rites of the Larentalia were performed. Conceived as going about on baleful errands or with evil intent, they were called *lemures* or *larvæ.* At the festival of the Lemuria, beans were dedicated to them to ward them off from the house. The spirits of ancestors in relation to their *gens* were known under the name of *di parentes;* their festival was the Parentalia, held in February. The ancestral spirit of the family proper, the *lar familiaris,* received his worship in the home. Family religion, the *sacra familiæ,* thus comprised the cult of the *genius,* of the *lares, vesta,* and *penates.* The continuity of this religion was bound up with the possession of male posterity. If there were no sons in a family, the continuance of its cult was secured by the adoption of a son. This is the original explanation of that practice both among the Romans and the Greeks; it was to keep alive ancestor-worship in the family.

These are the most important, though by no means all, of the ancient Roman deities and observances which cannot be proved to have been influenced by the Etruscans or Greeks, although, as we shall see, such influence made itself felt as time went on. On the other hand, Saturnus, to whom the festival on the 17th of December, known as the Saturnalia, was dedicated, was apparently of Etruscan origin and corresponded to the Etruscan god Satre; his original character, however, was so greatly altered by his being subsequently identified with the Greek Kronos that it is no longer possible to gain a clear idea of it.

The most striking characteristic of the Roman religion in its oldest period was the absence of personality in the deities, the lack of any tradition regarding the details of their personal life and experiences. This holds good for later time also, although perhaps to a lesser degree. Ancient Roman religion knew no mythical histories of personal gods, no genealogies, no marriages or children, no heroic legends, no worship of legendary heroes, no cosmogony, no conceptions of life in the underworld — in a word, nothing of that which Homer and Hesiod had so abundantly supplied for the Greeks. This remained essentially true of it throughout its entire history. Many of the deities never attained personality at all, but continued to be impersonal forces, *numina*. As a result they were never pictorially represented. Indeed, the idea of images was borrowed from Etruscan and Greek sources. The absence of a factor such as the Greeks had in the epos and all that it involved is one of the essential distinctions between Greek and Roman religion, and reflects the difference that existed between the imaginative Greeks and the phlegmatic Romans, a warlike and agricultural people. It was the interests of the tiller of the soil and the warrior that dictated the nature of the Roman religion. It was pre-eminently the religion of a unified state, not of numerous city-states with different cults. It was strictly prescribed, and its control lay in the hands of priesthoods. Sacrifices, festivals, and prayers were all carried through in accordance with fixed ceremonial, and the spheres of influence of the deities were as strictly defined as the functions of the priests and other officials. The nature of a deity was in keeping with his name, which either indicated his activity or, as in the case of Janus and Vesta, an object which was originally itself the fetishistic deity. Of course, the state religion, which is familiar to us from Roman literature, was somewhat juristic in character, but the customs of the private cults are not so well known, and of those of some of the individual *gentes* we hardly know anything at all. But even private religion followed fixed lines and employed fixed formulas of prayer which had to be learned and recited word for word, and this rigidity of ritual was never relaxed throughout the centuries.

The narrowness that marked the geographical and intellectual horizon of the Romans of the sixth century was reflected in the spheres within which their deities exercised control. As, however, the powers of the gods kept pace with the increase of material and intellectual civilization, and were adapted to the changes in the lives of their worshippers, so the expression of Roman dominion and the consequent multiplication of needs necessitated a similar expansion of the powers of the gods. These were no longer confined to war, agriculture, stock-raising, and the needs of domestic life. The Romans themselves, however, contributed little to this heightened conception of their gods.

Just as they drew their higher culture from outside sources, chiefly from the Greeks, so it was under Greek influence that their gods developed during the centuries that followed. By the end of the sixth century, at the end of the kingdom, Rome had become the chief city of Central Italy. It had extended its dominion over the larger part of Latium. Two and a half centuries later, in the time of Ptolemy II, fifty years after the death in Babylon of Alexander the Great, its power extended over all Italy south of Pisa and Ariminum — that is to say, over the Greek colonies in Italy; and ere many years had passed its Hellenistic empire rivalled the Diadochoi empires of the Antigonides, the Ptolemies, and the Seleucids, till by and by these also were incorporated, in the reign of Augustus, in the Roman world-empire. Thus the end of the sixth century or the beginning of the fifth saw the Hellenization, as the end of the third saw the Orientalization of the Roman religion. On the other hand, Rome through her colonists sent her own cults all over Italy and even beyond.

It was not merely the tolerance of the Romans that induced them to grant admittance to alien cults. Similar tolerance was exhibited by the Greeks, and it was the universal belief of antiquity, down to the Christian Middle Ages, if not beyond that time, that the gods of foreign peoples really existed. The Romans not only suffered alien gods — they sought them out. By their *evocatio* they summoned to Rome, with the promise of new temples, the gods of the cities they were about to conquer, and considered themselves under obligation to preserve the cults of the states they subjugated. In times of need and special danger they vowed temples in Rome to foreign gods. Thus to the circle of ancient Roman gods, the *di indigetes,* were added an ever-increasing host of new deities, the *di novensides.* In most cases, however, these newcomers lost on their arrival in Rome some of their former characteristics.

As far back as the sixth century the number of the gods had begun to increase. At that time Rome was extending her power over Latium, and was on the eve of important political changes. Toward the end of the sixth century was introduced, probably from Etruria, the Capitoline triad, Jupiter Optimus Maximus, Juno Regina, and Minerva, thus displacing the ancient trinity of Jupiter, Mars, and Quirinus. An Etruscan artist from Veii had undertaken the adornment of the temple, and had fashioned the clay image of Jupiter. An idea of its appearance is given by the recently discovered clay statue from Veii (Fig. 84). On the Alban Mount now rose a large new Temple to Jupiter Latiaris, and from Aricia, about the beginning of the fifth century, came the Latin Diana to her new sanctuary on the Aventine. Most important of all, however, was the introduction into Rome of the collection of oracles known as the Sibylline Books. These were kept in the cellar of the temple of Jupiter on the Capitol, and for their interpretation a new order of priests, the *duoviri sacris faciundis* — their number was afterwards increased to ten and later still to fifteen — was founded. These were the guardians of the "Greek ritual," and their researches in the sacred books led to the introduction of numerous Greek cults into Rome.

The first Greek cult — that of the Dioscuri, Castor and Pollux — came to Rome independently of the Sibylline Books. Nor did it come directly from the Greek colonial sphere, but probably from the Latin Tusculum. The same is to be said of the cult of the originally Greek hero Hercules, which also came from a city of Latium — perhaps Tibur. Both had temples inside the precincts of the city. The first deity to be directly adopted from the Greeks was Apollo. He was closely associated with the Sibylline collection of oracles, and seems to have reached Rome at the same time as they did, probably from Cumæ. Like all the other deities adopted from Greece, Apollo lost some of his qualities, and came to be regarded chiefly as the god of healing. In the first decade of the fifth century he was followed by Demeter, Dionysos, and Kore; at a time when the crops had failed a temple was dedicated to them under the names of Ceres, Liber, and Libera and adorned by Greek artists. This is one instance of Greek deities being identified with ancient native Roman gods; another is found in the

FIG. 84. THE APOLLO OF VEII
From " Antike Denkmäler "

case of Poseidon, who was introduced into Rome in the fifth century and identified with the Roman Neptune. Almost contemporaneously with Demeter, Dionysos, and Kore, Hermes was adopted in Rome. He was worshipped in his quality as god of commerce, and in accordance therewith received the name of Mercurius.

It was in the fifth century that these deities were adopted in Rome. For more than a hundred years after that date nothing is heard of similar temples to other Greek gods. It was not till the beginning of the third century, when

Rome was visited by a pestilence, that, on the advice of the Sibylline Books, a foreign deity was introduced. This god came from Greece itself. He was the god of healing, Asklepios of Epidauros, whose sacred animal, the serpent, was brought to Rome with a stately escort. The serpent itself selected an island in the Tiber as the site of the future temple of Æsculapius. During the dark days of the Second Punic War the Hellenization of Roman worship made further advance. At that time the cult of Aphrodite of Eryx, in Sicily, was introduced into Rome, and this goddess was identified with the ancient Latin Venus. Needless to say, all these deities were worshipped in Rome in accordance with Greek ritual.

This Greek ritual included the *lectisternia* dedicated to the gods — in some cases regularly, in others in special cases of need. Lying on couches, the gods partook of the banquet set before them. The first banquet of this kind took place in the year 399, on the advice of the Sibylline Books. The deities thus entertained were Apollo and Latona, Hercules and Diana, Mercurius and Neptune. As time went on similar banquets were provided in the temples (in the first instance) of those deities which were worshipped in accordance with Greek ritual, and later in the temples of Roman gods. This custom found easy entrance into Rome, because it had long been a practice to set food before certain deities.

But about this time some Italic observances again found their way to Rome. These included — in the fourth century — the cult of Venus, who was identified later with the Greek Aphrodite; several cults of Juno, such as those of Juno Regina of Veii and of Juno Sospita Mater Regina of Lanuvium; and, in the third century, the water-nymph Juturna of Lavinium and Vortumnus from Volsinii in Etruria.

To these, Rome added new deities of her own creation. The spheres of influence of the various ancient gods were extended, a new deity being created alongside the ancient one to watch over the new extension. The new deity either bore the name of the ancient one, being differentiated by an added epithet indicative of his activity, or received an entirely new name. In these latter cases personifications of abstract ideas were regarded as deities. Jupiter, the guardian of loyalty, was worshipped in a new temple on the Quirinal in the year 406 as Dius Fidius, and about the middle of the third century a temple was erected to a separate goddess named Fides. As the god of victory Jupiter Victor was worshipped, and by and by this aspect of his activity was separately deified as the goddess Victoria. Juno, the goddess of parturition, was worshipped under the name of Juno Lucina, but other cults were added in her honour as Juno Regina, Quiritis, Moneta, etc. The goddess Fortuna, whose cult, like that of the Greek Tyche in the Hellenistic period, became prominent about this time, extended her sway, and assumed a large number of other names. New sanctuaries were dedicated to her to ensure the success of any undertaking or to acknowledge her claim to homage in her new spheres of influence.

Their growing acquaintance with Greek literature and mythology brought home to the Romans their lack of national traditions regarding their past history. They now realized that they had no stories, or myths, or cults of legendary heroes. This lack was in due time supplied under Greek inspiration. Of course, they could not hope to produce anything to equal the epics of Homer and Hesiod; the poems of Virgil and Ovid, written in the time of Augustus, were simply imitations of the Hellenistic poetry of writers like Apollonios, Kallimachos, and Lykophron. Roman religion had, however, already reached a stage higher than that which these men represented, and their works had little creative power.

The fact that the Romans had no hero-cults, although they had ancestor-worship and worship of the dead, is explained by this absence of an epic tradition; without heroic legends t h e r e could be no heroic cults. As soon, however, as the traditions of the coming of the Trojans under Æneas, of the foundation of Rome, and the stories of ancient days in Rome had had time to strike root, the ground was prepared for a kind of hero-worship, but it was a matter of erudition rather than of piety. The names of the legendary heroes of the past were associated with existent cults. The eponymous Latinus — a Greek invention — was now believed to have been snatched away during a battle and to have been worshipped as Jupiter Latiaris.

FIG. 85. THE TRANSPORTATION OF MAGNA MATER TO ROME

From Ernst Schmidt, " Kultübertragungen "

Similar tales were told of Æneas, Romulus, and Hersilia: since their abduction they had been worshipped as Jupiter Indiges, Quirinus, and Hora Quirini. To these euhemeristic interpreters the gods Janus, Saturnus, and Faunus were kings of long ago, their cults going back to the time of their death. Other prehistoric figures, like Tiberinus, and Aventinus, and perhaps also Remus, Argus, and Pallas, were deduced from place-names or associated with them on the ground of phonetic resemblance. Stories were invented to explain why some of the seven kings of Rome had no cult. In fact, this whole tradition lived only in books, and had hardly any effect on religious observance.

Toward the very end of the third century B.C. the East also began to influence Roman religion. This was a natural result of the historical events that drew the Romans to the East. In the year 204, toward the end of the Second Punic War, the Sibylline Books decreed that the sacred stone of Kybele at Pessinus, in Phrygia (Fig. 85), should be brought to Rome, and in the year 191 a temple on the Palatine was dedicated to her under the name of Mater Deum Magna Idæa. The Eastern campaigns of the Romans in the first century made many Oriental cults familiar to the soldiers, and through them to the people of Rome. Some of these were adopted by private individuals, and then found their way into the state religion. Lower Italy also, where Oriental observances had become widespread, was another source from which these found their way into Rome. In this manner, one after another, came Isis, Sarapis, and other Egyptian deities, the cult of Mâ from Cappadocia, Adonis, Atargatis, and others from Syria, Mithras from Persia, Judaism, and Christianity. Alike over the Greek world and over Italy and Rome poured the originally Babylonian belief in the influence of the stars on human affairs, which the science of astrology claimed to interpret. Even the reforms of Augustus could do nothing to stem this flood of foreign beliefs. It was from political rather than religious motives that that emperor tried to infuse new vigour into ancient Roman religion and ancient Roman *virtus,* and similar motives guided him in trying to find in religion a basis for the Imperial power.

FIG. 86. PLATO

From Bernoulli, " Griechische Ikonographie "

III. THE RELIGION OF HELLENISM

The Greeks had connexions with the East as far back as the fourteenth century B.C., when, as we learn from inscriptions from Boghazköi recently deciphered by Forrer, a Hittite King addressed a king of the Achæans as " my brother." At the time when Ionian commerce was at its height the Greeks made extensive voyages of exploration, and the results of these were assimilated by the new sciences of geography and ethnography. Skylax of Karyanda even sailed up the Indus and round Arabia. They had also intercourse, both in peace and in war, with the Lydians, Persians, and Egyptians. With a tolerance equal to that of the Romans they welcomed foreign cults; that they did so to a less extent than the Romans was due to the fact that they had so many of their own; but although their own deities sufficed to meet their religious needs, they had no objection based on principle to the admittance of foreign deities. Their knowl-

FIG. 87. ALEXANDER THE GREAT
From Arndt, " Griechische und römische Portraits "

edge of them was derived in part from the numerous foreign traders who came to Greece in connexion with the extensive commerce carried on in the Ionian cities and in Athens, and partly from their own foreign travels and their colonies. The foreign gods were worshipped by religious societies whose membership included both foreigners and Greeks, but some of the cults were officially adopted. When Grecian civilization was at its height Kybele from Asia Minor and Ammon from Egypt were well known in Greece, and even the Thracian Bendis, the goddess of a 'barbarian' people, was familiar to many. The actual opening-up of the Far East and of India, however, dates from the campaign of Alexander the Great in the fourth century—a century that constituted a turning point in the civilization of antiquity. To that century belong the two men who did most to usher in the new era—Plato (Fig. 86) and Alexander the Great (Fig. 87). Intermediate between the two was Aristotle (Fig. 88), the pupil of one of them and the teacher of the other.

FIG. 88. ARISTOTLE
From Arndt, " Griechische und römische Portraits "

These three men can be described in the same words: all three were founders of a new and great empire. Plato was the discoverer of the world of ideas, that changeless world that lies apart from the shifting world of phenomena. Aristotle, the historian, philosopher, and organizer of science, recognized the unity that underlies all the sciences, and thus made a discovery which has borne fruit down to our own days, although the world was slow in understanding its value. Alexander the Great discovered the East, threw it open to the influences of the West, and founded one united political empire extending from the city where Plato taught to the land where Buddhism prevailed. All these three empires had one feature in common—the aspiration toward unity that we have already seen in another connexion.

Behind the infinite variety of outward things Plato sought to find the one unchangeable, eternal idea, the unity that lay behind the multiplicity. Aristotle, the greatest systematic thinker of all time, raised a structure in which all the sciences found their due place. Alexander the Great laboured to achieve the unity of the inhabited world, to bring about a world-empire that should include Greeks and barbarians and unite them in one civilization. All three, each in his own sphere, finished what Greek colonization had been trying to do since the eighth century, what Ionian science had been labouring to do since the sixth.

Alexander's empire fell to pieces immediately after his death, but his life-work had secured the Hellenization of the world. By this achievement he became in a real sense the pioneer of Christianity. It was he who broke down the barriers that separated one petty city-state from its neighbours. Men could now lift their eyes beyond their narrow horizon to the earth's utmost bounds with the feeling that their home was wherever Hellenistic civiliza-tion prevailed. The sense of cosmopolitanism grew apace. By means of a universal Greek language, the *koine*, which replaced all local dialects, men everywhere could understand each other; it became the medium by which Greek civilization, and at a later time Christianity, was spread over the whole world. Large commercial cities, like Alexander's own city, Alexandria, became the connecting links between East and West. Other cities, like those founded by the Seleucids, were centres of Hellenistic civilization in the interior of Asia. This world-empire, becoming increasingly Hellenized and unified, found its champion first in Alexander, then in the Diadochoi and in some of the Roman emperors. It thus stood for international commerce, unified civilization, one world-language, cosmopolitanism, one world-empire, one monarchy. This was the outcome of Alexander's labours. It lacked only a unified religion, and even the germs of this were present. Thus Alexander had in outward matters prepared the way for Christianity. The world had to be Hellenized before it could be Christianized.

But changes had also taken place in human hearts, and men were seeking new ways of deliverance from the shackles of the world. In this sphere it was Plato who voiced the thoughts of his time. It was he who left the deepest impress on the thoughts of the ensuing age, and prepared men's hearts for the reception of Christianity. All who came after him found the nucleus of his teaching in his theory of ideas, his doctrine of the two worlds: on the one hand the world of phenomena, of the material, of becoming, of eternal flux, a world in which there can be no true knowledge; on the other hand the world of ideas, the true existence and nature of things, immaterial and immutable, to see which is the only true knowledge. The human body is a part of the world of sense; it is the medium of the deceptive sense percep-tions. The soul is immortal, and the noblest part of it — viz., the organ by which true knowledge is attained — belongs to the intelligible world, but is cribbed and confined by the desires and appetites of sense. This leads to an epistemological and ethical pessimism. The body is the grave of the soul, and in its efforts to attain to goodness and truth the soul is retarded by that which is earthly.

In following up these doctrines it was inevitable that the idea of fleeing from the world should occur to men's minds. It was not expressly taught by Plato, but it had already been mooted in the older mysteries and in mysticism. It was only logical that this world, which Plato, faithful to the ancient Greek view, declared in one of his latest works to be the best of all possible worlds, should by some men be despised; that the chasm between the Here and the Hereafter, between God and the World, Body and Soul, should be considered impassable; that men should long for deliverance from the world of appearance and set all their hopes on redemption from this world and on the world to come. Asceticism, which at first was a secret practice confined to sects like the Orphics and Pythagoreans, or took the form of fasting and refraining from sexual intercourse as apotropæic and cathartic measures previous to certain celebrations, now began to spread. Under the influence of the Oriental mystery religions it continued to gain ground, and assumed more and more the form of antagonism to this world and its pleasures. These conceptions were not confined to the educated classes; they penetrated to the lower ranks of the people, where they found ready response, and the proselytizing activities of mendicant preachers of the Cynic school, who called on men to fight their appetites and practise virtue, did much to extend their popularity.

All these views and conceptions were more or less alien to the Greek mind before the Hellenistic period. To that mind only one world was present, the earth, on which human life was spent. It was for this world only that Homer's heroes lived and fought. Battle and victory and the strong will to live constituted their life and their hope. What, after all, had the world beyond to offer them? A shadowy existence in the underworld, without power or consciousness. This joy of life, this will to live, was always strong in the genuine Greek, and the allurements of the hereafter as presented by the Mysteries had little attraction for him. Only very rarely do we hear words like those of the captive Silenos: " Not to be born is the best of human lots "; but they were almost unheard because of the troubled time that elapsed between the migration period of the Greek Middle Ages and the battle of Arbela, with the intermediate stages denoted by the names Miletus and Athens, Marathon and Salamis. It was only after Plato's time that such thoughts met with an ever wider response, till they found expression in the words " What is a man profited, if he gain the whole world, and lose or forfeit his own self? " [2] At the close of his most perfect work Plato makes Socrates utter the prayer: " Dear Pan, and ye other gods here, grant me beauty within." This prayer, an expression of personal longing, is a landmark in the history of Greek religious life. Albrecht Dieterich, who taught us so much about Greek religion, had them chiselled on his tombstone.

The increased importance of the individual finds expression in a stronger sense of personal religion. Though individualism was not the product of the time of the Sophists, these thinkers encouraged its growth, and gave it a philosophical basis and justification. It now became very noticeable in the

[2] Luke ix, 25.

religious sphere. The personal aspect of religion gained increasing prominence, and exerted a reflex influence on religion as a whole. The chains of the petty city-states were burst asunder, and this loosened the tie that kept the gods of the *polis* together as against those of the neighbouring cities. The *polis* had collapsed, burying in the ruins the gods who were inseparably bound up with its existence. The individual, now no longer a citizen of one city, but a member of an empire and a citizen of the world, could freely choose the deity in whom he would place his trust, and was no longer restricted to worship, as the city desired him to do, " after the manner of his fathers." And the field of choice was wide. There were the ancient native gods and heroes, deities of later date, and the foreign gods, whose number was being constantly increased. The longing of the individual for salvation, his hopes for the hereafter, sought and found deities who undertook to rescue him from the dangers of this life and promised him a life of bliss beyond the grave. He sought and found a saviour, a *soter,* the mystery. Religion as a civil duty was replaced by personal religion.

In these circumstances it was in a different frame of mind that men regarded the native gods, the sacred tradition, and the myths. From the close of the fifth century onward *naïve* acceptance of the contents of the sacred books became rarer and rarer. Philosophers and historians gathered courage to criticize and explain, and under the influence of this new spirit Euripides brought on the stage legendary heroes who had little in common with the brave men of the epos and who uttered thoughts which the Sophists had made familiar to the cultured Athenians. The old tales of heroes became more matter of fact, and the same process was repeated in the case of the gods. The legendary heroes had once been regarded as gods, but in Homer's pages, they had become men of long ago. So similarly the " twilight of the gods " had arrived for those figures who till now had retained their divine rank. Even Kronos and Zeus, Apollo and Poseidon, and all the rest were now regarded as men who had gained their divine eminence by their outstanding gifts. Zeus's grave was in Crete, Apollo's in Delphi. It was in this spirit that Euhemeros in the beginning of the third century wrote for his contemporaries the history of the gods. Extended to include the deities of Rome and the East, this interpretation found ready acceptance, and was gladly used by the Church Fathers as a weapon with which to assail the ancient religion. Historians no longer began their histories of mankind with the legendary heroes; they began farther back, at the time when Uranos, Kronos, and Zeus reigned on earth, when Janus and Saturnus lived in Italy and Osiris in Egypt. Universal history now included that of the East, and Eastern historians themselves penned it, in order to give the Greeks a trustworthy account of a history and a religion, a sacred tradition and a civilization, much more ancient than their own. It is significant that these Oriental historians were also priests — the Egyptian Manetho of Heliopolis and Berossos of Babylon, the priest of Bel, both contemporary with

Euhemeros. In the East science was mainly in the hands of the priests, and was regarded as divine revelation. This close connexion between science and religion now spread to the Western world. Eastern sciences became familiar there, especially that most peculiar branch of it, half science and half religion, that was called astrology; and the whole system of magic, which had always flourished in Greece among the lower strata of the people, now became a pseudo-science. The magic papyri which have been preserved provide clear evidence of this. Philosophy too was Orientalized, and gradually became a substitute for religion. This process can be traced from the first century B.C. onward, till it reached the height of grotesqueness in the system in which syncretistic neo-platonism sought to infuse new life into the philosophy of Plato. Similarly, the works of Hermes Trismegistos, which circulated in Greek as early as the second century A.D., were regarded as a divine revelation of Oriental wisdom, religion, science, and mysticism.

Although science in ancient Ionia had also originated in close connexion with religion, it had almost from the very beginning thrown off its allegiance. Owing to the absence of a unified dogma, a unified priesthood, and a unified religious organization, there had never been in Greece anything like a serious breach between religion and science. It is not between science and religion, but between science and the Church that controversies arise. Attacks launched by philosophers against a myth or a religious practice met with no resistance from religion, because religion was not organized. But now, under the influence of the priestly science of the East, and with the rise of religious communities and churches with fixed dogmas, uniting intolerance with proselytizing zeal, conflict could not have been avoided if science had still been as strong as it was in the time of Aristotle. But if we except Poseidonios the Stoic, that comprehensive intellect had left no successor who could take all knowledge for his province. The separate sciences had indeed continued to flourish for a time, but ere long the scientific gains of antiquity were buried in manuals more or less imperfect, and were handed down in the form in which they had been received and for the most part merely in extracts. In that rigid form, fixed and definitive, they were kept and used as weapons of the Church, mostly by men who were both scholars and ecclesiastics. From the side of science, therefore, there was little prospect of attempts being made to stem the flood that poured in from the East. On the contrary, all the science that still survived was yoked to the triumphal car of religion and the Church. Sober criticism, such as the ancient sage had demanded from the scientist, gave place either to a barren scepticism or to a faith that claimed to stand above all reason. The Syrian Poseidonios himself, who, like Aristotle, had mastered all the sciences and produced a unified theory of the world that governed men's views during the era that followed, was not strong enough to break with the traditional religion, and bent his energies to the reconciling of science and religion.

Thus Greece, which had begun to Hellenize the East, was in great danger of being itself Orientalized. Its complete domination by the East, however, was averted by a power which now began to play a decisive part in the history of the world. That power was Rome. We have already seen how in the third century B.C. Rome had grown into a state which ranked with the Hellenistic Oriental empires, how it had come into conflict with them and had ultimately incorporated them in its world-empire. It had itself been Hellenized, although it had retained its own language. The chief theatre of Rome's colonial activity was in the West; Gaul and Spain were Romanized; Germany and Britain were also opened to Greek and Roman civilization. But Roman troops and Roman officials also came eastward, and here a remarkable spectacle is seen. While Eastern religions were adopted by the Romans and carried by them westward as far as Spain and Germany, the cults of the Western peoples, of the Celts, Iberians, and Teutons, were as a rule adopted only by the soldiers who came personally into contact with them, and carried by them to the various places to which they moved; they were not adopted by the Romans themselves. One exception is the Celtic goddess Epona, who was worshipped by individuals in Rome. Nothing shows more clearly the superior attractiveness and dignity of Eastern religions. The unity of the Roman world-empire was split into two — the Roman-Greek West and the Hellenistic East, the former speaking Latin, the latter speaking Greek.

At this point, amid the multifarious phenomena of the Hellenistic-Roman religion, we come upon one feature that stands out prominently not only in Rome, but also throughout the provinces of East and West. We mean the religious worship paid to monarchs. The best account of this is that of Kaerst, to whom we also owe the most illuminating description of Hellenism as a whole. In itself this worship of kings was not a new thing. As we have seen, the conceptions underlying it had always been present in the Greek faith. It rested on the belief that in every human being there lives a *daimon* — in outstanding men a specially potent *daimon*. The worship of kings was therefore merely a form of homage paid to the orenda of a man during his life and after his death. Even in Homer we find honour paid to the orenda of the king, who is acknowledged as king only so long as his strength remains unimpaired. He is a favourite of the gods, who bestow on him this power, which carries with it the privilege of being worshipped by his subjects. In token of his power the king wields the sceptre, the staff charged with potency. We find no example in the epos of homage being paid to a king in his lifetime, although there are numerous examples of worship of dead monarchs; but that in historical time the *daimon* of a living man required and received homage is indicated by many kinds of phenomena. For one thing, the celebration of birthdays points in this direction. It was an act of homage to the *daimon* of a man who was still alive. The number of those who took part in such homage varied with the eminence of the person concerned. The earliest example of a public celebration of this kind belongs to the fourth century, when the birthday of Timoleon, the liberator of Syracuse, was celebrated throughout Sicily. Further, the festivities held in honour of the victors in the great national games were likewise based on this belief. Songs of victory and hymns were sung in their honour, and they were conducted to their native cities by solemn processions. Frequently, indeed, a portion of the city-wall was thrown down, and the entry of the victor resembled the epiphany of a god. Additional proof that worship was paid to rulers in their lifetime is provided by Sicily in the fifth and fourth centuries, and at the close of the fifth century sacrifice was offered to the Spartan general Lysandros as to a god, and pæans were sung in his honour. Even outside the ranks of kings there were others, ' god-men,' whose marvellous powers were told in legends. In some cases there was a substratum of history — e.g., in those of Abaris and Aristeas, Pythagoras and Empedokles — and later times recounted the miraculous doings of Apollonius of Tyana, Alexander of Abonuteichos, Peregrinus Proteus, and Simon Magus. King Pyrrhus worked miracles of healing, as did also the emperor Vespasian and Jesus Christ and his Apostles.

But it is when we come to Alexander the Great that the worship of kings gathers more widespread significance. His father, Philip, had been worshipped in his lifetime, and Alexander's friend Hephaistion had been deified after his death. To the subjugated Egyptians and Persians Alexander, as the successor of the Pharaohs and Achæmenids, was a god on the throne, and Oriental *proskynesis* was ere long demanded from the Greeks. Both Egyptians and Greeks saw in Alexander the son of Ammon Zeus. After his death his divinity became even more clearly recognized. His remains were taken from Babylon to Alexandria, and his name was officially entered among those to whom the Empire paid divine honours. The first of the Diadochoi, Ptolemy I and Seleucus I, were likewise deified. This apotheosis took the place of the ancient Greek ceremony of enrolling great names among those of the heroes — a ceremony that had gradually lost its place in public esteem because in many parts of Greece almost every dead man had come to be regarded as a *heros*. Such apotheosis was not altogether without precedent in the older Greek religion: according to Greek belief heroes like Herakles, Achilles, and many others had been translated — they had no grave on earth where homage could be paid to them, and their worshippers had to look for them where they were believed to dwell, in heaven. It was, that is to say, a uranic cult like that offered to gods, not a chthonic cult like that paid to the mortal dead. From the time of Ptolemy II onward the ruler in his lifetime was regarded as a god on earth, and the epithet Epiphanes, which has this meaning, was applied to many Hellenistic rulers. The ' advent ' of such a deity, whether he were a Hellenistic king, a high Roman official, or a Roman emperor, was solemnly hailed as the epiphany of a god. Augustus, who had once more given peace to the world, was worshipped as the saviour of the world, especially in the East, and after his death a decree of the Senate placed him among the gods; in the same way, a temple was built in the Forum to Julius Cæsar after his death. From that time onward Roman emperors received worship in their lifetime and the Romans, resuscitating ancient conceptions, officially worshipped them as *divi*. The first cult of this kind was that awarded to the *genius* of Augustus. This official Imperial cult was a part of unified religion, observed throughout the whole Empire, and while anyone might decline to do homage to any other god, it was the bounden duty of every one to bear a part in the worship of the emperor. This cult of the living emperor was the visible counterpart to the teaching of Euhemeros. He taught that the Olympian gods had once been men: the Imperial cult implied that the gods still dwelt on earth in human form. The teaching of Euhemeros thus supplied a theoretical foundation for the worship of the emperor.

This one great religious innovation of the Hellenistic period, which was bringing about a unification of religion, took place simultaneously with the introduction of a number of new gods, the gods of the East. This seemed to nullify the attempt to achieve unity. The multiplication of cults thus produced was, however, only apparent, for most of these faiths were not aiming at the institution of new cults by the side of others. They claimed to be the one true religion, and fought for sole dominion. They were international, and claimed to belong to all men. And to them, with their appeal to each individual, the individual attached himself — Hellene, Roman, barbarian, bond or free. For here he found what he longed for, what the ancient gods could give him only in incomplete measure (though it was vouchsafed to him in some degree by Asklepios, the god of healing, whose cult was once more flourishing, and by the ancient Mysteries, which still retained their attraction) — here he found deliverance from the dangers of this life, purity by means of religious observances, penances, and asceticism, union with God, a priest who cared for the individual soul, and a blessed life in the world beyond. All this was offered to him amid a magnificent environment and presented in a ritual that appealed to every sense and deeply stirred the heart. The dogmatic teaching added a view of the world which, in a pseudo-scientific dress, met the demands of his intellect and defined the moral life.

These Oriental cults made headway by means of their own missionary activities, and by commercial intercourse, which extended from India to the Pillars of Herakles, bringing into personal contact merchants of all nations, and gathering Egyptians, Syrians, and Jews in all the commercial centres. Other bearers of propaganda were Roman soldiers and officials passing from province to province. Many of the older Greek and Roman gods were identified with one another, and this gave them to some extent a new life. For example, Sarapis was now Zeus, now Asklepios or Dionysos; the Egyptian Thoth was Hermes; the Phrygian Sabazios was the Jahve Zebaoth of the Old Testament. Some of the new gods, however, claimed to unite in themselves all the old deities, and Isis was at one and the same time Magna Mater, Demeter, Persephone, Hera, Aphrodite, Artemis, Hekate, etc.

We saw that some Oriental cults had found entrance into Rome as early as the end of the third century B.C. In the two centuries before and after the beginning of the Christian era these Oriental cults spread with great rapidity. Rome resisted for a time, and even took measures to repel some of them. Augustus decreed that Egyptian deities should be worshipped only outside the Pomerium. It was not till the beginning of the third century A.D. that all restrictions were removed even in Rome. It was chiefly the gods of Egypt that competed with the Greek gods, especially Sarapis and Isis. Next in influence were Osiris, Anubis, and Horus; then came the Phrygian Kybele, who was identified with Attis, the Thracian-Phrygian Sabazios, and Syrian deities like Jupiter Dolichenus, Jupiter Heliopolitanus, Dea Syria Atargatis, Adonis, and Sol Invictus. The two religions, however, which fought most keenly for dominion, and on whose victory depended the faith of the Western world in days to come, were the Persian religion of Mithras and Semitic Christianity. One of these gained the victory over all the others, although in order to gain that victory it had to adopt many features from the faiths which it conquered. The causes that led to that victory constitute a problem which research has not yet solved.

BIBLIOGRAPHY

Wide and Nilsson, *Griechische und römische Religion* (reprinted from *Einleitung in die Klassische Altertumswissenschaft*, vol. ii, 3rd ed.) (1922). For Greek religion: Samter, *Die Religion der griechen* (1914); Moore, *Religious Thought of the Greeks* (1916); Pettazzoni, *La Religione nella graecia antica fino al Alessandro* (1921); Nilsson, *A History of Greek Religion* (1925); Kern, *Die Religion der Griechen*, vol. i (1927). For the Roman religion: Wissowa, *Religion und Kultus der Römer* (1902; 2nd ed., 1912); Fowler, *The Religious Experience of the Roman People from the Earliest Times to the Age of Augustus* (1911). For the religion of Hellenism: Wendland, *Die hellenistisch-römische Kultur in ihren Beziehungen zum Judentum und Christentum*, vol. ii of *Handbuch zum Neuen Testament* (2nd ed., 1907; 3rd ed., 1912); Kaerst, *Geschichte des Hellenismus* (vol. ii, 1909; 2nd ed., 1926); Cumont, *Die orientalischen Religionen im römischen Heidentum* (1910); 2nd ed., 1914); Reitzenstein, *Die hellenistischen Mysterienreligionen* (1910; 3rd ed., 1927); Geffcken, *Der Ausgang des griechisch-römischen Heidentums* (1920).

7. CELTIC RELIGION

by Carl Clemen

Neither France, England, nor Spain was the original home of the Celts. They had migrated thither from beyond the Rhine, from North and West Germany, and to these settlements they had gathered from South Germany, Switzerland, Bohemia, Moravia, and Hungary. In the year 390 B.C. they advanced against Italy and in 368 against Greece, but their only lengthy stay was in Asia Minor, in that part of it which was named after them, Galatia. They were the chief representatives in Europe of the so-called La Thène civilization. Our main sources for their religion are the references in Greek and Latin writers and the monuments from Gaul. Indeed, all our detailed knowledge of their beliefs and observances refers to Gaul. What is known of them in other countries will be dealt with incidentally.

That the primitive Celts, like other peoples of that period, worshipped stones we have already seen. In fact, in some places they worship them still. The same holds true of springs and rivers. The Gauls also cast into lakes gifts to the higher powers, and several specimens of such offerings have been recovered. The sea also was apparently regarded as a higher, but in this case a hostile, power. As to trees, inscriptions have been found which indicate that the beech and the oak were regarded as deities. The oak was specially sacred when a plant of mistletoe grew on it. In England this plant is still considered lucky. Of animals, the serpent and the bull were worshipped. On the so-called Altar of Notre-Dame in Paris (Fig. 89) there is a figure of a bull with three cranes on its head and back, but that is probably due to a misunderstanding of the Greek name for the three-horned bull, which was worn as an amulet (Fig. 90). A bear-like monster which was found at Noves, in the department of Vaucluse (Fig. 91), has its forepaws resting on two human heads and a human arm protruding from its maw. This probably indicates that human sacrifices were offered to it. We shall refer to it again later. It may be remarked here that the Gallic custom of employing animal figures as military badges and helmet ornaments and the British practice of tattooing animal figures on the person not only originated in the worship of these animals, but still bore this significance at a later time. Probably the same meaning is to be read into the Gallic practice of using various animals for purposes of divination. Certain animals are always represented along with deities who have a human shape, and the fact that the animals are usually larger than the deities seems to indicate that the animals were originally objects of worship.

According to Cæsar, among the Gallic deities there was one outstanding figure, whom he calls Mercury. Numerous inscriptions contain the name. Probably Cæsar used this appellation because the Romans first came into touch with the Gauls in the way of commerce, and thought that the chief Gallic deity must, like Mercury, be a god of commerce. What his actual name was we do not know, and the other deities, whom Cæsar calls Apollo, Mars, Jupiter, and Minerva, were no doubt various Gallic deities whose names appear on inscriptions as epithets accompanying the Roman names. Cæsar further tells us that the Gauls traced their origin to Dispater, the Roman god of the underworld (or to his Gallic equivalent). This statement is supported by an Irish source, which declares that the Gauls had an ancestor who was also the god of the dead, but here again we do not know the Gallic name of the deity referred to.

FIG. 89. TARVOS TRIGARANUS, FROM THE ALTAR OF
NOTRE-DAME IN PARIS
From Clemen, " Religionsgeschichte Europas "

Other Gallic deities whose representations have come down to us are always mentioned by their Gallic names. One, of whom we have numerous images, and who is always shown with one or more hammers, was called Sucellus or Sucælus (Figs. 92 and 93) — *i.e.,* " the Deft Striker." He was probably a rural deity, and is therefore frequently associated with a goddess of abundance, whose name occurs once — Nantosuelta. Esus, who is shown on the Altar of Notre-Dame in Paris already mentioned, in the act of hewing branches from a tree with a hatchet (Fig. 94) — possibly he is clearing ground for tillage — was perhaps a god of fertility. This was certainly the case with Cernunnos, who is depicted on an altar found at Reims in the act of pouring grain from a sack to feed a bull and a stag (Fig. 95). He is shown on the altar at Saintes (Fig. 96), together with two goddesses who are holding a cornucopia in their hands. Epona is not only always accompanied by one or more horses, but often has a cornucopia on her arm or a basket of fruit in her hand. She was therefore the goddess of fertility both in animals and in

FIG. 90. THREE-HORNED BULL
From Clemen, " Religionsgeschichte Europas "

FIG. 91. MONSTER FROM NOVES
From Clemen, " Religionsgeschichte Europas "

plants. There were also mother-goddesses. These were worshipped throughout the whole Celtic territory and in the later Teutonized territory on the right and particularly on the left of the Rhine. They also were represented with fruits in their laps or with cornucopias, and were fertility deities — perhaps for one family or one district. These mother-goddesses are usually three in number (Fig. 97), like other deities already mentioned. After Christianity had been introduced these fertility goddesses were occasionally interpreted as the three Marys, and as such they were adored in Metz till well into the eighteenth century.

The worship paid by the Gauls to fertility deities other than the mother-goddess took that peculiar form which we have already found among some primitive peoples and among the Persians. They were killed in order that, instead of dying of old age, they might be replaced by another of the species, or in order to utilize or preserve their powers. This must have been the meaning of the custom of burning a huge hollow human effigy, made of twigs or laths, in which human beings or animals were placed. The practice is mentioned by Poseidonios. In earlier times the victims were probably burnt without such ceremonies. Both they and the later colossal human figures represented the spirit of vegetation. This is the explanation of Strabo's statement that when there was a large number of men who had been condemned to death — these provided the human sacrifices — it was

FIG. 92. GOD WITH A HAMMER

From Clemen, " Religionsgeschichte Europas "

believed that the harvests would be abundant. This is to say, the sacrifice would promote fertility and fulfil the same purpose as was served by the killing of the spirit of vegetation. Of course, the latter sacrifice had to take place annually, whereas the former was offered up only every five years. The reason probably was that a later time felt it to be an excess of cruelty to burn human beings every year. Among the ancient Gauls, however, and at a later time — isolated cases occurred as late as the last century — certain animals were burned every year on Midsummer Day, and in the district round Grenoble to this day a goat is slaughtered at harvest-time. Its flesh, with the exception of one piece, which is kept for a year, is eaten by the reapers, and out of its skin the farmer has a coat made, which is believed to have healing virtue. In Pouilly an ox is killed, its skin being kept till the next seed-time. Undoubtedly these animals represent the spirit of vegetation. In former days in Brie on the 23rd of June, and down to the year 1743 in a certain street in Paris on the 3rd of July, a human effigy was burnt, the people fighting for the *débris*. This custom had a similar origin. Finally, there are certain phrases still current in many districts of France which contain an allusion to the killing of a human being or an animal at harvest-time. When the last sheaf is being garnered or threshed the people say, " We are killing the old woman," or " the hare," " the dog," " the cat," or " the ox."

Another remarkable custom mentioned by Strabo, and which was probably Celtic, was intended originally to enable the deity to aid man. A holy place on an island at the mouth of the Loire was roofed in one day every year by the priestesses in charge. Any priestess who during the operations let her load fall was torn to pieces by the others, and the fragments of her body carried round the sanctuary. Indubitably the purpose was to impart the powers of the dismembered body to the sanctuary, and thereby to reinforce the potency of the deity. It is not certain, however — perhaps it is improbable — that this meaning was still understood in later days. It is much more likely that in this case, as in the other just mentioned, it was merely a conservative retention of an ancient custom.

It is also impossible to say whether the cannibalism ascribed to the Celtic invaders of Greece, England, and Ireland, or the custom of using the skull of a slain enemy as a drinking-cup or at least preserving it, was believed to be a means of transferring to the living the superhuman powers of the dead. Numerous relics of the La Thène period show that parts of the skull were made into personal ornaments. They must, at least originally, have been worn as amulets. We have already seen that the custom of tattooing the person with animal figures, or using such figures as military badges or helmet decoration, could even at a later time have had a magical meaning. Pliny mentions a curious custom of British women that points strongly in the same direction. On certain occasions they dyed themselves brown with an infusion of plantain, and at such times also went naked. That practice was also followed in connexion with magical ceremonies, the purpose being that the emanations passing from one person to another should not be impeded by clothing. This is in line with Cæsar's statement that owing to religious scruples the Britons ate neither hares, hens, nor geese, although they bred them. We have found at least traces among the Gauls of animal-worship, and it is legitimate to infer that they considered many other animals as taboo.

It is also doubtful whether certain practices which were originally intended to keep the dead at a distance and which are attested among the Gauls — such as making a trench round the grave or beheading the corpse — continued to be understood

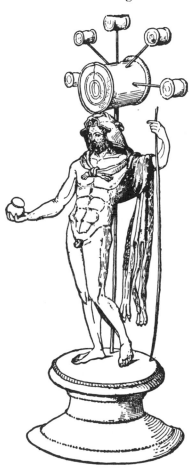

Fig. 93. God with Hammers
From Clemen, " Religionsgeschichte Europas "

in this sense. In some cases at least they were probably further examples of conservative continuation of ancient custom. The attempts of the Celts to appease the dead or to gain their goodwill took the form of dedicating to the dead all that they valued in their lifetime. Cæsar tells us they did so, and the statement is corroborated by the grave-finds. These also prove that not only slaves and dependents, but also women were buried with the dead, the women being in many cases younger than the dead man. We shall see later the light this custom casts on the Celtic conceptions of the life after death.

Excavations also show that the sacrifices offered to the gods included many of the objects which people in the Stone and Bronze Ages were wont to

FIG. 94. ESUS, FROM THE ALTAR OF NOTRE-DAME
IN PARIS
From Clemen, " Religionsgeschichte Europas "

bury with the dead, and which were originally regarded as higher beings or at least as symbols of such — axes, wheels, and things of that sort. Valuables were also offered. Ancient writers make frequent mention of this fact. Even gold was thus dedicated. The animal figures that have been found were undoubtedly intended to serve as substitutes for the actual animals. They were presented before or after a hunting expedition in order to appease the guardian deity of the animals in question. A similar interpretation is to be put upon the effigies of children and imitations of certain members of the human body. They were meant as substitutes for human sacrifices. But human beings also were actually sacrificed, and such sacrifices took place even after the emperor Claudius had forbidden them. The victims were frequently criminals who had done something to deserve death, but if these were not available innocent people were sacrificed. The explanation of all this we shall see later.

The worship of the gods was performed either at home — and many of the images referred to have been found in the houses — or, if more than one

FIG. 95. CERNUNNOS FROM THE ALTAR AT REIMS
From Clemen, " Religionsgeschichte Europas "

family was concerned, in groves or temples. Many of these latter consisted of several buildings — *e.g.*, the temple of the matrons at Pesch, in the Eifel district, although this was probably also used at a later time for the mystery cult of Kybele.

It has already been mentioned that some of these temples were served by priestesses. These were believed to possess numerous powers outside of their professional calling, including that of foretelling the future. Similar gifts were ascribed to the female seers of whom we also hear. The male priests also claimed to be able to reveal secrets of all kinds, by means of dreams and visions, observation of cloud-movements, the direction taken by the flame or smoke of the sacrifice, and especially by the flight or cries of birds. They could also read omens in the entrails of the sacrificial victims, and, when these were human beings, in the manner in which they fell and shed their blood. This last method of soothsaying had been employed by the pre-Celtic Iberians, and was perhaps borrowed from them. The Druids too, apart from those who came from Britain, were mostly drawn from the pre-Celtic population. There was this difference between them and the ordinary priests. They took part in the election of kings and princes, marched into battle, and acted as legates or ambassadors. They also met once a year in the territory of the Carnutes — *i.e.,* near Orleans, at a spot which was considered the centre of the country — and there they settled all the private and public disputes that were laid before them. Whoever refused to acquiesce in their decision was excommunicated. These later arrangements are all connected with the customs with which we are now dealing. At the head of the Druids was a

FIG. 96. ALTAR AT SAINTES
From Clemen, " Religionsgeschichte Europas "

high priest. When he died the most outstanding of his colleagues succeeded him, or, if there were several of equal eminence, the other Druids elected one of them as his successor. Sometimes the office was filled after a series of combats between the rival candidates. This seems to show that the Druids were originally something more than priests only. Before they were received as Druids they had to pass through a period of training, which sometimes lasted for twenty years. Their doctrines were not in written form: they had to be learned by heart. According to Cæsar, the Druids " discussed the stars and their movements, the size of the world and of the various countries, and argued about the nature of things." Later writers go even farther, but we have the less hesitation in pronouncing the descriptions fanciful, seeing that the statements of Cæsar and others regarding the teaching of the Druids about the after-life are far from correct.

Cæsar and others declared that the Druids and the Gauls as a whole believed in the transmigration of souls, but according to more trustworthy accounts they only believed that the dead survived in another world. Like so many other peoples, they located this other world in the west, where the sun goes down. Claudian says of it:

> There soft movements are heard of shades that uncertainly hover,
> Moaning and sighing in sadness: there too the peasant sees ever
> Beings with faces so pale, figures of those who have gone hence.

According to Procopius, the settlers at the mouth of the Rhine believed that their dead lived on islands, or on one particular island named Brittia,

FIG. 97. MATRONS

and to this day the Bretons believe that the dead pass from Cape Race to the island of Tevennec or live in the " Bay of Souls." The Irish too believed in a realm of the dead in the south-west, while a few specially privileged men were thought to pass *without dying* to the Isles of the Blest. The offerings dedicated to the dead, of which we have already spoken, prove that the Gauls conceived of life hereafter as a continuation of the life on earth. This is further illustrated by the discovery in a grave in Berry of a pair of smith's tongs which the dead man had been wont to use, and by the fact that chieftains sometimes had their horses and war-chariots buried with them. The practice of having a war-charger led in the funeral procession of its master has lasted down to our own time in what was originally Celtic territory. The dead were entrusted with letters to be delivered to those who had predeceased them, and were even expected to collect debts which had been left unpaid. In fact, as a Latin poet puts it, death was the middle of a long existence. This explains why human victims were so often sacrificed, and why relatives of the dead frequently committed suicide. To the Celts death on the battlefield was preferred to death on a sickbed, but it does not appear that the life lived in this world affected a man's lot in the hereafter.

Alexander the Great is said to have asked the Celts what they most feared. The answer was: "Our greatest dread is lest the sky should fall on our heads." According to Strabo, the Druids expected that fire and water would one day swallow up everything. A conversation between two Irish scholars in the time of the Vikings also discusses the ultimate destruction of the world by fire and water. It is possible that the Celts expected that the gods themselves would perish, and that the Teutonic belief in the same catastrophe was learned from them. But this is another subject on which our information is incomplete.

BIBLIOGRAPHY

Renel, *Les Religions de la Gaule avant le Christianisme* (1907); MacCulloch, *The Religion of the Ancient Celts* (1911); MacBain, *Celtic Mythology and Religion* (1917).

8. TEUTONIC RELIGION

by Franz Rolf Schroeder

Teutonic religion is as old as the Teutons themselves. It is here that the problem lies. No problem exists, of course, for those who believe with Tacitus that the Teutons have lived from time immemorial in the countries they still occupy, and who look for the primeval home of all the Indo-Germanic peoples somewhere on the shores of the Baltic Sea, in North Germany, on the Danish islands, and in the south of Sweden. This opinion, however, can hardly be maintained. The question is extremely complicated, but so far as it is possible to answer it to-day we may say that South Russia has the best claim to be regarded as the earliest home of the Indo-Germans. A part of the original people must have left that early home about the middle of the second millennium B.C. or a little later, and moved to the north-west, subjugating the far more numerous aborigines of that region, imposing on them their language, and gradually completely amalgamating with them. It was from this mingling of the Indo-Germanic hordes with the aborigines that the Teutons sprang.

Thus it will be seen that it is impossible to decide with certainty what part of the Teutonic religious conceptions goes back to the aboriginal population and what was introduced by the Indo-Germanic ruling class. On the whole, however, the differences between the civilizations of conquerors and conquered can have been but slight, and therefore we may assume that in all essentials the same religious conceptions prevailed among both. The thoughts of both dealt with the matters that constitute the chief germs of religious life everywhere — viz., the phenomena of nature, beliefs regarding the dead, and the concerns of agricultural life. Water, earth, and air were full of spirits and demons of all kinds. Some of these beliefs endured side by side with higher manifestations of religion all through the millenniums, but others have ever and anon been begotten anew by the unchanging ' soul ' of the race.

It is with Cæsar and Tacitus, about the beginning of the Christian era, that our historical attestations begin. Tacitus' *Germania* (*c.* A.D. 98) opens with the story of the origin of the Teutons. According to it, all the Teutonic peoples are descended from Tuisto, a scion of Earth and his son Mannus. Tacitus names as the three highest gods of the Teutons Mercury, Hercules, and Mars, meaning by these Wodan, Donar, and Ziu. He tells of the sacred grove of the Semnones, which no one enters till he has been bound with a chain, and of the Alci, two brothers worshipped by the Nahanarvali. This pair is probably a part of the ancient Indo-Germanic inheritance, and akin to the ancient Indian Ashvins. Tacitus then gives a detailed description of the ritual of the goddess Nerthus, who was worshipped by Germanic tribes on the shores of the Baltic. In addition to these pieces of evidence we have a number of votive stones erected to their native gods by Germanic soldiers in the Roman service. Most of the names of the deities are replaced by the corresponding Roman names (the so-called *interpretatio Romana*), but many of the epithets employed are explicable only from Germanic linguistic sources and show that Germanic deities are meant (*e.g.,* Hercules Magusanus, Mercurius, Cimbrianus, Mars Thincsus, etc.). Scanty as these attestations are, they are invaluable to us, especially as they show that we may carry back over more than a thousand years a great deal of what has come down to us from Nordic sources of a much later date.

The later centuries tell us very little, too, about pagan religion on the Continent. Here and there, in ancient writers or in the lives of saints and other sources of a similar kind, we come upon a brief mention of a heathen ritual. For example, we are glad to have in the *Merseburger Zaubersprüche* (*Incantations of Merseburg*) at least two attestations (on which suspicion has recently been unjustly cast) of Germanic heathen beliefs, and to find mention made there, in the Saxon baptismal vow, of the gods Thunaer, Wôden, and Saxnôt, but we have practically no knowledge of the religion itself. The early Christian missionaries attempted to extirpate root and branch all that savoured of heathenism, and where they found that impossible they contrived to give the tenacious heathen conceptions a Christian colouring. For these countries, therefore, we have to fall back upon deductions from popular customs of the present day and upon the abundant relics of superstition. Such deductions are of course not always reliable, and they concern only the conceptions that were current in more primitive mythology.

Fortunately, however, we have an abundance of Nordic tradition; without it we should know next to nothing of Germanic religion. But this too raises many problems — far more, in fact, than it helps us to solve.

The chief sources are the two Eddas. The poetical Edda, an Icelandic collection of the thirteenth century, contains, besides heroic lays, about a dozen songs to the gods, and is of great value, because it contains the only specimens of Teutonic songs of this kind that we possess. The age of these songs has been the subject of much dispute. Each one demands separate investigation, and some of the suggested dates differ by five hundred or nearly a thousand years. Then we have the prose Edda, a sort of *ars poetica,* a manual for young poets, written by Snorri Sturluson, the greatest scholar and statesman of Iceland at the beginning of the thirteenth century. This work contains a large number of myths. Some of these are otherwise quite unknown, while others have been handed down in other versions or are alluded to elsewhere. Snorri's version, however, is not always a reliable rendering of ancient popular tradition. He has frequently altered his material and supplied additions of his own.

These are our most important sources, but there are others. Numerous Icelandic sagas provide valuable details, and the gorgeous poetry of the scalds, which abounds in quaint periphrases of simple expressions, the so-called *kenningar,* frequently draws its material from mythology. One example will suffice. In the oldest scald lay that has come down to us the shield is called " the sole of the foot of the thief of Thrud." This would be unintelligible if we did not know the Nordic myth of the giant Hrungir, who ran off with Thor's daughter Thrud. This myth tells how, while awaiting the angry god, Hrungir stands on his shield, because he has been warned that Thor will emerge out of the ground to attack him. Further light is also cast on our subject from Germanic runic writings, and some help is found in the religion of the Lapps and Finns, who borrowed from the Teutons numerous words, as well as many important religious conceptions. Finally, recent research into Scandinavian place-names compounded with names of deities has added greatly to our knowledge of the distribution of the various cults.

When we pass from the scanty tradition of the Continent and the British Isles, we find in the North an almost confusing multitude of gods and goddesses, and it is not always easy to distinguish the most important deities from the great crowd of *dii minorum gentium.*

Adam von Bremen, canon and head of the cathedral school, who wrote his *Hamburgische Kirchengeschichte* in the second half of the eleventh century, gives a brief but very valuable description of the most celebrated sanctuary of the North, the temple of Upsala. He says:

> In this temple, richly ornamented with gold, the people worship the images of three gods. Thor, the mightiest of the three, stands in the centre of the church, with Wodan and Fricco on his right and left. Thor, they say, holds the dominion of the air. He rules over the thunder and lightning, winds and rain, clear weather and fertility. The second deity, Wodan, *i.e.,* Rage (*Wodan id est furor*), wages wars and gives man courage to meet his foe. The third is Fricco. He gives to mortals peace and delight. . . . All their gods are provided with priests, who offer the sacrifices of the people. When plague or famine threatens, sacrifice is offered to Thor; when war is imminent, to Wodan; when a wedding is to be celebrated, to Fricco.

Here we have in the temple at Upsala three of the most prominent gods combined into a kind of trinity. From the standpoint of late Nordic paganism we can call them *the* three principal gods. Thor is the German Donar; for the second Adam of Bremen employs the German form of the name, Wodan (the exact North Germanic counterpart is Odin); and Fricco is the Nordic Freyr.

The position occupied by the images is worthy of notice. Thor stands in the centre, the two others on either hand. This is somewhat remarkable, because we know that in later pagan times Freyr (Fricco), not Thor, was the chief deity of the Swedes, and as such bore the additional name " god of the Swedes." The fact that Thor occupied in Upsala the place of honour points back to an older time when the god of thunder was the chief object of worship throughout the whole of the North. With the tenacity that is characteristic of every form of religion, this arrangement has preserved a trace of the older faith.

There was a time — not very long ago — when the opinion prevailed that all myths about the gods had their origin in myths about nature, and it was believed that every detail of every myth could be explained in this way. The most outstanding representative of this school was Ludwig Uhland. With the poetic delicacy that so greatly distinguished him, he took these Nordic myths to his heart, found in all of them myths of nature, and — no other words will express it — remade and reinterpreted them. To-day this is recognized to be a mistake. It was a complete misreading of primitive thought, though it would be equally erroneous to deny that some features of the Nordic myths can be explained in this way.

For example, the figure of Thor undoubtedly has its roots in the thunderstorm. It was, of course, not the natural phenomenon as such that primitive man worshipped, but the hidden, higher power that roused fear and dread when it revealed itself in thunder and lightning. It was only very gradually that this conception materialized into a deity with a human form, the god of the thunder and of the fertilizing rain, the god of agriculture, the red-bearded Thor, as the Edda describes him, driving along in his chariot drawn by he-goats. It was in this guise that he was worshipped by the Teuton.

From the lands lying along the lower Rhine and coterminous with the Celtic territory the cult of this god spread among all the Teutonic tribes. On the runic clasp of Nordendorf, near Augsburg, which probably belongs to the seventh century (Fig. 98), Thor's name occurs along with that of

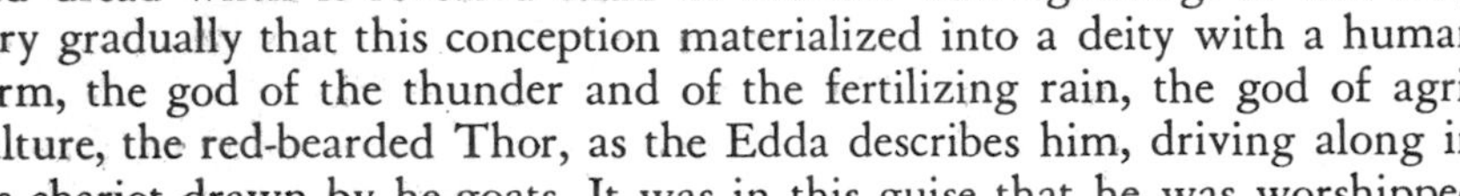

ᛟᚷᚨᚦᛟᚱᛖ   ᚹᛟᛞᚨᚾ   ᚹᛁᚷᛁᚦᛟᚾᚨᚱ

o g a th o r e   w o d a n   w i g i th o n a r

FIG. 98. THE GREAT RUNIC CLASP OF NORDENDORF
From Haas, " Bilderatlas zur Religionsgeschichte "

Wodan, and at Geismar, in Hesse, Boniface felled with his own hand the Oak of Thor, which, like the Oak of Zeus at Dodona, was believed to be the abode of the god of storms. It is chiefly from the North, however, that the evidence comes which proves how deeply the worship of Thor had struck root there, and whereas in Sweden he came to yield pride of place to Freyr, in Norway and in Iceland he continued to be the favourite deity of the people as long as paganism endured. An irrefutable proof of the high position occupied by this deity is provided by the fact that one in four of the population of Iceland bore a name compounded with Thor, while few names contained that of Freyr and none that of Odin.

In the Teutonic religion the relation between the gods and men is entirely different from that which prevails in Christianity and the numerous other Oriental religions. No doubt, especially in earlier days, the Teuton too entertained the sense of fear and awe in the presence of the divine, and Tacitus' account of the sacred grove of the Semnones undoubtedly suggests this. Yet when the Teutonic race had reached its manhood it stood before its deity with reverence, but boldly and without fear. The Icelandic sagas tell of many a man who entered into close friendship with this or that deity, and chose him as his confidant (in Icelandic *fulltrúi*). One such zealous worshipper of Thor was the Norwegian Thorolf Mosterbart, of whom we read in *Die Geschichte vom Goden Snorri,* when called on to decide whether he should come to terms with King Harold of the Beautiful Hair, who had subjugated the whole of Norway in the year 872, or should seek safety elsewhere, he asks his "beloved friend Thor" for guidance, and is directed to betake himself to the newly discovered isle of Iceland. Thorolf makes all ready, orders the temple to be demolished, and carries away with him most of the timber with which it was built and the earth on which the altar of Thor had stood. Accompanied by numerous friends, he puts to sea, and in due time they near the west coast of Iceland. Then Thorolf throws overboard the pillars of the altar that had stood in his temple, and on one of which Thor's image had been carved. Thorolf declares that he will settle wherever the pillars drift ashore, and at that spot he builds a new temple to the god. Very illuminating is the detailed description given in the saga of the building of this new holy house. It constitutes the *locus classicus* for the appearance presented by a Teutonic place of worship.

A mighty structure it was. In the side wall, near one gable, was a door. Within the door stood the pillars. In them were nails, called "divine nails." In the interior was a large space for sanctuary. Farther in, nearer the other gable, was a room resembling the sacristy or vestry in churches of to-day, and in it, in the centre of the temple floor, was an elevation like the site of an altar. On the altar lay a ring with unjoined ends, twenty ounces in weight. On it all oaths had to be sworn, and the priest wore it on his arm at all meetings of the Thing. On the altar stood usually also the sacrificial bowl for the blood, and in it was a sprinkler like a holy water sprinkler. With it was sprinkled the blood, called the sacrificial blood. This was the blood that was shed when the animals dedicated to the gods were killed. Round the altar in the separate room stood the images of the gods.

It is not surprising that we possess a large number of myths, some of them in the ancient form of lays, regarding Thor. They tell chiefly of his combats with giants, who find in him their fiercest foe. The majority of these myths, however, are late, and the plots are those usually found in folk-tales and romances. They have gathered round the figure of this deity, but they have no genuine religious content. One of them at least is certainly ancient — the myth of Thor and the Midgard serpent, which lies out in the ocean and coils itself round all countries. In a similar manner into the late Eddic lay of Hymir has been interpolated the myth which tells how Thor sits in a boat with a giant and, with a bull's head as bait, angles for this world-serpent. In his "Art of Poetry" Snorri vividly describes how these irreconcilable enemies gaze into each other's eyes. They will meet each other again when the destruction of the world comes, and fall, each mortally wounded by the other. On the gravestone at Gosforth the same scene is depicted (Fig. 99). This Northern Midgard serpent is to be classed with the Babylonian monster Chaos, Tiamat, the Jewish-Christian Leviathan, and the monster cat of Celtic saga, with which King Arthur does combat, with varying result.

FIG. 99. THE CROSS AT GOSFORTH
From Montelius, " Vara Forntid," 1919

From small beginnings the worship of Thor overran a very large part of the Teutonic world. It is a disputed question whether it overran it entirely. No doubt there were also other storm-gods before and contemporary with him. The East Teutons had one, Fjörgynn, of whom we know hardly anything but his name. He is akin to the Lithuanian Perkuna and the Indian Parjanya. Like so many other local deities, he must have been ousted by Thor. In Upsala also there seems to have been another deity, earlier than Thor — viz., Ullr, whom later Icelandic pedantry transformed into Thor's stepson. We know little about him, but the few hints that do exist seem to indicate that he too had to give way to Thor. According to Adam of Bremen, there stood beside the temple at Upsala a sacred tree whose wide-spreading branches were green summer and winter. It has been suggested that this was a yew-tree. As a verse of an ancient Edda calls Ull's abode "Yew valley," and local names near Upsala (such as Ulltuna) prove that the worship of the god was known in that district, the suggestion is perhaps not too far-fetched.

These examples show that in the Teutonic religion, even in prehistoric time, changes were in progress. In many places local cults spread beyond their own narrow bounds either because of political events or in virtue of their own religious power. For example, the worship of the radiant sky as a personal deity must have reached the Teutons at a very early period, and of the ancient Teutonic sky-god Tyr, as he is called in the Norse form (it is the same name as the German Ziu and the English Tiw, which still survives in the word ' Tuesday '), it can be definitely said that he was not known to the aboriginal population, but was introduced by an Indo-Germanic tribe. This is, indeed, proved by his name, which is linguistically akin to that of the supreme deity of the Indians, Greeks, and Romans (Dyaus, Zeus, and Jupiter). At an early time, however, Tyr lost his supreme position and became the god of war — a transformation which was quite likely to happen among a people so warlike as the Teutons of those times. Even Tacitus hints at this development when he calls Tyr by the name of Mars. His chief rival was Wodan.

We have already seen that in the North Thor had become the god of agriculture, and it is not difficult to understand the high esteem in which he was held by an agricultural people. In all ages fertility and good crops have been two of the most important needs of mankind. Men's eyes have always been turned to sky and earth. Golden sunshine and the rain from heaven had to render the soil fertile if ripe harvests were to be secured. And primitive man sees everything in the mirror of his own daily existence. He constructs the macrocosm after the fashion of his own microcosm. Heaven and earth thus become for him the divine spouses living in " divine wedlock," the fertilizing heaven being mostly regarded as the husband and the conceiving earth as the wife. " Hail to thee, O earth, Mother of Men," runs an Old English alliterative prayer. " Bring forth fruit in the divine embrace, filled with food to feed mankind." And as late as the seventeenth century Friedrich von Logau says of the month of May: " This month is a kiss bestowed by heaven on earth, making her now a bride and by and by a mother." This is the meaning of the myth regarding Zeus and Hera, which tells how " beneath them as they lay couched in love on the crests of Ida the divine earth sent forth fresh new grass " (*Iliad*, XIV, l. 347); of the myth of Zeus which tells how he shed a rain of gold on Danae; and of the myth of Zeus and Semele, for the latter name is the Thracian word for earth. Similarly, the ancient Teutonic Tyr, the god of the sky, was the husband of the earth-goddess, who was also called " the Darling " (of the god of heaven), for that is the meaning of the name Fria (Norse Frigg). Only a few traces of Tyr's marriage to the earth-goddess have been preserved. One is found on Hardanger Fiord, in Norway, and even this only becomes intelligible when we call in the aid of place-names. Ousted by Wodan from his predominant position, Tyr had also to yield up his spouse to that deity, and Paulus Diaconus, the historian of the Langobardi, has a droll tale of Wodan and Frea which strikingly recalls the Homeric story of Zeus and Hera which has just been mentioned.

Many of the customs of rural life which are still tenaciously retained in many country districts, although their meaning is no longer understood, go back a thousand years. The setting up of a maypole on the first of May or on Whit Sunday or on Midsummer Day seems to be depicted on rock-drawings in Sweden belonging to the Bronze Age, and reflects primitive conceptions. The maypole is the demon of vegetation in tree form. It was only gradually that the tree or tree-trunk developed into a god with a human form, and then we have the vegetation god shown with the tree which originally was itself the deity. The same holds true of Attis in Asia Minor with the pine, and of Osiris in Egypt with the sycamore. The Whit Sunday brownie or bogie-man who also appears in present-day rural observances, a young lad dressed in foliage, is also a representation of the demon of vegetation in human form.

In the annual cycle of nature vegetation pushes up in spring from the fertile earth, in summer it clothes itself in rich foliage and blossom, and in autumn, after yielding its fruits, it fades and withers away, to awake to new life in the new spring after the long sleep of winter. Out of this natural phenomenon arose the belief in a god who, born in the spring-time, grows up as a beautiful youth, is slain by an evil spirit, the demon of winter, and next year resumes, amid festivities, his previous career. This is the explanation of many Christian customs (for example, the Easter celebrations of Notker the Stammerer, a monk of St Gall in the ninth century, are clearly connected with the myth of the seasons), and also of the myths of Adonis, Attis, Osiris, and many others. The most outstanding Teutonic myth of this kind is that of Balder, to which we shall return.

Above all others, Freyr is really the god of fertility, in men, animals, and plants. Adam of Bremen tells us that when paganism was passing away he was still represented *cum ingenti priapo*. (See Fig. 100.) His female counterpart is Freyja, who is both his wife and his sister. In these two, Freyr and Freyja, whose names mean simply " lord " and " lady," various conceptions have been intermingled. Sometimes they are thought of as a heavenly couple, but most frequently they are spirits of vegetation, Freyr being the male and Freyja the female element. All life arises from the union of male and female. Present-day popular customs everywhere include vegetation couples of this kind — May King and May Queen, count and countess, or, in more primitive form, corn-man and -wife, he- and she-goat, or simply old man and old woman. All these couples, however, are not mere survivals of the two Teutonic fertility deities, Freyr and Freyja; they represent an older, lower stratum, from which Freyr and Freyja were developed, but which they transcended.

There is only one lay — but that one of the finest in the whole Edda — that sings the praise of Freyr. It is the lay of Skirnir. It tells how the god, afire with love for Gerd, the giant's daughter, sends forth his servant Skirnir to seek for him the hand of the maid. Only after using dire threats does Skirnir gain the consent of the shy Gerd and her promise to meet Freyr in the grove of Barri after three days. This is simply a new myth of the wooing of the earth-goddess by the god of the sky, whose part is here taken by Freyr. The chosen rendezvous indicates this, for Barri means " among the corn." The union is to be consummated there. A similar practice is still followed in connexion with popular marriage customs. It is a sort of analogy magic. The embraces of the human couple represent the bridal union of sky and

earth, resulting in abundant yields. The meeting of Freyr and Gerd is represented on a number of rectangular plates of thin sheet-gold w h i c h were found in the county of Jäderen, on the coast of Norway. These depict a man and a woman, the latter holding in her outstretched hand a stalk with a blossom or a leaf (Fig. 101).

We have s e e n t h a t F r e y r became the national deity of Sweden. The Swedish royal dynasty claimed d e s c e n t from him, but his original home was rather Jutland or Denmark — perhaps in the districts where the kindred cult

of Nerthus arose. This latter cult also came northward, but at a very early date the female deity Nerthus was changed into a god of the same name (in Norse, Njörd). According to the Norse myth, Njörd married Skadi, and became the father of Freyr and Freyja. Together they constitute the divine dynasty of the Vanir, whereas Thor and Odin are the heads of the family of the Æsir. Very complicated problems are involved here, which cannot be further discussed owing to limitations of space. Different cycles have been intermingled, and there are numerous contradictions, of which probably the people of that time were unaware. There was no rigid dogma that combined them into a coherent, harmonious structure.

From Sweden the cult of Freyr was carried into Norway, but evidently it was confined to certain localities, of which Drontheim was the chief. We are also told that this deity was worshipped in Iceland, but there too Thor ranked far above him. One zealous worshipper of Freyr was Thorgrim of Iceland. The saga tells that when he died the south side of his grave-mound was always free of snow, and people said that Freyr loved him so dearly that " he would allow no coldness between them." Another saga tells how

FIG. 101. FREYR AND GERD
From the Bergens Museum, Aarbog, 1909

Hallfred built a temple to Freyr, dedicated to the deity a steed named Frey-faxi, and forbade any man to ride it on pain of death.

Besides Freyr and Freyja, there were of course a great many other local fertility deities. This was probably the original character of Loki, who in his after development borrowed some of the features of the Christian devil. He was the Mephistopheles among the Norse gods, the chief figure of the *Loka-senna,* or *The Scoldings of Loki,* in which he satirizes the weaknesses of all the gods and goddesses to their faces. It is an excellent satire, full of high spirits, comparable perhaps with Seneca's *Apocolocyntosis* or with Lucian's *Deorum Concilium*. Lucian's Momus vividly recalls Loki.

Especially numerous were the female deities of fertility, and there are many traces of the "ritual of matrons" in the regions lying between Celtic and Teutonic territory. These goddesses included Volla (who is mentioned in the second Merseburg incantation, and whose name in the north was Fulla), Gefjon of Zeeland, Idun, the keeper of the rejuvenating apples of the gods, and many more, of whom we shall mention only Frau Holle. Her worship was mostly confined to Central Germany. She was the giver of fertility, and also the guardian of the spirits of the departed, just as Freyja, according to a lay of the Edda, received half of those who fell in battle, Odin receiving the other half. We see here the same close connexion between the vegetation deities and the gods of the underworld which we have already noticed in the myth of the deity that died and rose again. The earth is the source of life, but it is also the realm of the dead.

The beliefs regarding the dead are even more significant than the conceptions revealed by the agricultural rituals. The present-day acceptance of the dualism between soul and body dates back to very early times. It has been suggested that the Teutons received this dualism from Christianity, but that is very unlikely, for the same belief is found all over the world. Not only at death, but also during sleep and in dreams does the soul leave the body. It is now only a metaphor when we speak of Iphigeneia's soul seeking the land of the Greeks, but in olden days it was a fixed belief. In the shape of a bird (often a pigeon), a serpent, or a mouse the soul leaves the body and passes through varied adventures. It is sufficient to recall the legend of the Frankish king Guntram, related by Paulus Diaconus.

More ancient still is t' ' conception of the living corpse — the belief that a man's life does not   se at death, but that in the guise of a vampire, spectre, or apparition h . can return to disturb his relatives. Only when the body has completely decayed can death be said to have really taken place, and primitive thought ascribes this process of decay to the action of invisible demons who devour the corpse. There are hounds of hell, eagles, wolves, and demons of horse-shape who tear the dead to pieces. The name of the giant Hräsvelg ("Corpse-devourer"), the wind-demon who lives in eagle form at the north end of the world, betrays his original connexion with this type of thought. In course of time this animal-shaped demon was conceived as possessing a human shape, and the horse or wolf or dog merely indicates a feature of his character.

It was thus that arose the conception of Wodan and the story of how he gallops along on his eight-legged horse Sleipnir. Originally Wodan and his steed were identical, and if the rider of the eight-legged steed shown on the gravestones in Gothland (Fig. 102) represents a dead man being carried away by the horse-demon, and not Odin mounted on Sleipnir, this conception was still current in Gothland at a much later time.

It seems to me to be one of the most certain results of research into Teutonic religion that the figure of Wodan originated in the beliefs regarding the dead. The conception of the god, however, did not grow only out of the conception of the horse of the dead. It is, in fact, impossible to derive from one single source any of the great figures of the more advanced religions. In many districts we still find the belief in the wild hunt, the fierce army, the host of spirits who rush through the air during the " twelve

FIG. 102. GRAVESTONE AT TJÄNGRIDE, GOTHLAND
From the Bergens Museum, Aarbog, 1909

nights " under the leadership of Wode. The relationship between Wode and Wodan is similar to that which we have met between the vegetation deities of modern popular customs and Freyr and Freyja. Wode is more primitive than Wodan. And here again we have the conception of the storm-demon. When the air is full of the noise of the storm, is it the souls or is it the wind? They cannot be separated. It is the soul that speaks in the roar of the wind, and thus the god of the dead becomes also the god of the wind.

Like the worship of Thor, that of Wodan originated in lands bordering on Celtic and Teutonic territories. In my opinion this older view is to be preferred to that of those scholars who hold that the cult of Wodan was common to all Teutons or was derived from the south-east. It was the last of the three great cults to reach the North, and it never became widespread among the Nordic peoples. This was due to his quality as god of the dead, to whom human sacrifices were offered. Although later poetry had much to say about him, the average man must always have thought of him with a shudder. He was not a god of the common people, but the god of the upper classes, the war-god of rulers and their Courts, who led his favourites from victory to victory, but who also at the critical moment might suddenly withdraw his favour and doom them to ruin in order to carry them off to Valhalla. Valhalla was originally the hall of the dead, and was regarded and depicted as a battlefield where the warrior lived on just as he had fallen, with bleeding wounds and shattered cuirass. By and by this hall of the dead was transferred to the bright realms of the sky, and there Odin and his faithful ones lived a life of pleasure. His warriors, however, the Einherjar, are at all times armed, and ready, when the end of the world shall come, to fight the last great battle with the hostile demons. " The notables who fall on the field pass to Odin, but the vassals pass to Thor," says the poet in a lay of the Edda. That poet was a devotee of Odin, and seeks thus humorously to contrast the intellectual superiority of Odin with the clumsy boorishness of Thor. Odin is the god of all intellectual powers, the inventor of runic writing, the father of magic, and the source of poetry.

All advance in civilization, taking the word in its narrower sense, comes from a few select minds. The mass of the people is and ever remains uncreative. They continue to think and feel in primitive ways. It is the same in the sphere of religion. The religious life of the multitude is still in essentials what it was thousands of years ago. True, Christianity has changed and recast it, but every one knows to what extent superstition still rules in the hearts of men to-day. And what is superstition but primitive religion? Even the religion of educated people originated in primitive ideas and is inconceivable without them, although it has transcended them and finds expression in higher forms. These forms, however, are the work of individuals gifted with special capacities. By virtue of their more intense religious experience, which is the source of their creative power, by virtue of their inward impulse, which is frequently reinforced and strengthened by external influences, they raise the religion of their day to a higher standard. And there is a further consideration. While the religion of the multitude remains essentially unchanged, the religion of the more educated undergoes changes. It is determined and coloured by the great inward and outward experiences to which chiefly the upper sections of the people are exposed. When we look at Teutonic religion from this point of view we should expect that the centuries which shook the Teutonic world to its foundations would also have been of decisive importance for the religious ideas of those peoples. I mean the time of the migration of the nations. I think it can be shown that this was actually the case, and in the history of Teutonic religion we can distinguish two strata differing clearly and essentially from each other.

The older stratum I should like to call the Teutonic, but this does not mean that it contains nothing but what was indigenous to the Teutons. It was at this stage that the outstanding divine figures which have been mentioned gradually emerged and attained importance beyond that of the hosts of demons. This emergence was not a mere mechanical development; it was a series of creative acts. It has been suggested that the emergence of personal gods among the Teutons was a result of contact with the far older civilizations of the near East. It is difficult to adduce proof for this, but it must now be admitted that even at this stage, which we are calling Teutonic, influences from the near East which afterward proved to be enduring were already at work, especially in connexion with the deities of fertility.

There are a number of religious conceptions of an entirely different character, which, I think, can be completely explained only as the result of influences emanating from the countries lying round the Mediterranean Sea during the centuries immediately before and after the opening of the Christian era. We may therefore call this the Hellenistic stage. The influences referred to include those of Christianity so far as these existed at this early date. (As a matter of fact, it is not always easy to say which of these Christian influences were early and which were late. Iceland was perhaps first affected.) In the first centuries of our era Southern lands were under the influence of the -astral cult, which after Alexander's death poured like an irresistible flood over the whole of the inhabited world. According to this cult, the secret of existence lay concealed in the starry firmament. The constellations were the invisible gods to whom supreme honour must be paid. This belief found acceptance among the Teutons also, and especially affected, as I believe, their ideas of Valhalla. In face of this fatalistic belief in the inescapable stellar powers men began to seek comfort in the mystery religions. These almost without exception go back to ancient rituals of fertility and burial, but from being mere agrarian cults they developed into religions that promised salvation. Traces of the earlier stage are everywhere clearly apparent, but they had lost all reality and power in the minds of pious men. The old ideas were spiritualized. It was "salvation" that men were now seeking, and although the ancient customs survived outwardly unchanged, they had taken on a new and more profound meaning.

In the belief of the devotees of these mystery religions the life of the universe unrolls in a series of "great years" or world-periods — what the Greeks called αἰῶνες. When such an æon reaches its culminating point appears the deliverer, the saviour, who redeems himself and all mankind from the dominion of the material world. The ascension of this saviour into the higher celestial regions is the signal for the dissolution of the present æon. The world passes away, overwhelmed by fire and water, to rise again like a phœnix from its ashes into a new existence.

The southern Teutons fell under the spell of these conceptions, and Hellenistic influence on Teutonic religion is in some instances plain and palpable. Not only is there evidence that the Teutons were familiar with the idea of great world-periods. According to a method of calculation that had its origin in Babylon, an æon comprises 432,000 years, and we meet with this identical number among the Teutons. A strophe of the Edda says that Valhalla has 540 gates and that through each of these pass daily 800 Einherjar on their way to battle. That gives a total of 432,000 Einherjar. This cannot possibly be a mere coincidence.

It is in this connexion that we come upon the figure of Heimdall and the more important figure of Balder. The Nordic myth tells how evil dreams warned Balder that danger was threatening him. Frigg, his mother, made all things swear that they would do him no hurt, but, thinking it too insignificant, she overlooked the mistletoe. Loki discovered this, and plucked a sprig of mistletoe; when all the Æsir had assembled to hurl all kinds of missiles at Balder — although none of these could harm him — he approached the sightless Höd and handed him the sprig, telling him to throw it at Balder. Mortally wounded, Balder had to go down into the realm of Hel. The goddess Rind, however, bears a son to Odin, who grows up to avenge Balder. The latest researches have clearly proved that Balder was originally a fertility god closely akin to Freyr. The myth, as has been already said, embodies the idea of the god who dies and rises again. (Balder's avenger is really the risen god in person.) But Balder passed beyond this stage of being a fertility deity. The special ethos and the unique note of the myth have always been profoundly felt, and this can be explained only by the influence of the mystery religions during the period of the migrations of nations. It was the work of a Teutonic priest who desired to reconcile the faith of his fathers with the new thoughts. Balder's figure henceforth occupies the central place in all that happens in the cosmos. This is the view of the world that is given in the opening poem of the Edda, the *Völuspa,* or *The Prophecy of the Sibyl.* That great poem, the greatest of all the alliterative poetry of the Teutons, describes the course of a world-period, an æon extending from the creation of the world to its destruction and the rise of a new earth. Balder's death is the point round which all that happens in the world turns. It is he who gives the signal for its overthrow, and the mental vision of the sibyl sees the approach of fresh hosts of malevolent demons who seek the destruction of gods and men. Thor, Odin, and Freyr fall before them, and all the elements are thrown into disorder. " The sun goes out, the land sinks into the sea: the bright stars fall from heaven: smoke and fire rage everywhere: the heat rises to the sky." But after all the old things have passed away, out of the waters rises a new earth, and a blessed day dawns. The choice of words betrays that a Christian poet of Iceland has added many touches to the poem, but the whole lay is the product of nearly a thousand years. The East contributed incidents like that of the Wolf Fenris, who, having broken his fetters, dyes with blood the seats of the gods, and later centuries interwove Celtic material, but the nucleus of the poem, with its tinge of Hellenistic and Christian ideas, carries us back to the times of the migration of nations.

It has become increasingly clear that Teutonic religion is to a large extent a religion that has been Teutonized. We may mention two other examples. The myth of the creation of the world out of the separate members of the body of the primeval giant Ymir is of foreign origin. The closest analogue to it is found in the doctrine of the Persian Gnostic sect of the Manichæans. And there is the profound but obscure myth of Odin's self-immolation on the world-tree. On it he hung for nine nights, with a spear wound, a sacrifice to Odin — i.e., Odin himself a sacrifice to himself. Although the connexion has been strenuously denied, this myth cannot be dissociated from Christ's death on the cross.

We have thus seen that, long before the Teutons were definitively converted to Christianity, many Christian thoughts had found their way among them. In Germany and England that conversion took place early, in Denmark and Norway not till toward the end of the tenth century, in Iceland in the year 1000, and in Sweden last of all, at the beginning of the twelfth century. But it was long before the " white Christ " expelled the ancient gods from the hearts of the people. Thor was the last to go. To this day he survives in the national saint of the North, St Olaf, who is depicted with a red beard and with an axe in his hand, after the manner of Thor with his hammer. The saga, too, of the Norwegian king Olaf, son of Tryggvi, tells how that hero met Thor on the high sea. " The people of this land," says the god, " continued to call on me for aid in their times of need, till thou, O king, destroyedst all my friends. Does that not call for vengeance? " With these words he turned his head and looked at the king with a bitter smile. Then he threw himself overboard as quickly as if an arrow had been shot into the sea, and was never seen again. The sorrow and pain caused by the disappearance of the ancient gods could not be more tellingly expressed.

BIBLIOGRAPHY

Mogk, *Germanische Religionsgeschichte und Mythologie* (1906; 2nd ed., 1921); Axel Olrik, *Nordisches Geistesleben* (translated by Ranisch, 1908) and *Ragnarök, Die Sagen vom Weltuntergang* (translated by Ranisch, 1922); Helm, *Altgermanische Religionsgeschichte* (vol. i, 1913) and " Die Entwicklung der germanischen Religion, ihr Nachleben in und neben dem Christentum," in *Germanische Wiedererstehung* (edited by Nollau, 1926); Neckel, *Walhall, Studien über germanischen Jenseitsglauben* (1913) and *Die Überlieferungen vom Gotte Balder* (1920); Naumann, *Primitive Gemeinschaftskultur* (1921); F. R. Schroeder, *Germanentum und Hellenismus* (1924) and *Altgermanische Kulturprobleme* (1928).

9. SLAVIC RELIGION

by Karl H. Meyer

At the time when the conversion of the Slavs to Christianity began, they already occupied territory extending from the Baltic Sea and the river Elbe to the Adriatic and the Black Sea, and in the East to beyond Kiev and Novgorod; that is to say, they were no longer one homogeneous people. The process of conversion began in the south-west, in Pannonia, in the sixth century, and about the end of the ninth century Christianity was introduced among the southern Slavs (Slovenes, Croat-Serbs, and Bulgarians). The conversion of the Slovaks and Czechs began about the ninth century and that of the Poles and Russians toward the end of the tenth century. The Slavs on the Saale, the Elbe, and on the shores of the Baltic Sea became converts to Christianity in the course of the eleventh and twelfth centuries.

Our information regarding the expiring pagan religion of the Slavs does not come from a pagan source. We possess no hymns in honour of Slavic gods, no epic that tells us of a Slavic Olympus. In other words, we lack the source which is of greater value than any other because it reveals the depths of the heart, where religion lives. Apart from a few scanty notes of Arabic travellers, our information is derived chiefly from Christian writers. Some of these were either not interested in Slavic paganism or ignorant of it, like Procopius in the sixth century; others were hostile foreigners, like Thietmar of Merseburg, who died in 1018, Saxo Grammaticus, who died about 1110, Helmold, who died after 1177, Ebbo, Herbord, and an anonymous writer in the biographies of Otto, Bishop of Bamberg, in the twelfth century; still others were Slavs, like the Kiev chronicler, the so-called Nestor (1110), the translator of the Greek *Malalas,* and some sermon-writers (*slova*). They all tell us very little about Slavic paganism. This left all the more room for the play of imagination, and the scholars of the seventeenth, eighteenth, and the beginning of the nineteenth centuries claimed to know more about the religion of the pagan Slavs than anyone will pretend to know to-day. The purely archæological sources are very inadequate. The origin and genuineness of the few statues which have been found on ancient Slavic territory have been called in question, and some of them are so late that, like the ruined temples, they must be regarded as proofs of outside influence on expiring Slavic paganism. Therefore they cannot be used as sources for a description of ancient Slavic paganism, and we do not reproduce them as illustrations here. Present-day popular customs and beliefs no doubt reflect many elements of ancient Slavic paganism, but it is even more difficult than usual to draw inferences from Slavic folklore and to reconstruct from it the beliefs of the pagan Slavs. On the other hand, an excellent source for our purpose is provided by the Slavic language, and in the absence of the usual aids we shall use it freely in our description of the religion of the ancient Slavs. The current conceptions of a people necessarily find linguistic expression — *i.e.,* they find their way into speech. If, therefore, we come upon words used by the original people which express definite religious ideas, we are justified in inferring that these ideas existed; and, *vice versa,* if certain words are entirely lacking it is extremely probable that the corresponding conceptions were unknown. Further, for a people like the ancient Slavs, who were almost entirely untouched by other civilizations, religion is predominantly a matter that calls for care (*religere* as contrasted with *neglegere*), attention, and caution. Therefore conceptions that belong to the sphere of religion are usually expressed with special caution or by means of circumlocutions. As a result, the words used to express religious ideas frequently do not conform to the ordinary laws of phonetics or linguistic form. They are either weakened or appear as composites whose simple elements have vanished. Examples will be given as we proceed.

Although widely different opinions are held regarding the religion of the pagan Slavs, it is generally agreed that the period lying between the separation of the small original Slav people, which till the end of the fourth century A.D. occupied the territory that now forms the republic of Poland, and the conversion to Christianity of the various Slav peoples was marked by an unusual degree of change and development in religious conceptions. The chief feature of this development was the emergence of individual deities. Hitherto the only religious conceptions current among the people were those of spirits, demons, dread powers of darkness, and the mysterious powers of nature as collective beings. The original Slavs had no Olympus, or at most only the germ of one. In the period after the Slavs became a separate people this germ developed into the beginnings of personal gods, and even in some cases into actual personal deities. The stages of this evolution were very unequal in the east, south, and west, and the progress was greatest in those districts where the new faith, Christianity, was latest in arriving. It is therefore easy to understand why the Slavs on the Elbe and on the Baltic have a fuller Olympus than the Russians, and why the Russians have more deities than the southern Slavs, who, so far as we know, did not possess even one single personal deity. The fact that this great development took place not only helps us to understand the descriptions that have come down to us of a very well-furnished Slavic Olympus, but also warns us not to carry back to the primitive period even the best-attested facts adduced by the early writers already named.

Ancient without any doubt is the idea of and the word for 'god' (*bogŭ*).

Probably this is derived from the Iranian language. That the word originally meant 'wealth,' 'abundance,' may be inferred from the adjectives *bogatŭ*, 'rich,' *nebogŭ* and *ubogŭ*, 'poor.' From meaning 'rich' it came to mean 'owner of wealth' and then 'giver of wealth,' and this specific meaning was probably long retained, just as the Greek name Pluton never lost its connexion with πλοῦτος, 'wealth.' Whether the word *bogŭ* originally meant a person — like Pluton in Greece — or was used in the plural to mean 'higher beings,' 'gods,' or finally 'deity' in the abstract, like τὸ θεῖον, cannot be decided offhand. Probably it included all three meanings, for there is no doubt that from the very beginning of the tradition the same word was used to indicate the heathen gods, the Christian God, and abstract deity.

Very ancient, too, are both the idea of and the word for 'demonic being.' The word is *běsŭ*, meaning something 'disagreeable,' 'ugly,' or 'horrid.' It is the word used in the oldest Slavic writings for the 'devils' cast out by Jesus. The demoniac is *běsĭnŭ — i.e.,* a person who has a *běsŭ* or several *běsy*. On the other hand, the devil who took Jesus up to a high mountain is never called *běsŭ*, but *dijavolŭ*, a word borrowed from Greek. This shows that the Slavic conceptions of the time did not include an individual demon as opposed to deity and that therefore the word *běsŭ* was collective. But as soon as we try to deduce from present-day popular Slavic beliefs the nature or the separate types of *běsy* our difficulties begin. Among these is the belief in a power possessed by the spirits of the departed. The word for 'spirit,' *duchŭ*, is very old. The original meaning is 'breath,' and it has a female doublet, *duša*. This is not the same as, though it is very similar to, the Latin doublet *animus* (Greek ἄνεμος) and *anima*. Both Slavic words meant and still mean the breath and the soul of a living as well as of a dead man. The ancient Slavic graves, with the numerous utensils given to the dead, speak an unambiguous language. And to this day there is a widespread faith in the power possessed by spirits and souls that is utterly at variance with Christian conceptions. Similarly, it is widely believed that the soul of the dead man flies out through the window or by some other exit in the form of a bird (swallow, nightingale, cuckoo, pigeon, or crow), a bat, bee, fly, wasp, butterfly, or mouse, and that the spirits of the departed continue to exist as *ubozĭje* ('poor fellows'), *dědŭ*, or *dědŭko* ('grandfather' or 'little grandfather'), *roditeli* ('ancestor'), or *baba* ('grandmother'). They are conceived as having the form of an old man — more rarely that of an animal (a serpent) — and their place is behind the stove. As evil spirits they can bring upon the house illness, poverty, and wretchedness, and become vampires or apparitions. They are easily irritated, and it is important to avoid mistakes in dealing with them. The werwolves (wolf-men), who are known in the south under the name of *vĭlkodlakŭ* and elsewhere under various other names, were perhaps originally a species of demons. They were souls of the dead in animal-form, and inflicted injury on mankind. But if the souls of the dead were kindly remembered and provided with food and drink, if their due festivals were observed — the third and the ninth days after burial were important dates — then they acted as guardian spirits (in Russian *domovoj*), looked after the house, barn, and stables at night, and shared in all domestic joys and sorrows. In short, they might be either harmful or helpful. There are still some districts where wooden or clay images of the dead are set up in a corner of a room and are called " gods."

As a matter of fact, death occupied a very prominent place in the minds of the ancient Slavs. To them death seemed something violent and uncanny, and as a result it was spoken of not by its own name of *mirtis* (compare the old Indian *mrtih* and the Latin *mors*), but by an indirect name, a compound, *sŭmĭrtĭ*. This points to taboo. It will be remembered that as far back as Homer the Greeks personified death and called it " the brother of sleep," and made it a demon. The first Slavs also had the conception of a realm of the dead, which they called *rajĭ*. In the historical period this was regarded as a happy place, analogous to the Christian Paradise. The place of punishment, *pĭklŭ*, seems to have been a later conception, due to foreign influences. *Pĭklŭ* means ' pitch.' In the Christian terminology it occurs less rarely than the borrowed word *geona* as a translation of the Greek γέεννα. Sometimes the Greek word is rendered by *rodĭstvo*. This is simply an error due to the confusion of γέεννα with γενεά, and shows that the earliest Slavs knew nothing of a hell as a place of torment for the dead.

A special place among the demons, who probably owed their existence to the belief that the spirits of the dead possessed certain powers, was occupied by the Vilen and Rusalken. The Vilen perhaps go back to primeval times. There is no explanation of their name, but they were analogous to the Valkyries. They were maidens, treacherous and full of malice toward their enemies, well inclined toward their friends, fond of dancing on the greensward, bellicose and scheming. They were young and fair, but could change themselves into serpents and birds. According to the poets, they were children of the dew and rain, and preferred to live in springs, rivers, and the sea. This hardly justifies us in thinking that they were water-nymphs, for, in contrast to what we know of the Indians, Persians, Greeks, and Teutons, there are no sure indications that the earliest Slavs considered water to be in any way sacred. The Vilen were often found far away from water, in rocks or woods and on mountains. Some of them even had their home in the stars.

Judging from their name, we should say that the Rusalken were of later origin. The name is derived from *rosalia,* an old festival name, but it is quite possible that they displaced older types of similar demonic beings. Their worship was very deeply rooted among many of the Slav peoples, and the prohibitions of the Christian Church have failed down to the present day to repress festivities in their honour. Food is offered to them, and garlands and pieces of cloth are thrown into the water or hung on trees, practices which seem to show that they were believed to be departed spirits. They live beside or in the water. They bathe at night in the sea or dance on the shore. They use the branches of trees as swings or rest among growing crops, and bewitch or mock or hurt people passing by. The fanciful descriptions of these two kinds of demons given by later poets have masked many of their original characteristics, but it is difficult to deny that they had their origin in the beliefs regarding the souls of the departed.

It was not till a comparatively late period that the Slavs came to believe in an actual god of the dead, like the Greek Hades or the Indian Yama. We can trace the actual development from demon to personal deity. The figure that thus arises is that of Volos, who is so frequently mentioned in Russian sources. His name is phonetically identical with the Veles of the west. There is no trace of him in the south. In the west, among the Czechs, Veles is not an individual deity, but a generic being who can be called either a devil, a dragon, or a goblin. In the east — in the *Kiev Chronicle* and elsewhere — Volos is the name of the god of cattle or stock-raising, although as a rule the task of looking after the cattle and the household falls to the house-spirit, the departed ancestor. Further, repeated and emphatic mention is made of the fact that solemn oaths are sworn " by Volos," and this inevitably recalls the practice of the Greek gods of swearing " by Styx." When we also take into account the facts that the cognate Lithuanian word *vėles* means ' images of the dead ' and the old Norse *valr* means ' those who died on the battlefield,' we can have little doubt as to the real nature of this Volos who attained the rank of deity only among the East Slavs. Veles or Volos was originally the dead ancestor, a demonic being, who in the last centuries of paganism became in Russia a personal deity. In the *Kiev Chronicle* we are told that Vladimir after his baptism ordered the image of Volos to be thrown into the river, and in the life of St Abraham of Rostov we read that the saint destroyed the image of Volos worshipped by the Finns there. Długoš, Canon of Cracow (died 1480), says that the heathen Poles worshipped Nyja as god of the underworld and guardian of the souls of the dead, guiding them into fairer fields. But this is all that we know of Nyja, and we hesitate to draw inferences from it.

Among other demons of primeval Slavic paganism were the female Fates. Sacrifices in the shape of green corn, honey, cheese, and bread were made to them till far on in the Christian period. Vigorously but vainly, both by tongue and pen, the Christian priests opposed this practice, but it exists to this day among many of the more ignorant Slavs. These Fates were called *rožanicė* among the East Slavs; this is their name still in the east and south; in the west they were known by other names. They are female demons, sometimes old and sometimes young. They spin the thread of life and determine human fate. They are thus analogous to the Roman Parcæ or the Norse Norns. What they were originally we do not know, but the etymology of the name may cast some light on the matter. The usual explanation is ' mothers,' but this is very doubtful for various reasons. The word is derived from *roditi,* ' to beget ' or ' to bear,' a derivative, causative verb, not from *rodŭ,* the root of that verb. The chief meaning of this word at the present day is 'race,' 'tribe,' or 'lineage,' sometimes 'birth,' sometimes 'fruit.' The Slavic (not the Baltic) language has lost the old stem for 'giving birth' or 'birth' (*gen-, gon-*), and therefore this can be only a secondary meaning of the stem *rod-.* Further, old compound words, which frequently retain original meanings best, show that the oldest meaning of the word *rodŭ* was 'fruit' in the botanical sense. For example, in Ukrainian *urod* means 'rich harvest,' *nerod* 'bad harvest'; the Russian *urožoj,* the Polish *urodzaj,* means 'good harvest'; in Czech *úroda* means 'fertility.' Finally, it frequently happens that 'fruit' in the botanical sense takes on a secondary meaning applicable to organic life, and comes to mean 'birth' (as the result of begetting), whereas I am not aware that the reverse process ever occurs in language. Indeed, in view of the primitive man's method of thinking, it is more improbable, although it should be remembered that primitive man looks upon natural objects and human beings as being very closely related. If, therefore, the Slavic *rožanicē* had their origin in primeval belief, and not — which can hardly be supposed — in later Slavic time, they were fertility demons, distantly related to Demeter and Ceres. If this is correct, the later, wider meaning of the *rožanicē* is easily understood. To an agricultural people like the ancient Slavs fertility and abundance are synonymous with fortune and fate; Ceres develops into Fortuna. Besides, it is very natural that in view of the change of meaning of 'fruit' to 'descendants,' with the derivative *roditi,* 'to beget' or 'to bring forth,' the *rožanicē* should be associated with this meaning, and, especially in women's minds, come to denote the deities of female fertility.

Besides these demonic beings the East Slavs had a male personal deity, Rodŭ. So far as is known, his nature was in no respect different from that of his female companions. His name, which probably meant 'giver of fruit,' points to great antiquity. And as Rodŭ and the *rožanicē* seem to go back to primeval Slavic time, so they continued to retain their position more tenaciously than any of the other pagan elements in the Christian period. To be sure, neither Vladimir nor any other built temples either to Rodŭ or the *rožanicē.* Their roots lay less deep in the centres of civilization than in human hearts. It is no wonder that Procopius had never heard of them, and declared that the Slavs did not believe in a *heimarmene.* His Slavic informants prudently kept as deep silence regarding these forms of darkness as did his non-Slavic sources. Dlugoš identifies with Ceres the Polish personification of dying nature and death, the figure of Marzana decked with corn ears and flowers, but we need not attach great weight to the statement. It must also be left an open question whether, as some of his functions seem to suggest, Svantovit, whom we find (he is mentioned in Helmold and Saxo) at Arkona, in the island of Rügen, was originally a fertility deity.

Among the prehistoric Indo-Germans, so far as we can gather from Aryan,

Greek, Teutonic, and also Baltic tradition, the most important part of religion lay in the worship of natural objects like the sky and the earth, sun, moon, water, wind, and fire. In ancient Slavic mythology, on the other hand, there is no indication whatever that such homage was paid to the sky, earth, or water. The original word for 'sky' has disappeared. It has been replaced by the word for 'cloud' (*nebo* — compare the Greek νέφος). And even although a few Russian songs speak of " Moist Mother Earth," that does not prove the existence of earth-worship in ancient Slavic times. Water once meant a taboo in the Slavic tongue, but that might be explained by phonetic and formal peculiarities of the Slavic word *voda*.

The wind is indicated by a word of active meaning, *vētrŭ,* 'that which blows,' and the air by late compounds like *vŭzduchu* ('exhalation') and *povētrĭje,* but this gives no foundation for mythological combinations. Nor can we build on the fact that present-day Slavic superstitions personify the winds. It is significant, however, that late Polish and East Slavic tradition mentions the wind as a personal deity. In Polish it is called Pogwizd (pronounced 'Pochvist'), in South Russian Pozvyzd. According to the lay of Igor, where the winds are addressed as " Stribog's grandsons," the wind-god's name is Stribogŭ. There was an image of Stribog at the Kiev Court. Finally, Długoš mentions a Polish goddess Pogoda, " Temperies," the giver of favourable wind.

Our sources indicate that the worship of the sun was far more prominent than that of the wind. That it goes far back is proved by the linguistic form of the name — it is a diminutive. The Slavic word is not the equivalent of the Lithuanian *Sauli* or of the Latin *sol* or of the Greek ἥλιος; it is the term of endearment *sŭlnĭce.* This is, indeed, a characteristic feature of Slavic forms of worship: the gods are addressed in terms of this kind. The Slav came into the presence of his god not with solemnity or awe, but with filial affection. Among the West Slavs the name of the fire-god Svarogŭ was used exclusively in the diminutive form of endearment, Svarožič (Svarožic). It is only among the East Slavs that we find certain attestation of the sun as an individual deity — viz., Dažĭbogŭ, to whom, as the *Kiev Chronicle* tells us, Vladimir consecrated a statue. He is called a son of (the fire-god) Svarogŭ (*vide infra*), and in the lay of Igor the Russians are poetically called " Dažĭbogŭ's grandsons." The name Dažĭbogŭ is ambiguous. It is doubtful whether it is genuinely Slavic or a foreign name transformed by popular etymology. If it is Slavic it means 'liberal giving'; if it is of later origin it means 'the god of giving' — either meaning would suit a Slavic Helios. On the other hand, it must be remembered that an Indo-Germanic root (*dhegh* or *dhōgh-*) means 'burn,' 'heat.' In Slavic this would take the form of *dag, daž-* and it occurs in all Indo-Germanic languages that are spoken in the countries that surround the Slavic territory. In the Slavic south the form *dabog,* 'lord of the earth,' is found, so this lack of agreement among the Slavic languages themselves means, as it does in so many cases, that there has been borrowing.

The moon too was worshipped as divine, although this aspect of the religion was not so widespread. The ancient appellation *měsęcĭ*, which is cognate with the Latin *mensis,* etc., occurs only in the diminutive form meaning ' dear moon,' whereas the actual moon is called *luna,* which is cognate with the Latin *luna,* the latter a name with no religious associations. If we are correct in thinking that the diminutive form for moon indicates that that luminary was worshipped, then there is no reason for doubting the statements of ancient Russian and South and West Slavic sources that the pagan Slavs worshipped the moon. A few sources speak of a worship of the stars, but the fact is not widely attested.

Among the powers of nature, fire was held in great reverence by the pagan Slavs. The best ancient sources state that it was worshipped, and to this day on exceptional occasions, when cholera or plague is raging, when important events are happening, or on the festival days of certain saints, the primeval custom is followed by producing ' living fire' by friction. Whether Iranian influence has been at work here must be left undecided, but there is no doubt that, as may be inferred from the etymology of the word for fire, the Slavs inherited fire-worship from prehistoric times. The Slavic word for fire, *ognĭ,* is not directly cognate with either the Lithuanian *ugnis* or the Latin *ignis,* but it is related to both, and this indicates that the word for fire had a special meaning and denoted a taboo. The god of fire was Svarogŭ (or, in the form of a term of endearment, Svarožič, Svarožic), identified by the Russian gloss on Malalas with Hephaistos and by later Russian sermons with fire itself. That the Obodrites on the Baltic worshipped this fire-god is confirmed by Thietmar and others. Especially in Retra his image was honoured above all others. It is a matter of dispute whether the worship of the personal fire-god goes back to primeval Slavic days or whether his worship in Russia and on the Baltic is the result of later intercourse and is indigenous only in one of these two places. Both opinions are supported by authorities on Slavic mythology. If we keep in mind that the original small Slavic people had no temples, with the necessary priests, altars, and other appurtenances, and that personal deities require all these; further, if we take into account that, though it cannot be proved, it is highly probable that there was commercial and therefore also cultural intercourse between the cities on the Baltic and Kiev and Novgorod; and, finally, if we remember that there is absolutely no trace of the deity among the Southern Slavs, Czechs, or Poles, then, it seems to me, we must conclude that either the Russians or the Baltic Slavs must have borrowed the practice. Which of them borrowed from the other is uncertain. Seeing that fire-worship is indigenous in Russia, while the only indication of it among the Baltic Slavs is the worship of Svarožic just mentioned, probably the latter were the borrowers. The form of the name is a matter on which opinions differ.

Possibly it is genuinely Slavic, meaning 'the quarrelsome person,' 'the brawler,' and as such it may be a tabooistic paraphrase for 'fire.'

We have still to consider those pagan religious phenomena of the Slavs which do not go back to the original Slav community, and a few others about which there is really very little to say. The name that occurs to the ordinary man of to-day when Slavic deities are mentioned is Perun. The word *perunŭ* is Slavic, and means literally 'beater.' It came to signify 'thunderbolt' and also, as the Polish language shows, 'lightning.' This seems to exclude the possibility that Perun was an original Slav deity, for it is quite out of the question that the name of a deity should be preserved and transferred to one of his attributes while the deity himself is forgotten, though the converse process has frequently taken place. There are numerous cases in which a natural phenomenon like lightning has been personified and transformed into a god. Therefore it is to be assumed that among the original Slavs *perunŭ* simply meant 'lightning.' Further, there is no indication that phenomena like storms, thunder, lightning supplied the original Slavs with permanent religious conceptions. Finally, as far as reliable attestations go, it was only in the east — indeed, only in Kiev and Novgorod — that Perun was worshipped as a deity. If the form Porenutius, which is given by Saxo Grammaticus as equivalent to Pomerania, means Perunic, the diminutive of Perunŭ, we should have here, as in the case of Svarogŭ, another example of borrowing by the Baltic Slavs from commercial centres in the interior of Russia. In the two Russian cities that have been named, Kiev and Novgorod, the Scandinavian Teutons exercised great cultural and political influence, and the supreme Teutonic god was Thor, the god of thunder. Therefore in my opinion the deity Perun was borrowed from the Teutons. Accordingly, Perun is a comparatively late Slav deity, who quickly came to occupy an outstanding position in Old Russia, and whose influence spread not only to the Baltic shores, but also perhaps into the Balkans (compare Pyrin, in Chatzon, and Porun, in the early Bulgarian Alexandreis) and to the Slovaks (as Parom). These changes in the form of the name indicate borrowing. According to the *Kiev Chronicle,* Perun, the god of lightning, was also the guardian deity of oaths. On a hill near Kiev there was a wooden statue of him, with a head of silver and a beard of gold. The people of Novgorod also made an idol in his honour. After the baptism of Vladimir (in the year 988) the glory of Perun began to fade. The statue at Kiev was tied to a horse's tail, disgracefully beaten, and thrown into the river Dnieper. A similar fate befell the idol in Novgorod. Among the East Slavs the place of the pagan god of lightning, Perun, was by and by taken by Elijah, the Old Testament prophet, who commanded the lightning, water, and the winds.

Before their conversion to Christianity the Baltic Slavs had adopted a considerable number of new gods. These were chiefly gods of war, who were supposed to give protection and help in the hard struggle for existence against the invading Teutons. In all probability they were merely local appellations of the one deity Mars rather than separate personalities. We know very little about either their origin or their later developments. There was Radogost in Retra, the chief centre of the Obodrites, where he had a temple and images till they were destroyed in 1068. There was Svantovit at Arkona, in the island of Rügen, where the ruins of his temple are still to be seen. Korvey monks identified him with their patron saint, St Vitus, who, they say, preached the Gospel in Rügen, but this is merely a monkish tale. In Wolgast we find an analogous deity in Jarovit (Gerovit); in Stettin and elsewhere there is Triglav ("the Three-headed"), and elsewhere still Bugievit.

Native Russian sources (and also the lay of Igor) mention along with Volos, Perun, and some others another noteworthy deity, Trojan. Of his sphere and functions nothing is said, but his origin is not obscure. He is none other than the Roman emperor Trajan, who in the years 101–102 and 105–106 subdued Dacia and received divine honours in the character of Cæsar Augustus. In the Balkans also we find "Zar Trojan" playing a part as the spectre of darkness. He is often depicted with wings of wax or with ass's ears, and these point to a connexion with the myths about Dædalus and Midas.

We may add here a few names of gods who were known in Russia, but regarding whom all details are lacking: Chŭrsŭ (mentioned in the lay of Igor as the sun-god), Mokoši (a female), and Simarĭglŭ, whose very name is so far quite obscure. Among Polish gods Dlugoš mentions Dzydzilelya, who was perhaps a guardian goddess of children, if her name is correctly understood. According to Dlugoš, she was a kind of Venus, a giver of children. There was also Drzewana, whom the present writer identifies for linguistic reasons with Diana, and Żywie, the god of life. Absolutely obscure are the names of the East Slav deities Rinovit, Turupit, Pizamar, Prove (worshipped in Stargard), Tiarnaglofi (probably "Black Head"), and various others.

It was after the breaking-up of the original Slavic unity that there appeared the temples, statues of the gods, altars, and priests of whom we hear so much in the sources when individual gods are named. There is no native Slav word for any of these. There are, it is true, Slav words for 'magic' and 'magicians,' who can control even the demonic powers. But the word even for the pagan 'priest' and the word for 'altar' had to be borrowed from the neighbouring non-Slavs. 'Temple' and 'image' had to be expressed by borrowed words or by native words which had originally a different meaning. Of ritual such as flourished in ancient India there was none, and could be none, among the Slavs, who lived scattered over their forests, marshes, and fields.

BIBLIOGRAPHY

The work in which for the first time the problems of ancient Slav religion are dealt with in a thorough, scientific manner, and with an exhaustive bibliography, is written in the Czech language: Niederle, *Život Starých Slovanu* (Part II, vol. i, 1916). It is chiefly a collection of sources that is given in Mansikka, *Die Religion der Ost-Slaven* (1922). Very meritorious are the critical — occasionally hypercritical and self-willed — works of Brückner, especially his *Mitologia słowiańska* (1918); it has been translated into Italian under the title of *Mitologia slava* (1923, with a preface and list of authorities).

10. JAPANESE RELIGION

by F. E. A. Krause

From the point of view of their civilization the Japanese are a young people. Whereas the origin of Chinese civilization is hidden from our sight in the mists of prehistoric time, what can be called civilization in the islands that constitute Japan dates only from about the year A.D. 400. It arose under the strong influence of China, and in historic times Japan must be considered as having been intellectually completely dependent on China.

Our present theme is the religion of the Japanese previous to their contact with a superior alien civilization. We shall see that it is in this sphere that the ancient Japanese mentality is most clearly displayed, although as time went on all forms of religion underwent profound changes.

Going back to primitive times, we find that the national religion in Japan, as in China, consisted in nature-worship and the worship of ancestors. The manner of the rise and development of these two ideas, however, was entirely different in the two countries. It was not the observation of nature and the complete inclusion of human life in the great harmony of the universe that gave rise to religion in Japan; it was the child of the youthful imagination that knows nothing of logic. The first expression of Japanese thought is the fairy-tale.

In the oldest literature, especially in the *Nihongi,* which was reduced to writing after the year 700, we read the fanciful story of the creation of the world by the divine pair Izanagi and Izanami. Thereafter their children took over the *rôles* of the gods of nature. The story is told with complete *naïveté,* and, as might be expected in view of the low level of civilization of the people among whom it originated, the behaviour of the gods is at times highly obnoxious. This absence of definite moral ideas is a pronounced characteristic of the oldest Japan.

Although ancestor-worship in Japan has many features in common with that in China, it is understood in an entirely different manner. It originated not in a desire to find a fitting place for the departed souls in a unified nature charged with all manner of potencies, but in the feeling of fear of the dead. In ancient Japan ancestor-worship was not based on the conception of an enlarged family including both the living and the dead; on the contrary, the desire was to be separated from the dead, and the purpose of offering them worship was to gain their goodwill.

We obtain here a glimpse of that dread of uncleanness which was one of the most powerful factors in the religion of old Japan, and of which we shall see many examples. The dead are unclean. The dead body, instead of being cared for, is hurriedly disposed of. The dwelling in which the deceased man died is abandoned by the survivors. This also explains why, in the oldest time, the rulers always sought another place of residence, until a different way of thinking made possible a permanent home for the emperors.

After the house where a man died had been abandoned by his kindred it became a temple in which worship had to be paid to his spirit. All the national Japanese temples retained the form of a simple wooden house roofed with rushes, even the temples in which the deities of nature were worshipped.

As time went on Chinese customs began to affect ancestor-worship. It became a domestic rite, and it was carried through on lines that closely imitated the Chinese practices. Its character was thus profoundly altered. The Japanese adopted the ancestral shrine from China. There the spirits of the dead were supposed to dwell, and it stood on the *kamidana* with the symbols of the gods. The practice of burial was abandoned in favour of the Buddhist custom of cremation. The vague Japanese ideas regarding a realm of the dead gave way to the Buddhist conceptions of various hells and heavens. In ancient Japan there was no thought of reward or punishment for human actions; indeed, religion had no bearing whatever on morality.

Whereas in China religion can in its entirety be called a system of morals, and every religious act was rooted in ideas that were universally binding, in Japan the very idea of morality and every application of it to religion were due to foreign influence. Japanese ethics were summed up in a dread of uncleanness — in a purely external sense. Cleanness was demanded, uncleanness meant sin, and the lost state of purity could be regained only by ritual performances. This view found its culminating expression in the Great Purification (*Ô-harai*), which was enjoined on all twice a year and which developed into a solemn act of ritual. The ethical system of a later day was entirely built up out of ingredients borrowed from Confucianism and Buddhism.

The attitude of Japanese thought to the world as a whole had a far-reaching effect on the forms of religion. Whereas the Chinese regarded their country and their people as the universe, and looked upon every human life as being related to the cosmos, the Japanese point of view was always limited to the nation. This is one of the main points of difference between the two peoples. This limitation of outlook has given Japan in historic time the strength it has displayed, and it could not fail to leave its mark on the national religion. We hear nothing of gods of nature, only of gods of Japan; we hear nothing of the sun as a power of the universe, it is the Japanese sun-goddess. Similarly, we hear of the Japanese god of the sea, of the deity of Mount Fu-ji, the protector of the Japanese rice-fields, and of others.

These gods were beings similar to men, and had definite proper names. They lived and acted like the Japanese themselves, and the national myths ascribed to them many actions that were all too human and extremely ungodlike. In complete contrast to the Chinese way of thinking, the Japanese conception of the divine was from the beginning and always distinctly personal and anthropomorphic. Unsophisticated popular belief created for every phenomenon a divine figure, with a name and definite qualities. Nature was animated not by impersonal powers, but by innumerable specific deities and corporeal spirits of every kind.

Not only was nature thus portioned out among deities, but all human affairs were placed under the care of special tutelary deities. These presided over the various crafts and callings, and even over inanimate tools and utensils. The *naïve* Japanese mind was continually busy constructing a petty deity for everything that met the eye. Similar activity was shown by a widespread superstition that invented for all aspects of Japanese life the drollest spirits and demons in human and animal shapes. Thus arose a Japanese pantheon the individuals of which it is impossible to enumerate. The Japanese themselves declare there are " eighty myriads " of them!

All these gods were called *kami,* higher beings, who inhabit a higher region. Worship was paid to them in the home, in the village communities, and at special sanctuaries. Some famous shrines, like that of the sun-goddess at Yamato, in Ise (Fig. 103), and the place of assembly of the gods at Kizuki, in Izumo, go back to the most ancient times. But in Japan there are none of the city-gods that are so numerous in China, because the Japanese cities came into existence at a later date, under the influence of alien civilizations.

The really characteristic feature of the national religion of Japan is due to a peculiar association between religious ritual and the civil government. Indeed, the Japanese word for ' government ' (*matsuri-goto*) really means ' affair of ritual.' This indicates that the office of ruler was originally a religious dignity. The head of a clan (*uji*) was the high priest of the distinctive god of that unit (*uji-gami*). *Vice versa,* the social classification of the people was based on the principle that those who worshipped the same deity constituted a clan. In the ancient clan-state the ruler of the district of Yamato, which was under the special protection of the sun-goddess, gradually obtained political hegemony over the numerous other chieftains, and thus became Emperor of Japan as a kind of *primus inter pares.*

In this manner the worship of the sun-goddess Ama-terasu became the most prominent in the whole country. To bring prosperity to the country by performing the rites due to her was the duty of the supreme head of the state, who, from being a clan-chief, had himself become the overlord of all. His political power was largely based on the supreme importance of the

religious duties that fell to him. The imperial palace became the very
centre of the national religion.

A further step was the linking-up of the lineage of the imperial family
with the sun-goddess, so that the emperor now paid homage to the deities
of nature as to his own ancestors. Similarly, other ancient clans traced their
descent from definite deities, preserving the ancient clan organization. The
position of the emperor in Japan was therefore entirely different from that

FIG. 103. TEMPLE OF THE SUN-GODDESS AT YAMATO
From Kern, " Das Licht des Ostens"

of the ruler of China. He was not " the Son of Heaven " and the sole representative of the world-mind on earth. He was merely the descendant of
the sun-goddess Ama-terasu, and, as chieftain of Yamato, had happened
to attain pre-eminence over the other chieftains, who were also descendants
of gods. It was under Chinese influence that this conception of the position
of the emperor in Japan was radically altered.

This conception that the leading families were descendants of deity
gave a different colour to ancestor-worship. Its one sole root had been fear of

the spirits of the dead. It now became linked with the realms of the gods of nature. The two aspects gradually coalesced, and by a subsequent process of development the conception of worship as a form of ancestor-worship gradually gained prominence at the expense of the homage that was paid to the gods of nature as such.

Belief in the gods, which, as we have seen, was at first without system, became systematized by being thus related to the central figure of the emperor. Japanese religion now had its centre in the State, and it was this that gave it its typically national form. The official cult paid homage to the ancestors of the emperor, and the emperor, as the descendant of the supreme sun-goddess, became himself divine. In the homage paid to the divine emperor the religion of the Japanese nation thus found a centre of gravity that gradually attracted all the centrifugal elements of its varied pantheon and its world of spirits.

The Japanese national character favoured a development of this kind, although it implied an entire reversal of the ancient beliefs. In the Japanese mind the tie that binds the people to the emperor is stronger than that which connects the members of a family with each other. A different view is held in China. In Japan loyalty to the emperor outweighs duty toward parents. This reveals a fundamental difference between the two peoples which has made itself felt throughout the whole range of social and political life. Indeed, this fact must be kept in mind when one considers the historical development of Japan. It is the one force that has counteracted foreign influence and prevented the complete preponderance of the Chinese civilization in the Land of the Rising Sun.

This strongly marked national consciousness also enables us to understand why, in addition to the emperors and their ancestors, men who have rendered great services to the State and the nation have been raised to divine rank. This practice has attained great dimensions in Japan, and throughout the whole country there have arisen local cults in honour of great generals, wise statesmen, and great patriots. Indeed, these deified heroes arouse extraordinary enthusiasm among the people, and are worshipped with as much fervour as the deities who preside over good fortune.

The national religion of Japan includes no dogma, no metaphysics, no ethics. The ritual is extremely simple. The temples contain no images. On the altar rests nothing but an (invisible) mirror — the symbol of purity. The oblation to the deity consists of prepared foods, *sake,* and flowers. The original Japanese ate meat, and before Buddhism was introduced the offerings included meat foods, chiefly game. But living sacrifices were never offered. Worship is paid to sacred trees, and many objects are regarded as fetishes.

The construction and furniture of the native temples (*miya*) are very unlike those of the Buddhist sanctuary (*tera*). The famous holy place of the sun-goddess is the temple at Yamato, in Ise. It is rebuilt every twenty years. To it and to many other shrines pilgrimages are made, and these processions form a characteristic feature of Japanese life. Celebrations in the temples assume the form of popular festivals, so that religious services present a joyous spectacle. Ritual and myth are intermingled. Dances and dramatic performances serve to disseminate among the people the old folk-tales. The religious customs retain some measure of connexion with an ancient phallic ritual.

There was a professional priesthood, strictly classified and graded. They conducted the temple services and performed the ritual, but otherwise were simple citizens. They were at liberty to marry, and could hand down their office to their sons. Callings were strictly governed by inheritance in ancient Japan. At the head of the national religious life stood the family or clan of the Nakatomi, whose modern representatives are the influential noble family of the Fujiwara. The priests wore their official dress only when doing duty in the temple. Very strict regulations were laid down to ensure purity and cleanness.

The national religion of Japan, whose chief features have now been described, is called Shin-tô ('the way of the gods'). It received this name only when it became necessary to distinguish it from the foreign Buddhism (Butsudô). The description given in the foregoing pages is to a large extent a reconstruction. Our knowledge of Japan as it was before it came into touch with China is very imperfect, and all the information that has come down to us bears marks of Chinese influence. This is the case even with the line of descent of the emperors. We must also keep in mind that within historical time there has never really been either a pure Shin-tô or a pure Buddhism, and that at all periods we find mixed forms and variations on the same theme.

The entrance of Chinese civilization into Japan was very soon followed by the introduction of Buddhist doctrine, which was the most effective of all the agencies that helped to spread Chinese influence. It was through Buddhism and its representatives that Japan received its entire civilization, and this is equivalent to saying that the spirit of that religion, in its peculiar Chinese form, also found entrance into Japanese life. In China itself Buddhism had never been of first importance, because it was strongly resisted by the State. The latter was based on Confucianism, which was essentially a State religion. In Japan, on the other hand, Buddhism was only the second and subsidiary religion of the country, next in importance to the indigenous beliefs, although it took first place in the political and intellectual life. It is never possible to separate what is purely Japanese from the framework of Buddhism in which it has been fixed by the development of a thousand years. Though we have done this to some extent in the foregoing pages with Shin-tô, it should be understood that in reality that religion has a strong Buddhist colouring.

Chinese civilization was introduced into Japan almost simultaneously with the coming of the Buddhist teaching. The Tai-kwa reform, which practically revolutionized the State constitution, implied also a conflict between the national Shin-tô and alien Buddhism. The extirpation of the Mononobe family by the clan of Soga meant the triumph of Buddhism, which soon became the State religion. Something now happened in Japan which would have been inconceivable in China. The emperor, who was himself the embodiment of the national religion, adopted an Indian religion which had been introduced in his empire in a Chinese dress. This decided both the political development of Japan and the character of its civilization. From the nature of things the influence of Buddhism could not fail to be infinitely more far-reaching in Japan than it had been in China.

The development of Shin-tô, the indigenous religion of Japan, has been greatly impeded by the strong influence of Buddhism. It can even be said that as a religion it has never reached completeness; the ascendancy of Buddhism has prevented this. In Japan, as elsewhere, Buddhism adopted into its own system the deities of the country, and the process of amalgamation proceeded exactly as it had done in China, where Taoism had been relegated to a subordinate position. The result in Japan, however, took an entirely different form, because, while Taoism in China was a faith rejected by the Government, Shin-tô was the actual national religion of Japan which had been exchanged by the imperial Government for an alien faith.

As early as the eighth century this amalgamation of Shin-tô and Buddhism was reduced to a rigid system by the priests Dô-shô and Gyô-gi. Ere long, through the labours of the famous sect-founders Den-gyô Dai-shi and Kô-bô Dai-shi (about the year 800), this system was completely unified under the name of Ryô-bu Shin-tô. It is characterized by the complete predominance of Buddhism. All later efforts to disentangle Shin-tô in its pure form from this amalgamation have failed. Even the great renaissance of ancient Japanese thought in the eighteenth century, which is associated with the names of Moto-ori Nori-naga and Hira-ta Atsu-tane, failed to achieve complete success in this direction. In the Meiji era of New Japan Shin-tô was at first declared to be the State religion, but the Government was not able to make this decree effective, and was finally compelled, in the new constitution of 1889, to grant the nation complete religious liberty. This proved that among the people at large Buddhism had more living power than Shin-tô. The old religion was only a shadow of its former self, and it has now little more than an archæological interest.

It is not a part of our task to inquire how this amalgamation of Shin-tô and Buddhism was carried out, nor to examine the attitude of the various Buddhist sects to the national religion. Nor can we here enter into details regarding the transformations through which the various deities have passed. Even some of the national heroes have been affected by the change, and of the gods of good fortune worshipped by the common people three are of Indian and two of Chinese origin.

The historical problem of the Japanese religion has been entirely different from that of the Chinese. In China it was a question of establishing and maintaining an orthodox form of religion suitable in all respects for the purposes of the State and capable of meeting its needs. All other forms of religion — native or alien — were definitively relegated to a subordinate position. In Japan, on the other hand, there was a complete fusion of the national faith with Indian doctrine, and the new religion made its influence felt in every sphere of life. Its effects were not confined to the sphere of what was strictly religious, and it profoundly influenced and changed the whole intellectual life of the nation. The result was not, as in China, a syncretistic religion consisting of an almost pure national religion with an admixture of foreign elements. In Japan the national spirit was completely permeated with Buddhism, and the result has been an entirely new civilization for the Island Empire.

BIBLIOGRAPHY

Florenz, *Japanische Mythologie* (1901) and *Die historischen Quellen der Shinto-Religion* (1919); Aston, *Shinto, the Way of the Gods* (1905); Rathgen, *Staat und Kultur der Japaner* (1907); Schiller, *Shinto* (1911); Krause, *Ju-Tao-Fo, die religiösen und philosophischen Systeme Ostasiens* (1924).

IV. THE WORLD RELIGIONS

1. RELIGION OF THE HEBREWS

by Leo Baeck

With the Hebrew religion an entirely new formative principle appeared among mankind. In the history of religions it stands for a revelation or, what is the same thing, a revolution, and as such it has been one of the most powerful forces of civilization and become a world religion.

Revolution — of course we are using the word not in a political, but in its intellectual and spiritual meaning — is not the same thing as mere reform. The latter aims only at a new form. It seeks to secure continued validity for something that already exists; and this it does either by bringing it back to its true and original meaning or by leading it on to better and more unambiguous results. Reform is new only in a qualified sense; it is a new expression of an old way of thinking. In revolution, on the other hand, we hear the voice of something that is fundamentally new. It is the first expression of an entirely different way of thinking. It claims to be an absolute beginning, and therefore it completely rejects all that has hitherto existed. It demands a breach with the entire past, with all that has been and with all, other than itself, that is. It claims to be, not an evolution, but a new creation. Even from a purely historical point of view, therefore, and apart from the supernatural, a religion that thus appears on the scene as a revolution bears the character of a revelation, a new beginning from which everything must proceed.

But also in a supernatural sense — and this is another respect in which it differs from mere reform — such a religion comes into the world as a revelation. It is able to stand up for the One Thing, and therefore to oppose everything else, only because it knows itself to be the working of the sole higher power that exists, the Word that comes forth from God. A mere reshaping of something that exists, however thoroughgoing it may be, is felt to be merely a work of man. It is the perfecting of a talent, or of a moral code, or of a form of piety. It never claims to be anything else. But when the way is being prepared for something that is quite new and different, for the One and Absolute, there is a disclosure of the Beyond, a revelation. Into the heart of the man who experiences this comes that which is higher than he. He now knows something whose origin is hidden. His light and strength come from the Beyond. Confident of his prophetic office, he proclaims to men the message that has come to him from God, the Eternal.

It was through men who had had this experience that the Hebrew religion came into existence. Its nature and its results are due not only to its contents, but also and in equal measure to the fact that it was shaped and formulated by men of revelation, by prophets. These men were prophets in a quite special sense; they have no peers. They had, like others, their mysterious experiences. Like others, they were often in the grasp of ecstasy. The consciousness that they were touched by God overwhelmed them, body and soul. But it was not that, or it was least of all that, which made them prophets of Israel. All these things they shared with seers of a different kind. What made them the unique prophets they were was something else. It was the call which they experienced, the commandment that came to them to carry out the work of God, to form anew humanity and the future. It was the realization that they had been appointed to stand up for the one, the essential thing, against their nation and their time that constituted their unique quality and gave them their importance for the world.

This also distinguishes the Hebrew prophet from the mystic. The mystic too has his moments of ecstasy; he knows what it is to be rapt away; it is in such hours that he has his knowledge of God. But he lacks the impelling conviction that God has laid a task upon him. He has his place, and there he stands rapt in the Divine, but he knows nothing of a path that he must prepare, a road that he must tread. To him his experience is an end in itself. It is both beginning and end. He never advances beyond it. To the prophet, on the other hand, his experience is a summons, an equipment for his mission. It is only a preliminary to his activity, and it is in his work that he becomes a prophet of the Eternal. In spite of the mystery that breathes in them no words could be less mystical, less ecstatic, than those in which Jeremiah tells how God laid hold upon him. "The Lord said unto me, Say not, I am a child: for to whomsoever I shall send thee thou shalt go, and whatsoever I shall command thee thou shalt speak."[1]

Here, too, on the very threshold, lies the explanation of what is often called the ethical character of Hebrew prophetism. The prophet is conscious of having been called of God to proclaim to men the one absolute message that comes from God, and it is with it and its demands on his lips that he comes forth to men. What distinguishes him is not that he claims to predict the future, nor even that he is under compulsion to speak. These would not mark him off from others. What sets him apart is that it is the *commandment of God* that he must preach to men, and his predictions refer only to that future which is determined by the fear of God and disregard of Him. He is "full of power by the spirit of the Lord,"[2] so that his theme is and can only be righteousness and wickedness. The

---

[1] Jer. i, 7.　　　　　[2] Micah iii, 8.

inward compulsion and the inward conviction have assumed a moral character. Therefore it is always the categorical imperative that he utters. He cannot soften it down nor omit any part of it. He never bargains with the world nor concludes a compromise with it. He can afford to be indifferent to what men call facts, to what they regard as success and victory.

In turn, this ethical character implies the universalism that ultimately reached maturity within the Hebrew religion and made it a religion for the world. It is to men as such that the message of the Hebrew prophet is addressed. It is the moral imperative that he preaches, and that demand knows no limits, no bounds such as are set by States and peoples. It is addressed to every man whoever and wherever he may be. The prophet, it is true, is the prophet of Israel, for everything that concerns men arises and grows within the confines and even within the barriers of a definite human community. But he is not the prophet only for Israel. The word that laid bare to Jeremiah the meaning of his call was heard by all the other prophets of Israel also. " I have appointed thee a prophet unto the nations. . . . See, I have this day set thee over the nations and over the kingdoms." [3] They addressed, it is true, their message first to their own nation. Their ardent love constrained them to abide with their own people. But their eyes and their words were always directed to all nations. This expression " the nations," " all nations," or, as it sometimes runs, " all the families of the earth," " all the ends of the earth," came from the mint of the prophets. It is this expression and the prominent place it occupies in their activity that gives the religion of Israel its character of a world religion.

With perhaps even greater clearness this universal character comes out in that revelational, that revolutionary element which is inherent in prophetism and therefore in the religion of Israel. The mere reformer confines his efforts to the sphere with which he is immediately concerned. He creates new social or ecclesiastical or political structures, but these, however important they may be, are limited to their own range. But religious revolution aims at permeating the world with a new religious principle, and it is into the whole world that the new ferment is poured. It aims at a new world. This imperative that comes from the Beyond; this great contradiction of the world as it is, is one that seeks the ear of the whole world. It is the power that resides in this idea, not the power of numbers; not its extension, but its intension; not its success or expansion, but its nature and its aim, that make it a world religion. This inward power, this capacity to produce and shape and grow, is peculiar to the religion of Israel. It is this that makes it a world religion. At an early stage it became conscious of it, and this consciousness found expression in the assurance that Israel was an elect nation and in the conviction that the goal of all history was contained in that election.

This commandment, addressed to the world and claiming the ear of the whole world, could of course find expression only when Israel's horizon

[3] Jer. i, 5, 10.

began to expand and wider distances came within their view. Only then was it possible to hold the conception of a history of the world. The world Israel knew was Nearer Asia and the adjacent countries of Africa and Europe — the territories covered by the names given in the tenth chapter of Genesis. The peoples there enumerated are regarded as a unit appointed by God. They are all descendants of Noah and his sons, the sole survivors of the Deluge. The knowledge that these peoples existed enabled them to rise to the conception of a world of men and of a history of it, and to formulate the idea that all peoples, however much they differed in face and in speech, and however different their history and their countries, were parts of one whole. And the territory which their horizon thus embraced was veritably a world. It has been of outstanding importance for the history of our own civilization. From it we have derived all our essential powers, and the most important manifestations of these powers have come to us from it.

The country in which the Hebrew religion passed through the critical days of its birth and growth was Canaan, or Palestine. It lay in the very centre of that world of which we have spoken, in the midst of the great civilizations that flourished there. To make itself known to them, and yet to cling to its own peculiar revelation, was at all times the task set before the Hebrew religion. By virtue of its physical features and geographical position Palestine seemed to have been specially destined for that task. That country was shut off from the world by mountains and deserts and a harbourless coast-line. And yet it lay open to the world, because the great commercial highways that connected the east and the west, the north and the south of that world passed through it. Palestine is not one of those countries which, so to speak, open their arms wide, but neither does it unduly segregate its own inhabitants. It is not easily divisioned, yet it is not devoid of form. It fosters first the life of its own people; intercourse with others is secondary. The country was such that, though surrounded by other religions and other civilizations, the conviction of its people that they possessed a unique revelation could gather strength, and their determination to cling to their own thoughts and pursue their own purposes could be carried through when the time was ripe and when the people were ready.

In what forms the people of this revelation manifested their faith in higher powers before their great hour arrived it is difficult to say. The accounts we have from later days do not tell us; indeed, they hardly enable us to conjecture. According to the poetical narrative, the national leader, speaking of the nation's ancestors, says: "Your fathers dwelt of old time beyond the River . . . and they served other gods."[4] The ancient tradition mentions as the actual forefathers of the nation Abraham, Isaac, and Jacob, and according to the same tradition this beginning of the nation was also the beginning of the religion. From the Euphrates Abraham journeys to

[4] Joshua xxiv, 2.

Canaan, and at the outset of this journey is set like an omen the word spoken to him by God, the word that is itself ominous of revolution: " Get thee out of thy country, and from thy kindred, and from thy father's house." [5] And a further stage in the development is recorded in the word addressed to Moses, the " servant of God," to whom the whole tradition points back as the man who made the religion (and by means of it the people) what it became. Laying upon him this task, God says to him: " I am Jehovah: and I appeared unto Abraham, unto Isaac, and unto Jacob, as God Almighty [El Shaddai], but by my name Jehovah [I am that I am] I was not known to them." [6]

This man Moses stands out as the first clearly defined figure, the first historical person, in the religion of Israel. Careful as we must be not to carry back to his time the thought or language of a later century, we can plainly recognize his figure and his work through all the poetry of the narratives. All later time — on which clearer light shines — points back to him as the definitive founder of the national religion, and it should be remembered that the date of the earliest literary attestation of an event or a law is not necessarily the date of what is thus attested. This at least is certain: that Moses laid the foundation for the history and the religion of the nation; he gave to both an inner unity by giving the national genius for religion its close connexion with life, its strength of character, and by setting before the people as their life-work the task of serving Jahveh, the one living and true God, and none other beside Him. He thus made religion " the heroic form of life." He sanctified the national life, and to him it is due that the Israelites, when they settled in Canaan, did not become Canaanites. The religious leaders who succeeded him experienced for themselves, in their own way, what was so marked in him. They accentuated it in their own way. They had their own share of the revolutionary spirit that came from the revelation, and, like him, they preached it. They too were prophets, but they were prophets after Moses. His personality and his work stand at the beginning of Israel.

It was from Moses that this religion derived not only its external forms and ritual, but also its living power, meaning by that its power to grow, its power to regenerate the human spirit. This capacity for inward development really constitutes its history. External development, needless to say, co-operated with the development within. Just as preliminary stages had to be passed through before the new principle could struggle into life, so other formative stages had to precede the time when it could take definite shape. In matters of this kind the external and the internal, or, shall we say, the material and the spiritual, frequently interact. The Hebrew language itself had to reach a certain stage of development. All higher religion is *inter alia* an attempt to find a name for something that has no name, to give utterance to the ineffable. The thought is prior to the word in which it

---

[5] Gen. xii, 1.   [6] Exod. vi, 2–3.

seeks to utter itself, and language has to be fought for. The book of Israel, its Bible, contains passages in which this contest is plainly seen. This is especially the case when a name has to be found for God, the One, whose name must to some extent be both a proper name and a generic name. The most characteristic example is found in the ancient narrative that recounts the call of Moses. He asks to be told God's name. " And God said unto Moses: I am that I am: and he said, Thus shalt thou say unto the children of Israel, I am hath sent me unto you." [7] " I am that I am " — that means, He for Whom no word or name is sufficient. The fight for language here becomes the fight *against* language.

There is another respect in which the man with thoughts that crave for utterance has to wage war with language. The original word is a sign or token; it appeals not only to the ear, but also to the eye; it sets forth an image, and that image is in part mythical. It has been justly said that mythology is the shadow cast by language on thought. From the time of Moses men had known the commandment " Thou shalt not make unto thee a graven image, nor the likeness of any form." [8] But the very words that men used contained both image and likeness, and men had to strive to reach words that were full of life and yet free of myth. The image in the word must not be really an image, but only a hint, a parable. It must represent the thought and also hold it up to view. It was a constant struggle, this fight for parable, for poetry, for ideas, and it had to be fought again and again. Every prophet fought it anew, and it is a fascinating sight to see that battle taking place before our eyes in the pages of the Bible, to see the prophets fighting for a new language and fighting with it after they have attained it. It was the outcome and the expression of that revolutionary element in the new principle whose demand that everything should be new included a new language. Although at first Hebrew religion had much in common with the religious languages of the great contemporary civilizations, yet the peculiar element in it, that which made it entirely different, ultimately forged its way through, and created a language for humanity. It provided words in which men could pray and express their faith. It made a language suitable for a world religion.

But it was not only in the language which they inherited and into which they were born that men found mythology. They met it in many conceptions, forms, and images, in many of the rites and practices current in the surrounding civilizations. Palestine lay, as we have seen, in the centre of these, and, intellectually as well as in the spheres of economic activity and technical achievement, these were the dominant civilizations of the time, ancient, impressive, and often aggressive. And besides, sometimes of its own accord and sometimes perforce, Israel came into close touch with these peoples. Traces of this contact can be plainly seen in all the ancient sources. It is all the more remarkable that the peculiar and essential features of the

[7] Exod. iii, 14.   [8] Exod. xx, 4.

religion were neither stayed in their progress nor deflected from their own path by these strong influences. In one way or another the Hebrew religion always maintained its ground. The personal element in it retained its independence and its determination to be different, nor did the nation ever lose sight of its destiny. Nothing reveals more clearly the revolutionary character of this principle and its unique origin, with its resultant unique living power.

And yet, as we have already said, it is not in this encounter with what they had inherited, nor in the contest with what they met as time went on, nor was it even in the constant endeavour to find means of self-expression, that we see the most significant development through which this religion passed. The truest development was in the actual progress of its thoughts and the ever-new forms in which these thoughts found expression. It is an essential characteristic of all that is truly original, of every product of genius, that it means more than it actually says, and implies more than it expresses. It transcends itself by continually forcing the mind and conscience that receive it to wrestle with it. Again and again in different eras men are laid hold of by it, and they cannot let it go until it blesses them. This power of constant renewal is inherent in it. It creates new men, and is in turn reshaped by them. Wherever the revelation, the new principle, enters, history ceases to be a mere series of events, a mere continuation, a mere coming and going of men, a mere recurrence of attack and resistance. It becomes the encounter of the principle with new individuals, the reciprocal meeting and grappling of revelation and man. The principle is always the same, and yet there is always something specifically new. God reveals Himself to men, and man reveals himself to God. They speak to each other and, as it were, contend with each other. The problem that underlies the principle is thus ever personified afresh. It receives notes that were never heard before, an accentuation that is in each case new. That is what history now means. It is the history of man's wrestling for the problem and with the problem. The history of a reform may mean a gradual amelioration of conditions, but the history of a revolution is a reshaping of personalities.

In this struggle revelation is being continually born again, and history becomes the history of a perpetual renaissance. Each period and each personality in which the idea is thus reborn and personified afresh has its own importance and its own value within this history. It is therefore idle to ask, as is sometimes done, what man or what period is greater or less than another. The only relevant question is whether any period or any man has grasped the problem afresh and whether the problem has been set in a new light. When the problem has fallen on silence, it means that a period of death has come. If the problem is the same as it was before, it denotes a period of decline. History resumes its course only when the problem makes its voice heard again in man's ears, when men discover it again, and thus discover what they themselves are in their inmost nature. Whatever a man may then say, provided he contributes his own note and therefore a fresh note to the problem, in that man history has reawakened. Therefore it is equally an error to try, as is so often done, to separate the religion of the Hebrew from the religion of the Jew, to contrast the period before the Babylonian Exile with the period that followed it or to set against each other the periods before and after the second destruction of the temple. It is always the same problem that is in question. It rings through all the periods; only the accent has changed. The history of revolution — that is, of revelation — is this constant revivifying and repersonifying of the problem. The religion that goes back to Moses has a history, because the new principle that is associated with his name has from the very beginning and throughout its whole course exhibited this power of being born again. This is another quality that makes it a world religion.

The One God. What, then, is this new principle, this force that means revolution? Put in its briefest form, it is the idea and the challenge of the One. This challenging idea is firstly the One Thing, the one thing that alone is needful, that which has been commanded, the good, the right. Secondly and mainly it means the one Being who has proclaimed this One Thing and demands it from men, the One God, beside whom there is none else. And finally it means the unity and totality of man. It means that through this One Thing, and therefore with his whole heart and soul, man is to serve the One God and Him only. All that the prophets from Moses downward have taught, all the ways in which the religion has tried to express itself anew, are, however different the ways in which it has been expressed, just this: that there is only *one* reality — the One God, His commandment and the doing of it; that only *one* knowledge and *one* trust are of any avail — the knowledge of the One God and trust in Him; and that only *one* decision and *one* life are set before men — the decision regarding the *One* and life in the *One*.

The new principle is often succinctly called ethical monotheism. This name is meant to denote that the root of this doctrine is ethical. The psychical origin and the certainty of the faith are found in the experience of the absoluteness and indivisibility of the claim on conscience and of the commandment that knows no limitation. The unity and exclusiveness of the moral demand imply the unity of God. When men came to see that good and true and holy are only different names for one thing, that to this one thing all men are to devote themselves and for its sake turn away from all else, God was recognized as the One, the Holy. It is not so much that ethical monotheism was *taught,* but that it was made the central thing in life, determining all else; it is this relationship of man to God, the fact that human life is theocentric, that is the outstanding feature in this aspect of the Hebrew religion.

In each man, therefore, there is a unity, or, to speak more accurately, a totality, that corresponds to the unity of God. This is an essential element in the doctrine of ethical monotheism. From man is demanded conduct that is exclusively and absolutely related to God. To the One and only valid Thing man can give himself only if he yield up to it all that he is and all that he has; only thus can he serve the One God and acknowledge Him as the only one. All half-measures, all that savours of neutrality toward the Good, all bargaining or making of terms with it, is thus excluded, as well as all lethargy and all mere pose, all that antiquity regarded as the ideal of the wise man. This demand for definite decision, this sternness, this " Thou shalt, thou shalt not," is the core of this religion. Here the Good is not, as it was for Plato, a mere idea to which man can rise by contemplation of it; nor is it, as Aristotle taught, the golden mean or *via media* between two extremes. It is something quite different. It is the imperative, the categorical. It demands the man wholly and absolutely. It demands that his will be set toward the One and Only and against the Many and the Manifold, and this it claims to the end, even to martyrdom. " Thou shalt be wholly for the Lord thy God." The sentence " Hear, O Israel: the Lord our God is one Lord " [9] is immediately followed by another — a sentence in which a later age read the call to martyrdom which is addressed to every man — " Thou shalt love the Lord thy God with all thine heart, and with all thy soul, and with all thy might." [10] To the Hebrew mind these two sentences are inseparable, because the certainty of the unity of God is inseparable from the certainty of the unity of commandment and from the certainty that man achieves his own unity by keeping the commandment. All three taken together constitute the revelation.

Thus morality, in its absoluteness and in its unity, is an essential attribute of God, and we have here the decisive contrast to polytheism, to all the gods of nature and of fate. Belief in these gods has had its stages and its varieties. It has undergone development, especially in the direction of attributing morality to the gods. Men came to regard them as the guardians of the laws of the family, the tribe, and the state. But these gods are moral only in as far as their *behaviour* is not immoral: morality is not essential to their divinity. Despite all subsequent developments, this type of faith never led to ethical monotheism, to faith in the one holy God who lays His commandments on men. No gods of nature or fate, notwithstanding all the ethical features that have at any time been attributed to them, ever developed into Him. It is not by way of an evolution or by a transition, but only by way of a breach that men ever pass from the many gods to the one God. Faith in Him is not even the result of a reform, but only of a revolution. The difference between them and Him is not a difference in number, but a difference in nature. The value and power that are inherent in Hebrew monotheism are not due to a numerical unity, but to what that unity stands for. The significance of Hebrew monotheism does not lie in the fact that the one God is greater than the many gods, or that He by Himself is what they all taken together

[9] Deut. vi, 4.　　　　　[10] Deut. vi, 5.

are, but in the fact that He is different from them. He is the Holy One, the cause and guarantee of the One Thing, the Good, the Righteous, and to Him man can draw near only through the One Thing, only by " doing justice, loving mercy and walking humbly with God." [11] That is the new principle.

This new principle stands opposed to all mythology and to all belief in Fate. Mythology is full of biography and of an appointed lot. It tells of the coming and going of gods, their birth and growth, their fall and defeat, their unions and separations. Even distinctions of sex exist among them. And the destinies of the gods are reflected in the destiny of nature and of men. The theogonies are reflected in the cosmogonies. Fate among the gods, manifold and multifarious as are its forms, is always reflected in a Fate that governs the world. In the Hebrew religion this is replaced by the moral law. There is no room left for mythology, and therefore no room for idol-worship. It is, indeed, a characteristic feature of the Hebrew religion that the Bible has no word for " goddess." The God of the Hebrews is neither Fate nor the World. He is exalted above them, because He is the just and holy One. Therefore the contents of the religion are entirely different. Here there is nothing of that coming and going of gods which involves a coming and going of worlds. It speaks of what God is for man and what man should be as before God. Man, on whom is laid the command to become holy, has the duty and privilege of making his personal decision and living his life in the presence of the one holy God, Who has called him into being. In this religion tragedy is not, as in other religions, the tragedy of Fate, but the tragedy of man's will. In other words, the essence of this religion is piety, righteousness of life. The attitude of man, to whom God has given life and the commandment, to his God, the only God, is the essential thing — this piety with its two poles, the certainty of being God's handiwork and the certainty that he is called to live and work for God.

The first certainty just mentioned is the certainty that, like all else in the midst of which he lives, man is a creation of God's hands. It was only gradually, after a struggle with language and its images, that this peculiar conception of a creation took shape in the Hebrew religion. There it holds the place occupied in other systems by the myths of origin and destruction; indeed, traces of such myths have survived in a few passages of the ancient Hebrew literature. The idea of creation is necessarily involved in monotheism. The One God is different from all else, and in relation to Him all else can only be His creation, His handiwork. That is the meaning of the statement with which the Bible opens — a statement which was the starting-point for further reflection: " In the beginning God created the heaven and the earth." The same statement forms the close of the first exhortation of the great prophet of the Babylonian Exile: " To whom then will ye liken me, that I should be equal to him? saith the Holy One. Lift up your eyes on high and see who hath created these." [12] A prophet had already prayed: " Thou

[11] Micah vi, 8.   [12] Isaiah xli, 25–26.

art the God, even thou alone, of all the kingdoms of the earth; thou hast made heaven and earth." [13] And seeing that God and God alone is the Creator, all the beings whom the peoples call their gods are idols, or to use the striking Biblical word, " things of naught " or " nothings." " For all the gods of the peoples are things of naught, but the Lord made the heavens." [14] Therefore those who go after these go after naught, as Jeremiah says: " They . . . have walked after vanity [naught], and are become vain [naught]." [15] Things of naught also are all the images by means of which the people seek to please God or serve Him. This contest against the gods and idols is a feature of the religion in its early period. It finds its classical expression in the first two commandments of the Decalogue. At a later time the absence of images in the national worship was one of the things that impressed other peoples and gave later minds food for thought. It was one of the features that led the world to realize the pure spirituality of the God of the Hebrews.

As the Creator of the world, God is to the religious mind greater than all that is great and mightier than all that is mighty. He is far more than all that seems to men to be mighty, greater than all lands, greater than the whole world. Compared with Him the nations are as the " dust of the balance "; [16] the continents are as " grains of sand." " For a thousand years in thy sight are but as yesterday when it is past, and as a watch in the night." [17] The sense of infinity and eternity and mystery was awakened by the faith in the One God, and led to search and reflection. The Hebrew mind divined Him as present in the mysterious and as living on into a Beyond. " The Lord hath said that he would dwell in the thick darkness," said Solomon in his prayer at the dedication of the temple, [18] and a later writer makes one of Job's friends try to end all argument and dispute by saying: " Teach us what we shall say unto him; for we cannot order our speech by reason of darkness." [19] The One God is the Exalted One, Whose greatness is veiled in mystery. It was from this source that the conception of sublimity gathered its entire contents and its whole symbolical power, and it was here that the reflection of the sublime — viz., the poetical conception of the world and of the universe as the handiwork of God — was disclosed. Further, the sense of humility that awakens in man's heart in the presence of the sublime grows and finds expression — the consciousness that in God's presence man is petty, insufficient, and impotent, merely a work of His hands and yet a work of *His* hands, one born of God and therefore akin to Him. " I am but dust and ashes," [20] says Abraham to God, and yet he argues and remonstrates with Him. The same note is heard in the Psalter: " What is man, that thou art mindful of him? and the son of man, that thou visitest him? For thou hast made him but little lower than God and crownest him with glory and honour." [21]

[13] Kings xix, 15.	[16] Isaiah xli, 15.	[19] Job xxxvii, 19.
[14] Chron. xvi, 26.	[17] Ps. xc, 4.	[20] Gen. xviii, 27.
[15] Jer. ii, 5.	[18] 2 Chron. vi, 1.	[21] Ps. viii, 4–5.

These passages show that the Hebrew had an equally strong consciousness of these two — the sense of distance and the sense of nearness. Here lies the paradox of Hebrew piety. Humbled as he is by his sense of creaturehood, deeply conscious as he is of the sublimity of God, the Ineffable, Unsearchable, Infinite, and Eternal One, yet he is no less conscious of the relation in which all men stand to the living God. He knows he derives his being from the source of all life, and in that knowledge he finds the meaning of his own life and confidence to live it. The thought of being the work of God's hands is always accompanied by the consciousness of being in safe keeping. For him the world is no longer in the hands of Fate, nor is it merely the scene of chance happenings. All that happens takes place according to the will of God, for " the whole earth is full of his glory." [22] All that happens in it is for the Hebrew mind the doing of the One Eternal God. As the ancient phrase has it, between God and the world, as between God and man, a covenant has been made. This means that God abides, is omnipresent, ever near. The pious heart knows what is real and what is the basis of all life. In all that is transitory he sees the eternal, in all that is of earth he sees the infinite, in all that lives he sees the presence of God. The world and his own life are eloquent with messages of revelation.

But all this becomes still more personal. It is the personality of a man, his *ego,* that is conscious of it all. God is the God of man, and man may and should speak to Him. " Thou art my God." [23] All the words that men can find to denote union, security, intimacy, and nearness are in place here. To man God is protection and help, a refuge and strength, hope and consolation, light and health, shepherd and keeper, the merciful one and redeemer. Here Hebrew piety has displayed most clearly its power to invent the language it needs, and its poetic genius has sounded the most intimate depths of the human heart. It calls God the " father " of men; it speaks of His " love " for them. The first personal pronoun is laden with all the meaning it can hold: " *My* God." Especially the Psalms and the prayers of later Judaism are full of this poetry and these metaphors. All that is involved in the Nature of God is used to express this deep sense of personality. The " nature " of God, His " attributes," were summed up for later Judaism in the words of the prayer of Moses: " The Lord, the Lord, a God full of compassion and gracious, slow to anger, and plenteous in mercy and truth; keeping mercy for thousands, forgiving iniquity and transgression and sin: and that will by no means clear the guilty." [24] But hardly ever in the history of the Hebrew religion did God become a God made up of attributes, an abstract deity, a mere " god " of philosophy and dogma. At all periods He was the *personal* God to Whom man could pray and speak. He was always felt to be personal, and faith in Him found expression in all the moods and feelings that the heart can know. To be sure, there were times when Hebrew minds brooded

[22] Isaiah vi, 3.   [23] Ps. lxiii, 1.   [24] Exod. xxxiv, 6–7.

and reflected on the divine nature and endeavoured to construct a conception of God. The Middle Ages of Judaism had their profound philosophy of religion. But the characteristic feature of the Hebrew religion has always been the personal, living God, to Whom men can come with their longings and their love, their tears and their praises, their fears and their hopes. He is in verity God, the Exalted One, but man knows he is safe in His hands: he speaks and prays to Him. With his mind full of abstract conception man cannot pray: he cannot place his hopes in logical definitions. In God's presence he cannot think at all without rising to poetry.

Of course this personal language was not always proof against the tendency to speak of God in terms applicable to man. In the days when thought and speech were still naïvely aiming at vividness the contradiction was not felt. Words were pictures, imagery was inseparable from them. But the case was different when in the Hellenistic period the actual contents of the religion became the avowed subject of reflection. All descriptive imagery was felt to be like reducing God to the level of man. It was an anthropomorphism which ought to be avoided. The truly spiritual God should be spoken of spiritually. How deliberate and determined this effort was is clearly seen in the Aramaic translations of the Bible made in Palestine and Babylon — the so-called Targums. But this way of thinking, stressing as it did the purely transcendental aspects of the Divine, ran the opposite risk of reducing the living God to an abstraction. Religion was in danger of becoming abstract, and this involved the further danger that religion might be replaced by reflection about religion. The inwardness and immediateness of faith in God were in danger of being lost, and God was removed to a far distance. In the heart that longed for nearness to God the desire inevitably arose to fill up, as it were, the chasm that thus seemed to yawn between God and man, and it is easy to understand how ideas of all kinds were suggested. On the one hand, the *naïve* imagination of the people sought to secure their connexion with God by interposing intermediate figures as His servants and messengers; on the other hand, philosophic thought postulated a sort of quintessence of all creative and efficient powers, a *Logos,* or even spheres and elements, as helpers and overseers proceeding from God. This seemed to be a way of preserving a connexion between God and man. The history of Hebrew thought shows repeated endeavours of this kind, and on the basis of these, some have attempted to divide that history into periods. The real nature of the religion was at times obscured by such endeavours and the door was opened for the entrance of mythology. The straight path was regained only when men's hearts again became conscious of the living God and realized afresh the paradox of sublimity and immediacy, God's distance and His nearness.

After all, however, the danger of thus sublimating the Divine was never really formidable, because in the Hebrew mind the conviction of man's creaturehood was always balanced by the other characteristic conviction, that man is a moral being, gifted with the capacity for action and called upon to exercise it. The Hebrew mind has never lost sight of the truth that man receives from God not only his life, but also the commandment. The God of love, Who calls man into being and maintains him in life, is also the God Who demands from him righteousness, tests him and judges him. To man He says: " I am the Lord thy God. . . . Thou shalt . . ." [25] Before man God sets the categorical, irrefragable, unconditional commandment. It is by fulfilling the commandment that man can serve God and prove his love to Him. This love to God is the first of all the commandments. " And now, Israel, what doth the Lord thy God require of thee, but to fear the Lord thy God, to walk in all his ways, and to love him, and to serve the Lord thy God with all thy heart and with all thy soul? " [26] Human behaviour is thus filled with meaning, and life itself becomes the path that leads man to God. Man is declared to be an ethical personality. Hebrew religion becomes the religion of God's commandments — the Bible is full of them — and the piety it demands is the piety of the moral life. That is what is meant by the " activism " of the Hebrew religion, but the characteristic feature of it is not this laying of commandments on men taken by itself. What is distinctive in it is that man's knowledge of the commandment is conjoined with his consciousness of being the work of God's hands. The fact that man is God's creature and the fact that he is under law to God belong inseparably together. Both convictions were present in the Hebrew mind. The emotional and the conative elements go together.

All this implies, therefore, that man is not only a creature, but a creature with a moral personality. What he is reveals to him what he is meant to be. He can and ought to do something as toward God. He is to serve Him actively, not merely to sit humbly charged with emotion and consciousness. The significance that God has put into human life is to be reinforced by the significance that man should give to his own life. " See, I have set before thee this day life and good, and death and evil; . . . I have set before thee life and death, the blessing and the curse: therefore choose life." [27] Man thus stands free before God, he " chooses the will of God," chooses the world in which he means to live. He can make his own life. He can " walk with God." In virtue of what he is, he makes it his task to fulfill the commandment; he acts as a moral being. What he does he can claim as his own act, and it discloses to him what he is capable of. As is said in the Talmud — the so-called " oral torah " — i.e., the oral teaching, the explanation and completion of the written or Biblical torah — " Everything lies in God's hands, except the fear of God in the heart of man." Human life is thus raised above all necessitarian theory and all control by Fate. This conviction was so deeply felt that later mystical Hebrew writers went so far as to say that the human will and human action had cosmical force; they could affect the fate of the world and bring about either the salvation or the destruction of the world. The

[25] Exod. xx, 2 ff.   [26] Deut. x, 12.   [27] Deut. xxx, 15, 19.

Hebrew mysticism of the Middle Ages of Judaism and the ensuing centuries rests largely on this conception. And even in an earlier period the Talmudic poetry, the Haggadah, had said that owing to the wickedness of seven generations God had left the world and only in the days of seven just men had He returned to His place in it.

But it was not only mystical writers who uttered thoughts like these. In the earliest Talmudic period a thought similar, and indeed identical, found expression in words that became classical. The words occur in the Bible, but it is in the Talmud that their full meaning is brought out. The words are: "the hallowing of the Divine Name." Every time a man chooses the good, says the Talmud, he "hallows the name of God," for he thereby demonstrates the reality of the nature and commandment of God, "the Holy One"; and all wickedness in thought or deed "desecrates or defiles the Divine Name," because it implies that a piece of life has been left unconsecrated. "When ye sanctify yourselves, God is sanctified." "I will be hallowed among the children of Israel." [28]

This became one of the most familiar phrases in Israel. This thought of the creative power that has been given to man and enjoined upon him received a further interpretation — viz., that man makes a place for God and builds a kingdom for Him on earth. The phrase coined by religious language to express this thought is "the Kingdom of God." It means that the sphere of good created by man is a sphere in which, so to speak, God does not set man, as He sets him in his environment in life, but in which man sets God and which he gives to Him as His dwelling-place. There is another classical expression for the same idea, the *shechinah*.[29] Again and again with varying words it is declared that whenever men make and perform the vow, "All that the Lord hath spoken we will do," [30] then the Kingdom of God has come on earth. Wherever good men meet together, there is the *shechinah,* the dwelling-place of God here below. The conception of the election of Israel also assumed this form. Wherever Israel is and turns to the Father in heaven, there is a Kingdom of God, there is the *shechinah*. And whenever men longed for the "end of the days" and wished to see it realized they thought of it as the time when the whole earth would be a Kingdom of God. In this picture of the future the Hebrews saw the meaning of their election. Theirs was the task of bringing about this kingdom. A prayer that belongs to the third century of the Christian era and is used at the Hebrew New Year services runs: "Our hope is . . . that we may make the world a Kingdom of God and that all the sons of men may be thine."

The emotion that fills the heart of a man who knows the commandment and is conscious of his own freedom is reverence, the emotion that is inspired by the moral imperative, by what is morally lofty and holy. It is the

[28] Lev. xxii, 32.
[29] This is the Talmudic word for "the divine presence."
[30] Exod. xix, 8.

emotion that is felt by the free man who can look up when he is clearly conscious of the commandment and of his responsibility. The fine Bible word for this is " the fear of God." " Thou shalt fear " were the words used to children to remind them of their due attitude toward their parents, and in a later time this same attitude was enjoined toward teachers; but the word was used chiefly of man's attitude toward God. " Fear thy God " [31] is the closing injunction of the commandment. This is the emotion felt by the man who comes into the presence of the Holy One, to serve Him in goodness and with uprightness, and it is therefore synonymous — although the emphasis is different — with the other phrase, " love to God." To " love God and fear Him " is almost *one* word in the Bible. Both in humility and in this " fear of God " there is present a sense of infinity and eternity; for the commandment, being God's commandment, is for man always unfinished. But whereas humility always has its eyes fixed on the unsearchable and the mysterious, reverence has in view what is manifest and definite — viz., the commandment, which is always clear and always binding. In the light of duty the reverent man recognizes the endless path on which, as he passes from commandment to commandment, from act to act, he is to work out his life-task.

But here again, in the significance thus put on human conduct, lay another danger — viz., that human action as such, or the commandment in itself, should be regarded as all-sufficient, and that the sense of reverence should gradually fade away and finally be lost sight of. Already in the Book of Isaiah it is said that " their fear [of the Lord] is a commandment of men which hath been taught them." [32] Again and again it seemed as if the commandment had ceased to be God's commandment — that is to say, it had lost its note of eternity and infinity, and become a mere convention or legal enactment: obedience to it was merely external and formal. This meant that religion, although it might have much to say about God, was a matter of this life merely, unconnected with the Infinite and Eternal, that it had been so externalized that it was in danger of becoming a form without contents. It threatened to become a mere rule of conduct, uninspired by reverence. Further, the thought which is almost always associated with the commandment, the thought of the blessed and happy reward that follows its fulfilment, thus becomes meaningless. Many passages of the Talmud show how keenly this danger was felt. Again and again it is reiterated that God desires the heart, that the commandment demands worship and a suitable disposition, that man is to seek the good " for God's sake," or, as it is sometimes put, " for its own sake." At the beginning of the second century a rabbi used the phrase: " The reward of the commandment is the commandment and the punishment of wickedness is wickedness." And more than three hundred years earlier another rabbi, whose words have also come down to us in the Talmudic " Sayings of the Fathers," uttered the exhortation: " Be ye not like servants who serve in the hope of receiving reward, but be like servants

[31] Lev. xxv, 17.					[32] Isaiah xxix, 13.

who serve without hope of reward. Let the fear of God in heaven be upon you." It is in the last words of this exhortation that the real significance lies. Reverence involves assurance of fulfilment and satisfaction, promise and consolation — these are the reward. When the commandment loses its reverence in men's eyes, their assurance of reward suffers the same loss. The true commandment, this new principle, this revelation, is recovered only when this injunction: " Fear God," has again become a living word.

Thus just as Hebrew piety combines the consciousness of creaturehood with the consciousness of being under the commandment, so it combines into a unity reverence and humility. Every aspect of the commandment speaks of something that is hidden, of the Eternal and Infinite; all that is hidden and secret speaks of the commandment; and the ground of our life speaks of the path we are to tread, just as the path that we are to tread speaks of the ground of our life. Or, to use the terminology of a later time, all faith implies law and all law implies faith. The one cannot be understood without the other. Their complete unity reveals the meaning of life and guarantees piety and union with the One God. Some have declared that the Hebrew faith is a religion of this life, but the statement is only partially true. It is true in the sense that the paths on which God's commandment is fulfilled are here, on earth and in the life on earth. But the statement is also incorrect, because it overlooks the fact that this path that man is to tread originates in the Beyond, in the depths of life. All that is transcendent enters into this life as the appointed way for men, as the divine commandment which it is man's life-task to fulfill. Therefore there is here no opposition between Immanence and Transcendence, or, to put the same meaning into other words, between that which is to be felt and that which is to be lived, between the Mystical and the Ethical. It is only in thought that these should be distinguished: in Hebrew religion they are essentially one and the same. Of course, in view of the many minds that have been occupied with the subject we may freely admit that differences have emerged, and that the emphasis has been laid now on one and now on the other aspect. But the characteristic attitude of the Hebrews is abandoned only when it is claimed that either aspect is the only valid one, when faith is so emphasized that no room is left for law, or when law is made so supreme that it denies a place for faith. Either attitude abandons the principle, the revelation which became history in the Hebrew religion.

Man. It is through the one God that man, in the Hebrew religion, gains his religious significance. Created and called by God, he is not only *a* man, but *man,* the *one* man that lives in all men. He is the man of God, or, as the Biblical metaphors, which transcend their original meaning, put it, he is " made in the image of God," he is " the child of God." That is to say, man — not merely this or that individual, but man generically — is capable of manifesting the divine. This implies a new principle of humanity, a new dignity and unity of the human race, and it involves the status and the value of every human soul, its uniqueness and personality. Each individual is the image, the child of God. " Know that for thy sake the world was created " is the Talmudic rendering of this thought. Self-reverence is here enjoined on man.

This idea of being made in God's image, of being the child of God, constitutes the supreme injunction that is laid on every individual — viz., the injunction to show himself divine. The utmost is required from each. The classical expression of this in the Bible is " Ye shall be holy: for I the Lord your God am holy." [33] This call to holiness, or, as it is also called, to purity of heart, is addressed to every man. An ancient prayer bids each man say: " My God, the soul which thou hast given me is pure: it is Thy breath in me." In this purity lies man's whole task, the whole potentiality that is latent in him, the whole liberty that is opened up to him. The word " live " becomes a commandment: " Thou shalt live." And it is a commandment that is endless. If man is to be holy as God is holy, or, as another Biblical expression has it, if he is " to walk in all his ways, and to love him," [34] if his life is to be thus measured by the supreme, divine standard, his task is never finished. The commandment comes to him as something that is ever new; commandment follows commandment; man is never done with it. The ideal continually rises up before him, demanding to be realized, and yet it ever recedes before him into infinity. This is another characteristic difference between the Hebrew religion and the ideal of antiquity, when men fondly believed that they had reached the goal of virtue and wisdom and thereby achieved perfection.

To the Hebrews their distance from perfection was evident not only because of their lofty conception of the ideal, but also and especially from their knowledge of human nature. The infinite task has been laid on finite human life; or, as a somewhat trite sentence from the " Sayings of the Fathers " puts it, " The day is brief and there is much to be done." Man's capacity, which can never overpass the limits of the earthly, is called upon to fulfill the commandment that is infinite. He is to be holy as the Lord his God is holy, and yet no man on earth is holy. Still this commandment rises up unceasingly before him. To quote once more from the " Sayings of the Fathers ": " It is not within thy power to finish the task, nor is it within thy liberty to abandon it." This contrast is very keenly felt in the Hebrew religion — the contrast between man's greatness and his limitations, between his task and his powers, between the divine and the human, between the Beyond and the Here in his life. And it becomes all the more deeply felt because of the continual reminders of man's personal responsibility, of the obligation that rests upon him to choose and decide, of his accountability to God, and of the stern thought of judgment. God is " the Judge of all the earth," [35] He " searcheth the heart, and trieth the reins." [36] The more man learns about himself, the

[33] Lev. xix, 2.   [35] Gen. xviii, 25.
[34] Deut. x, 12.   [36] Jer. xvii, 10.

more clearly he is conscious that he comes short of what he is meant to be as the image of God, a man pure and free. And this consciousness becomes clearer still, because it proclaims not only the human limitations which cause him to come short of what is demanded, but also the fact of his *guilt*. For he can also resist the commandment and refuse to walk in the way of God. He can deny the holy: he can choose what displeases God: sin can enter into his life. And each sin he commits is *his* sin. This is another feature that is peculiar to Hebrew religion. Disdaining all mythological explanations of sin, and rejecting all theories that attribute sin to Fate, it emphasizes the personal part played by man in his sin and the personal fate which he brings upon himself by sinning. Keenly and clearly felt as are the links that connect the days and the generations of men, the influences of environment and heredity, the weaknesses, temptations, and difficulties of life, little is said about sin in the abstract, about original sin or inherited sin. The emphasis is on personal sin: " Thou hast sinned: it is thy sin." It is not Fate, but the individual man that is here involved. The word " sin " is the word of judgment concerning the personal act. The responsibility lies with man.

This raises the most important question presented by the religion of Israel. Is not the soul, created pure by God, rendered impure by sin? And does not man, created free, forfeit by reason of his sin the liberty that was his? Does he not, indeed, cease to be a child of God? This question is answered by the characteristically Hebrew conception of conversion or return — the Biblical word for it is often wrongly translated by " penance " — and of the *reconciliation* which is brought about by the return. This means that man is never a lost soul; it is always open to him to begin afresh and to get back to the path of life. In the words of the prophet, he can " make for himself a new heart and a new spirit " [37] — " new " is another characteristic Bible word — and thus recover his purity and his liberty. Or, as the Talmud says, " Seeing that he makes his behaviour new, God makes him a new creature "; he is born again; his life is given to him anew. This Bible teaching contradicts all theories of fatalism. The sinner can return. " Let the wicked forsake his way, and the unrighteous man his thoughts: and let him return unto the Lord, and he will have mercy upon him; and to our God, for he will abundantly pardon." [38] Or, in still other words, which lay greater emphasis on the personal relationship between God and man, man can " purify " himself before God and " become clean " again, and thereby become reconciled to God, and God forgiveth " iniquity and transgression and sin." [39] He " sets free " and " delivers " man. " As far as the east is from the west, so far hath he removed our transgressions from us." [40] Sin no longer means Fate. After man is thus reconciled, sin is recognized as error or mistake. Man had gone astray and has now returned. God's covenant with man abides. To quote the Talmud once more, " Ye are children of the Lord your God, even when ye behave

[37] Ezek. xviii, 31.
[38] Isaiah lv, 7.
[39] Exod. xxxiv, 7.
[40] Ps. ciii, 12.

not as his children." " God says, What I was before man sinned, I still am after he has sinned."

The religion of Israel thus proclaims how the merciful, pardoning God, the God of righteousness and of love, receives back man thus reconciled. But this reconciliation is not conceived as being exclusively the work of grace. It means here more than a miracle of deliverance wrought for one of the elect. It lays the emphasis on the *decision made by man* and on the path that *he* now treads. It was *his* sin; it is *his* return. He may and ought to have faith in the forgiving God, but this faith alone cannot guarantee his reconciliation. The sole guarantee of that is his own actual return. The deliverance in question is not a deliverance from the task of exercising his will and living his life: it is not a deliverance from the world and from life in it: it is a reconciliation of man's will with God, an at-one-ment, a coming to be at one, a condition in which man " makes God's will his own." Hebrew mysticism also has always maintained this position. And something more is implied — viz., the moral directness and immediacy of the reconciliation which thus comes to man. No one and nothing intervenes between him and God: man must purify himself, and God readmits him to His fellowship after he has done so. No one can relieve man of this necessity: no one can do this task for him: no one else can acquit him. " Return unto me, and I will return unto you, saith the Lord of hosts." [41] This doctrine of reconciliation has always been set forth by the teachers of Israel as their own peculiar faith. It has been deliberately proclaimed as such ever since it became necessary to differentiate the Hebrew exposition of it from that of other expositors. A leader of Jewish thought in the early years of the second century said, " Blessed are ye, sons of Israel! who is He in whose sight ye purify yourselves, and who is He Who purifies you? He is your heavenly Father." The Jewish religion was proclaimed to be the religion of reconciliation and reconciliation was proclaimed to be the ultimate meaning and goal of humanity. It is the crown of the belief that man is the image and child of God. Along with New Year's Day and " the Day of Judgment," and combined with them into a unit, " the Day of Atonement " is the culminating point of the Jewish ecclesiastical year.

Of course, this thought of reconciliation or atonement could be fully developed and understood only when the ancient sacrificial forms of service had lost their meaning for the people — only, indeed, when these forms had ceased after the destruction of the second temple. Sacrifice was an inheritance from the past, and its symbolism had taught the people many important truths. But the danger was always present that something which was essential would be inseparably associated or even identified with something that was merely external; and the danger was all the greater because the expiatory sacrifice was understood as in some way a mediation between man and God.

[41] Mal. iii, 7.

The prophets had therefore frequently attacked the importance attached to sacrifice, and all the pathos of their ministry had been manifested in this connexion. Again and again they had declared that God desired not sacrifice; [42] that he desired " faithfulness and truth," [43] obedience to His voice; [44]

FIG. 104. READING FROM THE LAW
After a painting by St Bender, Munich

that He desired " mercy, and not sacrifice "; [45] and like a grateful response to their message come the words of the Psalm: " The sacrifices of God are a broken spirit: a broken and a contrite heart, O God, thou wilt not despise." [46] When the service of sacrifice had ceased, and especially when its true mean-

[42] Hosea vi, 6.
[43] Isaiah xxv, 1.
[44] Deut. xiii, 4.
[45] Hosea vi, 6.
[46] Ps. li, 17.

ing was seen to be the sacrifice of return, the sacrifice of righteous life —
"return" and "doing good" constitute one idea in the Talmud. When
worship had come to consist only in prayer and the reading of the Scriptures; when sacrifice had ceased and no sacrament had taken its place,
then the conception of reconciliation as a new beginning, a new life,
a rebirth, attained its full purity and sublimity. Henceforth it was the
centre of the religion. It could even be said, "Where the men of the
return stand, perfectly just men cannot stand." As the religion of reconciliation with God, the religion of Israel came to know its profoundest
meaning.

This assurance of reconciliation also provided the key to unlock the mystery of the grave. The Bible mentions death for the most part merely as one
of the facts of life. Man "goeth to his long home." [47] It has therefore comparatively little to say about a life after death, especially as its chief purpose
is to bring men face to face with the commandments that refer to life
here. But this silence is also a tacit protest against all the figures and
images with which the neighbouring religions had peopled the world
beyond. The words of the Decalogue, "Thou shalt not make unto thee
a graven image, nor the likeness of any form," were conceived as applying
to any world above or below, to heaven and hell. Therefore it is probably
not fortuitous that the thought of the Beyond began to find expression only
when idol-worship had definitively vanished from the national life. It was
only then that men began to speak of the "life to come," of "everlasting
life," [48] of "the world to come," of which this present world is only the
"outer court," and of the man who knows that he is "a child of the world
to come." And in this assurance of eternal life with God the longing heart
now found its ultimate goal and its complete consolation. The word "peace"
becomes the word for eternal life, and, using another word that was also
employed to designate the Day of Atonement, men spoke of this peace
as "the sabbath, which is all sabbath." The life everlasting is conceived as the
great reconciliation of this life, as deliverance from all that is finite and
earthly, defective and impure. It is the world in which there is nothing
unhallowed, nothing unsabbatic. Men could now say, "Death reconciles."
Here and there, it is true, especially among the mystics, the Beyond was
objectively depicted, but the ancient spiritual conception always predominated. "The world to come, no eye hath seen it, save thou, O God,
alone." These words are in the Talmud, and the same source contains
another sentence that constitutes a paradox: "One hour of return and of
good works in this world is more than all the life of the world to come;
and one hour of bliss in the world to come is more than all the life of
this world." This shows once more how in the religion of Israel the
Beyond and the Here are closely connected, how each is the answer to the
other. Life here takes its meaning from the life beyond, and our knowledge

[47] Eccles. xii, 5.   [48] Daniel xii, 2.

of the life beyond advances *pari passu* with our knowledge of the meaning of life here, with its commandment and its reconciliation.

This attempt to connect the Here with the Hereafter, Time with Eternity, which is so characteristic of the religion of Israel, becomes especially prominent when the Sabbath, to quote the Talmud once more, "is felt by the pious man to be a parable or image in this life of the life beyond." Hebrew piety finds its fulfilment not in a deliverance from the world, but in a deliverance *in* the world, through the hallowing of the world. To the Hebrew mind there is nothing that is only of this world, nothing that is merely secular. This is the thought that is expressed in the Sabbath, and the Sabbath is one of the great blessings which Israel has brought to all men, especially to the poor and the oppressed. To the Hebrew himself it is the great symbol, "the token between God and the children of Israel." More and more their love has turned to it and rediscovered in it the central feature of the religion. Again and again it has lifted man above the toil that besets him behind and before and preserved for the toiler his personality. Into the fret and rush of life it comes as the day on which man can look within. Week by week it calls a halt to the activities of the working day and confronts man with that which is holy, giving him an opportunity to look into his own heart and see the meaning of his life, sanctifying him again after his immersion in the secular. It claims to be a day in this world and yet not of this world; in the haste and press of this world it is a day of quiet. For quiet is not here synonymous with mere rest. It has the new, peculiar meaning that comes from God. Rest is an earthly thing: this quiet is religious, reconciling. The Sabbath is thus a world that comes week by week from above. "A sabbath unto the Lord "[49] it is called in the Decalogue. The prophet calls it a "delight"; [50] the day "when the soul expands," says a rabbi in the Talmud. It is the token of surety for all that is included in the "blessing from the Lord." [51]

The commandment concerning the Sabbath illustrates another aspect of the new principle — viz., that religion has a *social* side. The commandment in question has come down to us in the Decalogue in a twofold form.[52] In the one it is associated with the Creation; in the other it is connected with the right that belongs to those who serve others. According to the latter form, the purpose of the Sabbath is "that thy manservant and thy maidservant may rest as well as thou." [53] They have their part in the commandment: it is meant for them. The conception of man, the man of the Sabbath, implies that conception of "fellow-man" which is also a product of Israel's religion. If man is made in the image of God, if he is the child of God, then every human being is included, and the whole significance of the one man is extended so as to embrace every man. Every man is fellow-man to every other man, or, to use another word, every man is "thy brother."

---

[49] Exod. xx, 10.
[50] Isaiah lviii, 13.
[51] Ps. xxiv, 5.
[52] Exod. xx and Deut. v.
[53] Deut. v, 14.

He is a brother even if till this moment we have been ignorant of his existence, even though he live far away, even if he be a foreigner, so that the Bible can speak of "thy brother whom thou knowest not" and of "thy brother . . . as a stranger and a sojourner." [54] Every man belongs to us, he is given to us, so that the Bible can again say, emphatically, "thy poor," "thy needy," "thy stranger." The well-known passage in Leviticus which is usually translated "Thou shalt love thy neighbour as thyself: I am the Lord" [55] means literally: "Love thy neighbour: he is as thou"; and in this "as thou" lies the full meaning of the commandment. In the same chapter it is repeated and extended still further. "The stranger that sojourneth with you shall be unto you as the home-born among you, and thou shalt love him; he is as thyself; for ye were strangers in the land of Egypt: I am the Lord your God." [56] Not this man or that man, therefore, but the man who is ourself — that is the meaning of the expression "as thyself." Thus it includes not only the stranger, but also the enemy. He too is this fellow-man. Hence the same injunction includes him. "If thine enemy be hungry, give him bread to eat; and if he be thirsty, give him water to drink." [57] "If thou meet thine enemy's ox or his ass going astray, thou shalt surely bring it back to him again." [58] And perhaps the most characteristic feature of all is that this thought of our fellow-man is extended into the conception of the life beyond. A sentence of the Talmud which has become almost symbolic says: "The pious among the heathen have their share in the world to come." Piety and its consummation in the Hereafter are thus open to the human race. Wherever a man's lot may have been cast, he is a man, and the way is open to him to be a good man.

Thus the title fellow-man applies to every man. "Thy brother may live with thee." [59] And he is our fellow-man by God's appointment. It is not our goodwill nor our kindness, nor is it any social convention or legal enactment that makes him so. He is so by the appointment of the One God, and therefore no one must deprive him of his standing or reduce its meaning. Every human right means a claim that our fellow-man has upon us as his birthright given to him by God. The commandment to "do justly and love mercy," which is announced to man and demanded from him, is to govern all behaviour toward our fellow-man. What we owe to God is to be paid first and chiefly to His children. In our relationship to them we find the sum of the duties which God has laid upon us: in our relationship to them we can manifest our love to God and our delight in His service. The Talmud says: "Love God in the men whom he has created." The appointed path to God is by way of our fellow-man. The social element is therefore an essential part of religion. To the Hebrew mind there can be no religion without our fellow-man. There is no religion in fleeing the world or in separating oneself from it. The leading teachers of the Talmud have therefore declared that

[54] Lev. xxv, 35.   [56] Lev. xix, 34.   [58] Exod. xxiii, 4.
[55] Lev. xix, 18.   [57] Prov. xxv, 21.   [59] Lev. xxv, 36.

this recognition of our fellow-man is the "essence of the *torah.*" From it everything else follows. To use the language that was specially minted to express this teaching, the good man can be properly described only by the words "just" and "loving," which involve social relationship.

As it is a divine commandment, this duty to our fellow-man is absolutely binding. He is entitled to it; he has that claim on us; as the Bible elsewhere says, he is "the owner of the benefit." [60] This is expressed in another word from the Hebrew mint, one which denotes, far more clearly than any exposition could do, what we owe to our fellow-man, to the needy, the suffering, the weak. That word is "justice," and it implies that he who helps and encourages another has done no more than his duty. He has rendered to him only what was his due. He who refrains from helping has, as the same passage says, "withheld" something that is due. As one of the ancient rabbis puts it, he has "robbed" him, deprived him of something that was his by the appointment of God and by the claim of humanity. No warmth of feeling, no sentimental goodwill, no barren sympathy, no empty love can be a substitute for it. Therefore this "justice" has been expounded in numerous Bible passages. The statutes on this subject aim at securing protection for the stranger, who has the same rights as the home-born, for the slave, who is regarded merely as a servant, but whose personal standing as a human being is recognized in the stress that this religion laid on the dignity and blessing of labour, and for the needy and the poor. In the Bible the word "poor" has a religious connotation. The poor man is the child of God and our fellow-man in a special degree. He is *par excellence* the fellow-man whom we must not pass by. Not only the Bible, but all later Hebrew literature emphasizes these demands.

It is here that we find the great social task grasped for the first time. The thought that human society is a community pervaded by human duties, a moral confederacy and solidarity, is here seen taking shape. And it is from the Bible that the social commandment has again and again gone forth into the world. There is still another important aspect of it. This social order, this great community, includes the animal world. The help and support enjoined by all the commandments are claimed for the lower creatures, for it is said: "O Lord, thou preservest man and beast." [61] The two are frequently mentioned together in this way. Still more remarkable is another peculiar phrase which occurs twice in the Bible: "to know the heart." On the first occasion it refers to the stranger: "Ye know the heart of a stranger, seeing ye were strangers in the land of Egypt." [62] The second reference is to animals: "The righteous man knoweth the heart of his beast." [63] Luther's

[60] Prov. iii, 27 (in the Hebrew); the Revised Version renders this as "to whom it is due."

[61] Ps. xxxvi, 6.

[62] Exod. xxiii, 9.

[63] Prov. xii, 10. This proverb is frequently quoted inaccurately: "The merciful man is merciful to his beast." Our Authorized Version reads: "A righteous man regardeth the life of his beast."

translation, otherwise so masterly, in this case comes short of the meaning. He renders it: " The righteous man has mercy on his beast." To understand the animal, not to neglect or overlook it, is included in the law of justice.

This " justice," in its positive, social sense, with its unequivocal demand to be translated into action, is the first and plainest element of what we are called upon to offer to our fellow-man. To this the Hebrew religion immediately adds love toward our fellow-man. For it is not only external aid, aid that passes from hand to hand, and which is frequently a matter of mere legal enactment, but the aid that goes from heart to heart that our fellow-man needs. His heart must receive from us its due. According to a saying of the Talmud, " ' justice ' has value only in so far as there is love in it." This love is called " the beginning and end of the *torah.*" Without it men are said to be idolaters. Three things are mentioned by which a professor of the Hebrew religion can be known: mercy, chastity, and love to man. Love is included here, while the positive social righteousness of which we have been speaking is omitted. It is omitted because there are many of our fellow-men who do not need it at our hands. As the Talmud says: " Justice can be shown only to the living, but love to both the living and the dead. Justice can be shown only to the poor, but love to both rich and poor. Justice can be shown only by means of what we have, love by what we have and by what we are. Justice and love outweigh all the commandments in the Bible."

Here again the enemy is included. Hate and vengeance are condemned. The Bible proverb runs: " Say not, I will do so to him as he hath done to me; I will render to the man according to his work." [64] All hate is called in the Talmud " hate without a cause." One of the old sages bids us pray: " Grant, O Lord my God, God of my fathers, that in no man's heart hate may rise against us, and that no hate may rise in our heart against any man." And another saying from the same source runs: " Those who are injured and return no injury; those who hear despiteful things said against them and answer not; those who act in love and joyfully bear their trials; these are they of whom the Scripture saith, ' They who love the Lord are as the sun rising in his strength.' " In the matter of punitive justice, moving words ascribe to God alone [65] the right of vengeance, as of anger and jealousy. Anger and jealousy must be holy. They must evince nothing but the solemnity, the deep pathos of the ethical, burning opposition to wrong and wickedness. And though at times Hebrew hearts were invaded by anger and hate, though one of the Psalmists — one who was keenly conscious of the omnipresence and judgment of God — was tempted to cry, " Do not I hate them, O Lord, that hate thee? and am not I angry with those that rise up against thee? " [66] the cry was answered in the prayer of another Psalmist in the older version of his word: " May sins disappear from the earth; and then there shall be no wicked men." [67]

[64] Prov. xxiv, 29.   [65] Deut. xxxii, 35.   [66] Ps. cxxxix, 21.   [67] Ps. civ, 35.

There is still another element in this love, an element that is also at variance with human vengeance and hate — viz., that aspect of love toward our fellow-man that is expressed in sincerity, in candour. We are not only to speak the truth, but also to offer it to our fellow-man, to help him to the good and lead him to the right. " Love men and bring them into touch with the *torah*." That is another call laid upon man in relation to his fellow-men. The commandment to love him thus becomes the duty of caring for his soul, and it is enjoined on every man as part of his duty to his fellow-man. This prophetic task is assigned to every one. " Thou shalt not hate thy brother in thine heart: thou shalt surely rebuke thy neighbour, and not bear sin because of him." [68] This points to the great moral responsibility that lies upon a man for his brother — the brother's sin may become his. As the Talmud says: " Ye are all sureties, one for another." This completes the conception of the human society. It is a community of moral suretyship. To live with one another means to lead each other on the path to God, the path to reconciliation. This is the meaning of the ancient prayer used on New Year's Day and the Day of Atonement: " Vouchsafe, O God, to all whom thou hast created, thy fear . . . that they all may be brought together to do thy will with all their heart." These words give expression to reverence toward our fellow-man as well as to reverence toward God.

This reverence toward man as such implies the last aspect of the new principle — the conception of history and human responsibility for it. God is the God of history: man whom God has called into existence and enjoined to keep the commandment, has his place in history. He is the man of history, or, to use other words that mean the same thing, he is the man who is in humanity and for it. This idea was part of the religion of Israel from the beginning. At the opening of the religion and decisive for all time stood a historical event, the deliverance from Egypt. That taught the Hebrews to hear the voice of God in history. It kept alive their memory for history and fed their religious confidence. The prophetic writings as a whole are a commentary on the meaning of history. Its meaning had to be thought out, for at all times the successes and the majorities were on the other side, and the enemies of Israel could appeal to what seemed to be the verdict of the centuries. To meet these appeals the true reading of history had to be discovered and set forth. How different that reading was! It took no account of what men called success: to give heed to it meant to be guilty of idolatry. It is this new reading of history that is contained in the Bible. Whereas all other conquerors not only laid down laws to justify themselves at the time, but also caused history to be written to justify them in the eyes of future generations, whereas, that is to say, laws and history were in these cases whatever the conqueror determined they were to be, the standpoint here is essentially different. In the Bible the laws are framed to meet the case of the weak and the needy, and history is conceived and described from the point of view of the

[68] Lev. xix, 17.

conquered. The ethical meaning of history was here discovered, the meaning of all that happens by the commandment of God. In particular the Bible expresses with imperishable pathos opposition to a double code of morality. It opposes the laying down of different codes of morals for the great and for the humble, for rulers and for ruled, for individuals and for states, for private life and for public or political life. All history is now conceived as the history of the struggle for what is good and just, for the one thing that is needful, and it thus becomes in the true sense world history, the revelation of the eternal, living God. It now attains its unity and its completeness.

The men of whom we are speaking were able to realize and maintain this because they had the living conviction that they had been called of God. He who is conscious of such a call feels that he has been sent to the future, and he is therefore able to wait for and appeal to the future. He has in mind " the day that is to come." This conception of the future is another especially Hebrew thought. It is implied in the conceptions of Creation and of the commandment. What the One God has created is a life that will abide and attain its fulfilment; what He has ordained will have its day, " the day of the Lord," when it will be justified. That alone is permanent and real which has come forth from God. In this sphere the future does not mean primarily that which will be, but that which has been ordained, that which will come to pass as surely as the Lord liveth. He has commanded it: it shall be. The future is thus the great promise, the great certainty. The Bible also calls it the great " consolation." Despite all disappointment and failure, it points to the goal, to that which surely is, and it consoles for all the disappointments of the present. This assurance of the final outcome implies an abiding conviction of the task, the path, and that conviction is another comfort in the midst of the failures of the present: For every true task is infinite. It constantly transcends itself; it is the path that ever leads to the path. This infinity of the commandment, the impossibility of fulfilling it, could hardly fail to produce a keen sense of spiritual need. At critical moments in the history of Israel it was acutely felt, and awakened a longing for something that could be called fulfilment. But the real content of this idea has always been positive, not negative, a promise, not a denial. It proclaims that the commandment of God lives, not for a time only, but, to use the language of the Bible, " unto all generations." [69] This gives to the commandment its full breadth and sweep and to history its wide horizon. It indicates the goal toward which all men can press and at which they finally meet. The existences of the individual and of a generation are fitted into a totality, and filled with corresponding depth of meaning. The totality of the human individual has become the totality of the human race. In face of the success of their enemies, in face of all hostile bragging and boasting, the irony of the prophets can find voice; their ability to see eternity behind the years and the centuries, the sublimity of God behind all human greatness, enables them to despise success and cling

[69] Isaiah li, 8, and often.

to the future. This future therefore connotes nothing historical; it is a faith. God's call and the future condition each other, and give the lie to all mythical and fatalistic theories of history.

This idea of the future is usually called " Messianic," because it originated in the hope of a Messiah — *i.e.,* an Anointed One, a descendant of David, a king by the grace of God, a man on whom rests " the spirit of the Lord, . . . the spirit of wisdom and understanding, the spirit of counsel and might, the spirit of knowledge and of the fear of the Lord." [70] He is the man who is to come; in him the history of the future gains personal form and colour. He will usher in a kingdom of fulfilment, a kingdom in which wickedness or destruction, dispute or war, finds no place, an era of peace and reconciliation, the time when " the earth shall be full of the knowledge of the Lord, as the waters cover the sea." [71] This Messiah is called by God to be the " judge of all the earth." " He shall not judge after the sight of his eyes, neither reprove after the hearing of his ears: but with righteousness shall he judge the poor, and reprove with equity for the meek of the earth." [72] This picture of the Messiah passes into that of his people, the people of Israel, whose path is the path to this future, and whose history therefore becomes Messianic history, the history of the future. The destiny of humanity is Israel's destiny, and Israel's destiny is that of humanity. The obligation that has been laid upon it is also the promise that has been given to it. Therefore the people of this religion comes to be the Messiah. " I the Lord have called thee in righteousness, and will hold thine hand, and will keep thee, and give thee for a covenant of the people, for a light of the Gentiles; to open the blind eyes, to bring out the prisoners from the dungeon, and them that sit in darkness out of the prison house." [73]

But side by side with this personal interpretation of the Messianic king and the Messianic nation, and by and by transcending it, emerges that idea of the future of which we have spoken, the Messianic conception of the life of the " days to come," the world that is to be, the realization of the ideal, the appearance of the Beyond in the Here. This is the future which is brought about by the freedom and piety of men, by their " return " to God. To it was applied the name which was used to denote the dwelling-place which man prepares for God in the world, the " Kingdom of God." The Kingdom of God now becomes the kingdom of the future, and to it men's longings turn. It is not a kingdom above or beside the world in which men live, but the hallowing, the reconciliation, of this world. It is the world in which " God will be Lord over the whole earth, he who is the one and whose name is the one." It will have come when all men " hallow the name of God," when God " gives the peoples pure lips that they may all call on the name of the Lord and serve him shoulder to shoulder." The daily prayer will then be: " Hallowed be his name: his kingdom come." There have been

[70] Isaiah xi, 2.
[71] Isaiah xi, 9.
[72] Isaiah xi, 3–4.
[73] Isaiah xlii, 6–7.

times in the history of Israel, times of adversity, when men were inclined to picture this future as they had the Life Beyond, or to "compute the end." But even at such times the ideal finally prevailed. However prominently the stress was laid on the Messiah, on the Messianic people or on the Messianic era, it was always the thought of the "Kingdom of God" that men had in mind.

It was this Messianic idea that brought out into clearness Israel's message for the world. In it Israel's task and Israel's responsibility found clear expression. Israel now began to see that every "call" is to service. Every one to whom such a call comes is, as the Bible says, a "servant" of God.[74] This title is applied especially to the Messiah, whether he be regarded as a person or as the nation. Israel now also learned that every "call" means suffering. To have a task for humanity laid on one means to take on oneself a heavy burden and bear it for men. The "Servant of God" is a sufferer; his path is a tragedy. The thought of suffering had already been illumined by the faith in the One God. Humility was seen to mean submission to God's will and trust in His love. Reverence had seen in it a test, a training to endure and overcome. But now suffering is set in a Messianic light. There is a suffering for the sake of the future, a suffering for the reconciliation of the world. One of the prophets saw the "Servant of God" in this very guise as the suffering Messiah. He is the despised and rejected one, who "bears the sins of many" and "bears their griefs and carries their sorrows."[75] And even in this suffering servant of God the two ideas of individual and nation coalesce. This Messianic fate of the nation is voiced in still another Bible word, "the remnant." It had already been understood that decision for God means a great election or selection among men, in which only a few of the many remain. "A remnant shall return."[76] But now it was felt to be the great consolation, the profound meaning of the world's history, that these few are they to whom the future belongs. They are "the holy seed."[77] "And the remnant that is escaped of the house of Judah shall again take root downward, and bear fruit upward. For out of Jerusalem shall go forth a remnant, and out of Mount Zion they that shall escape."[78]

The Messianic idea also completes the conception of reverence toward man: it culminates in the idea of reverence toward humanity. The grand style here enters into history. This is the source of the optimism of Israel's religion. It is not the optimism of the man who is satisfied with everything because he is satisfied with himself. It is the optimism that is contained in decision for God, the optimism that becomes the commandment and therefore sometimes demands heroism and martyrdom. It is also the capacity and the determination to make the great resistance, to be zealous and earnest, to do and dare to the end. For the sake of the Messianic ideal it can take up a stand against the year and against the century. For the sake of God

---

[74] Isaiah lii, 13, et al.   [76] Isaiah x, 21.   [78] Isaiah xxxvii, 31–32.
[75] Isaiah liii, 3, 4.   [77] Isaiah vi, 13.

it is able to deny, to despise, to reject. It cannot but be at times pessimistic at the thought of things as they are in the world, but what is peculiarly Jewish in this pessimism is that it never leads to resignation or indifference toward things as they are. It is only the " No " that is the downstroke of the " Yes," [79] the negative side of the optimism, the courage that is determined to " prepare the way." This optimism is the steady setting of the will toward God: it is the " and yet " of faith in the meaning of life. And in it we hear the voice of the new principle that in Israel's religion has become world history.

The Individual and the Community. Like all other religions, that of Israel is a religion of the individual. He is the subject of it. Its gifts are bestowed on him, and it is to him that its demands are addressed. But each individual is brought by his religion into touch with a larger whole — viz., the community consisting of those who profess the same religion as he — and so the desire of the individual heart to possess the religion is reinforced by the desire that it should be the abiding possession of the community from generation to generation. This need for the larger whole makes itself felt in all religion except that of the hermit. Anything that is calculated to preserve the believing community rouses the interest and demands the support of the individual, and finally becomes a fixed tradition. Thus, if we may use the expression here, the religion of the community, of the church, is superadded to that of the individual. This wider aspect becomes fraught with more significance as the individual realizes what he owes to the community, the help and strength it affords him. Through it he gains increased assurance of his religion. He realizes that he does not stand alone either in space or time, and his fellowship with others is a constant source of strength, assurance, and confidence. He becomes still more conscious of all this when the existence of the community takes on in his mind the Messianic, worldwide meaning, and thus seems to guarantee to him, individual though he be, a place in history. Its life and its outward forms are full of interest to all who claim to belong to it. Like the individual, the community also should learn the meaning of sanctification and have its own future. To those commandments which personal religion lays on the individual are added those duties which arise from the existence of the community.

As we have seen, it is a peculiar feature of Israel's religion that it demands definite behaviour from the individual. In a similar manner interest in the continued existence of the community calls for definite forms of worship and determines their nature. This interest was embodied in varied enactments, observances, and forms, as, for example, in the ordinances regarding food and the observance of the Sabbath. These have often been called the ceremonial legislation or " the Law " of Israel's religion, but the name is unsuitable, for it does not indicate what is essential and it is apt to mislead. More accurate and more illuminative is the name that was applied to the observances of an early period. They were called " the hedge round the *torah*," and this name

[79] These are expressions used by the philosopher Hegel.

clearly expresses their real nature and purpose. They were meant to preserve and secure the doctrine, to delimit and hedge round the community of the *torah*. That is why they became more numerous in proportion as the community had to fight for its existence in face of persecutions and allurements to disloyalty. The service rendered by the Pharisees, if we may allude to that sect in this connexion, can be understood only when it is realized that their great object was to preserve and guard the community at a time when the foundations of its life were shattered. The special importance of the Jewish ordinances lies in the fact that the religion of Israel lacks the means employed by other religious communities to secure unity and provide protection. In consonance with its whole nature, it lacks a definite, rigid creed. It knows no dogma. Dogma has never had any place in it, because it knows no definite, restrictive " facts of salvation," with their sacraments, and because it has no official body with authority to make the articles of the creed binding. And, further, lacking sacraments and dogmas, it does not constitute a church which is a channel of salvation and in which the individual merely accepts the faith of the church. It recognizes only the religious community composed of individuals who accept the faith and undertake the obligations. The Jewish community is thus " congregational " and democratic in character.

But just on that account this " hedge round the instruction " is all the more important. Needless to say, these enactments have always been distinguished from the religious commandments proper. Obedience to them has never been regarded as " good works," disobedience to them has never been condemned as sin, and, what is still more significant, it was unhesitatingly declared that their validity would cease in the Messianic time, when the great purpose for which the community had been maintained was accomplished. Nay, more; it has been only at rare times, in certain periods of transition, that they have been felt to be a burden or restriction. Speaking generally, they have been gladly observed, and the ancient phrase " thy law is my delight " [80] has been exemplified in them. Only one danger has threatened them, the danger of losing their content and their meaning, of being regarded as something merely ' legalistic,' so that men have sometimes kept them merely for the sake of keeping them and with a feeling of having thereby *done* something. There was also, perhaps, another danger, the danger that their importance would be overrated. They have sometimes been looked upon as being the whole of the religion, and as a result personal piety has sometimes been relegated to a subordinate place or been lost sight of altogether in comparison with this congregational religion. At such times it has been necessary to emphasize what personal religion really means.

Nevertheless, on the whole this ' Law ' has been fraught with rich blessing. Its precepts are far from being matters to which a religious man can be indifferent; they are by no means merely outward or external. They are all related to religious thoughts and life and longings. They are meant to be

[80] Ps. cxix, 77, 174, *et al.*

symbols that point hour by hour to God and His commandment, to remind men of something that transcends the ordinary and the mean, and they have therefore always nourished religious activity and pious sentiment. The passage that enunciates their meaning and purpose is " That ye may remember and do all my commandments, and be holy unto your God." [81] The ' Law ' represents the great and successful attempt to bring religion into daily life, and thereby to bring man into day-long touch with God. All the small and prosaic things of life, even eating and drinking, thus received their note of worship, all the dull and trivial things their note of poetry and spirituality. The ' Law ' also ensures that human life contains a touch of that asceticism with which no religion can dispense. It has taught self-control, moderation, sobriety, and liberty as against license, thought as against impulse. It has in view the goal indicated by the words which stand at the beginning of Israel's history, the words spoken at Sinai: " Ye shall be unto me a kingdom of priests, and an holy nation." [82]

This ' Law ' has served to maintain in the community of Israel an ever-ready piety, a moral purity, and even a courage to face martyrdom. For many a long day this could not fail to be an essential part of the task set to the community and to each individual member of it. The commandment that enjoined a sense of responsibility for the fellow-man necessarily and from the beginning involved the commandment to missionary work, and at many periods the religion of Israel had its Apostles and made numerous proselytes. Centuries of oppression and persecution, such as no other community has ever been called upon to suffer, aimed at shutting out the Jewish people from all contact with other nations, and the Jews were forbidden to preach to them. But they came to see that their existence and their tenacity in holding fast to their faith were in themselves a message to the world, a missionary enterprise. Religion should speak to the world through the lives of its adherents. The greatest commandment of all was to show by word and deed what the religion of Israel is, what it demands and secures. The ancient phrase that speaks of the " hallowing of the divine name " now gathered new meaning. To bear witness to the religion in daily life was seen to be its meaning. The restrictions and prohibitions lasted right through the Middle Ages, down to the beginning of the nineteenth century, when liberty began to be restored; but during all that time, and in spite of all repressions, spiritual life and scientific work were cultivated by the community. An abundant and varied literature testifies to their activities. And, what is still more, that work was followed with interest by the whole community, which contained no illiterates nor uneducated. This too was a source of strength, but the most important matter in this period of trial was the continued existence and loyalty of the community.

This religion can be said to have a twofold history — the history of Jewish thought as affecting the Jews themselves and the history of that thought

[81] Numbers xv, 40.   [82] Exod. xix, 6.

and its results in other religions and in the world. There too Jewish faith has manifested its life and its power, working like leaven and exerting a compelling influence. Indeed, a history of the Christian Church might be written from the point of view of the prominence of the Jewish element in it. At no time has the Jewish religion been important in respect of the numbers of its adherents. With its (roughly speaking) fourteen million members it is a small body compared with the great religions of the world. But in this very fact it has descried one of its tasks. It has read in it a commission and call to give voice to the moral conception of minority, to the idea that justice is really justice only when the few and the weak share in it. The importance of the religion of Israel lies not in its extensive, but in its intensive aspect, not in its geographical expansion, but in its living power. It has never been able to boast large numbers, but it has been the most influential religious principle in the world. This principle has lived and worked for two thousand years in other religions and philosophies, but its truest content and value have been evinced within the Jewish community itself. It is a world religion both in other religions and apart from them. Its adherents have always felt it to be their God-given task to be loyal to their own community; to gather from the past courage to face the future; to cleave to the great principle which was revealed among them and which, like all revelation, has ever become and will ever become new; to cleave to the determination to serve the One God and do their duty by all that He has created and commanded; to continue in this faith and fear.

BIBLIOGRAPHY

Graetz, *Geschichte der Juden* (11 vols., 1853–75, some of them in a 2nd or 3rd ed., 1888–1900); Kittel, *Geschichte der Hebräer,* his *Geschichte des Volkes Israel* (2 vols., 1888 and 1892; 5th and 6th ed., 1923 and 1925); Wellhausen, *Israelitische und jüdische Geschichte* (1894; 7th ed., 1914); Lazarus, *Die Ethik des Judentums* (2 vols., 1898, 1911); Bousset and Gressmann, *Die Religion des Judentums im neutestamentlichen (späthellenistischen) Zeitalter* (1903; 3rd ed., 1926); Baeck, *Das Wesen des Judentums* (1905); Elbogen, *Der jüdische Gottesdienst* (1913; 2nd ed., 1924); Buber, *Vom Geist des Judentums* (1916); Cohen, *Die Religion der Vernunft aus den Quellen des Judentums* (1919); Dubnow, *Weltgeschichte des jüdischen Volkes* (10 vols., 1925 ff).

2. BUDDHISM

by Heinrich Hackmann

At the point where the railway-line from Calcutta to Darjeeling in the Himālayas begins to climb from the Indian plain to the mountains the train crosses the so-called Terâi or Tarai. This is a marshy lowland, sloping gently toward the south. Its average elevation above the sea is 650 feet; the breadth varies up to thirty miles. Much of it is bush interspersed with a few tall trees; some of it is covered with long grass, with an occasional tilled field and a few scattered settlements. The whole district is moist, swampy, un-healthy, and fever-stricken; and its only inhabitants are a few poverty-stricken survivors of pre-Aryan tribes. The British Government has laid a few light railways through this frontier district that lies between the Ganges plain and the Himālayas. In December of the year 1896 a memorial column was dug up in this territory. It had been erected about the year 250 B.C. to mark the birthplace of Buddha. It bore the still legible inscription: "Here the Sublime One was born." Not far off, in the same Tarai district near the place called Piprāvā, a grave-mound was discovered in 1898. When the grave was opened it was found to contain several vessels filled with all kinds of valuables. A steatite urn bore the inscription in ancient writing and ancient language: "This urn with the relics of the sublime Buddha, of the family of Sakya, is reverently placed here by his brethren, sisters, and wives."

Thus not far apart we have attestations of the birth and death of the man who gave his name to Buddhism. Next to the religion of Israel, Buddhism is the oldest of the world religions that still survive, and in the opinion of many it is the most profound and precious wisdom that has ever been conceived.

Buddha must have been born about 560 B.C., and his death must have taken place about 480 B.C. We know very little about him that is reliable, except broad outlines and a number of names. His father was Shuddhodana; he ruled over a small dominion, of which Kapilavastu was the centre and capi-tal. The name of Buddha's mother is given as Māyā, and she is said to have died seven days after he was born. The princely line to which Buddha belonged bore the name Sakya, and therefore the famous son is sometimes called Sakyamuni, "the Hermit of the Sakya Family," or Sakyasimha, "the Lion" of that family. His personal name was Siddhārtha ("the Success-ful") or Sarvarthasidda, which has almost the same meaning. The family name, by which he is frequently called, was Gautama. 'Buddha' is not a proper name. It is the designation of a special dignity which he acquired when he had gained the profoundest knowledge (bodhi), and it means " the Awakened " or " the Enlightened." Another title frequently applied to him is Tathāgata, which is sometimes translated as " He who has gained the Truth " and sometimes as " the Perfect One."

Prince Siddhārtha grew up as the son of an Indian royal house, and received the best education that was possible in his time. When he attained manhood he married Yasodhara, who bore him a son, Rāhula. Ere long, however, he broke away from the life he had led. Against the wishes of his relatives, and while still in the freshness of early manhood, he left his father's palace and betook himself to the wilderness. This step was the result of an unconquerable longing to think out the mystery of human life, a longing which he could not satisfy in the environment and ˄ ˙d the duties of his home. At first he sought the guidance of renowned Brahmans, but, finding no satisfaction in their teaching, he devoted himself to an ascetic life, in which at that time many believed the path to the profoundest knowledge was to be found. Here again he was disappointed, and after years of self-torture he abandoned that path. Then suddenly came the day when the veil fell from his eyes. As he sat engrossed in thought under a pipal-tree (the Bodhi druma or, as it is sometimes called, the Bo-tree) the secret of the world and the right path were suddenly revealed to him — he became the Buddha.

From that time he went about the country as an itinerant teacher, preaching his new truth and gaining disciples. He defined his teaching with the greatest care, and defended it against objections and attacks. He solicitously watched over the studies of his disciples, organized them into a band of seekers after the new path, superintended their efforts, and guided their steps. The number of his followers grew, and included, it is said, his own family. Twenty-four years he spent in this way, seeking to perfect and extend his teaching. The scene of his labours was his own native land and the two larger kingdoms, Kosala and Magadha (Behar), which adjoined it on the west and south — that is to say, roughly the territory between the eighty-first and eighty-seventh degrees of longitude, of which Benares is the centre. He is said to have died, at the age of eighty, at Kusinagara (Oudh), in a copse on the bank of a river.

These are the only incidents in his life which can be said to be historical, but many legends have grown up round his name. Some of them may be based on facts, but it is hardly possible to say more precisely what historical basis there is for many of the stories that are told.

With regard to his teaching, however — and it is with it that we are chiefly concerned here — we possess fairly complete and reliable information.

The teaching of the Buddha is closely bound up with the philosophy and religion of India, which had been developed before his day, and it will be helpful to recapitulate briefly some of the fundamental conceptions into which, if we may put it so, the Buddha was thus born.

The ancient Vedic gods of nature had, at least for thinking minds, passed away, and men were searching for a new, comprehensive power as a basis on which existence might rest. This single universal power was conceived in two ways, and was designated by two names, Brahma and Ātman. The Brahma — *i.e.,* the power of the sacred word used in sacrifice by the officiating Brahman — is itself a supra-divine entity, and finally becomes the creator and sustainer of the universe. The Ātman, on the other hand, the self or ego that dominates the personality, leads to the conception of an ego in the universe. These two, Brahma and Ātman, were gradually identified with each other; they are the same absolute world power looked at from different points of view. But this ultimate world power is very vague and abstract. The idea of God is faint; the idea of an impersonal power is prominent. Further, this ultimate world principle awakens all kinds of questions which are not easy to answer — as, for example, in what relation Brahma or Ātman stands to empirical individual existence. The mysteries that abound here are deliberately overlooked in order not to arouse uncertainty in the mind, or the whole conception of God is resolutely rejected. The school of Sāmkhyam, which postulates an atheistic dualism of spirit and matter, follows the latter method.

In proportion as the conception of God loses its clearness, the idea of deliverance becomes more prominent. This had already happened in India before Buddha's time. The suffering that is inherent in existence gradually comes more prominently into view. Existence is conceived as the entanglement of a spiritual principle in matter, a condition of restraint which results in misery. The processes of empirical life are more and more clearly seen to be aspects of suffering, obstacles, confusion, deception. All the defects and imperfections of mundane things, disease, pain, privations, bodily decay, passions, disappointments, and ultimately death, are so many proofs that the spiritual principle is under the dominion of matter. Thus there arises an increasing desire for deliverance from this subjection and torture. Death does not bring the desired deliverance, for reincarnation (the transmigration of souls, metempsychosis) was a fixed article of faith. Death is only the end of one chapter of life. The decay of the body is necessarily followed by the rise of a new body, and in this regard the barriers between human beings and animals are broken down: a man may be reincarnated in the body of an animal. This belief naturally gave added intensity to the sense of the suffering that is inherent in existence. It implied that this suffering was endless, that life was a ceaseless passage through bodies and existences, all of which involved a captivity of suffering. This was called *saṃsāra,* the ceaseless moving through various existences, the dread cycle of births and deaths. The varieties of incarnations, however — *i.e.,* the difference that did to some extent exist between human or animal life and the separate kinds of existence —

were associated with moral self-consciousness and moral self-judgment, and led to the thought that the kind of reincarnation, with its greater or less degree of suffering, represented a verdict on the life that a man had led. This is what is meant by *karma,* literally ' act ' or ' deed ' (ritual performance). It is the resultant of all the deeds of a life. After death these make themselves felt in the kind of reincarnation that ensues. There is no question here of a divine judgment on life. The tribunal of *karma* proceeds as by a law of nature. This conception of the law of *karma* of course increased the sense of the misery of existence and strengthened the desire to find a way of deliverance from it. Even before the time of Buddha various answers had been given to the question how man could be delivered from life. These answers represent two outstanding views. According to the first of these, the way to deliverance is found in enlightenment or knowledge. As soon as a man recognizes that existence is essentially an evil, and sees clearly what his life essentially is — that is, the entanglement of a spiritual principle by the allurement and power of matter — he brings his slavery to an end. By looking frankly and resolutely into the depths of this mystery he cripples, as it were, its power, and thus steps outside the circle of its spell.

According to the other view, the means of deliverance is found in peculiar spiritual exercises, called Yoga. This denotes an abnormal inward condition (Yoga means literally ' tension ' or ' strain '), in which the ordinary mental level is transcended and new exceptional experiences are made. Many peculiar means were employed to induce this state of mind, chiefly self-flagellation and asceticism (*tapas,* literally ' heat '), as well as many other physical and mental exercises — control of respiration, bodily attitudes, and control of thought. By the use of these methods unusual states of mind were created, which were associated with peculiar sensations of happiness and peace and in which the symbol of deliverance was seen. The Yogi (*i.e.,* he who practises Yoga) attains complete purity and peace, deliverance from the suffering of the world. This condition was called (even before the time of Buddha) Nirvāṇa(m). We shall consider it in greater detail later.

These are in brief the main types of thought on the subject of human life which were common in India before Buddha was born and with which we must assume him to have been familiar both by teaching and study. But these thoughts, as they were set forth and translated into practice at that time, did not commend themselves to him as a solution of the riddle of life. Much of this teaching he accepted, but he combined with it his own original conception of existence, and thus produced something that was quite new. In many of its details, of course, his teaching showed affinity with former speculation, but it had features of its own, and its compactness, its depth of thought, and the religious force and warmth with which he preached it invested it with a power which has lasted through the centuries.

" Existence is suffering ": the Buddha wholeheartedly accepted this statement of earlier thinkers. It was the starting-point of all his thought, but he read into it a much profounder meaning. To him suffering is not merely what is usually understood by that word — pain, privation, bodily and mental defect — though it includes all these. The suffering that is inherent in existence is much more deeply rooted. It manifests itself in three aspects which are present in all existence. These are sorrow (*dukkha*), transitoriness (*anicca*), and unreality (*anattā*). Under the first are included the painful experiences through which all men are called upon to pass and in which the suffering of existence becomes patent to all. Most prominent among them are disease, age, and death. But these are, so to speak, merely symptoms: something more serious lies behind them. This is *anicca,* the instability and perishableness of all that is. Everything changes: nothing abides. The destroying worm is present in everything. In the words of the German poet:

> for all that from the Void
> Comes forth, deserves to be destroyed.[1]

The period of existence may be longer or shorter in different cases; strength, beauty, greatness, and glory may seem to be greater in one case than in another, but all are alike doomed to pass away. Anyone who really thinks must see that birth is the beginning of death, that every beginning is the first step on the path to the end. But there is a third and still more grave defect in all existence — *anattā* (the ' non-self '), illusion, the unreality that inheres in all that appears to exist. The perishableness of all things implies that they are not, for it involves the notion of non-existence. A true existence could not perish, for how could it be transformed into its opposite, non-existence? The perishable is necessarily illusory; it is a coming and a going, an appearing and a disappearing, with a shorter or longer interval between. If for the sake of illustration we imagine the interval to be infinitely short, we see the nothingness, the illusoriness, of anything that is subject to change.

In his blindness, however, man thinks that this unreality, this changeableness, is a reality, a permanent thing, and allows himself to become engrossed in it, for he feels himself drawn to the things around him. He desires to possess and enjoy them: he cleaves to them. This cleaving to the illusory things of the world constitutes, indeed, all human effort. Man grasps at this or that grosser or more refined object: he would like to possess or hopes to gain it. But they are all illusions! He is grasping at shadows! There is a contradiction in this endeavour to attain things that do not really exist, in this cleaving to what dissolves in smoke. We realize this, and, realizing it, continually experience anew the suffering that is inherent in life. The true satisfaction that we hoped for is never attained: what we seem to have gained and enjoyed turns out to be an unexpected emptiness. Our thirst is never quenched. What seems to quench it always turns out to be a *fata morgāna* which brings no satisfaction. Full of this unrest, man dies, finish-

---

[1] Goethe, *Faust,* " Studierzimmer," l. 985. Said by Mephistopheles.

ing this life only to awaken in a new life marked by the same unrest. From existence to existence he is thus hurried through endless eras, through repeated incarnations on higher or lower planes of existence, borne along by the current of perishable, unreal phenomena that bring him nothing but sorrow and suffering, the ocean of births and deaths (*saṃsāra*).

But the ever-renewed pain of this vain ' cleaving ' arises not only from the illusoriness of the world, but also and in equal degree from the illusoriness of one's own ego. All that has been said about the things outside us — that they are all fraught with pain, perishable and unreal — is equally true of man himself. In man there is no permanent, abiding element, no imperishable substratum, no " immortal soul." On the contrary, man himself is composite and changeable. He is a structure, endowed with functions, which has its day and then completely dissolves and disappears. Man can be called an assemblage of parts, just as a carriage is an assemblage of parts. When these are taken asunder, nothing remains. The component parts of man are the so-called " five groups " or " five collections " — (1) corporeity, (2) feeling, (3) perception, (4) judgment, (5) consciousness. When these five groups are conjoined you have a human being. So long as they cooperate the human being exists. When they are dissociated the human being passes away. None of these component parts is permanent, and, as they constitute the whole man, there is no permanent, abiding element in him. To assume that there is an abiding basis for human existence, such as an immortal soul, is, according to Buddha, a very dangerous error, and he often combats it. He was fond of setting forth the absence of any permanent substratum, and of illustrating this by two analogies. One was that of running water; the other was a burning flame. In both there seems to be a permanent object present, in the one an unchanging stream and in the other a uniform light, but in reality they are only two ever-changing but constant processes.

But if man completely passes away in death, how can we conceive of a reincarnation, which after all must be in some way or other a " transmigration of souls " ? The Buddha postulates a reincarnation, but for him there is no transmigration of souls. Nothing of the vanished being passes into the new one. There is no real connexion of that kind between the different incarnations. It is the total result of the extinct life which calls into being a new existence of a definite kind. The new existence is connected with the former life in a decreed way, just as an effect is connected with its cause. A living being originates through the action of a casual connexion: the efficient causes lie in the former life. This causal nexus (the *nidāna* chain, or connecting chain with its twelve links) is one of the most obscure points in the teaching of the Buddha. But he finds in it the proof that a rigid inner necessity connects the history of any life with the origination of a subsequent one. The law of *karma* obtains here. The fact that a former life has run out, that a definite result was achieved in it, that this result was of a certain character — that is the sufficient cause why, even after that life has completely vanished, it should produce a new life corresponding to it. In this causal connexion the most important factor is the 'thirst' or the 'cleaving' to which the vanished life was subject, that eager grasping after the world and its objects which desires the unattainable. And this 'cleaving,' this 'thirst,' is due to something that lies still deeper, to man's ignorance of the nature of things. Its ultimate root is *ignorance*.

If this continuous generative process, this ever-new procession of one existence from another, is to cease, then the 'thirst,' the 'cleaving,' must be completely subjugated, and as the ultimate root of this 'thirst' is in ignorance, this too must be overcome. When a man has learned the truth about the world, when he has come to see how profoundly the happenings of life are interconnected, and when thus the fatal urge, which makes him long for the illusions of existence, has been completely extirpated, his life has no further causal effect — the *karma* nexus has been broken. Even before Buddha's day the goal thus reached had been called Nirvāṇa(m), and he retained the name. The word means 'extinction' — that is, the extinction of the flame of desire which had found its fuel in the 'thirst' and 'cleaving.' When the fuel has been withdrawn that flame can burn no longer. The continued existence of the body has no relevant connexion with Nirvāṇa; its dissolution (*i.e.,* the separation of the five groups which had been brought together by a previous *karma*) may be postponed; that is to say, the attainment of Nirvāṇa and death are not necessarily simultaneous. When death does come (and a man attains Parinirvāṇa, perfect Nirvāṇa) this excarnation is followed by no reincarnation — deliverance has been found. (The question whether there is not some kind of positive " eternal bliss " beyond Nirvāṇa is entirely unbuddhistic: it was raised by later speculation. In Buddhist doctrine Nirvāṇa is the final end. Of course, it is frequently lauded as a place of blissful refuge from all suffering, as a state of peace, but this idea involves no contradiction. The certainty that escape has been found from all the suffering of existence fully justifies positive expressions of this kind.)

But how is this final goal attained? In particular, what agency is there to help men to subdue the 'thirst,' the 'cleaving' to life? The path to it is a *via media,* a middle path; that is, it avoids the two extremes of devotion to enjoyment and asceticism. Between these two Buddha has pointed out a path which he calls the Eightfold Path. His practical directions for finding the true path and living the true Buddhistic life are set out under eight heads: (1) right belief (or right view of life); (2) right purpose; (3) right speech; (4) right behaviour; (5) right calling (or occupation); (6) right endeavour; (7) right contemplation; (8) right concentration. This list, of course, requires further elucidation. Its contents are sometimes grouped into three categories — viz., understanding, morals, concentration. A correct, profound understanding of Buddhist doctrine must be reached by study; further, by obedience to the moral precepts one must bring oneself into the right state of body and mind; lastly, by the practices of meditation and concentration one must unloose the chains that bind him to existence. The demands made under the categories of understanding and morals are closely akin to each other. They include both theory and practice. By following them a man brings himself mentally and bodily into complete accordance with the Buddhist conception of the world. Contemplation and concentration are of another kind. The two words denote a comprehensive system of spiritual exercises. It opens with " devout contemplations." These can be directed to objects of any kind, and help, as it were, to saturate the mind with certain conceptions (say, of perishableness, the loathsomeness of the body, death) or to objectify mental processes and disconnect them from the self. The culmination of the system is reached in the ' meditations ' or ' concentrations.' By means of certain methods of mental discipline, peculiar, abnormal mental conditions (*dhyāna*) are experienced, in which one rises above all that is phenomenal to ineffable heights of liberty.

For anyone who desired to follow the precepts of the Eightfold Path ordinary civil life was full of distractions, and therefore the Buddha called upon all his serious disciples to abandon it. They had to forsake family, occupation, and society and lead a solitary life either as anchorites or as members of a monastic community. Almost from the beginning the latter mode was most frequently adopted. Buddhistic monasticism was a protective measure whose aim was to render possible the mode of life that was suitable for the purpose in view: in itself it had no special value, and no special merit attached to it. The Buddha laid down numerous rigid rules for these monastic communities. The dwellings had to be simple — in many cases they were mere rock-caves — and they had to be away from cities or villages. The dress of the monks was strictly prescribed. It consisted of three garments — an under-garment, a kind of coat, and a cloak. The hair of the head and the beard were shaved off. As the monk must be free from the necessity of earning his bread by toil, he had to beg his food, and for this purpose he made a mendicant round every morning. He was not forbidden to eat meat if he found it in his wallet, but later Buddhism strictly prohibited all meat diet. The rules for the monastic life were summed up in ten (negative) commandments, as follows:

(1) Refrain from killing.
(2) Refrain from stealing.
(3) Refrain from unchastity.
(4) Refrain from lying.
(5) Refrain from intoxicants.
(6) Refrain from solid food after midday.
(7) Refrain from dancing, music, and theatrical representations.
(8) Refrain from using garlands, perfumes, and salves.
(9) Refrain from using high and broad couches.
(10) Refrain from accepting gold and silver.

This decalogue, however, indicated only the broad lines of behaviour. Further regulations covering the minutest details were added, and this process was continued long after Buddha's time. The oldest document containing these detailed regulations is the *Prātimoksha*, a list of about two hundred and fifty contraventions by which the monks had conjointly to test their consciences twice every month. The day appointed for this searching of hearts was called *upavasatha* (*uposatha*) — *i.e.*, "day of fast." The procedure was strictly regulated, and this observance was the sole trace of cultus practised in ancient Buddhism.

Anyone, without restriction of caste, was eligible for admission to this monastic order. The only bars to acceptance were certain grave sins (such as parricide), some forms of disease, and lack of personal liberty. There were two stages in the process of admission — the 'exodus' (*i.e.*, the forsaking of domestic associations) and the 'entrance' (*i.e.*, admission to the order). Both were carried out with the utmost simplicity, the one essential requirement being a declaration made by the applicant in the presence of witnesses. This declaration did not bind for life, and a monk who saw reason to change his mind was free to leave the order at any time.

It was not till a later time and, as it would seem, against his will that the Buddha consented to the formation of nunneries, but these were expressly and emphatically subordinated to the monastic communities.

The man who set out to follow the right path advanced by stages. Of these there were four. The entrant was known as "one who has stepped into the stream" — *i.e.*, a novice; then he became "one who returns once more" — *i.e.*, one who will return only once more (here on earth); then "one who returns no more" — *i.e.*, he will not be reincarnated as man, but in a higher world (a 'heaven'), and thence enter into Nirvāṇa; the highest stage is that of the *arahat* ('venerable' or 'saint'), who passes immediately from his present existence into Nirvāṇa.

All who did not become members of the monastic (or conventual) communities thereby excluded themselves from full discipleship of Buddha and from attainment of the final goal. It was possible, however, to occupy a certain relationship to the teaching of the Buddha as a lay disciple. Buddha laid down instructions for these lay brethren too. They had to endeavour to lead a moral life in keeping with the demands of the time, and to fulfil all duties toward parents, teachers, wives and children, servants and subordinates, ascetics and Brahmans. The first five commandments of the monastic decalogue were especially enjoined upon them, as well as the duty of supporting the monastic communities by gifts and in other ways. All these endeavours could not procure for lay brethren the highest salvation, entrance on Nirvāṇa — that was practically, if not in theory absolutely, impossible for a layman sharing in the life of the world — but they would help to procure a favourable reincarnation, in which it would be possible for them to do what had been denied them in their present existence —

i.e., become members of a monastic community and ultimately attain the rank of *arahat*.

All the instructions, precepts, and ordinances of the Buddha were originally in the form of oral tradition. For a considerable time nothing was put into written form; indeed, it was only after the lapse of centuries that the teaching was written down and a sacred literature began to take shape. That literature seems to have consisted at first of two parts, the rules for the monastic life and the oral teaching of the Buddha. Later a third section was added, treatises of a philosophical, or, rather, psychological, nature. These three parts together were called the *Triple Basket* (*Tripiṭaka*) — *i.e., The Threefold Tradition*. The separate parts were called respectively *Vinaya Piṭaka* (*The Basket of Monastic Rules*), *Sūtra Piṭaka* (*The Basket of Instructions*), and *Abhidharma Piṭaka* (*The Basket of Commentary on the Instruction*). The oldest form of these canonical writings has come down in the Pāli language. In course of time, when Buddhism had spread to other countries, the literature was translated into numerous other tongues. This diffusion was accompanied by a considerable amount of rearrangement and expansion, and much supplementary matter was added, so that to-day it exists in different countries in very various forms.

When we look at the entire system founded by Buddha the following seem to be the chief characteristic features.

In its essentials the doctrine has a distinctly Indian character. Its affinity with older Indian thought lies everywhere on the surface, and the Western mind is at once struck by the singularities that abound in it. To begin with, the fundamental assumption of transmigration or reincarnation strikes a note that is strange to us. The emphasis with which it is declared that life is suffering; the sensitiveness that regards all taking of life as a wrong; the strength with which it is asserted that the world is unreal because it is perishable — these are features which have their origin in Indian mentality and which are perhaps ultimately due to the climate and the history of India. Again, the manner in which philosophical and religious thoughts are intermingled is peculiarly Indian. This intermingling is specially prominent in the conception of *karma,* in which the religious need for a future retribution is satisfied by philosophical argument (the *nidāna* chain). In this combination of philosophy and religion the stress is plainly laid on the former, so that the teaching of Buddha demands considerable mental ability and training — another feature which it shares with Indian systems generally. From the point of view of religion, we find in original Buddhism a very rarified air, in which it is not easy to breathe. The gods are dethroned; their heavenly seats are transitory places of reward; a deity, in the complete sense of the word, does not exist; worship or cultus, in which the individual can participate, has no place; there is no room for prayer. On the other hand, abstract ideas abound. To know or not to know, that is the question, and it is significant that deliverance can be found only in the narrow circle of monks or anchorites. The great world outside is excluded. It must be left behind. The path to salvation leads not into the world and through the world, but away from it. In a life of seclusion each individual must take upon himself the heavy task of working out his own salvation by self-discipline, self-purification, study, thought, meditation, and concentration.

This predominantly philosophical and abstract character of original Buddhism has made it, in spite of its Indian colouring, extremely attractive for thoughtful minds in all lands and among all peoples. It has aspects in which it comes into touch with philosophic thought of a quite different kind. It was a message for men as such, not only for the Indian (hence its entire rejection of caste distinctions), and it has found listeners beyond the bounds of India. Most of these, it is true, are men of unusual mental power, and it would seem as if a special temperament were also necessary to appreciate its profound appeal. Buddhism, in its original form, found no response among the masses. These, as we shall see, had to be reached by indirect means.

For some centuries after Buddha's death the community which he founded led an existence of which few details are known to us. Presumably his teaching gradually spread in the territories where it originated and in those that were adjacent to them. We do know that numerous disputes arose within the community and that attempts were made by great councils to settle these differences. It has to be remembered also that Buddhism was only one school of thought among others and that in many points it resembled these others so closely that it can hardly have been clearly distinguishable from them. At the same time, it is worthy of note that the first Greek writer who has given us detailed information about India — Megasthenes, the ambassador of Seleucus Nikator at the court of Pāṭaliputra — mentions two schools of philosophic thought, the Brahmans and the Sarmans, the latter being in all probability the Buddhist monks (*Sramana*). In that case Buddhism had already become a widespread movement in North India about 300 B.C.

A great impetus was given to the young religion by King Asoka, who ruled over an unprecedentedly large Indian dominion from 273 to 233 B.C. It was only after he had ascended the throne that this prince came under the influence of Buddhism, but he became a zealous adherent and a keen champion of the faith. This is established beyond doubt by a large number of inscriptions, recently rediscovered, which he ordered to be cut in rocks and on pillars. Asoka was a Buddhist by complete and profound conviction. For a time he himself lived the monastic life. In the year 249, under the leadership of Upagupta, the monk to whom he owed his conversion, he undertook a pious pilgrimage to the most famous centres of Buddhism, and on that occasion he erected on the spot where the Buddha was born the memorial pillar to which reference was made in our opening paragraph.

Asoka's zeal brought about a great revival of Buddhism. He laboured earnestly to purify the religion and to deepen its spiritual life. He also conceived it to be his duty to spread the Master's teaching in all directions, and even beyond the confines of India; that is to say, he felt the call to missionary effort. These aims found clear expression at the Council of Pāṭaliputra, which met by the King's command about the year 245 B.C. At that Council the Buddhist organization was thoroughly purged from heresy and heretics, and a number of Buddhist missionaries were sent forth to proclaim the message in all parts of Near India and adjacent territories. This was probably a pet project of the King himself, for we know from one of his edicts preserved on a rock that he was specially interested in the spread of Buddhism beyond India and sought to promote it by personal correspondence with Western kings like Antiochus II of Syria, Ptolemy Philadelphus of Egypt, Antigonus Gonatas of Macedonia, and others. At the Council of Pāṭaliputra nine different countries were suggested as suitable theatres of missionary effort. Some of them lay within the borders of Near India, though outside the dominion of Asoka. Besides Near India proper, mention is made of Kashmir and Gandhāra (Punjab), Bactria, certain Himālaya districts, the 'Goldland' (Suvarnabhūmi, the coastal district of Farther India), and Ceylon. In all these countries at a later time Buddhism actually came to hold a predominant position. The missionary to Ceylon was Asoka's own son Mahendra, and ere long Mahendra's sister Sanghamitrā followed him to found a conventual order. As a result of these efforts of King Asoka Buddhism became to all intents and purposes what its character and nature fitted it to be — a world religion. From this time onward, by ways and routes that we can now hardly follow, it made its way into foreign lands, till finally it overflowed like a deluge the whole of Southern, Central, and Eastern Asia. Before that happened, however, it had to undergo another great transformation, charged with a significance that has endured to the present day, and to this we must now turn our attention.

The centuries that followed the reign of King Asoka were a period of revolution and profound unrest in North India and the adjacent regions. Mighty racial movements were in progress, beginning at the frontiers of China and continuing as national migrations and displacements right through Central Asia as far as the north-west of India. These resulted in the formation, by nomadic tribes of presumably Turkish blood, who gathered together like an avalanche, of a new great empire on the frontiers of India. This was the Indo-Scythian empire, which gradually annexed large stretches of North-west India. The mightiest monarch of this empire was Kanishka, who ascended the throne about the year A.D. 78. This Indian king stands next to Asoka not only in renown and might, but also in respect of influence on the fortunes of Buddhism. His dominions embraced North-west India as far as the river Jumna and stretched beyond India as far as Khotan, Kashgar, and Bokhara. Apparently it was long after he had ascended his throne that Kanishka was converted to Buddhism, but his influence on its history was very great. In his time that religion underwent a radical transformation, and his personal influence was reinforced by the altered conditions of his empire and the state of Buddhism at the time.

In the period between Asoka and Kanishka Buddhism had come into touch with all kinds of new influences. Its missionary activities had carried it to foreign countries and to peoples hitherto unknown, where life and thought were still at a primitive stage. The Ceylon of that day, Farther India, and the Himālayan territories were peopled by half-savage tribes, and it was to them that the ideas of the most profound thinker of India on the ultimate problems of existence were now to be presented. Further, the population of Kanishka's own empire consisted largely of people of the same primitive type. This condition of things was bound to react on the manner of propaganda. On the other hand, since the time of Alexander the Great some elements of Western life and thought had been introduced into India, in particular those of Greece and Macedonia. Mention has already been made of the presence of the Greek ambassador Megasthenes in Pātaliputra. Asoka had maintained diplomatic relations with Syria, Egypt, Macedonia, Epirus, and Cyrene. After the time of Asoka there grew up on the western frontiers of India mixed empires (Indo-Greek and Indo-Parthian), in which various currents of civilization intermingled. In these circumstances there can be no doubt that both Greek and Persian ways of life and thought had become familiar, and Buddhism cannot have escaped their influence. During these centuries, therefore, Buddhism had come into touch with both foreign civilization and foreign barbarism, and it had to take account of both in order to make headway under the new conditions.

Now, in India, even before the time of Asoka, it had been found that the pure teaching of the Buddha had little attraction for the great mass of the population. It presumed too great a capacity for philosophic thought. As a result recourse was had to other, more effective manifestations of religion, such as the relic-worship practised by Asoka himself and the erection of commemorative monuments. This tendency became more prominent when primitive populations had to be dealt with; their cruder needs had to be taken into account. This did not present much difficulty, because in some respects Buddhism is a very adaptable faith. In particular, its doctrine of reincarnation was capable of being adapted to the unenlightened views of the populace. A man's fate is not irretrievably fixed all at once: by a long series of reincarnations one can gradually come to a knowledge of the truth. A temporary admixture of truth and error is therefore not so fatal. Wrapped up in vague conceptions that appealed to the people the doctrines could be presented in a way that they could understand, and the rest could be left for the future. This adaptation to alien ideas has often been practised by Buddhism when entering on new fields. It is one of its most characteristic features, and it was practised with great success in the age of Kanishka.

It is also to be kept in mind that every higher religion in course of time clothes its inmost and most sacred thoughts in the dress of theological speculation, partly to protect and preserve them, and partly to follow out and supplement certain conceptions. The impulse to recast what has come down to us is never extinguished. In particular, later speculation loves to busy itself with the founder of the religion and to connect him with its other religious conceptions. It also endeavours to reach dogmatic clearness regarding his person and to justify the adoration offered to him. These tendencies have also manifested themselves in Buddhism.

In the period between Asoka and Kanishka all the factors that have been mentioned co-operated to bring about a great fermentation and transformation in the religion of Buddha. By the time of Kanishka they had produced a new type of Buddhism, which showed great missionary activity. This new type is usually called Mahāyāna Buddhism.

Mahāyāna means " the Great Vehicle." It had always been a favourite metaphor in Buddhism to speak of the sacred teaching as a ship in which man could cross the ocean or stream of *samsāra,* the cycle of sorrow-laden existences, and reach safety on the further shore in Nirvāṇa. The new type of Buddhism now took the name of " the Great Vehicle," implying that it was a ship that could contain many travellers and carry the mass of the people. The older type of original Buddhism, which retained numerous adherents, and still retains many to this day, was called Hīnayāna, " the Little Vehicle," meaning a vessel that can carry comparatively few. Certainly these names aptly describe the outstanding distinction between the two types. Mahāyāna is a Buddhism modified to meet the needs of the masses, and by its adoption of many new conceptions it has gained adherents among many peoples and in many countries far distant from the land of its birth. Hīnayāna is less widespread, and confined to those territories that were accessible to the original disciples of the Buddha. It need hardly be said that the adherents of Hīnayāna dislike this appellation, as it seems to convey a suggestion of inferiority.

It ought also to be added that many Mahāyāna Buddhists, especially the Japanese, deny that their type of religion is a late modification called forth by a change of conditions, and claim that it goes back to Buddha himself. They maintain that he taught his doctrine in various ways according to the kind of hearers he had before him and the kind of people he had in view. He taught the Mahāyāna version for the great masses, but at first it was kept in the background and became generally known only at a later time. Historically this claim is untenable, but many Japanese Buddhists cling tenaciously to it and assert the right of Mahāyāna to be regarded as possessing originality and authority equal to those of Hīnayāna.

The following are some of the aspects in which Mahāyāna Buddhism differs from Hīnayāna.

Original Buddhism had no room for a deity, and had therefore no doctrine of God. To it the ' gods ' of the Indian populace and the ' heavens ' in which they dwelt were only other, happier kinds of existence — the rewards of a good *karma*. Of a deity in the full sense of the word, as the principle and ruler of the world, the teaching of Buddha knows nothing. Mahāyāna therefore introduces the idea of deity into the religion, and it does this in two ways: in a profoundly *speculative* way, which belongs more to philosophy than to religion, and in a *popular* way, more akin to the polytheism of the populace.

The speculative form of the theism of Mahāyāna starts from the thought that the emergence of an earthly Buddha has a hidden background in eternity. Out of this the Buddha comes as a kind of emanation. It is specially peculiar that the later development of this idea ultimately led to a tenet which is akin to the Christian doctrine of the Trinity. This Buddhistic tenet is called the doctrine of the *trikāya* — i.e., " the Triple Body." The sole background of it is the *bodhi*, " the knowledge," the attainment of which made Gautama the Buddha. In the Mahāyāna this *bodhi* becomes a metaphysical principle: it is, so to speak, the substance of the Buddhist trinity. The *bodhi* manifests itself in a threefold body — viz., *dharmakāya, nirmāṇakāya,* and *sambhogakāya. Dharmakāya* means the true existence of the world, the eternal and indestructible element that lies behind the transitory appearance of empirical existence, the true world substance that pervades all. When this *dharmakāya* manifests itself within the life of the world and assumes a form, it is the *nirmāṇakāya,* the embodied form. The historical Buddha was such a *nirmāṇakāya.* The third body, *sambhogakaya,* " body of the blessing," is the power of the blessing that resides in the *bodhi,* which works through the Buddha in the believer; it is the saving power of the Buddha community. Though the *trikāya* is thus to some extent analogous to the Christian doctrine of the Trinity, it is nevertheless possible that the Buddhist doctrine grew up quite independently, and developed out of the three entities Buddha, *dharma,* and *sangha* (*i.e.,* Buddha, doctrine, and community), which were an integral and important part of the religion from the very beginning.

The popular form of the theism of Mahāyāna Buddhism was the *bodhisattva* doctrine. The name ' bodhisattva ' (" a *bodhi* Being " — *i.e.,* one whose whole nature is pervaded by *bodhi*) is mentioned in original Buddhism. It means anyone who is just about to enter on the supreme incarnation as a Buddha. For example, Prince Siddhārtha, leaving his father's palace or living his ascetic life in the desert, was a *bodhisattva.* This was the only meaning of the word in early Buddhism. It was the last stage in the progress toward becoming a Buddha. But in Mahāyāna the *bodhisattvas* are of prime importance. There are many of them. Throughout the wide world and in the course of past ages a very large number of noble men have trod the path of the Buddha, and all of them had to pass through the *bodhisattva* stage ere they could attain the dignity of Buddha. But Mahāyāna teaches that these stopped at the *bodhisattva* stage, and did not take the final step that would have made them Buddhas, because they were filled with infinite pity for the suffering world. In their love and compassion they preferred to remain in a position in which they could still help sufferers in their times of need, and therefore they postponed for a time the last stage to the rank of Buddha. At the end of the Buddha path lies Nirvāṇa, where existence and all possibility of helpfulness ceases. The *bodhisattvas* prefer to wait and continue their ministry of help and protection to those who are in need. They dwell in the heavens, where they sit enthroned in glory and whence they look down in love and compassion on the world of suffering beings. From time to time in their desire to succour the oppressed they leave their heavenly seats, and appear on earth in all kinds of incarnations as a company of ministering angels. Of many of them it was said and believed that in their loving-kindness they had solemnly vowed to help in some way or other those that suffered, and numerous legends recounted the innumerable deeds of mercy in which the *bodhisattvas* had touchingly and marvellously manifested their inexhaustible and unwearied kindness and readiness to aid.

These *bodhisattvas* are the peculiar creation of Mahāyāna Buddhism, and the conception transformed the religion in numerous directions. The centre of gravity of Buddhist doctrine was completely shifted. The motive power of love and pity finds here ardent expression. The Buddha had also on occasion spoken of love and sympathy, but there was an element of coldness, a leaven of theory, in that love (*maitrī*): in his teaching the first and most important thing was one's own salvation, and love to others was left somewhat in the background. Buddha also taught that love to others was best shown by teaching them the truth about salvation, by seeking their conversion. Ordinary human pity for the sufferings and privations of existence was, so to speak, overborne and swallowed up by the axiomatic presupposition that " existence is suffering." It is an entirely different spirit that inspires the *bodhisattva*. His love, which is infinite pity (*mahākarunā*), glows and throbs and wins the heart. It is bent on alleviating all actual suffering, bodily and spiritual. The *bodhisattva* intervenes and saves from dangers and from death. He protects the weak and helpless, frees the captive, fights plague and famine, consoles the sorrowful, and comforts those who are ready to despair. Thus the *bodhisattvas* are energetic beings, full of practical help in face of the sufferings of life, and are thus in strong contrast with the monks of original Buddhism. The *bodhisattva* has the qualities of the knightly hero, who was ever ready to ride forth to aid the oppressed. Of course, he too cherishes the desire to lead all men to the truth as it is in Buddhism, but this end is usually achieved easily and simply as a result of his helpfulness. Those whom he delivers cannot but open their hearts to the message of their saviour.

In these *bodhisattvas* the Buddhist missionaries who laboured among for-

eign peoples had an efficient means of preparing the way for the introduction of other religious conceptions. With the help of these *bodhisattvas*
polytheism, belief in demons, and other heathen ideas could be readily assimilated to Buddhism. That is to say, the gods and demons of the peoples
whom the missionaries were seeking to convert were declared to be incarnations of the *bodhisattvas*. In this way it was comparatively easy to secure
the transference of the faith of the heathen to other objects. It was unnecessary to uproot their faith; the *bodhisattvas* were simply put in the place of
the old gods. It is still possible to trace in the case of numerous *bodhisattvas*
of various countries features of former gods or demons or legendary figures.
It is easy for us to understand how in this manner the *bodhisattvas* figured
prominently in the minds of the masses, who saw in them gracious and
helpful deities.

Buddhist thinkers were meantime doing their utmost to provide for the
bodhisattvas a definite place in Buddhist religious doctrine, and here again
we find thoughts that closely resemble a trinitarian doctrine. According to
this teaching, each *bodhisattva* is an emanation of a Buddha. This Buddha,
being a supra-real being belonging to another world, was known as a
dhyāni-Buddha (" Buddha of the World of Meditation "). For every *bodhisattva,* however, there was a human Buddha in this world (*e.g.,* the Buddha
Gautama of Kapilavastu), in whom the special task of the earthly Buddha
was fulfilled. Thus every *bodhisattva* stands midway between a *dhyāni-
Buddha* and a human (*manushi*) Buddha, with whom he forms a compact
(theoretical) unit.

The conception of the *bodhisattva* also profoundly changed the moral side
of Buddhist teaching. In original Buddhism the chief end was one's own
salvation, growing ripe for Nirvāna. He who had attained to this was
arahat, the perfected one. There was no more for him to do. The rest of
mankind had to look after themselves. The welfare of his fellow-men had
no place in his thoughts. In Mahāyāna this ideal was replaced by the ideal
of the *bodhisattva* who labours unweariedly in the cause of those who suffer.
The adherent of Mahāyāna finds here the pattern of what life should be
and receives the impulse to make that pattern life his own. Love and readiness to help become the true aim of the faithful follower of Buddha.
The adherents of Mahāyāna declare roundly that the goal set before men
in original Buddhism is simply narrow-minded selfishness. It teaches that
man's sole aim is to deliver himself from the chains of *saṃsāra*. Surely
that is not true life. The *bodhisattva* ideal, on the other hand, summons
men to live helpfully, to be kind and unselfish toward their suffering
fellow-men. This is a nobler goal. The *bodhi*-heart (*bodhi-citta*) must be
cultivated in every believer — the heart that beat in the breast of Buddha,
the great *bodhisattva,* the mind that feels one's kinship with all men (hence
it is also called *ekacitta*, " the unity heart "), enters into the cares of all as
if they were his own, and bears them lovingly in his heart. This emphasizes

the union that subsists between all men, and love to all is the bond of this union.

Every one must see that all this puts an entirely different face on original Buddhism. Instead of being absorbed in the task of achieving his own deliverance from the chains of perishable, worthless life, instead of striving to conquer his own thirst for and attachment to things of the world, a man should turn his face resolutely toward the world and undertake a self-sacrificing combat against evil. In fact, Mahāyāna here takes up a standpoint that is altogether new. Human passions and appetites (summed up in the word 'thirst') are not in themselves perverse and reprehensible: they are so only when they manifest themselves in ways that are selfish. They should rather be brought under law to *mahākaruṇā,* pity for all, and be thus purified and hallowed. Then they are not only justifiable, but good and valuable. Pity and love should pervade the world and sanctify its life.

As might be expected, the striving after Nirvāṇa which is so prominent in original Buddhism is replaced in Mahāyāna by a yearning after a more positive kind of Hereafter. The conception of a state of eternal bliss in a heavenly kingdom naturally has a stronger appeal to the masses of the faithful, and they speak of such Paradises, ruled over by Buddhas and *bodhisattvas,* where those who have trod the right path in life dwell for ever when they leave this world. But according to many Mahāyāna teachers entrance to Paradise depends mainly on the believer's faith in the Buddhas and in the *bodhisattvas,* faith in their gracious love and willingness to help. He who believes and trusts enters into bliss. This faith finds outward expression in calling upon the name of the helpful powers, and this worship, reduced to rigid, stereotyped formulas and recited with endless reiteration, is an outstanding feature of Mahāyāna Buddhism.

Naturally also a cultus — *i.e.,* outward forms of worship — which had been entirely absent from ancient Buddhism, grew luxuriantly in this new soil. It was especially to the *bodhisattvas,* who were regarded in the light of gracious, helpful deities, that worship was addressed. The monks now also became priests and performed the rites, and the monasteries became temples which were zealously attended by worshippers. The ritual of worship became very elaborate, and in some places it was performed in imposing edifices with all the artistic accompaniments that were available. The sacred literature grew by the addition of liturgical works and legendary narratives. Numerous celebrations, most of which were held in honour of certain *bodhisattvas,* and commemorated the days of their birth or death or some of their deeds, were held throughout the year, and took the form of special services of worship.

All that has so far been said about Mahāyāna concerns only one of its aspects. But it has two aspects — one for the common people, which has been described in the foregoing paragraphs, and one for thinkers and scholars. In the minds of these latter the rude religion of the common people, with its *bodhisattvas* and rites, its Paradises and eternal bliss, its legends and ideals of pity, is merely a concession to the needs of the ordinary man and has at best only a symbolical importance. On the other hand, the educated man treads the philosophical paths. These are also rooted in original Buddhism, but the Mahāyāna philosophers have modified them in a manner of their own.

No doubt the fundamental teachings of Buddha contained the germs of all kinds of profound philosophical speculation. What he had taught about the transitoriness and unreality of the world naturally gave rise to speculation on the nature of things, existence and becoming, causal connexion, the relation between the single and the compound. Similarly, his doctrine that there is no permanent ego or self, that man is a combination of five groups, was the starting-point for much detailed psychological study. It is therefore not surprising that even within original Buddhism (Hīnayāna) many different views were held on these philosophical subjects. In Mahāyāna these lines of cleavage remained. The questions raised are of the most varied kind, and are identical with the basal questions of Occidental philosophy. The detailed speculations of the Mahāyāna philosophy, however, are among the most abstruse and profound that are to be found in all the history of human thought, and we cannot go farther into them here. We can only indicate the kind of problems that were chiefly at issue.

Buddha laid down as the inevitable attributes of all existence the three qualities suffering, transitoriness, and non-reality. Among his successors, as has been said, these theses became the subjects of profound speculations. The recognition of the quality of transitoriness led to attempts to analyze the conception of time, and also raised the question how existence in the past and future was related to existence in the present. Some answered that only the present exists; others maintained that everything in the past, present, and future alike exists and that therefore what is called the lapse of time is merely a seeming. The other profound philosophical question, of the relation between individual existence and group existence, was also keenly discussed. Some maintained the absolute independence of separate entities; others claimed that all units of existence were inseparably connected and interdependent. Both views of course led to insoluble difficulties and had therefore to be modified. It was, however, chiefly on the attribute of non-reality that discussion was concentrated. What did it mean? The Mahāyāna schools maintained that the fundamental meaning was emptiness (*śūnyatā*): the seeming reality of things is empty — it has no true contents. But this raised a thousand problems. How far does this emptiness go? We do have some knowledge and experience of this reality that is alleged to be empty. Is not at least this inward, mental experience a reality? Can we not, from its effect in us, infer the real existence of our own consciousness? Some deduced from it the existence of an actual world external to ourselves, although its real nature is different from what our senses lead us to imagine. Others maintained that there is no objective world outside of us and that it exists only in our own mind. This mind, however, is regarded as really existent and as the sufficient cause of the apparently objective world. It was, of course, another long and difficult task to make plausible the derivation of the world from the mind. But others went still further, and maintained that even the mental world did not exist. They wiped out both object and subject. What then ultimately *is?* It is easy to understand why these views have been designated philosophic nihilism. It is to be kept in mind that the three characteristics of all existence, according to original Buddhism — that it is full of suffering, perishable, and non-real — have been replaced in Mahāyāna by three other predicates — that it is empty (*śūnya*), without character (*animitta*), and without desires (*apraṇihita*).

This must suffice as an indication of the subject matter and the reasoning processes in the philosophical schools of Mahāyāna.

The spread of Buddhism beyond the frontiers of Near India began, as has been seen, in the reign of King Asoka. The new religion continued to extend uninterruptedly during the ensuing centuries, although we cannot now trace all the routes it followed. In Ceylon it quickly struck deep root. The missionary zeal of Mahendra, son of Asoka, resulted in the conversion of King Tissa and his court, and the people of Ceylon followed the example of their prince. Monasteries and stupas (dagobas) were built, and ere long Anuradhapura, the capital, was adorned by magnificent Buddhist buildings, which were famous in their day. The ruins of them can still be seen, and still arouse our admiration and wonder (Fig. 105). The north-west coastal districts of Farther India were also, it would appear, visited by Buddhist missionaries as far back as the time of King Asoka. By slow degrees the new teaching was carried by coast traders throughout these districts, and penetrated by way of the trade-routes and river-courses into the interior. The present-day countries of Burma and Cambodia (at least, their coast districts) were the first to be won over to Buddhism. Siam came next. The peoples of these countries at that time, however, were quite different from the races that inhabit them to-day, and in view of the numerous ethnological changes that took place from time to time Buddhism had many experiences of success and failure which we cannot follow in detail here. Suffice it to say that for centuries in all these parts of Farther India a weak type of Buddhism, largely intermingled with native elements, seems to have prevailed, till it was purified and revived (probably by missionaries from Ceylon). It should also be observed that Brahmanism, which in Farther India was older and stronger than Buddhism, greatly impeded the spread of the latter. It was not till the eleventh and twelfth centuries that these conditions changed and Buddhism became predominant in Burma, Siam, and Cambodia.

The case was the same in the East Indian islands. There too Brahmanism preceded Buddhism, and proved to be a strong rival. It was not till the eighth century that Buddhism made any headway in Java and spread thence to the neighbouring islands. In the fifteenth and sixteenth centuries, how-

FIG. 105. CAVE-TEMPLE STILL IN USE AT·ANURADHAPURA, CEYLON

ever, both Buddhism and Brahmanism had to give way to Islam, and to-day only a few adherents of Buddhism remain (*e.g.,* in Bali). Its traces can, how-ever, still be seen in its magnificent monuments and ruins (Fig. 106).

At a time considerably earlier than that of its appearance in Farther India Buddhism entered China and made important conquests. There had been some slight contact with that country as early as the third and second centuries B.C., and echoes of it are found in various tales, some of which are clearly legendary. The route by which Buddhism reached " the Middle Kingdom " passed through Central Asia, and its way seems to have been pre-

FIG. 106. BOROBUDUR, IN JAVA

pared both by trade intercourse and military expeditions. Later historians of Chinese Buddhism ignore these first faint points of contact and date the introduction of Buddhism into China about the middle of the first century A.D., or, to give exact figures, in the years 64-67. They say that the Emperor Ming Ti, of the (Later) Han Dynasty, saw in a dream a divine form, whose body had the colour of gold and whose head gleamed like the sun. It flew into his room. He was thrilled with joy, and asked his courtiers next morning what it might mean. They referred him to the Buddha who was worshipped in the Far West. The Emperor sent twelve delegates to the land of the Yüe-chï (Indo-Scythians) to bring back credentials of that divine one. They brought back two Buddhist monks and all kinds of objects. The monks remained in China and became the first representatives of Buddhist teaching in that country.

This tale exists in a large number of different versions, and is patently a folk-tale of dubious historicity. There is, however, a certain confirmation of its main contents. A Buddhist document has come down to us which is said to have been written by one (or both) of the Buddhist monks referred to and which is incontestably the oldest attestation of Buddhism on Chinese soil. The folk-tale just given also connects this writing with the introduction of Buddhism.

In China the new religion was faced by a condition of affairs different from that which it had found in the Himālaya districts, in Ceylon, and in Farther India. On the Hoang-ho and the Yangtse-kiang lived a people with an ancient, distinctive civilization of their own, with established religious views and institutions, and with a highly developed type of thought. As a result the new teaching met at first with little success. The strong patriotism of the people caused them to refuse to listen to any foreign teaching. Further, in a country like China, where family life was so highly prized, the monastic character of Buddhism was an additional obstacle to its reception. And, still further, the foreign language in which the sacred books of Buddhism were written presented another great difficulty, and the first task of the apostles of the new religion was to provide suitable translations. Almost the only information we have about Buddhism during its first centuries in China is that some immigrant monks translated various writings into Chinese. The first translators included no native Chinese, and tradition says that for a long period the Chinese were forbidden to become monks. From the middle of the second century onward Buddhism began to gather strength. There is occasional mention of native monks and translators. In the course of the fourth century the door was opened more widely, and permission was given to natives to enter the monastic life. Of course, equal progress did not take place in all districts. Between the years 220 and 618 China was divided into numerous separate small states, some of whose rulers were friendly, while others were hostile to the Indian religion, while the educated classes offered relentless opposition. In spite of all this, the four centuries between the close of the Han Dynasty and the beginning of the Tang Dynasty witnessed the definitive triumph of Buddhism. In that period its most outstanding champion was Emperor Wu Ti, of the Liang Dynasty (502–550), who himself on three occasions became for a time a monk. In his zeal for his Buddhist faith he even forbade the offering of living victims at the Confucian celebrations, and animals made of dough had to be substituted for them. He is even said to have enacted that dress ornamentation should not include figures of animals or human beings, lest they should be severed by the tailor's shears and thus be, as it were, deprived of life. He also put a stop to executions and corporal punishment. His support of Buddhism was of course highly approved in the distant home of Buddhism, and ambas-

sadors from Farther India came to offer congratulations and to pave the way
for closer relations. It is highly significant also that in his reign the famous
Indian teacher Bodhidharma, who under the title of 'Patriarch' had been
the leader of Buddhism in India, left his native land and settled in China.
With him the patriarchate passed to China, and this Bodhidharma has long
been one of the most popular heroes of legendary stories among Chinese
Buddhists.

No sooner had Buddhism become firmly established in China than it
began to spread farther eastward. First of all it reached Korea. In the fourth

FIG. 107. THE GREAT BUDDHA OF KAMAKURA, JAPAN

century and the years that immediately ensued the new religion was successively adopted by the three states that made up the Korea of that time. The
first apostle was a monk belonging to the Chinese petty state of Tchin. He
met with little opposition, and was greatly helped by the superiority of
Chinese civilization, which the Koreans looked up to with great respect.
We hear nothing of opposition or difficulty. Indeed, within a century and a
half the small peninsula was itself furnishing missionaries for the conversion
of its eastern neighbour, Japan. A Korean embassy visited the Mikado to
commend to him the religion they had received from China, and handed to

him various objects used in the cultus and some of the sacred books. At first vigorous opposition was offered by the adherents of Shintō, the Japanese native faith, who thus voiced the national patriotic sentiment against the introduction of any foreign worship, but it was a prince of the Imperial family, Shōtuku Daishi (died in 621), who, after long and obstinate struggles, brought victory to the intruding faith. Buddhism gradually assimilated Shintō by adopting its chief deities as *bodhisattvas* and giving its temples and temple services a Buddhist colouring. Ere long the thriving Japanese Buddhism, ignoring Korea, got into direct touch with China and requested its guidance and instruction in the fundamental teachings of Buddha. For a long time Japanese Buddhists continued to be docile disciples of the Middle Kingdom, and the journeys made by gifted Japanese monks to China for purposes of study did much to promote the education of the Mikado's empire, until finally the Japanese had sufficiently mastered the Buddhist system and were able to walk alone.

Chinese Buddhism also reached Annam, although that came much later. Progress here was slow. It may seem strange that Annam, a part of the East Indian peninsula, should not have felt the influence of the Buddhism at its doors in Siam and Cambodia. But it had remained unaffected. To the south and south-west lay long-standing foes of Annam — viz., the ancient states of Khmer and Tshampa, in the present-day districts of Cambodia and Cochin-China — whereas to the north it lay open to the influences of the mighty Chinese people. It was in the wake of these influences that Buddhism reached Annam from China. It was, however, weak and superficial; it never attained to vigorous life, and was always less influential than the Chinese State religion and the Confucian philosophy, both of which had found entrance into Annam, giving the population their spiritual backbone. In fact, to this day Buddhism in its Chinese forms plays a very subordinate *rôle* in the life of the Annamese.

There remains another important region whose conversion to Buddhism we have still to chronicle — the Central Asiatic plateau of Tibet and the adjacent territory of Mongolia.

It is a sufficient indication of the secluded character of the hill-country of Tibet that, at a time when Buddhism had long become predominant in the west, south, and east, this country was still, and long continued to be, absolutely untouched by that religion. No Buddhist missionaries found their way into that inhospitable country, either from the Himālaya states or from Turkestan, or even from China. It was the personal influence and the political sagacity of a ruler who had succeeded in welding a number of savage tribes into one state that brought about the entrance of Buddhism into that country in the seventh century A.D. This prince was Srong Tsan Gampo. About 640 he sent ambassadors to India, and introduced the new religion into his kingdom. Through his two wives, one a daughter of the Chinese Imperial family and the other a princess from Nepal, he was acquainted with both Chinese and Indian Buddhism. The fact that Srong Tsan Gampo sought to get into touch with Indian Buddhism proves that Tibet, as was natural, gravitated more towards the Himālayan countries and Northern India than toward China. This was mainly due to the fact that the southern districts of Tibet lent themselves more than the others to agriculture and a certain amount of civilization. Besides, Lhasa, which Srong had made his capital, lay in the south. The most civilized and most influential districts of his kingdom were thus adjacent to the Himālaya states, which had been built up by Indian civilization, while between these districts and China stretched great deserts and mountainous solitudes.

Tibetan Buddhism has assumed a distinctively Indian cast. The fact that the Indian writing (the Devanāgarī alphabet used for Sanskrit) was suitable for the Tibetan language was typical of other conditions. But at that time the prevalent religion of Northern India and the Himālaya states was Mahāyāna Buddhism, and for the most part the Mahāyāna of the Tantra system, which combined the philosophic nihilism (see p. 318) of Mahāyāna with a very robust if sensuous type of worship. Magic and miracles, priestly authority and superstitious tomfoolery, predominated in the popular aspect of this system, and sexual ideas were strongly accentuated. Certain deities (bodhisattvas) were provided with female 'complements' (śakti), and some of the religious exercises symbolized sexual relations, so that the religion had a pronounced erotic side. All these features were taken over by Tibet, and because of the low civilization of the population the grossness that characterized them was greatly intensified.

It was only slowly that Buddhism advanced in Tibet. The native religion (Bonpa), a primitive worship of nature-gods and spirits, was one obstacle; another was the incapacity of the backward people to understand the Buddhist teaching. For the first hundred years no progress whatever was made. But about the middle of the eighth century the arrival of the Indian Padma Sambhava brought about a revival of energy, and from that time onward, with the constant encouragement and aid of Indian teachers, the new religion steadily gathered strength. From the tenth century onward the country was dominated by religious authority to an extent that has perhaps never been equalled elsewhere. Even secular affairs were completely under the control of the religious authorities and the monks or lamas. Organized religion, indeed, monopolized authority in all that concerned intellectual life and civilization, while outside of it stood a completely uneducated, helpless, indolent populace, the ready prey of the clergy. These latter were not only keen students of Buddhist doctrine; they also developed an interest in administration and a strong tendency toward an organized hierarchy. In the higher ecclesiastical ranks the idea of the reincarnation of famous bodhisattvas played an important part. At the head of the hierarchical organization stood the two great lamas of Lhasa and Tashi Lhumpo. The former has become universally known under the title of " Dalai Lama," and although the latter,

" Pantshen Erdeni," is not so well known in other countries, he is regarded by the Tibetans themselves as equally sacred and venerable. The power of the Dalai Lama rests chiefly on the secular and political position which he attained with the help of China in the middle of the seventeenth century. He is looked upon as the incarnation of the *bodhisattva* Padmapāni, who is a kind of guardian god of Tibet.

The power of Lamaism (as Tibetan Buddhism is usually called, after its monks or lamas) was greatly increased when the religion spread throughout Mongolia and even beyond. This took place in the thirteenth and fourteenth centuries, which saw the sudden rise of those mighty Mongol states to which even China was for a time in subjection. The famous emperor of the Mongols, Kubla Khan, at whose Court the Genoese explorer Marco Polo was long a guest, did much to aid the extension of Lamaism among the Mongols. It became so firmly established among them that it has continued to be the only religion of the people to this day.

In conclusion let us pass in review the Buddhist countries as they are at the present day.

The entire Buddhist world of to-day can be divided into three parts, marked by numerous differences — viz., Southern, Northern, and Eastern Buddhism. The first comprises Ceylon, Burma, Siam, Cambodia, and all the small Buddhist communities in the East Indian islands. It is worthy of special note that there is no longer any Buddhism in Near India. Between the eighth and eleventh centuries it began to disrupt and decay. Again and again its adherents were persecuted, and it disappeared entirely when Islam invaded Near India in the twelfth century. Northern Buddhism includes the Himālaya states (Nepal, Bhutan, Likkim, Kashmir), Tibet, Mongolia, and some districts of Siberia. Eastern Buddhism prevails in China and Manchuria, Annam and Cochin-China, Korea and Japan.

Between these three groups there are noticeable differences, whereas the countries included in each present on the whole a similarity both outwardly and inwardly. It is better, therefore, to divide the Buddhist world into these three provinces instead of, as is usually done, into two — Northern and Southern Buddhism.

Southern Buddhism has preserved to a larger extent than the other two the features of ancient Buddhism. This is partly because Hīnayāna has maintained its ground here, and partly because the climate and the external conditions of life are the same as those of the land in which Buddhism arose. The monks can still wear the costume of three garments originally prescribed. Their usual shelter is still a " hut of leaves," with one or two inmates — *i.e.,* they live more or less as anchorites. Where the monastic communities are larger the houses are still primitive buildings partitioned into cells which contain merely the barest necessities of life. Only the monasteries in larger cities, like Colombo and Kandy in Ceylon, Rangoon in Burma, and Bangkok in Siam, are solid structures of several stories with rooms furnished in modern European style. The monks still beg their food in accordance with the injunction laid by Buddha on his disciples. At early morn they proceed, in larger or smaller companies, to the houses of the people, till their mendicant bowls are filled. (Fig. 108.) Of course, in the case of large and wealthy monasteries this is now a mere formality. The meals of the monks are prepared in the monastery, and what is received on the mendicant rounds is given to the poor and to animals. The monks following the Southern form

FIG. 108. BURMESE MONKS ON THEIR DAILY MENDICANT ROUND

of Buddhism take no solid food after midday. During the three months of the rainy season they follow the ancient ordinance and remain within the monastery, and what they require from outside is brought in to them.

In addition to the quarters of the monks the larger monasteries contain other buildings which are at the service of those who do not belong to the order. These contain images and pictures of Buddhas and their disciples, as well as figures taken from Brahmanic mythology, and many outsiders come to meditate and pray in front of these. (Fig. 109.) There are also apartments where the sacred books are read aloud both to monks and visitors and in the rainy season the canonical texts are read for edification. Most of the monasteries are distinguished by one or more dagobas, those memorial

columns sometimes called stupas, under which relics have been buried. These
are tower-like erections of various shapes. The main column is conical in
form, tapering rapidly upward and crowned by an umbrella-like coping,
which is often lavishly adorned. Some dagobas stand apart by themselves, and
these give a picturesque touch to the landscape. To build one of these brings
great merit.

Speaking generally, the common people in Southern Buddhist countries
regard the monks with great veneration. This is especially the case in Siam,
where the king is himself a model of devout Buddhism, and members of the

FIG. 109. AN APARTMENT IN A BURMESE MONASTERY, WITH STATUES OF
BUDDHAS

royal family are the heads of the religious system. On the other hand, the
behaviour and character of the monks are on the whole dignified and unob-
jectionable, although, of course, men who really understand and value the
more profound truths of their religion are the exception. Southern Buddhism
has at least some share in the education of the people, and there are monastic
schools in which primary instruction is given. Further, it is the usual practice
for every youth, even if he is not to become a monk, to spend a period in a
monastery. This forms a kind of transition from youth to manhood. During
that period, and in many cases in his actual school-days, the child is taught
by the monks to read and write. He learns the forms of prayer, and becomes

acquainted with the stories and legendary history of the far past. This stay
in the monastery usually creates a bond of personal goodwill between monks
and laymen. It must not be imagined, however, that the religious ideas
current among the people in the lands of Southern Buddhism are purely and
wholly Buddhist. There is a large admixture of primitive conceptions, demon-
worship, and pre-Buddhist nature-worship, so that the Buddhist doctrine is
understood only in a confused and distorted fashion. Even many monks can
be found whose Buddhism is largely adulterated with primitive beliefs.

On the whole, therefore, the impression conveyed by Southern Buddhism
is an agreeable and pleasant one. The picture presented by Northern
Buddhism (Lamaism) is entirely different. The religion here is coarser and
harsher, and it lies like a yoke of slavery on the people who conform to it.

FIG. 110. LAMAIST MONASTERY IN THE GOBI DESERT

As has been said (p. 324), it was in the guise of a late and distorted type of
Mahāyāna that Buddhism entered Tibet; and it was a backward, primitive
people with coarse habits, living amid inclement surroundings, who adopted
it and the civilization that came with it. Therefore the religious life that
developed here was coarse and sensual. Hardly anywhere else has a religion
so completely dominated and permeated the entire life of a people as
Lamaism has done and still does in Tibet and Mongolia. The monasteries are
the fingerposts of the entire intellectual life. They are everywhere, even on
the storm-swept, snow-clad heights of Central Tibet and amid the solitudes
of the deserts of Mongolia. Massive and gloomy most of them are, shutting
out the world. With their broad, high walls, pierced by long rows of small
square window-openings, they suggest fortresses with shooting embrasures.
(Fig. 110.) Many of them, indeed, were fortresses down to the days of the

British expedition against Lhasa. Many of these monastic enclosures resemble small towns with lanes and streets, and contain thousands of monks. The actual monastery consists of buildings for worship and dwellings for the monks (Fig. 111). The environs are adorned with structures for worship, pagodas (called *tshortas* in Tibetan), with long, rampart-like walls (in Tibetan, *mendong*). (Fig. 112.) Niches in these walls hold lighted candles and sticks of incense. In the grounds are also huge prayer-cylinders containing large prayer-rolls. The cylinders are turned with the help of gigantic beams. Merit is gained by turning them; to revolve a prayer-roll is equivalent to saying a prayer. The buildings devoted to worship, which contain many images and altars, stand in the middle of a square, on the sides of which are

FIG. 111. PRINCIPAL PLACE OF WORSHIP IN A TIBETAN MONASTERY

the dwellings of the monks. These dwellings are simple cells of varying size, with a veranda opening on the inner courtyard.

The Lamaist pantheon contains a bewildering number of deities. In addition to many Hindu deities, there are numerous creations of the speculative imagination of Mahāyāna, as well as deities that go back to the primitive nature-worship that prevailed in Tibet before the coming of Buddhism, local deities, personal tutelary spirits, etc. (Fig. 113). The monks hold stated services of worship in honour of most of these higher beings. These services follow a carefully drawn-up ritual, and the monks wear splendid vestments. A large part of the service consists of music, although most Westerners would call it an unbearable noise. There are five regular daily services, and, in addition to these, extra services on holy days or on other special occasions. The time of the monks is thus largely taken up with religious duties. The lama (Fig. 114) is also frequently called to the homes of the people, to give advice and aid or to exorcise evil spirits by reciting the sacred texts. The monks have also many secular duties, for the monastic communities constitute considerable establishments. The various offices, including those of treasurer, superintendent, overseer, kitchen assistant, clerk, guest-attendant, are apportioned every year among members of the order. Many monks devote a large part of their time to the study of the sacred books and other theological writings. The younger brethren, whose education

FIG. 112. PAGODAS IN THE VICINITY OF A TIBETAN TEMPLE

is still unfinished, have to study hard, and their work is tested by occasional examinations.

The whole monastic order is carefully organized. The " pupil " is promoted to " novice," then to " junior monk " (*gets'ul*), then to " full monk " (*gelong*), then to " graduate monk " (*geshe*). The next rank is " head monk " or abbot. In the larger monasteries he is called Khampo, and properly speaking it is he alone who is entitled to be called lama ("superior"), although in practice that title is now used as a general designation for all the clergy. There are many other learned titles and monks of distinction besides these. There are also grades of sanctity. The lowest grade includes men who are

regarded as reincarnations of Tibetan saints. Then come the reincarnations
of Indian saints. Last in order — *i.e.*, the highest — are the reincarnations of
bodhisattvas, like the Dalai Lama and Pantshen Erdeni. This rigid organiza-

FIG. 113. TIBETAN TUTELARY DEITY WITH OTHER OBJECTS OF WORSHIP

tion adds greatly to the power of Lamaism. It has perhaps one element of weakness. Tibetan Buddhism has split up into several ' schools,' who have again and again taken up an attitude of active hostility toward each other.

Over the masses of the people Lamaism wields an almost unlimited power. Beyond all question it is Buddhism that has raised the population of Tibet to their present level of civilization and made their history. In return for this it holds the people in its grasp and compels strict obedience. There is no secular power in the country to be a rival to it, for China has practically no authority over Tibet, and the will of the lama is the law of the land. After all, the monks themselves are the *élite* of the nation, and throughout Tibet

and Mongolia a son of every family becomes a lama. In many districts, indeed, the monasteries have legal authority to see that this duty is fulfilled. The interests of the people are thus closely bound up with those of the monasteries. The religious education, which is in the hands of the lamas, has remained at a low level. Fear of hell, the desire to be born again in the Paradise of Amitābha, belief in reincarnation, fear of evil spirits, confidence in the magical efficacy of the sacred writings and exorcist charms— these practically sum up the faith of the average Tibetan. But all these items of his faith place him at the mercy of the lama. With a magnetic attraction the monasteries draw men and women and induce them to bring whatever they can, gold and jewels or, if these they cannot give, even a small piece of butter, in order to win the favour of the gods through

Fig. 114. Tibetan Lama   their representatives, the lamas, or to protect their families and homes from the wiles of evil spirits. Without the lama a man is helpless. Needless to add, under conditions like these even matters that have no direct connexion with religion are completely under the power of the priests.

In what we have called its eastern province (China, Japan, Korea, Annam) Buddhism does not occupy anything like the same predominant position. Here it is only one religious current among others. In fact, the civilizations and religions which existed in these countries when Buddhism came to them have left clear marks on its forms. For instance, the most popular *bodhisattva* in these countries, Kuanyin (in Japanese, Kwannon), is, in spite of its association with an Indian Mahāyāna figure, mainly a Chinese product. (Fig. 115.)

FIG. 115. KUANYIN

And ancestor-worship, which is really altogether alien to Buddhism, has been universally adopted in this province, and is carried on both inside and outside the monasteries. Inside the monasteries it is observed officially at certain times, and in private houses the monks readily take part in it at or after funeral services. Many other instances of modification and innovation could be mentioned. On the other hand, Buddhism has set its stamp on the religious life and the religious forms which it found on its arrival. Chinese Taoism and Japanese Shintō have both borrowed many features from it. The monastic life, the pantheon, and the sacred literature of Taoism show clear

FIG. 116. SMALL BUDDHIST MONASTERY IN CHINA (P'U T'O)

traces of Buddhist influence, while Shintō borrowed so largely from Buddhism that, under the names of Ryōbu-Shintō ("Mixed Shintō") or Ryōbu-Buddhism ("Mixed Buddhism"), it almost became a mere sect of Buddhism, until at the great rebound in the years 1867 and 1868 the combination was disrupted and Shintō was zealously restored.

In China the Buddhist monastery (Fig. 116) exists side by side with the Taoist monastery, with the temples of the deities of the State religion, and with the temples devoted to ancestor-worship. Buddhist sanctuaries are most numerous in the middle coastal districts and in the valley of the Yangtse (Fig. 117). They vary in size from very small settlements to those that house more than a thousand monks. The buildings used for worship (Fig. 118) are separate from the quarters inhabited by the monks, and occupy as a rule the centre of a square formed by the latter. At fixed hours every day the monks perform the ritual. (Fig. 119.) The more important monasteries are visited by numerous suppliants and pilgrims. The most famous and imposing

FIG. 117. CHINESE PAGODA AT SHANGHAI

monastic settlements are four in number, situated in four different districts, amid magnificent natural surroundings. These are: in the east the island of P'u T'o, off the coast of Chiang; in the west Mount O Mi, in the province of Szechwan; in the north Wu T'ai Shan, in the province of Shansi; in the south Chiu Hua Shan, on the middle reach of the Yangtze. These four establishments are known all over China, and numerous pilgrims find their way thither from all parts of the country, not only at special seasons, but throughout the whole year.

These pilgrims belong for the most part to the lower classes of the people, and the majority of them are women. The educated classes look down upon the " bald heads," and make them a frequent subject of jest. But among the higher classes too there are devout worshippers of Buddha, like the well-

FIG. 118. CHIEF PLACE OF WORSHIP IN A LARGE CHINESE MONASTERY (P'U T'O)

known Empress-Mother Tze-hsi. Most of the monks belong to the lower orders, especially to the peasant farming class. Many of them are taken to the monasteries in their early childhood, and grow up there. The ordinary religious routine is easily learned, and the religion of most of them ends there. Earnest and zealous monks, or even monks who possess any real culture, are rare exceptions. There have been times when the intellectual life of Chinese Buddhism was vigorous and found expression in various lines of educational work. But that is long past. For the last six or seven hundred years Chinese Buddhism has lived on tradition and formal routine.

Conditions are quite different in Japan. While Japanese Buddhism is of the type that prevails in China, in this sphere, as in so many others, the Japanese have filled the borrowed moulds with contents of their own, and their religion is still a living power in the national life. While it must perhaps be admitted that the best period of Japanese Buddhism now also lies in the past (in the Middle Ages, an era of remarkable intellectual activity and of outstanding men), much of that formal intellectual life still survives. Especially since 1868, when the State abandoned Buddhism and that religion had to depend on its own resources, it has given many proofs that it is still a living power. In the last decades Japanese Buddhism has shown beyond all doubt that it is the most fruitful branch on the tree of that religion. It has evinced

FIG. 119. ABBOT AND MONKS OF A MONASTERY ON THE ISLAND OF P'U T'O

a keen appreciation of the religious ideal, a real concern for the welfare of the people, and a strong interest in scientific study, although there are some schools of thought in which these signs of life are not so clear. Japanese Buddhism has even taken a share in infusing renewed vigour into the religious life of Buddhism in other lands (China and Korea) and in carrying on missionary work in America and Europe. Any future revival or extension of Buddhism will most probably originate in Japan.

Of Buddhism in Korea and Annam to-day there is little to be said. There is neither vigour nor power in it. In Annam it has all along been merely a faint echo of Chinese Buddhism. In Korea it was full of vitality for centuries (900 to 1400), but to-day shows few signs of life. The monasteries are few in number and small in size; in many instances the buildings are in a ruinous condition, while the monks are both few and uncultured. The Koreans of to-day pay little heed to Buddhism, and have reverted to their ancient, primitive worship of nature and demons. Even after Buddhism had been introduced into Korea these ancient conceptions continued to survive as an undercurrent, and now that Buddhism has lost its hold on the people they have resumed their old power over men's minds. Recently, however, as has been already said, Japanese Buddhism has been endeavouring, not

FIG. 120. BUDDHIST SANCTUARY IN KYOTO, JAPAN

altogether without success, to revive that religion in the neighbouring peninsula. Since the annexation of Korea by Japan the Japanese are realizing their duty to the people. What the result will be time alone can show.

BIBLIOGRAPHY

Oldenberg, Buddha (1881; 8th and 9th ed., 1921); Kern, Der Buddhismus und seine Geschichte in Indien, translated by H. Jacobi (2 vols., 1882 and 1884; devotes special attention to the legends); Pischel, Leben und Lehre des Buddha (1908; 3rd ed., 1917); Hackmann, Der Buddhismus, " Religionsgeschichtliche Volksbücher" (3rd series, Nos. 4, 5, and 7, 1906; 2nd ed., 1917; gives special attention to the present-day features of Buddhism in the various countries); Lehmann, Der Buddhismus als indische Sekte, als Weltreligion (1911); Beckh, Der Buddhismus (2 vols., 1916); Hillebrandt, Buddhas Leben und Lehre (1925).

3. CHRISTIANITY

by Erich Seeberg

1. Christianity arose in a world in which religion was already a living power. Just as Greek thought was pouring in streams large and small to the utmost limits of the Farthest East, so broad waves of Oriental religion were flowing over the Western world, and Christianity may be regarded as the climax of this general Orientalization of the West. It is a fact of prime importance that Christianity is an Oriental religion.

It is now beyond doubt — for it has been proved by long, laborious research, whose history is itself full of interest — that the Christian religion, born into the midst of this movement, was profoundly influenced by the religion of the time, and that its pre-natal history must therefore be sought not merely in the teaching of the prophets and in late Judaism, but also in the various Oriental religions, whose meaning and importance we are gradually learning to appreciate, notwithstanding all the difficulties that surround the interpretation and the dating of the sources. This influence is not confined to mere matters of ritual; nor is it limited to explaining the connexions between the construction of dogma and the ethical-theistic or the mystical-monistic schools of philosophy. Its effects can be still more clearly seen in what is far more important — in the very spirit of the religion.

By its very nature Christianity is concentrated round the thought of deliverance, salvation, redemption. Momentous political struggles, economic crises, artificial social conditions had intensified the need for deliverance, just as the sceptical-eclectic view of the world propounded by philosophy deepened the longing for something trans-subjective and positive in religion. It was for deliverance that men prayed to Asklepios; it was for deliverance that men looked to the saviour of the world who, when this world had passed away, was to reign in the new age over a new humanity; and all the faltering, cheerless pronouncements of antiquity regarding death and its meaning, variously conceived and variously expressed, were met by Christianity with its assured hope of immortality and of a felicity that can be known even in this life. Men longed for deliverance from the impersonal power that determined their lot, from the cycle of rebirths, from the inexorable influence of the stars, from the relentless power of Fate; man found deliverance when, freed from himself by asceticism and raised above himself by ecstasy, he entered into a conscious union with God and became himself divine. Reitzenstein's researches into the mystery of redemption have led us to ancient Iran — *i.e.,* Persia — and proved that two ideas of supreme importance for the history of religion originated there. The first of these was the idea of a judgment of the world, which forms the core of the virile religion of Zoroaster, with its clarion call to strenuous life. The great struggle between the two powers that contend for the mastery of the world and of man is to close with the great judgment on individuals and on the world; and this judgment is to usher in the new world of the redeemed. As Bousset and Eduard Meyer have already pointed out, this circle of ideas influenced late Judaism and through it Christianity also. The second idea was the myth of the first man, with its mystical turn as reconstrued by Reitzenstein. According to this myth, the redemption of each human individual is a copy or even a component part of the metaphysical lot of the original man. The divine original man has sunk into the material world. Parts of him form the souls of men, and these live, so to speak, as strangers in this world. But by and by the original man rises out of his corporeity, resumes all souls into himself, and returns to his heavenly home. But herein is also our salvation, for which we should prepare ourselves by awakening from sleep and nursing into flame the divine spark within us.

Although the Hellenistic Mystery religions — the cults of Attis, Isis, Osiris, and Mithras — began as gross and fetishistic nature religions, they developed into faiths in which the primitive elements were gradually spiritualized, and as opposed to the juristic character of the religion of Rome and the æsthetic character of the religion of Greece, they attracted in a time of decadence, scepticism and mysticism large numbers by their gorgeous ritual, the magic spell of their Mysteries, their demand for an ascetic life, the blissfulness of the ecstatic state, and their promise of deliverance and immortality. In these Mysteries all distinctions of class and of nationality were obliterated. Religion was individualistic, and therefore open to all; more than that, it was tolerant. The worshipper stood there as a man, not as a barbarian or a Hellene, a bondsman or a freeman. The only distinction recognized was that of nearness to God, and the worshippers constituted a new community in virtue of their common experience. Further, a man could become an initiate of all the Mysteries. In the centre of them all stood the incarnate God, with whom the initiate, by means of a cultus full of dramatic moments and by means of the sacraments, attained to a fellowship that was partly sensuous and partly spiritual. The myth of the God who died and rose again, and that of the saviour who was born of a virgin — these and other conceptions were distinctly present in these Oriental religions long before the appearance of Christianity. They had both the god and the myth. Further still, they included the promise of deliverance, which was to be attained in their union with God through regeneration by means of mystical experience. Above all, assurance of this deliverance could be secured through the sacraments. And here we come upon primitive, semi-material, semi-spiritual religiosity — the ancient conception that man can assimilate deity by eating or by the sexual act. He into whom the holy substance has entered himself becomes an incarnation of the deity, and can transmit to others its powers in sacred formulas. Finally, these Mystery religions included astrological and magical speculations that culminated in a religious philosophy of nature. Although the shafts of the early Christian apologists were aimed not at the Mystery religions, but at the officially recognized heathen gods, that does not imply that the former were unimportant, for at the very same time Christianity was waging its great war against the Mystery religions in its polemics with Gnosticism.

As has already been pointed out in connexion with Hebrew eschatology, Judaism too felt the influence of Oriental as well as of Greek thought, so that it is no longer possible to draw a sharp line of distinction between Jewish and Greek elements in Christianity. Indeed, the question whether Christianity is more deeply rooted in Judaism than in Greek thought should not be put in that form, because Oriental elements abound both in Hellenism and in late Judaism. Judaism too is an Oriental religion, and the Palestinian pietism in which Jesus grew up bears clear traces of gnostic influence. In the forefront of Jewish religion stands prophetism, with its insistence on inwardness and righteous life, on conversion and obedience, with its universal and spiritual view of God, according to which He is the living Lord of history and yet the Father of each individual who seeks Him. God is at work in all things, and He is the Holy One into whose presence man comes conscious of his distance by reason of his sin and guilt. Then, intensified during the Exile, came legalism — *i.e.*, unquestioning regard for the Law, which contained not only the moral commandments and the ordinances governing worship, but also the law of the nation. This implied that God's favour could be gained by good works; morality was split up into a multitude of separate commandments, and religion hardened into a legalistic relationship. On the other hand, however, it was just this moral-legal piety that preserved the spiritual character of the religion. In a world that was full of sacramentarianism Judaism knew nothing of sacraments. Finally we have to remember the attitude of the Jewish religion to its literature. In that religion the sacred book and tradition played an all-important part — Jewish theology was exegesis. But it was just this effort to spiritualize the religion that led to its rationalization. Religion came to be based on knowledge and culture; the prophet was replaced by the scribe, who was both jurist and theologian. Of course (though we cannot go into details here) there were various stages and strata in Judaism, and much might be said about Jewish metaphysics and Jewish speculations concerning hypostasis, about the development of Jewish eschatology and Jewish conceptions of immortality. But we must be content here with a glance at the religious temper that characterized Judaism. One prominent feature of it was the feeling of trembling reverence in the presence of God, who was Lord of the living and of the dead. Another was the utilitarian view of practical conduct based on the belief in a retribution in this life, even although all hopes were projected to the life beyond and the world to come. True, Judaism reached the sublime thought that the fear of God is the beginning of religion and of morality, but — and this is the dark side of it — all conduct was judged from the standpoint of the Law and the performance of its requirements; and the fellowship of man with God was determined by the balance between obedience on the part of man and the corresponding dealings of God.

2. This was the atmosphere in which the Christian religion was born, and it cannot be denied that it acquired suggestions, forms, conceptions, and rites from its environment. Yet it would be an utter mistake to say that Christianity was simply a specimen of syncretistic religion. On the contrary, the task of its historian is just that of trying to understand and set forth what is peculiar to it amid all its relations and similarities to others.

The *Gospel of Jesus* — nothing is to be said here about the critical problems of the sources — preaches a conception of God which, notwithstanding all its points of contact with prophetism, is peculiarly its own. This conception includes His omnipotence, His holiness, and His goodness. In the forefront of Jesus' faith regarding God stand fear toward Him and obedience to Him, and the moral basis of Jesus' message is expressed in the conception of reward and punishment. But this does not mean that it inculcates service for the mere sake of reward; it expresses the conviction that nothing good and nothing evil in this world is without its consequences, and that God causes good to bring forth good and evil to come out of evil in order to show forth His truthfulness. It further implies that good and evil are eternal and absolute opposites, and raises the question whether good or evil is the ruling power in history. Jesus therefore emphasizes the thought of judgment and utters the conviction that, when history has closed, eternal salvation and eternal death stand waiting.

But together with this group of thoughts, and combined with it in a manner that is altogether unique, there is another. This holy and just God loves, not the ' correct ' and the virtuous, but sinners. He is the God of sinners: and Jesus Himself came to sinners. The profound meaning of this revelation is understood only when we take along with it the thought of the omnipotent and life-giving grace of God. God willeth not that the sinner should perish: He is ready to forgive, and through His forgiveness to give life. True, the immutable law says that only he that doeth the will of God can enter into the kingdom of heaven. But no man can of himself attain to this: divine power alone can free the sinner from the chains of evil and give him the power to live according to God's will. Thus judgment and forgiveness do not exclude each other: both are included in the life-giving will of the eternal love of God. The conception of God in which these thoughts arise is something entirely new, and it is just here that we see the distinctive character of the Christian religion. The consequences of it are most plainly seen in the

Christian ethic. As a matter of fact Jesus did abolish the Law, and destroyed the legal piety of Judaism and of every form of ' natural ' religion. And He did so, not by simplifying or making more inward those requirements of the Law which to Him were also expressions of the divine will, but by denying the inherent value of good works. The good man is not he who does good and thinks that he thereby has a claim on God, but only he does good whom God has withdrawn from sinfulness into His life and made good in his sin and guilt. Therefore, as has been justly said, Jesus reversed the ordinary way of looking at the relation of religion and morals. Man does not become good by doing good: good works do not build the bridge to God. God must first have made a man inwardly good before there can be any question of his doing good at all. Union with God is brought about solely through God's omnipotent grace. One does not come through morals to religion; it is religion that makes real morality possible. It is a logical deduction from this that moral life is not the result of the organic unfolding and training of the germs of natural good in man, nor of the kindling and developing of a divine spark in the soul. It implies a breach and a conversion. The first step is regeneration, being " born again." To enter at length into the ethical teaching of Jesus does not come within our present task, and a few general observations must suffice. In the first place, it would be a complete misunderstanding to look in the teaching of Jesus for ideas on social reform or to place Him among the great social reformers. Secondly, His teaching is not confined to negatives like the injunction: " Resist not him that is evil." [1] The ethical requirements of Jesus are stern and searching beyond measure, demanding entire devotion and complete consecration. Perhaps the briefest summary of them is found in the double commandment: " Thou shalt love the Lord thy God with all thy heart . . . and thy neighbour as thyself." [2] This whole-hearted love, which when it manifests itself as love to one's enemy actually overcomes the world, has nothing in common with sentimentality or ' acosmistic,' aloof indifference. What greater thing can there be than this willing and obedient devotion to the will of God, which in all circumstances and conditions, in weal or woe, with renunciation and surrender of self, aims only at conformity to the will of God? What can surpass in worth this fight in the cause of good and against evil — the commandment to love one's neighbour by no means suspends this contest — but with no hate in the heart against men, and with love even toward one's personal enemies? Here we have something that is supremely matter-of-fact, yet not frigid, but ardent, a love founded in God, love that sees even in an enemy a fellow-man and a brother because he is a creature of God. Lastly, the ethical demands of Jesus are timeless and absolute. Eternity, fellowship with God, is the source and the goal of all human conduct. Where that exists men cannot but do right, for the Kingdom of God implies service to God on the part of man. Here all that is earthly becomes petty, and yet it is immediately seen to be great; and

[1] Matt. v, 39.   [2] Luke x, 27.

we must approach the peremptory words of Jesus without the artificial exegesis that vainly strives to reconcile them with actuality. The goal remains high, uncompromising and clear: " That ye may be sons of your Father which is in heaven . . . ye therefore shall be perfect, as your heavenly Father is perfect." [3]

The gospel of Jesus includes a third set of thoughts. These are centred in the expression " the Kingdom of God." Jesus uses the term without its traditional national and secular colouring. Jesus is not thinking of the question whether Rome must be overthrown. The signs of the kingdom of which He speaks are that Satan, demons, and sin are rendered powerless, that the miraculous powers of God give life to the miserable and the poor, that God's spirit triumphs over all that is evil and demoniacal. The Kingdom of God is entirely personal: the core of it is personal fellowship with God, manifested in the doing of His will, a fellowship whose results will be seen in a world of men religiously and morally renewed. This kingdom does not lie in the far-off future. It is not a kingdom whose signs can be read by astrological calculations or whose life can be described by far-fetched, romantic dreams. It is at hand: the end is near: nay — in a definite group of His sayings Jesus taught this — it is already here. That is a superhuman thought, that this last, perfect stage, the goal of history, has been reached here and now, and reached, too, through the power of God, Who works according to His good pleasure, and in view of which our only question can be, whether we are ready for it. To this Kingdom of God Jesus Himself of course belongs. He was not merely the preacher of a new, paradoxical view of God. Faith in His person is an essential part of the Gospel; without this it would lose its profoundest meaning. His own work is to Jesus a proof that God has begun to inaugurate His kingdom. He Himself is the Messiah, not in the sense implied in the national hopes, but as the Saviour who has come to serve His brethren, heal their wounds, and lead them to fellowship with God. This constitutes the profoundest mystery in the person of Jesus — His relation to the Father. As man He had those profound experiences whose outlines can be learned from the narratives of His baptism and temptation, in spite of all the difficulties raised by the nature of these records. Jesus was conscious of being the representative of God on earth in His power and in His judgment, and this consciousness implies a unique combination of the divine and the human. To come to Him was to come to the Father: His work was God's work: He Himself was preparing the way for that reign of God which was to transform humanity into the Kingdom of God. Jesus had the Spirit of God — that is, He lived continually in that close fellowship with God which we can experience only in rare moments vouchsafed to us. That involved a tremendous elasticity in the human soul of Jesus, enabling Him to realize the presence of the Eternal in every moment of His life and to see even in His own death something that was not merely fortuitous, but

[3] Matt. v, 45, 48.

was divinely appointed to serve divine ends. This thought, that He was destined not to life, but to death, lay like a load even on the soul of Jesus, but He found comfort in the assurance that at long last the Kingdom of God would prevail and that He Himself would come again as the Man from Heaven, justified by God, to judge the world. On principle, therefore, we cannot accept the view that insulates the Gospel of Jesus and seeks to disentangle a moral or religious kernel from a later accretion of dogmatic conceptions. Nor can the Gospel of Jesus be separated from the theological ideas current in Oriental piety: on the contrary, it is suffused throughout with them. In it is already implicit that " dogmatic Christianity " which unfolded later in the history of Greek and Oriental Christianity mainly under the formative influence of Greek thought. Jesus transferred to Himself, the historical person, the myth of " man " — *that* is the root of the Christological dogma, and a telling example of the difference between myth and dogma in Christianity.

3. The *reassembling of the disciples who had been dispersed by the death of Jesus* took place amid marvellous experiences, which are usually spoken of as the " appearances " of Jesus. For the historian it is a matter of comparative indifference whether these appearances should be regarded as visions and auditions or as objective manifestations of divine powers. The disciples saw their Lord, transfigured, but bearing the stigmata of the cross, just as the privileged three had seen Him transfigured in His lifetime. It was these appearances, the first of which was interpreted as the Resurrection — the theological idea of the justification of Jesus by God was still at work here — and the last of which was interpreted as the Ascension, that produced the decisive revolution in the minds even of the disciples. The appearance to Peter was of special importance because of its effect on the history of Christianity, and it was probably this appearance — for it had a place of its own in the early Christian ' faith ' — that gave Peter his prominent position in early Christianity and afterward in the Christian Church. In passing, it may be pointed out that there are traces of connexion between the Last Supper and the appearances — a connexion that throws light on the original meaning of the Supper — and that both Christian traditionalism and Christian ecclesiastical law have their roots in these pneumatic phenomena.

It was in the atmosphere created by these tremendous experiences — experiences which show more graphically than anything else the personal power of Jesus in His lifetime — that arose the theological ideas which influenced so decisively the history of the Christian religion. At first the disciples had seen in Jesus a man who had the Spirit of God; they believed in Him now as the power of the Spirit who had taken to Himself the Man Jesus. Jesus had now become identified with the Spirit of God; He was the Lord, whose everlasting Gospel could never be lost. It is on this estimate of Jesus, which can be traced back to Jesus' own estimate of Himself, that all that goes by the name of Christology is based. It was not the cultus that created the divine standing of Jesus; on the contrary, the recognition of Jesus as divine necessarily preceded the cultus. The faith came first, the cultus followed. It is likewise a mistake to interpret the designation of Christ as κύριος, the Lord and King of Heaven, after the analogy of the κύριοι who were worshipped as divine in the Hellenistic Mystery religions. The invocation Maranatha,[4] and its authentic New Testament translation, " Come, Lord ";[5] the sharp distinction drawn by Paul between " God " and " Lord," which he probably learned from his rabbinic teachers; the early designation of the Christians as those " that call upon the name of our Lord Jesus Christ in every place "[6] — all these are indications that the name " Lord " and the implied interpretation of the Person of Christ arose among the original Aramaic-speaking Christian community. The Person of Christ thus became an object of faith, and the resurrection on the third day and the appearances to Peter and to the Twelve show on what this faith was based. Simultaneously, in the same early community in Jerusalem, arose a number of other theological ideas which expressed, as from one central point, the new interpretation of the events that had happened. The death of Christ was no accident, but a dispensation of God. The sacred Scriptures of the Old Testament had predicted it as well as the Resurrection; and it had taken place " for our sins." [7]

It is usual, when giving an account of early Christianity, to include prominently among its outstanding features its enthusiasm. When we recall the tremendous results of these visionary experiences, or the loving communism that prevailed at the outset among the early Christians, we must admit that this prominence is justified. And yet this enthusiasm was only one feature of early Christianity. Equally marked — and characteristically Jewish — was the steadfastness or tenacity which marked both their religious thinking and their social life. It has already been indicated that it was in the sphere of the charisms, in the " appearances " of the risen Jesus, which were regarded as having ceased at a definite time, that Christian tradition began to form. Confining itself to what was Apostolic, tradition showed a determination to cling to and retain these revelations, restricted as they were to a certain period of time, and to concern itself with them only. Even Paul found traditional items of this kind, loosely formulated and attributed to Christ, already in existence, and these he communicated to his churches. Among these we must include not only stereotyped statements like the valuable one preserved in I Corinthians, xv, 3 ff. — which is the nucleus of the Apostles' Creed — the tradition of the Last Supper as given by Paul,[8] or the outline of early Apostolic preaching which can be seen in the addresses contained in the book of Acts,[9] but also the " two ways "[10] which Paul taught wherever he went, and which constituted a sort of syllabus of ethical instruction. There can be no doubt that this traditional material was of surpassing importance for the future

[4] I Cor. xvi, 22.
[5] Rev. xxii, 20.
[6] I Cor. i, 2.
[7] I Cor. xv, 3.
[8] I Cor. xi, 23–26.
[9] Acts ii, 14 ff.; iv, 8 ff; vii.
[10] Cf. the Didache.

development of the Christian religion. It determined the thinking and the sentiment of the large masses of the Christian 'people,' whereas the Gospel of Jesus came into prominence in all its depth and greatness only in times of crisis. Similarly, there existed already in the early community at Jerusalem a fixed hierarchy and a Church that was regarded as an institution. James, Peter, and John, the "pillars,"[11] and next to them the Twelve, were at the head of affairs. This position they owed to the "appearances," which were, so to speak, their credentials. In the case of James, the Lord's brother, his relationship to Jesus no doubt counted to some extent — there is an example of the same kind in Islam. Further, the Church was strictly associated with the city of Jerusalem; none of the new Christian communities were self-governing, but were subordinate to the Church in Jerusalem, which on its part claimed the right to superintend the other communities. Even Paul's interest in the collections for "the poor,"[12] which was probably a name given to themselves by the early Christian community, seems to point to a kind of tax privilege claimed by the Church at Jerusalem.

The life of the first Christians continued to follow the lines with which they had been familiar. They attended as before the Temple services, they continued to observe the Law; though now Christians, they were still Jews. Out of this fact arose the epoch-making dispute between them and Paul, which ended in the latter's triumph.

By birth Paul was a Jew. In his own mind he had felt very deeply the contrast between Christianity and Judaism, and though he expressed himself after the manner of the Jewish dialecticians his thoughts were those of Hellenism. Jew though he was, he also belonged to the Hellenistic world. Greek was his mother tongue, and he grew up in Tarsus, a centre of Hellenistic education and culture. He was not the originator of Christian missions to the heathen, for the Hellenistic Christian church at Antioch was prior to Paul in that form of activity. But it was he who made Christianity de facto a world religion, and by his letters he made himself the doctor ecclesiæ and, next to Aristotle, the father of our intellectual and spiritual civilization. Very impressive too was his own large if rugged personality, in which a deep sense of religion, intensified by his visionary and ecstatic temperament, was combined with a power of profound theological thinking, passionate strength of will, and, one is tempted to add, diplomatic sagacity.

In the very centre of Pauline Christianity stand two things: first, the death of Christ, the Cross and the offence contained therein for every thinking mind, and, second, the position now occupied by the Law, whose fulfilment was for the Jew the guarantee of his fellowship with God. The problems here raised Paul solved by means of the fundamental thought of the Gospel. The atoning death of Christ was the proof of the gracious, loving will of God, who desires to draw to Himself the sinner on whom judgment has

[11] Gal. ii, 9.   [12] Rom. xv, 26; Gal. ii, 10.

been passed, not by way of the Law — the Law was a historically conditioned pedagogic measure — but by way of His pardoning and life-giving grace. Henceforth for the Christian only the law of Christ is valid, the law of liberty, which receives its contents from the life of the historical Christ. Here it is important to keep in mind the ethical character of Paul's doctrine as compared with the Hellenistic Mystery religions. For Paul — and this was the result of the 'appearance' on the way to Damascus, which Paul insisted was as real and important as the earlier 'appearances' to others — Christ Himself was the Spirit — *i.e.,* the divine power that pervades the world and shapes its history. From His heavenly existence before time began He came into the world, and overthrew Satan, the demons, death, and sin. He is the power of the revelation of God, and His work solves the problems of history. To all this must be added the set of conceptions which are usually called " Christian Mysticism " — Christ in us and we in Him; Christ, the head of Christendom, which is His body, and the soul of the history of the world. At the same time He is the " second man," [13] who, for the sake of this world, which was forfeit to death since the sin of the first man, seeks to accomplish His fate, His death and resurrection, and to redeem the world in virtue of this mystical union.

These are the fundamental notes of Pauline theology, and they show very clearly that Paul's message kept very close to the Gospel of Jesus, though it set forth that Gospel in a magnificent speculative system. They also make it clear that Paul is best understood from his Jewish side, although his thinking was profoundly influenced by Hellenistic Mysticism. It would be possible, indeed, to pick out from Paul's theology two great lines of thought which strike two distinct notes, or, to use another metaphor, we could thread his fundamental thoughts like beads on two strings. The one series strikes the Hellenistic note, and above it might be written the word 'redemption.' Here the most prominent element in the idea of God is love; Christ is the power of the Spirit that rules in history; sin is sensuousness and finitude; the sacraments, which are the media of the pneumatic powers of Christ, transfigure men; the end in view is to make men spiritual; the incarnation of Christ is the decisive 'fact of salvation,' the beginning of the actual process of liberation from sensuousness. The other series — put in a similarly compact form — strikes the Jewish ethical note, and over it might be set the word 'reconciliation.' Here the emphatic element in the idea of God is righteousness; in the Christology the human aspect of Christ is prominent, because it is He who through His Passion procures for us the righteousness which we need before God; sin is human opposition to God, and therefore involves guilt, of which man becomes conscious by the Law; the work of Christ culminates in His death; baptism and the Lord's Supper are parables and memorials of His death; the liberation of man from the power of sin is accomplished on the ground of His atonement as justification; the

[13] Cor. xv, 47.

end of the entire process is the judgment. In thus analysing Paul's system we must not overlook the fact that its unity is preserved by the 'Gospel,' by the estimate of the Person of Jesus, and by the proclamation made in Christ, especially in His death, of the grace of God, Who draws the sinner to Himself through forgiveness, not through the fulfilment of the Law. It was Paul the Jew who fought his way to these thoughts, but in setting forth his message he continually recurred to the ideas of Hellenistic Mysticism or to the forms of popular mythological conceptions. The Hellenistic element became progressively stronger in Paul, in Gnosticism and in Greek theology, but the very greatest minds in the history of the Christian religion, Augustine and Luther, fixed on Paul's doctrine of justification as the very kernel of the message. It was thence they drew the power to spiritualize and deepen the Christian religion, while they still left it true to the 'Gospel.'

The theology of Paul is in sharpest contrast to every type of legalistic piety. Works and reward have no place in it. Not a word do we hear of the opening of the heavenly books and the striking of a balance between debit and credit. God *gives* righteousness to the sinner, whom He forgives for Jesus' sake. Not in our own works, but in the divine will lies our salvation and our blessedness. "Boasting is excluded," [14] for we give God nothing. He gives us everything, even that which we give Him in return. Here Christianity attained its purest and profoundest form as the religion of deliverance and redemption.

Even in his lifetime Paul had to fight a stern battle in defence of his conception of Christianity. Both James and Peter opposed him.[15] Their differences came to a head in the two questions, whether the Christian converts from heathendom were to be obliged also to become Jews and whether the Law had lost its validity even for Jewish Christians. Into these practical questions came also the conception of the Church. Paul spiritualized the idea of the Church. In his view it was not on the Apostles, but on the Lord, who is the Spirit,[16] that the Church was based. Further, he held that the individual Christian, filled with the Spirit, had a direct, personal relation to Christ. Lastly, every separate congregation was part of the Church, and it was unjustifiable to restrict Church standing and authority to those locally connected with Jerusalem. With regard to the practical questions, history decided in favour of Paul, but in the matter of his doctrine of the Church it upheld the higher authority of the Apostles and instituted a new local tie — the Church at Rome.

There is perhaps some ground for holding that *the Jewish-Greek form of Christianity,* as set forth in a number of writings that belong to the end of the first century (*e.g.,* the epistle of Clement of Rome to the Corinthians, and even the Epistle to the Hebrews in the New Testament), was the outcome of the differences between the Pauline and the Palestinian types of Christianity. At least there is no doubt that this Jewish-Greek type, which

[14] Rom. iii, 27.   [15] Gal. ii, 11 ff.   [16] 2 Cor. iii, 17.

had assimilated primitive and popular elements of the Jewish and Hellenistic religions, was extremely widespread. It was a plain and simple Christianity, which in spite of its universalism had many points of affinity with Judaism. Faith in the one Creator God; Christ, the new law-giver and judge, Who must be regarded as divine and as having existed from eternity; the Christian life as *militia Christi* (subsequently a special emphasis came to be laid on un-Jewish ascetic demands in connexion with sexual matters, and this led to the setting up of a double code of morals); salvation, as essentially a deliverance from the power of demons, who have their abode in images and idols; the belief that the end of the ages was at hand, that Christians were citizens of another world, and would soon (for the moral philosophy and the eschatology supported each other) see the retribution and the victory of Christ — these are some of the features of this Jewish-Greek piety. It had lost not only the majestic, dualistic supernaturalism of Paul, his ethical conception of the Spirit, and his profound doctrine of sin, but also the conception of righteousness that was peculiar to the Gospel. In this Jewish-Greek piety, righteousness is no longer the gift of God, but a condition attained by man; and this defect is not counter-balanced by the fact that its ethics are determined by the precepts of Jesus — which is perhaps the most impressive feature in this Jewish-Greek type of Christianity.

Besides these three types of Christianity — the Palestinian, the Pauline, and the Jewish-Greek — there was a fourth, the *Johannine,* which should perhaps be located in Syria. Many problems regarding it are still unsolved. The question who ' John ' was cannot be settled by an appeal to tradition alone. Even if we regard the passage in Mark x, 35–45, as a *vaticinium ex eventu,* and if we rely on the statement of Papias, which finds some support in other sources, the disciple John suffered martyrdom along with James at a comparatively early date. But if we believe Irenæus, or, rather, the ' elder ' on whose authority Irenæus makes the statement, the author of our Fourth Gospel was John, the son of Zebedee, the disciple " whom Jesus loved ";[17] and the Gospel itself with its mysterious hint [18] seems (perhaps too deliberately) to point in the same direction. But there is a more important question — viz., to what stage in the history of Christianity does the Fourth Gospel (or the whole group of Johannine writings) belong? On the one hand, it has been suggested that the Johannine writings reveal a connexion with the Hellenistic Mystery religions, especially with the hermetical circle of writers; and attention has been called to the mystical features in the Johannine writings — to vision and deification by vision, to its terminology, ' light,' ' darkness,' ' life,' to its mystical views of Christ and God. On the other hand, there are many interesting points of difference between the thoughts of these writings and the conceptions of mysticism. Further, the presence of extremely archaic expressions, the intimate knowledge of the geography of Palestine, and especially the fact that the Fourth Gospel, as

[17] John xiii, 23 *et al.*   [18] John xxi, 24.

we have it, is clearly a translation from an Aramaic original, all point to a *milieu* different from that of the Mysteries. Another recent suggestion, which is at least worthy of consideration, is that the Fourth Gospel is perhaps connected with the Mandæans or Manichæans, and that it may represent a primitive form of Christianity with a Mandæic colouring, and may possibly go back to the circle of the Baptist. It is claimed that this suggestion finds support in the resemblances between the style of the Gospel of John and the Mandæic literature, and an attempt has been made to show that the myth of the 'first man' forms the background of the Johannine view of Christ. Jesus is there regarded as being 'man,' and His fate is the fate of the human soul. To say the least it is doubtful whether that touches the central point in the Johannine Christology, and it implies the entirely un-Greek and anti-docetic idea of the Logos who became flesh. It implies the incarnation of Christ in the literal sense, which involves the Virgin Birth and which has been opposed all down the centuries by the older Christological view — that the heavenly, spiritual Being assumed the man Jesus, with a corresponding stress on His baptism. But by the passionate energy with which John teaches that the historical Christ and the Christ of faith are identical he has saved the historical Christ as against all the speculations of Mysticism and Gnosticism. And, finally, the hierarchical and rigoristic features in the Christianity of the Johannine writings should be kept in view. These include the brusque accentuation of the 'commandment,' which must be obeyed; the deliberate, considered exclusion of heresy; the demand to " do righteousness," for only " he that doeth righteousness is righteous "; [19] and the austere attitude taken up toward the world and the State, which is so unlike the fundamental thought of Pauline sociology.

4. In the second and third centuries Christianity passed through two great crises — the Gnostic and the Montanist. *Gnosticism* is older than Christianity. It is not only related to Mandæanism — the names are synonymous — but it is a typical example of syncretism in religion. Even the New Testament writings contain polemic against Gnostics, and it was perhaps the theology of Paul that provided the openings through which Gnosticism penetrated into Christianity. The real nature of Gnosticism is to be seen not so much in its religious-philosophical and cosmological speculations as in the form of piety it advocated and produced. Gnosticism is theosophy. It aims at delivering men from the power of sensuousness, from demoniacal and stellar influences, so that the soul may attain a sublimated experience of God and a free ascent to Him. Sacraments and mysteries are the media of this deliverance, and Gnosticism may be regarded as a kind of secret society. The genuinely Oriental sharp dualism between God and the world, spirit and flesh, forms the basis of the Gnostic religious life. Salvation, therefore, is not the kindling of the extinct spark in the soul; it comes to man from without, as something alien to humanity. The work of salvation is

[19] 1 John iii, 7.

not carried through in a spiritual or ethical manner, but the metaphysically corrupted soul is physically and spiritually changed by the sacred substance of the sacrament. Nor does salvation rest on something that happened once for all in history; it consists in metaphysical processes, of which the happenings of history are a copy. Only the Pneumatic is content to stop short at history; the Gnostic goes behind history to find the original antitype, the deep meaning of history, and he repeats in his own life the eternal myth. There are various myths, which emerge again in manifold forms — the myth of the first man, of the heavenly mother-goddess, the fight of the saviour with the powers of hell, and many others.

Christian Gnosticism derives all its revelations and mysteries from Christus Soter, and thus claims to be a Christian religion, though in a sublimated and deepened form. There are various stages of it. The oldest stage is represented by Syrian Gnosticism, which gradually made its way westward. It exhibits in unmodified form the Oriental and primitive elements of Gnostic piety. The more advanced stages, though there are differences between them, show increasingly the influence of Mysticism and Greek philosophy. Their spokesmen are Basilides and Valentinus and their disciples. Basilides modified the dualism of Gnosticism, made the God of the Old Testament the instrument of the supreme God, relaxed the ascetic character, and based salvation on ethics, involving the doctrine of metempsychosis. He made a great effort to be scientific, and employed his theology as a dress for speculative ideas. But Valentinus approximated still more closely to Official Christianity, and under Platonic influence created a majestic speculative philosophy of religion. The profound experience of suffering on the part of the soul, which, though God-like, is held captive by the passions, he set forth in a magnificent mythological system. Resting on unmoved deity, far down and in silence surges eternal life. From it emanate pairs of æons, eternally differing in sex, but closely connected with each other. At the frontier of this æon-world, Wisdom, the most lowly link in the series of æon pairs, tears herself away from her husband in order to embrace in ardent desire the Primal Father himself. True, her way is barred by the eternal frontier, but a breach has been made in it. In order to repair this breach a new pair of æons, Christ and the Holy Spirit, are begotten. Wisdom is delivered from passion, which becomes the basic power of our world, and all the æons combine to contribute what is best in them to make a specially glorious, heavenly being, whom they bring to the Primal Father. This is the higher Saviour. He becomes betrothed to lowly Wisdom, and assumes human form in Jesus. Salvation is necessary, because a yearning for the higher has entered the world with the small piece of æonic glory that was projected into the world, and this longing finds an answer in the longing of the æons for the portion of themselves that was lost. Salvation is attained by the agency of the highest æon, the Saviour, who, being a man, also possesses pneumatic powers, and can thus save not only Gnostics, but also Church Christians (modifying the original dualism, Valentinus distinguishes three groups among men), who have been content with mere faith and mere morality and have not advanced to pneumatic experience. Even the Pneumatic needs the Christianity of the Church, though only as a transition stage, while the higher experience lies beyond. In this manner everything is harmoniously correlated, and all stages and forms of life are classed according to their longing after God. These speculations of Valentinus recall the lines from *Faust*:

> How each the whole its substance gives
> Each in the other works and lives!
> Like heavenly forces rising and descending
> Their golden urns reciprocally lending,
> With wings that winnow blessing
> From Heaven through Earth I see them pressing
> Filling the All with harmony unceasing!

Somewhat apart stands Marcion, whose efforts at organization made him a special danger to the Church. He also influenced Mani and Manichæism, which belong to this circle of Oriental-Hellenistic Gnosticism. Marcion's leading thought — it is ultra-Pauline — is the contrast between Law and Gospel, Righteousness and Grace. Christianity has nothing whatever to do with the Old Testament, for Christ revealed a God unknown to it, the God of grace and love and inwardness. There is therefore no historical connexion between Christianity and Judaism, and Marcion rejected the early Christian interpretation of history, which connected the Old and the New Testaments by conceptions of prophecy and fulfilment, of type and antitype. Christianity is a flat contradiction of human nature, and there is neither a natural nor a historical connexion between the two. Hence the strange Redeemer-God who appeared in Christ was neither the creator nor the guide of those who lived in Old Testament days. This truth the Catholic Church had falsified by carrying over the Gospel of Jesus into the Old Testament and confounding Law and Grace. The Church had sewn the new cloth on the old garment,[20] disfiguring and falsifying the New Testament writings, and interpreting Jesus and Paul in the sense of the mendacious Jewish Apostles. This idea, which expressed the religious experience of the contrast between nature and grace, was extended, perhaps under the influence of the Gnostic Cerdo, into the metaphysical sphere, and led to a doctrine of two Gods. The God of the Old Testament is the creator of the world. But what kind of being can He be, when we think of this senseless, worthless world, teeming with vermin, a world in which life arises by the disgusting process of procreation and ends in putrescence? Over against this being stands the good God, Who appeared in Christ. Christ differs from the Father only in name, He did His work in a pseudo-body —

---

[20] Mark ii, 21, *et parall.*

docetism is a fundamental feature of Gnostic Christology; He was not born. His activity began with His descent from heaven and His teaching in Capernaum. He preached the ' strange God ' by word and work; His ' beatitudes,' in their overflowing love, are especially expressive of His Gospel. By his descent into hell — upon which great stress is laid — He secured salvation for all, a salvation in which the heathen are more likely to share than the just men of the Old Testament. The contrast between nature and grace is carried further, into a contrast between matter and spirit, and salvation consists in the liberation of the spirit from matter — *i.e.,* from sensuousness — by means of strict fasting and ascetic celibacy. None but celibates were admitted by Marcion to membership in his church, and he insisted that the Church should be recruited not by procreation, but by missionary effort. As against the worthless Old Testament and the falsified Gospel Marcion drew up — perhaps he was the first to do so — a fixed canon of Scripture, which included a Gospel allied to our Gospel of St Luke and ten well-authenticated epistles of Paul. As a " marriage gift " to his canon appeared the *Antitheses,* a kind of dogmatic Biblical theology, which contrasts various statements from the Old and New Testaments and, by means of verbal exegesis, proves them to be irreconcilable.

Montanism was a movement within Christianity, or, rather, within the Church. The ardent zeal of the Montanists for rigorous asceticism, reinforced as it was by the belief that the end of the world was at hand, brought about a crisis in the Church, because it portended an outburst of the sectarian spirit which had all along existed in Christianity side by side with affection for the Church. Montanus came forward in Phrygia as a prophet, as the Paraclete whom Christ promised to send. Epiphanius has recorded one of his pronouncements: " I am the Lord God, the Almighty, who has condescended to dwell in a man." He preached that the end was at hand, that his hearers should leave the Church and the civil community and betake themselves to Pepuza and Tymion, where the heavenly Jerusalem was to come down to earth. Montanism was not a heresy except in one point — it regarded Montanus as the Paraclete, and esteemed his inspired statements as a new revelation of higher value than Holy Scripture. In other respects it revived elements of primitive Christianity which were on the point of disappearing in the progressive consolidation of the Church — *e.g.,* the eschatological expectation, prophesying, the yearning for martyrdom, ethical rigorism, with its tenet that post-baptismal repentance was impossible, strict exercise of discipline, the high estimate of woman as far as she possessed the spirit and her admission to public worship. But the distinctive features of Montanism were its unquestioning recognition of prophecy and its faith in Montanus as the Paraclete. The movement soon came into conflict with the episcopate in Asia Minor. Thereafter it penetrated into Europe. The Bishops of Rome long hesitated as to what attitude they should take up toward it, till finally Praxeas, a confessor of Asia Minor, brought about a breach with it, and thus sealed the doom of Montanism in the West. Nevertheless, Montanism gained the support of the most brilliant intellect of the Western world, Tertullian, probably because he found in its severe prophetic spirit the divine authority he required for his own views in favour of strict organization and ascetic morality. In any case, Tertullian's Montanism differed widely from the type that prevailed in Asia Minor. Ecstasy and its objectionable features were discouraged; the *nova disciplina* supplied the warrant for prophesying; the spirit took the place of the Law; but he retained the eschatology and the desire for a pure Church, consisting of members who justified their baptismal grace.

The *ordinary Christian piety* of the time was largely a syncretism, with its superstitions and its massive theological conceptions. When one reads the apocryphal Acts of the Apostles and similar popular Christian productions, such as the *Epistola Apostolorum* (published some years ago), one is amazed at the plethora of miracles and the attention paid to angels and demons. These writings show that the average Christianity of the day was an aggregate of the commandments preached by the prophets and confirmed by Christ; that Christ was naïvely identified with God; and that the eschatology — a sign that it had passed its meridian — abounded in glowing phantasies and vivid colours. But there was another feature that was specially characteristic of Christian piety and differentiated it from Gnosticism — the stress that it laid on the resurrection of the body, guaranteed by Christ and His work.

It cannot be said that the *positive 'ecclesiastical' features* of Christianity were the result of a reaction against Gnosticism and Montanism. It has already been shown that the elements of law and dogma were present in Christianity from the first, or at least since it began to form a community; but the conflict with Gnostic syncretism and with Montanist enthusiasm led to a strengthening of these elements of positive historical piety and to a transformation and displacement of the equally primitive pneumatic powers. This process can be seen at work in numerous details — *e.g.,* in the titles of the writings produced at the end of the second century, in the development of the conceptions of the martyr and the pneumatic, in the elimination of ecstasy from prophesying, which had now to conform to good order and be consciously done, in the varying attitude adopted toward women, and in many other points.

Of greater importance than these, however, are three things which definitively closed the door against heresy and syncretism, repressed pneumatism, and encouraged a return to the Bible and to history. The first of these was the *codification of the Holy Scriptures*. By a gradual process of sifting — collection and elimination — a fixed Canon was formed, containing the documents of the New Testament together with those of the Old. The principle that guided the selection was to confine the choice to Apostolic literature, thus drawing a clear line of division between what was primitive and what belonged to later time; and the Acts of the Apostles, which forms the bridge between the Gospels and the Epistles, is the key to the understanding of the idea of the Canon. It is difficult to overestimate the importance of this step. The fixing of the New Testament Canon put an end to the production of sacred writings and ensured the preservation of what were doubtless the most precious writings of the early days, and the Canon thus formed laid for all time a Biblical basis for Christian faith and life that included both Jesus and Paul; all speculative additions had henceforth to be confined to interpretation, chiefly in the form of allegorizing. Indeed, it was the formation of the Canon that determined the attitude to history that was adopted by Judaism. History was regarded as revelation, a permanent constituent of the Christian religion.

The second point calling for mention here is the fact that *theology was kept to traditional lines*. Here again the principle that was followed was the authority of the Apostles: this selection of a normative period made it possible to secure authority for the norms that already existed. The appeal of the Gnostics to Scripture and secret tradition was thus met by the setting up of the 'rule of truth,' which regulated the exposition of Scripture and the forms of faith. By this was probably meant the old 'baptismal teaching' — a more or less stereotyped complex of oral traditions, to which different importance seems to have been attached in the East and in the West. One part, perhaps the core, of this traditional material is the Apostolic confession of faith, the germs of which, as we have already seen, are to be found in the New Testament. The different structure of the separate articles — the first and third are dogmatic, while the second is historical in structure — and other important details indicate that the whole was composed of two older parts, one longer and Christological in character, the other briefer and Trinitarian. The welding of these two into the ancient Roman form of our present Apostles' Creed was probably the work of one man — perhaps Callistus of Rome. This supposition is rendered feasible, apart from other considerations, by the skilful composition of the second article, in which the sonship of Christ is based on the Virgin Birth and His divinity is made to rest on the so-called facts of salvation. The decisive importance of this fixation of the baptismal faith lies in the formulation of the belief in God as a Trinity, although of course the Trinitarian conception of God had been reached long before this time. Behind it lie speculations, whose history is still obscure, regarding the Spirit conceived as feminine — *i.e.,* regarding the Heavenly Mother, the Church. It acknowledges God the Creator and Father, God the Lord of history — *i.e.,* Christ — and God the Spirit, Who leads individuals through the Church to the resurrection of the body and to eternal life.

The third item to be dealt with here is the idea of *Apostolic succession*; this rounds off the idea of the 'rule of truth.' The living tradition of the successors of the Apostles and afterward of the officials of the Church was the guarantee, as against heretics, for the genuineness of the deposit of faith. The succession of the Apostles and afterward of the bishops thus guaranteed the purity of the doctrine on which the Church and salvation were based. Here we have another impressive example of the extent to which Judaism influenced Christianity. The first lists which were drawn up were lists of successors, not lists of bishops. Two considerations governed their preparation. First, the pure doctrine handed down by tradition was older than that of the heretics; and, second, parallel to the list of the successors of the Apostles ran a list of heretics. As the former of these was the germ of the Christian chronographies — the sacred history contained in Biblical tradition was older than the profane history contained in pagan tradition — so the latter was the germ of Augustine's philosophical conception of the two States, the State or City of God and that of the devil, which stand in opposition to each other.

The thought of the Apostolic succession led, further, to the first organization of the Church as a hierarchy. The churches founded by the Apostles ranked higher than the others, the latter being, as it were, 'daughters' of the former. Here we have also the germ of the position afterward adopted by Rome, a principle that can be traced back to the two chief Apostles. But only the principle can be thus traced, for the designation of Peter as the first Bishop of Rome started in Africa, and does not seem to go back farther than the third century. In view of our limited space we can only say here that the subsequent primacy of Rome in the West and that of Alexandria in the East were brought about by other considerations, some of which were in the nature of things, while others were due to the growth of the episcopate.

Although all these ideas, which gathered increased weight from the ever-growing sacramentarianism in the Christian life of the time, were tending to bring about a hierarchical conception of the Church, still the old pneumatic conception of it remained strong in the second and third centuries, especially in the minds of the great theologians. Even to a man like Cyprian, the episcopalian κατ᾽ ἐξοχήν, who held that the bond of unity which constituted numerous believers into a church was not faith, but the bishop and the unity of the episcopate, it was self-evident that the bishop is *spiritualis vir,* a man who lives a good life and is 'holy.' But his doctrine of the Church contained, along with the conceptions of succession and pneumatism, a decisive thought which afterward became an integral part of the doctrine of the Church — viz., the conception of sacrifice, and the idea that it is the bishop who in Christ's stead offers the sacrifice of the Supper. How fluid and inconsistent opinion still was within the Church at that time is shown by the fact that, in connexion with the dispute about the rebaptism of heretics, Cyprian vindicated as against Rome, which represented the institutional and sacramentarian view, an opinion that was more primitive and pneumatic.

5. The *development of theology* will be considered here only as far as it shows us the currents and influences that were present in the religious life of the time. We are met at the outset by a question that is fundamental. Is Christian theology a child of the Oriental mind or is it a product of Greek thought? Was Christianity Orientalized or Hellenized? When we recall the conclusions to which we have come in the foregoing pages we shall see that there is need of great caution before we give our support to the accepted opinion of to-day that Christianity has been orientalized. That opinion is based on the false assumption that there ever was a Christianity that was not essentially Oriental. We shall therefore do well to adhere to the older opinion that Christianity was Hellenized. That means that the fundamentally Oriental content of Christianity was shaped and moulded by the Greek mind, which loved to give logical form to conceptual thinking. This Hellenizing process has taken place again and again in the history of Western Christianity; indeed, the conflict between Oriental and Greek thought long continued to dominate the intellectual history of Europe and Nearer Asia.

The Christianity of *the Apologists,* who, in a manner that was neither creative nor original, sought to demonstrate the positive superiority of Christianity as compared with Stoic popular philosophy and the vulgar Jewish and pagan beliefs, might be regarded as a continuation of the Jewish line of Christian thought, were it not for the fact that it accepted the Greek philosophical doctrine of God and followed the rational method of Greek thinking. To the Apologists, the Christian faith was the absolutely rational religion. All the good and great thoughts that may be found in any philosophy are at bottom Christian, for Christ is the Logos, and the effects of this Christ Logos are present in germ even in the great thoughts of heathenism. On the other hand, revealed Christianity is not only older, but also more glorious than all pagan wisdom, which is merely patchwork, and is contradicted by revealed Christianity. The employment of the Logos idea, which goes back to the Gospel of John and the circle from which this came, serves to reconcile Christian monotheism with the worship of Christ, but it is also an indication of the universalistic feeling in Christianity, whose preparatory stage is found not only in Judaism, but wherever reason has been at work. The incarnation of the Logos in Christ was necessary in order to break the power of the demons who seduced mankind to polytheism, and then in His ministry Christ set forth to men (whose sin consisted in ignorance of the good and who receive along with their liberation the capacity for moral life) the commandments of God and showed how they should be fulfilled. All who obey Him receive the supreme reward — imperishableness. This last is not meant to be interpreted spiritually: it means, emphatically, the resurrection of the body. In this system of rational and moral piety there is no proper place for the paradox contained in the doctrine of justification or for the idea of salvation in its mystical and metaphysical depth. To the advocates of this piety religion is simply a mass of doctrines which differ from philosophy only in their universal validity and their comparative simplicity.

Of quite a different kind is the Christianity of *Irenæus*, who was influenced not only by the theology of Asia Minor — John's — but also by that of the Apologists. It reminds us of Hellenistic Mysticism, only there is no mention of sacramentarian magic or the piety of the Mysteries; and its almost Pauline manner of thinking gives the whole system a unique depth. We may perhaps distinguish three lines of thought in Irenæus. The first tackles the question why Christ had to become man. Irenæus' answer is, in order that man may become God. This brings the momentous conception of the deification of man into the centre of Christianity, and stabilizes a view of salvation which is based on the idea of type and antitype. The second line of thought interprets salvation as the restoration of the original state of the first man. This is accomplished by the incarnation of Christ, because Christ as the new man comprises in Himself the whole of humanity, communicates to it His spirit, fills it with His life, and thus destroys the disobedience and death that are in it. Christ has thus become the principle of a new life and a new humanity. The third line of thought interprets history as the history of redemption. The history of the relations between God and man has unrolled in the form of three covenants, and this gradual progress is an ascent, because in the course of it God works out the gradual education of the human race. This does not mean that salvation is simply a new creation or a restoration of man's original condition. It is something supernatural and miraculous, and "grace" confers more than "nature" contains in itself. Here we have already *in nuce* that peculiarly vague and indistinct system of nature and grace, evolution and revelation, which afterward became dominant in the theology of the Church.

Tertullian's Christianity is of special interest to us here, because it already contains the basal features of Catholicism. Paradoxical though it may seem to be, it is a fact that this great Catholic teacher was a Montanist. To Tertullian Christianity is not only the religion of reason, for which the human soul is adapted, it is also the religion of divine justice, which requires discipline and obedience on the part of man. This African theologian thus filled again with vitality ideas that ultimately go back to Judaism, but he recast them in polished formulas which have in them the spirit of Rome. His thoughts run on the following lines: the law of Christ must be fulfilled, and that law is all the stricter because humanity has now attained the age of manhood. It is our duty through obedience to acquire merit with God. To human merit corresponds divine grace, for only he is crowned who has obtained grace. But grace enables man to win eternal life and the resurrection of the body. In his doctrine of the sacraments Tertullian did not reach pure sacramentarianism. In this African teacher, therefore, we have the typical features of Latin Christianity — the religion of law, which prevails with God through obedience, and, as it were, intertwined with it, the religion of salvation and piety through grace, for it is God's grace that enables man to make the final ascent.

The great thinker in whom for a long time to come the problems of Oriental theology had their roots was *Origen*. His system may be compared with that of Plotinus, whose metaphysic of descent and ascent and whose mysticism, centred in the contrast between the One and the Many, have again and again influenced Christianity both directly and indirectly. Origen's system rests ultimately on the tradition of a Christian Gnosticism run wild, and the important question with regard to him and all who came after him is how far his theology was Greek or Oriental in character. Origen was fundamentally a Biblical theologian, and he was convinced that the teaching of the Bible was the same as the teaching of the Church. But it was just round the contradiction and the impossibilities in the Bible that his theological speculations turned, employing his genius for allegorical exegesis, and this double level of thinking resulted in a division of Christians into two classes — the " simples " and the " pneumatics," the latter being those who had passed beyond the simple, historical faith and had grown up into the wisdom which is life. The doctrine of the Trinity is interpreted by Origen as a theogonic process, and to each of the three Persons a special sphere of action is assigned. From all eternity God created a large number of imperishable, incorporeal spirits. Some of these fell away and became independent and free. Matter, which is eternally without form, serves to exercise and try the spirits. Corporeality and lot in life are the results of former choices. The world is thus a judgment before *the* judgment, and everything in human life is either guilt or merit, a consequence or a means of test. The cosmical drama decides what our life is to be, and the final end, after many worlds have come and gone, will be the return of all life into God. The original sameness will be restored, and the differences, which after all are merely the consequences of various pre-existences, will disappear in the One. It cannot be said that there is nothing specifically Christian in this system, because Origen, of course in his own speculative manner, not only dealt with the fundamental dogmas of Christianity, but also accepted and supported the tenets of the Creation and the resurrection of the body — meaning, however, the spiritualized body. Christ's work was necessary, because the harmony of the many spirits in the cosmos has been destroyed by too puissant evil. To restore this harmony is the work of the " God-man," and in this connexion Origen emphasizes the importance of Christ's death and of His fight with the devil. It is Christ and His work that make possible the gradual ascent of men's souls to God and, to some extent also, the retro-development of the Persons of the Trinity. In his Christology proper, Origen lays the stress on the soul of the man Jesus. It was with the pure soul, not with the body, of Jesus that the Logos united itself — the fate even of the soul of Jesus was decided in His pre-existence. In that union, which was maintained by the eternal urge of the soul toward the Logos, the Logos gradually changed the body into spirit, till in the resurrection body and Logos became one. With regard to the rest of Origen's system, we can mention only the following points. He spiritualized the doctrine of the Church; the Church reflects the harmonious gradation of the cosmos, and the pneumatic members take precedence in it. He also spiritualizes the sacraments and the eschatology. The following period abandoned the fundamental idea of Origen that theology is knowledge (gnosis), and thus deserted his great speculative ideas in favour of the teaching of the Church. Indeed, the Eastern Church ultimately condemned her greatest son as a heretic. But nevertheless the tendency to speculation continued, and burst forth in varying strength again and again, and enough survived of Origen's teaching — his doctrine of the Trinity, of the Logos, and of eschatology — to turn the 'rule of truth' into a philosophical theology. This can be seen in the work of a man like Methodius, the disciple of Origen who opposed his master. By the emphasis he laid on celibacy, and by the mystical-physical turn which he gave to the doctrine of salvation, Methodius had an important influence on the period that followed.

6. When, owing to the work of Paul, Christianity definitely parted company with Judaism and became a world religion it also forfeited the legal protection it had enjoyed throughout the Roman Empire along with Judaism. The Roman State, tolerant as it was toward private opinions so long as these did not touch the divinity of the State itself, seems to have proceeded against Christianity at a very early date, and it was not content with police and administrative measures. Although no mention of such a thing has come down to us, there seems to be good reason for postulating the issue of an edict that made it a crime to profess the Christian religion. Under Trajan and Hadrian the measures against the Christians were a part of the ordinary criminal procedure. No attention was to be paid to denunciations of the individuals, but *Christianity was a prohibited religion*; Christians were liable to be tried for high treason, and refusal by the accused to offer sacrifice was held to be proof of guilt.

Why did the tolerant Romans thus come to treat Christianity as a crime? The reasons were manifold. We are not referring here to the well-known calumnies that were spread concerning them, nor to the incitements that came from the Jews. The Christian religion itself was of a kind that made it difficult for the ancient world to regard it as a religion at all. The absence of images from its worship, the Apocalyptic expectation, which verged on hostility to the State and even seemed a threat against its life, the mode of life that menaced social fellowship, Christian exclusiveness and intolerance — all these told against it. But what roused still stronger opposition was the organization of the religion — *i.e.*, the Christian Church. It was a danger to the State that a strictly organized sect should carry on a zealous propaganda and deprive the State of officials, officers, and soldiers who were urgently needed. And as time went on the question became more and more pressing, whether there was not some inner connexion between the growth of the Church and the decline of the Roman Empire. Thus, although they had many features in common, the worship of Christ and the worship of the Emperor were in patent antagonism to each other: Christ against the one real Antichrist.

But, on the other hand, how are we to explain the rapid expansion of Christianity during the second and third centuries? Here we must remember that, favoured by the political turmoils of the time, the Orientalization of the West was growing apace and making itself felt in every sphere of civilization, and we must also keep in mind the aggregate policy of the Roman emperors, of which their attitude toward Christianity was an integral part. It is not the case that the ablest emperors were those who favoured Christianity. On the contrary, some of those emperors who had a leaning toward syncretism and encouraged the Orientalization of the Empire were also more or less friendly toward Christianity, while those who desired the restoration of the ancient, doughty Roman spirit persecuted the Christian religion and Church. It should also be remembered that it was not Mithras and the other Mystery deities that were brought into the field against Christianity; it was the recognized gods of the ancient Roman State. On the other hand, it must not be imagined that, amid the universal Orientalization that was going on, the Christian religion was really carrying all before it or achieving striking success. The notion that 'paganism' was everywhere threatened with collapse and was being everywhere replaced by the young and vigorous Christian religion is no longer tenable. Paganism was very far from being at its last gasp, and it can only have been the tremendous moral energies of Christianity and the human appeal of its historical Saviour that gave that religion the victory not only over the Roman official gods, but also over the rival Oriental religions. The severest persecution that the Church had to face took place under Decius, about the middle of the third century. Decius required all his subjects to prove their allegiance to the State by offering sacrifice to the emperor in presence of a competent authority, and refusal to do so was to be followed by severe and painful punishments. The result was catastrophic. There is no doubt that the large majority of Christians apostatized openly or secretly and that the organization of the Church was broken up. Still the Church clung to its ancient proud principles. True, it allowed its members to evade persecution by flight, but anyone who fell into the hands of the State was expected to declare his faith without reserve, and if necessary to suffer without flinching. To die a martyr's death was his duty. That genuine heroism was shown cannot be doubted. In the Diocletian persecution Bishop Peter of Alexandria issued instructions that those clergy were not to be deprived of office who had been gagged in order to render them unable to utter their confession of Christ or had been loaded with chains and forced to offer sacrifice with seared hands; and a similar dispensation was issued for those who, after having been tortured till they lost consciousness, offered sacrifice because they were powerless to resist.

As a result of these persecutions in the third and at the beginning of the fourth centuries the Church had to face difficult problems of organization. These led to repeated schisms both in the East and in the West. One troublesome question was, What was to be done with those who had apostatized? Were they to be readmitted after a profession of penitence? And who was entitled thus to readmit them—the bishop or the pneumatic—*i.e.,* the martyr? After serious controversies, into which we cannot here enter, these questions were decided in a manner that involved clever manipulations of former decisions. Apostates were readmitted after repentance and at the hands of the bishop. That meant a victory for ecclesiasticism in the Church; the "fellowship of the faithful" had now definitively become "the Church."

All these developments were gradually embodied in *constitutional* forms. The distinction between clergy and laymen had long been looming in the distance. Out of the forms of public worship—the idea of priesthood being strongly stressed—grew the ecclesiastical office, the bishop being regarded as the representative of God. The universal demand for ritual purity gave rise to a special standard of morals for the clergy, and by and by celibacy, in various degrees, came to be considered an indispensable requirement for the sacred office. The Synod of Elvira in the beginning of the fourth century prohibited all clergy, not from marrying, but from having marital intercourse, and this form of celibacy came near to being made a law of the Empire at the Council of Nicæa. It was only later, and only in the West, that all clergy were forbidden to marry, whereas in the East only marriage after ordination was forbidden. In the third century, however, the bishop was still far from being the absolute ruler of his diocese. Down to the fourth century all members took part in the most important questions of Church government, even in the election of bishops, and the ancient pneumatism survived not only in theory, but also in practice. The synods, in which at first all members of the Church took part, typified ecclesiastical unity, and the bishops were present at them, not as mandatories of the congregations, but as pneumatics—*i.e.,* possessors of the Spirit. Thus every synod symbolized the inward divine unity of the Church, and their decisions were not regarded as new law, but as ancient truth revealed by the Spirit. It is patent that danger of schism lurked here, especially when questions of dogma came before the courts, and the whole system thus seems to have been pervaded by the deep-seated contradiction between the growing autonomy of the bishop and the idea of ecclesiastical unity. It was because of this that the emperor had later to be invoked as the last court of appeal in the Church, and the calling of a great council by the emperor came to be the formal characteristic of an œcumenical council.

When we consider his religious policy as a whole we see that *Constantine the Great* had a forerunner in the Emperor Aurelian, who declared the sun-god to be a deity of the Empire as a rival to Christianity. His early death prevented his purposes from being carried out. But Constantine, who has justly been called " the Great," had the genius and the courage to come to terms with the Church and Christianity in face of the opinions of all law-abiding people in his Empire. This was a part of his policy as a whole. Like his predecessors, he had an eye on the East, and his policy was planned accordingly. Just as, reversing Diocletian's policy, he established the hereditary monarchy instead of the Imperial office, made numerous concessions to Hellenistic ideas of law, and with the insight of genius, made Byzantium, one of the pivotal points of political geography, his capital, under the name of Constantinople, so also, in a cleverly calculated way, he gradually discouraged the ancient religion, retaining for himself, however, the dignity and title of *pontifex maximus.* By these measures he made Christianity not merely a tolerated, but a privileged religion in the Empire, and fitted the Church into the general political organization. Throughout the Donatist and Arian controversies Constantine sought to leave the questions open and undecided till he had acquired a controlling power in the Church. Only a politician of genius, with an ear for the over- and under-tones of historical evolution, only a man who was ruthless enough to overleap all traditional barriers and dogmas, could have done this. As for his personal attitude, he continued to be a catechumen till shortly before his death, though this can hardly have been out of reverence for the Christian religion, whose representatives he had treated very cavalierly at times. His private life was that of an Oriental sultan rather than that of a Christian emperor. In his letters he speaks of God only in the ordinary conventional phrases, and hardly ever mentions the name of Christ. His religion may perhaps be compared with that of Napoleon. It was the faith of a man of action in an almighty Power which he had felt in the struggles and crises of his own life. " It is my steadfast faith that I owe my whole soul, my breath, my inmost thought, to the supreme God."

Constantine's policy was continued by his successors. The attempt of Julian, the Neo-Platonist on the throne of the Cæsars, to replace the Christian Church by the reformed Neo-Platonist Church was merely an episode, and under Gratian and Theodosius the Great the final victory of Christianity was assured. But this victory also meant the loss of the Church's liberty. True, the State bestowed possessions upon the Church, and granted so many privileges to the clergy that their calling became a desirable one (Constantine had even recognized the civil jurisdiction of the bishop), but at the same time ecclesiastical administration fell more and more into the hands of the emperor, owing to his influence with the synods and with the Patriarch of Constantinople, so that finally ecclesiastical jurisdiction was absorbed into that of the State, and the emperor elected by God — *e.g.,* Justinian — became master in the Church.

The question has often been asked how the new conditions produced by the ' conversion' of Constantine told upon the inner life of Christianity. It used to be said that Christendom had apostatized from Christianity and that paganism .now invaded the Church from all directions. It was this opinion that led after long scientific research to the now familiar conclusion that Christianity was " Hellenized." The subject must be approached to-day from the point of view of the history of the religion. In the course of its history the Gospel has had repeatedly to come to terms with two types of religious life, both of which go back to primitive times. The one, a spiritual-rationalist type, goes back to Judaism, knows no sacrament, and emphasizes history and morality; the other, the Hellenistic type, lays the stress on salvation interpreted sacramentally and conceives of holiness as belonging to things (not to persons). In proportion as Christianity spread and the primitive ideas about the Church gathered strength, the sacramentarian type of piety could not fail to flourish, and by and by it became the gateway through which pagan influences poured into the Church. The missionary activity of the great bishops, who utilized everywhere the forms of worship that appealed to the people, was deliberately directed so as to further this process.

It is in this light that the worship of saints and relics and various developments in public worship and in religious life should be viewed. The growth of the constitution of the Church, as well as its organization on lines which, while they were analogous to those of the State, did not exactly coincide with the latter at every point, was a result of the *rapprochement* between Church and State inaugurated by Constantine. To be sure, the Church had to purchase her security and her social prestige at the price of her freedom, and the emperor became the most powerful factor in her life. But it was not fortuitous that it was while this great change was taking place that monasticism came into existence. The ideal of monasticism, which was to some extent a continuation of the ancient pneumatism, and which has therefore all along been at odds with the Church, was set forth by Athanasius in his *Vita Antonii*. The culture of moral personality by means of asceticism (which was not merit, but duty), ardent zeal, subordination to the bishop, and the pastoral labours of the experienced monk — these are the main features of the ideal that was now cherished. Starting with the thought of the body of Christ,[21] and emulating the Apostolic life of the first Christians, Basilius lauded the monastic communal life as preferable to that of the solitary anchorite. Love of God, he said, must be conjoined with love of our neighbour — meaning by neighbour mainly one's brother monk. But his advocacy of communal monastic life did not succeed in abolishing the secluded life, and Justinian supported the view that the higher ideal was to be found in the anchoretic life within the *koinobion*. Ultimately the Areopagite drew monasticism into the orbit of his symbolical and graduated ecclesiastical and mystical piety, and thus weakened enthusiasm by extolling an emblematic and speculative mysticism. From time to time, however, there were reactions within monasticism in the direction of individual experience,

21 Col. i, 24.

toward personal touch with the divine and in favour of a direct, immediate view of the Divine Light that ignored mysteries and images.

7. There are perhaps three views of the *divinity of Christ* which may be now placed side by side. The first is a rational view, which sees in Christ the teacher and law-giver. The second is a historical-mystical view, which regards Christ as the inaugurator of a new humanity, Who fills with new life those who enter into mystical fellowship with Him. The third is a sacramental-mystical view, which emphasizes the saving powers of the in-carnate God, which have been committed to the Church, those powers which destroy decay and finitude and bestow immortality and deification. But the theological disputes which raged for several centuries round the doctrine of the Trinity and round the Person of Christ, and which forthwith became ecclesiastical controversies, were always decided on grounds of wider policy. The ancient feeling still survived that there could be no such thing as political fellowship without community of thought and opinion. But that was only one of the factors that were at work. Another factor, one that lay deeper than any of the differences that divided the schools of philosophy, was the inherent contrast between two types of religious life. Arius repre-sented the belief (which had its roots not only in philosophic thought, but in religious experience) in the transcendence of the absolutely unique God, Who is separated from the world by an impassable gulf, and in relation to whom even the created Logos and Christ, the organ of the Logos, are ranged with the world. On the other hand, the Alexandrians, starting from the idea of salvation, emphasized the unity in nature and the identity in sub-stance of the Father and the Son. If salvation is real, then also that must be real which brings it to pass; that is to say, the deification of man pre-supposes the incarnation of God. Here we see at work not only the sense of the immanence of God in all that is created and the view that the Logos had of necessity to take bodily form, but also the piety which regards the divine as immanent in all things, as well as persons. By taking bodily form God has come within our reach: Christ and God are identical. Only if the Son be the uncreated God and of one nature with the Father can His power deliver us from decay and give us immortality. Victory lay with the Alex-andrians just because their doctrine was more in keeping with the popular piety. Their victory opened wider the door for an inpouring of the Mystery religions into the Church, but it also concentrated Christian thought upon the Saviour and upon salvation, and thus prevented theology and religion from evaporating into mere speculation. All debate about God as the Primal Cause, all speculation on the existence that lies beyond existence, ceased. Men were content to say God is the God Who has been manifested to us: God is Christ.

These views, which became authoritative dogma at the Council of Nicæa, were built up by Athanasius, the first ecclesiastical Prince of the grand style, into a historical-mystical system of theology, resembling that of Irenæus.

In it not only the conceptions death and life, but also guilt and reconciliation have a place. The difficulty involved in his doctrine of the Trinity — that Christ is the Son of the Father and yet identical with Him — he tried to surmount by saying that he regarded the Son as the work of the Father. After Athanasius, the three great Cappadocians, Basilius, Gregory of Nazianza, and Gregory of Nyssa, tried each in his own manner to set forth the doctrine of the Trinity in a logical way, and after much heated controversy the orthodox watchword was no longer sameness of nature (*homoousia*), but similarity of nature (*homoiousia*) of the personally distinct Persons (*hypostaseis*) of the Trinity.

In the West, which was also drawn into the dogmatic controversies of the East, Augustine provided the final formulas. The Western doctrine of the Trinity differs from the Eastern in that it rests on the unity of God, and Augustine replaced the term *hypostaseis* ('persons') by the term relations. Thus Father, Son, and Spirit do not denote quantitative or qualitative differences in God; they are names for eternal relations or processes within the Godhead itself. We must keep in mind the religious intention of the Trinitarian doctrine of God, which expresses the life that is in the Godhead itself.

In the *controversy on the Person of Christ* (the doctrine was not logically formulated till well into the fourth century) the question at issue was that of the relation of the divine and the human elements in Christ. The Antiochian theology — represented by Theodorus, Theodoret, Chrysostom, and Nestorius — started from the conception of personality, which consists in moral disposition and conative power. Fundamental for this theology is the distinction between the divine and the human in the Person of Christ. The eternal Logos united Itself with the man Jesus at the moment of his conception in the womb in such a manner that that human being, who freely willed God and the Good, became the organ of the Logos. The Logos and the man became one; formally it was the man in Him that acted, but as a matter of fact His behaviour was determined by the Logos, to whom the man Jesus at all times submitted himself. This Antiochian theology thus stood for a rational type of piety, which emphasized the heterogeneity of God. On the other hand, the Alexandrians — among whom Cyril is the clearest and most intelligible — represented a sacramentarian type of religion supported by the need of intuition. In it the physical, strongly felt union of the divine and the human in Christ is brought into the forefront, and the double personality of Christ is rejected, thus invalidating salvation and disparaging the means by which it is secured. This Alexandrian theology does not seem to grasp the problem of personality at all. It deals rather with the two massive natures, and emphasizes the paradoxical union of the divine and the human in the historical Christ, which is such that in the frail human being the divine majesty can be seen and enjoyed.

But even the Christological controversy was by no means merely a spiritual

contest. It was also a struggle for power and hegemony between the Patri-
archs of Alexandria and Constantinople. Thrice did Alexandria, the most
powerful national Church of the East, triumph over Constantinople, which
represented the Byzantine State Church: Theophilus defeated Chrysostom,
Cyril overcame Nestorius, and Dioscurus triumphed over Flavian. But by
and by Alexandria was definitively conquered, and it fell because it abandoned what had been the traditional Alexandrian policy since the time of
Athanasius — that is, the policy of keeping in touch with Rome. It had even
tried to overmatch Rome. The Council of Chalcedon (451), whose pro-
ceedings were marked by the brutality of the methods employed and by
the cowardice of the Court bishops, condemned Nestorius and his Monophysite views. It also drew up a confession of faith that tried to combine
three tendencies — the Christology of Cyril, that sees the eternal God in the
finite man, the Antiochian view, which separates the two natures, in order
to safeguard the pure transcendence of God, and the Western view as
formulated by Leo the Great, which was content with the formula of
the two natures in the one Person. Thus the decision of Chalcedon placed
in the forefront the unity of the Person which was held by all three
groups. This unity of the Person was defined as consisting of two separate
natures, each perfect in its own way, but uniting to form one Person by
their action.

This decision of Chalcedon was followed by turmoil and ultimately by
schism. The Monophysite national Churches in the East broke away from
the Byzantine State Church, but immediately became involved in further
controversy as to whether Christ had had two wills or only one. These disruptions prepared the way for the invasion of the Arabs and the repression
of Christianity in the East. The Byzantine emperors endeavoured des-
perately, even at the cost of a breach with Rome, to restore unity. They tried
all kinds of measures. They issued edicts and procured the passing of synodal
resolutions. They granted concessions and had recourse to violent measures,
but even Justinian failed to achieve more than temporary success.

8. Before leaving this part of our subject we shall try to sum up the leading features of this *Greek-Oriental type of Christianity*. It represents a
special kind of Christianity not only from the confessional and national
points of view, but also in respect of its religious life. We shall leave out of
account here all questions of constitution and ritual, and confine ourselves
to the piety it produced.

The first point worthy of special notice is that although, like all forms of
religious life within Christianity, this Greek-Oriental type was based on
the Bible, the Bible was explained and expounded through tradition —
i.e., the resolutions of councils, the pronouncements of theologians, and the
oral tradition of the Church. This attitude toward tradition expressed the
felt consciousness of the living unity of the Church and the conviction of
a real connexion in the history of Christianity. The standard of truth was

thus not any formal juristic authority, but the self-witness of the Spirit Who lives in the Church. " The Church as a whole is infallible."

The peculiar nature of any type of piety is disclosed in its doctrine of God. Greek Christianity was dominated by the sense of the divine transcendence. God is simply the Transcendent One Who is exalted above the world, the Incomprehensible and Inaccessible. And, in the doctrine of *homoousia,* and to some extent also in the Monophysite view of His earthly life, Christ too is drawn into the sphere of transcendence. It is of course in the Christology that we see the other side of the matter, which resembles to some extent the Mystical Immanence of Oriental Christianity. In His goodness this absolutely transcendent God reveals Himself in the human figure of Christ as well as in the sacraments, symbols, images, and relics. Great as is our awe in presence of the far-off majesty of God, yet He is near in the holy

FIG. 121. THE LAST SUPPER, IN ST SOPHIA IN KRAL
From Kuhn, " Allgemeine Kunstgeschichte "

institutions and ordinances of His Church. In images and symbols, in sacrament and ritual, we experience the transcendent God, that living Power which is far off, yet near, to whose light only a few elect souls are raised in direct, immediate vision. Here we see the meaning of the Mysteries and the devotional mood that characterizes the entire Greek piety, and can also understand the high value attached to images, including those stiff and bizarre images of saints (see Fig. 121) that lack all movement and passion. The image is regarded as the manifestation of the saint in person. There is a mysterious relation between the image and the person it represents, which can perhaps best be explained as a ' sympathy.' The more theology became a scientific art and a political instrument, the more inevitable it was that ritual and mystagogy should produce this type of piety. High spirituality and material piety are thus intimately connected, and it was in this type of theological mysticism that the primitive Christian pneumatism, after passing through the various transformations that have already been described, found its ultimate resting-place.

It would therefore be unjust to say that the characteristic feature of Greek Christianity is the magical element that is so prominent in the ritual. That statement is not wide enough to cover the central religious mood of this form of piety — viz., the intense sense of the victory of life through Christ. The fact that God became man, and the fact that Christ rose from the dead, these transfigure human life and all its concerns, and eternal life has burst its way through death and corporeality. The victorious life that comes through the resurrection of Christ, and ennobles and elevates all that has been created, including suffering itself, *that* is the strength of Greek piety, and its cosmological postulate is unmistakable.

Greek Christianity is essentially concerned with salvation, but in order to understand its attitude here we must begin with its conception of sin. We at once come upon a peculiar intellectualism, which is connected with the tendency to cosmological metaphysic. Sin consists in the dominion of sense over reason, and the universality of sin is explained by the transmitted corruption of man's weakened and disordered natural life. The spiritual and personal aspect of sin, however, is preserved by the emphasis that is laid on the freedom of the will of sinful man. As children of Adam we are all disposed to sin, but it is our own act of will that makes us sinners. Sin is therefore not so much guilt as ruin, sensuousness, mortality. The defect in this theory of sin is its failure to recognize that sin is more than a series of single acts, that it is a power in history which gives a new direction both to the life of the individual and to humanity at large.

In keeping with this view of sin, the doctrine of salvation relegates the idea of reconciliation through the cross of Christ and His blood to a subordinate place, in favour of the view that regards salvation as bringing healing, new life, and immortality. But the deification brought about by the new man, Christ, is by no means conceived as purely physical; on the contrary, just as sin means the disturbance of the equipoise of the natural powers owing to the predominance of the senses, so salvation means the restoration of this harmony, and therefore of imperishableness. Thus we receive the life of the new creature. " The first things are passed away. . . . Behold, I make all things new." [22] That can of course be interpreted physically, especially when salvation is closely connected with the Mysteries; but it is also capable of a purely mystical meaning, and the strong emphasis laid on the good works which the saved sinner has to do in order to fulfil the moral law effectively exclude the physical interpretation. Justification is frequently referred to, but the Greeks never reached a real understanding of that profound doctrine. Their religious life revolves round two poles. On the one hand are genuine repentance, service to others, moderation in ethics, ascetic renunciation, and — in the great mystics — compassion and humility; the

[22] Rev. xxi, 4–5.

supreme good is peace with God, peace being understood not in the Quietist sense of repose, but as a supreme concentration of soul. The other pole is the joy that fills the heart of the man who has been sanctified and awakened to true life, who has received new eyes and new senses, and who even now sees the new life being poured over creation and witnesses the ennobling of all creatures, whose prototype is Mary, the Virgin Mother and Queen of Heaven.

This type of religion finds its culminating point in the Eucharist, in which the Christian enjoys the real presence of Christ. Through the invocation of the Holy Spirit — so it is believed — the miracle of Cana is repeated. The bread is changed into flesh, the wine into blood, although bread and wine remain. Just as the Holy Spirit once formed Christ in the Virgin, so He now continues to form Christ in the transubstantiation of the elements of the Supper. The miracle that takes place there is that of a continual incarnation, and the miraculous element is even intensified, inasmuch as the Christ thus formed on the altar is identical with the historical and transfigured Christ Who of course is omnipresent in heaven. The effect of the Eucharist is both spiritual and physical — it brings life both to the spirit and to the body — and seeing that the elements contain the body and blood of Christ, creation is also ennobled by them. There is one other feature, which comes out especially in the Eucharistic prayers — the stress laid on union, fellowship. The dead and the living, the Church on earth and the Church in heaven, are one great organic whole, in which the Spirit of Christ dwells. The Eucharist is thus the expression of the mystical fellowship of the body of Christ.

The doctrine of the Church leads to the same idea. True, all religious life is Church life: the Church guards the tradition, possesses the truth, and brings salvation. But the Church is not a state, and even the Kingdom of God is interpreted in a purely eschatological way by this type of piety, which at bottom is entirely metaphysical. The Church is also conceived as transcendental and mythical, and just on that account it was comparatively easy to adapt it to the State and to national life as such.

Again and again during its history the Greek Church in difficult days proved its living power. It faithfully preserved the old, and yet also adopted new features which really belonged to popular religion. In a certain sense this Church stands nearest to the ancient, Oriental, primitive Christianity. Perhaps the critical question for her to-day is that of the future of Christianity in Russia. There can be no doubt that Bolshevism, which in so far as it is an extreme form of Marxism is a direct continuation of the forcible Westernizing of Russia that began with Peter the Great, nevertheless contains a genuinely Russian element, which is bound in one way or other to lead to serious conflict with Christianity. All that has happened in Russia so far throws little light on the question of the form this settlement will take. All that can be said is that the Russia of to-day, whose political form no one can call permanent, has taken a step in the direction of Asia. Unconsciously prepared for by history itself, the question at issue is the future fate of Europe, and we can only dimly descry the part which the Greek Orthodox Christian Church will be called upon to play in the future shaping and transforming of our religion.

II

1. As we have seen, *Western Christianity* assumed an independent form and took a line of its own at a comparatively early date. There was little desire to speculate on dogma, and men were content with an intelligible exposition of the content of faith as provided in the Bible and the Confession. Specifically Western features included the sense of the universality of sin and interest in eschatology and in the philosophy of history. The real subjects of interest in the West were the practical questions of ritual and Church organization, although great questions, like the relation of pneumatism to the Church, were not completely settled. These were the specifically Western questions, which had been elaborated in Africa and in Rome, but Oriental influences found entrance at many points, and we can speak here also of a general syncretism. The chief factors were as follows:

(i) Manichæism, which in an ambitiously planned propaganda and in a strongly Christianized form preached the saving message of Mani, with its cosmological metaphysic. This was based on the ancient Persian conception of a contest between light and darkness, spirit and matter, good and evil, with its summons to the awakened soul to fight against the powers of darkness and of evil. (ii) Neo-Platonism, which had a flourishing school located in Rome and using the Latin language. This school of thought powerfully affected the speculations of Augustine. (iii) The Alexandrian philosophy, which, as set forth by Hilary, Ambrose, and Jerome, led to a speculative treatment of the Bible that made extensive use of the allegorical method of interpretation. (iv) The monastic ideal, which regulated and gave a deeper meaning to asceticism in the Western world governed by the Stoa. It was reintroduced by Ambrose in the Græcized form adopted by Basilius, and afterward assumed a specifically Western physiognomy by its concentration on work and on the reformation of the world. (v) Paulinism, which was impressively restated in the anonymous commentary (that goes under the name of Ambrosiaster) on the Epistles of Paul.

All these elements in the religious life and the culture of his time naturally influenced *Augustine*. It was he who gave the Christian religion the specifically Western form with which the Middle Ages had to deal, and he thus prepared the way for the metamorphosis of the Christian religion that resulted from the emergence of the Teutonic and Romanic peoples. Augustine was one of those great men in whom, as Dilthey says, there dwelt an "element of nature," and who have thus been able to surmount all conventions, desires, and traditions and to feel and face reality. He was not, properly speaking, a systematic thinker, but he was a man of many ideas, and in his mind one question gave life to the whole. He was also one of the greatest Latin writers, a master of words, with a fine sense of style, and yet he was almost meticulously thorough. His touching conscientiousness is shown most clearly in the work of his old age, his *Retractationes,* in which the aged Augustine revised his writings and eliminated their defects and mistakes.

The development through which Augustine passed reflects in summary fashion in the life of one man the transition from antiquity to the Middle Ages. It was Cicero who first summoned Augustine, like so many others, from the sensuous life of a keen lover of art to the ideal of the intellectual life. Augustine passed *via* Manichæism to Neo-Platonism, and there he not only learned how to explain the existence of evil, but also became convinced that it is only from the spiritual standpoint that the universe can be understood. This stage was followed by a brief period of scepticism, and then Augustine made up his mind to submit himself to ecclesiastical authority, and from that firm foothold to study life, religion, and philosophy. He was here acting on the principle *credo, ut intelligam.* This resolve was probably also to some extent the cause of his conversion, although other causes were at work there — for example, the experience he had had of the sensuous life and its attendant dispeace of mind as obstacles to the *fruitio dei.* Augustine's conversion presents a peculiar problem in so far as the books he wrote after his conversion are strongly influenced by the problems and ideas of Neo-Platonism, and this has led some scholars to say that that philosophy was the most powerful influence in his development. In my opinion, however, this overlooks two important points — that his deepest roots were in the thought and life of Carthage and that in the later writings referred to Augustine takes up the position that the truth is supernatural and must for that very reason be believed on authority. That position reveals the influence of the Church.

It was out of his own personal experience that Augustine drew his doctrine of the will. With all his borrowings from other quarters, even with all his debts to Neo-Platonism, this was genuinely his own. The will is the ruler of the soul. It is it that determines whether a man is good or evil, for the will is the only force in the world that can break away from the Absolute Substance and dispute its order. The evil will is the negative principle in the cosmos that resists the divine order of the world, though its resistance is vain. Knowledge cannot change a will which in itself is evil, a will which deliberately turns not to God, but to what is sensuous and merely apparent, a will that of its own choice takes a direction which is contrary to and not inherent in its nature, and that therefore brings upon itself guilt and punishment. The will is therefore the prime cause and seat of sin. At root sin is arrogance and desire. Its essence is deliberate enjoyment of the sensuous and non-existent in preference to the divine. But the divine order of the world is always carried out on man — he either does it or suffers it. The punishment of sin is not merely retribution and death; it takes the form of new sin, compulsion to sin, and ultimate inability of the will to choose the good. The task of religion is to change the direction of the will. The arrogant human will must be brought to turn away from itself and from the sensuous and devote itself, after the great example of humility — Christ — to God and the spiritual. As Augustine finely says at the beginning of the Ninth Book of his *Confessions*: " The whole matter was this — not to will what I was willing and to will what Thou willedst."

Although the Neo-Platonic idea of the Absolute Substance pervades his thought on this subject also, Augustine's doctrine of God reveals the influence of Paul in the emphasis it lays on the divine will and personality. The idea of Providence is carried over into it, and the Christian conception of creation may have deepened this conception of God as the omnipresent casual activity. With Augustine blessedness is not so much the union of two wills as contemplative rest in God. The supreme goal of religion is the enjoyment of God. It must be admitted that there is a eudemonistic touch in this interpretation of religion, and therefore we are not surprised to find that, for Augustine, love of self is perfected in the love of God — *i.e.,* human nature is perfected not in the breaking away from itself, but in the organic development of the self. On the whole, therefore, it may be said that Augustine has incised the Christianity of Paul into Neo-Platonic mysticism. Similarly, by adding the idea of the Imitation of Christ to the old mystical three paths to salvation Augustine has given to the mysticism of the Middle Ages the spiritual and ethical character which is found later in a man like Bernard. It must not be overlooked, however, that Augustine also brought Neo-Platonic mysticism into ecclesiastical positivism. According to him, the means which procure the blessed vision are the means of grace provided by the Church. The nature of grace becomes visibly clear in the ordinances of the Church; the Kingdom of God assures the experience of God. We cannot here go into the thoughts that occupied Augustine's mind in his earlier life. We cannot enlarge on his epistemology (doctrine of knowledge), which is based on Plato's theory of ideas, nor on his solution of the theodicy, which leads him to modify the contrast of good and evil and to postulate a gradation of good — another Neo-Platonic borrowing — nor on his doctrine of the Person of Christ, whose varying versions reflect different stages of development and which combines Neo-Platonic metaphysics and Christian piety. We must confine ourselves here to Augustine's doctrine of the Church and to his doctrine of grace and its appropriation by men.

It was in the contest with Donatus that Augustine elaborated his doctrine of the Church. Apart from personal antipathies and other merely temporary disputes, the point at issue between Catholicism and Donatism was the old question whether the sacraments were efficacious in themselves or whether their efficacy depended on the purity of the administrant. It was therefore a recrudescence of the double meaning of holy: holy because sacramentally connected with the Church, and holy as dependent on the free pneumatism of the person. To a certain extent both sides were able to appeal to Cyprian, who, while he based the unity of the Church on the episcopate, also regarded the bishops as possessors of the spirit.

The concrete problem here involved Augustine solved by maintaining the validity of the sacraments apart from the moral condition of the administrant, while he confined the efficacy of the sacraments to the Catholic Church, in which alone the spirit of love is effective. The sacrament confers on the recipient an indestructible character, and this is the basis of the claim of the Catholic Church on all who have been baptized. Again, the sacraments are efficacious in all cases where no human obstacle is put in their way. This seems to indicate that Augustine shared the magical view of the efficacy of the sacraments, and as a matter of fact he did much to promote this sacramentarian piety in its manifold manifestations. But on the other hand it was he who coined the expression " through the Word and the sacrament," laying the emphasis on the efficacy of the Word. The popular opinion that the divine working was shown in the empirical media used in the sacrament he did not hold: he maintained that the divine working transcends the earthly order, or is at least not completely shown in it, that above the chain of causality that obtains in the physical and psychical spheres there is a divine causality independent of it. The manifestation of this divine causality means a miracle, which is not something contrary to nature, though it is contrary to nature as known to us. Possibly, therefore, Augustine may have held the symbolical conception of the sacraments, but certainly he did not teach transubstantiation.

Augustine's doctrine of the Church is not a unified whole. Three concentric circles can be made out in it, the exterior circle including the intermediate one, while the innermost circle rises above the other two. To him " the Church " is sometimes the Catholic Church spread over the whole world, in which the Spirit of Christ rules in her ordinances and sacraments and guaranteed by the Apostolical succession of the bishops. At other times " the Church " is the fellowship of all true believers, who are held together not so much by knowledge as by the bond of moral love; that is the true Church, the Bride of Christ, which is found — and this came to be of very great importance — only in the Catholic Church, and which becomes real only in the fellowship of the sacraments. And at still other times " the Church " is the fixed and unalterable number of those who have been elected and predestinated by God to take the place of the angels who fell, although Augustine nowhere says how those who have been predestinated can influence each other or even recognize each other. The number of the predestinated is not identical with the fellowship of the saints, and may therefore apparently include others who do not belong to the Church Visible. Only a special revelation can bring certainty to anyone that he is one of the elect.

From this it follows that the *civitas dei* is not simply to be identified with the visible empirical Church, although that identificaton might seem to

follow from his premises. The *civitas dei* is rather the heavenly Jerusalem, the
Church as possessor of the Sacramental powers, as a mystical entity — which
again leaves room, of course, for a hierarchy. Further, the *civitas terrena* is
not simply the State. The State, indeed, is a counter-force to sin, inasmuch
as it paves the way for the Kingdom of God by helping to restore the
natural harmony of the powers of life. But the State must never become an
end for itself. Like the *civitas dei,* the *civitas terrena* is metaphysical in its
nature: it is the diabolical fellowship of egoists, who yet have no fellowship
and in that aspect it can of course be identified with the State, especially with
the polytheistic State.

Augustine's doctrine of grace was elaborated during the Pelagian controversy. It bears clear marks of Paul's influence, and that Apostle thus became
the teacher of the Christianity of the Middle Ages. In passing we may allude
to two points here. Augustine gave an æsthetic and philosophical turn to
Paul's conception of grace, and materialized it by his idea of its being " inpoured," and based his philosophy of history on Paul's attempt to interpret
history in the light of his fundamental conceptions of religion. It was Augustine's philosophy of history which, by placing the millennium not in the
future, but at the birth of Christ, encouraged that identification of the Church
and the Kingdom of God which largely determined the life and thought of
the Middle Ages.

Pelagius and Augustine were the two great protagonists of two fundamentally different tendencies in Western Christianity and, indeed, in religion as a
whole. The former emphasizes the freedom of men's moral action and the
law of obedience, by the fulfilment of which man can prevail on God; the
latter places in the forefront man's lack of liberty and the sovereignty of God,
Who of His own good pleasure provides salvation and bestows it on man.

Augustine's doctrine of sin concentrates attention on the first man, Adam;
but by sin, whose essence is arrogant self-love, he means not any isolated act,
but the taking of a wrong direction. And the punishment for sin, which is
also guilt, lies just in this, that man cannot but sin. Concupiscence, immod-
erate delight in the sexual act, paves the way for more sin, and also propagates
it as by contagion. That is the meaning of original or inherited sin and the
explanation of its universality. But Augustine did not regard even original
sin as involving either a physical or metaphysical determinism. The sinner
retains his psychological freedom of will, even although he is in the grasp
of a metaphysical necessity.

Only the grace of God, which became effective through the death of
Christ, gives the sinner the will to believe and the power to remain good.
It is grace alone, therefore, that snatches the sinner from his evil way and
makes him righteous, so that as a renewed man — this is a remarkable interpolation which looks like a concession to the common Catholic view —
he is able to act rightly and thus acquire merit, which God rewards with
eternal blessedness. And if not all those who are called attain to faith and

regeneration, there is only one explanation of it — namely, the will of God, Who is the ultimate, primal cause of salvation and of its successful achievement even in the case of the elect. Like Jesus and Paul, Augustine taught a predestination of which there is no outward distinguishing mark, so that fear and hope are always the basal notes in the life even of the elect. It was Augustine who thus stabilized for all time in the history of the religion of the West this great interpretation of the Gospel, that God acts in a free and sovereign manner toward man, and that man can give God nothing except what he has received from Him.

While it must be admitted that Augustine, under the influence of Neo-Platonism, placed the conception of grace in an important setting, the view of grace as a mysterious, impenetrable power of Fate is subordinated to its interpretation as being the attitude of God, the divine power of love that is revealed in Christ and which accomplishes our salvation by an act in history and by the effects that flowed from it.

Complicated and contradictory as Augustine's thinking is, it is possible to make out the three most important elements in his religion. These are: first, a voluntarist-personal-ethical piety, which culminates in God, who is conceived of as Will. It is to this element that his doctrine of grace as a whole belongs. Second, a Neo-Platonic, æsthetic piety, according to which God is the Sole Substance. This comes out in his epistemology or doctrine of knowledge and in his conception of evil, from which standpoint he looks on the sacraments as symbols. Third, his doctrine of the Church, which is so characteristic both for his development and for his personality. Here he favoured the limitation of the work of grace to the sacraments, and intensified the sense of fellowship and the appreciation of history by a stronger emphasis on the Church and the ecclesiastical doctrine of " the last things." All these elements were combined and unified by the ardent religion of a great man, who had known sin and the Church and the God Who is the cause of all things. It is difficult to say which of these weighed most with Augustine. Perhaps it was his doctrine of the Church that provided this restless spirit with his last and deepest foothold, and it was this that made this versatile thinker the guide of the Catholicism of the Middle Ages.

But the importance of Augustine in the history of religion lies in the fact that with the power of genius he restated Paulinism to his own age, and thus accomplished a work which, in spite of numerous condensations and embroideries, definitively introduced the Gospel in the Jewish-moralist type of Roman Christianity. This verdict on Augustine's place in history is not affected even when we remember that, ere many years had passed, the sharpest angles of his system were rounded off and that his teaching survived in the Church only in the form of Semi-Pelagianism or, rather, of Semi-Augustinianism. For in all times of crisis Augustine has come to life again, and has furnished with the weapons of his spirit all those who have attempted to reshape things — pneumatics, mystics, and reformers. If there has ever been in the history of Christianity a man of epoch-making influence, that man was Augustine. Various attempts have been made to divide Church history into eras and periods according to types, but all such attempts are vain. Any useful classification must take into account the two types in which the Christian religion has taken shape. These are the Oriental type, which has had its line of representatives from Jesus to Dostoieffsky, in which the Hellenizing of the Christian myth is only one feature, and the Occidental type, which began with the metamorphosis that was brought about by the emergence of the Teutonic peoples. The latter type became conscious of itself in the individualism of the twelfth century, and has been elaborated in an intensive, dialectical development of its essential features through the Renaissance, the Reformation, the Counter-Reformation, the Illumination,[23] and the philosophy of idealism. The prehistory of this type lies not only in the East, but also and chiefly in Africa and in Rome, where the organized Church had as its head, not an unwieldy council, but one individual mind. The man who brought about the union of these two types of Christianity and kept them together was Augustine. That constitutes his importance in the history of the world.

2. What we call the Middle Ages begins with the consolidation of the Teutonic peoples. In a sense that period was a new beginning of history, for this emergence of new nations in the centre of the world's history meant a change not only of the external, but also of the intellectual conditions of the time. A new ' mentality ' came upon the scene, and brought about a readjustment of all intellectual values. On the other hand, the Middle Ages provide a proof that there is no such thing as an absolute novelty in history, for these Teutonic nations, in taking over Christianity, Greek science, and fragments of Latin literature, took over the intellectual heritage of antiquity, which they laboured to work up and assimilate through a long evolution marked by repeated rapid advances. The period known as the Middle Ages thus provides a conclusive proof of the erroneousness of Spengler's theory that each civilization has had an independent life in its most pronounced form. For, equally with Aristotelianism and Platonism, the Christian religion — and that, too, in the form of the hierarchical Church — survived the cleavage that marked the times, and either as tradition, or *auctoritas,* or as *ratio* shaped and formed the men of the Middle Ages, their thought and their life, nay, their very individuality. Of course, this intellectual heritage had itself to undergo restatement, and in that process it was recreated; but the influence of the inherited forms was also extraordinarily great, and at some points the old contents were reproduced and infused with new life by men of religious genius.

It was in the form of a Church that stood above the nations that Christianity came to the new peoples. After the downfall of the Imperial Government it was the Church and its representatives that took charge both of the

[23] The German *Aufklärung,* represented by Leibniz. It is sometimes called the Enlightenment.

cultural and also of the administrative functions of political life. The Church, it was maintained, is not a society, but the State of God on earth. It demands subordination and obedience from its members, including the State and its head. It was from the standpoint implied in the name *civitas dei* that the struggle with the emperors was afterward waged. And it was no mere chance that it was in these troublous times that a start was made at various centres on the codification of ecclesiastical law. The teaching of the Church, whose truth was vouched for by Scripture, councils, the recognized Fathers of the Church, and the Pope, is the authority. The task of scholarship is limited to establishing this authority, understanding it, and proving its reasonableness. The Christian religion, which is in the keeping of the Church, brings the salvation which God bestows, but which nevertheless must be earned. Everything is of grace — so ran the formula — but even grace must be earned. These two great, complicated ideas, the Church and salvation of the soul, are brought together by the sacraments, in which the work of Christ is contained, and made available for the individual. The administration of the sacraments is in the hands of the hierarchy, and therefore belief in them is also actually necessary to salvation. But these groups of ideas, which led to a grandiose attempt to shape the world and to perfect a unified view of the world, contained two elements which, though in themselves inherently explosive, were robbed of their danger by being assimilated. These two elements were monasticism and asceticism. In monasticism there survived the ancient pneumatism, and in the spheres of theology, missionary effort, and popular eduction it rendered to the Church services that can hardly be overestimated, although it also gave birth to forces that led to the disruption of the ecclesiastical institutions of the Middle Ages. And asceticism, which had much in common with monasticism, was a great bulwark against the tendencies that existed within the Church to come to terms with the world; its watchword was to overcome the ego as well as the world in order to reach the world beyond. It was this pious idealism of asceticism that made so many ascetics — *e.g.,* Bernard — rulers of the world. It is always so; how should not he who has overcome himself also overcome others? This aspect of asceticism played a large part in the fight of Gregory VII for celibacy.

It can hardly be said that the Teutons had any special natural bent for Christianity. Their religion exhibited the same features as are usually found among other primitive peoples — belief in demons and in Fate. The *oldest Teutonic Christianity* (which has been described chiefly from Anglo-Saxon sources) shows in its very terminology how Christianity has been adapted to the Teutonic world of ideas. In illustration of this, special mention may be made of the Teutonic conception of Christ conquering Fate and its powers and advancing at the head of His vassals as a heavenly chieftain; and we may also point to the way in which the primitive sacramental aspects of the Christian religion were intensified when they came into contact with the uncivilized Teutonic and Romanic peoples. Most momentous of all was the collision of the Church with the Teutonic conceptions of the State and the community. The view that the community was a confederacy, which involved particularism and a feudalistic limitation of the power of the State, came into conflict with the conception of the Church, with its undeniable ancient Roman features. The general contrast, however, was displayed at another, quite special point. Religion, even the Christian religion, was regarded among the Teutons as a public matter, and therefore the monarch, or the lord of the soil on which the church stood, was looked upon as the head of the Church. In other words, among the Teutons the Church was a private Church, an idea that had some inner affinity with that of the national Church and patronage; and this view could not fail to come into collision with the supra-national and independent Catholic Church. The contest of the Catholic Church against investiture and against simony was at bottom a contest against the deeply rooted Teutonic ideas of the private Church and the sacred right of the ruler, although it afterward widened into the battle for the *civitas dei* and later still into the avowed struggle for the dominion of the world.

The form of Christianity which was first introduced among the Teutons was Arianism. That was due to an accident, to the fact that Ulfilas, who converted the West Goths to Christianity, was an Arian. Ulfilas, the son of a Cappadocian family which had been captured in war, was consecrated as bishop by Eusebius of Nicomedia in the year 341. By the West Goths this Arian Christianity was carried to the East Goths and other tribes, such as the Vandals living on the Danube. These Eastern Teutonic peoples carried it to the Suevi, Burgundians, and Alemanni. The predominant position occupied by the East Goth Theoderic probably increased the prestige of Arianism, especially in view of the breach of relations between Rome and Byzantium. There is no need to look for dogmatic differences and conflicting views behind the Arianism of the Teutons. The absence of theological speculation and the simple acceptance of the Scriptures were due rather to the incapacity of the 'barbarians' than to theological principles. And the fact that celibacy was not demanded from the clergy, nor virginity from the monks, indicates that Christianity was to some extent adapted to meet common practice and public opinion. It is in quite a different sphere, that of canonical law, that we find the characteristic feature of this Arian Christianity: the king is the head of the Church. The Church was in fact a dynastic Church, with the idea of the private Church as its basis.

Further milestones on the road traversed by Christianity were the 'conversion' of Ludwig to Catholic Christianity, which was mainly due to political reasons — Gregory of Tours likened it to the 'conversion' of Constantine the Great; the missionary work carried on among the heathen Angles and Saxons under the inspiration of Gregory the Great; the work of Irish and Scottish monks among the Franks and in Thuringia and South Germany, and the labours of Willibrord among the Frisians; the missionary, reforming, and organizing activities of the Wessex man Boniface, that faithful servant who really brought the Anglo-Saxon Christian civilization to the Germans and Franks, whose Christianity had been hitherto merely superficial, and who united them to each other and to Rome, thus paving the way for a uniform Western civilization. These were all stages on the road to that epoch-making union of the new nations with Rome and with the Catholic Church represented by it. A later step of tremendous importance was taken when the elevation of Pepin, a member of a petty dynasty, to the throne of the Merovingians was legalized and approved by the Pope. This was the first proof that the Church was now willing and able, if not to bestow a monarchical dignity, at least to give it its blessing. And in this connexion we may recall the coronation of Charles the Great as emperor at the hands of the Pope — a ceremony which in that form certainly took place against the will of Charles himself.

3. *Charles the Great* pushed the frontiers of his empire south to the Ebro and east to the Elbe, and prepared the way for a great extension of German civilization along the Lower Danube. His importance for the history of religion lies in the fact that, having been converted to the Anglo-Saxon conception of " ruler by the grace of God " and to that of the *civitas dei*, he guided the life of his empire into the paths of civilization and education. He clearly perceived that the life of a state should not be limited to waging wars and making annexations, nor should it demonstrate merely the will to live and the will to power of the nation and of its ruler. He held it to be the privilege and the task of a monarch to arouse in his people a sense of cultural values and to train them to appreciate education, morals, and religion. Charles the Great, who in this respect may be compared with men like Alfred the Great and Canute the Great, conceived this civilization, after the manner of Justinian, as a kind of theocracy. But he differed from his predecessors in this, that while they desired to see the Church subordinated to the State, he endeavoured to rule his empire in the spirit of Christianity. With this in view, he chose the leading clergy as his State advisers. This did not prevent him from exercising a despotic power in the Church. He held the ancient Teutonic view of law, and while he did not meddle with the constitution of the Church, he insisted on taking a leading part in its administration. In virtue of the royal authority bestowed on him by God he nominated bishops, heaped abbacies on one individual, punished offences by the clergy against discipline, sat in judgment on the Pope, systematically promoted the education of the clergy, even bestowed Church property in fief, while he also instituted an inventory of ecclesiastical possessions and strictly insisted on the payment of Church tithes. We must omit here all reference to many other of his administrative measures, important as they were. The outstandingly important fact is that during this whole period the Church allowed itself to be governed by the great Frankish kings and to be, in many aspects of its life, completely Germanized. It is a remarkable picture! For during the same

period the barbarian ancestors of the German people were diligently trying to master the dead book-lore of an expiring antiquity and putting in order the relics of a civilization that had passed away. Take, for example, the works of Alcuin, who was a kind of Minister of Education in the Cabinet of Charles the Great. With an entire lack of creative power, though with a certain gift of arrangement, he reproduced and gathered together what tradition had handed down. The really new books were manuals of instruction. Just as from the seventh to the tenth century there was no one capable of producing anything new in the realm of art, and as the scholars of the time could do no more than rearrange past knowledge, so in the sphere of theology they could only repeat, collect, and arrange what others had done. The theological writings of the time were anthologies and collections of excerpts from the expiring Patristic literature. There were certain efforts at systematization, some examples of logical treatment of isolated theological questions, but even these were largely borrowed from translations of Boethius, Porphyry, and Augustine. These efforts are the only productions that enable us to speak of a certain rationalism during this period. Augustine was the authoritative name, but Augustine's work was watered down in the weakened versions of the great regular Pope and orthodox theologian, Gregory I.

Otto the Great sought to counter the insurbordinate dukes by basing the organization of his empire on the bishops, and he deliberately encouraged their assumption of feudal lordship. The bishops were at once his feudal vassals and his State officials, the pillars on which his royal power rested. We are reminded here of Charles the Great, who had done something of this kind, but between his aims and those of Otto there was a profound difference. The great purposes which Charles had had in view were not shared by his descendant. Otto had no desire to use his capitularies to influence the inner life of the Church or to promote the education of his clergy or of his people. He was content to hold in his hand the executive powers of the Church. Nor was that all. The German Church, though it was now a national Church, was still the Catholic Church, and this implied a certain tension. The bishops were officials of the king, and at the same time servants of the Church and of the Pope. As soon as the Papacy should awaken this tension was bound to lead to a breach. That time was still far distant, however, and the manner in which in the eleventh century Henry II appointed Popes and deposed them proves the sovereignty and the assurance felt by the German kings in respect of the Pope, just as it also shows the false estimate they entertained of the moral power and of the conception of the Papal office. The life of the Church of this period is best seen in its missionary work. With the support — given for political reasons — of the German kings, the Church carried her message as far north as Hamburg, as far east as Magdeburg and later Gnesen, and south-east as far as Passau.

But even already, at first intermittently and then with ever-increasing frequency and loudness, could be heard the sound of the approaching storm.

It was heralded by two early forgeries, which were not unmasked as such till the time of the Renaissance and the Reformation. These were the Donatio Constantini, according to which Constantine the Great, out of gratitude for his recovery from leprosy, handed over the lordship of the West to Pope Sylvester, and the Isidorian Decretals, which were put forth as ancient tradition establishing the Roman system, the sovereignty of the bishop and the Pope, as against the idea of a national Church, the sovereignty of the king and the Metropolitan. In addition there was a movement on the part of the monks for reform. It began at Cluny, Brogne, and Gorze, and soon spread through the whole Church, including Italy and England. It was reaction of the ascetic ideal against the secular features that had crept into monasticism, owing, perhaps, to the employment of the monks in cultural tasks. Still further, although many of the German kings were in close touch with the brethren of Cluny, there arose a call for a reform of the clergy and of the Church itself, and ere long could be heard the watchwords of the parties — obedience to the canon law in the Church, insistence on celibacy, and opposition to simony. It is important to notice that the meaning of simony had changed. It had originally meant obtaining a spiritual office by the payment of money. Then it came to mean the exploitation of spiritual functions for gain, and finally the meaning was widened to include the bestowal of a clerical office by the secular power or the symbolical performance of such an action. To put it in the shortest form, investiture was now called simony.

Then came the struggle between Gregory VII — the name takes us back to Gregory I — and Henry IV. But it was not confined to Germany. Gregory VII, that fanatical champion of righteousness, refused to be satisfied with anything less than the restitution of the ancient right. He maintained that the Apostle Peter, who had, properly speaking, been Pope, speaks and acts in each of his successors. The Pope is *the* bishop; the other bishops are only his agents. But the Pope is also lord of the world, because this world belongs to Christ and the Pope is His representative, and because all earthly dominion is held in fief from God. Therefore the Pope can even deprive a monarch of his dignity should that step become necessary for the cause of God and of the Church. Papacy and royalty stand related to each other as the sun and the moon. In themselves these ideas were not new, but the man who now voiced them with daring idealism and in the spirit of ascetic piety had the courage and determination to translate them into action. Gregory VII, for whom Leo IX had in some degree prepared the way, tried to carry through this resolution in the Church with one bold stroke at the Lenten synod of 1075. The celibacy of the priests was to be immediately enforced. The people were called to rise up against married priests. Investiture at the hands of laymen was also forbidden. Feudal obligation was suspended, and the bond between Church and State was severed where canon law was not obeyed. This shook the Empire to its foundations. The struggle brought about the excommunication and deposition of King Henry IV, civil war in

Germany, and the walk to Canossa, but it ended in the personal defeat of the Pope, who clung to his principles with iron determination. Nevertheless, the pontificate of Gregory VII was the turning-point in the history of the Papacy, and the claims which he maintained to the end with a power that was reinforced by his manifest conscientiousness have never been surrendered. We must not forget that religious idealism underlay these claims. They were not dictated by a priestly thirst for power. How deeply the Popes were moved is best seen in the bold though impracticable proposal put forward by Paschal II, a successor of Gregory VII. He offered to surrender the possessions of the Church if the king would consent to cede the Papal claim to the investiture. The Church was willing to become poor in order to purchase her liberty. In the Concordat of Worms, which was made possible by the change of opinion that had taken place with regard to the legal position, a temporary compromise was reached. Though it was agreed that both king and Pope were to abandon their ambitions for the time, this Concordat paved the way for the absolute lordship of the Pope in the Church, and the independent Church of Gregory VII underwent, when years had passed, the ordeal of fire in the great struggle between Pope Alexander III and Frederick I (Barbarossa). Although the secular dominion of the Pope was not mentioned in the treaty of peace at Venice in 1177, and although the influence of the emperor was still paramount in the Church in Germany, still the emperor was compelled against his sworn oath to recognize both actually and symbolically the hated Pope, and the measures for the administration of Upper Italy suggested in the resolution of Roncaglia fell through.

The line of theological Popes of the type of Gregory VII was succeeded by a line of juristic Popes, the first of whom was Innocent III. Innocent held the same ideas of the nature of the Papacy and the position of the Pope as had been championed by Gregory VII, but he gave the central place to the claim to secular dominion. He claimed that the Pope was lord over all Christendom and that kings, while they occupied a sovereign position in relation to their own people, should submit their disputes to the arbitration of the Pope. The relation of kings to the Pope was that of fiefs — that is to say, the Pope had the right to invest even the German king with the *imperium*. The Pope, whose prototype was Melchizedek, stands between God and man — less than God, but more than man. He is the " spiritual man," who judges all, and is judged by none. He is also the absolute head of the Church. The aim of Innocent here was to abolish the election of bishops and to substitute their nomination. This would give the Pope an enormous influence in the affairs of the Empire, seeing that the bishops were now territorial grandees. As a matter of fact, Innocent succeeded in welding the greater part of Christendom — though only for the duration of his own pontificate — into a loosely constructed world empire. It is here that he is open to criticism. While he secured the secular power of the Pope by the only method possible — *i.e.*, by the use of political means — he also dragged the Church into the maelstrom of secular affairs and set her on a path which could not fail to bring her into serious difficulties when critical times should arrive.

It was Frederick II who resisted Innocent's attempt to place the Papacy on this lofty pedestal. He had ascended the throne as the ' Pope's man.' There were discordant elements in the personality of this emperor, which can be understood only when we remember his half-Arabian, half-Sicilian origin. That also helps to explain his vivid sense of his Imperial dignity, his belief that monarchical rule was a divine natural necessity, that Imperial power was an expression of the divine will and of human appointment, and that his own doings were divinely ordained. According to this faith, the emperor was divine; his power was immediately derived from God; he was the Messiah and the vicegerent of God. To rebel against the emperor was to rebel against God. That Frederick could entertain these views proves that, with all his versatility, his frankness, and his many gifts, he had not outgrown the mentality of the Middle Ages. In incalculable and passionate natures like his, scepticism, doubt, and scorn are frequently combined with acceptance of current opinion.

The struggle ended with the downfall of the Hohenstaufen dynasty and of the German Imperial dignity. It became more and more clearly a political contest for Italy, and Innocent IV pursued it with a brutal zeal that lacked the excuse of an ardent religious faith. There is no doubt that the Church was disorganized and demoralized by his ruthless use of her energies and her sanctions in a political controversy with the excommunicated emperor. Papal despotism had destroyed all law. The Papacy came near to losing its dignity, and the idea of the *civitas dei* had become a matter of secular politics.

Up to this point the Papacy, which in the struggle with the Hohenstaufen had made the momentous swing round toward France, and had itself received dire hurt in the Sicilian Vespers, was still at the zenith of its power. Proof of this is found in the Council of Lyons and the attitude taken by Rudolf von Habsburg. But the policy of Rudolf, whose chief interest lay in the national kingship and not in the supra-national Imperial dignity, and was centred in Germany and Austria and not in Italy, shows as clearly (though in a more veiled manner) as the course of events in England and France that the rising of the national states portended and brought about the limitation of politics to secular affairs.

Boniface VIII, the first of the Renaissance Popes, defined once more, in the words of the greatest and universally recognized theologians, the claims of the Papacy, and declared that faith in his absolute power was essential to salvation. Later, however, after he had applied to practical politics the ancient methods of the Curia and after he had treated the German king as a vassal, he fell a victim to the brutal violence of Philip the Fair, and it is symbolical of much else that this Pope, who asserted more crudely than any other the Papal claims to sovereign power, did not live in the doctrines of the Church; he devoted much interest to spiritualism and natural philosophy, and spent much time on matter which had no connexion either with his profession or even with religion.

It took the Papacy many years to recover from the blow it received during the pontificate of Boniface VIII. Then came the period of the exile in Avignon; the period of laborious consolidation in the midst of the conflict with the Conciliarist theories; and at last the disruption of the unity of Church and world that had marked the Middle Ages. The old arguments based on natural rights that had been used to support the claims of the Church were now turned against the Papacy. Then followed the Renaissance, the building up of the Church State in Italy, and the momentous struggle known as the Reformation. It was not till the Counter-Reformation, in which Catholicism assimilated the predominant spiritual and intellectual forces of the time, mysticism and humanism, that the Papacy was again able to raise its head. The eighteenth century, which might perhaps be called a period of decline, saw the victory of the Curia over the national Church represented by Gallicanism, and then after the romantic restoration the nineteenth century brought security to the Papal power within the Church through the dogma of Infallibility, the perfecting of the Church administration, the codification of the canon law, and the far-seeing attempt to impress on the world the universal moral authority of the Pope in a world rent by economic and political disputes and characterized by the mechanization and consequent impoverishment of life.

4. So far we have been dealing with the first period of the intellectual and religious history of the Middle Ages: the young nations, conforming in life and religion to the Church and to Christianity, absorbed like youthful pupils the spirit that breathed in Christian theology, which was for them authoritative. Even what we might call the personality of the time was profoundly affected by the authority of the model men sought to follow, so that it is difficult to find in this period or for many years later an individuality representative of the Middle Ages. The only exceptions were men like the monk Gottschalk, who revived out of his own deep experience Augustine's doctrine of predestination, or Scotus Erigena, who drew up a speculative system whose contents were reminiscent of Neo-Platonism and whose style recalled that of the Areopagites or of Maximus.

But already in the tenth and eleventh centuries we come upon a few men — for example, Odo of Cluny, Ratherius of Verona, Othloh of St Emmeran, and Gerbert of Reims — in whom was beginning to awaken that intellectual and spiritual self-confidence which not only ushered in a new spirit of piety, but gave new life to learning. We mean Subjectivism. It was at the end of the eleventh century that this new individualistic feeling of life appeared. It was the cradle of Scholasticism, and produced the three great attempts to make Christian truth a personal possession. These were, first, the attempt of Anselm, who sought to set forth as a living whole a comprehensive speculative system of Christian doctrine; second, that of Abelard, who sought to prove by a series of propositions the reasonableness of dogma; and, third, the experimental theology of Bernard of Clairvaux, which in its mystical representation of Jesus sought to transform dogma into personal experience. All these attempts have much in common, bitter as were the controversies that raged between their authors. Experience, logical thought, speculation, were merely three different paths to the same goal. They started from the same point and aimed at reaching the same result — the individual, personal possession of truth.

The *religious life of the twelfth century* presents three outstanding features. First, there was a resolute clinging to the Church, with its institutions, forms, and doctrines. That is to say, religious life was centred in the Church. The ancient Church creeds contained the truths essential for eternal life. The priest, performing the sacrifice of the Mass, giving absolution, and surrounding daily life with innumerable benedictions, was the mediator between God and man. But the ultimate basis of this Church piety — and this is the second feature — did not lie in Christian convictions, but in the vitality of the primitive pagan conceptions, which regarded 'holiness' as inherent in things, not in persons. This pagan piety united with Catholic Christian piety, which from its inception had combined with the Oriental nature religions and had adopted their myths and rites. This deep-seated mood furthered the adoration of saints and relics, which was so prominent in this period. Not only were the people continually creating new saints of their own, but, encouraged by the leaders of the reform movement, a ceaseless stream of holy relics was pouring from Italy into the North and the West, and, after the marriage of Otto II to the Greek Princess Theophano, Germany became acquainted with the cults of St Nicholas and St George. The third feature of the religious life of this period was the ascetic strain that pervaded it. Men had delight, no doubt, in the works of God's hand, and rejoiced in the beauty of nature, but stronger far was the conviction that the world, with all its beauty, was the battlefield where divine and diabolic powers were contending for man's soul. The opinion still prevailed that those who had entered the wedded state could only bring forth fruit thirtyfold, while widows were reckoned as among those who brought forth sixtyfold; and those who lived the virgin life were those who brought forth a hundredfold. Belief in devils, superstition, and witchcraft were widespread. Yet it was this ascetic strain in the religious life of the time that kept moral earnestness alive and prepared the way for the conception of the peace of God in an age when brute force was rampant and acts of violence abounded.

But there was still another feature that was very prominent in the religious life of the twelfth century, distinguishing it from that of the Carolingian period. We mean the awakening of Individualism and Subjectivism, the longing for personal certainty, for reflection and experience. 'Authority' now found a rival in 'experience.' And it can hardly be doubted that it was the natural disposition of the new nations, their own peculiar intellectual and emotional nature, that now broke through and gave the Christian religion the form it now assumed. Two ideas, which now emerged and soon dominated religious life, seem to me to illustrate best the change that was taking place. These were experience and conversion. No doubt, men felt, there is an obedient faith that comes before experience and is the beginning of the religious life, but then the contents of faith must be turned into experience if we are to transcend mere faith and attain to inward certainty and personal knowledge. Old monastic tradition and Augustinian thoughts are intermingled in this complex of ideas and feelings, which brought about a psychological sifting and deepening of the ' authority '

FIG. 122
BERNARD OF CLAIRVAUX
Detail from a painting by
Fra Angelico.

that had hitherto been obediently accepted. And this new Intellectualism and Rationalism were accompanied by a new Augustinian Voluntarism, which portended not merely a new psychology, but also a new comprehension of the world and of life.

There are various ways in which one might try to illustrate this new view of the religious life. We might point to the heretics of the time, to the new monastic order that now arose, or to the Crusades, and to the growth of the conception of repentance. But the best illustration is found in the man who dominated the intellectual and spiritual life of his time — Bernard of Clairvaux (Fig. 122). It is usual to emphasize his political influence; and it is a remarkable fact that this ascetic man, who revelled in the raptures of Mysticism, must be ranked among the world's greatest politicians, whose sure instinct and profound knowledge of human nature enabled them to shape affairs according to their will.

Bernard has been called the typical ecclesiastical politician, and the nature of his political activity is explained by his ascetic ideal. At heart he was really at one with the men whom he most passionately opposed. Like Arnold of Brescia, he preached the ideal of poverty; like Abelard, he longed for ' experience ' instead of ' authority.' But his belief in the Church led him to reject Arnold's spiritualism, and the voluntaristic-mystical view of religion which he had learned from Augustine made him oppose Abelard's Intellectualism, because it seemed to him to endanger the positivity of the divine revelation. In the centre of his faith stood not the heavenly Logos, but the man Jesus, in Whose humility and love he saw the sovereign power of God. Therefore it behoved men to follow the path of the lowly Jesus, that they might rise by self-surrender and service to the ecstatic experience of God and be kissed " with the kisses of his mouth." [24] And with Bernard this supremest of all forms of bliss was not a melting into the ' One,' but the union of two wills, in which the weaker will, overwhelmed and yet strengthened by the stronger, becomes capable of new service and new life. This voluntarist mysticism of Bernard runs side by side all through the Middle Ages with the Neo-Platonic doctrine of mystical union, which is found as early as the twelfth century, in Hugo of St Victor, though weakened by his insistence on the saving efficacy of the *life* of Jesus. And the interpretation which explains the ' bride ' in the Song of Songs not only as the individual soul, but also as the Church, which imparts to the individual her graces and gifts, was accepted all through the Middle Ages.

This Individualism determined the *theology of the twelfth century*. Apart from it the epistemological conviction of the similarity of nature between the finite and the divine spirit which was the basis of Scholastic thinking would be inconceivable. It is a magnificently *naïve* Idealism that reminds us of Hegel when it declares that the secret things of God are reasonable in a higher sense and can be understood by a reason that has been enlightened by God. But the contrast that runs through the theology of the twelfth century is not the contrast between Nominalism and Realism, but between dialectics and anti-dialectics; or, to put it differently, between a theology of experience and a theology of reason. That is the core of the contrast between Anselm and Bernard on the one hand, and between Abelard and Gilbert on the other, though there were mediating tendencies in Abelard's dialectical method of presenting his views.

The most telling theological attempt in this period was Anselm's brief monograph entitled *Cur deus homo?* It is written in the spirit of Augustine, and deals with the possibility of the forgiveness of sin and the efficacy of grace *sola ratione*. Its central thought is the atonement which was effected through the satisfaction offered by the God-man. Being voluntarily rendered, this satisfaction is ethical in its nature. But the two most prominent thoughts in the book are, first, the *civitas dei,* in which God's will is the sole law. The members of this divine state were the angels and — after their apostasy — mankind. The salvation of men was also decreed from all eternity, because God foreknew that men would fall. To bring about this eternal purpose, *that* is God's will, and His honour and majesty not only ensure its fulfilment, but determine the means whereby it is to be fulfilled. The second characteristic thought is that God's honour demands that righteousness should prevail throughout the cosmos. Even God Himself can do nothing that would contradict His righteousness, and rebellion on the part of the creature against the Creator calls for punishment or satisfaction. That is the argument. Then follows a detailed description of the nature of the satisfaction referred to.

[24] Song of Songs, i, 2.

5. It is still customary to speak of *High Scholasticism* — *i.e.,* systematic theology — since the thirteenth century as a unified system of thought dealing with theological themes on metaphysical lines. That to a certain extent it is so we cannot but admit when we recall the metaphysical bent of mind of Christian Scholastics and their view of truth — truth is a reality which exists; it is 'found,' not 'made' — or the Scholastic method, which, though first employed by the jurists, was now applied in setting out the arguments for and against an opinion, so that the separate problems were now discussed with a logical thoroughness that was unprecedented. But the diligent study of Scholasticism that has been carried on during the last twenty years has materially altered this opinion. It has disclosed behind an apparent unity an extremely attractive variety, and even an actual contrariety between the leading thinkers. The most marked feature in the intellectual history of the thirteenth century is the gradual mastering of the entire work of Aristotle and the introduction of the writings of Jewish and Arabian philosophers who were steeped in Aristotelian thought and in Neo-Platonism. In Spain and in Lower Italy, where the European and Arabian worlds came into contact, Aristotle, indirectly and with a Neo-Platonic colouring, became familiar in the translations of his Arabian commentators and through the efforts of Jewish philosophers. At the very beginning of the thirteenth century appeared direct translations from Greek into Latin, the most important being those of Robert Grosseteste, Bishop of Lincoln, and of the philologist William of Moerbeke, the friend and adviser of Thomas Aquinas. Moerbeke afterward also undertook the translation of Proclus. Compared with Albertus Magnus, whose work was far less systematic, it is Thomas Aquinas who seems to be the great innovator, for he recast theology and philosophy in the spirit of Aristotle, without, however, completely eliminating Neo-Platonism. It is a remarkable spectacle, this repeated Hellenization of Christianity, which, however, in virtue of its inherent Oriental elements, only deepened the unity of the Christian religion.

When we inquire how this introduction of Aristotle affected Scholasticism, we must take account of various things. In the first place, it meant a great increase of knowledge and of the material of knowledge. It also meant the introduction of the terms form and matter, actuality and potentiality, into metaphysics, psychology, and epistemology. And, thirdly, Aristotle's ethics (including his social ethics) deeply influenced the view of life that was commonly held in the Middle Ages. All this enables us to make a provisional classification of the currents present in High Scholasticism. For example, over against each other, with their representatives in the two great mendicant orders, we have Augustinianism and Aristotelianism, although both schools were at one and the same time Augustinians and Aristotelians, differing only in degree. The Aristotelians are subdivided into those who have a Greek and those who have a Neo-Platonic colouring. Lastly, there is the Neo-Platonic school, which was in touch with the school of Chartres, with the Neo-Platonic metaphysics of the Arabs, and with the theology of the pseudo Dionysius the Areopagite. This Neo-Platonic school gladly turned from its cosmological studies and took up the natural sciences, and its adherents in England showed distinct leanings toward empirical realism.

Augustinianism is represented by the great Franciscans *Alexander of Hales* and *Bonaventura*. Alexander's thinking, it is true, follows the rules of Aristotle — *e.g.,* his doctrine of grace is set forth in true Aristotelian form — but in him and in Bonaventura, as in the Franciscan school generally, there is a strong emphasis on the reality of ideas and on the practical character of religious knowledge. In them also we meet with Augustine's mystical and metaphysical epistemology, which is founded on the abrupt dualism of body and soul, emphasizes the spontaneity of the spiritual, and ultimately derives all truth — ideas — from God. Lastly, in this system we also meet a voluntarist psychology, which of course involves the accentuation of the merit of good works and of human freedom, as well as a tendency to a symbolical interpretation of the sacraments which was also learned from Augustine. As a correlate of the Mysticism of the Franciscan theology we find from Bonaventura onward a pronounced ecclesiastical Positivism.

Averroes, whose influence is specially apparent in *Siger of Brabant,* denies that the world was created. The world is an eternal process of becoming, without beginning or end, and governed by an iron causality that excludes both miracle and Providence. Every happening is merely a transition from potentiality to actuality and back again from actuality to potentiality. Averroes also teaches the unity of the *intellectus agens* — *i.e.,* the *anima intellectiva* is not a power of the human soul; that *anima* exists apart from all corporeality and is only temporarily associated by its activity with the human soul. It is thus one and the same entity in all men, apparent differences being due merely to the different dispositions of individuals. The results of this doctrine for immortality and the process of knowing are at once apparent. With regard to the doctrine of God in Averroism, God is the thinking entity, and Providence is denied. Taught explicitly by Avicenna and implicitly by Averroes is the theory of twofold truth, according to which what is philosophically untenable may be theologically true.

The most brilliant exponent of Aristotelianism was Thomas Aquinas (Fig. 123). He taught an epistemology (or theory of knowledge) according to which knowledge means the graphic understanding of a given reality which does not transcend experience. This theory thus emphasizes the passivity, not the spontaneity, of the knowing soul. The psychology is monistic rather than dualistic — *i.e.,* the soul is the form of the body. There are — controverting Averroes — as many souls or "forms of substance" as there are human bodies; and — as against the Franciscans — there is only one "spirit-soul," because the "form of substance" is single. The ontology (or doctrine of existence) employs the Aristotelian terms form and matter, potentiality and actuality, efficient cause and final cause, and it includes all existence between two poles — between pure potentiality (*materia prima*) and pure actuality (God) — and explains reality as a system of forms or entelechies which are individualized as separate entities by quantitative matter. Aquinas differentiated between theology and philosophy, and yet he combined them in one system. By our reason we know God as the First Cause by seeing its effects. All our other knowledge of Him is derived from the revelation contained in the inspired Scriptures and confirmed by the Church.

FIG. 123. THOMAS AQUINAS
Fresco by Fra Angelico in the Dominican Monastery of San Marco in Florence.

Owing to its supernatural quality, revealed truth cannot be grasped by our reason — it must be believed. Although faith is ultimately a function of the intellect, it can lay hold of what transcends the intellect, because by a creative act, by the inpouring of a *habitus,* God enables the weak human intellect to grasp the transcendent. Thus revelation and its comprehension form the second story of the structure which is built on the foundation of our natural knowledge. Revelation is not contrary to reason; it is only above it. *Gratia naturam non tollit sed perficit.* Thus a unified view of the world is attained. Theoretic knowledge, which is both faith and knowledge, is, as it were, the common denominator which enables us to add together faith and knowledge. It need hardly be said that this exposition of principles is supported on grounds that are purely intellectualistic. The will, which, like the rationalists, Thomas sees in free choice, occupies a subordinate position, and in an entirely Greek manner he conceives blessedness as the gradual satisfaction of the intellectual powers of the soul.

The *Platonism* of the Middle Ages, of which William of Moerbeke was an ardent supporter, has one line of connexion with the Arabians, with the *liber de causis,* and with the school of Chartres; its second line begins with Albertus Magnus and leads through Ulrich of Strasburg and Dietrich of Freiberg to 'German' Mysticism, to Master Eckart and Tauler. In Aquinas, and to a still greater degree in Bonaventura, there are pronounced elements of Neo-Platonism. The third strand is represented by Robert Grosseteste and Roger Bacon. Its interest lay in natural philosophy and " experimental science," and it anticipated many of the tendencies of the science of the seventeenth century. Among the features of this Platonism of the Middle Ages were the Neo-Platonic theory of emanation in connexion with creation; the metaphysic of light, whose history has been given by Bäumker from the standpoint of Witelo of Silesia; and its psychology, which maintains the unity and singleness of the *intellectus agens,* identifying it with the Logos or combining it with what it calls the " ground of souls " (*Seelengrund*).

The *theology of High Scholasticism* is gathered round its doctrine of God. The various elements of its thought and of its religion produced differences which led ultimately to the disruption of the theology of the Middle Ages. Side by side with the Biblical view of God as the Will that controls all things appears also the philosophical view, which sees in Him the Absolute Substance and the supreme First Cause. This philosophical view of God gradually prevailed over the other. No doubt in Aquinas the religious sense of the universality involved in the divine causality that controls all things is profoundly impressive, but omnipotence is again and again crowded out by his intellectualism — for example, in the relation between Providence and predestination. And although it would be unfair to say that Aquinas' doctrine of God represents God as idle — for God is *actus purus* — still this *actus purus* is ultimately God thinking of Himself. " God's existence is His thinking." The same is true of the doctrine of the divine attributes. These attributes are not so much the result of reflection on the attitude of God in the moral and religious process as the outcome of logical consideration of metaphysical questions. And logically consistent though this view may be in the system itself, still the variance is unmistakable when the attributes of God, Who is " the quite Other," " the entirely different," are, after the analogy of human psychology, disclosed by a theoretical extension of what is non-divine. The ontology of Aquinas, the metaphysic of existence, which reflects the impression of the universality of God, crushes all vitality out of His omnipotence. And there is still another difficulty. Into the view of God as the All-Existent there still comes, deflected by the Western idea of reward, the ancient Christian idea of God as the Law-giver, whose favour can be won by service in the moral order which He has ordained. In every type of nature religion there is an instinctive desire to move by some means or other the divine being who is the object of worship, and Scholasticism, while it puts in the forefront the absolute power and absolute existence of God — Aquinas is quite emphatic on this point — yet works into its system the other view of God as a law-giver who can be won over. This was done under the influence of the conception of merit and reward, and was reinforced by the rise of Individualism in religion and by the increased sense of the inwardness of morality. It caused, however, a breach both in the doctrine of God and in religion, and this juxtaposition of reverence in the presence of Him Who comprises all things and graciously discloses Himself in the sacrament and the righteousness by works that seeks for merit and reward is a characteristic feature of the religion of the Middle Ages.

The metaphysic of the Scholastics also determines their treatment of the doctrine of grace. They seem to regard grace as a material thing and to objectify it, but we cannot follow out their views in detail here. Suffice it to say that the metaphysics of the Scholastics allows only a subordinate place to forgiveness and to the word of God, which merely moves the heart; and it leads to the view that the soul is renewed by a divine creative act which becomes operative only in the Church, and by which love, like a supernatural quality, is inpoured into the soul. In place of the Gospel comes the sacramental grace, in which the work of Christ is effective. Of course, in keeping with their metaphysics, which loosens the strict causal nexus and allows some room for the free play of the human will, the Franciscans laid great stress on the psychological conditions under which grace works. Their teaching, although it is hedged about by many qualifications, is ultimately the co-operation of man with God, and although human merit is recognized only as the reason for the divine approval and is obtainable only by the power of 'preventing' grace, the Franciscans claim merit for the man who assents to "the World" and experiences penitence and fear. It is therefore just this emphasis on human merit that conserves the spirituality of the religion. To be sure, the chief end of the Franciscans also was not so much to bring about fellowship between God and man as to achieve man's moral transformation. This is clear both in their material interpretation of the forgiveness of sins and in their conjoining of grace with the sacraments. A similar peculiarity in their metaphysical view of God's working is shown in their conception of sacrament and of miracle. The sole efficacy of God is strongly asserted by Aquinas in his doctrine of regeneration. This is due to his determinist metaphysics, which leaves no room for any independent action of the so-called secondary cause alongside that of the First Cause which is at work in all things. There is no place here for merit in the natural man: God does all, both the willing and the doing. There is freedom only in so far as willing is by its very nature always free, but the willing is brought about by grace. It must therefore be admitted that Aquinas taught the omnipotence of grace in the clearest possible manner. But there is equal unambiguity about his sacramentarianism and the objectifying of grace. Indeed, he de-psychologized the conferment of grace by having recourse to the metaphysic of *habitus,* and he adopted the interpolation which Augustine made as a concession to popular Catholic opinion — viz., that what is thus created in man by grace merits the blessed vision.

Two things strike us at the outset in the *ethics* of Aquinas. The first is the close connexion (which is also found in Augustine) between morality and happiness. Just as evil arises from the desire for earthly things, so good springs from delight in the Eternal — *i.e., God.* It is this relation to the ultimate end that gives moral action its value. Only that is morally good which is motived by that love to God which comes by grace. And, second, there are grades of morality. A distinction is drawn between the active and the contemplative life, between commandments and counsels, between prohibitions which are eternally valid and commandments whose validity is not permanent. This elastic morality has of course the advantage that it suits actual life and does not make equal demands on every one. But it purchases this advantage at the cost of strict morality, and as a matter of fact the unqualified character of the moral demand is lost.

A similar classification into grades appears in the social ethics of Aquinas. Here he seems to set up a system intermediate between natural reality and the Christian ideal, and he employs the classification into grades as the basis of his theory of an architectonic organism in the world, side by side with the radical contrasts of Christian ethic. Like natural morality, the natural social world is the preliminary stage for grace and the kingdom of grace. They are connected, because both proceed from God and because the natural order evolves into the supernatural order in accordance with the will of God. The unfolding of the law of nature and the growth of reason are the preparatory stages on which the superstructure of grace can be built. The phenomena of human social life as such are therefore not the outcome of sin; they would exist even if there were no sin, but in that case they would work without friction, because there would be no selfishness, no sensuousness, no lust for power. The most important feature in this sociology, which regards the world as an organism and combines natural and Christian elements, is its introduction of the conception of natural right, that elastic and inconstant factor which still to-day lends to Catholic social philosophy and its attendant Catholic policy elasticity and adaptability. Of course, after the manner of his time Aquinas understood natural right in the patriarchal sense.

This great structure, with its combination of the natural and the supernatural in one uniform system, had been a creation of theology and the Church. It broke down both in the sphere of theology and philosophy and in that of Church and State. That marked the close of the Middle Ages.

The *last days of Scholasticism* were similarly dominated by the conviction of the incompatibility of faith and knowledge. This, however, did not lead to scepticism, but to ecclesiastical and Biblical *Positivism*. Reason cannot demonstrate the truth of the teaching of the Church. On the contrary, logical criticism proves that that teaching is irrational or against reason. That, however, does not affect revealed truth. It is guaranteed by the Bible and the Church. God, Who in His absolute power could have made everything quite different, has given us the Bible and the teaching of the Church, and faith must obediently accept the supernatural truths contained in them. Occam, a prominent representative of this nominalism, maintains that the task of theology is not to attain to a speculative knowledge of God, but to give a coherent, logical account of the accepted Church teaching. It follows that science has nothing to do with concrete things, but with the ideas and propositions which are symbolical copies of reality.

These principles also affect Occam's theology. His doctrine of God does not start from the first cause, but from the conception of the end, and is subjective and analytical. God, therefore, is ultimately unknown and unknowable. We have no terms that are adequate to define Him, and what we call His attributes are only reflections of our changing consciousness of Him. We cannot go further here into the intellectualism, eudemonism, and subjectivism of Occam's doctrine of God or into its historical connexions. And with regard to his doctrine of grace it must suffice to say that, while in itself it should regard grace in a purely spiritual sense as forgiveness and the gracious judgment of God, as a matter of fact it regards grace as being inpoured in the sacraments, and emphasizes the free, meritorious character of human action.

Occam's was the last of the great scholastic systems. Those who came after him were merely *epigoni*. They explained and interpreted the great works of the past. They debated the purely scholastic question of the real existence of universals. But their work had no life in it. It was mere dry-as-dust erudition, utterly unconnected with the springs of spiritual life.

6. The Mysticism of the best period of the Middle Ages was not merely an offshoot of the Neo-Platonism of the theology of the period. It was also an expression of a new sense of life that reached its fullness in the Renaissance. Individualism became so strong that the ego in its profoundest depths felt itself to be the dwelling-place of God and the vehicle of divine fate, and even the Church was at times relegated to a subordinate place. From this point of view the Middle Ages was the Christian continuation of " Teutonic piety," although it now voiced itself in the terminology of Neo-Platonism. Numerous as were the ' heretics ' among these mystical seekers after a speculative pantheism, many of the great nuns and *béguines* of the thirteenth century were loyal members of the Church, and in the Neo-Platonic hymns that sing of the One in the Many and of the innate union of the soul with God we hear echoes of the strains that called men to imita-

tion of the lowly life of Jesus and summoned them to the personal experience of fellowship with God that comes through Christ.

The Mysticism of the Middle Ages reached its zenith in the German mystics, although, as has been frequently hinted, the epithet 'German' constitutes a knotty problem. Its ancestry really goes back through Albertus Magnus and his followers to Arabianized Neo-Platonism. Though much of Master Eckart's psychology and epistemology is borrowed from Aquinas, his breach with the accepted teaching of the Church is unmistakable. Not only is the conception of a Creation given up through his identification of existence with God and the consequent replacement of causality by the divine immanence; even Christ, the Church, good works, and sin itself — these are at best nothing more than incitements, and they all disappear in the great quietude and solitude, in the imageless and workless emptiness, in which the soul finally realizes its unity with God and is 'remade' and transformed in Him: then the 'Son' is born in the soul. That is the soul's task, to get away from the world and from itself, in order to become God. Good works, even final blessedness, play no part here. Only he does good who is good, and only he is good who has become God. Eckart is just as little successful as Plotinus in deriving the multiplicity of creatures from the Absolute One who is conceived as an eternal process. Even suffering and evil, which, according to Eckart's metaphysics, are non-existent and become bliss in God, he still construes as self-will in the traditional Christian manner, and his theology has adopted the German position in its theory of evil.

Like Eckart, Tauler conceives the union between God and man as a union of substance, but he lays greater stress on practical considerations. It is not in works of asceticism, but in suffering that man finds God and the calm that overcomes the world, and the ego meets its ordeal of fire when a man joyfully endures even the pains of hell if he knows that this is the will of God. All that is done with an eye to reward is evil; only he acts aright in whom God acts. But man finds help and encouragement in the pattern set by Christ (which is not merely a moral help, but produces conformity to His image, death, and resurrection), and in gratitude, which urges him to desire even in the most modest of callings to return to God what he has received. Here the similarity to the standpoint of Luther cannot be missed. To be sure, the great cleavage which runs through all forms of Mysticism has not been bridged — the cleavage between the self which must be mortified and slain and the soul which is still the dwelling-place of God.

While this Neo-Platonic " Mysticism of Infinity " already shows traces of the relation to Christ insisted upon by Augustine and Bernard, still, there is another, later type of Mysticism, which conceives union with God not as an absorption into the One, but as a union of two wills. This finds its most beautiful expression in Jan van Ruysbroeck and in the *devotio moderna,* of which the finest specimen is the well-known devotional book *The Imitation of Christ.* Here religious feeling is not concentrated round the great contrast between the soul and God, the outer and the inner, flesh and spirit; the religious life is regarded as the moral fight in which the eyes of the combatant are fixed upon the Lord and Master. The scholastic doctrine of grace and sacramentarianism are retained, but the religious soul stands alone; and far more important than the Christ Who is present in the sacrament is

FIG. 124. FRANCIS OF ASSISI
Detail from the fresco by Cimabue in the Lower Church of Assisi.

the living Christ in the soul, with whom communion can be enjoyed at any moment.

The imitation of Christ—*that* was the ideal of Francis of Assisi (Fig. 124). Francis held up to the luxurious life of his time the ideal of the poor and lowly Jesus Who was obedient unto death. The aim of Francis was not the mystical shaping of life by Christ, nor was it pious contemplation, but the transformation of human life into the life of Jesus. Quite in the spirit of the Middle Ages, his ideal was at once the simplest and the most difficult of all tasks—viz., to imitate literally and actually the life of Jesus, and thus to set forth in actual life union with Him. This is no doubt the meaning of his long-concealed secret, that he bore on his body the stigmata of Jesus. His piety — the feeling that all he had was from God, and his readiness to surrender all — was no doubt influenced by his inborn Latin disposition, and it is this latter that explains the exuberant joy that marked his life, the immediacy of his emotions, his impulsive frankness, his chivalrous nature, and the greatness that was stamped on his every action. It also explains his keen feeling for nature, his peculiar habit of ascribing life to all the things which the average man regards as inanimate, so that nature became for him the garden of God. He could preach to the birds and lift out of danger the worms he found on his path. He was at once saint and poet.

The *early activities of the Franciscans* were not essentially different from those of the Waldensians. The *joculatores dei* aimed at resuscitating the itinerant preaching of the early Apostles, and sought to live in humility, poverty, mendicancy, and obedience. But it was not Ignatius Loyola, but Francis of Assisi who invented the phrase " the obedience of the corpse." Following a different policy from that which they had followed toward the Waldensians, the authorities in the Church approved the movement and gradually formed it into a strict order under the special protection of the Papacy. By doing so they imperceptibly altered the purpose of the founder, whose interest was all centred in the realization of his ideal and who cared nothing for organization. But in the history of the Order the ancient tension again and again made itself felt, and the Franciscan pneumatics continued to carry out the ancient strict observances and cherished spiritual ideals that were opposed to hierarchy and even to ecclesiasticism. These men lent a willing ear to the great Italian Apocalyptic Joachim of Fiore, with his preaching of the " everlasting Gospel " and with his eschatological views of history, through which shone the great thought of an evolution in history. In this evolution, he taught, there is nothing really new; out of the image develops the thing itself; out of the figure grows the reality.

7. The *Counter-Reformation* did not mean merely the victory of the reform party in the Catholic Church, a ruthless fight against disorders in the Church, and an insistence on discipline both for clerics and for laymen; nor were its violent methods in the stamping out of heresy and in its great political campaigns its only characteristic features. These can all be explained by the self-consciousness of Catholicism, which had been aroused and quickened by the Reformation. Indeed, Catholicism had already assimilated the two great spiritual forces of the time — Mysticism and Humanism. As a matter of fact, the spirit that animated the counter-reforming party in the Church was bent on advancing education and civilization, and, despite their profound differences, the Reformation and the Counter-Reformation moved on what was really the same plane, both furthering the dialectical development of Western Christendom.

The great figures in this movement were the Cardinals Caraffa, Gislieri, and Peretti and the Popes Paul IV, Pius V, and Sixtus V, other friends of reform in Venice, Naples, and Ferrara being Contarini and Pole, Valdez and Bernardino Ochino. But the most potent influence in that direction was the Order of Jesuits, founded by Ignatius Loyola. Loyola was a Basque, a man of remarkably primitive instincts, practical, sagacious, and distinguished by a profound knowledge of human nature. He passed through a spiritual experience which, like that of Luther, turned on the sacrament of penance. Following the path of German Mysticism, he had visions and auditions, but be kept these under strict control, and used them only as sources of inspiration to action. His strength of will and his determined nature kept him from being carried away by them, and he entered the service of the Church with a real desire to promote the glory of God. In his *exercitia spiritualia,* which owe much to his own experiences, Loyola provided a simple and practical, but impressive " book of drill " for Catholic Christians. It lays stress on the supremacy of the spiritual, kindles the imagination, and appeals for a free decision to follow the service of Christ in self-denial, self-control, and self-dedication. The Society of Jesus gradually took shape, and was organized with such rare sagacity and efficiency that it became the " spear head " or " shock troops " of the Papacy. By its missionary and educational activities (some of which anticipated the methods of modern Protestantism), by its work in school and university, among the educated and the illiterate, by its skilful use of the confessional, it practically produced and carried through the Counter-Reformation.

Jesuit theologians also took a leading part at the Council of Trent. While maintaining a clear attitude of opposition to Protestantism, that council reduced the various scholastic systems to uniformity, and declared the resultant doctrine to be ecclesiastical dogma. The Roman Catholic form of piety, combining an authoritative, legal morality with a mystical view of the sacraments, was now systematized, and became the basis for the later development of Catholicism. It is worthy of notice — and it is clearly evident from the debates between the schools of Duns Scotus and of Thomas Aquinas on the doctrine of justification — that the Thomist form of the Catholic faith, despite its rejection of the " merits of congruity," ultimately received the greater support. So the Council of Trent may be regarded as the starting-point of that retrogression from Nominalism to Thomism, which has borne the latter to victory in our own day.

Along with other Catholic Orders and with Protestant Humanist scholars, the Order of Jesuits took a highly creditable part in the foundation of historical science in the seventeenth century, and fought two campaigns of great importance in the history of thought — those against Jansenism and against Quietistic Mysticism.

Jansenism is the name given to the Augustinian reaction in the Catholic Church against Scholasticism and against the current semi-Pelagianism, whose main position was the defence of the ' natural,' legal element in Catholic religious life. After long controversy Jansenism was definitely overthrown in 1713, but the struggle helped to prepare the way for the Illumination, with its anti-Church attitude, which found so much support in France.

Quietistic Mysticism is characterized by a refined mystical method and by a system of elaborate and conscious introspection. The key to the understanding of the citadel of the soul with its many chambers lies in a recognition of its ruling motive. That motive is the fear of being misled by unusual religious experience. This explains the emphasis laid by Quietism on obedience to the Church and on good works. It also explains why this type of mysticism lauds sterility and death of the soul as the condition in which God is found. The supreme place is given to disinterested love, surrender of the will, and sheer self-abandonment. The ethical teaching of Quietism breathes the same harsh and ascetic spiritualism, which in the manner of Kant excludes all striving after reward and teaches men to find their happiness in pain. In Francis of Sales Quietistic Mysticism took a turn toward mystical theology, in Fénelon toward the Illumination, in Michael Molinos and Madame de Guyon toward a pure spiritualism that was specially opposed to natural and sacramental piety. It provoked the attack of the Jesuits and led to its speedy overthrow.

Quietistic Mysticism taught men the practice of introspection, the observation of their own souls. It left its mark not only in literature — it is seen even in Goethe — but also on the writing of history. It made itself felt as an undercurrent in the eighteenth century, conjoined with all kinds of Platonic ideas, and its fondness for reflection on darkness and death, as well as its purifying influence on the emotion of love, can be traced in the writings of the Romantic school.

8. In view of the limits of the space at our disposal we cannot attempt to describe here the constitution and ritual of the Catholic Church, nor can we even give a detailed account of Catholic religious life. The most important features of it have already been mentioned in our account of the historical development of Catholic Christianity, and we have seen that, while it was conservative in spirit, it was also capable of development. It must suffice here to consider briefly the present condition of Catholic Christianity, with a view to discovering its chief characteristics.

The life of our time is marked by a remarkable paradox. On the one hand, it exhibits a materialism, fed from many sources and pervading all classes of the people, which governs the practical conduct of men to such an extent that it even occasionally obliterates the strongest political differences. On the other hand, since the end of last century the intellectual life of Europe has witnessed the timid beginnings of a new ideal of life, which have found expression in manifold forms, both in science and in art. This new ideal has assumed a form of its own. In its conscious striving after a complete life and in its determination to realize it, it might be called quite generally the philosophical enthronement of the ideal and the religious longing for the absolute. This means a revival of religion. Again, there is the crisis that has overtaken civilization everywhere and finds support both in materialism and idealism. This crisis has raised all the moral and social questions that lie at the basis of our life. It is not yet possible to say how these various currents will affect each other and how the intellectual and spiritual tendencies will behave amid the ever-increasing mechanization and materialization of daily life.

There can be no question that amid these conditions Catholicism has gained a new ascendency. It has not adopted an attitude of pronounced opposition to the times, but has taken the line of reciprocal give and take. We need only look at the revival of monasticism. This revival has permeated all the Orders instituted since the Counter-Reformation with the spirit of the Jesuits, and has been specially felt by all the ancient Orders. Or we may look at the liturgical movement which, as against the vagueness of subjectivism, has insisted on form and order, and found points of contact with Young People's Movements and with the Circle of St George. Further, there is a new appreciation of Scholasticism and of the Middle Ages, which means that the verdict of the Illumination is no longer accepted. This is due not only to the labours of scholars and to the revival of interest in Mysticism. It is also seen in the reaction against Kant — the Logos comes before the Ethos, existence before conduct, truth before morality — and in the return to Plato, as, for example, in the problems of phenomenology. Here too the new sense of reality is the primary fact; that is to say, thinking does not produce its own object; the object of thought is objectively supplied. Hence arises the crisis of the positivist conception of truth and a new attitude to metaphysics, and even dogma is regarded not as a mystery and a burden, but as a helpful gift. The time is past when it was necessary for Catholicism to prove its claim to be the fount of " progress." Who to-day believes any longer in " progress " ? The prevailing sentiment of to-day is that contained in the lines from Goethe which Scheler once quoted:

> Long, long ago the truth was found,
> And noble hearts together bound.
> That old truth, lay ye hold on it!

And who can deny that powerful currents of our time, which has lost the buoyant faith in the creative power of the human mind and would fain find rest in obedience to the authority of the Church in which the eternal lamp is never quenched, are meeting these moods and thoughts? Lastly, there is the *policy that has been pursued by the Papacy*. Just as Leo XIII took a resolute step in the direction of socialism, and definitively enthroned Thomas Aquinas as the standard dogmatic theologian of Catholicism, so Pius X, whom only ignorant journalism can call " a pious fool," encouraged the liturgical movement in the Church, carried through a great reform of its administration, and decreed a new codification of ecclesiastical law, which has placed the reins of power more firmly than ever in the hands of the Pope. From the standpoint of the Curia and in view of the change that has come over the intellectual situation, the condemnation of modernism in the new Syllabus must be pronounced wise, although valuable and unique powers and gifts have been and will still be lost to the Church by that decree. And, further, the wise peace policy of Benedict XV during the Great War has probably increased the popularity of the Papacy and its moral prestige in the eyes of men generally. The Papal policy of the present day may be said to be pursuing three lines. First, it is endeavouring to strengthen the international Catholic sense of solidarity. Second, it is aiming at making the Catholic Church appear as the protector of international law and the Pope as the conscience of the world. Third, the Curia is seeking to win back the Eastern Churches. This is abundantly clear from various recent administrative measures.

In view of these facts the question is inevitable, What has made this sudden change possible? What is the secret of the power of Catholicism to attract men in our day? It is not sufficient to say that it is only another sign of the Neo-Romanticism of the time, with its tendency to mysticism and its longing for authority; nor is it enough to say that the metaphysical needs of our time are being satisfied by the metaphysic of dogma. These no doubt play a part, but the explanation lies deeper. The power of Catholicism in our time rests ultimately on the fact that it appeals to and satisfies certain innate cravings of human nature. Its primitively human and natural features are the secret of its abiding power. I should like in a few words to support this opinion from three points of view.

(i) Catholicism is the embodiment of sacramentarian piety and of the material conception of the Holy that underlies it. Just as our forefathers worshipped God in the sacred tree or sacred spring, so the Catholic worshipper realizes God in corporeal manifestation and feels the living presence of the Holy in the Church, in the relic, and in the sacrament. Look at Catholicism in all its sublimities and profundities and everywhere you come upon this essential feature, which has affinities both with mysticism and with magic. So long as this natural, innate aspect of religion abides in us, so long will Catholicism endure and flourish, especially in critical times. *Anima naturaliter catholica.* All that Catholicism teaches about grace, its power and its kingdom, is ultimately bound up with this basic principle. It gathers new strength with every increase in the emphasis that is laid on grace, and it has even made its way into Catholic dogma through the metaphysics of Neo-Platonism.

(ii) The second feature, which, if not so innate in the heart of man, is present in the very beginnings of human consciousness, is the Catholic morality, which moves along juristic lines. The moral theory of Catholicism is the rational complement of its sacramentarianism. Here are to be included all those complex conceptions which are expressed by the terms " merit,"

" works," " sacrifice " — the idea that man can prevail on God by doing the works ordained in His laws, that man must surrender and sacrifice if he is to take and receive, that the cosmical order demands an equipoise between renunciation and receiving.

(iii) Catholicism is the religion of history. It is the embodiment not only of faith in a revelation that was made once for all, but also of faith in the historical permanence and continuity of the divine revelation. This divine revelation is set forth in the organized Church, which, though legally constituted, is charged with living power. The Church is the great unity which binds together and gives inward meaning to all the changes of historical life, and it is the medium of the sacramental powers of Christ, which are bestowed on him who subjects himself to its rule. Thus sacramentarian mysticism and legalistic morality are combined in the conception of the Church. This enables us to understand the emphasis that is laid both on ecclesiastical authority, which has its basis in the sacraments, and on divinely given ecclesiastical law. It enables us to understand the peculiar nature of the Catholic social doctrines, which include a harmonious system of natural rules of expediency within the supernatural order of grace, and which, in the conception of natural right, have preserved a basis of immense adaptability and rationality. It also enables us to understand the tendency and the ability to direct actual daily life — a feature which is based on the teleological attitude of the Western mind.

These elements, which spring from separate sources, are all combined in Catholicism. None of them is valid apart from the others. Grace is connected with law, and law is perfected in grace, and the Church is at once the guardian of law and the medium of grace. The inmost nature of Catholicism is expressed in the ancient formula, *mereri misericordiam*. The central conception is that of the Church, and unquestionably it attains a double strength in a time like the present, which is seeking fellowship because it is weary of individualism and the culture of the personal self. And there is just as little doubt that the downfall of the old idea of the State as divine has been all in favour of the Church and its ideal of fellowship. The State is now being relegated to the sphere of utility and limited to the task of securing a free field for all competitive economic interests.

III

1. The word *Renaissance* means, not the rebirth of classical antiquity, but the rebirth of man, and practically the same idea is expressed by the word *Humanism*. At the heart of both movements was the search for the ideal type of the new man and for new human values, and although this ideal was pursued at a time when men were awakening to a new appreciation of antiquity and of national life, still it was Neo-Platonism and Franciscan spirituality that gave birth to that boundless longing for new life, for simpli-

fication and purification, that was the keynote of the Renaissance. That movement was thus an outgrowth of the individualism of the Middle Ages. Man, an intellectual and spiritual being — that was the ideal that hovered before the eyes of the representative man of the Renaissance. Ascetic piety was now recast and remoulded into an expression of the joy of living, the love of life and artistic form, and men's eyes were opened to see the laws of earthly life, the independence of the human soul, and the beauty of the human body.

This raised the question of the relation of Christianity to culture, and attempts were made to answer that question with the aid of humanistic and historical criticism and of Neo-Platonic speculation. Men had come to realize that intellectual and spiritual life existed outside of Christianity. The historical method was applied to the interpretation of the Christian sources. Men tried to reconcile Christianity with ancient philosophy. The Apologists, for example, sought to do so with the aid of the ancient Alexandrian theory of the dependence of Plato on Moses and with the aid of the Logos conception. They even built up a kind of eclectic natural religion derived from the teaching of Plato, Plotinus, and Christ. They placed in the forefront the simple, pure morality of the heart that existed in the classical epoch of primitive Christianity, and yet they felt that true culture and true Christianity belonged together. Though the Italian Humanists mocked at the Church, criticized tradition, and satirized the disorders that marked pneumatism, yet they submitted themselves to the rule of the Church, reposed blind faith in the sacraments, and were diligent in good works. Conjoined with much superstition there was a profound sense of its unreality, a mixture of scepticism and submission to constituted authority.

The movement known as Humanism spread over the whole of Europe. In Germany it took on a special religious colouring, which was largely due to the influence of the " new piety " in the Netherlands. The most outstanding figure was Erasmus (Fig. 125), the unobtrusive king of the intellectual life of the new era. He too, despite his views on the relativity of truth and his leanings toward scepticism, remained in the Catholic Church, probably because of his profound sympathy with one of the fundamental elements in Catholicism. He approved of its rational moral philosophy, and based on it his optimistic opinion of human nature and his religion of merit and reward. In the views of Erasmus, however, we find re-emerging the Universalism of the ancient Apologists, who found germs of the Logos even in the great men of pagan antiquity and saw preparations for Christianity outside the narrow confines of Judaism. This Universalism led him to see the essence of religion in the pious religious life that knows no dogma and to look on the positive elements and the sacraments of Christianity as symbols. Thus for Erasmus the central element in the Christian religion was not the "ecclesiastical " nor the " historical," but the psychical and the " universally human." His task was to find the kernel of Christianity, which had been obscured by the growth of dogma, to bring to light again the simple, practical, ethical

" philosophy of Christ " contained in the Bible and in the Fathers of the Church, and in this way to bring about a reformation in the Church. This " philosophy of Christ " lies in the preaching of that composure which overcomes the world, in genuine gentle toleration, in love of one's enemy, in contempt of death, and in assurance of a future life. That is the Gospel; it agrees with the best of ancient wisdom, and in its simplicity it is the copestone of the highest culture. That is life in the " war-service of Christ," in

Fig. 125. Erasmus
Painting by Holbein.

which the grace of God accompanies and strengthens us, so that we live and strive, and yet (as he puts it with a remarkable Nominalist turn of thought) we ascribe it all to God. This kernel of Christianity is reached, not by the method of logical speculation, but by means of critical historical research and rational judicial study. The authority for Erasmus was the Scriptures and the exposition of the good Fathers. Then came his critical labours on the text of Scripture and his historical studies. To him questions of dogma were historical problems. This helps to understand how Erasmus regarded the Church. It had apostatized and fallen into barbarism and externality. Yet it remained authoritative, because its true teaching agreed with the teaching of the classical period in the history of Christianity.

Erasmus inaugurates the *rationalist line in the history of modern thought*. The line was continued in the rationalist criticism of dogma by Socinus, in the theories of Bodin, Grotius, and Pufendorf on the natural right of the State, and in the changed conception of the Church that resulted from the labours of these men, who regarded it as analogous to a society or club; and in the " natural religion " advocated by Castellio and Coornhert, by the great philosophers of the seventeenth century, and by the Deists. Thereafter, through Melanchthon on the one side and Calvin on the other, Humanism began to affect Orthodoxy. It laid the foundation of the science of history in the seventeenth century, and taught men to think historically. It underlay the eirenical theology of the same century that aimed at the reunion of the Churches. Its 'liberal' theology influenced the solution of the question of toleration in the Anglican Church and the ecclesiastical policy of Cromwell, and thus Humanism played a part in preparing everywhere the way for the Illumination.

2. It was in the tense, uneasy Catholic religion that characterized the close of the Middle Ages that Luther grew to manhood. As the result of a personal experience he entered on the monastic life, seeking to attain perfection on the usual lines by self-mortification and surrender of his own will to the will of God. His difficulties on the subject of penance and the old question of Western theology regarding salvation led to his rediscovery of the Gospel. The controversies into which he was thus led, and which left him the thin, hollow-cheeked man seen in the early portrait of him (Fig. 126), turned on that deepest question of all religions: How can man attain that complete purity of will which God requires of him? Where can he find that true repentance which is the condition of God's forgiveness? The consolations of Scholasticism, especially in the Nominalist form, appealed to Luther for a time, but they brought him no rest; they rather increased his disquiet. Nor could he find comfort in Occam's counsel to " do what in one lies," nor in the confessional, in the comfortable Occamist theory of predestination, weakened by its doctrine of foreknowledge; and even the mystical Neo-Platonist experience of union with God failed to bring that harmony of will with God of which he was in quest. Full of the sense of the injustice and unfairness of the divine requirements, Luther began to fear that he was among those whom God had rejected from all eternity, and reached a state in which he hated the name of God. Like Paul, he found that salvation was impossible by the law. The shadows lifted a little when Staupitz pointed him to the wounds of Christ, in which God's mercy is manifested. Staupitz must also have shown him that hate against sin begins with love to God, and that it is a vision of Christ that makes it possible for us to love God. Somewhat later

Luther was impressed by Tauler's teaching that only he who has become reconciled to God can do good, because it is only in such a man that God works. The decisive influence in Luther's life, however, was Paul. From Paul he learned that man of himself can never win God's favour; that it is God who bridges the gulf, who in His goodness for Christ's sake forgives the sinner and gives him the power to act aright. In our extremity God seeks

FIG. 126. LUTHER
Engraving by Cranach.

us, and that man finds Him who in complete, humble surrender gives himself to Him. Suffering and death, sin and extremity, are no longer obstacles on the path to God; they themselves *are* the path on which God seeks us. In the *mortificatio* we experience the *vivificatio;* in the judgment we find the grace. In these scholastic words Luther expressed this liberating knowledge. It meant the rediscovery of the Gospel — *i.e.,* the view according to which God is not to be prevailed upon even by the fulfilment of His laws; of His own will and in His creative goodness He gives men all they need, even the power to serve Him.

It was with those profound thoughts that Luther stepped forth to face the authoritative teaching of his time. Many theologians have pointed out numerous similarities between Luther's teaching and that of Occam, but even these similarities — the anti-Aristotelian distinction between reason and revelation, transcendentalism, formal positivism and voluntarism, the criticism of the Church, certain aspects of the doctrine of God, of Christology, and of the sacraments, the germs of a non-substantial, spiritual view of grace — all show a difference of emphasis and an entirely different spirit. Indeed, Luther's views of God and of religion contradict the Unknown God of Occam and his eudemonistic, end-regarding conception of religion. In particular Luther rejected altogether the legal view of morality and the mystical efficacy of the sacraments, and this was tantamount to a breach with Catholicism.

With regard to his relation to Humanism, it may be said that, in spite of his interest in the translation of the Bible, and with all his zeal for reform in schools and universities, and despite that sense of German nationality which he shared with the Humanists, Luther differed more from that movement than he agreed with it. In saying this I have in mind not merely the superficiality and vagueness of the Humanists, their "natural" piety and their Catholic theory of morals. Luther's chief objection to the Humanists was that they regarded religion merely as one of the factors in human culture, and therefore, as at bottom a human and not a divine matter; and, further, their view of morals implied a growth and an unfolding of a natural germ in the human soul, which was good by nature. For Luther, on the other hand, religion was essentially a matter that concerned the relation of God to men, a matter that was far more vital than any other, a matter that lies on an entirely different plane from all that man desires for himself. And his view of ethics implied a breach with the "natural"; it demanded regeneration, a divine work that brings the life of man under the law of the spirit of Christ.

With German Mysticism Luther's relations were far closer. Tauler perhaps influenced him most. According to Tauler, the thought (which excludes all egoism and voluntarism) that the only good element in human conduct is that which God Himself creates and does is a direct, logical inference from the conception of the *unio mystica*. He also recognized the ethical value of the gratitude toward God that is felt by the regenerate soul, and he maintained that the hidden God works antithetically and seeks us in suffering — not in self-chosen suffering, but in that which He sends upon us. But even here Luther and Tauler do not accentuate the same points. The entirely different view of sin held by Luther — sin is not confined to the flesh and to the affections, but affects also the noblest parts of the soul, the reason and the will — and the absence of all Neo-Platonist metaphysics and of mystical theology from Luther's view of the moral and religious process, as well as the fact that it is founded on the Bible and on history, prove that the positions of Tauler and Luther, though apparently the same, rested on different foundations.

In answer to the question, what is the significance of the Reformation in the history of religion? three points call for special notice.

(i) When Luther rejected the Catholic mystical view of the sacraments, he was rejecting the age-long, primitive conception of the " divine." For him grace was not the heavenly medicine, but the attitude of the omnipotent and personal loving will of God revealed in the spiritual Christ and in the creative Word, of which we can lay hold in the spirit, in faith and obedience, and which finally unites us in the invisible spiritual world of which Christ is the King. In a new dynamic way of thinking, the ancient metaphysic of Substance is replaced by the conception of the personal, all-efficacious God. The other pillar on which Catholicism rested Luther also uprooted. The conception of religion as something rendered or something done, along with the profound idea of sacrifice, is replaced by the view of religion as a gift, something received, experienced, and undergone by man. This makes itself at once felt in the doctrine of God. There is nothing by which man can prevail on God, nothing man can do in which he can confidently trust. In man there is nothing but sin, and the best virtues of the great pagans were their deepest sins: the " whole man " is " flesh." The line in religion that leads from below upward is here cut away. The only thing that remains — and this position is no less radical than the religion that is based on works — is the creative power of God, which bestows everything that is in man, even the will and the power to do. The goodness of this creative power — God's " nature " — is shown in the fact that the holy God especially loves the sinner, breaks him that He may make him anew, forgives him that He may give him life. The hidden God reveals Himself in this very antithesis: when He destroys He creates; when He kills He makes alive; in the judgment lies the grace. The hidden God is the crucified God. Luther's doctrine of justification is thus the expression of the deep view that God Himself lays down the conditions on which He can tolerate the presence of the sinner — He bestows on him faith in Christ and in the Word, so that Christ and the sinner, united like bridegroom and bride, exchange what they have; and God, looking at the Christ in us, is able to take the beginning for the whole. It goes without saying that this faith in the sole efficacy of God, this faith that sees in all creatures and in all happenings the " masks and disguises " behind which God hides Himself, involves belief in predestination. Without the thought of " election," which explains why not all men believe, and which results in metaphysical, if not psychological, determinism, Luther's theology would be incomplete, and his position is made clear by what he said in his early manhood — and both Tauler and Occam would have said the same — that he would bow to the will of God even if he himself were not included among the elect. " If only I have Thee, nothing do I care for in heaven or on earth." [25] Luther's doctrine of God has some resemblance to that of the Scholastics. Nature and history reveal God as the all-working, hidden power that lives and moves in every stone and leaf. But what is thus in itself incomprehensible becomes intelligible, antithetically in the Cross and patently in the Word and in Him in Whom the Word became flesh. The Word which records and interprets the facts of history tells us where God, Who is everywhere and nowhere, desires to be found. In His lowliness Christ is thus the revealing power of God, and the Word, which is the record of salvation, solves the problem of life and history. It is at this point that the difference between Luther and the German Idealists clearly emerges. Luther also believed — one has only to read what he has written on the Lord's Supper — in the non-objective God. But while German Idealism found the guarantee of God's existence in personal experience, in " intellectual intuition," Luther found it " positively " in Christ and the Word — although the full reality of both is disclosed " transcendently " only in creative faith.

(ii) Luther's ideal Christianity was embodied in the Church. He did not aim at forming a new sect; he believed in the Church. He opposed both Catholicism and those whom he called " the fanatics," and desired to see a Church freed from all legalism and based on the priesthood of all believers. The Catholic view of the Church as a divine state constituted by divine ecclesiastical law he entirely repudiated. He believed in a spiritual Church, called into life by the Word and in which all believers are united in liberty. The Church exists only when the word is preached. The only essentials for the Church are the Word and the sacraments. By " Church " Luther meant the territorial or local community. It is an aspect of the civil community, thus involving the " national Church," although Luther insisted on the ideal " confessional Church." *Abscondita est ecclesia, latent sancti*. With the Church the sovereign as such has nothing to do. Only in special times, like his own, Luther admitted that the sovereign had a right to intervene, but any government of the Church by the sovereign was directly counter to Luther's ideas. The Church as such is free from error, but its membership includes mistaken teachers — in most cases they form the majority — so that the true Church is invisible. Controversy is the token of the living power of the divine Word that goes through the world like a sword. The world cannot endure the Word, but God cannot keep silence. Thus world and Word are at enmity, like Satan and God. This doctrine of the Church is based both on personal experience and on the view that it is not individuals who make the life of history: individuals are the outcome of human life as a whole. History is anterior to individuals. It is the great postulate, and it is within it that individuals find their place and their task.

(iii) There can be no ethics in the Christian sense till God has crushed the ego in man and formed his will anew; therefore for Luther there can

[25] Luther's rendering of Ps. lxxiii, 25.

be no autonomous system of ethics. His theory of morals, which excludes
both legality and neutral actions, has as its main postulates duty and human
freedom. Morality is unconditioned and absolute, and therefore it means
obedience to the unconditioned and is duty. But God re-creates man to enjoy
freedom, and fellowship with God results in a moral life whose essential notes
are freedom and joy. Therefore the goal of the moral life, in which gratitude
toward God is an additional motive to the service of one's neighbour, is not
calmness of mind or self-composure, but joyousness and delight in the thought
of being God's instrument and pleasure in serving God in one's daily calling,
be that what it may. God does not desire that we should seek artificial relations toward Him; our life is so ordered by Him that our work and our
calling are for us the path to God. This of course does away with the " graduated ethics " of the Middle Ages. The harshest feature of Luther's social
ethical theory is the fundamental dualism between Christianity and the civil
power. This dualism is retained by Luther — as against Catholicism and
Mysticism — for the sake of the truth of reality. Luther declined to lay down
Christian standards for the guidance of the natural life. He was afraid — and
this was one of the reasons why he opposed the peasants — that to do so
would make the Gospel an external law and lead to an increase of hypocrisy.
Therefore he maintained on principle that the State was a law unto itself
and had sole control of its own functions. Because of the wickedness of men
and because otherwise they would " devour " each other, State and State
law, compulsion and force, are necessary. These are part of the divine order,
revelations of the divine wrath, and channels of God's love, and they pave
the way of the Kingdom of God. And yet this view of the relation between
politics and religion does not mean that Christianity and the Church are to
take no part in public questions. Not only must the Christian man boldly take
his place in life and do his daily task as in God's sight, but the Church too
must do its part wherever it is a question of uplifting men, making them
better, and bringing them to God. The object in view is always the Kingdom
of God. But Luther did not expect salvation to come from the multiplication
of new institutions or of Christian sects and organizations. Men must become
better and more religious if conditions are to be permanently changed. There
is no doubt a lofty idealism in this attitude. It is not concerned with arrangements and organizations. It aims at changing men, and seeks in this way to
make a new world of new men, and its ultimate hopes are fixed on God.

These remarks will perhaps serve to explain the position occupied by
Luther in the history of Western Christianity. It will be seen that he stands
between the Middle Ages and the modern world, marking the close of the
one and the opening of the other. But Luther cannot be dismissed merely as
a link in the chain of Western evolution. He was not only the pioneer of the
German spirit in the intellectual life of the West; it was he who awakened
into life the profoundest influences of the Gospel and gave to certain elements of primitive Oriental Christianity a permanent place in the thought

and feeling of Western Christianity. In fact, we must keep in view both aspects of the great reformer's work. Further, Luther's influence was by no means confined to the sphere of religion; he has also left his mark on the history of civilization. He holds a commanding place in the history of the German people, to which he belonged in every fibre of his nature, and again and again his influence has guided and determined their attitude. If we are to estimate aright his influence on the civic and social life of the modern world we have to remember that he created a new conception of personality and of human fellowship. The line he laid down was interrupted, it is true, by Melanchthon and Calvin, but there are other respects in which his life and work have left a permanent mark. He laid the foundation broad and deep for freedom of conscience, the principle that there is a region of life in which no power on earth has any right to interfere. He roused the conscience of the State to face its civilizing and social tasks. And even Bismarck's political ideas — his attitude toward war, his non-imperialistic diplomacy, which respected the necessities of life of other nations, his realistic conception of the State — bear the impress of Luther's influence. It may even be said that the World War was a contest between Luther's and Calvin's views of the State. In the intellectual and educational spheres we should remember Luther's appeal for compulsory education, his ardent advocacy of universal education, which bore fruit in the seventeenth and eighteenth centuries, his achievements on behalf of the German language and of hymnody, his encouragement of the study of history, his work in the sphere of hermeneutics, his pleas for a sympathetic and discerning exegesis. Finally, it was he who prepared the way for the idealism of Leibniz and Böhme. The monadology of Leibniz has affinities with Luther's conception of personality, and Jakob Böhme, in his unmystical " metaphysic of contrast," and in his dualistic view of life, was clearly influenced by Luther's doctrine of God and his interpretation of life. Under the influence of Böhme, German Idealism conceived the Absolute as producing out of itself the contrast that obtains in the world and yet transcends it. As regards Luther's own philosophical foundation, we must keep in view how he rejected the metaphysic of Substance in favour of a peculiarly dynamistic transcendentalism, which was probably based on Occam; nor must we forget his basic view of the Christian religion, according to which the eternal must needs become subject to time, the spiritual become corporeal, and the Spirit become Word. Thus there was in Luther's thinking a nucleus of idealism which makes it unsafe to draw any sharp line of division between the Christianity of the reformers and German Idealism.

3. Mysticism is the one great root out of which grew both the *Baptists* and the *Pneumatics*. The difference between these two is mainly sociological. The Baptists represented the ancient sectarian type. They insisted that man's entire life should be reformed in accordance with the teaching of the Sermon on the Mount and on the lines of the *Imitatio Christi,* whereas the Pneumatics, despite their revolutionary radicalism, were indifferent to that aspect

of religion. Both were influenced not only by Humanism, but also by Luther. The Baptists, indeed, set out their teaching in a form that was intended to make clear how they differed from Luther. Like the Pneumatics, they regarded his work as not radical enough, as being a reformation of doctrine merely, and as not piercing deeply enough to reach the true inwardness of life. The Pneumatics, to whom, as to the Baptists, the Spirit was the essential element, the principle that spiritualized both Scripture and dogma, also came very deeply under the influence of Luther.

The main position of the Baptists was that of opposition to the secular spirit, which they professed to detect both in the sociology of the reformers and in the dogma of justification. They insisted on sanctification of the whole personal life and on personal experience of God. They recognized as members only those who had been born again and had received the rite of adult baptism in attestation of their religious experience. They declined to have anything to do with war, refused to take oaths, and refrained from taking part in civic affairs. Infant baptism they regarded as meaningless magic, and they declared that the whole Church had fallen away from the primitive Christian ideal. Their representatives, men like Münzer and Karlstadt, adopted so many of the doctrines of Mysticism that the lines of division between Baptists and Pneumatics were practically obliterated. The point of greatest interest is to understand how, holding the principles they did, the Baptists came to approve of revolution and the use of force. The explanation is found in their eschatological views, their teachings on "the last things." When the last days come the elect must be separated from the impure and gathered together into a visible Church and take vengeance on pseudo-Christians. The wicked cannot possibly be allowed to obstruct the path of good men to the gospel. The way must be cleared by the sword. All tyrants must fall, and the nation must be permitted to resort to force. It was not on economic grounds, but for religious reasons that men like Münzer and Rothmann became revolutionaries.

Spiritualism was a combination of Mysticism, that urge to reach the unity that transcends division which, anterior to all religion, is felt by the soul which has grown conscious of itself, and mystical theology. The nucleus of it is the ancient mystical doctrine of the soul spark. That spark is set free when we rid ourselves of the world and of self, and the spirit of God can then fan it into life and bring us to a knowledge of the identity between Him and us. Positive, historical Christianity is of itself a dead thing: the Bible is the Word of God attested and sealed with seven seals; dogma is religious experience that has become fossilized. They all come to life when the Spirit blows upon them and fills with life and meaning the dead letter and the fossilized Church. But none of them are really essential. "The Spirit bloweth where it listeth." Without any intermediary He works by way of direct personal enlightenment — even among Jews and heathens. Dogmas and rites are simply symbols and forms of expression of the one sole, uniform, simple religious experience. This remote and lonely Spiritualism takes no account of history and knows nothing of communion, and these features are common to mystical Spiritualism and rational Humanism. A religious experience which is thus independent of time and space, or a religious knowledge which is similarly independent and autonomous, resorts naturally to a comparison of the various phenomena of religion, and to critical investigations like those of Frank on the Spiritualist side and of Erasmus on the Humanist side. The various types of religion are thus reduced to a common level, to their psychological nucleus, and it is of comparatively little moment whether this nucleus consists in experience or in knowledge. It is hardly necessary to point out that this implies the relativity of truth and involves toleration.

It is this type of Spiritualism that dominates the splendid speculative philosophy of history which Sebastian Frank expounded in his numerous popular writings. The absence of cohesion in his thinking is due to the self-contradictory estimate of the soul found in Mysticism. History is the depravation or degradation of the divine, the disastrous apostasy from the Inward to the External, and its nature is shown by the manner in which good men have been persecuted and condemned as heretics. And yet history is the wonderful work of God, and throws light on His otherwise obscure Word. To be acquainted with it is like seeing God's back while the mystical knowledge is like seeing " His face at noon." But the unity of history becomes clear when we see that all its various aspects and happenings are nothing other than the life of the soul, which is stirred by the timeless opposition between the Christ in us and human selfishness. " All that is perishable is only a parable." " All men are but one man." The goal of Sebastian Frank is the " fourth faith," in which external Christianity entirely disappears and religion, freed from every semblance of historical form, becomes altogether the free experience of the human soul. It was Servetus, the scholar who was burnt at Calvin's instigation, who led Spiritualism in the direction of Socinianism by introducing the rational element. He was at once scholar, scientist, and philologist, and his object was to restore the original Christianity of the Bible by the use of critical exegesis. It was in this way he reached his attitude of criticism of the Church doctrine of the Trinity, which he declared to be an invention of the Platonized Church Fathers. He replaced it by an economic doctrine of the Trinity based on natural philosophy, and in keeping with it he adopted a speculatively realistic interpretation of regeneration, an intellectualistic conception of faith and of righteousness that comes by works.

The far-reaching effects of this Spiritualism cannot be gainsaid. The modern idea of toleration, the thoughts that lay behind the French Revolution, and the views that underlie the American Constitution are all rooted in it. Its insistence on experience — Paracelsus — its conception of man as a microcosm, the Neo-Pythagorean mystical theory of numbers, these all profoundly influenced the scientific work of men like Kepler and Copernicus. And, lastly, it would be easy to show a direct line of connexion from Spiritualism to Leibniz and Shaftesbury.

4. The greatest genius among the disciples of Luther was Calvin (Fig. 127). The Romanic form which he gave to the Reformation movement, at once systematic and rounded, had less resemblance to the Humanist, Protestant Christianity of Zwingli than to that of the South German Bucer, which was Biblical in its strict legalistic ethics, aimed at Church reform, and gave a prominent place to the tenet of predestination. Luther's disciples, Zwingli and Bucer, were much more in sympathy with Humanist Spiritualism than their master was. Zwingli was strongly attracted by the philosophy of the Renaissance movement, while Bucer had much in common with the Baptists. Both were far more eager than Luther to bring about reforms in the practice of the Church and to inaugurate a definite Church policy. Calvin's development, on the other hand, which culminated in a sudden conversion, took place not in the atmosphere of Scholasticism, but in that of Humanism, and the new teaching came to him in its full and complete form. Humanism was therefore an important element both in his thinking and in his personality. This outstandingly great man, strong in his self-control, downright and devoted, though he felt himself to be an instrument of God, yet never ceased to be the timid, reserved, and highly strung scholar. His personal charm must have been great. He did not produce anything that could be called a new system of theology. Most of his theological views had been learned from Luther, and he understood his master's teaching on justification better than Melanchthon did. But all

FIG. 127. CALVIN

Painting by an unknown master.

the same the result of his activity was a new type of reformed religion, whose chief difference from that of Luther was the stress laid on legalism. His insistence on " the world within " and his ascetic tendency still survive in the modern ' American ' style of life, and they have even left their mark on important schools of politics. Above all, it is owing to Calvin that the active, progressive aspects of Protestantism have had free scope, and his importance in the history of the Church is seen when we compare him with his greatest opponent, Ignatius Loyola. Calvin lived and worked in Geneva, in the midst of violent controversies which were concerned both with religious and political questions. He emerged victorious, and Geneva became the international centre of those who aimed at winning the world for Christianity. Calvin was the leading spirit of this movement, and his letters, in which he guided men's minds and discussed the relevant facts, did much to further the movement in France, Germany, and England.

The teaching of Calvin emphasizes two aspects of religion — the sense of absolute dependence and conscious active service to the glory of God. The obedience which the law of God demands involves such activity, and further motives to service are found in the Platonist yearning after a life beyond this world and in contempt for this world and all that belongs to it. His doctrine of God is akin to Luther's, but it lays greater emphasis on the rational conception of Providence or Foreknowledge — *i.e.,* divine omnipotence is working out a preordained eternal plan. One special application of this divine Providence is found in Calvin's theory of a double predestination — *i.e.,* the unfathomable double decree of God by which He has elected some to faith and others to unbelief. All things are included under the will of God, even the fall of our first parents. To ask why God has done this, or to call in question His righteousness in so doing, is vain and meaningless. It would imply the existence of a something higher than He Who created the world to be the " theatre of His glory." Our assurance of salvation has its sole basis in the will of God. This emphasis on Providence leads to a higher estimate of the Old Testament. The whole Bible is the record and expression of divine revelation, and it is therefore a binding authority even for the regenerate. Thus Calvin restores to the Law its prominent place as " a rigid, inflexible rule for life "; it lays down the order which regulates life in the Kingdom of the Sovereign God. It is here that Calvin clearly parts company from Luther. While Luther also believed in predestination, and regarded justification as the working out of it, Calvin held that predestination was the central dogma, and all other theological tenets were regulated by it. His conception, based on God's foreknowledge, that God deals with men according to a series of laws and covenants is absent from Luther's teaching. It cannot be denied that it is difficult to reconcile this combination of an irrational, spiritual view of God with legalism and that the danger of disruption was always present in Calvinism.

Two corollaries of Calvin's teaching still remain to be pointed out. First, there is his view of the constitution of the Church. By 'Church' Calvin means not any single congregation, but the Church as a whole. The Church is not, as with Luther, a human institution which can be changed; it is based on Scripture and exists by divine appointment. The Church is thus the Kingdom of God on earth, the divinely appointed medium of salvation. It is ruled by Christ in a system of ordinances, and neither force nor compulsion has any place within it. Theoretically it is entirely distinct from the State. State and Church are two separate independent entities. It is the duty of the State to secure not only the material well-being of its citizens, but also purity of doctrine, but it belongs to the Church to declare what the pure doctrine is; that is the only sense in which we can speak of the State — which Calvin conceives as essentially a republic — as being influenced by the Church. It was only in after days that Calvinism, under the influence of Spiritualism, abandoned or altered this basis. The second corollary is the fact that the emphasis in Calvinism falls on the practical behaviour of the Christian. The feeling that one belongs to the elect is transformed into the sense of obligation to promote the cause of God, and thus there enters into Christian conduct that element of impersonality, method, purpose, and discipline which Max Weber has designated as "asceticism in the world within." This inward attitude is identical with what is expressed in the modern phrase "Work for work's sake."

If we compare Calvinism as a whole with the teaching of Luther, three points may be noticed:

(i) Calvin belongs to the generation that followed Luther, and he is Romanic in spirit. This explains his gift and his fondness for stating his views in systematic order and for setting the new clearly and distinctly over against the old.

(ii) Calvin was a Humanist. It was because of this that his teaching was able to hold its own against the Counter-Reformation, and it also enables us to understand the eirenical, œcumenical, and international aspects of his doctrine, which enabled him to find acceptance for his teaching among peoples who differed widely in other respects.

(iii) Calvin had closer affinities than Luther with the Middle Ages. This is especially clear from the remarkable legalism of his system of theology, which also explains the frequent association of Calvinism with Protestant sects. This legalism and the conception of Foreknowledge are the points where rational tendencies — such as those of Arminianism — could emerge in Calvinism. And there were good reasons why at the great Synod of Dordrecht in 1618 the doctrine of predestination (in a slightly modified form) was firmly reasserted in order to be a bulwark against the inroads of Rationalism. It may thus be said that the specifically Western element is stronger in Calvin than in Luther, and it is certainly not fortuitous that outside of Germany Calvinism has been the soil from which democracy in politics has arisen.

We can devote only a small space to the *after history of Calvinism*. The leading events in it were the wars against the Huguenots, the clever, but harsh policy of Cardinal Richelieu, the prosperity of the Calvinistic Church in France and the great work done by its representatives in the science of history before it was brutally suppressed by Louis XIV. Calvinism was introduced into England in the reign of Edward VI, and entered into controversy with the High Church system of the English State Church, a system that oscillated between humanistic Liberalism *in theologicis* and royalist Absolutism *in politicis*. In England Calvinism split up into Presbyterianism, Congregationalism, and Puritanism. The separation of the Puritans was brought about by the influence of German Mysticism and of Mysticism generally. Then came the rise of Cromwell, whose chief supporters were the extreme Puritan Pneumatics. These parted company with the radicals on practical questions, and solved the problems of religious toleration by adopting some of the humanist ideas of the Anglican Church. A sort of universal Christianity was made the basis of the State Church, and the other denominations, except Catholics and Anti-Trinitarians, were tolerated in proportion to the measure of their agreement with the State Church. Then followed the founding of new Protestant settlements in North America, where the principles of Congregationalism led to a complete union of civil and ecclesiastical communities, and — through the labours of Roger Williams — brought about a complete separation of Church and State, the State being regarded as purely secular and as serving only material ends. Finally, there was the contest of the Netherlands with Spain, which resulted in religious liberty for North Holland, the great prosperity that attended the study of history and philosophy in the Netherlands, the rise of a humanist rational theology, the Church reform brought about by Precisionism, the partial popularity of Mysticism, and the new emphasis on "the history of salvation" in the Netherlands. All these events and phenomena were points of contact with the coming Illumination and with the rise of Pietism.

Neo-Calvinism, which lies at the basis of the Anglo-Saxon system, and in which all the rational elements of Calvinism except predestination have been retained and developed, is a rational supernaturalism. It combines individualistic Liberalism with free competition and with humanitarian care for the poor. It includes a conservative element that clings to the outward forms of life, and this explains the high esteem felt for the Church and the type of life approved by the Church. It is the high regard felt for religion and for religious conviction that lead to separation from the State. According to Jellinek, religious liberty is the root of the idea of human rights generally, which attained world-wide importance in the Constitution of the United States of America and in the French Republic. This sheds light on the English conception of the State, according to which the State as an association for certain ends is subordinated to the freedom of the individual and to his natural rights. There is also, of course, that power which dominates both

Church and State, and which enshrines Calvin's idea of the divine law — public opinion. This public opinion of Christian citizens presents the English method of life, based on natural rights and divine providence, as moral and in accordance with the will of God. It also casts light on the English view of war as a legal and punitive process and on the moral and Christian apologetics of English politics, which, in spite of the calculated frigidity and the *naïve* brutality that characterize them, it would be unfair to dismiss as mere hypocrisy.

5. The man who 'made' the Reformation in Church and school was Philip Melanchthon (Fig. 128). In his pellucid Latin and with his clear logic he wrote the manuals that guided men's minds. He carried through the university reform that made the humanities part of the curriculum of study and encouraged the pursuit of an ideal culture that combined Christianity and the learning of the ancient world. And it was he who actually laid the foundation for the system of national Churches in Protestant countries.

FIG. 128. MELANCHTHON
Copper engraving by Dürer.

Melanchthon began as a Humanist, and his first ambition was to re-edit Aristotle. It was Luther who led him to concentrate his attention on the Bible, but later he returned to his early love. His study of the Stoics and of Aristotle introduced him to the idea of the " light of nature," which is the psychological point of connexion between the efficacy of grace and the Gospel and which is conceived as a sum of 'natural' knowledge forming a kind of bridge between philosophical and Biblical science. It is at this point that Orthodoxy veers in the direction of the Illumination, which is reached at the moment when the idea of the ruin of human nature by original sin becomes obscured. The Humanist attitude of Melanchthon also underlies his other outstanding thought, that "pure ancient teaching" (by which he means the teaching of the Fathers of the first five centuries) is a binding authority for the Christian in addition to the Bible, which — differing from Luther — he looks upon as a law book. Bible teaching, as rediscovered by Luther, agrees, he holds, with the ancient Church teaching and dogma. It was at this point that Melanchthon drew a sharp line of division between his own position and that of Pneumatics of all shades.

This revolution in theological principles leads to a revolution in his theology as a whole. The conception of faith is understood more strictly owing to the prominence given to the 'historic' faith. The invisible Church is replaced by the Church conceived as the school in which true doctrine is taught. Predestination is weakened by being made dependent on human conduct. But the chief difference is seen in the modification of the doctrine of justification. Melanchthon viewed it exclusively from the human side, and understood it to mean the comfort derived by the alarmed conscience from the 'imputation' of the righteousness of Christ. But this excision of all 'mysticism' not only makes it difficult to see why the believer must continue to do good works, but also leads to the dilemma that either the justice of God is called in question or faith is credited with having a meritorious quality.

Melanchthon was also the father of the territorial Church of the seventeenth century. He held that the Church was essentially different from the State. The former was based on the clerical office and obedience to it, whereas the latter was founded on force and compulsion. But he also maintained that the magistrate was the "superior member" of the Church, and was bound not only in special cases, but regularly, to protect true doctrine and to suppress what was false. Of course, in spiritual matters, the civil authorities owed obedience to the clerical office, and were intrinsically bound to support Orthodoxy. But de facto it was this attitude of Melanchthon that put the government of the Church into the hands of the rulers of the State.

The long-drawn out controversies on the meaning of justification and of the Supper were ended by the formula of concord, which established a modified Lutheranism. Then came the *period of Orthodoxy*. Its centre was at Wittenberg. In it the Aristotelian view of the world was combined with Biblical theology into one system, which, however, was far from having the complete uniformity that some have claimed for it. Even from the point of view of method alone the period can be divided into two parts, and owing to the 'analytic' rearrangement of the dogmatic material the doctrine of God was so transformed that it prepared the way for the deistic conception of God. In fact, during the period of Orthodoxy that followed the Thirty Years War, a large amount of helpful, unostentatious work was done in the external and internal reconstruction of the Lutheran churches and in the religious education of the people. It was at this time that the hymn-book was produced, and the religious poetry of the period bears witness to the genuine religious life that existed. It must also be kept in mind, however, that religious life within the Church at this time had assumed the character of a 'policed' life and had been degraded by compulsion. The head of the State, in virtue of his exalted position, controlled the external affairs of the Church, and that meant practically everything except doctrine.

In the midst of this official orthodox piety arose men — especially in Rostock — who desired to see a *reform of the Church* and who in some details anticipated the programme of Pietism, although they desired to preserve the Church. These men insisted on the importance of a personal experience of justification as interpreted by Luther. They were not content with a theoretical understanding of it: there must be a personal experience of it either in repentance for sin or in a sense of God's love. This, they thought, would revive and strengthen the sense of fellowship which in their judgment the religious life of the time lacked.

At this point appeared a revival of *Mysticism* throughout the whole Lutheran Church. The most prominent figures in this connexion were the subjective idealist Weigel, who was also a Neo-Platonist; Jakob Böhme, who borrowed both from Luther and from Paracelsus, and who, in order to counteract a mere 'historical' and literal faith, produced an elaborate system of dualistic metaphysic and voluntarist Mysticism; and, lastly, J. Arnd, who was, indeed, the moving spirit of this great revival of Mysticism in the seventeenth century and who sought to combine the most varied types of it. It was, indeed, the old Lutheran reading of history, which had lauded the mystics of the Middle Ages as "witnesses to the truth" during a time when the Church had fallen away from the Gospel, that prepared the way for this entrance of Mysticism into Lutheranism.

6. The seventeenth century witnessed the revival of the tendencies of the Renaissance, which had been interrupted or diverted by the Reformation. Its chief importance for the history of Western thought perhaps lies in the fact that it not only paved the way for, but also carried through, the rupture of the specifically Western tendencies in the rhythm of historical evolution, and pushed the Oriental and Christian elements into the background. The "system of nature," which cast aside all theological fetters and asserted the principle that the different departments of life are autonomous, rest on three bases: first, the science of history, which was the child of the seventeenth century, the historical century *par excellence*; second, natural science, which started with Neo-Platonist conceptions and Neo-Pythagorean mysticism of numbers, and gradually attained an independent position; and, third, philosophy, which in Descartes had definitely turned its back on the metaphysic of existence in favour of the philosophy of consciousness, and thus involved the two great characteristics of modern thought — viz., historism and naturalism. In turn this "system of nature" gave birth to the new science of

religion. It applied historical criticism and the methods of secular philology. to the Holy Scriptures, and two of its results were Hobbes' attack on the very conception of a Canon and Spinoza's historical criticism of the Bible. This new science of religion, in the hands of Herbert of Cherbury, maintained that the essence of religion was outside the sphere of reason; other thinkers reconstructed natural religion by putting together the essential elements of the historical religions, and, *vice versa,* these religions were held to represent the various modifications of natural religion under the influence of temperament and climate. The use of the same secular methods led to a new conception of the State. Starting from the idea of natural human right men now looked on the State as an agreement entered into by individuals. Its essence consists in sovereign power. It exists for the purposes of State and not for the preservation of religion. Similarly, the idea of the Church was revolutionized by the substitution of the idea of an association. The Church was regarded as an association consisting of individuals who have combined for a common purpose. The metaphysical fellowship, the invisible Church, the Body of Christ, is replaced by the ecclesiastic society, the local community. As time went on, the difference between Church and Sects became uncertain, and the very idea of the one and only Church was altogether lost.

These are the fundamental ideas of what has been called the *Illumination,* the intellectual movement that now spread over all Europe. The human mind had been roused as from sleep, and its intellectualism acknowledged no limits. Confident of its strength, it sought to distinguish in thought between Reason and Reality, between Inward and Outward, between History and the Present, between the Ego and the World, and thus to understand them all. This meant a new attitude toward history. The central ideas were now those of human solidarity and human progress. The ideal was now no longer conceived to lie in the past, but in the future, and the human race was believed to have attained a stage higher than any that had been reached in the past. Historians arranged their material according to the 'ideas' of their own day, and the ultimate subject of their study was individual men, the agents of the evolution that was proceeding. This belief in the supremacy of Reason in nature, in history, and in the human heart meant the dissolution of the historical religion. Its place was taken by the natural religion of Reason, whose essence lay in the moral effort to attain perfection. This emancipation from religion meant of course that the great time of the Church was past. From this point onward we come upon theologians, and we even meet with saints, but we no longer find outstanding leaders.

The Illumination movement presented a different aspect in the various countries of Europe. In *England* it exhibited a strain of sensuous empiricism, which gradually found its way into France. The religious philosophy of Deism — which was in itself far from being uniform — derived the positive religions, which it regarded as the creations of priestly cunning, from the normal religion of Reason, but was in turn overthrown by the æsthetic, optimistic Neo-Platonism of Shaftesbury and the sceptical Rationalism of Hume. According to these thinkers, the deistic religion of Reason is a fiction. In his psychological sketch of the history of religion Hume claimed that religion began with animism and gradually evolved into polytheism and monotheism.

The *French* Illumination exemplified the French leaning to scepticism, its fondness for criticism, and its delight in definite formulas. The movement in France was radical, not liberal. Its typical spirit was Voltaire, the Erasmus of the eighteenth century. But even Voltaire was no atheist. In spite of all his criticisms of church and dogmas, he remained all his life a believer in the religion of Reason, and wrote an interesting history of religion, including Christianity. His hatred was reserved for the Church. In France the Illumination veered noticeably in the direction of materialism, but Rousseau, the first representative of the Romantic school, wrote a criticism of civilization that passed the bounds of the Illumination, and gave to the word ' nature ' a new meaning of energy, passion, and emotion. His history of philosophy betrays more than anything else he wrote the discordance of his thought, and he vacillates between a glorification of the primitive state of nature and a worship of democratic ideals.

The leading spirit of the *German* Illumination was Leibniz. His pneumatism laid down the lines on which German theological thought was to move, and it was he who made it impossible for German thinking to move in the direction of materialism and scepticism. He was, so to speak, the hinge on which the attitude in West Europe to natural science turned toward an interest in idealism based on history. The connexion between Leibniz and German Idealism is unmistakable, and Spinoza, with whom post-Kantian speculation had many points of affinity, had drunk deep of the spirit of Leibniz. The *death-blow to the Illumination in Germany* was delivered by the greatest son of the movement, Kant. Seeing that all knowledge presupposes consciousness, and even the law of causation is nothing but a function of the understanding dealing with material supplied to it, metaphysics has no claim to be a science. There can be no knowledge apart from sensuous perception, which is arranged in accordance with the pure forms of cognition. Kant's reconstruction of knowledge starts with the most personal element in his system — viz., the categorical imperative, the absolute demand. " Here everything sinks beneath our feet." The categorical imperative is the *a priori* of the practical Reason, and its postulates are not the projections of a desire that is unsatisfied in this life, but the recognition of a reality which compels men's allegiance against their natural desires. From this Absolute Kant comes to the subject of religion. The battle in his own soul is to him only an episode in the great battle of humanity which is recorded in the Bible tradition. Then he proceeds to set forth the philosophy of the Christian religion. His theme here is the battle of good against evil, the bringing about of the Kingdom of God in the world, but he fails to solve the problem of history.

Looked at from another point of view, the Illumination, which was the working out of essential tendencies of Humanism, was a mighty movement of emancipation. It meant the emancipation of Church and of morality. It meant more naturalness, personality, humanity, and joyousness, although it also meant more luxury, more immorality and selfishness. Also, no doubt, the improved education of the people had produced a profound cleavage between the classes — the different classes had ceased to understand each other — which brought to the front the social problem, and furthered a materialistic view of life. The breach with the old civilization that was based on authority meant perhaps more loss than gain. And even with regard to the Church the dark side of the liberty of the individual and of individual toleration was the widespread tendency to regard the Church as a State. The ideal of the Illumination, however, was not merely the training of the understanding, but also the education of the heart — " Humanity." This carried with it the ideal of universal education, which in turn implied the study of sociological questions and the popularization of the sciences. At first this ideal was affected by French and English influences, but after Lessing and Winckelmann had stemmed these, it revealed an artificial naturalism and included erudite Chinese speculations which penetrated even into religious thought.

The *religion of the Illumination* was all-comprehensive. Its eyes were bent on nature. There it read harmony and adaptation of means to ends, and saw therein tokens of the wisdom and goodness of God. This created a joyousness of spirit, and awakened a sense of gratitude to God, Who thus makes " all things work together for good." [26] " How precious is thy loving-kindness, O God." [27] The reverse side of this is seen in its anthropocentric character. God's creation is designed for man's benefit, and fully justifies man's longing for bliss. This view omits important elements of Reformation thought, and even undermines the doctrine of justification. The intellectualism in this religion is less critical than positive, for it regards the truths of religion as the most reasonable things in the world. But it is also clear that the mysterious element in religion, its incomprehensibility, has vanished. Again, this strong sense of blissfulness involves an almost exclusive interest in the practical side of religion. Its truth must be simple and clear, accessible to every man, and bringing happiness to all. Simplicity is the highest quality of truth. Therefore history ceases to be the agent of the eternal; something that has happened but once can no longer be regarded as expressing the infinite; eternal truths of reason, and history conditioned by time, no longer belong together. As a farther consequence, morality is the ' purpose ' or ' end ' of religion, as well as its test, and belief in future retribution is the most powerful sanction of moral conduct. But this is to forget the inherent

[26] Rom. viii, 28.   [27] Ps. xxxvi, 7.

value and the characteristic quality of religion. Religion becomes merely one factor of civilization along with others. It loses both its roots and its contents. This conjoining of religion and bliss — Christianity is called the doctrine of bliss — this optimistic faith in Providence, this 'synthesis' of civilization and religion, are all features of the religion of the Illumination which obscure the stern tensions and contrasts that are inherent in Christianity — sin and grace, the gap between natural and supernatural, the contrast between the manifest and the hidden God. It is not unfair to say that in its harmony and rationality the piety of the Illumination is more akin to Catholicism than to Lutheranism, although the two former differ widely from each other as to the importance that should be attached to the validity of history.

But the Illumination never at any time enjoyed undisputed dominion in Germany. Side by side with it — at one with it in its individualism, though differing from it in the emphasis laid on objective and subjective irrationality — stood Pietism. This religious movement again and again influenced the German Illumination, and ultimately brought about its decline. Like the Illumination itself, Pietism was not a national, but a European movement. It was a protest against the coercion of the State Church and against the otherworldliness of Orthodoxy and the Aristotelian forms in which it was set forth. It laid special stress on sanctification of life and on personal experience of religion. All types of Pietism contained a large leaven of mysticism, in the form of " mystical theology." It was based on the teaching of Arnd, and at all times it numbered among its adherents various types of mystical Pneumatists, followers of Jakob Böhme, who revived in a splendid and scientific manner the ancient ideas and ideals of spiritualistic mysticism. Among these was Gottfried Arnold. Some of them gradually veered round to Rationalism. But Pietism proper had little in common with this radicalism, and it was probably owing to the influence of sectarianism that Pietism adopted this attitude. The various sects were made up of men who attached importance to conventicle assemblies, demanded preachers who had been " born again," emphasized the importance of teaching on the subjects connected with the future, insisted on the sanctification of their adherents, on independent Bible study without Church control, on the confirmation of their members, and practised a strict morality that came near to asceticism. Compared with the sects Pietism paid little attention to social and political questions. The complete reorganization of the social order in accordance with Christian teaching was not one of the aims of the Pietists. They maintained that it was not the world but religion that required reformation. The Pietists were thoroughly loyal, and the prevalent type of life and morality found in them a strong bulwark. Where disruption did occur, it was necessitated by local conditions.

As has been already indicated, there were various types of Pietism. One of its first advocates was *Spener*. His aim, which in keeping with the time was individualistic and therefore successful, was the renewal of the Church and the completion of the Reformation movement by the cohesion of regenerated Christian men and women. Secession from the Church had no place in his thoughts. In fact, he was in entire agreement with the ideas expressed by Luther in his preface to the German Communion service. But, all the same, these *ecclesiolæ in ecclesia* gradually became estranged from the public worship of the Church. Their minds were concentrated on punctilious scrupulousness and sentimentality, and ultimately they adopted an attitude of spiritual superiority to the organized Church. In his theology Spener followed the lines of Luther's teaching as interpreted by mystical theology, but his dogmatic positions are confined to what he calls the "fundamental truths," and by his insistence on the necessity of "experience" he dismisses quite a number of doctrines as being purely theoretical, with no bearing on "practice." It is undeniable that in other respects also there is a certain similarity between Spener's thoughts and those of the Illumination, but his real importance does not lie in the sphere of theology at all. Spener was the tutor of the Lutheran Church, and his influence on the religious thought and life of the clergy endures to this day. His whole life-work had a mediating tendency. He introduced mysticism into the Church, but it was a mysticism with a leaven of Lutheranism. It is to this mediating influence that he owes the veneration with which he is regarded as a Father of the Protestant Church, but it also implies that there was an element of incoherence, irresolution, and a lack of clarity in this good and gentle man. He was "timidly careful," and always sought the *via media*.

The Pietism advocated by the fearless and energetic *A. H. Francke,* of Halle, was based on the usual Pietist foundation, but it was characterized by a pronounced interest in practical efforts, such as education, missionary work, and the distribution of the Scriptures. Like the Quietists, Francke laid stress on a personal conversion which could be dated, and therefore he drew a line of distinction between Christians who had been born again and those who had not experienced this change. His lectures on theology aimed largely at edification and neglected — perhaps unduly — systematic theology. Partly owing to Francke's personal friendships, his Pietism was more akin to pneumatic mysticism than was that of Spener. It is also worthy of notice that the Prussian Government thought that by supporting Pietism they could best promote the policy of unity which was all along one of their own essential interests. This royal support led to considerable personal intercourse between the Franckes (father and son) and Frederick William I.

It was Spener who introduced Pietism into Württemberg. Its adherents were drawn mainly from the lower classes. The sagacious Church leaders in Württemberg kept Pietism in that country in close touch with theological learning. One outstanding representative of this tendency was *Bengel.* He gave more prominence to the Bible than to personal experience, and he laid a firm and lasting foundation for the textual criticism of the New Testament. To him the Bible was a living system governed by one idea, dealing not with Church doctrine, but with the history of God's dealings. Another distinguished son of Württemberg Pietism was Reuss. He inaugurated a new period by adopting a sober, apologetic supernaturalism. Octinger, another representative, was an intermediate link between Böhme and Schelling. He combined into an elaborate realistic metaphysic of revelation Bengel's Biblical idealism and Böhme's theosophy.

The Pietism of Zinzendorf was a remarkable combination of intense ecclesiasticism with Luther's teachings and with Moravian sectarianism. Zinzendorf himself had no leanings toward separation from the Church. He desired to see the Philadelphian community forming an integral part of the confessional Churches. That is to say, he advocated a voluntary association of Christians who loved the Saviour. Nor had he any sympathy with pneumatism as such, although he preached a mystical union with the Christ who was manifested in the historical Jesus. And yet in the strong emphasis he laid on the "universal spirit" in Christianity and in his philosophy of history, which regarded the Protestant confessions as God's methods of education, there was something œcumenical, something that transcended the confessions. And after the union with the Moravian emigrants his teaching on ethics and on the Church presented the typical features of sectarianism and reflected the early apostolic ideal.

Orthodoxy brought two charges against Pietism. It accused it firstly of subjectiveness and enthusiasm and secondly of so overestimating the value of good works that it seemed to advocate righteousness by works and libertarianism. These charges were perhaps justifiable, but Pietism continued to flourish in spite of them. The manner in which it emphasized personal and living Christianity and insisted that religion must be individually experienced and translated into life; its reprobation of confessional controversy and the importance it attached to the universal and unifying elements in the Christian faith; its strong insistence on the importance of practice; its opposition to the orthodox institutional and legalistic interpretation of Christianity — these were the features that contributed to the victory of Pietism, although unquestionably it undermined the sense of Church fellowship and weakened the foundations of the Church theology. Its individualism, its formal and æsthetic piety, are no doubt in many respects artificial, sentimental, and unreal. But it once more brought out into clear light the great thoughts of the Reformation — that faith cannot be subjected to a logical system, but must be the outcome of personal experience, and that the Church has duties toward those who are outside it. Pietism also exercised a profound influence on the intellectual life of the German people, not to say of the world. This influence extended to education and social life, and the pietist conviction that human life was divinely guided found eloquent expression in the letters, autobiographies, and novels written by its representatives. But the culminating

point of Pietism was reached in its practice of introspection of the soul, including what is subconscious, and in its resultant convictions that the human
heart cannot be understood by logical analysis of the conception of humanity
as a whole, that each human being is a separate entity, that the distinctive
element in personality is emotion and intuition.

7. It was the German poets who brought about the downfall of rational
culture and ushered in *a new Irrationalism*. Genius and intuition — these
are the two conceptions which indicate the meaning and the direction of
the new sense of life that emphasized individuality, life, and sympathy.
Hamann and Herder, the Romantic school of poetry and Goethe — the last-
named being no doubt profoundly influenced by the glorification of antiquity
which was inaugurated by Winckelmann — are the outstanding names most
closely associated with the development that set in at this period. Needless
to say, the attitudes of these men toward religion and Christianity differed
widely. Hamann advocated a deliberate return to Christianity, which was
subsequently continued by the poets of the Romantic school and roused
opposition on the part of the " legalistic" Illumination. Hamann's Christianity, which had much in common with Pietism, and was even more akin
to the teachings of Luther, was based on the Bible, and included a view of the
world that was centred in the idea of God. It was frankly irrational. In
Hamann's view God was not the meaning of life, but the mysterious principle of life which can neither be " created " nor " explained," but which must
be " accepted " and believed. Herder's position was the same. Just as Kant
had proved that the facts of the moral and therefore of the intellectual and
spiritual life have a surer foundation than those of the material world, so
Herder aroused the sense of the concrete and tried to " understand " the
world from the standpoint of the human soul, with its emotions and its
faculty of imagination. It was on this he based his interpretation of history,
in which he saw the ideal of humanity realized in a gradation of individual
types that varied in value. According to this morphological view of history,
history is the outcome of cosmos and nature; it is throughout miraculous and
transcendent. Herder found allies in the Romantic poets, whose enthusiasm
burst through all artistic forms and was hailed as the principle of art and of
science. These poets, awakened by Schleiermacher's lectures on religion, gave
a central position to the problems of the infinite, of the universe, and of
religion, and their most important work was done in the sphere of psychology
and the history of thought. It was in this direction also that Schelling's work
became important for the organology of the German historical school. Lastly,
Goethe was in deep sympathy with all the intellectual and spiritual forces of
his time. His interests included engineering, the study of antiquity, emotional Christianity, Kantianism, the natural sciences, and the newly revived
special sciences, and his creative imagination enabled him to combine them
all in his unique personality. Likewise in his view of the world he shared in
the consciousness of unity that prevailed during this period, which con-

ceived the Universal One as pervading all contrasts and consciously working out the creative evolution that tends ever upward. Spirit and matter are not opposites, but complementary to each other, and Goethe's theory of organic nature may be described as a synthesis of Platonism and Realism. His attitude to religion varied at different periods of his life, but, if we inquire what features were present in it at all periods, the following may be mentioned. He laid great stress on the immanence of the divine, although he was not a pantheist. He insisted on the realism of religion, although he found God in nature more than in the Christianity of the Church. He had a profound sense of reverence that had much in common with Schleiermacher's sense of dependence, and combined the sense of individuality with a respect for the mystery of life. He believed in a peculiar determinism which allowed an equal place to the demonic principle of self-preservation that is inherent in every living being and to the exhortation to " get rid of self." *Nemo contra deum nisi deus ipse.* There was a Protestant strain in Goethe's religion throughout, but his theory of the moral life as idealized nature or as a reconciliation of nature and spirit and his commendation of consistent character stand outside all the confessions. It is well known that under the influence of various motives Goethe modified his opinion of the Catholic idea. Human nature, purified and radically changed, and thus atoning for all mistakes, active piety, redeeming love that has been delivered from self — these constituted the Christianity of Goethe. It culminated ultimately in profound metaphysical mysteries which are only faintly adumbrated in his reflections on the future life, on the putting off of the mortal coil in monadic immortality, on regeneration through death, on the transmigration of souls, and on union with the cosmos.

German Idealist philosophy is based on Kant's theory of knowledge and on Spinoza's interpretation of the philosophy of Leibniz, and cannot be dissociated from the great poetry of the period. Despite the idiosyncrasies of the various thinkers, this idealist philosophy is ultimately a unit. Its characteristic note is its procedure from the general to the particular. It presupposes the primacy of the mind in reality, so that the unity of reality is reached in the mind by intellectual perception. With this is combined opposition to the ontology of Realism and to the " objectifying " of the mind. Schelling, for example, conceived the world as an unending process of evolution, which originates in and returns to the Absolute and in course of which the Absolute becomes conscious of itself. The " indifference " of subject and object, the identity of nature and spirit, is the Absolute: it is Reason, and becomes differentiated in order to become conscious of itself in subject and object. In the universe there is movement, and in the evolution of Absolute Reason Schelling distinguished two series — that of nature, in which the " real element," and that of mind, in which the " ideal element," preponderates. As matter unconsciously reproduces itself in ever loftier forms of nature, and as man is the point of equilibrium between the natural and the spiritual, so the evolution of the subjective proceeds with an increasing diminution of the objective in man. But nothing is purely subjective and nothing is purely objective. There are only " quantitative differences." Whatever exists is always a unity of the two. Hegel, who had been a profound student of theology and history, stands on Schelling's shoulders. But his thought was conceptual and systematic and was based on reality. He did not regard the Absolute as the " indifference of opposites," but, under the impression of the " tremendous power of the negative " he construed it as that which becomes apparent in separation and afterward unites identity and non-identity. The characteristic thought in his " phenomenology of mind " is that the transcendental history of consciousness is also at the same time the history of the upward steps of humanity. The history of the world is the self-explanation of the Absolute Mind, and the path which consciousness follows is the path of the Absolute Mind. The evolution of the world is the self-evolution of the divine idea, for the real is the reasonable and the reasonable is the real. Dialectic is the copy of the evolution of the Absolute Mind, and the history of the world is the " true theodicy." From these thoughts Hegel proceeded to work out his comprehensive and unrivalled philosophy of history. Central in it is the dialectic logic of movement based on his metaphysical view of the nature of mind. With unprecedented power Hegel arranged the material supplied by history and produced a universal history which seems to solve even the great material problems — Orientalism and Westernism, Greek thought and Christianity, European thought and Christianity.

At the centre of the Idealist philosophy is the idea of God. He must not be conceived objectively, for the Absolute is Mind. The supreme act of human cognition and of divine self-cognition are therefore one and the same. Seeing, however, that the Absolute Mind evolves as life in the world, God cannot be conceived merely as pure mind, but also concretely as the fullness of life. At the same time, the relation of God to the world is understood dialectically — that is to say, the unity of God and man implies a dialectical distinction. The contradictions are based in and disappear in the unity. As the history of the world is regarded as the self-development of Mind, and as Mind is alive in each individual, Christianity can be described as the absolute religion, the positive realization of the idea of religion. Against the background of Hegel's fine interpretation of the history of religion, Christianity is the reconciliation of God with man, in which the defects present in consciousness apart from Christianity are overcome by the knowledge of the unity of God with man. Fichte places the divine consciousness of Jesus in the very centre of the Christian religion. Hegel gives that place to the incarnation of God, in which Spirit becomes conscious of itself and thereby becomes the self-consciousness of the Christian community. He held, however, that it is not in the events of history, but in the construction put upon them that the Absolute is found. In other words, it is found in dogma. And in the same way, although Idealism regards a breach with the past and a new birth as the conditions of the new life, it conceives evil as something natural and finite, without definite content.

In this system religion and philosophy are not regarded as opposed to each other. What religion contains in the form of conception, philosophy contains in the form of idea. Idealism is believing philosophy. But religion and the Church are not ultimate ideas. Philosophy is " the rose in the cross of the present," and the juridical and moral aspects of the State are the true " subaction of worldliness."

At the beginning of the nineteenth century, however, Idealism found a rival in the *Restoration movement*. At that period, favoured by the political conditions and helped by the intellectual forces of the time, the reaction of Irrationalism against the Individualism and Liberalism of the Illumination was extended to all spheres of life. This reaction manifested itself not only in the revival of Catholicism, in the formation of the Protestant national Church in Prussia, and in the universal reawakening of ecclesiasticism and orthodoxy, but also in the great thinkers of the time, in Fichte as well as in Schleiermacher, in Schelling as well as in Hegel. The sociologically important idea of the racial mind as representing the Absolute Mind, and the profound " positive philosophy " of Schelling, which turned Idealism into the direction of Schopenhauer and has borne fruit in the most recent theological and philosophical movements, come under the same category. The same reaction is seen especially in the awakening that continued the line of Irrationalism. This movement of awakening attained great strength after the wars of liberation, and finally parted company with Idealism over the controversy with Hegel. Nearly all its representatives professed a romantic and mystical form of religion, and it paved the way for the revival of Lutheranism, of the Church, and of the Bible.

8. It was on Idealism, the Restoration, and the Illumination that the thought of the nineteenth century was based. The most important aspects of it were Neo-Humanism, Neo-Romanticism, Christianity, and Liberalism. That century also witnessed a revival of the natural sciences, which started from the mechanical explanation of nature that was current in the seventeenth century, and a development of the historical sciences, which was due to Idealism and to the national prosperity, although it fell more and more under the influence of Positivism, which favoured the various sciences. What specially characterized the nineteenth century, however, was the increasing influence of political and economic factors on the life and thought of the people, with the result that the Illumination took a materialistic direction both in Germany and elsewhere. Idealism gradually lost its speculative tendency, and Humanism and Romanticism alone remained. Since the opening of the twentieth century these mechanical and technical aspects of life have aroused a many-sided criticism. A new sense of life has recast the various sciences and made them more subjective, and has emphasized in all spheres of life the " idea," " totality," and " the Absolute." Owing, however,

to the increase of the population and to the industrialization of economic life, this criticism does not seem in any way to have weakened the influence of capitalism, socialism, and imperialism. The questions that still await future settlement are the clarifying of the " new spirit " by all the renaissances and by the historicity of its own consciousness and the contest of that spirit with the powers that dominate actual life and that have assimilated many of the features of the ancient ideology.

FIG. 129. SCHLEIERMACHER
Engraving.

In the midst of this intellectual and cultural *milieu* the science of theology had been quietly pursuing its way. Its leading figure was Schleiermacher (Fig. 129), although it was no part of his purpose to found a school. His work in dialectic and in ethics alone entitles him to be ranked among the leaders of German Idealism, but his most influential achievements lay in another sphere. His influence rests on the manner in which he emphasized the historical method of approaching the Christian faith; on the positive ecclesiastical direction which he gave to theology; on the definiteness which he claimed for Christian truth; on the stress he laid on the independence and separateness of religion in the intellectual life; and on his masterly adjustment between the value of religion in general and that of the religion whose contents are based on Christ. All the theologians of the nineteenth century have been indebted to Schleiermacher, and not only those who sought to adjust the differences between the various schools and prevented the dogmatic teaching of the seventeenth century from gaining the victory that seemed to be imminent owing to the influence of the Restoration and the Awakening. Even modern experimental theology and religious psychology have felt the influence of Schleiermacher's work. And Ritschl himself, who disliked the religious psychology of Pietism, betrayed Schleiermacher's influence in his doctrine of ' value-judgments,' although in other respects he disagreed with that great teacher's attitude toward the Bible. Beneath this broad current of Schleiermacher's influence flowed the weaker current of speculative theology, which was based on Hegel and which was represented by outstanding men in the second half of the nineteenth century. The influence of this speculative theology was greatly restricted by the application of the historical method to the Christian religion and by the disintegration of Hegelianism by Feuerbach. A third current, which was largely absorbed by the other two, was that of positive Church theology, which had its roots in the Restoration and Illumination movements. Full of the Romantic spirit, it subordinated the subjective to the objective factors on which faith rests, especially the Bible. With their empirical conception of experience, borrowed, perhaps, from the natural sciences, Hofman and Frank came very near to Schleiermacher's position, but they claimed to prove the objective, metaphysical, and historical bases of religious experience from that experience itself, without, however, being able to reach the particular and the individual. The most momentous fact in connexion with the theology of the nineteenth century was its invasion by historical science, which has borne such splendid fruit both in wider and narrower fields. It approached the fundamental question of the historical object of Christian faith by the purely historical method and with the help of comparative religion, and thus gradually brought into prominence not only the amount of adjustment that is necessary to arrive at the nature and reality of the Christian religion, but also the validity and reality of its contents. The Ritschlian school may be regarded as an attempt to reconcile the claims of historical theology and the teaching of the Church. Ritschl's views coincided with Neo-Kantianism as against Hegelianism, and many of his positions are founded on the former philosophy, but Kant's specifically theological opinions are given more prominence in the Ritschlian theology than in Schleiermacher's teaching, and the revelation of God in Christ is the source of Ritschl's dogmatics. Thus, while the history of dogma is freed from all restrictions, the teaching of Jesus and His ethics, interpreted as applicable to His own time, are isolated, withdrawn from critical discussion, and used as the basis of dogma.

The twentieth century opened with a great extension of the historical method of studying Christianity. The history of dogma was widely regarded as a part of the general history of thought and of religion, and even the development of Christian ethics was looked upon as co-operating with other general factors that are at work in civilization and sociology, and therefore the Ritschlian isolation of the Person of Jesus and of Christian ethics is regarded as impossible. Further, there are unmistakable signs that in this sphere, as in that of historical science generally, there has arisen a retrograde tendency with regard to the use that can be legitimately made of important sources, and under the influence of systematic tendencies the interpretation of the historical Jesus is beginning to move away from that which prevailed in the days of early Christianity. At the present time this obsession of history is manifested in two directions. On the one hand, it is giving renewed prominence to the attitude taken up by Schleiermacher in connexion with the phenomenon of religion as a whole. While it looks upon Christianity as the most important type of religion that has appeared, it regards it as possessing only a relative validity, and claims that its truth depends on the extent to which the presuppositions of religion are admitted to be naturally consonant with human reason. The main supports of these views are mystical and metaphysical. On the other hand, deliberate emphasis is again being laid on the specifically Christian and theological aspects of Christianity. Christianity and Idealism are declared to be opposed to each other. A new type of Irrationalism, advocated by Kierkegaard and variously expounded by different thinkers, is widely held. On various grounds they proclaim the necessity of a " diastase " of Christianity and civilization. Others see in Christianity the crisis of every civilization. By a leap from history into a sphere that transcends history, and by a flat rejection of Rationalism and Psychology, they reach their " objective " truth only in the sense of a nominalist dialectic. Lastly, there is still another school of thought, which is avowedly theological and theocentric. It draws its inspiration from Luther and German Idealism. It co-operates with the great science of history, but claims a large place for the " mystical " and " experimental," and seeks to set forth the nature of the Christian religion by speculative arguments, chiefly derived from the philosophy of history. It need hardly be said that within all these ' schools ' there are various differences and shades of thought, including different attitudes toward the Church. It must be admitted that, like other sciences, the theological thought of our day has been drawn into the universal " Irrational " reaction; in theology, as in other spheres of thought, the historical and critical methods are being replaced by the systematic method that takes due account of the history of thought.

The Protestant Church also is faced by many problems of surpassing importance. Its separation from the State necessarily raised many questions of organization and policy, but the " œcumenical " movement has brought forward other questions that affect not only ecclesiastical policy, but also religion itself. These form only a part of the problems which have resulted from the change of opinion regarding the sense of fellowship — a change brought about by theories of imperialism and democracy and which in itself has been favourable to the " Church." These problems include the attitude of the Church to the social question, to ethics in general, and to the ethics of work in particular. Owing to the increase of population, the mechanization of labour, and the general breakdown of civilization and morality these have all become burning questions, even from the religious point of view. There is also the problem of missionary effort and its task of bringing Christianity into touch with foreign peoples and thereby paving the way for the great future synthesis between Western Christianity and the East.

Most important of all is the question whether the Gospel in the form rediscovered by Luther, will display its powers in the present crisis of thought and civilization. The essential features of the Christian faith are perhaps these: the personal God, the creative Author of all — of grace and works, willing and doing; Christ, Who is not only the Revealer of this God, but also His Agent in all His work; the contradiction that underlies human life — the fact that the human ideal of " living for others " is contradicted by the egoistic impulse to " live for self "; the moral life, which is not a law to itself, but is based on a fellowship with God that presupposes a previous breach, and whose essence is expressed in the profound thought of " freedom from the law "; society or the community, which is anterior to the individual, which produces and educates him, and which is founded on the free and spiritual union of its members in God; and the recognition of personal standards of justice and politics, which does not, however, exclude the slow Christianization of public life by individual influence. There can never be a new religion for European civilization, because both the increasing complexity of life and the loss of the " spiritual " call loudly for the " simplicity " of religion. Our task is to preserve the profound thought and the historical certainty of the essentials of Christianity, and to permeate with these the thought and life of the nations and of all mankind. Christianity aims at a culture of the mind, of love, and of deed, a culture that embraces the innumerable ramifications of life and reaches the profound contradiction that underlies human life. The tasks that lie before the nations of Europe are far from being finished, but their powers are not yet exhausted, and a future world composed of new peoples and races will take up the intellectual and religious inheritance of Europe and bring it to a new birth.

BIBLIOGRAPHY

Harnack, *Lehrbuch der Dogmengeschichte* (4th ed., 3 vols., 1886–90); Loofs, *Leitfaden zum Studium Grundriss der Dogmengeschichte* (1889; 3rd ed., 1907); R. Seeberg, *Lehrbuch der Dogmengeschichte* (1895–98; 3rd ed., 1922 ff.); Meyer, *Ursprung und Anfänge des Christentums* (3 parts, 1920 ff.); Reitzenstein, *Die hellenistischen Mysterienreligionen* (2nd ed., 1920); Reitzenstein, *Das iranische Erlösungsmysterium* (1921); Cumont, *Die orientalischen Religionen im römischen Christentum* (translated by G. Gehrich, 1910; 2nd ed., 1914); Reitzenstein and Schaeder, *Studium zum antiken Synkretismus aus Iran und Griechenland* (1926); Weber, *Der Prophet und sein Gott* (1925); Holl, *Urchristentum und Religionsgeschichte* (1925); Bousset, *Die Religion des Judentums* (1903; 2nd ed., 1906); Bousset, *Kyrios Christos* (1913; 2nd ed., 1921); Weiss, *Das Urchristentum* (1914); Kittel, *Die Probleme des Palästinenischen Spätjudentums und des Urchristentums* (1926); Wernle, *Jesus* (1917); Bultmann, *Jesus* (1926); R. Seeberg, *Der Ursprung des Christusglaubens* (1914); Deissmann, *Paulus* (1911; 2nd ed., 1925); Ed. Schwartz, *Charakterköpfe aus der antiken Literatur* (vol. ii, 1910; 3rd ed., 1919); Holl, *Der Kirchenbegriff des Paulus in seinem Verhältnis zu dem der Urgemeinde* (1922); Leitzmann, *Messe und Herrnmahl* (1926); A. Seeberg, *Der Katechismus der Urchristenheit* (1903); Feine, *Die Gestalt des apostolischen Glaubensbekenntnisses in der Zeit des Neuen Testaments* (1925); Haussleiter, *Trinitarischer Glaube und Christusbekenntnis* (1920); Caspar, *Die älteste römische Bischofsliste* ("Schriften der Königsberger Gelehrten Gesellschaft," 1926); Bousset, *Hauptprobleme der Gnosis* (1907); von Harnack, *Marcion* (1921); Müller, *Kirchengeschichte* (vol. i, 1892; 2nd ed., 1924 ff.); von Harnack, *Die Mission und Ausbreitung des Christentums* (1924; 4th ed., 1924); Achelis, *Das Christentum in den ersten drei Jahrhunderten* (1912; 2nd ed., 1925); Geffcken, *Der Ausgang des griechisch-römischen Heidentums* (1920); E. Schwartz, *Kaiser Konstantin und die christliche Kirche* (1913); Mullert, *Konfessionskunde* (1926); von Arseniew, *Die Kirche des Morgenlands* (1926); von Arseniew, *Ostkirche und Mystik* (1925); Ehrenberg und Bubnoff, *Östliches Christentum* (1925); Masaryk, *Zur russischen Geschichts- und Religionsphilosophie* (1913); Nötzel, *Die Grundlagen des geistigen Russland* (1917); Scheler, *Krieg und Aufbau* (1918); Mausbach, *Die Ethik des heiligen Augustin* (1909); Scholz, *Glaube und Unglaube in der Weltgeschichte* (1911); Troeltsch, *Augustin, die christliche Antike und das Mittelalter* (1915); von Harnack, *Augustin, Reflexionen und Maximen* (1922); Holl, *Augustins innere Entwicklung* (1925); Salin, *De civitate dei* (1926); von Schubert, *Geschichte der christlichen Kirche im Frühmittelalter* (1921); von Schubert, *Geschichte des deutschen Glaubens* (1925); von Schubert, *Der Kampf des geistlichen und weltlichen Rechts* (1927); Hauck, *Kirchengeschichte Deutschlands* (1887–1904; 4th ed., 1904 ff.); Hampe, *Deutsche Kaisergeschichte* (1919); Burdach, *Vom Mittelalter zur Reformation* (1913); von Ranke, *Die römischen Päpste* (5 vols., 1834–36; 10th ed., 1900); von Pastor, *Geschichte der Päpste* (1895 ff.); Grabmann, *Geschichte der scholastischen Methode* (1909 ff.); Overbeck, *Vorgeschichte und Jugend der mittelalterlichen Scholastik* (1917); Überweg and Heinze, *Grundriss der Geschichte der Philosophie* (vol. ii, 1864; 10th ed., 1915); Bäumker, "Die europäische Philosophie des Mittelalters" (fifth article in *Kultur der Gegenwart*, vol. i, 1909); Bäumker, *Der Platonismus im Mittelalter* (1916); Grabmann, *Die Philosophie des Mittelalters* (1921); Grabmann, *Mittelalterliches Geistesleben* (1926); Seeberg, *Die Theologie des Duns Scotus* (1900); Ritter, *Studien zur Spätscholastik* (1921–1922); Troeltsch, *Die Soziallehren der christlichen Kirchen und Sekten* (1912); Preger, *Geschichte der deutschen Mystik* (1874 ff.); Otto, *Westöstliche Mystik* (1926), Lehmann, *Mystik in Heidentum und Christentum* (1918); Thode, *Franz von Assisi* (1885, 1904); Sabatier, *Das Leben des heiligen Franz* (1895, 1897); Gothein, *Ignatius von Loyola und die Gegenreformation* (1895); Böhmer, *Die Jesuiten* (1904, 1907); Holl, *Die geistlichen Übungen des Ignatius von Loyola* (1905); Wiegand, *Die Jesuiten* (1921); Rückert, *Die Rechtfertigungslehre auf dem tridentinischen Konzil* (1925); Wieser, *Deutsche und romanische Frömmigkeit* (1919); E. Seeberg, *Zur Frage der Mystik* (1921); Adam, *Das Wesen des Katholizismus* (1926); Heiler, *Der Katholizismus* (1925); Hermelink, *Katholizismus und Protestantismus in der Gegenwart* (1925); Mirbt, *Quellen zur Geschichte des Papsttums und des römischen Katholizismus* (1895, 1924); Bergsträsser, *Der politische Katholizismus, Dokumente seiner Entwicklung* (1921); Burdach, *Reformation, Renaissance, Humanismus* (1926); Mestwert, *Die Anfänge des Erasmus* (1917); Dilthey, *Gesammelte Schriften* (vol. ii, 1914); Scheel, *Martin Luther* (1917); Holl, *Luther* (1921, 1923); Böhmer, *Der junge Luther* (1925); Ritter, "Martin Luther" in *Kämpfer* (1925), also published separately; Bornkamm, *Luther und Böhme* (1925); Brieger, *Die Reformation* (1914); Weber, *Gesammelte Aufsätze zur Religionssozialogie* (vol. i, 1920); Koehler, *Die Geisteswelt Zwinglis* (1920); Müller, *Kirchengeschichte* (vol. ii, 1919); Bauke, *Die*

Probleme der Theologie Calvins (1922); Holl, *Calvin* (1909); Hirsch, *Die Reich-Gottesbegriffe des neueren europäischen Denkens* (1921); Doumergue, *Jean Calvin* (1899 ff.); Schrenck, *Gottesreich und Bund im älteren Protestantismus* (1923); O. Ritschl, *Dogmengeschichte des Protestantismus* (1908 ff.); Holl, *Die Rechtfertigungslehre im Lichte der Geschichte des Protestantismus* (1906, 1922); Holl, *Die Bedeutung der grossen Kriege für das religiöse und kirchliche Leben im deutschen Protestantismus* (1917); Leube, *Die Reformideen in der deutsch-lutherischen Kirche zur Zeit der Orthodoxie* (1924); Koepp, *Johann Arnd* (1912); Ritschl, *Geschichte des Pietismus* (1880); E. Seeberg, *Gottfried Arnold, Die Wissenschaft und Mystik seiner Zeit* (1923); Troeltsch, *Gesammelte Schriften* (vol. i, 1912; vol. iii, 1922; vol. iv, 1925); Unger, *Hamann und die Aufklärung* (1911, 1925); Unger, *Herder, Novalis und Kleist* (1922); Obenauer, *Goethe im seinem Verhältnis zur Religion* (1923); Lehmann, *Die deutsc'en Klassiker* (1921); Kroner, *Von Kant zu Hegel* (vol. i, 1921); Lütgert, *Die Religion des (utschen Idealismus und ihr Ende* (1923 ff.); Hirsch, *Die idealistische Philosophie und das Christentum* (1921); Rothacker, *Logik und Systematik der Geisteswissenschaften* (1926); R. Seeberg, *Zum Verständniss der gegenwärtigen Krisis in der europäischen Geisteskultur* (1923); Elert, *Der Kampf um das Christentum* (1921); Kattenbusch, *Die deutsche evangelische Theologie seit Schleiermacher* (1924); Weber, *Das Geisteserbe der Gegenwart und die Theologie* (1925); Frick, *Religiöse Strömungen der Gegenwart* (1923); Tillich, *Die religiöse Lage der Gegenwart* (no date).

4. ISLĀM

by Franz Babinger

According to a careful estimate the adherents of Islām, or Muhammedanism, number 250,000,000. Of these, 170,000,000 are in Asia, 76,000,000 in Africa, and about 12,000,000 in Europe. According to these figures, Islām is the religion of something like one-sixth of the human race. It is the youngest of the great world religions. It originated in Arabia, that country which seems to have sent forth all the Semitic migrations. It has been suggested that the monotheism of the Prophet Muhammed was the result of the magnificent monotony of the desert on an Arabian imagination, but a closer study of the religion called Islām proves beyond dispute that it has only an external resemblance to the religious ideas either of the desert Arabs or of those who live in settled communities, and that as a matter of fact it contains numerous elements that have been borrowed from Judaism and Christianity. In recent years Tor Andræ, the distinguished Swedish student of Islām, has given good grounds for believing that Muhammed borrowed a great deal, if not directly from the Nestorian monasticism of Syria, then certainly from an ecclesiastical religion which was strongly influenced by that form of faith. In any case, there can be no doubt at all that Muhammed drew his inspiration not from the Arabian heathenism that flourished in great strength in his native district, but from the thoughts that are fundamental in the other two world religions. With our defective knowledge of the history of South Arabian thought, we are unable to say how far Hubert Grimme is justified in maintaining that Islām was strongly influenced by the conceptions that prevailed in South Arabia. It is of course undeniable that the religion of Muhammed was profoundly affected by the civilization of the southern part of the Arabian peninsula. Taken as a whole his religion was a great advance when compared with the worship of the powers of nature and of the stars that was indigenous in extensive regions of Arabia. Muhammed took those religious ideas of his people which seemed to him to be defective — *e.g.,* worship of the constellations, fetishism, misunderstood elements of Judaism and Christianity, some features of Zoroastrianism — and combined them into a unity and a monotheism that leaves a magnificent, not to say a terrible impression. Even those elements of idolatry which seemed serviceable and suitable for his purpose Muhammed adopted and purified and reinterpreted. Thus it is not unfair to say that, leaving out of account South

Arabia (Yemen) and the northern part of the peninsula, where contact with Judaism and Christianity had already produced a higher stage of moral and religious civilization, the view of the world that underlay Muhammed's teaching was altogether different both from the religious conceptions and the social arrangements that prevailed in the Prophet's immediate environment.

The name of the religion, Islām, which means ' submission ' or ' resignation ' (that is, to the will of God), succinctly describes its central principle. To exemplify complete submission to Allah's will and precepts is its supreme goal. To obtain the favour of the one omnipotent God by unquestioning obedience is the main task of every believer. God is All Will and All Power. In His hands every creature is helpless — man and beast no less than plant and stone. This characteristically Islāmic conception of man's relation to God has been declared by some to be the result of the " divine slavery " that was practised in South Arabia. That is perhaps doubtful, but the eschatological ideas of Islām, its conceptions regarding the resurrection of the dead, the last judgment, hell, and paradise, are unmistakably borrowed from Judaism and Christianity. Muhammed had hoped that by borrowing Jewish customs he would gain the Arabian Jews for his cause, and he had expected that both Jews and Christians would hail him as the promised Messiah. It was not till a later time that he deliberately broke with Judaism. One day, shortly before the battle of Badr (A.D. 624), he turned his face in prayer not to Jerusalem, as had been his custom, but to Mecca. This was the outward sign that he had parted company with Judaism. Henceforward the eyes of the Prophet and of his followers were turned to the still unliberated Ka'ba at Mecca, from which with two hundred adherents, often erroneously called the " companions of his flight," he had fled in the year A.D. 622 to Yathrib. This city of Yathrib was from now onward called simply Medīna, " the city." This meant a very important change. The tribal association which had prevailed in Arabia since primitive times was replaced by the fellowship of the faithful. Muhammed left his kith and kin. The significance of this departure or Hegira, which is often wrongly called his ' flight,' is clear from the fact that since the time of the Caliph 'Omar the Islāmic world dates the beginning of its new era from it (July 15 or 16, 622). Simultaneously with this Hegira of the prophet to Medīna came also the transformation of the religious into the political Islām. The new fellowship of faith was organized, and the ancient tribal classification was definitively abandoned. A house of prayer (in Arabic *medjid,* hence the English word ' mosque ') was to be henceforth the meeting-place of the united believers. The bitter feeling between Mecca, the birthplace of the prophet, and Medīna, his new headquarters, grew more and more intense. In order to keep this tension alive in the hearts of his followers and associates Muhammed declared the primeval sanctuary of Mecca, the Ka'ba (Fig. 130), to be Allah's chosen holy place. There stood the black stone, which had for ages been an object of special veneration. There, too,

stood the image of Hobal or Hubal. This Ka'ba (literally ' dice ' or ' cube ')
became the centre of the faith. Round it revolved the actual worship, which
consisted of a special pilgrimage, and the sacred rite, which took the form
of a sacrifice and repeated processions round the stone. In course of time
Mecca inevitably fell into the hands of the Prophet and his followers, and
when after years of fighting and dispute that city submitted to his sway the
ancient idolatry had disappeared. The Ka'ba remained, and the religious
customs connected with it were continued. Indeed, with certain modifications the so-called ' pilgrimage ' (hajji) has lasted down to the present day.
After a short illness Muhammed died at Medīna on the eighth day of June

FIG. 130. THE KA'BA
From Mann, " Der Islam "

in the year 632. He was just over sixty years old, and had shortly before made
his last pilgrimage. He had, it is true, established a political dominion over
the tribes of Arabia such as no other ruler before him had ever possessed,
but his life-work remained incomplete. Nothing shows this more clearly
than the contents of his message.

Muhammed was far from being a logical or consistent thinker, and it is
therefore impossible to present his teaching in a systematic manner. In the
course of his life, in obedience to outward constraint or inward impulse, he
played many parts. At one moment he was a fanatical visionary, at the next
he was announcing the end of the world; now he was a patient martyr, now
a savage warrior; to-day an astute statesman and legislator, to-morrow he
was pouring contempt on worldly possessions and denying all value to

earthly life and its concerns. His incoherent thinking is clearly reflected on every page of the Korān (literally, ' recitation '), the book of the Moslem faith, written in the Koreishite dialect as spoken in Mecca. It embraces all the revelations which were regarded as passages from the divine book of wisdom and were therefore received as the Word of God. Both in language and style it is far from being uniform. The book contains 6206 sentences, the shortest consisting of one single word, the longest of sixty-eight words. It is divided into 114 chapters, called suras (Arabic *Sure*), the shortest comprising three and the longest 286 verses. It is the Bible of the Muhammedan

FIG. 131. THE GREAT MOSQUE WITH THE GRAVE OF THE PROPHET IN MEDĪNA
From Mann, " Der Islam "

world, and its language and phraseology have impressed themselves on all Moslem literature. As might be expected in a book written at widely different times and reflecting different influences, the Korān contained many contradictory and absurd statements, which gave rise to controversy and dispute. When we remember the importance of the Korān, and the fact that its commandments and prohibitions (and, indeed, all its presuppositions) are binding on every believer, it is not surprising that the prophet's immediate successors in the leadership found it necessary to purge the sacred book, to remove its confusing and contradictory readings, and to provide a purified and standard text. This was done by the Caliph 'Osmān (644–656), and it is to him we owe the present version of the Korān.

As time went on the contents of the Korān were classified, in a manner that did not always command acceptance, into two parts, called 'Meccan' and 'Medinic' according as they were believed to have been composed in Mecca or in Medīna. Even the Prophet's contemporaries could not fail to see that many of the expressions used in the Korān were ambiguous, while others were unintelligible, and already in Muhammed's lifetime it was felt that the book needed elucidation and explanation. This led to what was called the *Tafsīr,* or exposition of the Korān, which claimed to be based on authentic utterances of the "Apostle of God." Further, owing to the fact that it had been left unfinished, the Korān could not be used as a law book, and therefore, in order to regulate the religious exercises of believers and meet their social and political needs, recourse was made to another source, the so-called *Hadīs* or 'tradition.' From time immemorial the court of appeal among the Arabs with reference to what was right and legal had been traditional custom. All that was in accordance with it was regarded as true and right. This traditional custom (Arabic, *Sunna*) was the accepted rule of conduct. Although, as we have seen, Muhammed broke away from the ancient views and suspended this ancient code, he could not simply abolish this *Sunna.* He had to adapt it to the requirements of the faith he had founded, so that in Islām *Sunna* came to mean whatever had been done or approved by the Prophet and his companions and by the first generation of the faithful. The received accounts of their words and conduct and desires constitute the contents of the tradition known as *Hadīs.* In the course of the centuries this material swelled to an enormous size, and, as can be easily imagined, it included, along with well-authenticated testimonies, numerous contradictions, inventions, and additions. At first, of course, these traditions were handed down orally, but they were afterward committed to writing, with an exact statement of the authority on which they rested. Out of these collected traditions arose the well-known canonical books, which are treasured along with the Korān as sacred scripture by every adherent of Islām. The compilations of Bukhārī and of Muslim are the most esteemed, but the works of four other compilers of the traditions are received as hardly less authoritative. As can be imagined, the scholars of Islām, faced by this mass of material, justly consider it one of their supreme tasks to sift out what is genuine and expose what is unauthorized. The scientific value of these compilations, as C. H. Becker says, is that they provide us with authentic documents which enable us to see how the new religion was adapted to the new mentality that had appeared. Although Muhammed is throughout represented as the chief actor and speaker, the pronouncements are of course not to be referred to his time, but to the time when they were composed. The only historical element in them is their tendency, and, as a matter of fact, a careful study of the *Hadīs* material reflects as in a mirror the intellectual history of the first three Muhammedan centuries in the utterances of Muhammed.

It is impossible for us in the few pages at our disposal to examine these traditions; nor shall we seek to trace the external and internal history of Islām. We shall rather try to describe the peculiar features of the religion, especially in their later forms. But as soon as we look at the religious doctrines and the law book of Islām we are met by the question how this medley of religious disputation, this "rank growth," as C. H. Becker calls it, was reduced to anything like order or arrangement. The answer to the question is that the order was the result of the so-called concord or *consensus doctorum* or *ecclesiæ,* without which the consolidation of Muhammedan doctrine and practice would be completely unintelligible. *Vox populi vox dei,* or, to quote an utterance of the prophet, "My people will never be unanimous in error." This is the principle that underlies the whole development of Islām. Therefore "it is not so much by what the Korān and the *Sunna* say that we must judge the religious life of Islām, but by the accepted interpretation of the text and the meaning" (Ignaz Goldziher). It is not, however, the mass of the people who determine what this interpretation is, but the spiritual guides of the people, the scribes or lawyers. They are "those who bind and loose." It is they who expound and set forth the law. Only a correct appraisement of this *consensus ecclesiæ* explains how, in the after history of Islām, certain movements in the Moslem world have been stigmatized as heretical, although they were manifestly intended to restore the ancient pure doctrine. We shall return to this curious phenomenon when we come to speak of the Wahabis. As C. H. Becker says: "The 'catholic instinct' of Islām is a marvellous thing. This *consensus* enables it, without the intervention of councils, to attain a healthy uniformity."

The momentous importance of this consensus comes out with especial clearness in connexion with the four orthodox schools of jurisprudence, of which we shall afterward speak. Along with the Korān and the *Sunna,* this consensus determined the rule of conduct for the followers of Islām. The State, civilization, and religion were not regarded by Muhammed as different conceptions. All the actions of the faithful were guided by their religion. It governed all the activities of life.

Seeing that there was room for differences of opinion with regard to the true meaning of numerous texts, it soon became evident that it was not sufficient to know the contents of the sacred writings that determined faith and conduct. On the lines of the Canonical law of the Christian Churches in the East, a new special science arose whose task it was not only to expound the sacred texts, but also to derive from them regulations that would be legally valid. This science, which was increasingly restricted to what came to be called the doctrine of duty, led ultimately to the foundation of four schools of jurisprudence, which to this day are regarded as authoritative by all Muhammedans. These schools, which are often wrongly called sects, differ from each other in many details both of matter and of method, but chiefly in their approval or condemnation of certain acts. All four, however, are regarded as orthodox, and they practise toleration toward each other. The oldest school goes back to Abū Hanīfa, and is named after him the Hanafitic school. Then came the Malikitic, the Shafi'itic, and the Hanbalitic schools. The last-named is the most orthodox and the most rigid. So little importance is attached to the differences between them that a Muhammedan who finds that a contemplated action is forbidden by one school is at liberty to follow the decision of another school that approves it, provided he then faithfully and consistently observes the directions of the school he has chosen. The scribes (or lawyers), who are usually called in Arabic 'ulemas and in Persian *mollas,* may belong to several schools, and they are of course at liberty to give professional advice to adherents of different schools. They do not, however, constitute a religious profession in Islām. Any such professional opinion, *fetwā,* is given in accordance with the accepted law books. The chief officially appointed scribe who gave opinions of this kind was the Sheik Ül-islām, of Constantinople. These lawyers are not to be confounded with the judges (*cadis*) who administer the law in secular affairs. Another most important formal source of religious authority was what was called the " process of inference." Where the sacred writings themselves did not provide material for deciding a question of religion, recourse was had to reasoning from analogy, and decisions were borrowed from analogous cases. Thus, alongside of the Koran and the *Sunna* and the *Hadīs* there came to be a fourth source of doctrine. Needless to say, when Muhammedanism continued to spread, great toleration had to be exercised toward the customs that prevailed in the countries thus invaded. In various parts of the Muhammedan world numerous local habits and customs have survived from earlier days and have offered stubborn opposition to the new version of the faith. For example, saint-worship in Islām is to a large extent a survival of pagan practice. We shall refer to it again later. It is a difficult but fascinating task to pierce through the Muhammedan covering that has been thrown over practices that go back to primitive times and thus disclose the ancient forms of worship. Of course, similar phenomena are also found in other religions.

It will be convenient to give at this stage a short account of the religion of Islām according to the Sunnite version. The current catechisms, of which the best known is that of Birgevī (sixteenth century), usually present the religious doctrine in six articles, which treat respectively of God, the angels, the sacred books, the prophets, the resurrection and judgment, and predestination. We shall take these *seriatim.* (1) The Muhammedan idea concerning God is most briefly expressed in the words of the Korān: " Speak! Allah is the one God, the eternal God: He begets not, neither is He begotten, and there is none like unto Him " (*Sura* 112). God has therefore no local habitation. He is invisible, and has neither form, nor colour, nor parts,

He has life and knowledge; He hears all and sees all. The one God has seven eternal attributes, by which He unceasingly manifests Himself. These are life, knowledge, omnipotence, will, hearing, sight, and speech. The divine nature, clothed in these attributes, possesses forty-one qualities. These must not be confused with the ninety-nine so-called "beautiful names" of Allah, which are collected from the Korān and from tradition and are recited with the help of the Muhammedan rosary. They are frequently used to form Muhammedan names with the prefix 'Abd — *i.e.,* ' servant ' or ' slave.' The evil deeds of men, which, like their good deeds, are done with the knowledge and will of God, are classified into serious and venial sins. (2) The Muhammedan doctrine on the subject of angels is clearly borrowed from Jewish and Christian sources. These spirits are divided into various classes, and they act both as messengers of God and as guardian spirits of men. Jibril (or Gabriel) was the agent in the revelation. Another angel, who at the Creation refused to worship Adam, although he had been endowed with divine light, became the devil, Satan (Arabic, Iblis, from the Greek διάβολος). The jinn (Latin, *genius*), a name familiar to every reader of the *Thousand and One Nights,* are classified into good and evil and, in anthropomorphic fashion, into believers and infidels. They are a relic of ancient Arabian paganism. They climbed up to heaven and endeavoured to pry into the divine councils. The balls of fire which the indignant angels hurl at them are the falling stars. This indicates clearly the figurative, imaginary character of the jinn. (3) The third article of religious doctrine deals with the sacred books. These were communicated to mankind from the beginning by angels, prophets, and other messengers of God. The Law of Moses, the Psalter of David, the Gospel of Jesus, have been superseded by Muhammed's Korān, because they were misunderstood or tampered with by the so-called "guardians of the Scriptures." The Korān, on the other hand, will never be abrogated. It was revealed by Allah to Muhammed through the archangel Jibril, and communicated to men by the Prophet piece by piece in the course of twenty-three years. (4) Many prophets have been sent by God to men, but not so many Apostles. These latter were entrusted with a special mission — viz., to bring to the world the divine revelations in written form. But whereas the other Apostles of God were sent to special peoples, Muhammed's mission was to the whole world — of men and spirits — and therefore his laws and revelations will remain valid till "the end of the days." By his numerous miracles — he cleft the moon in twain, travelled to Jerusalem in a night, and ascended to heaven (Fig. 132) — Muhammed showed himself to be the greatest ·of the prophets, whose ' seal ' he is. The prophets have special endowments, chief among them being veracity, loyalty, infallibility, and sinlessness. They have the privilege of interceding with God for men. In this connexion we might refer to the worship of saints in Islām, but as the subject will be discussed later it may suffice here to say that it was absolutely unknown to Islām originally and that the Korān

(*Sura* 18, 102) expressly condemns it as polytheism. But when Islām spread to other lands and suppressed or, rather, absorbed other religions this feature was adopted, and grew all the more rapidly because Muhammed's rigid

FIG. 132. THE ASCENSION OF MUHAMMED
From " Biblioteca Asiatica "

doctrine, which admitted no mediator between the inaccessible deity and man, was not everywhere acceptable. Subsequently the worship of saints was universally approved by the consensus. It was ultimately legalized by all the four orthodox schools, and has now a recognized place in the Muhammedan religious system. Abū Bekr, the greatest of the saints, has a special position along with the other first three caliphs in this hierarchy of saints. (5) Seeing that human actions, although they are the work of God, are in their moral character determined by man himself, and are accordingly rewarded and punished in the future life, the Muhammedan conceptions of the future life were shaped by this doctrine. After leaving this world — indeed, during the first night after burial — the dead are examined by the two angels of the grave, Munkar and Nakir, as to their orthodoxy. They are required to recite the confession of faith — hence the funeral custom by which some poor men (usually blind men) walk in front of the *cortège* and recite the confession in order to assist the memory of the deceased. In the Korān and also in later speculation the doctrine of the resurrection has been greatly embellished, and various elements have been borrowed from Christianity. This is clear from the *rôle* that has been accorded to Jesus. He introduces Islām as a world religion. He is accompanied by the Mahdi and the beast of the earth. The Antichrist (*daddshal*) precedes the event. The first trumpet blast of the angel Israfīl (Fig. 133) lays all low in death; the second blast is the signal for the resurrection. Then comes the Last Judgment. The good pass over a bridge, which is as narrow as a razor edge, into the Beyond, while the wicked miss their footing and fall into the pit of hell. Paradise and hell, the narrow bridge just mentioned, the scales in which men's good and evil deeds are weighed, and the pond of the Prophet are the chief features of Islāmic eschatology. The judgments passed on men are determined in accordance with the books of the recording angels. The record of his life is given into the right hand of the good man; in the case of the wicked man it is tied on his back. All this shows that, in keeping with his type of mind, the Prophet expressed himself in great detail on this theme of "the last things." (6) According to the Korān, bliss and condemnation, like all things else in the human lot, are predestined and written down on the eternal tablets of Fate. At a later time attempts were made to modify this terrible idea, which underlies the fatalism of the Muhammedan. The scribes and lawyers differ in opinion with regard to the place of sojourn of souls till the last day. The souls of the prophets and martyrs (on the latter of whom Islām has much to say) pass immediately into Paradise, and thus escape the terrors of the Last Judgment. This explains the extraordinary "courage unto death" displayed by loyal Muhammedans in battle and in other dangers. The confident belief that he will forthwith enter on the delights of Paradise, with its countless pleasures and enjoyments, upholds the courage of the follower of Muhammed and enables him to face death undismayed. All infidels, without exception, pass straight into hell, while every one who has in his heart even a grain of faith — that is, of Islām — is delivered from hell after he has expiated the punishment pronounced on him, and may then enter on the joys of Paradise.

The chief duties that are incumbent on the faithful, the "five pillars" of the Muhammedan religion, are as follows: the recital of the creed, prayer after ceremonial ablutions, giving of alms, fasting during the month of Ramasān and the pilgrimage to Mecca. A few words may be said on some of these. The washing that precedes all prayer except private prayer can, in

FIG. 133. THE ARCHANGEL ISRAFĪL
From Kühnel, "Miniaturmalerei"

the absence of water, be performed with sand, and has therefore a ritual character. Prayers must be said five times every day — before sunrise, at noon, in the afternoon, at sunset, and two hours thereafter. On Friday, which corresponds to the Christian Sunday or to the Jewish Sabbath, the noon prayer is replaced by a more extended service of worship, which includes two sermons. In other respects Friday is like any other day — *i.e.,* it is not observed in the Western manner or as a day of rest. At the public service on Friday there must be at least forty worshippers present, and every male Moslem of full age is required to attend unless he is prevented by sickness. The hours of prayer are announced from the minaret — an imitation of the Christian belfry — by the official (*mu'essin*) whose duty it is thus to call the people to prayer. Turning in all directions he calls in long-drawn-out musical tones the words: "*Allāhu akbar* [repeated thrice] *ashadu anna lā ilāha illallāh va-Muhammadun rasūlu'llāh*"; that is to say: " Allah is great. I declare that there is no God but Allah, and that Muhammed is the Apostle of Allah." He concludes with the words: "*Hajju 'ala's-salāt*" — *i.e.,* " Hither to prayer." Each of the five daily prayings is accompanied by various bodily movements (see Fig. 134), which are strictly prescribed as to number, nature,

FIG. 134. MUHAMMEDAN ATTITUDES OF PRAYER
From Grimme, " Mohammed "

and order. The prayers consist of invocations to God and the recitation of certain passages from the Korān. With regard to the recital of the creed, it should be said that the utterance of the words, " There is no God but Allah, and Muhammed is the Apostle of Allah," implies the acceptance of Islām and binds him who utters them to the observance of the entire law. It is not necessary that he should know all the articles of the creed, but he must accept them as true. The prescribed almsgiving may be regarded as a kind of property or income tax. On movable property, such as cattle, goods, gold, and silver, it amounts usually to $2\frac{1}{2}$ per cent., on farm crops to 10 per cent. The money is used for the following purposes, which are specially laid down in the Korān — for the poor and needy, for the cost of collection, for missionary propaganda, for the redemption of slaves, for debtors who are unable to pay, for the " way of Allah," and for travellers (*Sura* 9, 60). The commandment to fast holds good for the entire month of Ramasān, the month in which the Korān was sent from heaven. During that month from early dawn till sunset the faithful must neither eat nor drink nor smoke. The practice is based on the Christian Lenten season, and is binding on all except the aged, the sick, those absent from home, pregnant women, and mothers with unweaned children. These may either purchase exemption or keep the fast when the emergency is past. The end of the month of Ramasān is celebrated by the festival which the Turks call "Little Bairām." It lasts several days, and is a time of high revelry. With regard to the pilgrimage to Mecca, every free Moslem, who is of full age and possesses the necessary means and strength, must make it once in his lifetime. He is further under obligation to observe those ceremonies associated with the pilgrimage which have survived from the heathen period. The chief of these are to wear the pilgrim dress, to spend a night on Mount Arafa, to walk seven times round the Ka'ba, and to run seven times between the hills Marwa and Safā. Further, both men and women have to shave their heads, or at least cut off their hair. This last takes place on the tenth day of Dsulhije, the month of the pilgrimage. Throughout the whole Muhammedan world an animal is sacrificed on that day, which is called the "Great Bairām."

According to the Muhammedan religious law, all things are divided into clean and unclean. As is well known, pork and wine are forbidden, but it is not so well known that music is also prohibited. There are also a large number of rules of etiquette, some of which can be traced back to primeval religious customs. This subject has not yet been fully investigated, but many of the rules are interesting. For example, salutations must be given with the right hand only, because the left hand is used for unclean purposes. The use of toothpicks is recommended, and circumcision is highly praised. Although this last-named rite is not obligatory, it is universal in Islām. It is probable that many of these customs were borrowed from Judaism. The catechisms that have been mentioned enumerate many of these rules of etiquette. It is quite erroneous to suppose that images are forbidden in Islām. Dislike of images, especially of those that cast a shadow, is occasionally expressed, but it is due to an exaggerated interpretation of Muhammed's polemics against the idolatry that prevailed among his compatriots. Pictures of trees, plants, and inanimate things were never at any time forbidden.

The juridical and political principles of Islām are also of great importance. The "sphere of Islām" (*dār al-islām*), meaning the territory under Muhammedan rule, is contrasted with the "sphere of war" (*dar al-harb*). According to the Korān, the inhabitants of the latter have legal rights only when treaties have been made with them. Jews and Christians, who are designated as "possessors of the writings," must be treated as enemies until they pay tribute or tax; heathens must be similarly dealt with until they accept Islām. Even Muhammedans themselves are not all equal before the law. Their status varies according to their age, sex, standing, and state of health. The free Moslem may have four wives at the same time; the slave is allowed only two. Marriage between those who are of the same kin is forbidden. There is no community of property, and the wife retains all that is her own. The husband is entitled at any time to send his wife away, and is responsible to no one in the matter. Children of slave wives are counted as legitimate, and the slave mother herself cannot be sold; when her husband dies she is a free woman. The law that compels women to be veiled is of late origin; it seems to have been unknown to ancient Islām. The law of in-. heritance is very complicated, and the estate of the testator and that of the heir are not regarded as being the same. The heir is not responsible for the debts of the testator. Buying and selling, gifts and bequests, cautions and writs, letting, leasing, and lending are all strictly regulated by religious law, although theory and practice do not by any means always coincide. In fact, there are very few Muhammedan countries where the ancient Muhammedan law is in force to-day. It has been replaced almost everywhere by European legal practice. A conspicuous example is provided in Turkey, where within the last thirty years Western legal methods have been gradually introduced, and hardly anything of the old system remains. At the present time — leaving Arabia out of account — Afghanistan is the only Muhammedan country which still retains the ancient, barbaric religious laws of early Islām and thus to some extent cuts itself off from the rest of the world. In view of this restricted range it is unnecessary to say more about this side of Muhammedan law. With regard to the political constitution of Islām, the supreme head of the Muhammedan world is the Caliph. He is elected by the faithful. To be eligible for election he must belong to the Koreish tribe, be of blameless life, have no physical deformity, be versed in Moslem doctrine, and be capable of defending the faith and of waging the holy war. As is well known, the last Caliphs belonged to the house of 'Osmān. The 'Osmānic caliphate began in 1517 and lasted till March 1924, when it was brought to an end by Mustafā Kemāl Pasha, the creator of New Turkey. Recent researches, especially those of the Russian scholar W. W. Barthold, have proved conclusively that the claims of the house of 'Osmān to the caliphate were unfounded, and it may be added that the recognition of the Sultan of Turkey as caliph was far from being universal throughout Sunnitic Islām. How little influence the Sultan had, at least in recent years, on the Muhammedan world at large is clear from the poor response that was made to his call for a holy war. In the Great War Moslem fought against Moslem and paid little heed to the *jehād* proclaimed by the Caliph.

A glance at the history of Islām from the beginning of the caliphate to its close in 1924 shows that Islām acted with very great tolerance toward the laws of custom that prevailed in the various countries that had accepted the religion. But while this amazing adaptability of Islām to foreign races, manners, customs, and religions adds greatly to the interest of the study of its history, it also increases the difficulty of presenting a clear view of it. The most important features in its long history are the gradual growth of the Moslem faith into a theological system, the rapid rise of Persian influence, and the dogmatic differences that soon arose within Islām itself. We cannot enter here into the external history of Muhammedanism, because even a short account of it would carry us beyond the limits of the space at our disposal. With extraordinary rapidity — indeed, within a few decades — the religion founded by Muhammed spread over the whole of Arabia, Nearer Asia, North Africa, and Persia. Everywhere it had to face long-established religions, chiefly Oriental Christianity and Zoroastrianism. It had perforce to take over many foreign religious opinions, which affected all aspects of life, political and economic, artistic, and literary.

As is well known, Muhammed left no male heirs. His successor, the first Caliph, was Abū Bekr (632–634). Then came 'Omar (634–644), 'Osmān (644–656), and Muhammed's son-in-law 'Alī (656–661). Thereafter the Omayyads seized the caliphate and made Damascus their city of residence, till they were overthrown about 750 by the 'Abbāsids, who transferred the chief seat of the empire from Damascus to Bagdad. It was from Bagdad that the 'Abbāsids ruled the Arabian empire from 750 to 1258. It was from Bagdad that the Caliph Hārūn al-Raschīd sent to the Court of Charlemagne at Aix-la-Chapelle that embassy round which so many legends have gathered. When the caliphate of Bagdad fell at the hands of the Mongols the Muhammedan empire broke up into separate states, whose history cannot be followed here. The Mongols themselves accepted Islām, and infused it with a new strength that manifested itself in many directions. It was mainly due to them that the religion of Muhammed found entrance into India and even into the lands farther east. By and by the Ottoman Turks became the most powerful Muhammedan state. Expelled from their home in Central Asia, they continued to force their way westward till they subjugated the whole Balkan peninsula and came up to the very gates of Vienna.

This brief *résumé* shows that in the course of the centuries Islām was adopted by various peoples who had little or nothing in common. In some cases this was done voluntarily, in others it was brought about by force, and each people adopted it in its own way. It need hardly be said that Islām was no exception to the usual fate of all religions — viz., that of being split up into sects. This process began as soon as it passed the frontiers of its native Arabia. In particular Persian influences made themselves felt. I. Goldziher justly says that the Muhammedan occupation of 'Irāk and the centres of Persian civilization was one of the most momentous events in Moslem history. "Persian religious leaders," he says,

> carried over into the newly adopted religion the mentality they had inherited, and as at the time when Islām was accepted by the Persians it was still an incomplete system, the new converts had an opportunity of adding to it many features which were destined to become very prominent.

For example, the original hours of prayer in Islām had been three in number; under Persian influence they were increased to five. The early Muhammedan ideas of ceremonial cleanness and uncleanness were profoundly modified when they came into contact with the religious customs of Persia. As so often happens, the religious divisions of Islām were the result of political differences. In this case they were due to the secularization of the caliphate under the Omayyads, whose rise to power was unacceptable to many of the faithful. From the doctrine that whatever Allah permitted to happen must be patiently borne by man, many drew the conclusion that the new secular power should be obeyed. Discussions on the freedom of the human will led to still further disruptions. Some asserted that the human will was free, and these formed a party which sought to gain adherents to their views. Nor were these the only subjects of controversy among the religious leaders. The doctrine of predestination and the authenticity and authority of the Korān were keenly debated. Differences of opinion on these and other questions led to the founding of schools, which were constantly occupied in disputation with each other. It is impossible to follow here all these dogmatic discussions and dialectical and casuistical disputes. They were intolerably prolonged, and the appearance of Ghazālī (who died in 1111) came like a deliverance. He declared that religion should be regarded as an inward experience, and condemned all merely scholastic treatment of religious questions. He published a complete system of the Moslem religion in a book to which he gave the proud but justified title, *Revivication of the Religious Sciences*. Ghazālī has been deservedly called Muhjī ed-din, "the Restorer of Religion." He is the greatest "Church Father" of the Muhammedan world.

Of far greater and more lasting importance than these long-buried dogmatic controversies is the schism known as Shī'a, the most important and profound deviation from the Sunnite form of Islām. Shī'a, which means "the party" (that is, of 'Alī) includes all degrees of 'Alī homage. As is well known, Muhammed left no instructions regarding his successor, and vehement disputes on the subject were the inevitable result of this omission. Abū Bekr, the Prophet's companion and friend, was declared by some to be the only legitimate successor, while others claimed the position for 'Alī, Muhammed's son-in-law, on the ground that only a descendant or relative of the Prophet was eligible either as successor or Caliph. Without having realized his ambition 'Alī was assassinated in the year 661, and his son Hasan was nominated as the Prophet's successor by his followers. Hasan, however, renounced the caliphate in favour of Mu'āwiya, the Governor of Syria, and the 'Alī party transferred their support to Hasan's brother, Husain. He too, however, along with his companion, was slain in 680 at Kerbelā by his enemies. The dead Husain now received a share of the homage paid to his father, and his grave at Kerbelā became the favourite place of pilgrimage of the Shī'ite party. From the constitutional point of view, therefore, the Shī'a is based on a renunciation of the caliphate, which in its turn rests on the *consensus ecclesiæ.* The Shi'ite party accordingly declare that the three Caliphs who preceded 'Alī were impudent usurpers. They also maintain that after 'Alī's death the caliphate, or, to speak more accurately, the *imamate,* belonged to the descendants of 'Alī by right of inheritance. For centuries this party sought to achieve their purpose by revolts and conspiracies. Meanwhile the 'Abbāsids had long been engaged in undermining the power of the Omayyads and seeking to step into their place. The Shi'ite party itself was not at one on the question of the succession. They believed that every period has its own Imām, but they could not agree as to his qualifications, nor as to the person who should hold the office. The party split up into numerous sects, and many aspirants to the throne — as apart from the caliphate — utilized these divisions to obtain a brief tenure of power. Some of these made use of the name of Mahdī (" the Rightly Guided One ") as a means of gaining their object, and this was the first of many similar Mahdist movements. The most recent attempt of the kind was the Mahdist revolt between the years 1881 and 1885, in the Egyptian Sudan. Neither Muhammed himself nor early Islām had anything to say about a Mahdī — that is, a Messiah — who was to come. Christopher Snouck Hurgronje has justly pointed out that all the Mahdist prophecies speak of a period of religious and political unrest which would only be ended by the Mahdī, the good and righteous Caliph. Needless to say, the Prophet could foresee neither these periods of unrest nor their repression. As a matter of fact, in Muhammed's day the end of the world was believed to be not far distant, and the early tradition saw in the mission of the prophet himself one of the signs of the approaching catastrophe. There can be no doubt that the idea of the coming Mahdī was borrowed by Islām from Christian teaching about the return of Jesus.

The essential qualities of the Imām include sinlessness and infallibility, and most of the differences between the Sunnites and the Shi'ites are solely concerned with the teaching about the Imām. It is not too much to say that the Shi'ite religious law does not differ from the Sunnite teaching more than any one of the four orthodox schools already mentioned differs from the others. Perhaps the most remarkable feature of the Shi'ites is their bitter intolerance of other sects. Their fundamental claim, that only direct descendants of 'Alī by his wife Fātima (Muhammed's daughter) can legitimately occupy the Moslem throne or hold the dignity of Imām, makes them regard any other holder of the caliphate as a usurper. This constant protest against the constitution as settled by the Idshmā of the Islām state found expression in countless revolts and struggles on the part of the 'Alī party. In spite of decisive defeats, they refused to submit or to give allegiance to any other than their own Imām of the age. But while they thus rejected the constituted authority, they adopted a policy of pretended submission to it, and under cover of this pretence they continued to carry on an extensive secret propaganda and founded secret societies of all kinds. Indeed, almost all the secret societies that have arisen within Islām can be traced to the

partisans of 'Alī. Ignaz Goldziher was the first to call attention to one remarkable result of the constant danger to which the adherents of the Shī'a
have always been exposed — it gave rise to the ethical theory that goes by
the name of *taqiya* (literally ' caution '). According to this theory, the Shi'ites
not only *may*, but *must* conceal their real faith. Living under a Government
that is hostile to their religious convictions, they maintain that it is their
duty to speak and act so as to deceive their enemies. In the midst of conditions that continually threaten their lives the Shi'ites not only allow, but
require their adherents to conceal their real convictions and to conform outwardly to formulas which in their hearts they condemn. Needless to say,
this injunction to conceal their true faith in the midst of a hostile environment, and even on occasion to profess acceptance of the heresy that holds for
the time the reins of power, necessitates a course of equivocation and deception that constitutes a blot on the principles of the Shi'ite sect. As we
shall see later, Leopold Weiss has endeavoured to explain this attitude as
the result of the history of Islām in Persia, but the psychology that underlies this doctrine of *taqiya* has not yet been investigated. The mere proof
that it exists does not go far to explain it. It seems to be the case, however,
that it is not found outside of Persia.

Numerous ramifications of the Shī'a have appeared and disappeared in
the course of the centuries. One of the most widely distributed is the so-called
sect of the Twelvers or the *Imāmiyya*. They are so named because the members believe that the twelfth Imām, who mysteriously vanished in his youth,
still lives in some secret place, and that he will reappear at the " end of the
ages " to purge the world from wrong and establish a kingdom of righteousness. This type of the Shī'a faith has been the State religion of Persia since
1502. A more moderate type, one that came much nearer to the orthodox
Sunna, was represented by the Zeidites. They maintained that the fifth Imām,
a grandson of Husain, Zeid by name, was the legitimate Imām. This sect
gradually split up into a number of subdivisions, one of which has still
numerous adherents in South Arabia, and several ruling dynasties, like the
Idrīsids, base their claims to royal power on their descent from Zeid. Much
more noteworthy are the so-called Ismāilis, also known as the Seveners, because they hold that the line of visible Imāms ended with the seventh Imām,
Ismāil. Their doctrines are an extraordinary medley, including a large admixture of apparently Neo-Platonist conceptions. They employ mysterious
formulas in teaching their religion, a practice which made the sect extremely
useful for political purposes. The Fatimid dynasty trace their origin to this
doctrine of the Seveners, and peculiar sects like that of the Druses seem also
to be offshoots of the Ismāili movement. The well-known murderous sect
of Assassins, which attained great prominence during the time of the
Crusades, was another side-shoot of the Ismāilis. It was founded by a certain
Hasan of Rai, near Teheran. In 1081 he began to gather round him a number of devoted Persian youths, whom he succeeded in inspiring with fanatical

zeal for himself and his ambitions. He made great use of a strong intoxicating liquor prepared from the leaves of the hashish plant. Among the Franks the name of these " hemp [or hashish] eaters " was corrupted into ' assassins,' a word which still survives in the Romance and other languages. The fearful outrages of these fanatics were brought to an end by the Mongolian Prince Hulagu in 1256. Traces of the Seveners can be found to this day in some parts of Nearer Asia, although the present adherents of Ismāili seem to have abandoned much of their chaotic secret doctrine. Western scholarship is faced with great difficulties in trying to study this system. Its doctrines are either concealed under an impenetrable cloak of mystery or deliberately misrepresented. An example of the boundless extravagances of this sect is supplied by the secret doctrine of the Hurūfīs, or " Letter-interpreters," who invented an extremely subtle symbolism of the letters of the alphabet and their numerical values. They were very numerous in Anatolia in the fifteenth century. The accounts of this system that have come down to us have been carefully investigated by E. G. Browne and others, but its origin and nature are still obscure. It has numerous points of contact with the doctrines of some of the dervish fraternities, especially that of the Bektashi order. Brief mention may also be made here of two other well-known sects. One is that of the Nusairis, who live in the valleys of Lebanon. To them 'Ali is actually divine, and forms along with Muhammed and a Persian saint called Selmān a divine trinity. Primitive heathenism, that has shown a remarkable tenacity of life in these Lebanon valleys, is conjoined in this sect with elements borrowed from Christianity and reclothed in a Muhammedan dress, and still survives in these secluded vales after thousands of years. The other sect referred to is that of the Jezīdīs, who live in the neighbourhood of Mosul, and are also found in Armenia, Persia, and even in Turkestan. They worship seven deities, and as Good and Evil are included in the number it has been justly inferred that Persian influence has been at work among them. Special interest attaches to the Ismāilis from the fact that their acknowledged head is the well-known Aga Khan, a man of great wealth, who lives in Bombay and who has recently become a conspicuous figure in Western society. He is the president of the All Moslem League, and is *persona grata* with the English Government, because he has done much to reconcile his adherents to the existence of British sovereignty in India.

Like Persia, India may claim a special place in the history of Muhammedanism. The remarkable diversity of races and religions that is found in India has given rise to a large number of special types that are worthy of notice, although most of them have now little in common with Islām. We have already referred to the influence exercised by India on the later development of Islām. The varied religious life of India, with its numberless sects, could not fail to leave traces on the religion of Muhammed as soon as the two came into contact with each other. It is the task of future research to bring out clearly the results of that contact. Indian and Central Asiatic influences undoubtedly underlie the appearance of Dervish orders and of Sufism within Islām. We can no longer shut our eyes to the fact that, in the later evolution of the Moslem religion, these influences have been at least as powerful as that of Arabia or of Nearer Asia. The more intensive study that has been directed to the subject in recent years has already proved that Indian and Central Asiatic doctrine has found its way into Islām to a far greater extent than even men like A. von Kremer and I. Goldziher were prepared to believe twenty or thirty years ago.

On the other hand, when Islām entered India it was inevitably affected by Indian thought. It has been justly said that nowhere else had the religion of Muhammed to digest and absorb so many non-Moslem features as in India, and that it is in India and the adjacent islands that the most striking mixture of Muhammedan and pagan religions is to be found. I. Goldziher says:

> Side by side with an Allah-worship that is purely outward, with a use of the Korān that is merely superficial, and with an unintelligent obedience to Muhammedan usages are to be found demon-worship and ancestor-worship and various other animistic practices.

The space at our disposal will not allow us to say more about these modified forms of Islām in India. Numerous special studies deal with the survival of Hindu faith in Muhammedan dress and with the mixed beliefs of the Moslem inhabitants of the East Indian islands. English and Dutch scholars have given special attention to these phenomena. *Vice versa,* the effects of Indian Muhammedanism on the native religions with which it came into contact are equally apparent. We need only refer to the doctrines of Kabīr, a weaver and one of the twelve Apostles of the school of Ramananda, and to the Sikh religion in Northern India founded by Nanak, a disciple of Kabir. The Great Mogul Abu'l-fath Jellāledin Muhammed, more widely known as Akbar the Great (sixteenth century), longed to unite all the various religions of his mighty empire into one. In his endeavours to realize this desire he sought to spread many of the fundamental ideas of Islām, but his system, which he called " monotheism " or " the religion of Allah," did not outlive its founder. What is probably the latest sect of Islām in India, arising at the end of the nineteenth century, will be described later.

All these varieties of Muhammedanism are of quite subsidiary importance when compared with what is called Sufism, a form of Muhammedan mysticism coloured by pantheism. It is the outstanding example of Indian influence on Islām. Recent research has established the fact that even in early days Indian elements were adopted by Muhammedanism, probably through literary channels, and there are incontestable proofs that at a later stage Indian thought influenced the leading minds of Islām. In the middle of the ninth century, especially in Mesopotamia, the Indian itinerant monks had already found imitators and it cannot be doubted that the Christian ascetic model was also at work here. The anchoretic spirit of the mendicant monks of Islām, as described in the accounts that have come down to us from the ninth century, seems to be closely akin to certain doctrines of Buddhism, and as is well known, the legend of the Buddha reappears in many of the stories told of Muhammedan saints. The problem of the origin and early history of Sufism has recently engaged the attention of several students of Islām. According to the instructive account of it given by Richard Hartmann, it seems quite clear that Sufism originated in Khorassan, and probably in the eastern part of that territory. In order to complete the history of Muhammedan mysticism it is therefore important to know what religions were indigenous in Khorassan and Turkestan before the Moslem conquest. Hartmann has pointed out that before that conquest Turkestan was the actual central point of the world's commerce. There lay the junction of the great caravan routes which united the distant East with Persia, and it was there that important trade routes branched off to India over the Hindu Kush. In Turkestan, therefore, there must have been a mixture of civilizations that included elements of all kinds. Of these influences, that of India will not have been the least powerful. Besides, it must be remembered that all the great religions of Nearer and Central Asia, especially Parseeism and Buddhism, were represented in Turkestan. Recent researches into the civilizations of Central Asia have shown that Nestorian Christianity and the Mani religion played a part whose importance is being increasingly recognized. With our present defective knowledge of the intellectual life of Central Asia and of Persia during these centuries we are unable to say exactly how far they affected Muhammedan mysticism. Sufism after all was a part of Muhammedan civilization, and that civilization was far from being a unified whole, and, besides, owing to its mystical character, Sufism can hardly be said to have a history.

Already at the end of the eighth century the advocates of the ascetic view of life had begun to meet together in houses and monasteries for penitential prayer. They laid down strict regulations for membership in the Sufi societies. The " reception of the dress and of the rule of the order," which symbolized admission to membership, has many points of resemblance to Indian practices. Also the mendicant orders of Islām, who do not live in monasteries, but go about singly, are palpable imitations of Indian and Central Asiatic orders, and it has already been said that the rosary, which has played a special part among the Sufi orders, came from India. The rules vary greatly in the different orders, and our knowledge regarding them is still incomplete. They seem to be as diversified as the orders themselves that have arisen in the course of the history of Islām. The oldest foundations seem to go back to the twelfth century, but at least one influential order, that of the Senusi, came into existence as recently as 1835. It would be a mistake to imagine that the dervish societies in any way resemble Christian monastic orders. Very few of them live together in monasteries. The fraternities resemble religious clubs, whose membership includes representatives of all classes and callings. Hence all attempts like that of Mustafā Kemāl Pasha to suppress the dervish orders in Turkey are likely to prove unsuccessful. These fraternities will continue to exist in secret, and cling to life all the more tenaciously because of the efforts to suppress them. It is a complete mistake to suppose that all the dervish orders practise those extravagant penitential exercises and impostures of which we read in books on Indian travel or in accounts of howling dervishes. The best and most ancient orders are entirely free from all such extravagances. It is true that the Mevlevis, who are perhaps the most distinguished fraternity, perform a curious whirling dance (Fig. 135), but the movements are not extravagant, and the dance is not accompanied by any of those self-castigations which are practised by other orders.

The same desire as is evinced in the Sufite love-union with God for intermediate beings who s h o u l d bridge the infinite gulf between God and man is apparent in another feature which is entirely alien to original Islām — viz., the worship of saints. It is this, along with the multifarious orders of which we have spoken, that gives the Muhammedanism of the present day its motley character. We know little as yet of the psychological presuppositions which favoured the intrusion of this new feature and even rendered it necessary. But there is no doubt that the native religions of the numerous lands over which Islām had spread assisted its introduction and fostered its growth to such an extent that in many instances it displaced divine worship proper. Like the worship of saints in the Christian Church, it was associated with ancient holy places and the graves of holy men, and it is one of the most fascinating as well as one of the most intricate problems

FIG. 135. DANCING DERVISHES
From " Biblioteca Asiatica "

to follow out the strange fusion of Christian and Moslem saints which is found everywhere. These ancient conceptions which Islām found and recast are perhaps nowhere so abundant as in Nearer Asia, especially in Anatolia. In no other sphere was there more adjustment of the original teaching of Islām to meet the needs of its new converts than in that of saint-worship. A competent scholar like I. Goldziher declares that it was " the 'Alī legend " which chiefly inspired the new worship of saints, because it supplied a framework for the fragments of religions that Islām had destroyed and of doctrines that differed from Muhammedan teaching. Even if that be the case, the worship of saints still calls for explanation. The original elements in matters of faith are neither doctrines nor conceptions, but experiences of a quite unique kind. The idolatrous worship of a living master could of itself easily lead to the Imām worship of the Shī'as. Every attentive reader of the Persian and Turkish *wilājetnāme* or lives of saints, which are full of the miraculous deeds of the so-called mystical sheiks, must have noticed this. But the 'Alī cult leads directly to Sufism, and the remarkable connexion between the dervish system and the Shī'a is therefore not at all fortuitous. The same can be said about saint-worship in Islām. Asia Minor is specially rich in holy places and in graves of pious sheiks and holy men (*baba* and *dede*), hidden away in the shade of ancient plane-trees and cypresses, and thither the faithful people resort to find help and strength in their times of need. Christian saints of olden days and even heathen idols, reclothed in Moslem raiment, are still worshipped. But in addition to these ' adopted ' saints there are also a number of what might be styled " utraquistic " saints both in Asia Minor and in Thrace and, indeed, throughout the south-east of Europe, to whose graves Moslem and Christians alike make pilgrimage. A few examples may be given here. North of Dishbudak, on the farther side of the Batova valley, below the level of the plain of Dobrudja, lies the village of Tekke, with a dervish monastery, of which K. J. Jireček tells the following curious tale.

> The saint of this monastery is a remarkable, utraquistic man. To the Turks he is Akjasyly Baba, to the Christians he is St Athanas. Both Christians and Muhammedans resort to him for advice when their cattle are stolen.

Another extremely curious figure in the 'Osmānic hagiography is the saint known as Sary Saltyk Dede, a reputed disciple of Hajji Bektash. He is said to have been born in Bukhara, and he is held in great honour to this day in the Balkan district. In his last will and testament he commanded his disciples to bury him in six or seven coffins in distant infidel lands, so that, being uncertain where his remains really lay, Moslems might make pilgrimages to all seven graves and thus gradually bring about the inclusion of these countries in the Mohammedan dominions! According to the story, one of these graves was in Danzig. A large number of similar examples is given by the 'Osmān traveller Evlija Tshelebi in his book of travels, which is a mine of detailed information about Turkish saints. He relates several stories about a Turkish saint whom the Christians call St Nicholas. Another famous saint in Sejjid Battāl, whose grave is a once famous Bektashi monastery in Anatolia, and whose connexion with Christianity was acknowledged in his fictitious biography. Lastly, mention may be made of St George, who was transformed into the Moslem Chisr Iljas and is worshipped in many places. There are also sacred springs, called *ajasmas,* which are visited both by Moslems and Christians on account of their healing virtues. When we follow the history of those Muhammedan saints whose holy places are situated in Nearer Asia we find that many of them were men who left East Persia for the West from the thirteenth century onward and finished their days in the odour of sanctity. Their graves became the resorts of pious pilgrims, many of whom came long distances to pray for their heart's desires. The nearer we come to the actual home of Muhammed, the more arid and rare becomes saint-worship, although there are many holy places scattered throughout Arabia. And the farther east we go, toward Persia, the more widespread it becomes. There must be special reasons for this, and it is instructive to consider a theory which professes to explain this aspect of Islām on Iranian soil. The theory in question seems to have been first put forth by Alfred Freiherr von Kremer. It was supported and developed by Baron Bernard Carra de Vaux, and has in recent days been formulated by a young Austrian traveller who was unaware of the fact that it had already been suggested. It is in itself so attractive and contains so much truth that it is worth while to consider it at greater length. It certainly deals with one of the most important questions in connexion with the later development of Islām.

Leopold Weiss, the author of a clever book of travel entitled *Unromantisches Morgenland,* recently delivered a lecture in which he supplemented his former statements about the psychology of the Persian people and brought out the connexion between that psychology and the conditions under which the Persian people adopted Islām as their religion. Every sensitive observer of Persian life immediately notices that the Persians are a melancholy people, a people who carry about with them a heavy, invisible Fate. Living inactive lives amid an atmosphere of indifference and *laisser aller,* they maintain an attitude of reserve toward outsiders in the most important affairs of life, and they are thus often regarded as suspicious and deceitful. A certain melancholic temper is common to them all, and varying grades and shades of this melancholy, together with geographical conditions, are responsible for all the differences between the racial types throughout the country, so far as these are of Persian origin. And yet it is easy to see that this sadness, or, to put it more accurately, this joyless quietude of spirit, is by no means a basic note of the Persian soul. There are times when these people, sad and dejected as they are, with their dark, shrouded eyes, respond like children to natural cheerfulness; yet, like so many Kaspar Hausers, divining the presence of light, but unaccustomed to it, they grope their way about awkwardly, and become stupid through embarrassment, although they betray hidden gleams of yearning. They are a people whose longings have been stifled. They have no desires beyond the day's life, and in their hearts there is neither hope nor despair. Their indolence is not of the expectant kind. It is that of men who have abandoned all attempts to improve their life and who are content to allow their real nature to slumber amid the shadows of their twilight existence. They are a people with a distorted visage, who do not show even to themselves their real face. It is possible, however, that from this, the darkest and, for Europeans, the most perplexing feature of Persian mentality — viz., its capacity for religion — a ray of light might come which would clear up conditions in Persia and elsewhere throughout nearer Asia. Leopold Weiss believes that the present condition of the Persians is due to the manner in which they came into possession of their present religion. At a time when Zoroastrianism had long lost its power and could no longer offer effective resistance to the triumphant Muhammedan faith Persia was *subjugated,* not converted, to Islām. It was then, says Weiss, that occurred that psychical breach which makes the Persians to this day the most enigmatical of all peoples. This compulsory acceptance of a new faith brought by an alien people could not fail to work like a hidden poison in the Persian body politic with its great history and, as a daily and hourly reminder of their national weakness, irreparably destroy all self-consciousness and all faith in their own capacity for a national life. This is what Islām has done in Persia. It is a strange play of powers which among the Arabs, on the one hand, have promoted so manifestly the growth of all rational qualities and among the Persians, on the other hand, have brought about the most calamitous results that can befall a people — the repression and death of their own characteristic qualities.

The Persians as a people have been forcibly dispossessed of all that is truly their own, and in this fact we find the explanation of all that is perplexing in their existence. Their historical continuity, the organic connexion between their past and their present, was suddenly broken. An Aryan people, with a deep strain of gentle romanticism, allowed the ethos of the desert to be forced upon them. The social and profoundly personal discipline of the Korān, confining individual liberty within a harsh legalism, was hardly compatible with the mystical rhythm of Persian life, which was based on the ideas of master and slave. Therefore life under law, the liberty of fettered power, could not fail to break out as fanaticism, which is at the other extreme from law. What to the Arab meant calmness and freedom, real life in the present, swung to the opposite extreme, transcendentalism and legend. The utterly alien Arabian religiosity had to run to extremes in the Persian soul in order to conceal its alien nature and hide from the Persians their subjugation and their loss. Thus Leopold Weiss sees in Shī'a, which is the dominant type of Islām in Persia, the revenge of Persia on Islām. He justly emphasizes the curious fact, familiar to every one who has talked with native Persians on religious subjects, that in Persia the Caliph 'Omar is the object of a quite extraordinary hate and contempt. "Cursed be 'Omar" is the strongest expression of Shi'ite hate against the Sunna. It was this 'Omar who subjugated Persia, and he has ever since been subconsciously remembered as the man who robbed Persia of her past, and the bestowal of the throne on the Shi'a was, it is asserted, nothing but a protest against victorious Islam. It is at any rate a remarkable fact that in the sixteenth century the Sefevids, the first purely Persian dynasty after centuries of Arabian dominion, evinced their awakening national self-consciousness by making the Shi'a the State religion of Persia. And the sanguinary Shi'ite tragedy that is performed in the month Muharrem in honour of the sons of Caliph 'Ali has become a Persian national festival. Grief for the murder of the house of 'Ali is a veil that hides hate against the usurpers, and in particular against the Caliph 'Omar. The entire history of the Persian nation since the reception of Islam has to be understood from this standpoint. That a nation can exert itself and manifest its powers only under its own impersonal law of life must be clear to anyone who has eyes to see; and it is equally evident that the torpor of a soul that has been so distorted as the soul of the Persian nation has been must be all the more profound in view of the abundance of "impersonal" energies which were crushed by the alien life that was forced upon it — i.e., by Islam. When it is considered how deep that sorrow must have been before it could imprint its stamp on the large majority of Persian hearts and make melancholy the racial characteristic of the people — when we consider this, only one conclusion can possibly be drawn. This people, this melancholic, inactive, lazy, indolent, clever, thoughtful people, who are living in a dream, must, within the barriers that separate it from its proper life, have gifts and talents in proportion to the measure of its unconscious sorrow. And that is not small. Leopold Weiss concludes his study by expressing the conviction that the puzzling and peculiar features of Persian mentality are due to what in an individual case psychoanalysis calls an "inferiority complex." Each reader will agree or disagree according to the attitude he takes up toward that science.

In reply to this theory that the present condition of the Persian is due to the manner in which they became Muhammedans, it may of course be said that other peoples besides the Persians have adopted Islam without having become ' Arabianized ' — e.g., the Turks and the Tatars. Among these latter peoples, it will be said, Islam had a positive and a strengthening effect, leading them to victory and expansion; whereas, according to the theory with which we are concerned, it has ruined Persian mentality. But the contradiction is only apparent. The Turks, for example, became Muhammedans without having been warred upon by the Arabs. They did willing obeisance to the spirit of Islam. They were not subjugated: they were converted. Besides, at the time of their conversion the Turks could hardly be said to have a past. They had neither to abjure nor abandon anything. They adapted their new national development to the new religious views. But the Persians at the time when Islām overran and subjugated them, had behind them a long history, full of change, heroism, and pain. With that they had to break.

No one can deny that Islām in Persia presents problems of exceptional difficulty. These cannot be solved by the aid of mere study of manuscripts and other literary remains; only a thorough investigation in the country itself will avail to settle them. To dismiss all these problems with a shrug of the shoulders and to try to solve the problem of the Shī'a by literary investigation is perhaps the easier course, but it is certainly not the right one. It is remarkable that while the history of Arabian Islām down to the thirteenth century has been repeatedly investigated and described by numerous Western scholars, little or no attention has been paid to the growth of Islām among non-Semitic peoples. Great importance attaches to the history of the Sefevids in Persia and to the amazing influence it exerted on its neighbours even before it extended its sway in Persia. This neglect is all the more inexplicable, because such a study is essential if we are to lift the veil of darkness that envelops the numerous sects and dervish societies which flourished from the fourteenth century or even earlier in the 'Osmān empire and in extensive regions of Northern Syria. Such a study will prove to anyone who is open to conviction that these sects and societies originated in East Persia. At the beginning of the fourteenth century that territory was the home of a peculiar religious life, of whose detailed features we are still almost entirely ignorant. From East Persia as early as the middle of the thirteenth century there issued numerous prophets who made their way westward, first to Azerbaijan, then to the very heart of the 'Osmān empire, to Anatolia. The influence of these holy men on the religious and political life of the people must not be underestimated. The strange revolts and uprisings of which we read in the period of the Rumselyukes — like that of Baba-Ilyas of Khorassan — may all be traced to the activities of these immigrants from East Persia, many of whom attained political importance and power. The dynasty of the Karamans, for example, which for a long time was the most dangerous rival of the 'Osmāns in Asia Minor, traces its lineage back to Nūre Sūfī, concerning whom little is known except that his success was due to his religious influence among the people.

What is perhaps the strangest of all these movements — viz., the rise of the Sefevid power in Persia — is to be ascribed to similar causes. In the first quarter of the fourteenth century there lived at Erdebīl in the northern part of Azerbaijan a great Sūfī sheik, Sefī ed-dīn. He traced his lineage back to 'Alī's grandson, and therefore claimed to be of 'Alidic descent. He died in the odour of sanctity on September 12, 1334, and was buried at the scene of his activity. His grave is still a famous holy place. The son, the grandson, and the great-grandson of this prophet also lived meditative lives, without seeking publicity or pushing their claims and ambitions. The fame of their holy walk and conversation spread as far as Brasa and reached the Court of the 'Osmānic sultan, who sent rich gifts and offerings every year to Erdebīl. Sheik Juneid, the son of Ibrāhīm, the great-grandson mentioned above, was the first of his line to enter the political field. His activities finally became so dangerous that the Prince of the White Wether, the Lord of Erdebīl, banished him from the country. He fled to the Court of Usun Hasan, the Lord of the Black Wether, who not only received him hospitably, but also gave him the hand of his daughter, whose mother was a Comnenian and therefore a Christian princess. Juneid moved about in the country and advanced as far as North Syria. Before he fell in battle he had gathered round him a considerable band of adherents, but his son Haider succeeded in raising a large army, each soldier of which wore a scarlet headdress, which became famous under the name of " the Haider crown." This was the origin of the name Kysylbash, or " Red-head," which was afterward given by the Turks to the Shi'ite Persians and to the 'Alidic sects in Asia Minor who made common cause with them. In the meantime a dervish order, which was originally composed of Sefevids, had grown into a powerful political party. Haider would certainly have carried things further and acquired a powerful position had he not been killed at the disastrous battle of Tabzerān. He left, however, a successor in his second son, Ismāīl, whose amazing energy enabled him to realize the empire of which his father had dreamed. When he came forward in 1499, at the age of twelve, he had about three hundred devoted followers. Ere long the number had largely increased, many coming from Anatolia. In the districts of Tekke and Hāmid in the south-west of Asia Minor, where the Sefevids had long had supporters, large crowds flocked to his banners. What was the attraction? Unfortunately, we know very little of the Sefevid organization. The Turkish accounts are of course biased, and the same may be said of the Persian accounts, few of which have been published. The Western accounts, which mainly consist of the *relazioni* of Italian consuls in the Levant, supply only a vague and sometimes unintelligible description of the movement. We do know, however, that in the eyes of Ismāīl and his followers money and rank were of no account; the one thing they valued was devotion to the new faith. The soldiers served without pay. Ismāīl preached the simplest communal life and liberal almsgiving. The Sunnite prohibition of wine and (it is said) of pork he repudiated, because his idol, 'Alī, could not possibly have approved of it. Toward Christians he seems to have adopted a benevolent attitude. Nothing is known of the religious doctrine advocated by Ismāīl, but it seems fairly certain that it was a mixture of ancient Persian beliefs and Christian practices. With Muhammed's Muhammedanism, and even with the ancient form of Shī'a, it had hardly anything in common but the name. The populace received the youthful Ismāīl with tremendous enthusiasm. He was their idol and their Messiah. His cause spread with incredible rapidity, especially in Asia Minor, and in the south of that peninsula his party soon attained a dangerous strength. In that region emerged the strange holy man Baba Shāhkuli (1510), who kindled a dreadful peasants' war and recommenced the series of revolts which a century before, under similarly suspicious circumstances, had plunged the country into disorder and shaken the throne of the 'Osmāns. This time, however, Constantinople perceived the danger. In 1502 Sultan Bajazet II had caused the Shi'ites of Tekke and Hāmid with their leaders and sheiks at their head to be branded on their foreheads and dragged to the European parts of the Empire, mainly to the Morea. Bajazet's successor, Selim I, recognizing the peril that threatened his empire, abandoned the tolerant attitude that had been adopted by the 'Osmān sultans toward the Persian dervishes and holy men who traversed Anatolia, preaching and setting up their hermitages everywhere. An opposite policy was now followed. An attitude hostile to Shi'ism was adopted, and the 'Osmāns became the bulwark of Sunnite Islām. In the subsequent hostilities between Selim I and Shah Ismāīl, who in the meantime had consolidated his power, the Sultan, thanks to his artillery and his janissaries, emerged victorious, and the young Sefevid State just escaped destruction. A limit, however, had been set to its extension westward. Thereafter, when once the Syrian and Egyptian empire of the Mamelukes, which had been a prominent part of the Muhammedan world, had been subjugated by the 'Osmāns (1517), the Shi'ite danger outside of Persia was practically overcome. There were still repeated religious risings in Anatolia, and resolute supporters of the Persian Shī'a continued their endeavours to regain lost ground, but the Turkish state was now in a position to meet all attempts of the kind. Only the dervish societies, which had established themselves in many parts of Asia Minor, and many of which, including the Bektashis, Kalends, Haideris, Edhemis, Babais, and Sheiads, were pronouncedly favourable to the Shī'a, could be regarded as centres of hostility to the Sunna. The connexion of dervishism with the Shī'a is far from being accidental: the two have a common psychological basis. It was neither the comfortable doctrines of the Sefevid Ismāīl, nor his good-humour that called forth that mighty religious movement and gave it its sinister power. The divine worship of the master had much in common with the devotion of the Shi'ites to their Imām. Nor is it merely fortuitous that the love-lyrics of Hafiz are referred by the Mevlevi (whirling) dervishes to Jehal al-Din, the sheik of the order. The worship of 'Alī or of Husain readily leads to Sufism. These matters cannot be discussed further here, and the numerous questions that are raised by the varied history of Islām in Nearer Asia during the Middle Ages can only be illustrated by a few examples.

The dervish orders of Asia Minor, together with the peculiar sects that arose in that country, are closely associated with the Shi'ite movement, which originated in East Persia and was valiantly supported by the Sefevids. In the east of Anatolia, close to the Persian frontier, the so-called Kysylbashes, sometimes also styled Tachtadshis or Tshepnis, are specially numerous. But even in the south-west, in Tekke, they have existed down to the present day. An eyewitness has stated that in this region down to recent days — the report is dated 1915 — the Tachtadshis were regarded as Persian subjects, and that the Turkish Government tacitly admitted this by not insisting on military service from members of the sect. The author of this statement was evidently unaware of the reasons for this exceptional position. The explanation has already been given above. But it is not only in Asia Minor that such 'Alidic sects are found. They are also met with in the Balkans. K. J. Jireček mentions Bulgarian Kysylbashes who live in scattered communities among the Turks near Alt-Zagora, in the Balkans, near Karnobad, and in the districts of Deli-Orman and Gerlovo. They are a peaceful agricultural people, who drink wine without any qualms of conscience, allow their women to go about unveiled, regard the shedding of blood as sinful, consider themselves superior to other Turks, and pay little heed to the precepts of the Korān. We shall not be far wrong if we suppose that these Shi'ite settlements originated at the beginning of the fifteenth century in those very districts where the sheik Bedr ed-dīn found so many followers and where he ended his troubled life on the gallows in 1416. The Behtashi dervishes have very numerous settlements in the south-east of Europe. Their distribution, which is clearly shown in a map drawn up by an English scholar, indicates how successful the propaganda of this order has been. They must have a very large number of adherents in Albania.

From what has been said it will be clear that Islām, at least as a national religion, had to adapt itself wherever it spread to the local racial and religious conditions with which it came into contact. A typically Semitic religion to begin with, it had to accommodate itself to every land and people, and thus it underwent great modifications. It is therefore not surprising that, in view of the excrescences and deteriorations that met the eyes of bigoted Arabian Moslems when they looked at Persia, India, and even Turkey, there should arise in Arabia, the actual birthplace of Islām, a desire to restore Muhammed's religion to its pristine purity and truth. It was only on purely Arabian soil and among genuine Arabs that a Puritan movement like that of the Wahabis could arise. Only there could it have any prospect of success. Outside the confines of Arabia it was bound to fail. Only at the source from which Islām long ago derived its vigour and power could the Wahabi movement hope to thrive. It would be a mistake to leave out of account this remarkable movement, which aims at the restoration of pure Muhammedan doctrine; it would be unwise to underestimate its importance. Its immense political power at the present time will ensure due consideration of it in wide circles not only of the Muhammedan, but also of the Christian world. If there is ever to be a revival of Muhammedanism it can only come from Arabia. The Wahabi movement, which, when it first appeared at the beginning of the eighteenth century, was erroneously regarded as an attempt to introduce some new kind of religion, has only one clear and definite end in view. It is frankly based on the Sunna, and, as Richard Hartmann puts it, it is a natural reaction against all those adaptations of Islām to complicated and alien civilizations which have sapped the strength of its founder's thoughts and resulted in the secularization of the religion. This reaction is natural and intelligible, because the social conditions in Arabia have undergone little change since the time of the Prophet, and it is based on the most conservative of the four Sunnite systems, that of Ahmed Ibn Hanbal.

The early endeavours of the Wahabis were known only from the accounts given by Western travellers like J. L. Burckhardt or from novels like Karl von Vincenti's *Die Tempelstürmer in Hocharabien,* but we have now fuller information regarding their latest activities, especially those of Abdul-asīs Ibn Sa'ūd. The Wahabis put into practice the Hanbaltic protests of the great religious teacher Ibn Teimiyya against all innovations that contravene the Sunna teaching. For example, they forbid the use of tobacco and coffee; the worship of graves and relics is a grievous sin; the erection of minarets on mosques and the use of the rosary (which was unknown to ancient Islām) are condemned. The gains that are claimed to have accrued from the historical development of the religion are stoutly denied by the Wahabis, whose eyes are turned exclusively to the past, to the time of Muhammed, the Apostle of God. They are ruthlessly opposed to all that seems to them to savour of heresy or innovation, and their methods are frankly iconoclastic. In recent years, in the wake of the World War, the movement broke out again, with a descendant of Ibn Sa'ūd as its leader, and owing to his outstanding abilities as a statesman and as a soldier it has become a burning question in Arabia, the cradle of Islām. Mention should also be made here of a phenomenon that is important from the sociological point of view, and absolutely novel to the Arabs. The attempt has been and is being made to gather together into new agricultural settlements Ibn Sa'ūd's adherents, his brave warriors, who are called Ikhwans — *i.e.,* " Brethren." When it is remembered that since primeval days the whole of Arabia, apart from a few city settlements, has been peopled by nomadic Beduins without any permanent domicile, we may imagine how profound may be the social and economic changes that may be imminent in Arabia if the founder of these Ikhwan settlements can persuade his subjects to abandon their roving life and if success crowns his efforts to create a great Arabian State.

While this Wahabi movement aims at restoring Islām to its original form, there is another recent movement which expressly seeks to develop the religion in accordance with present-day ideals. Its adherents are known as Babīs. Its particular object is the revival of Eastern Islām, and as a whole it reflects Persian and Shi'ite ideas. Its basis is the Mahdī creed of the Ismāilis. Its founder was a fanatical youth, Mirza Ali Muhammed, who first regarded himself as the door (Persian, *bāb*) or mouthpiece of the " hidden Imām," and then became convinced that he himself was the Mahdī, the literal embodiment of the supreme truth. He believed himself to be the reincarnation of

Moses and Jesus, and condemned all worldly aims and pretensions and the hypocritical holiness of the Persian priests. He aimed at raising to a higher and maturer stage the revelation of Muhammed, to which he gave a metaphorical interpretation. The exercises of Islām, the irksome laws of ritual purity, were either omitted or replaced by others. The Last Judgment, Paradise, hell, the resurrection, were interpreted on new lines. Mirza died a martyr's death in 1850, but his successors proceeded to develop their master's teaching. The threads of connexion between Babism and Shi'ite Islām were gradually severed, and the movement was avowedly proclaimed to be an attempt to found a redemptive religion *for all mankind*. In spite of the severe persecutions to which its Apostles were subjected, especially in Persia, the Babi movement has met with considerable success, although the number of its adherents has probably been exaggerated. It has spread not only in Asia, but also in Europe and North America. In all these territories there are Babi communities. They are gaining many new members from other faiths. On the other hand, they have broken up into various sects, and this cannot but impede the progress of the movement as a whole.

Still another Islamic sect has come into prominence in recent years. It originated in India, and is usually called Ahmediyya. It seems to have set itself the task of finding adherents in the West, among the subjects of Christian States. The movement belongs to our own time, for its prophet, Mirzā Ghulām Ahmed, died in the Punjab as recently as 1908. He too claimed to be the promised saviour. He spurned all warlike measures, and sought to gain the world to his cause by missionary effort, and was willing to adapt Islām to contemporary needs and conditions. His teaching was a mixture of Muhammedan and Christian doctrines, and he appealed to the writings of the Old and New Testament as well as to the Korān and to Muhammedan tradition (*Hadīs*). The Ahmedī sect, which seems to have plenty of money to spend on propaganda, is allowed full liberty by the English Government, probably because the sect favours the present English sovereignty in India. Its headquarters are in India, where many other influences are at work to bring about greater cohesion in the Moslem world. To reconcile the faith of Islām with Western civilization is the main ambition of leading men like Sir Sayyid Amir Ali and Sir Sayyid Ahmed Khan Behādur. The other extreme is represented by the bigotry of the Wahabis, whose eyes are fixed only on the past. The prospects of a united Islām are at the present moment less than they have ever been, and unless all the signs are deceptive the religion of Muhammed is face to face with serious internal difficulties. No one can say at present what the eventual result will be. The time of crisis through which Asia is passing is also the time of crisis for Islam.

BIBLIOGRAPHY

Müller, *Der Islam im Morgen- und Abendland* (2 vols., 1885 and 1887); Hartmann, *Der Islam, Geschichte, Glaube, Recht* (1909); Ignaz Goldziher, *Vorlesungen über den Islam* (1910; 2nd ed., 1925); Mann, *Der Islam einst und jetzt* (1914); Snouck Hurgronje, *Mohammedanism* (1916). For Muhammedan law, see Juynboll, *Handleiding tot de kennis van de Mohammedaansche wet* (1903; 3rd ed., 1925); the second edition was issued in German under the title *Handbuch des islamischen Gesetzes* (1910). For the mysticism of Islam see Nicholson, *Studies in Islamic Mysticism* (1914).

INDEX